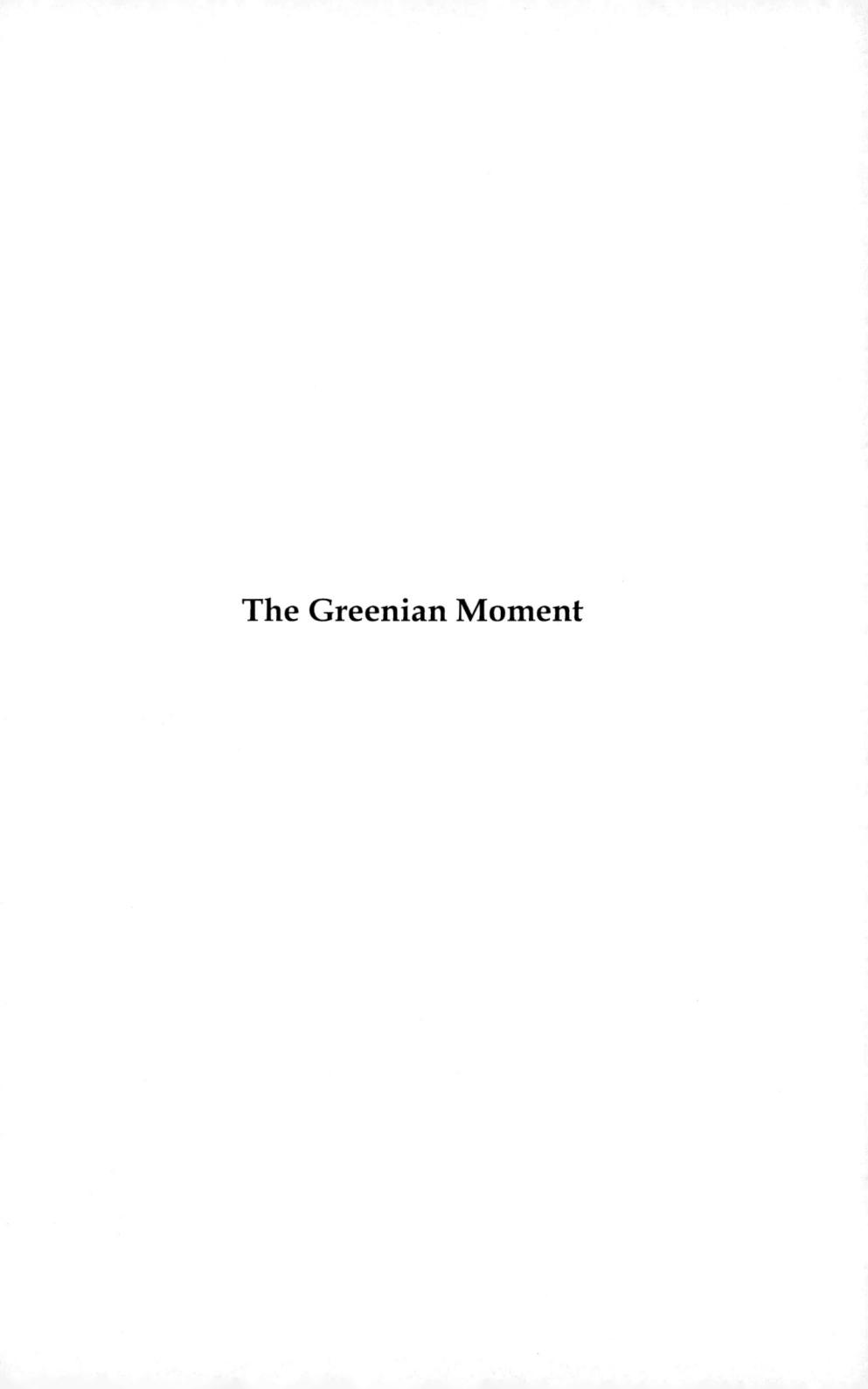

The Greenian Moment

British Idealist Studies Series 3: Green

1: Matt Carter, *T.H. Green and the Development of Ethical Socialism*
2: Denys Leighton, *The Greenian Moment*
3: Ben Wempe, *T.H. Green's Theory of Positive Freedom*

The Greenian Moment

T.H. Green, Religion and Political Argument in Victorian Britain

Denys P. Leighton

ia

IMPRINT ACADEMIC

Published in the UK by Imprint Academic
PO Box 200, Exeter EX5 5YX, UK

Published in the USA by Imprint Academic
Philosophy Documentation Center
PO Box 7147, Charlottesville, VA 22906-7147, USA

ISBN 0 907845 541

A CIP catalogue record for this book is available from the
British Library and US Library of Congress

www.imprint-academic.com/idealists

Contents

Preface

This monograph is adapted from a doctoral thesis entitled 'T. H. Green, Religion and Radical-Liberal Argument in Victorian Britain' (Department of History, Washington University in St. Louis, May, 2000). It responds to a vast literature on Green, modern ethics, Victorian political thought and British political history since 1789, while addressing questions about historical method and interpretation in the history of political thought. It is therefore a trans-disciplinary work that the author hopes will be of interest to readers of history, philosophy, politics and religious studies. Instead of interpreting Green's life and work with primary reference to British Idealism, the study examines the emerging culture of British academic philosophy, as well as the wider religious and political environments in which Green worked, with attention to both the formation and reception of Green's ideas. It explores religious ideas and themes in Green's work and examines the relation of religion to ethico-political discourse. In showing the persistence of religious ways of knowing in the Age of Darwin and Marx, this study suggests that the 'secularization of Western thought' was decidedly incomplete even by the opening of the twentieth century, when Green's influence was at its peak.

Research for the study was commenced during the early 1990s, when the historical view of Green had been effectively established by Melvin Richter's *The Politics of Conscience: T. H. Green and His Age* (1964). Although Richter's book was well received by historians, Green and British Idealism were unfashionable in an Anglo-American philosophical establishment dominated by the analytic or 'ordinary-language' school. Some political theorists attentive to the history of philosophy and political theory remained interested in Green's conception of 'positive liberty' and his theory of 'self-realization'. Richter had discussed Green's religious inspirations and his Liberal partisanship. One effect of *The Politics of Conscience*, perhaps unintended, was to reinforce the common perception of Green as a pioneering theorist of the Welfare State. However, by the 1970s scholars were eagerly reclaiming Green for the

Liberal Tradition, arguing that his philosophy illuminates a middle ground between 'socialism' (i.e. cradle-to-grave Labourism) and neoconservatism (with its agenda of systematically dismantling the Welfare State). Coincident with the communitarian turn of liberalism during the 1980s, Green's ideas appeared to be almost fashionable again in professional philosophical circles (see Chapter One).

In tracing Green's reception over the years by philosophers, political theorists, policy makers and politicians, I was struck by the great disparity of opinions and by the stated reasons on which those opinions were founded. Between 1880 and 1940 Green's writings were widely read and discussed, and their influence in many areas of British life has been amply documented. Nearly every Oxbridge-educated civil servant of the period would have been familiar with Green's teachings and would have formed some opinion of them. Not only within the British Empire and the Anglophone world but also among Westernized elites in China and Japan Green's ethical and political ideas were common currency and were taken as seriously as the ideas of J. S. Mill and Marx. In Britain itself, even after the Second World War there persisted a cultural memory of Green as perhaps less a good philosopher than a 'good man', a difficult philosopher to read but one who clearly wished to right social and political wrongs of Victorian Britain. On the other side, growing numbers of professional philosophers from the 1920s deemed Green a philosophical non-entity who clogged philosophical discourse with 'metaphysical' jargon and nonsense. Clearly, differing perspectives about the purposes of philosophy and changing fashions in ethical-political discourse had some bearing on deciding who the real Green was and on determining the historical significance of his thought.

Other issues concerning historical interpretation and the methods of study of political thought simultaneously caught my attention. The vanguard of the study of the history of political thought ca. 1980 was represented by linguistic contextualists like J. G. A. Pocock and Quentin Skinner, who were identifying the 'political languages' in European thought since the Renaissance. These and other scholars were tracing the emergence of new political and social vocabularies with the growth of Western commercial society from 1600, including natural rights, political economy, utilitarianism and evolutionism. Perhaps because T.H. Green had criticized uses of these vocabularies in his own time, and because he deployed an 'emotive' (non-analytical) vocabulary in his discussion of philosophical issues, political theorists and intellectual historians tended to regard him as a throw-back to an earlier 'moment' of inquiry (recalling Auguste Comte's division of thought into historical, stage-like theological, philosophical and scientific eras). Green was most readily categorized as a Hegelian Idealist, arguing for the primacy of spirit over matter and substituting, in a presumably un-English way, the 'real will' of society and 'the state' for God and the divine order. Many commentators ignored or glossed over the fact that Green spoke and wrote not only of an abstract Hegelian 'Spirit' but also of God and Christ.

Historians of politics and society could *trace* Green's influence in Britain ca. 1880–1920, yet historians of 'thought' could scarcely *account* for Green's impact. Why did Green's conception of the individual in society, with its theological trappings, gain currency in a world — or a section of the globe — that was supposedly becoming less religious and more secular? I concluded that the 'secularization thesis' associated with Weber, Tawney and others, and tacitly accepted by most intellectual historians, presented more hindrances than aids to understanding Green and his social significance. This difficulty was compounded by the fashionable historians of political thought identifying 'political thought' in a manner that emphasized elite discourses. These traced the movement of Great Ideas but effectively excluded ideas of wider social allegiance or those that influenced the thinking of 'the masses'. What was needed, I thought, was to reunite intellectual history, as the study of Great Ideas, with the social history of politics and language. I have consequently tried to recapture the sense of Green's relevance to his era by noting resonances between his teachings and popular attitudes and 'middle-brow' ideas. Among the latter were popular constitutionalism, revolving around the conception of the 'freeborn Englishman', and popular Protestantism, foregrounding Christian ideas of conscience, Godly community and social duty. Scholars of the history of political languages school have neglected such 'discourses'. The play in the title of my book on the influential work of John Pocock, *The Machiavellian Moment: Florentine Political Thought and the Atlantic Republican Tradition* (1975), is intended as a compliment rather than a swipe: the 'Cambridge School' of intellectual historians provide clues as to how Green and thinkers of the early modern and modern eras might be interpreted, but their assumptions about the social dimensions of discourse need to be reconsidered.

If there is a polemical note to this book, it includes the insistence that religious ideas and attitudes be taken seriously in comprehending an age of secularization. Green's era was marked by loss of faith *and* religious revivalism. In Western Europe and regions populated by Western Europeans ca. 1850–1900 people were renouncing *and* reaffirming orthodox Christianity in record numbers. Victorian Britain was a pluralistic society profoundly influenced by secular movements and currents of thought. Yet religious ideas and beliefs in the Age of Darwin and Marx continued to shape understanding of the body social, to promote social cohesion, and also to justify challenges to the social order. Christianity influenced most Britons' sense of right and wrong as well as their

sense of what was politically desirable and possible. Political Radicalism and Christian Socialism, both of which Green encouraged, were
forms of argument in which popular beliefs merged with 'High' ideas to
engender new conceptions of social purpose. Green's philosophical Idealism, even if imperfectly understood or disdained by philosophical
successors, complemented popular modes of social understanding in
his time.

* * *

The Introduction to *The Greenian Moment* discusses issues raised by
Green scholarship and recent contributions to the history of political
thought. Here I suggest why and how Green's life and work might be
re-contextualized in order to reveal broader and deeper relationships
between Green's ideas and popular as well as professional discourses
on ethics and politics. Chapter One is extensive, rather than intensive,
continuing examination of accounts of the significance and impact of
Green's teachings. The chapter contains biographical exposition and it
comments on Green's philosophical career in relation to contemporary
currents of European philosophy and science. Chapter Two provides an
account of Green's theory of the individual in society, including his conceptions of individuality and community, and indicates how an idea of
enlightened self-interest functioned in his system of ethics and
anchored his theory of polity. Chapter Three situates Green's ideas
within traditions of 'rational' and 'enthusiastic' religion since the seventeenth century. It establishes that the German theological movement
represented by Kant, Schleiermacher, Hegel, D. F. Strauss and F. C.
Baur, and transmitted to Britain via Benjamin Jowett and other liberal
Anglicans, was only one of many influences on Green's religious
thought. The chapter emphasizes connections between Green, evangelicalism and religio-political liberalism that have been neglected by
scholars focusing on the 'Germanic' features of Green's philosophical
work.

Chapter Four examines Green's cooperation with evangelicals, Broad
Churchmen and Nonconformists on religious issues, education and in
matters of social reform. It shows how Green's social outreach in this
respect had significant ramifications for 'advanced' or 'New' Liberalism
and other reformist ideologies of the late Victorian period. Green was
impressed by the phenomenon of English 'Political Dissent' (which
involved a striking expansion from the 1820s of Nonconformists' political participation) and the consequent changes to Victorian political and
public life. It is argued here that Green's Philo-Dissentism was a significant factor in channeling Dissenters' sense of mission into social reform
Radicalism. Chapter Five follows up on conclusions arrived at in the

preceding two chapters to demonstrate Green's role in the revival of 'moral' politics in the 1880s and '90s. The chapter examines the social and intellectual conditions for the ripening of a Greenian 'moment' and traces the religious and 'spiritual' impulses behind British campaigns for social reform and reconstruction down to 1914. Chapter Six considers Green's place in the political memory of Victorian and post-Victorian Liberalism. The chapter notes the influence of the Greenian outlook on non-Liberal thought and thinkers. It examines Green's advocacy of women's rights and his support for the political aspirations of marginalized social categories. It advances conclusions about Green as a role model in an age of democracy and 'collectivist' politics and about his continuing reputation as an activist intellectual.

* * *

Readers will be aware that Thoemmes Press has published a complete new edition of T. H. Green's writings in five volumes, including previously unpublished materials, letters and reprints of articles and reports from the contemporary press. This edition, prepared by Peter Nicholson, had not yet appeared when I first examined the Green Papers at Balliol College and other primary materials relating to Green in the Bodleian Library and the Oxfordshire County Record Office. For the convenience of readers, I frequently cite here letters to and from Green and newspaper articles as they appear in the Nicholson edition: *Collected Works of T. H. Green. Volume Five: Additional Writings* (Bristol: Thoemmes Press, 1997). In a very few instances where my reading of a manuscript source differs from that of Nicholson I have so indicated in my footnotes. As regards Green's previously published writings, I cite the edition of *Prolegomena to Ethics* edited by A. C. Bradley (1883) and I cite Green's other writings as they appear in the original *Works of T. H. Green*, ed. R. L. Nettleship (3 volumes, 1885–88). However, there are three texts I cite as printed in T. H. Green, *Lectures on the Principles of Political Obligation and Other Writings* (CUP, 1986), edited by Paul Harris and John Morrow. These are *Lectures on the Principles of Political Obligation*, the lectures originally published as 'The Different Senses of "Freedom"' and the lecture 'Liberal Legislation and Freedom of Contract'. Harris and Morrow have corrected these texts against the manuscripts in the Green Papers and have demonstrated variances between the manuscripts and the texts published by Nettleship in the 1880s.

For permission to quote from papers and letters, I thank the following: the Master and Fellows of Balliol College, Oxford; the Governing Body of Mansfield College, Oxford; the Bodleian Library, University of Oxford; the Honourable Mrs. E. A. Gascoigne (for letters in the Harcourt Papers); Lord Halifax and the Borthwick Institute for Historical

Research (for a letter of Arthur Boutwood). Every effort has been made to trace copyright holders and to obtain permission for the use of copyright material. The author and publisher apologise for any errors or omissions in the above list and would be grateful if notified of any corrections that should be incorporated in future reprints or editions of this book.

I have been fortunate in receiving extensive comments on my manuscript from Peter Nicholson and John Morrow. They have drawn my attention to errors of fact, misstatements and inconsistencies. Although I have not followed their advice on every point, this study has benefited from their critical acumen and constructive suggestions. They are of course not responsible for errors or problems that remain. Neither space nor memory permit me to acknowledge all those whose comments, advice and encouragement have helped me in preparing this book and the dissertation that preceded it. (I acknowledge assistance on particular points in footnotes.) However, I would like to thank some scholars with whom I have discussed the subjects of this study over the past two years: Avital Simhony, Gerald Gaus, David Weinstein, Maria Dimova-Cookson, Stamatoula Panagakou, Colin Tyler, Thom Brooks and Ben Wempe. I am grateful to Matt Carter for allowing me to read an advanced draft of his book, *T. H. Green and the Development of Ethical Socialism*, prior to its publication in the present series. It is with great pleasure that I thank once again Richard W. Davis, who maintained an interest in this project from its beginning as a dissertation prospectus, through dissertation and post-dissertation stages. Finally, my greatest debt is to my wife for her undiminished commitment to this book and to me.

List of Abbreviations

AHR	*American Historical Review*
AN	*Alliance News*
AW	*Collected Works of T. H. Green. Volume Five: Additional Writings*, edited and with an introduction by Peter Nicholson, Thoemmes Press, 1997
CUP	Cambridge University Press
DNB	*Dictionary of National Biography*
EHR	*English Historical Review*
GP	Papers of T. H. Green, Balliol College, Oxford
Harris and Morrow	*Lectures on the Principles of Political Obligation and Other Writings*, edited by Paul Harris and John Morrow, CUP, 1986
HJ	*Historical Journal*
HPT	*History of Political Thought*
JBS	*Journal of British Studies*
LPPO	*Lectures on the Principles of Political Obligation*
OCBBG	*Oxford Chronicle and Berkshire and Buckinghamshire Gazette*
OED	*Oxford English Dictionary*
OUP	Oxford University Press
PE	*Prolegomena to Ethics*, ed. A. C. Bradley, 1883
PP	*Parliamentary Papers* (United Kingdom)
VS	*Victorian Studies*
Works	*Works of Thomas Hill Green*, 3 vols., ed. R. L. Nettleship, 1885–8

For my parents and parents-in-law

INTRODUCTION

T. H. Green,
Philosophy and
Liberalism

T. H. Green's moral and political philosophies have been the subjects of many studies, not only due to his contributions to the discipline of political theory but because of the practical lessons about politics his contemporaries and successors drew from his teachings. Green was recognized in his lifetime as the leader of a new 'school' of philosophy, initially named (by the Oxford don Mark Pattison) the Oxford Hegelian school, and subsequently called British (or English) Idealism or Hegelianism.[1] A great deal of Green scholarship both old and new focuses on Green's relation to British Idealism.[2] Other studies have advanced claims about Green's impact on Liberal and Radical thought, on voluntary initiatives of social reform and on government policy during the late Victorian and Edwardian period. Indeed, Green was lauded by contemporaries and observers of subsequent generations as a model activist intellectual. The

[1]   M. Pattison, 'Philosophy at Oxford,' *Mind*, 1 (1876), pp. 82–97.
[2]   This literature includes: L. T. Hobhouse, *The Metaphysical Theory of the State* (London: Allen and Unwin, 1918); F. P. Harris, *Neo-Idealist Political Theory* (New York: King's Crown, 1944); A. J. M. Milne, *The Social Philosophy of English Idealism* (London: Allen and Unwin, 1962); A. Quinton, 'Absolute Idealism,' *Proceedings of the British Academy*, 57 (1971), pp. 303–29; D. Watson, 'Social Theory and National Culture. The Case of British and American Absolute Idealism, 1860–1900,' *Social Science History*, 5 (1981), pp. 251–74; P. Robbins, *The British Hegelians, 1875–1925* (New York: Garland, 1982); J. Morrow, 'Ancestors, Legacies and Traditions: British Idealism in the History of Political Thought,' *HPT*, 6 (1985), pp. 491–515; A. Vincent and R. Plant, *Philosophy, Politics and Citizenship. The Life and Thought of the British Idealists* (Oxford: Blackwell, 1984); P. Nicholson, *The Political Philosophy of the British Idealists* (CUP, 1990); D. Boucher, ed., *The British Idealists* (CUP, 1997); W. J. Mander, ed., *Anglo-American Idealism, 1865–1927* (Westport, CT: Greenwood, 2000).

present study pays due attention to his public and political life, especially to his work in areas of educational and social reform.

The study does not purport to organize comprehensively the data of Green's existence. However, it does utilize individual biography as a lens through which to view aspects of Victorian 'moral life' — more particularly, Victorian ethics and ethical culture at their intersection with politics and public life. In a sense, the study reverses the direction of previous approaches to Green by viewing his philosophical *opus* through his political and public commitments. It treats Green's life and work primarily in relation to Victorian Liberalism.[3] Victorian Liberals were preoccupied with *religious* questions to a degree that makes the liberalism of their time appear very nearly the opposite of what is today called liberalism. To be sure, many British Liberals ca. 1860 were as interested in neutralizing the authority of religious institutions — for instance, by effecting the 'separation of Church and State' — as are liberals of the present day. (Although disestablishment of the Church of England was a goal shared by only a minority of Liberals, commitment to some modification of the position of the established Church handily distinguished Victorian Liberals from Conservatives.) Unlike many modern liberals, most Victorian Liberals were convinced that religious belief did, and properly should, provide an ethical perspective from which temporal questions were to be considered.

To examine Victorian political culture and the life of a pre-eminent Victorian like Green is therefore to study politics in their relation to religious beliefs and attitudes. Even — or especially — when one regards famous Victorian agnostics, like Green's friend and philosophical rival Henry Sidgwick (1838–1900) or Leslie Stephen (1832–1904), and atheists, like George Jacob Holyoake (1817–1906), it is impossible to separate their attitudes toward secular issues from their beliefs about Belief. Although Holyoake's militant secularism represented a decidedly minority position within the Liberal fold, he was nevertheless a partisan in the Liberal interest.[4] Stephen, though he inclined later in life towards

---

[3]   Works on British liberalism and the Liberal Party I have found relevant to my investigation are D. Southgate, *The Passing of the Whigs, 1832–1886* (London: Macmillan, 1962); J. Vincent, *The Formation of the British Liberal Party, 1857–1868*, 2nd edn. (Hassocks, Sussex: Harvester, 1976); I. Bradley, *The Optimists. Themes and Personalities in Victorian Liberalism* (London: Faber and Faber, 1980); A. Hawkins, '"Parliamentary Government" and Victorian Political Parties, c. 1830–c. 1880,' *EHR*, 104 (1989), pp. 638–69; E. F. Biagini, *Liberty, Retrenchment and Reform. Popular Liberalism in the Age of Gladstone, 1860–1880* (CUP, 1992); and J. Parry, *The Rise and Fall of Liberal Government in Victorian Britain* (New Haven, CT: Yale UP, 1993).

[4]   Holyoake was a warrior of conscience as well as a great entrepreneur of Victorian secularism. He edited the *Reasoner*, fought for liberty of the press and advocated producer and consumer co–operatism. As Ian Bradley notes, Holyoake was the 'last person in Britain to be imprisoned on charge of atheism' (*The Optimists*, pp. 270–1).

political and social conservatism, maintained a worldview formed by his interaction ca. 1850–65 with other young intellectuals (students and dons) at Oxbridge, most of whom supported Gladstone's party as a force of progress and who, like J. S. Mill, viewed the Conservatives as 'the stupid party'.[5] Significantly, Stephen, Green and many other contemporary shapers of opinion did not regard their rationalism as antithetical to spiritual life.[6]

I examine here Victorian liberalism not as an ideology — for it was too diffuse to be understood as such — but as an ethico-political culture. 'Political culture' is not identical to 'opinion' or the 'public sphere' in the sense given those terms by Jürgen Habermas and others, but it is a definite social sphere.[7] I treat political culture or sub-culture as an intelligible, recoverable world of political acts and meanings, examining arguments used by Victorian Liberals and Radicals to make sense of events and enable collective action. I do not attempt to systematically assess Green's contributions to specific disciplines or areas of thought — that is, to hypostatized intellectual discourses like moral philosophy, political theory or theology. Although I engage in technical discussion of different philosophical viewpoints (e.g., idealism, empiricism, utilitarianism), I am not primarily concerned with Green's relation to British Idealism. Likewise, situating Green's social and political ideas within the intellectual construct called 'Western thought' — as a canon of texts — is not the main purpose of this investigation. As David Boucher and Siep Stuurman have observed, the *histories* of philosophy and political thought are recent inventions (at least in the English–speaking world), designed for didactic purposes with which we may not necessarily

---

[5]   Stephen was not the only Liberal of this generation to grow conservative with age. Sidgwick feared economic socialism. James Bryce and A. V. Dicey, both friends of Green, ended their lives on the right or 'individualist' wing of the Liberal Party. N. Annan, *Leslie Stephen. The Godless Victorian* (Chicago: UP Chicago, 1984); C. Harvie, *The Lights of Liberalism. University Liberals and the Challenge of Democracy, 1860–86* (London: Allen Lane, 1976); J. Kloppenberg, *Uncertain Victory: Social Democracy and Progressivism in European and American Thought, 1870-1920* (OUP, 1986), chap. 5.

[6]   On this point, see especially S. Collini, *Public Moralists. Political Thought and Intellectual Life in Britain, 1850-1930* (OUP, 1991), chap. 2.

[7]   See J. Habermas, *Strukturwandel der Öffentlichkeit*, 2d ed. (Neuwied: Luchterhand, 1965). People participate in a political culture as both producers and consumers of its meanings. A political culture is characterized by its participants' views of politics and society and may include assumptions about social rank or class, gender, ethnicity, and religion in relation to past, present and projected social orders. In the sense that by participating in political culture individuals have a proprietary relation to it, one may meaningfully speak of the political culture *of* Victorian Britons, as well as the culture of liberals (or of Radicals, socialists, Conservatives, and so on). It would be pointless, however, to speak of the *political* culture of British Theosophists or of the Social Democratic Federation.

agree.[8] My aim is to assess Green's work *across* disciplines and discourses in order to locate wider cultural meanings.

I am interested in Green not only as a social and political philosopher who may be of interest to present-day thinkers but as *zoon politikon*, indeed, as partisan and politician. Green considered himself and was acknowledged by his contemporaries as both a Liberal and a Radical. In using the terms 'Radical', 'Radicalism' and 'Radical-Liberalism', I refer to a political movement parallel to Liberalism, one allied with an older Whig tradition for political purposes during much of the nineteenth century yet antagonistic to it in fundamental ways.[9] This study reads Green's social and political ideas and his methods of realizing them against the ideas, values, and political objectives of Liberalism and Radicalism in Britain between ca. 1850 and 1914. Examination of T. H. Green and his work thus serves as an opportunity to explore a larger relationship between elite and popular liberalism during the High Liberal era, when the Liberal Party benefited from a high degree of ideological cohesion and attracted broad social support.

Whereas *political* historians have not ignored religious debates in Victorian politics, thorough consideration of religious expression has not been typical until quite recently of scholarship in Victorian intellectual history, history of political thought or history of political culture. For much of the twentieth century historians regarded religious controversy (and political arguments couched in religious terms) during the modern era as a quaint interest of theologians and denominational historians. Social historians in particular have tended to view denominational conflict as a cypher for class conflict. George Kitson Clark and Edward Norman are among the few historians of nineteenth-century Britain active since the 1960s who have considered religious ideas as

---

[8]   See D. Boucher, 'Histories of Political Thought in the Post-Methodological Age,' *HPT*, 14 (1993), pp. 301–16. The history of political thought emerged ca. 1860–1900 in the Anglophone world as a sub-discipline of history, 'largely philosophical in subject matter, emphasizing the timelessness of the issues; ... and highly practical in intention, highlighting the continuing political relevance of the thinkers discussed' (p. 301). Also S. Stuurman, 'The Canon of the History of Political Thought,' *History and Theory*, 39 (2000), pp. 147–66; and Gerald Graff, *Professing Literature. An Institutional History* (Chicago: UP Chicago, 1987).

[9]   'Liberal' refers to a national political movement since the 1830s, constituted as the parliamentary Liberal Party in 1859; 'liberal' (lower case) refers both to an ideology and a cultural outlook, including tendencies in social and economic thought and in religion. 'Radical' as a political label was simultaneously more and less specific than 'Liberal'. By way of illustration, many Radical MPs ca. 1820–1848 adhered to the specific doctrines of Benthamism or Philosophic Radicalism. Yet Radical was also used in a looser sense to indicate a person who took identifiably Liberal ideas or policies to *extremes*. For a succinct treatment of British Radicalism and issues involved in its definition, see D. Nicholls, 'The English Middle Class and the Ideological Significance of Radicalism, 1760–1885,' *JBS*, 24 (1985), pp. 415–33.

intellectual-cultural discourse in relation to social history.[10] Over the last decade or so historians defining themselves primarily as historians of ideas have begun to re-examine religious debate in the history of political thought and explore the roles of religious ideas and concepts in political ideology; in this they follow the lead of earlier generations of scholars, who recognized religion as one of the *sources* of Victorian political and social ideas or ideologies.[11]

By examining the place of religion in Green's theory of moral development and studying his conception of a liberal polity with reference to his religious inspirations and involvements, the present work casts new light on aspects of Green's thought noted by earlier scholarship. Green scholarship and even general studies of Victorian thought have indeed noted Green's religious cast or frame of mind, as did Green's contemporaries. Green's religiosity is a running theme of the memoir by Richard Nettleship, his student.[12] Benjamin Jowett (1817–93), Green's tutor at Balliol and one of the most influential Oxford dons after 1850, initially viewed his pupil as a typical product of a clerical household and Rugby School, which lay under the shadow of the liberal Anglican and Christian Socialist Thomas Arnold (1795–1842). With Jowett lies the primary responsibility for Green's introduction to German Idealism. Jowett drew an interesting inference from Green's enthusiasm for the thought of Hegel and other German philosophers, suggesting that Green's intellectual intoxication amounted to something like religious zealotry. To his friend Florence Nightingale Jowett wrote (on 15 December 1872), 'I . . . have persuaded the Revd Hegel Green to give up lecturing for a year and take to writing — whereby the minds of our undergraduates will be greatly clarified.'[13] (Green was not in fact a Reverend.)

Melvin Richter has suggested that Green's philosophizing was a substitute for religion, calling it a surrogate faith.[14] Yet attempts to elucidate

[10] G. Kitson Clark, *Churchmen and the Condition of England* (London: Methuen, 1973); E. R. Norman, *The Victorian Christian Socialists* (CUP, 1987).

[11] See especially B. Hilton, *The Age of Atonement: the Influence of Evangelicalism on Social and Economic Thought, 1785–1865* (OUP, 1988); D. Nicholls, *Deity and Domination: Images of God and the State in the Nineteenth and Twentieth Centuries* (London & New York: Routledge, 1994 [1989]); and A. M. C. Waterman, *Revolution, Economics and Religion: Christian Political Economy, 1798–1833* (CUP, 1991).

[12] R. L. Nettleship, 'Memoir,' in *Works of T. H. Green*, iii, ed. Nettleship (London: Longmans, Green and Co., 1888), pp. xi–clxi.

[13] *Dear Miss Nightingale. A Selection of Benjamin Jowett's Letters to Florence Nightingale, 1860–1893*, ed. V. Quinn and J. Prest (Oxford: Clarendon, 1987), p. 235.

[14] M. Richter, 'T. H. Green and His Audience: Liberalism as a Surrogate Faith,' *Review of Politics*, 18 (1956), pp. 444–72. See also P. Montagné, *Un Radical Religieux en Angleterre au XIXe Siècle ou la Philosophie de Thomas Hill Green* (Toulouse: Ouvrière, 1927); M. Richter, *The Politics of Conscience: T.H.Green and His Age* (London: Weidenfeld and Nicolson, 1964), chaps. 1–4; Vincent and Plant, *Philosophy, Politics and Citizenship*, chap. 2; M. Bevir, 'Welfarism, Socialism and Religion: On T. H. Green and Others,'

'Green's religion' for the purpose of interpreting his philosophy and political teachings have been insufficiently analytical, and ahistorical, because of their narrow contextualization of his thought. There is a paradox in Green scholarship: while many scholars have drawn attention to Green's religious interests, they have too quickly explained them away. One is left by many accounts of Green with the vapid impression of his religion as merely a rational conviction of a divine principle in the universe.[15] The ethical aspect of his religion is interpreted as a fervent desire — only slightly informed by particular doctrines, traditions or institutions — for the liberation of the individual in his or her temporal as well as spiritual existence, and for the prevalence in society of right thinking and living.[16] In *God's Funeral* (1999), the critic, novelist and biographer A. N. Wilson, represents Green as a theistic philosopher (an epigone of Jowett as well as Hegel) and practically disqualifies him as a Christian.[17]

Wilson's characterization of Green as a timid theist and unwitting ally of the Darwinists is consistent with that of more nuanced studies. Many Green scholars have discussed religion as something Green left behind; they consider his religious 'roots' and 'influences' chiefly in relation to attitudes he is supposed to have transcended. His thought is thereby regarded as an instance of Western thought's growing out of a religious and embracing a secular consciousness. While political and social historians today agree that religious beliefs greatly influenced Victorian social practice and that it was a major element of Victorian political culture, many intellectual historians continue to assume that

Review of Politics, 55 (1993), pp. 639–61; D. Boucher and A. Vincent, *British Idealism and Political Theory* (Edinburgh: Edinburgh UP, 2000), chap. 1.

[15] 'Idealism' presumes a form of theism. The view of individuals and their activities (including their thoughts) as manifestations of a Universal Mind or Spirit (or the Absolute) is characteristic of 'Absolute Idealism'. None of the British Idealists made reality and individuals' experiences of it *dependent* on the mind of God (George Berkeley's 'psychological idealism'). However, 'Personal Idealists' (including Green) gave more emphasis than Absolute Idealists to 'the point of view of the individual experient' (W. R. Boyce Gibson) in order to argue that reality was intelligible to individuals, not a transcendent realm of which humans could gain only occasional, indirect glimpses. Quinton, 'Absolute Idealism'; and Boucher, ed., *British Idealists*, pp. xii–xiv.

[16] The reduction and marginalization of Green's religion by specialized studies is perpetuated in more general works: e.g. E. Barker, *Political Thought in England 1848 to 1914* (Westport, CT: 1980 [orig. 1915]), chap. 2; J. Bowle, *Politics and Opinion in the Nineteenth Century* (London: J. Cape, 1954), Book 2, chap. 4. Mark Francis and John Morrow, however, allude to religious qualities of Green's thought in relation to contemporary movements of ethics and political theory: *A History of English Political Thought in the Nineteenth Century* (New York: St. Martin's, 1994), chap. 13. See also Nicholls, *Deity and Domination*, pp. 74–81.

[17] New York: W. W. Norton, 1999. The title of Wilson's book is from a poem of Thomas Hardy.

political thought, in Britain as elsewhere, was secularized during the Victorian period.[18] To trace Green's thought along a supposed trajectory of the 'secularization process' is to misread his thought and the contemporary enterprise of political theory in which he participated, and to misunderstand their relation to the ethical climate of the era. The present study points out the problematic nature of claims about the secularization process during the nineteenth century by treating religion, including its *evangelical* varieties, as in some sense a source of political–philosophical ideas rather than as rationalization for them.[19]

In the same vein, on the level of political and social history, the study indicates ways in which arguments for political and social 'reform' during the mid and late Victorian era were shaped by religious activists and agencies, and how reformers channelled the religious sensibilities of the British public into social and political action. It advances new claims about the significance for British Liberalism and a wider 'reform' agenda of Green's philosophy and his practical activities. On this point it should be noted that Green's teachings had arguably their widest and heaviest impact during the 1880s and '90s, or at the juncture where 'advanced' Liberalism and 'Socialism' were widely regarded in Britain as overlapping and complementary, rather than oppositional ideologies. A few days after Green's death, a young Oxonian inspired by him, Arnold Toynbee, delivered a lecture to the Leicester Liberal Association (which Green had himself addressed only a year before) entitled 'Are Radicals Socialists?' His answer to the question was a qualified Yes.[20]

[18] I have found instructive the following contributions to the continuing debate over the secularization of Western social and political thought: A. MacIntyre, *Secularization and Moral Change* (London: OUP, 1967); O. Chadwick, *The Secularisation of the European Mind in the Nineteenth Century* (CUP, 1975); K. W. Britton, 'John Stuart Mill on Christianity' in *James and John Stuart Mill. Papers of the Centenary Conference*, ed. J. Robson and M. Lane (Toronto: Toronto UP, 1976), pp. 31–42; E. Eisenach, *Two Worlds of Liberalism. Religion and Politics in Hobbes, Locke, and Mill* (Chicago: Chicago UP, 1981); L. Dickey, *Hegel. Religion, Economics, and the Politics of the Spirit, 1770–1807* (CUP, 1987); J. E. Crimmins, ed., *Religion, Secularization and Political Thought. Thomas Hobbes to J. S. Mill* (New York: Routledge, 1989); R. J. Helmstadter and B. Lightman, eds., *Victorian Faith in Crisis. Essays on Continuity and Change in Nineteenth-Century Religious Belief* (Palo Alto, CA: Stanford UP, 1990); R. Plant, *Politics, Theology and History* (CUP, 2001).

[19] 'Evangelical' refers to persons and a tendency within the Church of England; 'evangelical' (lower case) indicates a religious impulse at work both within and outside the established Church (e.g. among Methodists, Baptists).

[20] *Leicester Daily Mercury*, 29 March 1882; reprinted in A. Toynbee, *Lectures on the Industrial Revolution in England* (London: Longmans, Green and Co., 1884). On left or 'advanced' Liberalism and socialism during the period, see H. M. Lynd, *England in the Eighteen-Eighties: Toward a Social Basis for Freedom* (London: Frank Cass, 1968 [orig. 1945]); D. A. Hamer, *Liberal Politics in the Age of Gladstone and Rosebery: a Study in Leadership and Policy* (Oxford: Clarendon, 1972); H. V. Emy, *Liberals, Radicals and Social Politics: 1892–1914* (CUP, 1973); P. Clarke, *Liberals and Social Democrats* (CUP, 1978);

Without minimizing the novelty of his ideas, this study counters the charge, rehearsed in Chapter One below, that Green's ethico-political arguments and methods — because of their esoteric and often eccentric expression — were uncongenial to both other elite Liberals and the rank and file.

While Green criticized particular actions and attitudes of Liberal politicians, he supported the Liberal Party's wider 'mission' as articulated by William Ewart Gladstone ('The People's William'), John Bright, Joseph Chamberlain, Charles Dilke and others. Green had a higher personal regard for Bright, who during the 1840s, '50s and '60s seemed the Radical-democratic spirit incarnate, than for Gladstone, the Tory turned Peelite turned Liberal.[21] The Oxford classicist Henry Nettleship — one of the most astute commentators on Green — observed that if his friend had devoted himself more to public speaking 'his style would have come to resemble that of Bright.'[22] Yet Green was a thorough Gladstonian: he identified strongly with the mature Gladstone's conception of the nature and purpose of politics, and he approved of the Gladstonian mode of political action which, between 1867 and the late 1880s, bridged gaps between Radical and Whig sections of the Party. Green praised Gladstone's leadership in numerous political speeches delivered in support of Liberal candidates and policies between 1868 and 1882.[23]

M. Freeden, *The New Liberalism: An Ideology of Social Reform* (Oxford: Clarendon, 1978); P. Weiler, *The New Liberalism: Liberal Social Theory in Great Britain* (New York: Garland, 1982); Kloppenberg, *Uncertain Victory*, chaps. 6–8; E. F. Biagini and A. J. Reid, eds., *Currents of Radicalism. Popular Radicalism, Organized Labour and Party Politics in Britain, 1850–1914* (CUP, 1991), parts 2 and 3; J. Lawrence, 'Popular Radicalism and the Socialist Revival in Britain,' *JBS*, 31 (1992), pp. 163–86.

[21] Green met Bright and corresponded with him between 1860 and 1865, although none of the correspondence remains in the Green Papers at Balliol College. Green seems to have been influenced by Bright on the question of the proper Liberal stance towards the American Civil War. On visiting Oxford in 1864 Bright professed to be very pleased with the young Liberal set that included Albert Dicey, James Bryce and Green. Harvie, *Lights of Liberalism*, pp. 110–15; T. H. Green Papers [*GP*], 1(d), box 1: 'Notes by Mrs. Green. THG 1850–70 copies'. On the scheme of citation used here, see the Bibliography.

[22] *GP* 1(b): Nettleship to Charlotte Green (1882), transcription of a letter in CBG copybook, 23–65. On Green's Radicalism as influenced by Bright, see R. L. Nettleship, 'Memoir,' pp. xvi–xxxvii, xliii–xlv, cx–cxiii. Characteristic of Green's view of Bright was his description of a Commons speech by Bright on national defence (August 3, 1860) as 'that of a sober man among drunkards' (quoted in the 'Memoir,' p. xxiv).

[23] Green delivered an address on behalf of the Oxford Liberal Association to Gladstone upon the latter's visit to Oxford on January 30, 1878. (*Oxford Chronicle and Berkshire and Buckinghamshire Gazette [henceforth OCBBG]*, 2 Feb. 1878, p. 7 and supplement; the speech is printed in *AW*, pp. 317–19). This was shortly after the opening of Oxford's new Liberal Hall, and in the aftermath of the 'Bulgarian Agitation' which provided the occasion for Gladstone's most dramatic political come-back. *GP* 1(b): John St. Loe

What does Green's support for Gladstone indicate about prevailing values or ethical norms of the Victorian Liberal party? Jonathan Parry observes that Gladstone, in his manifestation as 'The People's William' (from the 1860s),

> was the man most responsible for developing the myth of 'the people' as a moral force, sharing essentially Christian sentiments, bound together in a spiritual campaign against injustice, and collectively charged with making responsible judgments about broad principles of government.[24]

It is unnecessary to take entirely seriously Gladstone's belief in a 'collectively charged' people moralized by Christianity. Many of his critics objected to his moralizing tone and political opportunism. Yet we should not dismiss the expressed religious sentiment of British Liberals in the age of Gladstone and Green. Nor are we justified in marginalizing religion as a source of collective identity and purpose. John Vincent observed more than thirty years ago that 'for many [Victorian] Liberals, politics was not an autonomous activity, but one deriving from a religious centre ...'.[25] The stalwarts of the Liberal Party might be adherents of political economy or another science of society yet take Christianity as their fundament and (in Vincent's words) 'as the conscious expression of their modernity and their sense of belonging to a revolutionary *élite* working for a newer and better civilization.'[26] Vincent refers on this point to men like the Edward Baineses (father and son), John and Jacob Bright, Richard Cobden, Edward Miall and Samuel Morley, most of them *non-metropolitan* ideologists and politicians proud of their origin in and association with the business classes — Matthew Arnold's 'Philistines'.[27]

Liberalism as a creed and political movement during the Victorian era may have been more decisively shaped by unsophisticated, 'Hebraic' Christianity — especially Dissenting or Nonconformist Protestantism — than by any other cultural current, religious or secular.[28] Polite and educated Victorians, as envisaged by Matthew Arnold, may not have

---

Strachey to Charlotte B. Green (1882), transcription of a letter in CBG copy-book, pp. 103–13. On the basis of Green's support, and that of other liberal intellectuals, for Gladstonian foreign policy, see R. T. Shannon, *Gladstone and the Bulgarian Agitation 1876* (London: T. Nelson, 1963), pp. 203–20.

[24] Parry, *Rise and Fall of Liberal Government*, p. 252.
[25] Vincent, *Formation of the British Liberal Party*, p. xxxi.
[26] *Ibid.*, p. xxx.
[27] In *Culture and Anarchy* (1869) Arnold indicted leaders of Liberal opinion for their Puritanism, Hebraism and Philistinism. Edward Miall (1809–1881) edited the *Nonconformist* and was a leader, between the 1840s and 1870s, of the movement to disestablish the Church of England. 'Mialism' was 'the inadequate conception of man's totality', flawed by exclusive attention to 'the worth and grandeur of the religious side in man' (from Arnold's 'Preface,' Yale University Press edition 1994, ed. S. Lipman, p. 22).
[28] I use the terms Dissent and Nonconformity interchangeably, as they were virtual synonyms in public discourse after 1828. Parry proclaims boldly, 'Popular enthusiasm

invoked religion in the manner of the 'Philistine' commercial classes or that of the masses, yet Liberals — including professors, Parliamentarians and pitmen, as well as preachers — viewed political questions in light of religious beliefs and preoccupations. As I seek to demonstrate, understanding of the political-cultural common ground they shared is vital to understanding Victorian liberalism and Green's place in it.

Gladstone, the dominant figure in Victorian Liberal politics, and Green, one of liberalism's great philosophical advocates, have not often been discussed together. They may have met on more than one occasion. One opportunity for their direct or indirect interaction was over the issue of religious tests: Gladstone was MP for Oxford University during the early to mid-1860s, when Green was campaigning against tests of religious conformity at the universities. Yet the Green who appears to have made an impression upon Gladstone was the *fictional* one, the Oxford tutor 'Henry Grey' in Mrs. Humphry Ward's best–selling novel of 1888, *Robert Elsmere*. Gladstone was critical of the liberal religious tendencies displayed by Grey and other characters in the novel, which he reviewed in the May 1888 issue of *Nineteenth Century*.[29]

The different temperaments of Green and Gladstone and their different paths in life have obscured some meaningful political and philosophical affinities. Green believed politics, like other human activities, to be something more than a complex process by which individuals satisfied animal impulses and acted out instincts.[30] In his view, the ascendant 'hedonist' theories of human psychology, rooted in the theories of John Locke and David Hume, could not explain the moral strivings of individuals. As Richard Nettleship observed, 'To Professor Green, Locke was not the seventeenth-century champion of free-thought and independence, but the logical father of certain views of experience

---

for the Liberal party derived its greatest impetus from nonconformist commitment...' Yet he is ambiguous as to whether Dissent galvanized Gladstonian Liberalism or vice versa: 'Very few nonconformists of any denomination were unaffected by the surge of enthusiasm within the Liberal party in the 1860s.' J. Parry, *Democracy and Religion: Gladstone and the Liberal Party, 1867–1875* (CUP, 1986), pp. 199, 200.

[29]   See *The Gladstone Diaries. Volume XII: 1887–1891*, ed. H. C. G. Matthew (Oxford: Clarendon, 1994), pp. 106–11 [16 March–11 April 1888]; and W. S. Peterson, 'Gladstone's Review of *Robert Elsmere*: Some Unpublished Correspondence,' *Review of English Studies*, n.s. 21, no. 84 (1970), pp. 442–61.

[30]   'Empiricism certainly inclined to the belief that man is a material organism, that thought is a function of the nerves, and that circumstances control action. Against this Green would assert that the nature of man is spiritual, that the physical body is not the cause of thought but its influence, and that circumstances are no more than occasions for the exercise of freedom in choice.' G. S. Brett, 'Green, Thomas Hill' in *Encyclopaedia of Religion and Ethics*, vi, ed. J. Hastings (New York: Charles Scribner's Sons, 1920), p. 436.

which he found dominant in modern England...'.[31] Nor could evolutionism, positivism, utilitarianism and other doctrines then in vogue explain the reasons for which people submitted to government, imposed moral responsibilities upon themselves and created new political obligations.[32] This conviction, as much as his technical theories of humans' being and knowing, marked Green as a philosophical Idealist.[33]

Green criticized 'positivism' as expounded by Auguste Comte (1798–1857) and Herbert Spencer (1829–1902), which purported to explain in evolutionary terms the origin and growth of sentiments of goodness and altruism, but he was more opposed to these thinkers' assumptions and methods than to some of their conclusions. Green held that religious truths, the 'laws' of political economy and principles of social evolution could be reconciled to a considerable extent, since natural laws and moral action were alike expressions of divine order. He understood the 'metaphysic of ethics' as fundamental to the disciplines of moral psychology, jurisprudence (literally 'science of right') and sociology (science of morals in social interaction).[34] Ben Wempe points out that in Green's philosophical system the science of political economy was formally separate from metaphysic of ethics, as the individual could resist economic laws no more than he could the laws of nature. Yet individuals' moral choices were not absolutely determined by nature and people exercised morality independent of natural causation.[35] Indeed, Green argued that philosophy was scarcely possible unless one granted the fact of free will. However, not all willing actualized freedom. He criticized as simplistic the view of liberty as a mere absence of constraint by law and authority, and he conceived of freedom ('positive

[31] R. L. Nettleship, 'Professor T. H. Green. In Memoriam,' *Contemporary Review*, 41 (1882), p. 862.

[32] 'Popular Philosophy in its Relation to Life [1868],' in *Works*, iii, pp. 92–125; 'Introduction to the Moral Part of Hume's "Treatise [of Human Nature]" ' [1874], *Works*, i (Longmans, Green and Co., 1885), pp. 301–71; *Prolegomena to Ethics*, ed. A. C. Bradley (Oxford: Clarendon, 1883), Book IV, chaps. 3–4; *Lectures on the Principles of Political Obligation*, secs. 17–31 (as printed in *Harris and Morrow*). The *LPPO* were delivered in 1879–80 and initially printed in the second volume of Green's *Works* (Longmans, Green and Co., 1886), pp. 334–553.

[33] Modern idealism defines itself against 'realist', naturalistic–materialist and utilitarian schools. A succinct treatment of these and other philosophical positions is provided by R. N. Beck, *Handbook in Social Philosophy* (New York: Macmillan, 1979). British Idealists took issue with a view of man that posited his split existence between animal (or natural) and spiritual being. See Boucher, ed., *The British Idealists*, pp. xi–xx; and M. Mandelbaum, *History, Man, and Reason: A Study of Nineteenth Century Thought* (Baltimore: Johns Hopkins UP, 1971), chap. 11.

[34] *GP* 2 (numbered philosophical manuscripts), MS 10a: 'Lecture on moral philosophy' (ca. 1868).

[35] B. Wempe, *Beyond Equality: T. H. Green's Theory of Positive Freedom* (Delft: Eburon, Netherlands, 1986), pp. 195–7.

freedom') as a moral-spiritual capacity of individuals as much as a legal-political condition.[36] He imagined a moral society as one in which individuals discover and actualize the 'spiritual principle' in themselves through both the pursuit of individual goods and collective experiments in 'the organization of life'.[37]

While Gladstone gave relatively little thought to philosophy or metaphysics (in a technical sense), his theological and historical interests inclined him toward a 'spiritual' view of life resembling Green's. In comparing the views of Green and Gladstone on politics, there emerges a set of assumptions about moral purpose that reveals the basic ethos of Victorian liberalism. Gladstone's revelation in the 1860s that virtually all adult male Britons were 'morally entitled to come within the pale of the Constitution' was a key episode in the history of the British Liberal Party and of liberalism.[38] He was instrumental in the passage of the Reform Acts that extended the parliamentary franchise to male urban householders (1867) and male rural labourers (1884–5).[39] Gladstone's youthful Toryism habitually set constitution, Church and State on one side, and popular opinion on the other. His Liberal populism appears to have been prompted by his recognition, during the 1850s and '60s, that 'intelligent' working men endorsed the proper policies of peace, free trade and financial retrenchment.[40] Whereas Gladstone came to embrace democracy only in late middle age, Green entered adulthood as a passionate political Radical. Hereditary privilege and class discrimination were to Green among the most deplorable features of British society. He perceived the Volunteer movement of 1858–9 — the formation of militias ostensibly to forestall French aggression — as one

---

[36] See 'Liberal Legislation and Freedom of Contract' (1881) in *Harris and Morrow*, pp. 194–212. 'Though of course there can be no freedom among men who act not willingly but under compulsion, yet on the other hand the mere removal of compulsion, the mere enabling a man to do as he likes, is in itself no contribution to true freedom' (p. 199).

[37] See Green's 1879 professorial lecture, 'On the Different Senses of "Freedom" As Applied to Will and to the Moral Progress of Man,' secs. 5, 23–24 (in *Harris and Morrow*, pp. 228-49). There is a similar treatment of freedom, spirituality and civil life in *Prolegomena to Ethics* [henceforth *PE*], Book III, chaps. 3–5.

[38] House of Commons speech, 11 May 1864. Quoted in P. Magnus, *Gladstone. A Biography* (London: John Murray, 1954), p. 160.

[39] On Gladstone's conversion to democracy see R. Shannon, *Gladstone. Volume I: 1809–1865* (London: Methuen, 1984 [1982]), chaps. 6–8; H. C. G. Matthew, *Gladstone. 1809–1874* (OUP, 1986), chap. 5; and Parry, *Rise and Fall of Liberal Government*, chaps. 9, 11.

[40] Gladstone promoted such policies as Chancellor of the Exchequer (1852–5, 1859–65). During the same period the Whig leader Lord John Russell argued that franchise reform was justified by 'the improvement and intelligence of the people and the general spread of information since 1832.' Quoted in E. J. Evans, *The Forging of the Modern State. Early Industrial Britain, 1783–1870* (London: Longman, 1983), p. 344.

designed to intimidate the British working classes. In a letter to his family Green remarked,

> Fools talk at Oxford of... [the rifle corps] being desirable, in order that the gentry may keep down the chartists in the possible contingency of a rising. I should like to learn the use of the arm that I might be able to desert to the people, if it came to such a pass.[41]

Though he was not, strictly speaking, a Chartist, Green advocated a much broader (more Radical) franchise than did Gladstone, and he regarded the vote as a civil right. As a young Oxford don he joined the Reform League, an extra-parliamentary pressure group, and publicly advocated parliamentary reform between 1866 and 1868.[42] Shortly before Gladstone formed his first (Liberal) government, Green proclaimed,

> We who were reformers from the beginning, always said that the enfranchisement of the people was an end in itself. We said, and we were much derided for saying so, that citizenship only makes the moral man; that citizenship only gives that self-respect, which is the true basis of respect of others, and without which there is no lasting social order or real morality.[43]

Green's commitment to popular government was more deeply rooted than Gladstone's, and he took democratic theory to lengths that disturbed some contemporaries. Green believed the scope of moral agency in society would be enlarged by popular participation in politics at both the local and national levels. The question for him was not, as it was for Gladstone and Lord John Russell, whether the disenfranchised masses — or any social category — deserved the vote. Nor, Green suggested, was electoral reform to be implemented with definite political results in mind: 'Untie the man's legs, and then it will be time to speculate how he will walk.'[44]

Green maintained that men denied citizenship were denied the means of achieving 'real morality': 'citizenship only makes the moral man.' For Gladstone, on the other hand, democracy was instrumental:

---

[41] Quoted in R. L. Nettleship, 'Memoir,' p. xxiv. This passionate announcement presents an interesting contrast to Green's anti-militarism: he opposed state military build-up and British military interventions in Continental politics. Henry Nettleship, one of Green's early associates at Oxford, remarked that the *Morning Star*, the pacifist daily paper issued 1856–69, formed a staple of Green's reading. H. Nettleship recollection (1882) in *GP* 1(b).

[42] The People's Charter(s) of the late 1830s demanded above all the widening of the suffrage. The English republican movement of the 1860s and '70s, one of the animating forces behind the Reform League, was greatly influenced by earlier Chartist agitations. Green was favourably impressed by the plebeian Radicalism of the 1850s and '60s. Harvie, *Lights*, pp. 125–6 (noting speeches by Green reported in the *Oxford Chronicle*); R. L. Nettleship, 'Memoir,' pp. cx–cxiii.

[43] Green at a dinner of the Wellington Lodge of Odd Fellows, February 1868, quoted in R. L. Nettleship, 'Memoir,' p. cxii.

[44] *Ibid.*

popular sentiment could be registered as endorsement of enlightened policies and leaders.[45] Despite these and other differences, Green's and Gladstone's political views converged in the cluster of sentiments Christopher Harvie, Jonathan Parry and others have identified as Gladstonian. Gladstonianism was a mode of politics that sought to harness enlightened leadership and popular moral enthusiasm to 'Reform', representing the latter as a matter of national destiny. Even before the peak of Gladstone's political career J. S. Mill identified the 'characteristic feature' of Gladstone's ministerial life as a zeal 'to seek out things that require or admit of improvement.'[46]

Though Victorian Liberals were fond of declaring that men could not be made moral by act of Parliament, many readily conceded that legislation could promote morality and inhibit vice. Indeed, doctrinaire 'laissez-faire'-ism or libertarianism was becoming unfashionable among Liberals by the late 1860s. Though *moral* was more important than material improvement, both might be advanced through legislative action. Most self-described reformers of the era assumed that appropriate legislative activity would support rather than weaken the moral life and that judicious state action was compatible with social voluntarism. The Congregational minister and Radical-Liberal R. W. Dale, with whom both Gladstone and Green were acquainted, remarked in 1878 that 'within the last thirty years a very great and remarkable change has passed upon the theoretical views of the advanced Liberal party': the doctrine of restraining powers of government 'within the narrowest possible limits' had been replaced by the conviction that 'government may contribute very much to the positive development of national life.' Despite their valorization of the individual, most Liberals agreed with Dale that improvement was manifested in 'national advance'.[47] National morality, formed in part by religious belief, was exercised and developed through popular political participation. Collective moral feeling could shape the political agenda, at least so far as the public could render 'judgments about broad principles of government'.[48]

Green's theory of individual freedom as self-realization or self-perfection was linked to his conception of the common good by the mechanism of a democratic imperative. According to Green, the task of

---

[45] On Gladstone as apostle or prophet, see R. Kelley, *The Transatlantic Persuasion. The Liberal–Democratic Mind in the Age of Gladstone* (New York: Knopf, 1969), chaps. 1, 5–6. On contemporary perceptions of the danger of Gladstone's populism, see Christopher Harvie, 'Gladstonianism, the Provinces, and Popular Political Culture, 1860–1906' in *Victorian Liberalism*, ed. R. Bellamy (London: Routledge, 1990), pp. 152–74.

[46] Quoted in Bradley, *The Optimists*, p. 200.

[47] Quoted in Bradley, *The Optimists*, p. 211.

[48] Parry, *Rise and Fall of Liberal Government*, p. 252.

ruling oneself — in a negative sense, taming self-defeating desires and anti–social passions — was correlative to ruling others. Although he by no means discounted the role of self-interest in politics, as in private life, Green believed conscience and altruism would be activated in individuals allowed positive political rights. Without full (male) citizenship there could be no firm commitment to the social order and no workable consensus as to the moral purposes of the state. Indeed, as we shall see in Chapter Two below, Green held sovereignty itself to be contingent not upon the state's use or threat of force, or even upon the authority of determinate persons, but upon a moral consensus ratified in the everyday activities of society's members.

Like John Dalberg, Lord Acton (1843–1902), the eminent liberal Catholic historian and critic, Green saw a positive correlation between true liberty and conscience.[49] Conscience, as an element of moral judgment, was at once the individual's comprehension of a spiritual principle in the universe — as held by the Stoics, for whom conscience was in man's nature — and the effect on him of socialization (internalizing social norms and habits). Yet conscience by itself could not moralize the individual or make him free. As individuals participated in public life, in effect testing each others' moral capacities, the more 'freely' and completely would they be brought to 'consciousness of the absolutely desirable' (as opposed to the arbitrary and 'irrational') in themselves.[50]

Green's commitment to liberty in a social context, or what he called 'positive freedom', was not founded on purely abstract reasoning; he believed his optimism was justified by historical example. One was the 'ethical life' of the ancient Greek city-states. G. W. F. Hegel (1770–1831), in lectures posthumously published as 'Introduction to the Philosophy of History', stated that the ancient Greek 'Idea of freedom' 'was not yet a conscious morality, but a spontaneously ethical life in which the will of the individual stands firm upon the unmediated custom and habit that prescribes what is right and lawful.' In *Philosophy of Right* (1821) Hegel observed that it is in the Greek *poleis* 'that we see the principle of personal individuality arising,' along with 'the ethical life of freedom and happiness,' among citizens ('free men', not slaves or women).[51] For Hegel, of course, the story of human history was a growing realization of the meaning of freedom.[52] Green agreed with Hegel that moral freedom, insofar as it could be experienced collectively, had been invented,

[49] Acton stated, 'Liberty is that condition which makes it easy for conscience to govern' (Cambridge University Library, Add. MS. 4939). Quoted in G. E. Fasnacht, *Acton's Political Philosophy. An Analysis* (London: Hollis and Carter, 1952), p. 32.

[50] Green, 'Different Senses of "Freedom",' secs. 5–6.

[51] Hegel, *Introduction to 'The Philosophy of History', with an Appendix from 'The Philosophy of Right'*, trans. Leo Rauch, Indianapolis, IN: Hackett, 1988, pp. 95, 104.

[52] Acton's view was similar: 'Liberty is the one common topic of ancient and modern history. Every nation, every epoch, every religion, every philosophy, every science'

if only partly achieved, in the *polis*. 'The man … entering into the idea of the *polis* was equally qualified to rule and be ruled.'[53] Although Green did not *define* positive freedom as self-rule, the conception was clearly shaped by the classical Greek idea that the person who both ruled himself or herself and adjusted personal desires to accommodate the good of others had advanced beyond an immature condition of license.

The idea of freedom had been advanced as well by the growth of Christianity. Green shared with Hegel a belief in the 'positivity' of Christianity, that religious ideas and religious modes of knowing had governed progressive political change in the West.[54] Indeed, many of Green's contemporaries ignorant of Hegelian philosophy tacitly accepted this as well. In 'Four Lectures on the English Revolution' (1867), Green depicted Oliver Cromwell as a pioneer of freedom of conscience. The real heroes of Green's lectures, however, were the Independents (non-Anglican Protestants), believers in an 'inward light' whose 'spirit' refused to be 'bound' by ecclesiastical and civil laws.[55] This view of conscientious dissent and civil disobedience as premonition of modern liberty resembled that of Acton and of contemporary Nonconformist leaders (see Chapter Three below). More generally, the philosophy of history expressed in Green's English Revolution lectures and other writings was accepted by Victorian believers and unbelievers alike — namely, that social groups, societies and states were defined, and judged by posterity, by their religious and moral 'character'; and that mankind's spiritual and political quest for freedom was both origin and goal of history.

Benjamin Jowett and Mark Pattison mischievously and somewhat misleadingly characterized Green as a disciple of Hegel (see Chapter One below). Like Hegel, Green claimed to discern in the history of the Christian West the enlargement or extension of the conceptions of freedom and the common good. The 'conscientious citizen of modern Christendom' develops powers of judgment (Kant's *Urteilskraft*) which carry with them the recognition 'that every human person has an absolute

---

(Cambridge University Library, Add. MS 4941, quoted in Fasnacht, *Acton's Political Philosophy*, p. 6).

[53] Green, 'Different Senses of "Freedom",' secs. 5-6. Cognition of 'the sense of "autonomy of will"' in the *polis* was possible only in 'some favoured individuals' — i.e., *citizens* enjoying some degree of economic independence. See also *PE*, Book III, chap. 5, on the limitations of Greek freedom.

[54] Hegel claimed that the Christian character of European states remained even as the specifically Christian content of civil institutions was altered. See 'The Positivity of the Christian Religion' (1795–1800) in *Hegel. Early Theological Writings*, trans. T. M. Knox, with an introduction by R. Kroner (Philadelphia: Pennsylvania UP, 1971), pp. 67–118. Green cannot have read Hegel's essay, which was unpublished until the twentieth century, but Hegel's understanding of religion and social change was evident in those writings of Hegel with which Green was familiar.

[55] *Works*, iii, pp. 277–364.

value; … that every one has a "suum" which every one else is bound to render him.'[56] The positivity of Christianity, for Green, lay not only in the fact (as he saw it) that the Christian nation-state was the political community in which the highest degree of human freedom had hitherto been achieved; Christianity continued to shape the larger culture in which individuals in Western democracies were moralized and politicized:

> In modern Christendom, with the extension of citizenship, the security of family life to all men (so far as law and police can secure it), the establishment in various forms of Christian fellowship of which *the moralising functions grow as those of the magistrate diminish*, the number of individuals whom society awakens to interests in objects contributory to human perfection tends to increase.[57]

Green was convinced that Christian sociability and forms of fellowship helped produce a type of individual of higher moral potential than the subject of a despotic state or a member of a 'savage' society — an individual able to reconcile the apparently conflicting demands of self-perfection and the common good. The evolution of Christian thought and the progressive realization of Christian principles had led to and were continually improving modern 'free' society.[58]

Despite the esoteric formulation of Green's ethico-political philosophy, it coincided on many points with the convictions of contemporary Liberals about faith and moral progress. Victorian Liberals were convinced that the nation's well being depended as much on the moral 'health' of individuals as on the balance of trade or the efficiency of the Army and Navy. For Green and many Gladstonians, regardless of specific religious beliefs, it was inconceivable that individuals could behave morally without grounding in some positive faith. Comte imagined a secular-scientific stage of social evolution succeeding and obliterating the vestiges of Christian society, and 'Positivism' (the Comtean motto was 'Love, Order, Progress') held considerable attraction for some

---

[56] *PE*, sec. 217 (in the section titled 'The Extension of the Area of Common Good').

[57] 'Different Senses of "Freedom",' sec. 5 (emphasis mine). The paragraph continues: 'So far the modern state, in that full sense which Hegel uses the term (as including all the agencies for common good of a law-abiding people), does contribute to the realization of freedom, if by freedom we understand the autonomy of the will or its determination by rational objects, objects which help to satisfy the demand of reason, the effort after self–perfection.'

[58] Acton had noted the significance of the 'discoveries' of natural law (12th–13th centuries) and conscience (by Socinius and the Independents, 16th–17th centuries) and commented in 1862, 'Reverence for conscience is the germ of all civil freedom, and the way in which Christianity served it.' Quoted in Fasnacht, *Acton's Political Philosophy*, p. 31.

members of the British educated classes around mid century.[59] Yet despite their anticlericalism, few British Positivists were sanguine about the withering away of Christianity and its replacement by a superior ethical system.[60]

When Gladstone examined ancient and modern history he became convinced that the survival of a complex commercial-industrial state depended on a shared faith rooted in the nation's history (i.e. *not* a synthetic, scientific philosophy).[61] The idea of national faith, however, gradually became detached in his mind from a national (or state) church, as he came to conceive of the visible church as the nation of Christian citizens.[62] Gladstone's faith, like that of John Henry Newman, had been founded on dogmas, guarded by one catholic church.[63] During the 1830s and '40s Gladstone was an almost fanatical upholder of Anglicanism as he understood it. Like Newman and other members of the Oxford Movement (or Tractarians), Gladstone prophesized the moral dissolution of the British nation with the erosion of the religious Establishment.[64] As late as 1865, when campaigning to retain his Parliamentary seat for Oxford University, Gladstone insisted that the ancient

[59] F. W. Knickerbocker, *Free Minds: John Morley and His Friends* (Cambridge, MA: Harvard UP, 1943); W. Irvine, *Apes, Angels, and Victorians. Darwin, Huxley, and Evolution* (Cleveland, OH: World Publishing Co., 1959 [1955]), chaps. 14–18; C. Kent, *Brains and Numbers: Elitism, Comtism and Democracy in Mid-Victorian England* (Toronto UP, 1978); and T. R. Wright, *The Religion of Humanity: the Impact of Comtean Positivism on Victorian Britain* (CUP, 1986).

[60] T. H. Huxley, while a member of the London School Board in 1870, referred to his own faction in the struggles of that body as the Third or Scientific Party (neither Protestant nor Catholic). Yet, as Helen Lynd puts it, 'Huxley, Spencer, Frederic Harrison, and Matthew Arnold conceived that in criticizing the churches they were not abandoning religion but laying the foundation for a more living religion and morality' (Lynd, *England in the Eighteen-Eighties*, p. 341). Huxley insisted that children in the Board Schools read from the English Bible — and not merely, as is sometimes maintained, because he believed in its 'literary' value.

[61] Bradley, Colin Matthew and Parry have suggested that Gladstone's Classical researches (including the three-volume *Studies on Homer and the Homeric Age* [1858]) led him to the conviction that a civilization required a core religious belief, cherished by the masses as well as the elite, if it was to avoid going the way of the ancient Greek states. Bradley, *The Optimists*, pp. 78–9; J. P. Parry, 'The State of Victorian Political History,' *HJ*, 25 (1983), pp. 479–80; Matthew, *Gladstone. 1809–1874*, pp. 152–5.

[62] D. Schreuder, 'Gladstone and the Conscience of the State' in *Conscience of the Victorian State*, ed. P. Marsh (Syracuse, NY: Syracuse UP, 1979), pp. 73–134.

[63] Newman took the independent or 'free' intellect as the greatest peril to salvation (not to mention temporal order): 'Liberalism is the mistake of supposing that there is a right of private judgement, that is, that there is no existing authority on earth competent to interfere with the liberty of individuals in reasoning and judging for themselves.' J. H. Newman, *Apologia Pro Vita Sua* (1864), quoted in Bradley, *The Optimists*, p. 86. Gladstone, however, believed in man's sinfulness *and* his freedom.

[64] Gladstone went so far as to argue (in *The State in its Relations with the Church*, 1838) that the state should purge heterodox clergy in order to allow the Church to moralize society. Shannon, *Gladstone I*, pp. 50–7, 76–87. Gladstone's fantasy of a national clergy was

universities should be kept orthodox: he would rather see 'Oxford level with the ground than its religion regulated in the manner which would please Bishop Colenso' (Colenso being only the most recent Churchman to question the veracity of Biblical narrative).[65]

Though Gladstone remained in his own religious habits a High Churchman, ever ready to criticize the heresies of liberal Protestantism, he became a proponent of undenominational Christianity — at least in part because he came to appreciate its political and social uses. In one of his characteristic shifts of attitude combining political expediency and emotional conviction, Gladstone began to listen carefully to Dissenting Protestant leaders during the 1860s.[66] Like his 'conversion' to democracy, his embrace of Dissent had powerful political repercussions — first registered in educational policy and the question of Irish Church endowment. Gladstone was impressed (or pretended to be) by leaders of Dissenting opinion, made appeals to their followers during his first Liberal premiership and helped ensure Dissenters' traditional loyalty to the Liberal Party.[67] In effect, Gladstone had concluded that a sort of free trade in Christianity would better facilitate the moralization of society than the ministrations of an Established Church. This view of the *civil* and social functions of religion was surprisingly close to Green's.

Green's religious creed was quite different from Gladstone's, and in essential matters his view of religion changed less drastically over time. Son of a moderately evangelical country rector (gentleness and lack of ambition were two of Valentine Green's qualities affectionately recalled by his son), he became a Broad Churchman, opposing doctrinal narrowness in any and all sects. Green was in this sense a successful product of Rugby School, an institution dedicated, in the mind of its most famous

---

an unintentional parody of certain ideas of S. T. Coleridge: see B. Knights, *The Idea of the Clerisy in the Nineteenth Century* (CUP, 1978), and J. Morrow, *Coleridge's Political Thought: Property, Morality and the Limits of Traditional Discourse* (New York: St. Martin's, 1990).

[65] Gladstone to a Dissenter (J. Baldwin Brown), July 29, 1865: letter reprinted in *Correspondence on Church and Religion of W. E. Gladstone*, ed. D. C. Lathbury (London: Macmillan, 1910), pp. 219–20. John William Colenso, Bishop of Natal, South Africa from 1853, was illegally deposed for heresy in 1865. Author of *Commentary on the Epistle to the Romans* (1861) and *The Pentateuch Examined* (1862–3). On the Colenso controversy, see especially G. Faber, *Jowett: A Portrait with Background* (Cambridge, MA: Harvard UP, 1958), chap. 14.

[66] G. I. T. Machin, 'Gladstone and Nonconformity in the 1860s: the Formation of an Alliance,' *HJ*, 17 (1974), pp. 347–64.

[67] See discussion in 5.6–5.7 below. Gladstone's title 'apostle of Liberalism' (Kelley, *Transatlantic Persuasion*, chap. 6) is apt. He 'claimed to discern in the public mind ... [a] commitment to the "laws of eternal righteousness" which the leading Dissenting preachers ... expounded in the sermons which he read and approvingly scored.' His 'conception of Liberalism as a joint and zealous struggle for economy, self-government and Christianisation was massively powerful and massively influential.' Parry, *Rise and Fall of Liberal Government*, pp. 251–2, 254.

headmaster, Thomas Arnold, to the production of self-governing 'Christian gentlemen'.[68] With his Classical education and indoctrination in liberal Anglican, 'latitudinarian' Christianity, Green might be expected to have regarded Dissent as theologically crude and Dissenters as uncultivated. Yet he openly sympathized with Dissent, which was at that time more evangelical (on the whole) than the Establishment. An anti-dogmatist, he believed that the English universities, like all institutions of civil and political life, should be thrown open to individuals without regard to religious affiliation, and he fought alongside University Liberals to repeal tests of conformity in the Ancient Universities. Green conformed to the Thirty-Nine Articles of the Anglican creed in order to take his Oxford fellowship in 1860. According to Henry Nettleship, Green believed it politically naïve to refuse such pledges: to be scrupulous about the letter of the articles when one accepted the spirit of Christian teachings would leave the colleges to High Churchmen and Tories.[69] Green became thereafter a chief representative of the anti-doctrinal sensibility at Oxford.

The particular qualities of Green's religion will be discussed in subsequent chapters, but it bears mentioning here that Green emphasized the moral and social *utility* of religion. Like liberals of his own and other times, Green saw that doctrinal controversy eroded morality and civility as well as religion. As for the constructive dimension of religion, Green and Gladstone shared the view that 'faith' was the basis of the best in human nature. Both defied the naturalistic spirit of the age by denying that religious belief could be reduced by science or philosophy to a more fundamental instinct or mental phenomenon. That Green viewed religion as an irreducible quantity is revealed in a statement in 1872 to his former pupil Henry Scott Holland, subsequently a Canon of St. Paul's and a founder of the Christian Social Union. Green avowed, 'I have never dreamt of philosophy doing instead of religion. My own interest in it, I believe, is wholly religious ...'. He explained:

---

[68] D. Newsome, *Godliness and Good Learning. Four Studies on a Victorian Ideal* (London: Cassell, 1961), especially chap. 1; and A. Briggs, 'Thomas Hughes and the Public Schools,' *Victorian People. A Reassessment of Persons and Themes 1851–1867*, 2nd ed. (Chicago, IL: Chicago UP, 1970), pp. 140–67. Certain of Green's contemporaries nevertheless noted his resistance to the Rugbeian mould. As a sixth former Green rationalized absenting himself from compulsory chapel and he was squeamish about exercising prefectural power. Algernon Grenfell, who went up to Oxford with Green from Rugby in 1855, described him as ever 'a boy apart ... a plant growing, not a brick being moulded.' *GP* 1(b): Revd. Algernon Grenfell to Charlotte Green, 10 October 1882, letter transcribed in CBG copy-book, pp. 141–9.

[69] *GP* 1b: H. Nettleship to C. B. Green, 1882. On the issue of religious conformity at Oxford at mid century, see W. R. Ward, *Victorian Oxford* (London: Frank Cass, 1965), chaps. 11–12; Harvie, *Lights of Liberalism*, chaps. 3–4, 6; H. A. L. Fisher, *Life of James Bryce*, i (London: Macmillan, 1927), chap. 3.

> There can be no greater satisfaction to me than to think that I at all helped to lay the intellectual platform for your religious life; and that, not merely because if I were only a breeder of heretics I should suspect my philosophy. If it is sound, it ought to supply intellectual formulae for the religious life whether lived by an 'orthodox' clergyman or (let us say) a follower of Mazzini ... [Philosophy] is to me (not exactly, in the popular phrase, 'the handmaid of religion') but the reasoned intellectual expression of the effort to get to God.[70]

Certain of Green's contemporaries — notably, Sidgwick, John Morley and Leslie Stephen — lapsed into agnosticism because faith seemed to impose demands incompatible with those of intellect.[71] Green not only refused to view religion as an inferior means to the true and the good but he habitually rejected the opposition of faith to reason as false. He was completely unsympathetic to burying skepticism in obedience to ecclesiastical authority, as did Newman, E. B. Pusey and Gerard Manley Hopkins.[72] Intellect, reason, the attempt to understand the natural world by comprehending its laws — all served an overarching spiritual purpose. Green stated in his 1878 lay sermon 'Faith',

> The human spirit is one and indivisible, and the desire to know what nature is and means is as inseparable from it as the consciousness of God and the longing for reconciliation with him.[73]

Green was intent upon demonstrating the impact of religious belief on individual behaviour and social life, which was manifest in 'the development of the moral ideal' (*Prolegomena to Ethics*). As we shall see in subsequent chapters, Green's personal faith informed his moral theory, even if some contemporaries chided him for his religious heterodoxy. Henry Nettleship expressed puzzlement that Green's refusal to believe in the miraculous aspects of the Gospel had not apparently disturbed 'the basis' of his 'evangelical piety'. He never doubted Green's 'complete belief in the code of ethics universally accepted as Christian as a practical guide for conduct.'[74] Green was but little concerned with reconciling specific Christian teachings, much less dogmas; nor was he especially interested in comparing religious ideas to some universal moral code. Rather, he explored the epistemology of Christian belief,

---

[70] The letter (dated October 6, 1872) was occasioned by Holland's ordination. S. Paget, ed., *Henry Scott Holland. Memoirs and Letters* (London: J. Murray, 1921), p. 65.

[71] See especially Annan, *Leslie Stephen*.

[72] Interestingly, Daniel Brown has argued that Hopkins was susceptible to many aspects of Green's thought: see *Hopkins' Idealism: Philosophy, Physics, Poetry* (Oxford: Clarendon, 1997).

[73] Printed in *Works*, iii, pp. 253–76. Quotation p. 264.

[74] The adjectives 'complete' and 'practical' are significant here. 'Of the *pain* of doubt, so far as I know, he felt very little ... He knew nothing of mental cataclysms, and had none of the qualities which make interesting converts.' GP 1(b): Nettleship to Charlotte Green (1882). Nettleship implicitly contrasted Green's case to those of the conscientious doubters of his time, like Stephen, Sidgwick and A. H. Clough.

emphasizing the moral and mental habits of individuals who experienced Christian piety — habits which underlay their efforts at self-realization and consequently governed their social interaction. In Green's view, the proper channelling of moral sentiment, including religious belief and practice, was to lead to a liberal millennium.

Many other Radical-Liberals during the last three decades of the nineteenth century sought to employ religious belief in the service of political and social 'reform' — preaching and often practicing what Melvin Richter calls a 'politics of conscience'. Many of the most active of these were liberal Anglicans and Dissenters.[75] Green's religiously informed liberalism was as pragmatic as it was principled, insofar as it promoted the social cohesion of the Liberal party in an emerging age of mass politics. Like Gladstone, Green recognized that shared religious 'spirit', if not common adherence to specific religious observances, could constitute the basis for lasting social and political cooperation. Through the practice of free faith individuals explored the boundaries of their nature and learned how true freedom entailed both resistance to authority and adherence to shared principles ratified in social and political practice. Green's optimism about the spiritual consciousness of the 'common people' was partly based on his awareness of how popular Protestantism buttressed the 'Englishman's birthright': popular religion reinforced a sense of constitutional inheritance (e.g. the right to resist oppression) that lent itself to Liberal goals.[76] This spiritual consciousness was experienced not merely 'negatively' — as identification of restraints to be thrown off in the name of justice or freedom — but positively, as a zeal for social improvement, in the quest for which citizens might agree to impose upon themselves new social obligations. Although Green's conception of liberal society and polity was sometimes expressed in esoteric terms, it was congenial to many of his contemporaries because of rather than despite its religious resonances.

Shared appreciation of the transformative power of religion and democratic citizenship was a significant factor in the social cohesion of the Liberal Party, although this was not enough — in the long run — to

[75] See W. J. Rowland, 'Some Free Church Pioneers of Social Reform,' *Congregational Quarterly*, 35 (1957), pp. 134–45; K. S. Inglis, 'English Nonconformity and Social Reform, 1880–1900,' *Past and Present*, 13 (1958), pp. 73–88; Peter d'A. Jones, *The Christian Socialist Revival, 1877–1914* (Princeton UP, 1968), pp. 86–94, 421ff; R. J. Helmstadter, 'The Nonconformist Conscience' in *The Conscience of the Victorian State*, ed. Marsh, pp. 135–72; W. M. King, 'Hugh Price Hughes and the British "Social Gospel",' *Journal of Religious History*, 13 (1984), pp. 66–82; S. Meacham, *Toynbee Hall and Social Reform, 1880–1914: the Search for Community* (New Haven, CT: Yale UP, 1987).

[76] P. Joyce, *Visions of the People: Industrial England and the Question of Class, 1848–1914* (CUP, 1991), especially Part Three; Biagini, *Liberty, Retrenchment and Reform*, chaps. 1, 4; and J. Vernon, *Politics and the People. A Study in English Political Culture, c. 1815–1867* (CUP, 1993), chaps. 7–8, conclusion.

avert the disintegration of traditional Liberalism. When Green died in March 1882, the Liberal Party was in the seat of power yet dividing within itself.[77] A vacillating tactic combining agrarian reform with coercion in Ireland was strengthening the forces of nationalism at the expense of liberalism. (In May 1882, Charles Stewart Parnell, the 'Uncrowned King of Ireland', was released from Kilmainham Gaol, where he had been imprisoned on a charge of seditious conspiracy.) Britain's quashing of Arabi Pasha's rebellion in Egypt (1881–2) was not domestically popular and chilled relations with other Great Powers, especially France. Orthodox Liberals championed 'just' struggles for national liberation — such as the Magyar, Italian and Polish struggles earlier in the century — yet deplored militarism. British agriculture and land values declined as foreign imports increased, hastening the decay of landed society. To a greater degree than had been the case during the preceding thirty years, Capital and Labour seemed to represent conflicting political interests.

Liberals' departure from the party of Gladstone after 1886 over Irish Home Rule, whether quiet or ostentatious, often masked their disagreement over wider issues, such as imperial relations, labour law and social reform.[78] They disagreed about remedies for the 'labour unrest' of the later 1880s, which involved male artisans and (more alarmingly) unskilled male labourers, women and juveniles.[79] Radicals disagreed with Whigs and among themselves over the nature and extent of 'state intervention'.[80] By ca. 1900 some of Green's moderately Liberal contemporaries had come to view the 1860s and '70s as liberalism's Golden Age. Some who could not follow the late Victorian and Edwardian shift of Liberal ideology and practice found in 'memorializing' Green a con-

---

[77] On late Victorian political instability and the challenge to democracy, see especially R. Shannon, *The Crisis of Imperialism 1865–1916* (London: Palladin, 1984), parts 2–3; and M. Bentley, *Politics Without Democracy 1815–1914* (London: Fontana, 1984), Part 2.

[78] J. F. Glaser, 'English Nonconformity and the Decline of Liberalism,' *AHR*, 63 (1958), pp. 352–63; S. Koss, *Nonconformity in Modern British Politics* (Hamden, CT: Archon, 1975), pp. 8–10.

[79] Labour unrest among hitherto non-unionized workers (e.g. the London dockers in 1889) and the 'sweated trades' has long been recognized as a factor of late Victorian liberal crisis. See H. Pelling, *The Origins of the Labour Party, 1880–1900*, 2nd ed. (Oxford: Clarendon, 1965). Judith Walkowitz has broadened this assessment by pointing to male fear of female (especially working-class) indiscipline and violence: *City of Dreadful Delight. Narratives of Sexual Danger in Late-Victorian London* (Chicago: UP Chicago, 1992).

[80] See e.g. E. Bristow, 'The Liberty and Property Defence League and Individualism,' *HJ*, 18 (1975), pp. 761–89; Shannon, *Crisis of Imperialism*, chaps. 5, 8–9; M. Barker, *Gladstone and Radicalism: the Reconstruction of Liberal Policy in Britain, 1885–94* (Hassocks, Sussex: Harvester, 1975); T. A. Jenkins, *Gladstone, Whiggery and the Liberal Party, 1874–1886* (Oxford, 1988); and M. Taylor, *Men Versus the State: Herbert Spencer and Late Victorian Individualism* (Oxford: Clarendon, 1992).

venient means of emphasizing the constructive and redemptive role which liberalism had claimed for itself. Liberals who moved beyond what Green's philosophy explicitly endorsed, and who came to identify themselves as Radicals, Socialists and even Conservatives, were also eager to claim Green's moral legacy. This study attempts to show not only how T. H. Green contributed to Victorian liberalism but how Green as a cultural construct intrudes upon present understanding of him as a historical figure.

SOME OBSERVATIONS ON HISTORICAL METHOD

As I demonstrate in Chapter One, Green scholarship and general accounts of modern British thought reveal ambivalence about Green, or uncertainty about how to situate him within the movements of his own time or within the canon of political philosophy. I have observed already that the attribution to Green by some contemporaries of 'Hegelian' ideas has perhaps been one of the chief factors encouraging modern scholars to locate Hegelianism and German Idealism as the most immediate or the governing context of Green's thought. (This line of inquiry has of course resulted in important findings about congruence between Hegelianism and British Idealism.) Likewise, the marked anti-naturalistic bias of Green's thought (see 1.4–1.5, 2.2–2.3 below) and his criticisms of Locke, Hume and Spencer appear to have led some scholars to assume that Green was either hostile towards or unimpressed by 'British thought'. Others regard Green's writings and his public activities as unproblematic realizations of thought, as conscious, deliberate applications of theory (like Marxian *praxis*) or as natural derivatives of his social position.[81] These approaches have led to some interesting insights about Green's stated or unstated intentions and thereby to imputation of historical significance, but they also disregard the tentative or exploratory character of, for instance, Green's civic activities and the extent to which his ideas were worked through in his social practice.

Other interpretive tendencies have, I believe, served to obscure the picture of Green. Historians have more often resorted to 'functional' than to 'meaningful' analysis of Green and his work. Functional analyses focus on questions of precise causality, purporting to explain why X thought or did Y, or how (in what way) A was able to influence B. Melvin Richter has argued that Green's evangelical upbringing accounts for the tone of his thought; subsequently, scholars have

---

[81] See C. Jenks, 'T. H. Green, the Oxford Philosophy of Duty and the English Middle Class,' *British Journal of Sociology*, 28 (1977), pp. 481–97; and Melvin Richter, 'Intellectual and Class Alienation: Oxford Idealist Diagnoses and Prescriptions,' *European Journal of Sociology*, 7 (1966), pp. 1–26.

claimed, without elaboration or careful justification, that Green's thought assumed a particular form because of this evangelical upbringing. But this claim raises questions about how evangelicals thought and whether they all thought alike. Functional explanations also assess beliefs and actions according to their social utility and rationality *from the viewpoint of the modern observer*: because a person wanted to accomplish X, he thought or did Y; or, given a particular social condition or situation, it was reasonable for him to believe or do specific things. But this approach begs the question of why Green perceived conditions as he did, and why others similarly positioned may have perceived them differently, and it limits cultural analysis to sociology of knowledge. Functional analysis can go only a short way towards revealing the social dimensions of meaning.

I try to engage in my assessment of Green in a form of 'cultural meaning' analysis that has been employed effectively by Stefan Collini and Laurence Dickey. In his richly contextualized study of Hegel, Dickey argues that

> A Christian theology of history rather than an Hellenic ideal constitutes the 'motivational situation' within which the [i.e., Hegel's] writings of the 1790s were written ... *Sittlichkeit* [a Protestant conception of morals and right living] was an ideal — an inspiration for, and telos of, religio-political activism.[82]

Hegel did not simply reflect upon the ideas of the great ethicists and philosophers of the Western tradition; his work was informed by the narrower, more homely cultural ideas of German Pietist Protestantism. Hegel scholars had already noted how Hegel's thought bore the imprint of his Swabian and Lutheran background, but none had decoded that constitutive culture as systematically as Dickey. This is more than to state that Hegel's philosophy did not occur in a cultural vacuum. It is to recognize that analysis of culture, to paraphrase the American literary critic Kenneth Burke, produces meanings for us as we place objects of study 'in contexts of varying scope.'[83] Dickey borrows the term 'motivational situation' from Max Weber's *Theory of Social and Economic Organization*, observing that Weber 'always tried to use contextualism to assess the "motivational situation" of historical actors and to illuminate what he called "the subjective-meaning complex of action". "Meaningful", not "causal", relationships were what Weber was trying to establish.'[84]

I am likewise interested in the cultural situations that informed Green's ideas and actions and shaped the social constructions of meanings. This involves paying attention to his 'life-world', including the broad ethical and political culture in which he participated, as well as

[82] Dickey, *Hegel*, p. 149.
[83] K. Burke, *A Grammar of Motives* (Berkeley, CA: California UP, 1969), p. 77, quoted in Dickey, *Hegel*, p. 298.
[84] Dickey, *Hegel*, p. 299, n. 18.

the narrower academic-professional culture he helped create.[85] 'Life' must be given as much weight as 'text', even in the ascription of textual meaning: not only a writer's stated concerns and goals must be considered but also those of the people to whom he was responding. One must also take under consideration a wider range of 'texts'. Until recently historians have given remarkably little attention (during the Victorian or other periods) to relationships between political theorists (or 'thinkers') and political participants, or between high theory and plebeian political opinion.[86] Except for Green's lecture 'Liberal Legislation and Freedom of Contract' (1881), Green scholars have neglected his ethical and political statements delivered to, or intended for consumption by, popular audiences—occasions when Green often eschewed the technical language of Idealist philosophy for the purpose of more effective communication.[87] Examination of Green's contributions to 'middle-brow' or non-specialist publications such as *North British Review* and *Contemporary Review*, and of his speeches at public meetings or to working men's clubs, provides insight into Green's relation to popular liberalism.

Even terms and idioms used by Green the philosopher—*ex cathedra*, as it were—may carry cultural meanings that remain unnoticed when his statements are read exclusively against those of other Great Thinkers or in relation to 'political languages'. Practitioners of 'linguistic contextualism', such as John Pocock, Quentin Skinner, Anthony Pagden, Stefan Collini and Donald Winch construe political-philosophical texts by 'locating' them in political languages or discourses.[88] They interpret texts by demonstrating the orderly, conventional and derivative nature of individual acts of speaking and writing. By comparing linguistic practices of political thinkers across time, they have categorized the symbolic content of political languages according

---

[85] The notion of a life-world as a surrounding medium of intellectual activity was employed by Edmund Husserl and Martin Heidegger and has been revived by Dominick LaCapra: *Rethinking Intellectual History: Texts, Contexts, Language* (Ithaca, NY: Cornell UP, 1983).

[86] On 'plebeian' political thought and discourse in the Victorian period, see especially Biagini, *Liberty, Retrenchment and Reform*; and Vernon, *Politics and the People*.

[87] A notable exception is Peter Nicholson's 'T. H. Green and State Action: Liquor Legislation,' *HPT*, 6 (1985), pp. 517–50 (reprinted in *Philosophy of T.H.Green*, ed. A.Vincent (Aldershot, England: Gower, 1986), pp. 76–103), dealing primarily with Green's reported speeches to temperance audiences. On intellectuals' widening sense of public life, see J. Stapleton, *Political Intellectuals and Public Identities in Britain Since 1850* (Manchester: Manchester UP, 2001).

[88] E.g. J. G. A. Pocock, *The Machiavellian Moment: Florentine Political Thought and the Atlantic Republican Tradition* (Princeton, NJ: Princeton UP, 1975); Q. Skinner, *Foundations of Modern Political Thought*, 2 vols. (CUP, 1978); A. Pagden, ed., *The Languages of Political Theory in Early Modern Europe* (CUP, 1987). An early statement of the approach is Skinner, 'Meaning and Understanding in the History of Ideas,' *History and Theory*, 8 (1969), pp. 3–53.

to discourses (e.g., civic humanism), and this approach to intellectual history has produced interesting insights into the work of Machiavelli, James Harrington, Locke and others. The categories ('paradigms') themselves can be refined or disputed insofar as the autonomy of conceptualized languages can be challenged by demonstrating variations within the posited languages or divergent rhetorical intentions or political goals within a language community.[89]

I need not rehearse here the various objections of historians and philosophers to the method of the 'Cambridge School' of intellectual historians, but one broad issue deserves mention here because of its relevance to the present study. This concerns the historical significance of speakers' and writers' conformity (or nonconformity) to the posited discursive paradigms. Mark Bevir and Mark Francis have noted how 'hard contextualism' (which Bevir associates with Pocock in particular) pre-selects the supposedly autonomous and specialized discourses within which acts of speech and writing are rendered meaningful, so that unconventional speakers/writers become marginalized.[90] Indeed, it is difficult to imagine any imputation of textual or contextual meaning being possible at all without some process of selection and comparison, but focus on discourse as the bedrock or irreducible reality of social and political thought can obscure the relations of speakers/writers to their societies. While discourses do establish 'communities' of authors often far removed in time and space, focus on discourse may arbitrarily preclude comparison of statements by speakers/writers inhabiting the same social and political environment. One effect of this is that language is effectively rendered *asocial*, insofar as the discourses traced by linguistic contextualists appear to assume the roles of independently thinking entities, divorced from human agency. Another is that social meanings of arguments are artificially narrowed: by focusing on *textual* traditions (and texts of High Culture at that), linguistic contextualism situates social and political ideas in discourses maintained by comparatively small numbers of elite thinkers, while ignoring other informing cultures. Traditions, textual and otherwise, constitute culture, yet culture cannot be interpreted as a sum of traditions or discourses.

---

[89] M. Francis, 'The Use and Abuse of Paradigms in the History of Political Thought,' *Politics*, 18 (1983), pp. 93–9; Larry Dickey, 'The Pocockian Moment,' *JBS*, 26 (1987), pp. 98–107; D. Harlan, 'Intellectual History and the Return of Literature' and D. Hollinger, 'The Return of the Prodigal: The Persistence of Historical Knowing,' *AHR*, 94 (1989), pp. 581–621; and M. Richter, 'Reconstructing the History of Political Languages,' *History and Theory*, 29 (1990), pp. 38–70.

[90] Francis, 'Uses and Abuses of Paradigms'; M. Bevir, 'The Errors of Linguistic Contextualism,' *History and Theory*, 31 (1992), pp. 276–9; M. Bevir, 'Review Article: English Political Thought in the Nineteenth Century,' *HPT*, 17 (1996), pp. 114–27; M. Bevir, 'Begriffsgeschichte,' *History and Theory*, 39 (2000), pp. 273–84.

In the interest of demonstrating congruence between Green's intellectual and practical work and contemporary shifts in ethical and political attitudes, this study most often considers Green's statements with reference to the 'argument' of mid and late Victorian Radicalism. By Radical argument I mean the discursive expression of a Radical world-view as used to achieve political ends. My use of the term argument is similar to that employed by Stefan Collini in his study of Leonard Hobhouse. Despite the somewhat disconcerting vagueness of his definition of 'argument' as 'a certain level of discourse,' a 'medium ... in which ... thought moved and had its being,' I have adopted Collini's method by considering the arguments of Green and his contemporaries in terms of the 'forensic resources' furnished by the political culture from which the arguments were generated and to which they contributed.[91] Although I cannot attempt here a reconstruction of Victorian political culture, I do at least refer to social contexts of argument and try to indicate how moral and political vocabularies employed in elite debates related to underlying beliefs and *moeurs*.[92]

Analysis of argument entails reconstructing what Collini calls '"the context of refutation" — that is, an account of the theories which [a writer or speaker] was attacking, the arguments he was rebutting, the assessments he was challenging.' Furthermore, it requires sensitivity to the 'overriding [rhetorical] force' of discourse, familiarity with 'the emotional resonances of key terms', and awareness of 'the exploitable tensions within accepted beliefs.'[93] This requires not only close reading of texts but knowledge of idioms and rhetorical functions characteristic of the cultures in which arguments are embedded. (Thus Collini's method might well be termed 'soft contextualism': it situates speech-acts in political and popular culture as well as literary culture.)[94] One must know, in effect, what contemporary audiences of texts/speeches knew:

> Political arguments ... must, if they are to have any persuasiveness, deploy, re-work, or otherwise make use of the shared evaluative language of those to

[91] S. Collini, *Liberalism and Sociology: L.T. Hobhouse and Political Argument in England, 1880–1914* (CUP, 1979), p. 9. Ronald Formisano comments usefully on the use and abuses of the political culture concept: 'The Concept of Political Culture,' *Journal of Interdisciplinary History*, 31 (2001), p. 393–426. I am indebted to Professor Jack C. Knight for his comments about my references to political culture in the dissertation on which the present work is based.

[92] Recent studies attending to 'forensic resources' of argument and culture include P. Joyce, *Democratic Subjects. Self and Society in Nineteenth-Century England* (CUP, 1994); D. Wahrman, *Imagining the Middle Class. The Political Representation of Class in Britain, c. 1780–1840* (CUP, 1995); and J. S. Meisel, *Public Speech and the Culture of Public Life in the Age of Gladstone* (New York: Columbia UP, 2001).

[93] Collini, *Liberalism and Sociology*, p. 9.

[94] On refining the 'hard contextualist' approach, see Francis and Morrow, *A History of English Political Thought in the Nineteenth Century*, introduction; and Bevir, 'Review Article: English Political Thought in the Nineteenth Century'.

whom they are addressed, and hence must appeal to the ideals and aspirations which that language represents. In this sense, political theories are parasitic upon the less explicit habits of response and evaluation that are deeply embedded in the culture.[95]

Thus, we must acknowledge the ethico-political preoccupations of Green's audiences as a way of hearing how terms, ideas, even styles of delivery would have been received. Some of Green's most cogent ethical and political statements were not written for philosophers, nor even for university students, but were presented to audiences gathered for particular purposes, such as temperance agitation or mobilization of support for candidates for public office. We can easily imagine that the first audiences of Green's lectures on political obligation at Oxford in 1879–80 might have suspended judgment in order to listen to an argument to the end; whereas the clergymen, temperance enthusiasts and provincial political activists who heard 'Liberal Legislation and Freedom of Contract' at Leicester in 1881 must have attended to Green's words in a very different, partisan manner. The social meanings of Green's statements were determined, to some extent, by the nature of his audiences.

Although I am indebted to the work of pioneering linguistic contextualists like Pocock and Skinner, I attempt to frame ethico-political language within debates occurring in social rather than literary space. Because of the passage of time, some of those debates are — from our current vantage point—every bit as esoteric as narrowly 'literary' ones. Yet only by acknowledging the obscure as well as the familiar contemporary debates can we grasp what situations and circumstances motivated Green and what factors shaped the reception of his ideas by others. This is similar to the 'archaeology of knowledge' approach of Michel Foucault:

> Such an analysis does not belong to the history of ideas or of science: it is rather an inquiry whose aim is to rediscover on what basis knowledge and theory become possible; within what space or order knowledge was constituted; on the basis of what historical a priori, and in the element of what positivity, ideas could appear, sciences be established, experience be reflected in philosophies, rationalities formed, only, perhaps, to dissolve and vanish soon afterwards.[96]

Foucault was primarily interested, of course, in exposing instances of exclusion and the creation of 'hierarchies of knowledge', by which dominant classes or social elements have deemed discourses unacceptable or irrelevant in explaining the world as they see it. It may well be that bringing to light suppressed or neglected discourses is different from

---

[95] Collini, *Public Moralists*, pp. 4–5.
[96] M. Foucault, *The Order of Things [Les mots et les choses]*, trans. A. Sheridan (London: Tavistock, 1970), pp. xxi–xxii.

examining concepts *in* discourses across time and with attention to social situation, as recommended with different emphases by Melvin Richter, Mark Francis and Mark Bevir. Yet the two approaches, 'archaeology of knowledge' and rich contextualism, share a common purpose — to highlight the subjective rationality in the deployment and contestation of concepts, and to reveal the social meanings of ideas. Eugenio Biagini, Boyd Hilton, Patrick Joyce and other historians whose work is cited within these pages have illuminated Victorian political and social life by showing the importance of moral vocabularies and arguments marginalized by many intellectual historians.

In examining the subjective-meaning complex of the ideas of Green and his contemporaries, I do not mean to ignore major informing discourses like Hegelianism or ideologies such as liberalism. However, one needs to look beyond the constituent elements (or what A. O. Lovejoy called 'unit-ideas') of 'political theory' and 'history of political thought' in order to appreciate how Green's teachings resonated with the moral assumptions of his contemporaries.[97] Although he was activated by a desire to philosophize religion, Green was not attempting to transcend it. Many later commentators have lost sight of the Greenian 'moment' in accepting the claim that modern political theory, properly so called, is secular. Theological elements of ethico-political discourse, so pronounced in the writings of Richard Hooker and John Locke, were certainly less evident in Western political thought by the second half of the nineteenth century. Yet the Christian element in the thought of Green (and of some other British Idealists), and the religious contexts of its reception, should make us wary of marginalizing religious ideas in modern political thought as vanished rationalities.

---

[97] A. O. Lovejoy, *Essays in the History of Ideas* (Baltimore: Johns Hopkins UP, 1948).

CHAPTER ONE

Career, Influence, Reputation

Between 1880 and 1914 no other thinker exerted a greater influence upon British thought and public policy than did T. H. Green.[1]

[Green] is a philosophical radical, but of a very peculiar kind. Almost all his definite opinions might be endorsed by Bright or Cobden, but neither Bright nor Cobden could understand the process by which Green's opinions are attained, nor the arguments by which they are defended ... He argues for the most utilitarian of political schools, on idealist principles, and, attaching the greatest importance to national life, constantly expresses a contempt for so-called 'national' honour and imperial greatness which might perhaps offend the patriotism even of Mr. Cobden.[2]

[Green] had no firm grasp of what philosophy was about. Repeatedly, when he appears to confront some major issue — free will, the rationality of morals, the place of 'character' in moral conduct — one encounters, not an argument, but a resounding phrase.[3]

1.1. IDEALISM, ANALYTIC PHILOSOPHY AND RELIGION

These three quotations illustrate some important points of contention about Green's life and work. The first is a statement by a political scientist who has made important contributions to the study of intellectual history and the history of political thought. Melvin Richter believes that a direct line of influence can be traced between Green's ethical and political teachings and later Victorian and Edwardian reform efforts, relat-

---

[1]   Richter, 'T. H. Green and His Audience,' p. 444.

[2]   A. V. Dicey's journal entry, summer 1862. R. S. Rait, ed., *Memorials of Albert Venn Dicey. Being Chiefly Letters and Diaries* (London: Macmillan, 1925), pp. 37–8. Richard Cobden (1804–65): Liberal MP, pacifist and 'free trader'; created the Anti–Corn Law League in 1839 and negotiated the Anglo–French Commercial Treaty of 1860.

[3]   Geoffrey Warnock, 'A sage for a time,' *Times Literary Supplement*, 3 June, 1988, p. 606: review of G. Thomas, *The Moral Philosophy of T. H. Green* (Oxford: Clarendon Press, 1987). Sadly, Warnock says little here about the book ostensibly under review.

ing especially to the Poor Law, education, taxation and industrial relations, and culminating in the legislation of the Liberal Governments between 1906 and 1915. The second quotation is an evaluation of Green's manner and mode of thinking by A. V. Dicey (1835–1922), a distinguished historian of law, but offered (in 1862) when neither the evaluator nor the person evaluated had any authority or influence to speak of. Green's philosophical idealism appeared to Dicey similar in its goals to the 'Philosophic Radicalism', or Utilitarianism, of Bentham, James and J. S. Mill, John Austin and others.[4] Dicey's testimony to his friend's 'peculiar' combination of philosophical and political radicalism has been cited in many studies of Green.

The third quotation is an observation by a recent philosopher about another philosopher whose reputation he deplores. In company with analytic, linguistic and 'ordinary language' philosophers, Geoffrey Warnock maintains that Green and other 'metaphysical philosophers' put the venture of philosophy on the wrong track. In a classic expression of this view, A. J. Ayer contends that any verbal proposition concerning 'relations of ideas' which cannot be construed as 'some possible sense experience' (or related to 'the phenomenal world') is metaphysical and 'is neither true nor false but literally senseless.'[5] Even philosophers who have been impressed by Green's insights suggest that his ideas require liberation from his (Idealist) idiom. Harold Prichard, who is inclined to take Green's philosophy seriously, suggests that Green's language spoils otherwise defensible ideas:

> By expressing his view in ordinary language [Green] gives it a plausibility which it does not deserve, by making it seem consistent with our ordinary ideas although in fact it is not. This being so, the only useful plan is to take the statements to which Green would seem to attach most importance, and ascertain what he is really implying in making them, and then to formulate his doctrine in accordance with these implications, regardless of whether or not the formulation agrees with his ordinary method of expressing himself.[6]

---

[4]   Bentham's utility principle entailed the question, does it (e.g., institution, law, practice) bring about 'the greatest happiness of the greatest number?' John Stuart Mill founded a 'Utilitarian Society' in 1832: 'To belong to it, it was necessary to accept the principle of utility, and also certain fundamental corollaries which Bentham and James Mill had drawn from it ...' E. Halévy, *The Growth of Philosophic Radicalism* (Boston: Beacon, 1955 [orig. English ed. 1928]), p. 480.

[5]   A.J. Ayer, *Language, Truth and Logic*, 2nd ed. (New York: Dover, 1952 [1946]), pp. 31, 33. Furthermore, since a sentence either 'expresses a genuine empirical hypothesis' or does not, 'there is nothing in the nature of philosophy to warrant the existence of conflicting philosophical "schools"' (pp. 31–2). Therefore, the alternative to analytic philosophy is pseudo-philosophy.

[6]   H. A. Prichard, *Moral Obligation. Essays and Lectures* (Oxford: Clarendon, 1949), pp. 55–6 (from the lecture 'Green's Principles of Political Obligation' [1935–7]). Geoffrey Thomas reports Prichard as saying, with reference to Green's teachings, 'You can

Ayer and Warnock, among others, represent Green's philosophical value as wholly negative; by clogging philosophical discourse with jargon and invalid propositions, Green and the British Idealists ushered in the ordinary–language philosophy of Moore, Russell, Ryle and Wittgenstein.[7]

To whom did Green's ideas and actions matter, and why? What was the nature of his 'influence'? How did Green emerge as an authoritative figure if, as Dicey asserted, he was out of step with dominant trends in British thought and opinion? What might explain the development of such contradictory evaluations of Green's thought and its significance? These and related questions raised by the statements of Richter, Dicey and Warnock are the immediate subject of this chapter. The now vast scholarly literature about Green reveals substantial disagreement about the validity and applicability of his ideas, and about Green's relationship to philosophical, ethical and political culture. The philosophical part of Green scholarship — the responses to Green by those primarily interested in the coherence of his philosophy, his deployment of terms and concepts, in short, in the validity of his efforts *as* philosophy — amounts to several hundred items, including unpublished theses, monographs, essays and journal articles in English and other major languages (including French, German, Italian and Japanese).[8] In addition to the philosophical literature are scores of essays and monographs discussing Green in relation to law, education, social reform, international relations, and to the disciplines of political studies, sociology, theology and other fields of inquiry.[9] Brief accounts of Green are found in historical period surveys, encyclopedias and reference works in the social sci-

approach the truth only through the ruins of what is false' (*Moral Philosophy of T. H. Green*, p. 3).

[7]   P. Hylton, 'The Nature of the Proposition and the Revolt Against Idealism,' in *Philosophy in History*, ed. R. Rorty, J. Schneewind, Q. Skinner (CUP, 1984), pp. 375–9.

[8]   Recent contributions include C. Tyler, *Thomas Hill Green and the Philosophical Foundation of Politics: An Internal Critique* (Lewiston, NY: Edwin Mellon, 1997); M. Chrétiene, ed., *Le nouveau liberalisme anglais* (Paris: Economica, 1999); and M. Dimova-Cookson, *T. H. Green's Moral and Political Philosophy: A Phenomenological Perspective* (Basingstoke, Hampshire: Palgrave, 2001). Extensive bibliographies of the philosophical literature are included in Thomas, *Moral Philosophy of T. H. Green* and Nicholson, *Political Philosophy of the British Idealists*.

[9]   B. Harrison, *Drink and the Victorians: The Temperance Question in England 1815–1872* (Pittsburgh, PA: Pittsburgh UP, 1971), chap. 9; P. Gordon and J. White, *Philosophers as Educational Reformers: The Influence of Idealism on British Educational Thought and Practice* (London: Routledge and Kegan Paul, 1979); Nicholson, 'T. H. Green and State Action: Liquor Legislation'; B. M. G. Reardon, 'T. H. Green as a Theologian' in *The Philosophy of T. H. Green*, ed. A. Vincent, pp. 36–47; P. Rich, 'T. H. Green, Lord Scarman and the Issue of Ethnic Minority Rights in English Liberal Thought,' *Ethnic and Racial Studies*, 10 (1987), pp. 149–68; O. Anderson, 'The Feminism of T. H. Green: A Late Victorian Success Story?,' *HPT*, 12 (1991), pp. 671–94; V. Bailey, 'English Prisons, Penal Culture, and the Abatement of Imprisonment, 1895–1922,' *JBS*, 36 (1997), pp. 285–324.

ences, theology, and so forth, and some of these offer original insights, not merely derivative assessments.[10]

Given the concerns of the present study, it is pertinent to note here the gap that began to emerge after 1920 between discussions of Green conducted by theologians or philosophers of religion and those conducted by 'pure' philosophers. Particularly between 1945 and the early 1980s there was an evident reluctance among many academic philosophers and political theorists to address the ethics of religious belief, much less to argue for positively relevant implications of Christianity to philosophy.[11] A. C. Ewing, H. D. Lewis and Alasdair MacIntyre were among the few recognized philosophers who brought unapologetically religious concerns to bear in discussing the British Idealists' (including Green's) ideas about personality, obligation, community and the purposes of the state.[12] Not only did many analytic philosophers disdain British Idealism as a superannuated school of thought, they were indifferent to or hostile towards the history of philosophy.[13] By delegitimizing metaphysical language, they have implied that we are simply not obliged to engage in discussions of religion as philosophy.

Another reason for philosophers' avoidance of Green, and indeed of British Idealism generally, until relatively recently, has to do with the ideological hegemony of liberalism and the problems with which most philosophers and political theorists in liberal societies have concerned themselves since Green's time. Green, as shall be seen, was more con-

---

[10] J. T. Merz, *A History of European Thought in the Nineteenth Century*, iii–iv (Gloucester, MA: P. Smith, 1976 [orig. 1912]): iii, chap. 5, and iv, pp. 215ff, 370–1; Brett, 'Green, Thomas Hill', pp. 435–40; W. H. Walsh, 'Green, Thomas Hill' in *Encyclopedia of Philosophy*, iii, ed. P. Edwards (New York: Macmillan/Free Press, 1967), pp. 387–9; W. H. Greenleaf, *The British Political Tradition. Volume Two: The Ideological Heritage* (London: Methuen, 1983), chap. 4.

[11] On the relationship between the communities of philosophical and theological scholars, see A. P. F. Sell, *The Philosophy of Religion, 1875–1980* (London: Croom Helm, 1988), introduction.

[12] H. D. Lewis, *Morals and Revelation* (London: Allen and Unwin, 1951), chap. 3; MacIntyre, *Secularisation and Moral Change*, p. 28 and *passim*; A. MacIntyre, *After Virtue, A Study in Moral Theory* (Notre Dame, IN: Notre Dame UP, 1981, 2nd ed., 1984), p. 10.

[13] The late Geoffrey Warnock was simply incorrect in stating that Green's 'reputation survived only feebly' into the twentieth century ('A sage for a time'). Rather, it was only the 1950s and '60s that saw 'the general repudiation of the historical mode of understanding within analytic philosophy.' Peter Hylton, *Russell, Idealism, and the Emergence of Analytic Philosophy* (Oxford: Clarendon, 1990), p. vii. The Idealist G. R. G. Mure cites pretended ignorance of past philosophy as a characteristic of the analytic school. 'As Green and the idealists were well aware, the sympathetic study of past thinkers is a *sine qua non* of learning to philosophise; in a barren period some understanding of the great philosophers is the only gift of certain value which a teacher can pass on to his pupils. But few of our academic philosophers know this.' G. R. G. Mure, review of J. Pucelle, *La nature et l'esprit dans la philosophie de T. H. Green, Philosophy*, 37 (1962), pp. 279–80.

cerned that individuals have access to institutions through which they might express their personalities, than that material wealth be evenly distributed throughout society. In the liberal West, generally speaking, prosperity rendered disputes over distribution of goods and services somewhat less violent by the 1950s (Daniel Bell's 'end of ideology'), while debates over social discrimination (i.e. unequal citizenship) became more acute. By the 1960s and '70s, many liberal philosophers were absorbed in discussions about the needs of social groups, and about the rights of individuals to pursue their own conceptions of the good and to resist having the values of others imposed upon them. Indeed, such concerns were hardly alien to J. S. Mill, Green and other philosophers of their day.

However, it can be argued that prosperity in the Western liberal and social democracies since the Second World War framed the debate over rights and pursuits of the good in a new way. The claim that all citizens of democratic, industrialized states might easily enjoy freedom from want (in the Rooseveltian formulation) helped socialist and labourist elements into positions of unprecedented political influence, in part because the experience of war had generated in the victor populations a powerful sense of entitlement; whereas among the defeated (e.g. Germans, Italians) there prevailed the conviction that economic and political reconstruction could only be successful with an overhaul of the pre-war social order. In Western democracies and democracies-under-construction, then, social reconstruction and social welfare were on the agenda, and in a more broadly based manner than had been the case before 1939. As political commitment to social reform became less partisan, the centre of debate in political philosophy came to be occupied by the entities 'rights' and 'entitlements', and ethical debate became the articulation of justification for individual or group claims.[14]

Because liberalism historically has enshrined scepticism about values, resulting in 'toleration' and compromise, it has usually undergirded ethical pluralism. This would seem to rule out of hand an ethical theory tethered to a Christian metaphysic, concerned as it is with a specific notion of the Good and a *telos* (purpose and end) of human activity and history. If forbearance, or agreement to disagree, is the keystone of all values (more or less freely chosen), what becomes of the habit of individual and collective commitment to any distinct set of values? How could a Christian ethic be appealed to as the correct value in a pluralistic

---

[14] Contributions to 'rights talk' include J. Rawls, *A Theory of Justice* (Harvard UP, 1971); C. B. Macpherson, *Democratic Theory. Essays in Retrieval* (Oxford: Clarendon, 1973); R. Nozick, *Anarchy, State, and Utopia* (New York: Basic Books, 1974); R. Dworkin, *Taking Rights Seriously* (Harvard UP, 1977); J. Feinberg, *Rights, Justice, and the Bounds of Liberty* (Princeton, NJ: Princeton UP, 1980).

society composed of religious and areligious communities?[15] It is no coincidence that increasing numbers of scholars have turned to serious appraisal of religious dimensions of British Idealism, as being of positive relevance to political philosophy, since the 'communitarian turn' of the 1980s. Communitarian liberals responded to criticisms (by Marxists, conservatives and others since the 1960s) of the anomie and purposelessness of capitalist societies (and even quasi-socialist ones), and sought to correct what they perceived to be the excessive rights-orientedness of liberalism's dominant proponents. Communitarians have objected to a version of liberalism in which social duty is reduced to mutual non-interference; they argue — as Green did — for the social constitution of the self and emphasize the importance of a common good in maintaining a sense of social identity and collective purpose.[16]

Despite Warnock's dismissal of them Green's ideas are the subject of expanding political-philosophical and historical discussion. Compelling claims for the importance of Green's thought have been advanced during the past twenty years. It is not only that recent scholarly literature on Green has been more generally favourable towards his thought than that of thirty years before. Contextualization of his thought has become both wider and more nuanced. That is to say, Green is now readily claimed, flaws and all, for the liberal tradition and his ideas discussed in terms of the wider motions of philosophy.[17] Peter Nicholson finds lasting relevance in Green's 'distinctive and valuable account of the self–realisation by all human beings of their spiritual natures in a non-competitive and cooperative manner.' He hazards, 'It may be that the political philosophy of the British Idealists ... can test the value of

---

[15] For presentations of the problem of religious values for the liberal viewpoint, see G. F. Gaus, 'Ideological Dominance through Philosophical Confusion: Liberalism in the Twentieth Century,' in *Reassessing Political Ideologies: the Durability of Dissent*, ed. M. Freeden (London: Routledge, 2001), pp. 23–5; and Plant, *Politics, Theology and History*, chap. 1 ('Liberal Society and Political Theology').

[16] Key statements of the communitarian liberal position include M. Sandel, *Liberalism and the Limits of Justice* (CUP, 1982); N. Rosenblum, *Another Liberalism* (Cambridge, MA: Harvard UP, 1987); W. Kymlicka, *Liberalism, Community and Culture* (Oxford: Clarendon, 1989); and S. Kautz, *Liberalism and Community* (Ithaca, NY: Cornell UP, 1995).

[17] R. Bellamy, *Liberalism and Modern Society: A Historical Argument* (Oxford: Polity, 1992); S. Den Otter, *British Idealism and Social Explanation. A Study in Late Victorian Thought* (Oxford: Clarendon, 1996); M. Freeden, *Ideologies and Political Theory: A Conceptual Approach* (Oxford: Clarendon, 1996); D. Boucher, 'British Idealism and the Just Society' in *Social Justice from Hume to Walzer*, ed. D. Boucher and P. Kelly (London and New York: Routledge, 1998), pp. 80–101; A. J. M. Milne, *Ethical Frontiers of the State: An Essay in Political Philosophy* (London: Macmillan, 1998); J. Morrow, *A History of Political Thought. A Thematic Introduction* (New York: New York UP, 1998); R. Hudelson, *Modern Political Philosophy* (Armonk, NY: M. E. Sharpe, 1999); Boucher and Vincent, *British Idealism and Political Theory*; P. Fairfield, *Moral Selfhood and the Liberal Tradition: the Politics of Individuality* (Toronto: Toronto UP, 2000).

socialism or capitalism or the welfare state.'[18] Geoffrey Thomas defends Green's philosophy as a unique synthesis of Aristotelian, Kantian and Hegelian ideas which might be salvaged for use as a guide to modern liberalism. Ben Wempe argues more boldly that Green's conception of positive freedom can justify state action to ensure social justice. Avital Simhony is interested in Green's ideas about individuality and community for their bearing on democratic citizenship.[19]

Yet a more respectful reception of Green by academic philosophers will not necessarily prepare society to reap the harvest of Greenian ideas. In a review of Nicholson's study of the British Idealists, intellectual historian James Kloppenberg contends that

> Resurrecting Green's ideas ... would require more than a clear understanding of his principal arguments. It would require the far broader, and much less likely, reorientation of contemporary culture toward the moral ideals ... that animated Green himself.[20]

Kloppenberg, though himself appreciative of the accomplishments of the British Idealists, implies that while the ideals animating Green were congenial to many ethical thinkers of his time and place, they might be less compelling to us. As Andrew Vincent has recently observed, 'The problem for the contemporary reader of Green is that the language of the "protestant state" and "Christian citizen" appears remote and anachronistic.'[21]

It is significant that many of the most recent reassessments of Green and 'New Liberalism' (i.e. the shift in British thought, ca. 1880–1914, away from classical, atomistic liberalism) are conducted in a manner that can be described as quasi-historical and historicist. Michael Freeden, Gerald Gaus and Andrew Vincent have observed that the aforementioned rights-talk during the last four decades of the *twentieth* century was 'impoverished' by an ahistorical (and as Freeden suggests, essentially American) misunderstanding of 'the liberal tradition'. The liberal tradition, so understood, sanctified a 'sequence from Locke to Kant to [J. S.] Mill to Rawls' — a configuration privileging individualistic and rights-centred elements of liberalism — and denigrated thinkers

[18] Nicholson, *Political Philosophy*, pp. 3, 5. See also his commentary on Green's *Lectures on Political Obligation* in *The Political Classics: Green to Dworkin*, ed. M. Forsyth and M. Keens (OUP, 1996), pp. 17–36.

[19] Thomas, *Philosophy of T. H. Green*; Wempe, *Beyond Equality*; A. Simhony, 'Idealist Organicism: Beyond Holism and Individualism,' *HPT*, 12 (1991), pp. 515–35; A. Simhony, 'T. H. Green and the Common Good Society,' *HPT*, 14 (1993), pp. 225–47; A. Simhony, 'T. H. Green's Complex Common Good' in *The New Liberalism: Reconciling Liberty and Community*, ed. A. Simhony and D. Weinstein (CUP, 2001), pp. 69–91. See also Fairfield, *Moral Selfhood and the Liberal Tradition*.

[20] Review of Nicholson, *The Political Philosophy of the British Idealists*, *Albion*, 24 (1992), p. 152.

[21] Boucher and Vincent, *British Idealism and Political Theory*, p. 53.

(including, ironically, Mill, but also Green and L. T. Hobhouse) representing communitarian and republican ideals, or attending to common goods and collective conditions in order to counter-balance individualistic demands.[22] Many recent assessments of Green and liberalism, therefore, proceed from the assumption that a more historical approach to the study of liberalism can provide theorists of the present day with useful cues and insights into liberal problem-solving. Vincent points out that Green's contribution to philosophy and to liberalism was not only to provide certain ideas or articulate principles but to demonstrate how 'the function of the philosopher is to understand the historical development of the ideas.'[23]

The primary purpose of the present study is to depict Green in relation to intellectual issues — and thus to social, political and economic problems — of his *own* era. Prerequisite to this, the present chapter reviews significant assessments of Green's thought, for the purpose of demonstrating how a century of Green scholarship has framed questions about his teachings and the meaning of his life itself. An historiographical approach reveals interpreters' biases which, I contend, continue to shape our understanding of Green, and in the present study this approach complements standard techniques of scientific history — for instance, bringing new and neglected information about Green and his milieu to bear. Although much biographical exposition and historical contextualization are left for subsequent chapters, relevant facts of Green's life and career (or careers) are offered here, and points of posthumous controversy examined.

1.2. THE EDUCATION AND CAREER OF AN ACADEMIC PHILOSOPHER

Understanding Green's life as an academic philosopher, including the conditions and constraints of the career that consumed the greatest part of his time and energy, is essential to evaluating his historical significance. Richter, in *The Politics of Conscience* (still unmatched as an intellectual biography of Green), traced in detail Green's intellectual development and academic career, but labelling him an academic explains less than might be supposed. The term itself today has connotations different from those of Green's day, and Academe at Green's death had changed significantly from the community of his student days. Above all, Oxbridge had become more 'secular'. When Green went up

[22] Simhony and Weinstein, eds., *The New Liberalism*, chaps. 1, 6, 9 (essays by the above mentioned authors). The quoted material is from Chapter One (M. Freeden, 'Liberal Community: An Essay in Retrieval'), pp. 26, 30–1. See also Freeden, *Ideologies and Political Theory*, chap. 5.
[23] Boucher and Vincent, *British Idealism and Political Theory*, p. 54.

to Balliol College, Oxford, in 1855, all of its tutors and most of its resident Fellows were in holy orders, potential if not actual functionaries of the Established Church. During the period when Green was successively a student, tutor-fellow and professor at Oxford University, Oxford was being transformed from an Anglican seminary and finishing school for English gentlemen into an institution less avowedly sectarian and more truly national, whose purposes included the education of public servants and the promotion of scientific learning.

Churchmen or clerical–statesmen have made important contributions to British thought: consider Thomas More, Richard Hooker, Joseph Butler, J. H. Newman and, in more recent times, the Christian Platonist W. R. Inge.[24] Increasingly from the seventeenth and eighteenth centuries, the pre-eminent social and political thinkers were statesmen (Sir Edward Coke, Burke), counsellors to power (Hobbes, Locke), and 'scientists of morals' (Hume, Smith) — men whose concerns and goals were rather more secular than religious. The triumph of the market during the eighteenth and nineteenth centuries produced the man of letters (Gibbon, Carlyle, Macaulay, Leslie Stephen) and his close relation, the independent intellectual (Bentham, Frederic Harrison, Matthew Arnold).

Green can be counted among the first of a new breed of English university intellectual. He was in a certain sense an academic *instead* of a 'don'.[25] Arriving at Oxford during a period of reform, his social consciousness was unlike that of most senior fellows and tutors.[26] Dons such as Newman and John Keble, who came of age during the political and social upheavals of the 1820s and '30s, concerned themselves with such questions as the proper role or 'idea' of the University. Yet many of

---

[24] The philosophical influence of Bishop Butler (1692–1752) extended well into the nineteenth century. See Hilton, *The Age of Atonement*, p. 163 and *passim*. Inge (1860–1954) was a Classicist and theological modernist, and Dean of St. Paul's, 1911–34. In *Christian Ethics and Modern Problems* (1930) and *God and the Astronomers* (1933) he asserted a Christian humanism similar to that of T. S. Eliot, but attacking more directly egalitarianism, materialism, and scientism. See D. L. Edwards, 'Inge, William Ralph' in *Twentieth-Century Culture. A Biographical Companion*, ed. A. Bullock and R. B. Woodings (New York: Harper and Row, 1983), pp. 353–4.

[25] 'Don: 3. a distinguished man; a leader; an adept (colloq.) 1634. 4. Hence, in the English Universities: A head, fellow or tutor of a college 1660' (*Oxford Universal Dictionary*, 3rd ed. [1944], an authorized abridgement of the *OED*). On the conditions of Victorian intellectual production, see especially T. W. Heyck, *The Transformation of Intellectual Life in Victorian England* (London: Croom Helm, 1982), and Collini, *Public Moralists*.

[26] 1850 conveniently marks the beginning of an era of reform at Oxford. In that year Royal Commissions were established to investigate the conditions of Oxford and Cambridge universities and official reports appeared in 1852. By 1854–5 important changes had been made in Oxford's collegiate and University statutes. Ward, *Victorian Oxford*; W. J. Reader, *Professional Men. The Rise of the Professional Classes in Nineteenth–Century England* (London: Weidenfeld and Nicolson, 1966), chap. 9.

them remained content to regard themselves as members of private foundations (the constituent colleges of the University) or of a club of adepts.[27] Green rejected this insular, guild mentality. It would be convenient to characterize his idea of a university as a secular one, and even to describe it as part of a larger secularist project. After all, Green was among the 'infidels' who tried to remove clerical restrictions on academic life and promote 'free' intellectual inquiry. Undergraduates and scholars, Green believed, should be free to recognize any religious creed or none. While he was junior Dean at Balliol, undergraduates were excused from compulsory chapel. Yet, as we shall see, Green was not a secularist in an unambiguous sense. He believed that the character of the University was and should remain essentially religious, but to a degree unusual for a mid-Victorian don he identified with intellectual, moral and social purposes beyond those of Balliol, Oxford and the Established Church.

Green left Rugby in the spring of 1855 and entered Balliol College in October, at the same time that fellow Rugbeian Henry Sidgwick, who emerged as Green's formidable neo-Utilitarian philosophical opponent, went up to Cambridge.[28] Green was among the first Oxonians specifically *not* required to pledge conformity to the Thirty-Nine Articles of the Anglican creed upon matriculation. He was not an introvert but was certainly a serious student — in Oxbridge argot, a 'reading man' rather than a 'hearty' (athlete) or 'Pass man' (student seeking a Pass degree). He belonged to the 'Old Mortality' and 'Essay' Societies and debated in the Oxford Union, often defending unpopular positions.[29] ('Old Mortality' referred to the novel of the same name by Walter Scott, set against

---

[27] Many undergraduates and dons in early nineteenth-century Oxford scarcely recognized the existence of a university beyond the colleges. Consciousness of membership in 'The University of Oxford' was increasingly formed by inter-collegiate clubs (of undergraduates and of tutors) and by the Congregation of the University (effectively after 1854, all faculty, examiners, and resident Masters of Arts). A. J. Engel, *From Clergyman to Don: The Rise of the Academic Profession in Nineteenth-Century Oxford* (OUP, 1983).

[28] Biographical details are gleaned from two chronologies by Charlotte Green in the Green Papers 1(d), Box 1: labelled 'CBG to RLN. Biographical Details for RLN's life of THG' and 'Notes by Mrs. Green. THG 1850–70 copies'. These were compiled for Richard Nettleship's use in preparing his published 'Memoir' of Green. Also *Alumni Oxoniensis, 1715–1886*, ii (Oxford, 1888); and Bodleian Library, Western Manuscripts, MS.Top.Oxon.d.517 (a register of Oxford dons ca. 1840–1900 and their University distinctions, degrees, and offices).

[29] Dicey recalls, 'His two or three [Union] speeches, though badly delivered, were the most remarkable I heard during my residence at Oxford. Anyone who knows the Union will not need to be told that a society which could applaud claptrap, personality, flippancy, and impertinence to the echo, would hardly give a hearing to Green' (Rait, *Memorials of Albert Venn Dicey*, p. 38). On 22 November 1859, Green moved abolition of the Church rates; on 4 February 1861, he vindicated Mazzini and Italian fed-

the backdrop of religious and political conflict in Scotland during the seventeenth and eighteenth centuries.) Green moved into a circle of young aspirants to literary and scholarly distinction that included A. C. Swinburne, J. A. Symonds, A. V. Dicey, James Bryce, John Nichol and Walter Pater. These 'Lights of Liberalism' — as Matthew Arnold called them — fraternized with Benjamin Jowett, Mark Pattison, Goldwin Smith, J. E. Thorold Rogers, John Conington, Henry Smith and other dons counted among the Oxford reformers and liberals. Green's young associates and many of the older dons who encouraged them took an interest in wider social and political issues; as children of an Age of Reform, they were concerned about their own usefulness to society. In contrast to the Tractarians, the Oxford liberals of Green's time sought to accommodate change in British society rather than protect the University from it.[30]

Green was ranked in the First Class of the Honours School of *Literae Humaniores* in the summer of 1859. *Literae Humaniores* (or 'Greats') was one of six areas of study in which candidates for honours degrees were examined via written and *viva voce* exercises after their twelfth term (normally four years) but no later than their sixteenth term following matriculation. The final exams of the 'Greats' school included 'the Greek and Latin Languages'; 'the Histories of Ancient Greece and Rome'; and 'Logic, and the Outlines of Moral and Political Philosophy' (sharply skewed ca. 1830–70 towards Classical authors).[31] Green also took the final Honours exams in the School of Law and Modern History later that year but scored only a Third. His satisfactory combined performance made him a likely candidate for a Balliol fellowship open in 1860, to which he was duly elected. He justified his religious conformity upon taking his fellowship as smuggling 'the new wine in the old bottles,' but in contrast to many others of the time he never took Holy Orders (i.e.

---

eralism; in February, 1863, he spoke in favour of the American Union and against the Confederacy.

[30] Harvie, *Lights of Liberalism*, pp. 9–18. The authors of the pamphlet series *Tracts for the Times* — including Newman, Keble, Edward Pusey and W. G. Ward — were alarmed by the attempts of the post-1832 political establishment to alter the status of the national church. Mrs. Humphry Ward observed of this generation, 'How [sic] little the leading ideas of that seething age of social and industrial reform, from the appearance of *Sybil* in 1843 to the Education Bill of 1870, mattered to Pusey or to Liddon, compared with the date of the Book of Daniel, or the retention of the Athanasian creed' (*A Writer's Recollections* [1918], quoted in Richter, 'T. H. Green and His Audience,' p. 454).

[31] *The Student's Handbook to the University and Colleges of Oxford*, 6th ed. (Oxford: Clarendon, 1881) refers to alterations of curricular requirements and academic rules and statutes since 1854–5, the year of a critical parliamentary Act relating to Oxford University.

received ordination).[32] Green remained a Fellow of Balliol until his death. Due to changes in University and collegiate statutes he was not forced to renounce the fellowship upon his marriage in 1871 to Charlotte Byron Symonds (1842–1929).[33]

Green's tutorial duties at Balliol were initially more historical than philosophical, but in 1866 he was entrusted with teaching Classical texts — e.g. Aristotle's *Nicomachean Ethics* — for their philosophical content; this was his rationale for lecturing on the history of ethics, modern as well as ancient.[34] When Green was elected to his fellowship the Balliol Senior Common room was a centre of liberal theology and political thought at Oxford. The most notorious of this liberal faction was Benjamin Jowett, Green's tutor and Master of the college after 1870. Other Balliol liberals included Edwin Palmer and W. L. Newman, and the influence of these men within the University after 1850 was reinforced by ties with Balliol men at large, like A. C. Tait and Frederick Temple (both subsequently archbishops of Canterbury).[35] Green's first decade at Oxford coincided with the now obscure ecclesiastical and theological controversies which shook educated society at mid century, battles in the 'war' between science and religion.[36] In 1860 *Essays and Reviews* appeared and Jowett, whose essay on Biblical scholarship suggested that the Bible be read 'like any other book', was attacked by High Churchmen and Evangelicals, both within the University (three of the Essayists were dons) and without. Though Green retrospectively dismissed these battles as parochial and unnecessary, he was at the time an intimate of Jowett and a partisan of the comprehensive or 'Broad Church' party.[37] He witnessed the public attack on the Essayists (vilified as 'the Seven Against Christ') by Samuel Wilberforce, the Bishop of

---

[32] H. Nettleship recollection (1882) in *GP* 1(b).

[33] Fellows had also traditionally been bound to clerical celibacy. Green was technically *re*-elected to his fellowship following his marriage. His marriage landed him a comfortable income. Charlotte was the daughter of a prosperous Bristol physician and the marriage settlement netted the couple between £750 and £880 p.a. from 1871 onward. *GP* 1(a): letters of C. D. Cave to THG, 6 October 1871, 4 December 1877.

[34] Wempe cites the Balliol Deansbook, indicating the creation on October 12, 1866, of an 'Ethical Lectureship' for Green with an annual stipend of £100 (*Beyond Equality*, pp. 189, 311).

[35] W. L. Newman to C. Green (27 November 1882): recollection in *GP* 1(b). Like Green, Newman (historian and classicist) was interested in larger social, political and economic questions: see W. L. Newman, 'The Land Laws,' *Questions for a Reformed Parliament* (London: Macmillan, 1867), pp. 79–130. On the liberal Balliolites, see Ward, *Victorian Oxford*, chap. 7; Harvie, *Lights*, pp. 57–66; Parry, *Democracy and Religion*, pp. 66–72.

[36] P. Appleman et al (eds.), *1859. Entering an Age of Crisis* (Bloomington, IN: Indiana UP, 1959), Part One.

[37] Geoffrey Faber claims the term 'Broad Church' was invented by Arthur Hugh Clough (1819–61), pioneer of conscientious doubt and a Balliol man, to whom Green was occasionally compared (Faber, *Jowett*, pp. 315–16). In Green's day it was common to

Oxford, at St Mary's.[38] While Green presumably did not attend the famous Oxford debate on evolution between Wilberforce and T. H. Huxley ('Darwin's Bulldog') on June 30, 1860, he would almost certainly have sided against the clerical party.[39]

Historians have recognized the important role Green played in the Victorian reform of Oxford University, the construction of a philosophical curriculum and the 'professionalization' of philosophy in Britain.[40] Green argued, along with Mark Pattison (Rector of Lincoln College, 1861–84) and other champions of the 'endowment of research', that the collegiate tutor-fellow should be afforded greater opportunity to advance his own knowledge if he was to be an effective teacher, much less a qualified candidate for a university professorship.[41] Green complained that tutors were too restricted to teaching the same classic texts in a superficial manner to advance very far beyond the intellectual capacities of a clever undergraduate. These and other of Green's beliefs about the purposes of academic enterprise were grounded in mature reflection upon his own experiences as a tutor and fellow.

Green was dissatisfied during his first years as a college fellow and tutor, doubting both his competence as a teacher and the importance of

---

speak of religious parties at Oxford: e.g. Tractarian, Evangelical. The Broad Churchmen denied that they constituted a party.

[38] *Letters of John Addington Symonds. Volume I: 1844–1868*, ed. H. M. Schueller and R. L. Peters (Detroit: Wayne State UP, 1967). Symonds' letters 162–4 (31 January 1861, 2 February 1861, 4 February 1861) to his sister Charlotte give details of Wilberforce's orations and the commentary of the press.

[39] Green spent July 1860 with a reading party including his former tutor John Conington and John Addington Symonds, his future brother-in-law. The Huxley–Wilberforce debate was almost certainly a topic of discussion among the party.

[40] Richter, *Politics of Conscience*, chaps. 3, 5; J. B. Schneewind, *Sidgwick's Ethics and Victorian Moral Philosophy* (Oxford: Clarendon, 1977), introduction, pp. 401–3; Heyck, *Transformation*, pp. 172–5; P. Hinchliff, *Benjamin Jowett and the Christian Religion* (Oxford: Clarendon, 1987), pp. 76 and *passim*, 150–1. On the subject of Victorian university reform I am indebted (in addition to works already cited) to J. Sparrow, *Mark Pattison and the Idea of a University* (CUP, 1967); S. Rothblatt, *Revolution of the Dons: Cambridge and Society in Victorian England* (New York: Basic, 1968); and E. G. W. Bill, *University Reform in Nineteenth Century Oxford: A Study of Henry Halford Vaughan* (OUP, 1973).

[41] Pattison was author of *Suggestions on Academical Organization* (1868). Another radical proponent of research was Charles Appleton (1841–79), Green's student and founder of the journal *Academy*. Green gave evidence to the Royal Commission on the University of Oxford in 1877 (the published report of this is reprinted in *AW*, pp. 199–215). Green's knowledge and experience in matters of university organization and administration were recognized by W. V. Harcourt, Liberal Home Secretary, 1880–5. Harcourt solicited Green's advice about candidates for the secretaryship of the commission responsible for preparing a new Oxford University reform bill in 1880–1. Green to Harcourt, 16 November [1880], and Harcourt to W. E. Gladstone, 22 November 1880. Bodleian: Harcourt MSS. dep. 8, fols. 26–9.

his work.[42] He did not at first regard his Balliol fellowship as a definite step towards a collegiate career or a professorship. Although some fellowships at Oxford and Cambridge colleges had been thrown open to competitive examination after 1854, many were still essentially sinecures. Fellowships were effectively rewards for undergraduate performance and provided means to careers in the Church, law, letters and politics.[43] Until the 1870s most fellowships carried no teaching responsibilities, and the fact that some fellows were competent teachers cannot obscure the time-serving and dilettantism of others. Sir William Hamilton's criticism of Oxford in 1831 still held some truth thirty years later:

> Tuition is not solemnly engaged in as important, arduous, responsible, and permanent occupation; but lightly viewed and undertaken as a matter of convenience, a business by the by, a state of transition, a stepping-stone to something else.[44]

Even before his matriculation Green had assessed the University's members as amateurish and the institution as undeserving of its intellectual reputation. To David Hanbury, a Rugby friend, he wrote, 'The Dons appear corrupt and selfish … The temptations to idleness seem innumerable.'[45] Like his contemporary Algernon Swinburne, who was expelled from Oxford before he could take his degree, Green never abandoned a certain prejudice against the place; above all, Green resented the institutional arrangements conducive to idleness and

---

[42] Green complained to his Rugby friend David Hanbury in 1863, '[pupils] do me no good (they did me some at first), and I do them precious little' (*GP* 1a: THG to David Hanbury, 26 January 1863). In the spring of that year he informed his friend Donald Crawford, a fellow of Lincoln College, 'Altogether I am hanging loose on Oxford, and must seek escape somehow. Perhaps the best thing to do would be to get on the staff of a daily paper. But this would involve living in London, and hanging about clubs, which of all things I should hate' (*GP* 1a: THG to Crawford, 30 May 1863).

[43] *Student's Handbook*, pp. 76–83. Fellowships were originally established 'for the promotion of religion and learning' and were worth between one hundred and fifty and three hundred pounds per year before 1871 (and up to twice that by the 1880s). By Green's time most fellowships were awarded to men who had already taken degrees. 'Prize' fellowships enabled graduates without independent means to reside in college or to leave (residency requirements were lax or non-existent).

[44] 'Universities of England — Oxford,' *The Edinburgh Review*, 53 (June, 1831), reprinted in *Reform and Intellectual Debate in Victorian England*, ed. B. Dennis and D. Skilton (London: Croom Helm, 1987), p. 185. Heyck estimates that only twenty per cent of Oxbridge fellows taught ca. 1830 (*Transformation*, p. 71). By 1860 the proportion of tutorial fellows was perhaps one-third. On the opportunities of a late Victorian Oxford fellow, see C. Oman, *Memories of Victorian Oxford* (London: Methuen, 1941), chaps. 11–13.

[45] *GP* 1a: THG to Hanbury, [1854?]. The date of this letter is uncertain, but in it Green refers to his visit 'on our [i.e. the Rugby] whole holiday' and Oxford as his 'future alma mater'.

snobbery.[46] Practices and traditions both ancient and recent made Oxford a less serious and productive place than it might otherwise have been, and in the late 1870s Green was proposing specific remedies for these perceived defects.[47]

Before 1866 Green supplemented his fellowship income through private tuition. He joined the Oxford Tutors' Club, a group of salaried college tutors and private 'coaches', in 1862, when he took his MA.[48] Even a non-fellow, a Bachelor of Arts with First or Second class Honours, might earn a decent living as a tutor (or 'coach' or 'crammer'), and a fellowship plus coaching at Oxford or Cambridge was potentially quite lucrative.[49] The main task of official tutors and private coaches alike was to prepare undergraduates for their 'Mods' (Moderations, the first public examination normally taken in the second year after matriculation) and the 'Schools' (subject exams constituting the final academic requirements for the BA). Permanent Private Halls under the direction of Masters of Arts had been allowed at Oxford since 1855, gradually increasing stable teaching opportunities for graduates. The proliferation of 'unattached students' at Oxford from the later 1860s might have resulted in a parallel growth of unattached tutors, except that colleges and halls from that time kept larger numbers of resident fellows and tutors.

Green was fortunate never to be entirely dependent on private tuition for his bread, yet despite his tenure of one of the best fellowships in the university he felt his position to be a marginal one. In 1863, he was offered the editorship of the *Times of India*, which he turned down. He spent January 1864 with his uncle David J. Vaughan (vicar of St. Martin's, Leicester), apparently assisting Vaughan with the Working Men's College established there in 1862 (see 3.3 below). Green was occupied in the spring of 1865 and of 1866 with his work as an assistant commissioner (i.e. regional inspector) for the Taunton Commission on education. The Taunton Commission had been charged with investigating 'middle-class' endowed and proprietary schools not investigated by the

---

[46] Swinburne too was one of Jowett's favourites. Though Green's criticism was more ethical and Swinburne's more aesthetic, both men were passionate in their denunciation of Oxonians' dullness and apathy. They were associates rather than friends, but one of their bonds was Romantic politics. D. Thomas, *Swinburne. The Poet in his World* (OUP, 1979), chaps. 2–3.

[47] Details of Green's idea of the university are revealed in his testimony before the University of Oxford Commissioners in 1877–8 ([c.2868], [House of Commons] *Sessional Papers*, 1881, vol. 56, pp. 200–5), the manuscript notes for which are contained in GP 1(c): 'Evidence given before the Commission'.

[48] The entry for Green in Bodleian MS.Top.Oxon.d.517 (p. 44), written in his own hand, indicates membership in the 'Club'.

[49] In Leslie Stephen's time at Cambridge a high Wrangler (ranked high in the first class in final exams) was likely to win a fellowship at Trinity or St Johns and would have excellent coaching credentials. Stephen estimated the value of a First or Second Wrangler during the 1850s at £5000 over a lifetime. Annan, *Leslie Stephen*, pp. 24–8.

1862 Clarendon Commission (one of whose members was Matthew Arnold).[50] Green appears to have given serious consideration during the mid-1860s to leaving Balliol and Oxford. He applied unsuccessfully for a professorship at St Andrews that had fallen vacant in 1864 with the death of J. F. Ferrier (a very competent expositor of German philosophy). Green's letter to James Bryce in March 1866, announcing his interest in shifting to Owens College, Manchester, reveals the dilemmas he faced:

> I have felt drawings toward Owen's College, but Jowett urges me to stop here [at Oxford]. In the teaching way I suspect I can do more here. Manchester clerks would want some shorter cut than my Hegelian philosophy, and whereas here I expect increasing success with my pupils. I am beginning to be sought after by men reading for fellowships, with whom I can expatiate. At the same time I am beginning to fear that I shall never be properly well here. The practical openings at Manchester are the great attraction, but they wd. be poor compensation for failure in one's proper line of work as a teacher.[51]

Green applied in 1867 for the Wayneflete professorship of Moral and Metaphysical Philosophy at Oxford. He was drawn closer to the administration of Balliol in October 1865 upon appointment as junior Dean. He was a University Local Examinations Delegate in 1866 and a Public Examinations Delegate in 1870.[52] While Green had reason to view Oxford collegiate teaching in the 1860s as a grind, with little opportunity for scholarly accomplishment, financial security or family life, he was also aware of Oxford's prospects. Enrollments at the Ancient Universities stagnated between 1820 and 1860; thereafter they rose steadily.[53] Jowett and others had rigourized the Oxford examination system and, with the Oxbridge curricula in mind, made recommenda-

---

[50] The Clarendon Commission had reported on the condition of nine 'public' schools including Eton, Harrow and Rugby. The schools investigated by the Taunton Commission were boarding schools and day schools supported by pupils' fees and by endowments; their pupils were generally of lower social position than those of the Clarendon Commission schools. The Taunton Commission report [c.3966, VII–XV] was published in 1867–8, and it included Green's 'Special Report on Birmingham Free School, and General Report on the Counties of Stafford and Warwick' [c.3966-VII: Volume VIII, pp. 91–252].

[51] T. H. Green to James Bryce, 23 March [1866], Bodleian Library, MSS. Bryce 73, fols. 63–4. Printed in *AW*, pp. 419–21.

[52] Charlotte Green maintained that her husband had shaken off his disillusionment over his Oxford career by 1864–5 ('Biographical details for RLN's life of THG', *GP* 1c). Perhaps Green's assuming the sub-deanship of Balliol was an indication of this.

[53] Rothblatt, *Revolution of the Dons*, chap. 2; Heyck, *Transformation*, chaps. 3, 5. Student enrolment at Oxbridge and all other examining universities combined remained less than one percent of the national age–group 18–22.

tions about recruitment into and promotion within the Civil Service.[54] As government service began to become meritocratic after 1854, and since the aspiring political-grade civil servant was required to have a solid grounding in the liberal arts, a degree from one of the Ancient Universities took on new practical value.

Internal debate at Oxford at the time of the 1850–51 Royal Commission revolved around the question of the relationship between the University and its colleges. Many 'Liberals', including A. P. Stanley and other admirers of the German higher education system, advocated strengthening the supervisory authority of the University and giving more power to the professors. 'Tories' and some Liberals maintained that the University was merely a weak confederation of colleges and insisted on the 'beneficial relation which the college system establishes between tutor and pupil' (Mark Pattison). Throughout the century Oxbridge's claims of superiority over the universities of London, Edinburgh, and elsewhere rested on the argument that the liberal arts could be taught only in a collegiate and residential system.[55] More than any other action of the Victorian state, these civil service reforms raised the status of liberal arts education, and with it the standing of Oxbridge tutors and examiners. The function which Oxbridge came to play in constituting, for example, the home and colonial civil services, gave a more powerful focus to its role of training gentlemen to govern, and it is in this sense that Jowett's early biographer Lewis Campbell referred to the 'nationalization' of the Ancient Universities.[56]

Green's teacher Benjamin Jowett has been mentioned here frequently and the relationship between the two men deserves further comment. Jowett had detected great potential in the undergraduate Green and, along with Charles Parker and John Conington, encouraged Green's unorthodox intellectual interests.[57] It was due in large part to Jowett's urging that Green remained at Oxford during the 1860s. Green repaid

---

[54] In 1853 Jowett had served on a committee set to work out criteria for selection of personnel for the Indian Civil Service. He also advised Sir Charles Trevelyan, assistant Treasury Secretary, who in 1854 published the historic *Report on the Organisation of the Permanent Civil Service* (Reader, *Professional Men*, chap. 6).

[55] M. Pattison, *Memoirs* (Fontwell, Sussex: Centaur Press, 1969 [orig. 1885]), pp. 255–9; Ward, *Victorian Oxford*, chaps. 5, 7.

[56] *The Nationalisation of the Old English Universities* (London: Chapman and Hall, 1901). See also R. Symonds, *Oxford and Empire: The Last Lost Cause?* (Oxford: Clarendon, 1988). R. Soffer, *Discipline and Power. The University, History, and the Making of an English Elite, 1870-1930* (Palo Alto, CA: Stanford UP, 1994) contains an excellent bibliography on the voluminous literature relating to modern university education in the West.

[57] 'I get awfully bullied by the Dons, all of whom I dislike more or less, except Jowett, who is my Tutor and kind to me, and for whose book [*The Epistles of St Paul to the Thessalonians, Galatians and Romans*, 1855] I have a profound respect' (*GP* 1a: Green to D. Hanbury [undated letter: probably late 1855]).

Jowett's confidence by proving an effective intellectual and political ally.[58] The Master of Balliol appears to have viewed Green, if not as a disciple, as his representative. As Peter Hinchliff observes,

> Green was instrumental in propagating much that Jowett stood for ... What Jowett tried to do for Green as his tutor had been worth doing. Green's life had been a kind of vindication of Jowett's determination to make Balliol a centre of liberal religion.[59]

In later years Jowett became averse to Green's mature philosophy and to his style of intellectual mentoring; he accused Green of foisting a 'system' on immature minds.[60] Thus he wrote to his friend Florence Nightingale on 29 March 1882, 'I have just returned from Prof. Green's funeral. He is a terrible loss (notwithstanding his metaphysics).'[61] Envy may also have played a part in Jowett's attitude towards his pupil from the 1870s. When Jowett became Master of Balliol, Green became principal classics tutor of his college as well as Senior Dean. Charlotte Green wrote in her notes for R. L. Nettleship that in 1870–1 virtually the entire 'subordinate management' of Balliol fell to her husband. While Jowett was widely known during the 1860s as a translator of the ancient classics and victim of clerical bigotry, by the 1870s the scholarly reputation of the student was beginning to overshadow that of the master.[62] Green's view of scholarship and of the function of the university was more in line with that of Pattison and other proponents of the endowment of research; Jowett, while approving some curricular innovation,

---

[58] Green became, like Arthur Hugh Clough and Arthur Stanley in the previous Balliol generation, one of Jowett's picked men. During the *Essays and Reviews* scandal, a pamphlet appeared entitled *Statements of Christian Doctrine, Extracted from the Writings of B. Jowett* (Oxford: J. H. and Jas. Parker, 1861). A copy is in the Green Papers. J. A. Symonds attributed the pamphlet to Green and Eleanor Elizabeth Smith, and its unsigned preface to Stanley, then professor of ecclesiastical history (*Letters of Symonds*, i: JAS to C. Symonds, 4 March 1861, and 10 March 1861).

[59] Hinchliff, *Benjamin Jowett*, pp. 157, 159.

[60] Faber, *Jowett*, pp. 356–9. 'Jowett continued to criticise him, even in the sermon he preached to mark his death' (Hinchliff, *Benjamin Jowett*, p. 166). Symonds commented on the friction between Jowett and Green in his recollection in the Green Papers. Green felt it necessary to caution *his* picked man, Andrew Bradley, 'If you have gathered any impression (throu' Nettleship or otherwise) that there is any serious want of agreement between me and the Master as to the way in which I should do my business, please put it aside' (GP1a: Green to A. C. Bradley, 16 December [1873]).

[61] *Dear Miss Nightingale*, ed. Quinn and Prest, p. 282.

[62] Jowett's most enduring literary efforts were the Clarendon Press translations of Plato's *Republic* and *Dialogues*. After *Essays and Reviews* Jowett had been forced by the Vice-Chancellor to re-subscribe to the Thirty-Nine Articles and his salary as Regius Professor of Greek had been held up for a few years (Hinchliff, *Benjamin Jowett*, chap. 4).

believed that faculty research cheated students.[63] This said, however, had Green not been associated with the most famous Oxford don of the nineteenth century, his academic career as well as his impact on society might have been quite different.

Much of the present investigation concerns Green's politics. Green's intellectual interests before 1870 were rivalled, if not overshadowed, by his political ones. Dicey, James Bryce, John Symonds and other contemporaries remarked on how Green's political interests combined Romantic and idealistic attitudes with the practical and material: he was as concerned about Italian unification as about the taxes paid by the British lower classes. Like many contemporary Liberals and Radicals, Green was attentive to European movements of liberal nationalism. Radicals believed that a foreign policy based upon 'free trade' and diplomatic restraint was preferable to 'meddlesome truculence cloaked under the guise of the patriotic "national" policy.'[64] Yet he was no isolationist: in an essay written ca. 1857–8 Green satisfied himself that Britain might justifiably intervene in European and world politics in order to uphold international law.[65] He was dismayed by intra-Italian struggles and by the aggressions of France and Austria between 1859 and 1861, but was hopeful for a 'Mazzinian' or federal solution to Italian nationalism. Green visited Switzerland and Germany in the summer of 1862 and again in 1863 and displayed a lively interest in German social and political conditions. He was worried by Bismarck's press ordinances but characteristically envisaged an alliance between the artisans and the educated middle classes as the basis of a strong and responsible German Liberalism.[66]

Since his days at Rugby Green had identified with the political aspirations of British artisans and had even expressed sympathy for the 'militant' suffragists. He was active in the Reform League in 1866–7 and rejoiced in the passage of the Second Reform Act. Green championed the Federal cause in the American Civil War against a 'slave-holding, slave-breeding, and slave-burning oligarchy, on whom the curse of God

---

[63] Hinchliff, *Benjamin Jowett*, chap. 2, pp. 149–51, 163–7. Pattison had by the 1860s reversed his view of the collegiate-tutorial system and held that students and tutors alike were deprived by the system: 'a tutor could thoroughly master only a single branch of classical learning even; and then there was the whole field of knowledge outside classics to be furnished with teachers who could only be professors of the University' (Pattison, *Memoirs*, p. 259). Most progressive dons of the 1870s and '80s adopted some version of Pattison's view, while Jowett appeared conservative in comparison.

[64] So Richard Shannon describes the oppositional (i.e. anti-Palmerston and anti-aristocratic) view of the Radicals, Gladstone, and even some moderate Conservatives during the late '50s and early '60s. *Crisis of Imperialism*, p. 40.

[65] 'Can interference with foreign nations in any case be justifiable?,' Undergraduate Notebook #2, GP 2(b). Printed in *AW*, pp. 15–19.

[66] R. L. Nettleship, 'Memoir,' pp. xli–xlii.

and humanity rests.'[67] Also typical of his high-toned political attitude was his response to the 1865 outrages in Jamaica sanctioned by the colonial governor: with J. S. Mill and other members of the 'Jamaica Committee' Green urged the prosecution of the brutal Governor Eyre to the full extent of the law. The Jamaica Committee and its opponents included many leading academic and literary men of the time; Carlyle was among Eyre's defenders. The sentiments and actions of the Jamaica Committee were reminiscent of those of the anti-slavery and anti-militarist movements of the period ca. 1815–48. However, as Bernard Semmel and Richard Shannon have noted, the engagement of Green and many other liberals in the Eyre prosecution anticipated a more systematic anti-imperialism (see 5.6 and 6.5 below).[68]

Green's interest in Reform included the English universities. By the 1850s and '60s reform of Oxford and Cambridge had attracted the attention of such leading politicians as Gladstone, Salisbury, Robert Lowe and John Bright. Gladstone, Salisbury and Lowe recommended change of some university statutes in order to preserve the Anglican and intellectually conservative character of Oxbridge. In contrast, Green, James Bryce and other young Liberals regarded the University Tests of (Anglican) doctrinal conformity as both an intellectual nuisance and a great political and social wrong.[69] Green attended the important meeting of University men, clergy, journalists, and politicians at the Freemasons' Tavern, London, on 10 June 1864, and he attended a Parliamentary debate on the Tests as late as 1866.[70] Although his father, maternal grandfather and maternal uncles were Anglican clergymen, Green urged disestablishment of the Church throughout the 1860s.

As was the case with other University Liberals, Green's interest in the Tests was connected to his interest in social reform. Reform of education at all levels was a social necessity. Following abolition in 1868 of college

---

[67] Green was commissioned to write an essay on bribery in elections for a book to be published in 1867 by Macmillan's (*Questions for a Reformed Parliament*) but he never delivered (Harvie, *Lights*, pp. 129–30). Green's words against the Confederacy are from his February 1863 Oxford Union speech (quoted in Nettleship, 'Memoir,' p. xliii).

[68] Henry Nettleship's recollection (in *GP* 1b) comments on Green's participation in the agitation against Eyre. See also [Jamaica Committee], *Facts and Documents Relating to the Alleged Rebellion in Jamaica, and the Measures of Repression: Including Notes of the Trial of Mr. Gordon* (London: Privately printed, 1866); B. Semmel, *The Governor Eyre Controversy* (London: MacGibbon and Kee, 1962); and Shannon, *Gladstone and the Bulgarian Agitation*, pp. 206–9.

[69] Henry Nettleship recalls that he, Green, Sidgwick, Bryce, Edward Caird, and a few others contemplated publishing a volume of essays on the Tests Question as early as 1862–3, but they gave it up because 'the question ripened so soon' (Nettleship Recollection, *GP* 1b). Sir Edward Strachey, letter to C. Green [June, 1886] in *GP* 1b; Harvie, *Lights*, chaps. 2, 4.

[70] Letter (23 March 1866) to James Bryce cited above.

residency requirements at Oxford, Green was warden of the new Balliol Hall for 'unattached' students. (The latter were relieved of many of the fees that made the collegiate system so expensive.) He was interested in primary and secondary education and had ideas about their improvement. By 1872 he was a temperance activist of some importance, believing that alcohol abuse was one of the endemic miseries of the working classes. Green's attention to the Drink Question during the 1850s and '60s had an important personal dimension: his brother, Valentine, Jr. (four years his senior), was a binge drinker who had been expelled from both Oxford and Cambridge universities for disciplinary infractions.[71]

Green's serious engagement with political and social problems during the 1850s and '60s did not divert him from the practice of philosophy — more specifically, the clarification and advancement of Idealism. Despite his indebtedness to Kant and post-Kantian German thought, it is impossible to characterize Green as an imitative Kantian or Hegelian. He merits recognition as the founder of the 'Oxford Hegelian' school not because he initiated serious study of German Idealism but because he persisted in it longer than his Oxford predecessors. Between the 1840s and Green's time Jowett, Frederick Temple, T. C. Sandars and Goldwin Smith had lectured and written about Kant and about Hegel's logic, legal philosophy and historical method. More generally, of course, the educated British public had become familiar with German thought since Kant principally through the literary and critical writings of Coleridge and Carlyle. A landmark was the translation by George Eliot of D. F. Strauss's *Das Leben Jesu* (1835–6), published in 1846. Eliot's work clearly demonstrated to British readers the Hegelian basis of the 'Higher Criticism', as German philological, literary and historical criticism came to be called (whether or not it derived from Idealist philosophy).[72]

As early as 1861, by which time he was a tutor and a fellow of Balliol, Green had embarked upon serious study of Kant and Hegel, perhaps in

---

[71] The brothers roomed together at 58 St John's Street in Oxford for seven months in 1861–2. Charlotte Green noted ominously to R. L. Nettleship that in April 1862 Green's 'efforts to reclaim his elder brother from drinking had ended unsuccessfully.' Wempe, citing letters I have not consulted, claims 'Arthur [sic] left for London on 28 March 1862 and Green went to live in College for the Easter term of that year' (*Beyond Equality*, p. 207, n. 59). J. A. Symonds (recollection in GP 1b) notes these Green family difficulties.

[72] Dozens of English writers, and even more Scottish ones, since the 1820s had remarked on the development of German philosophy and other scholarship. Oxford was more benighted than other learned academies. Edward Pusey reported that during the 1820s 'there were only two men in Oxford believed to know any German' (Faber, *Jowett*, p. 179). J. Bradley, 'Hegel in Britain,' *Heythrop Journal*, 20 (1979), pp. 1–24, 163–82; K. Willis, 'The Introduction and Critical Reception of Hegelian Thought in Britain 1830–1900,' *VS*, 32 (1988), pp. 85–111; H. G. Reventlow and W. Farmer, eds., *Biblical Studies and the Shifting of Paradigms, 1850–1914* (Sheffield: Sheffield Academic Press, 1995); Den Otter, *British Idealism and Social Explanation*, chap. 2.

continuation of Jowett's interrupted efforts.[73] Ben Wempe has meticulously traced Green's reading, establishing that Green turned seriously to Hegel in 1861 while on a reading party with John Conington. A manuscript in the Green Papers at Balliol labelled 'Analysis of Hegel' dates, by Wempe's reckoning, to 1866, and a translation/summary of Hegel's *Philosophische Propadeutik* (his lectures at the Nuremberg Gymnasium) in Green's hand dates also to the 1860s.[74] Green's earliest published writings, 'The Force of Circumstances' (1858) and *An Estimate of the Value and Influence of Works of Fiction in Modern Times* (Chancellor's English Prize essay, Oxford University, 1862), show no specific impress of Hegel, nor indeed of other Idealists.[75] Green's two *North British Review* essays — 'The Philosophy of Aristotle' (1866) and 'Popular Philosophy in Its Relation to Life' (1868) — indicate both knowledge of and engagement with Idealism.[76] Green's 'Notebook of School Inspection', relating to his Taunton Commission activities in 1865–6, includes a list of books by Ritschl, Trendelenburg, Meyer, Schwegler, Ewald and others. Whether this represents texts lent to or borrowed from colleagues, the list suggests the range of German philological, theological and historical scholarship to which Green had been exposed before 1868 (see 3.4–3.5 below).[77]

Green's religious thought, and the influence of Idealism on it, will be discussed at length in Chapters Two and Three below. It should be noted at this juncture that it was in thinking about religion and spiritual matters that Green first became convinced of the value of Kant and post-Kantian thinkers. One of his earliest (though uncompleted) scholarly endeavours was a translation, commenced about 1863, of Ferdinand Christian Baur's *Geschichte der christlichen Kirche*.[78] Baur

---

[73] Hinchliff observes, 'Jowett and [Frederick] Temple had set out — in the 1840s — to translate some of Hegel (probably the *Wissenschaft der Logik*) into English, though the enterprise was abandoned when Temple moved from Balliol in 1848' (*Benjamin Jowett*, p. 80). Early published renderings of Hegel into English included *The Subjective Logic of Hegel*, trans. H. Sloman and J. Wallon (London: J. Chapman, 1855) and *Lectures on the Philosophy of History*, trans. J. Sibree (London: G. Bell and Sons, 1857).

[74] Wempe refers to 'MS.4' in *GP* 2(a) and 'Analysis of Hegel' in *GP* 2(b), Box 1. *Beyond Equality*, pp. 21–32, 59–64.

[75] 'The Force of Circumstances,' *Undergraduate Papers*, no. 3 (Oxford, 1858), pp. 147–54, reprinted in *Works*, iii, pp. 3–10; the prize essay was read in the Sheldonian Theatre, Oxford, 2 July 1862, and reprinted in *Works*, iii, pp. 20–45.

[76] Reprinted in *Works*, iii, pp. 46–91, 92–125.

[77] Notebook in *GP* 1(c). The notebook includes material relating to Green's activities through 1868 or 1869 (as inferred from events and persons noted).

[78] 60 pp. mss. in *GP* 4, marked 'T. H. Green'. Letter of THG to Mrs. A. H. Clough, 12 December 1869: Bodleian MS.Eng.Lett.e.76, fols. 195–7. Mrs Clough was the widow of the Balliol poet Arthur Hugh Clough. R. L. Nettleship ('Memoir', pp. xxxvii–viii) notes Green's translation but makes no mention of Clough taking part in it. Apparently Green and Mrs Clough embarked on separate projects and each subsequently

(1792–1860) was David Strauss's teacher, an esteemed German theologian in the line of Hegel. In reading Baur's *Geschichte* sympathetically
Green implied his own agreement with a Hegelian view of Christianity
— that a Divine spirit was 'immanent', revealing itself not only in the life
of Jesus of Nazareth and the functions of an apostolic church but in the
actions of individual human beings in historical time.[79]

Green was unusual among his British contemporaries in regarding
critical study of Kant and his successors as a necessary step towards
putting philosophy on a more secure foundation. What Peter Hinchliff
says of the Idealist Edward Caird (1835–1908) applies as well to Green:
'he took Kant as the starting-point for all his philosophy, but he did so
because he believed that Kant proclaimed the essential truth, that life is
moral.'[80] Green believed that the version of empiricism originating with
Locke and Hume could not provide a plausible explanation of moral
life. This most important negative argument of Green's philosophy
emerged in the 1860s and remained unchanged: empiricism reduced
ideas to sensations and stimuli produced by an objective (external)
world, a world set aside, conceptually, from the human mind.[81] As Kant
and others taught, there is no experience without mind, and mind establishes relations among facts. The phenomenal world is only an aspect of
reality, and 'reason, if abstracted from ideals like system, coherence,
truth, and intelligibility, is incapable of discharging its function of grasp-
ing reality.'[82] The 'hedonist' empiricists of Green's own era, including
J. S. Mill, Spencer and Sidgwick, were simply 'anachronistic'.[83]

Some of Green's early pupils recognized the unconventional nature
of his views and the intellectual costs of propagating them. C. A. Fyffe,
who passed his Greats finals in December, 1867, recalled that Green's
serious pupils of the period 1864–7 (including R. L. Nettleship) were
inclined to overlook Green's lack of clarity in expressing himself

---

learned of the other's efforts. James Bryce recalled that Green began the translation of
Baur during their 1863 travels in Germany. Letter printed in *AW*, pp. 431-3 and n.50.

[79] On Baur and German Biblical criticism, see Merz, *History of European Thought in the
Nineteenth Century*, iii, pp. 170–5; Georg Schwaiger, ed., *Historische Kritik in der
Theologie: Beitraege zu ihrer Geschichte* (Goettingen: Vandenhoeck & Ruprecht, 1980);
Ulrich Koepf, ed., *Historisch-kritische Geschichtsbetrachtung: Ferdinand Christian Baur
und seine Schueler: 8. Blaubeurer Symposion* (Sigmaringen: J. Thorbecke, 1994).

[80] Hinchliff, *Benjamin Jowett*, p. 211. Caird is best known for his *Critical Philosophy of
Immanuel Kant* (1889) and *The Evolution of Religion* (1893); he succeeded Jowett as Master of Balliol. Green reviewed Caird's earlier work on Kant in *Academy* (September 22,
1877), reprinted in *Works*, iii, pp. 126–37 ('The Philosophy of Kant').

[81] On Green's critique of empiricism and his recognition of differences between Locke's
account of experience and that of Hume, see Hylton, *Russell*, pp. 21–31.

[82] Beck, *Handbook in Social Philosophy*, p. 89. Kant referred to constituting 'categories' of
the mind, Green to 'conceptions'.

[83] 'Introduction to the Moral Part of Hume's "Treatise [of Human Nature"]' (1874), in
Works, i, pp. 370–1. Henceforth 'Hume II'.

because they were aware of his struggle to define an original position.[84] Green's attention to Kant and the German Idealists was all the more unusual in the 1860s, at least for a regular tutorial fellow, because these scholarly interests did not correlate with the Oxford undergraduate curriculum.[85] For the first public examination, students were examined in mathematics or Classics, and in neither area were they required to work up 'modern' texts.[86] The second and final examination for Pass (not Honours) candidates required no specific knowledge of modern philosophy apart from what might be included under the rubrics of medieval and modern history (conceived in narrowly political terms), modern languages, political economy or legal studies. The most recent books for which candidates for the final Honours School of *Literae Humaniores* were responsible were Bacon's *Novum Organum*, Locke's *Essay Concerning Human Understanding* and Bishop Butler's *Sermons on Human Nature*.[87] Only after 1870 — due to the influence of Green, Jowett and a few others on the Boards of Studies — were Greats students required to read Hume, Kant and other modern thinkers for examination in the 'outlines of moral and political philosophy.'[88]

It is clear that at the beginning of his scholarly career Green felt his research agenda to be restricted by the Oxford curriculum.[89] It was in the process of preparing an edition of Aristotle's *Nichomachean Ethics*

[84] C. A. Fyffe recollection (undated) in *GP* 1(b): pp. 115–39 in CBG copybook.

[85] Goldwin Smith, appointed Regius Professor of Modern History at Oxford in 1858, referred to Hegel in his 1859-61 lectures and articulated a quasi-Hegelian philosophy of historical progress. Willis, 'Hegelian Thought in Britain,' pp. 103–4; Soffer, *Discipline and Power*, p. 84. Still, students and tutors alike in the collegiate system had little incentive to read Kant or Hegel. Green's own undergraduate coach, Charles Parker, claims to have set Green on this track in 1857-8. 'I was impressed and interested by the ability, as well as earnestness with which he reasoned.' Parker also testifies to the Oxford dons' scanty knowledge of German Idealism before 1870 (*GP* 1b Recollections: C. S. Parker to C. Green, 26 September 1888).

[86] The discussion of curricular requirements in this paragraph is derived from *Student's Handbook*, chap. 4. 'Those who do not seek Honours' were examined at Mods in the four Gospels in Greek; logic, or mathematics; translation of English into Latin; and 'three books, of which one at least must be Greek, and one either a historical or a philosophical work' from a list of about twenty ancient texts.

[87] By the later '70s students were allowed to offer, as 'special subjects', papers on Hume, Berkeley, and modern political economists (*Student's Handbook*, p. 142). In theory students could have offered as subjects of special papers Rousseau, James and J. S. Mill, Reid, Bentham, John Austin, William Hamilton, and others, but they did so only rarely, and no doubt to the chagrin of their examiners. Green himself had 'optionally' read as an undergraduate Berkeley, Hume, Reid, Kant, and Hegel (C. S. Parker recollection cited above).

[88] *Student's Handbook*, pp. 140–2; Pattison, 'Philosophy at Oxford;' Richter, *Politics of Conscience*, pp. 151–3.

[89] Some of his friends recognized this. Henry Nettleship complained to James Bryce, 'Would that he [Green] would get [sic] to and write a book — but Oxford is not favourable to such things' (Nettleship to Bryce, 17 September 1866, Bodleian MSS. Bryce 110, fols. 33–6).

between 1863 and 1866 (but not completed) that Green became better acquainted with philosophers since Bishop Berkeley.[90] The essay which issued from this project, 'The Philosophy of Aristotle', published in *North British Review* in 1866, represented Aristotle as a proto-idealist.[91] His 1868 essay 'Popular Philosophy in Its Relation to Life' (also published in *North British Review*) indicates the real beginnings of an independent line of philosophical thinking and anticipates his more extensive critique of Locke and Hume (1874–5). Green's unpublished lectures dating to 1866–8 are significant as well for their departure from pure exposition of and commentary on the texts with which Oxford examinees were expected to be acquainted. The 'Lecture on Moral Philosophy' (ca. 1868: MS 10A in GP 2a) contains a discussion of 'pure' versus 'practical' reason in Kant (and, running on the reverse sides of pages from back to front, a critique of Kant's theory of intelligibility). The 'Lectures on Moral and Political Philosophy', which F. H. Bradley (1846–1924) and (possibly) G. M. Hopkins heard as undergraduates in 1867 or 1868, discuss moralists and philosophers as various as Plato, Marcus Aurelius, Butler, Bentham, Hegel, Comte and J. S. Mill. Green concludes here that 'All important modern ethic is from Kant to Hegel.'[92]

More than his publishing activity, Green's teaching of modern texts, particularly German ones, made him vulnerable to criticism from Oxford dons convinced of the superior didactic usefulness of Classical literature and the foundational texts of Anglican Christianity. Tractarians like E. B. Pusey, Canon of Christ Church and Regius Professor of Hebrew, maintained that religious scepticism was a foreign influence, 'imported [into Oxford] by Germanising liberals.' H. P. Liddon and other heirs to Tractarianism kept such intellectual conservatism alive at Oxford into the 1890s.[93] Perhaps if Green had limited himself to

---

[90] With regard to Berkeley, Green reviewed *The Works of George Berkeley, D.D.*, ed. A. C. Fraser, 4 vols. (Oxford: Clarendon, 1871) in *Academy*, 3, no. 40 (January 15, 1872), pp. 27–8. He concluded that Berkeley's destiny and historical function was to show the necessity of Kant.

[91] Green took the appearance of an edition by Sir Alexander Grant as occasion to expound his view of Aristotle. (Nettleship, 'Memoir,' p. xxxvii.) The *North British Review* ran from 1844 to 1871 and achieved a maximum circulation ca. 1865 of 3,000 copies. It was taken over in 1869 by a group of liberal Catholics led by Acton, who expanded the journal's reviewing of books by foreign, especially French and German, writers. J. H. Newman and High Anglicans regarded the Review as hopelessly liberal. *Wellesley Index to Victorian Periodicals, 1824–1900*, vol. i, ed. W. Houghton (Toronto: Toronto UP, 1966), pp. 663–6.

[92] *AW*, pp. 105-182 (quotation p. 180): notes of F. H. Bradley, Merton College, Oxford (IA1). Nicholson (like Wempe) dates these to 1867.

[93] Ward, *Victorian Oxford*, p. 129. See also Pattison, 'Philosophy at Oxford'; Heyck, *Transformation*, p. 160 and *passim*; Hinchliff, *Benjamin Jowett*, pp. 168–81. Clergy outside the universities were probably even less tolerant of German scholarship. Even before the controversies over *Essays and Reviews* and Colenso, Bishop Blomfield of

uncontroversial commentary on standard authors his way to scholarly distinction would have been less arduous.

A turning point occurred in 1874–5, when Green published (with T. H. Grose) a four-volume edition of Hume's *Essays, Moral, Political and Literary* (including the *Treatise of Human Nature*, 1739–40), to which he provided a lengthy introduction. The introduction was an assault on Hume and Locke but also indirectly on nineteenth-century 'hedonistic' theories of mind and morals. Since the eighteenth century various British thinkers had attacked Hume's version of utilitarian ethics.[94] Green, however, observed that Hume's assumptions had survived in the thought of J. S. Mill, Henry Sidgwick, and contemporary natural scientists of the mind. These and other modern thinkers were children of Hume, 'misunderstanding our passivity in experience — unaware that it has no meaning except in relation to an object which thought itself projects.'[95] The page heading of Green's conclusion to the second introduction is 'Hume terminates an epoch', and there he expresses his hope that the attentions of Englishmen might be diverted 'from the anachronistic systems hitherto prevalent among us to the study of Kant and Hegel.'[96] Virtually the entire tradition of British empiricism was being attacked from behind the smoke screen of an introduction to a standard edition, and some recognized the challenge for what it was. It was in no small part due to Green's 'Hume and Locke' that the British public formed some conception of philosophical idealism.[97]

London inquired of each candidate for ordination, 'I trust, sir, that you don't understand German?' (H. N. Oxenham [1861], quoted in Willis, 'Hegelian Thought in Britain,' p. 95).

[94] See Schneewind, *Sidgwick's Ethics*, chaps. 2–5.

[95] Evidence of particular contemporary thinkers Green meant to implicate in 'Hume and Locke' lies in his 1874–5 Balliol lectures. The unpublished Green MSS. 6A, 7A, 12 (in GP 2a) deal primarily with Hume, Kant, and Mill; these date to the period 1867–74. The published 'Lectures on Logic' [1874–5] (*Works*, ii, pp. 157–306) contain critiques of J. S. Mill and H. L. Mansel which relate to criticisms made in the edition of Hume. Mansel, a Churchman, had delivered the 1858 Bampton lectures on 'the limits of religious thought' and debated with F. D. Maurice (a theologically heterodox Anglican) questions of the possibility of human knowledge of the divine. Green's lectures also referred to Sir William Hamilton, a mid–century representative of the Scottish 'common–sense' school of Reid, James Beattie, and Dugald Stewart. Hamilton's reputation had been seriously damaged by Mill in 1865. R. V. Sampson, 'The Limits of Religious Thought: the Theological Controversy,' in *1859: Entering an Age of Crisis*, ed. Appleman et al., pp. 63–80; Schneewind, *Sidgwick's Ethics*, chap. 2.

[96] 'Hume II', pp. 370–1.

[97] W. H. Walsh, 'Green's Criticism of Hume' in *Philosophy of T. H. Green*, ed. Vincent, pp. 21–35. Pattison was the first authority to connect Green to an Oxford Idealist movement (see his *Memoirs*, pp. 165–7; and 'Philosophy at Oxford,' pp. 94–6).

In December, 1877, Green was elected to the Whyte's Professorship.[98] As the position carried with it a seat on the Hebdomadal Council, the main governing body of Oxford University, the zenith of Green's academic career coincided with his dominance as a university politician. In the year preceding the appointment he published in *Academy, Contemporary Review, Journal of Education* and *Mind*. The *Mind* and *Contemporary Review* essays expressed his views about some of the most contemporary versions of scientific materialism, including 'evolution', as applied to study of the human mind and morals.[99] Of Green and the evolutionists G. S. Brett remarks,

> Between Green and those writers who laid emphasis on the physical substratum of the mind, the natural history of morals, and the continuity of animal and human natures, there was hardly sufficient sympathy to make the antagonism interesting.[100]

This assessment is true in the sense that Green consciously toned down his polemical early attacks on the Spencerian evolutionists and the utilitarians, and, by the later 1870s, was formulating a complete alternative system. In 1878, Graham Wallas (1858–1932), budding sociologist and future member of the Fabian Society, attended Green's lectures. Wallas asked on one occasion whether the Professor's argument about the 'continued existence of a conscious mind' applied to the mind of a *dog*. Green replied tersely that he was not interested in dogs.[101] Elsewhere he was willing enough to smite his enemies. As much as T. H. Huxley and Spencer, Green saw himself as the representative of a great cause, and consciousness of a mission made him an eager controversialist.

Even before publication of what are today regarded as his major writings, Green was known to a sizeable reading public concerned with philosophical issues. That Green chose to publish in the *Contemporary*, a large-circulation review of general culture (with approximately 10,000 copies per month in 1878), as well as in the philosophy journal *Mind* indicates something about his intellectual intentions. The *Contemporary* had been launched in 1866 to counter the *Fortnightly Review*'s moderate

---

[98] J. R. T. Eaton, appointed in 1874, resigned the professorship in the autumn of 1877. See J. Symonds to Charlotte Green, 13 November 1877 [letter 1075], in *Letters of John Addington Symonds*, ii.

[99] 'Hedonism and the Ultimate Good,' *Mind*, ii (1877), pp. 266–9; 'Mr. Herbert Spencer and Mr. G. H. Lewes: Their Application of the Doctrine of Evolution to Thought (Part I),' *Contemporary Review*, 31 (1877), pp. 25–53 [reprinted in *Works*, i, pp. 373–409]. Parts two and three of the Spencer/Lewes critique appeared in *Contemporary Review*, 31 (pp. 745–69) and 32 (pp. 751–72) [both reprinted in *Works*, i].

[100] Brett, 'Green', p. 437.

[101] M. Wiener, *Between Two Worlds. The Political Thought of Graham Wallas* (Oxford: Clarendon, 1971), p. 8. Green concluded in *Prolegomena to Ethics*, 'If the animals have a consciousness corresponding to that which we exercise in knowledge, at any rate we cannot enter into it' (sec. 84).

agnosticism and rationalism. The special province of the *Contemporary* until the early 1880s (whence it 'assumed a more [politically] activist tone') was 'religious problems' as enlightened by 'current philosophy and science.' *Mind*, the first professional journal of philosophy in Britain, commenced in 1876 as one kind of reaction to the great reviews. Its founder, the Scottish philosopher Alexander Bain, felt that the *Contemporary*, the *Quarterly Review* and others were not devoting enough attention to serious philosophy.[102] It is fair to say that Green, in sending essays to the *Contemporary Review* and *Mind*, sought to propagate his ideas via the middle-brow as well as the high-brow press and to influence opinion beyond Academe.

The work for which Green is perhaps best known to other philosophers is his *Prolegomena to Ethics*, which appeared in 1883 and remained in print until 1949. Although seen through the press by his former student A. C. Bradley, the *Prolegomena* had nevertheless been conceived as a single work, a systematic treatise on the basis of knowledge and the moral formation of the individual. By demonstrating 'the practical value of a theory of the moral ideal,' the *Prolegomena* was an attempt to supplant 'hedonistic' empiricism with an effective 'theory of the good as human perfection.'[103] Roughly one-quarter of the material in the *Prolegomena* had appeared in three successive issues (January, April, July, 1882) of *Mind* ('Can There Be a Natural Science of Man?').

Richard 'Lew' Nettleship, another of Green's students, assembled for publication most of the remainder of his professorial lectures. Appended to these were previously published materials, including the aforementioned critique of Hume, the majority of Green's published reviews and short essays (some dating to his undergraduate years), and two 'lay' sermons (the latter were also published separately with a preface by Arnold Toynbee). To all of this were added previously unpublished speeches and essays and Nettleship's 'Memoir' of the master. The collected *Works of T. H. Green* were published in three volumes between 1885 and 1888. Green's *Lectures on the Principles of Political Obligation*

---

[102] Quotations from Houghton, ed., *Wellesley Index to Victorian Periodicals*, i, pp. 210–13. See also J. Roach, 'Liberalism and the Victorian Intelligentsia,' *Cambridge Historical Review*, 13 (1957), pp. 58–81; Heyck, *Transformation*, chap. 2; Annan, *Leslie Stephen*, chaps. 2–3; Collini, *Public Moralists*, pp. 52–7, 211–12.

[103] The first edition of Henry Sidgwick's *Methods of Ethics* appeared in 1874, the year after Mill's death. While Schneewind contends, 'it is a mistake to view the book as primarily a defence of utilitarianism,' he concludes that since Sidgwick prioritized 'the demands of rationality' in moral–ethical speculation, he was convinced 'that there is no alternative principle satisfying these demands as well as the utilitarian principle' (*Sidgwick's Ethics*, pp. 192, 422). The second (1877) and third (1884) editions of *Methods of Ethics* responded to Green's and others' criticisms of Sidgwick's conception of moral action. See the prefaces (pp. ix–xiv) to *Methods*, 7th ed., with foreword by John Rawls (Indianapolis, IN: Hackett, 1981). Also, Sidgwick's important critique of Green's *Prolegomena*: 'Green's Ethics,' *Mind*, 9 (1884), pp. 169–87.

were published in the second volume of *Works* (1886) but appeared in 1895 in an edition compiled by fellow British Idealist Bernard Bosanquet.[104] The *Lectures* went through eleven reprintings down to the 1960s and remain Green's best known contribution to political theory.[105] Peter Nicholson has ventured to rank them towards the bottom of the ten or twelve most important works in the history of (Western) political philosophy.[106] *Prolegomena* and 'Hume and Locke' were readily available in abbreviated form through the 1970s, and Green's works have appeared in recent collections and anthologies.[107] Denigration of the 'school' of Green became popular among academic philosophers after the Second World War, yet more than a century after Green's death *Prolegomena* and *Lectures on the Principles of Political Obligation* remained standard reading for philosophy students at Oxford.[108]

1.3. THE QUESTION OF INFLUENCE

In what ways do consciously propagated teachings, as well as ideas generally, affect 'real life'? How does one ascertain the beginnings and endings of the influence of a person or group? I contend that with regard to Green these are meaningful, not futile questions, although the answers given by some Green scholars have been unhelpful or misleading. No one can deny that Green found a receptive audience, particularly during the time (ca. 1880–1914) when Britain was the pre-eminent world power. Historians continue to demonstrate how men and women consciously applied Green's teachings to their investigation of problems, both speculative and practical.[109] To support his claim about Green's

---

[104] In his preface to *Principles*, Bosanquet indicates that Green's lectures presented themselves as an obvious 'text-book for a projected course of instruction on political theory, to be given in London' (*LPPO* [1955 imprint], p. v.).

[105] See *Harris and Morrow*, p. 321 (containing a publishing history of Green's writings).

[106] 'A Moral View of Politics: T. H. Green and the British Idealists' [review essay], *Political Studies*, 35 (1987), p. 116.

[107] Paperback editions of Green's writings include *Thomas Hill Green's Hume and Locke*, edited with an introduction by R. M. Lemos (New York: Thomas Crowell, 1968); and J. R. Rodman, ed., *The Political Theory of T. H. Green* (New York: Appleton–Century–Crofts, 1964). The compilation by Harris and Morrow cited above remains in print. Green's 1881 essay 'Liberal Legislation and Freedom of Contract' is probably the most widely read of his writings today. It has been reprinted in *Harris and Morrow* (pp. 194–212); in David Miller, ed., *Liberty* (OUP, 1991); and in J. Stapleton, ed., *Liberalism, Democracy, and the State in Britain: Five Essays, 1862–1891* (Bristol: Thoemmes, 1997).

[108] When I first examined Green's manuscripts at Balliol in the spring of 1991, the *Prolegomena* was included in the standard reading of the Oxford 'Modern Greats' or PPE curriculum (School of Philosophy, Politics and Economics).

[109] See especially J. Harris, 'Political Thought and the Welfare State, 1870–1940: An Intellectual Framework for British Social Policy,' *Past and Present*, 135 (1992), pp. 117–39;

intellectual and moral authority, Richter observes that in the 1906 General Election — the 'Liberal Landslide' — '31 Balliol graduates were elected to the House of Commons' and the Cabinet included four Balliol men.[110] Among the latter was the Chancellor of the Exchequer, Herbert Henry Asquith (Prime Minister, 1908–16). Asquith had earned First Class Honours in Greats, was elected in 1874 to a Balliol fellowship and enjoyed a successful career as a barrister before turning to politics. Asquith recalled, 'Although I never "worshipped at the Temple's inner shrine" I owe more than I can say to Green's gymnastics, both intellectual and moral.'[111]

Stefan Collini detects a 'misplaced individualism in explanation' in adducing such testimony as evidence, as Richter does, of the transmission of Green's influence. Rather, Collini argues, Green's considerable impact can be explained by the fact that many 'assumptions' of his philosophy were already widely shared.[112] Sandra den Otter similarly concludes that Green's philosophy and British Idealism generally were 'so persuasive because … [they] provided a foundation for community.' In an era when forms of social dysfunction, such as chronic poverty among the working population, were being attributed to rampant individualism, Green's socially conscious theory of human perfection was bound to appeal.[113] Yet in assessing Green's influence it would be a mistake to ignore his institutional location. His association with Balliol College was a crucial determinant of his impact. John Bowles has remarked, 'the tradition of Victorian Balliol made an impact on society probably unique in the history of a British academic institution.'[114] This assertion gains plausibility if one substitutes 'the official mind' or 'the mind set of the governing elite' for 'society'. Balliol was one of the largest Oxbridge colleges and the largest producer of higher public servants by 1880. As

---

and H. G. Williams, 'Arthur Acland, Tom Ellis and Welsh Education: A Study in the Politics of Idealism,' *Welsh Historical Review*, 17 (1995), pp. 387–410. Victor Bailey notes that Evelyn Ruggles-Brise, chairman of the Prison Commission from 1895, referred specifically to Green's ideas about 'realization of the best possible self.' Ruggles–Brise helped effect a 'sea change in prison policy and practice between 1895 and 1922' by contesting the prevailing 'positivist paradigm', including the accepted typology of criminality and the notion of hereditary criminality. Bailey, 'English Prisons,' pp. 310–15, 324.

[110] Richter, 'T. H. Green and His Audience,' p. 444.

[111] *Memories and Reflections: 1852–1927*, i (Boston: Little, Brown, 1928), p. 24. See also the more reverential comments in his Romanes Lecture of 1918, *Some Aspects of the Victorian Age* (Oxford: Clarendon, 1918). Green ranked Asquith below Andrew Bradley in the 1874 Balliol fellowship competition. *GP* 2(b), box 2: notebook marked 'Analysis of Politics (Aristotle)' and 'Few Notes on philosophical paper in Fellowship Examination (Bradley and Asquith)'.

[112] Collini, *Public Moralists*, p. 83.

[113] Den Otter, *British Idealism*, p. 208.

[114] Bowle, *Politics and Opinion in the Nineteenth Century*, p. 274.

Harold Perkin notes, for the entire period 1832–1914 no less than ninety-four percent of Balliol graduates 'went into government service or the learned professions.'[115]

Even before his appointment as Whyte's Professor Green had a wide student audience due to Balliol's regular tutorial arrangements with half a dozen Oxford colleges in philosophy, theology and ethics. Green's March 1866 letter to James Bryce cited above hints that some of his early serious listeners were advanced undergraduates from outside Balliol and men already holding BA's competing for fellowships. F. H. Bradley had been an undergraduate at Merton when he heard Green's lectures on the history of moral philosophy. (His younger brother, Andrew, became one of Green's literary executors.) The economist J. A. Hobson (1858–1940) apparently attended Green's lectures ca. 1878–9 while an undergraduate at Lincoln College. L. T. Hobhouse (1864–1929), who tempered Green's metaphysics with Jamesian empirical psychology, went up to Corpus Christi College in the year Green's *Prolegomena* was published.[116] D. G. Ritchie (1853–1903), who must be ranked among the major British Idealists, had studied under Green in the early 1870s. Among Green's immediate but informal audience were wives, sisters and daughters of dons. Women were not admitted to Oxford University as degree-earning students until after the First World War. Green had been among those dons who formed a 'Lectures for Women' committee in 1873. He and Charlotte Green were among the founders in 1879 of Somerville Hall, one of the first colleges for women in Oxford. By the time of Green's death women at Oxford had access to some of the same educational resources as male undergraduates.[117]

Memoirs attest that for six or seven decades men and women went forth into the world from Oxford under the impression that Green's teachings deserved serious consideration. Alfred Marshall (1842–1924), the pre-eminent British economist between the reigns of Mill and Keynes, was slightly jealous of Green's hold on undergraduates. Mar-

[115] During the same period only twenty-nine Balliol graduates went on to business careers, and all of these into the genteel reaches of banking and land agency (Harold Perkin, *The Rise of Professional Society. England Since 1880* (London: Routledge, 1989), pp. 369–70).

[116] J. A. Hobson, *Confessions of an Economic Heretic*, ed. M. Freeden (Hassocks, Eng.: Harvester, 1976 [orig. 1938]), p. 26; and Collini, *Liberalism and Sociology*, pp. 54–6.

[117] See 6.6 below. Charlotte Green served on the Somerville College Council between 1884 and 1929. Somervilleans in the twentieth century included Indira Gandhi, Iris Murdoch and Margaret Thatcher. P. Lynn, 'Thomas Hill Green and His Involvement in Victorian Education' (B.Ed. thesis, Manchester Univ., 1976); G. Sutherland, 'The Movement for the Higher Education of Women: its Social and Intellectual Context in England, ca. 1840–80' in *Politics and Social Change in Modern Britain*, ed. P. J. Waller (Hassocks, Sussex: Harvester, 1987), pp. 91–116; J. Sutherland, *Mrs. Humphry Ward. Eminent Victorian, Pre-eminent Edwardian* (OUP, 1991), pp. 63–4; P. Adams, *Somerville for Women. An Oxford College, 1879–1993* (OUP, 1996).

shall was under the impression that in Green's lecture-room 'a hundred men, half of them B.A.'s ignoring examinations, were wont to hang on the lips of the man who was sincerely anxious to teach them the truths about the universe and human life.'[118] It is curious that Melvin Richter cites Marshall's statement as unstinted praise of Green, when it was intended as a judgment on Sidgwick, lecturing in Trinity College, Cambridge (Marshall claimed), to a 'handful of men ... bolting down what they regard as useful for examinations ...'[119] Marshall believed that Green's manner of teaching was a crucial ingredient of his influence.

By 1900 Green's reputation as a moral and political philosopher extended throughout the British empire, Europe, the United States, and even to China and Japan.[120] The wider influence of British culture might help to explain Green's popularity in Anglophone (or, in some cases, unconsciously Anglocentric) intellectual environments, even to the present day. Around the turn of the twentieth century the British Idealists — and their political ideas specifically — exercised considerable authority in Australia and New Zealand.[121] The longevity of British Idealism in South Asia is also noteworthy. Sarvepalli Radhakrishnan (1888-1975) taught philosophy at Madras, Calcutta, Benares and Oxford. His interpretation of Vedanta and classical Indian thought systems bore the imprint of Kant, F. H. Bradley and Andrew Seth Pringle-Pattison; his work had been introduced in English philosophical circles during the First World War by J. H. Muirhead (Green's student).[122] British Idealism's influence on academic philosophy in India via Radhakrishnan and his students was decisive as late as the 1970s and '80s.

---

[118] From a letter of Marshall to Henry Sidgwick, quoted in Richter, 'T. H. Green and His Audience,' p. 445. Marshall passed most of his academic career at Cambridge but was elected a fellow of Balliol in 1883.

[119] *Ibid.* See Harvie (*Lights*, p. 200) on the Green–Sidgwick rivalry.

[120] N. Abbagnana, *Il nuovo idealismo inglese e americano* (Naples: Società Anonima, 1927); K. R. Hoover, 'Liberalism and the Idealist Philosophy of Thomas Hill Green,' *Western Political Quarterly*, 26 (1973), pp. 550–65; H. Atsuko, 'Self–Realization and the Common Good: T. H. Green in Meiji Ethical Thought,' *Journal of Japanese Studies*, 5 (1979), pp. 107–36; Watson, 'Social Theory and National Culture'; B. Kuklick, *Churchmen and Philosophers. From Jonathan Edwards to John Dewey* (Yale UP, 1985), chap. 16.

[121] Boucher and Vincent, *British Idealism and Political Theory*, introduction.

[122] Radhakrishnan's first philosophy teacher had been a student of Andrew Seth Pringle-Pattison (who was loosely associated with Green through Edward Caird and William Wallace). Radhakrishnan delivered the Hibbert lectures in England in 1929, reprinted as *The Idealist View of Life*, and was subsequently appointed Spalding Professor of Eastern Philosophy and Religion at Oxford. Following Indian independence Radhakrishnan was a UNESCO delegate and Ambassador to Moscow before serving as Vice President and President of India. Robert Minor, *Radhakrishnan: a Religious Biography* (Albany: SUNY Press, 1986).

Green and the British Idealists, however, had only a modest impact on Continental European thought, not to be compared with that of J. S. Mill, Spencer, or even Samuel Smiles. Major French and Italian thinkers in the Idealist mode — like Alfred Fouillée — sympathized with Green's views but were not inspired by them. Benedetto Croce, one of the few twentieth-century Idealists of consequence, appears not to have been impressed by Green.[123] The British historian and philosopher Robin Collingwood (d. 1943) 'resituated' Idealism, as handed down to him by Green and others, with the aid of Croce's insights into the relation of philosophy to other forms of human experience, including history.[124]

Later in the present chapter I make some observations about how scholars of T. H. Green, British Idealism and British Liberalism have understood Green's influence. In Chapters Five and Six below I examine in greater detail Green's impact —both that of his teachings and of his personality—on various social and professional circles, as a way of correcting the received view of Green. Preliminary to this, however, there must be some further consideration of the intellectual currents which formed Green's ideas and to which he responded.

1.4. EMPIRICISM AND NATURALISM IN THE NINETEENTH CENTURY

As has been indicated by the quotation from Albert Dicey at the head of this chapter, some who witnessed the formation of Green's ideas and understood his later teachings perceived that Green cut across the grain of contemporary British thought. What intrigued Dicey was the resemblance between Green's reformist enthusiasm and Utilitarianism, which since the end of the eighteenth century had provided intellectual backing to various demands for the reform or abolition of inefficient institutions. Dicey recognized the intellectual provenance of Green's ideas, inspired as much by Wordsworth, Coleridge and Carlyle, as by any German thinkers Green or Dicey were then acquainted with. But because of Green's advocacy of the reformism of Cobden (the Manches-

---

[123] On Fouillée (1838–1912), see Kloppenberg, *Uncertain Victory*, pp. 35–7 and *passim*. Croce (1866–1952) absorbed the influences of Vico, Hegel, Marx, and Dilthey in developing a philosophical history. 'It would be a great error to call Croce a Hegelian. But one can argue that Hegel was responsible for the most doubtful features of Croce's thought — its tendency toward a schematic rationalism and its insistence on the pervasive role of a quasi–deity called "the spirit".' H. S. Hughes, *Consciousness and Society. The Reorientation of European Social Thought, 1890–1930*, revised ed. (New York: Vintage, 1977), p. 208 (quotation) and chap. 6.

[124] As tutor and professor at Oxford from 1912 to 1941, Collingwood bore the brunt of an assault on metaphysics led by Gilbert Ryle at Oxford and G. E. Moore at Cambridge. See Collingwood, *An Autobiography* (OUP, 1939); Fred Inglis, *Radical Earnestness. English Social Theory 1880–1980* (Oxford: M. Robertson, 1982), chap. 4 ('Resituating Idealism'); A. Quinton, 'Collingwood, Robin George' in *Twentieth-Century Culture*, p. 154.

ter School of 'free trade' and 'laissez-faire') and Bright (who encouraged franchise reform and employer–worker cooperation), he appeared to be linked historically and by temperament to the Benthamites, to the new (or 'professional') political economists like J. R. McCulloch and David Ricardo, and to the *Westminster Review* radicals including J. S. Mill. Green's earliest contributions to social theory were even more destructive than those of Philosophic Radicalism, offering less in the way of positive formulations and injunctions than criticism of the prevailing empiricism and positivism.

In 'Popular Philosophy in its Relation to Life', Green argued (*pace* Edmund Burke) that the 'moral sense' of the eighteenth-century Scottish Enlightenment was deeply flawed; it was at least inferior to that of the best evangelical reformers. The philosophy of David Hume and the felicific calculus of Jeremy Bentham constituted

> not merely, as theoretical, a different attitude of the spirit from the religious life, as practical; it was incapable of a theory of that life. Its 'moral sense', however construed, could account for nothing beyond distaste at an observed predominance of unsympathetic over generous passions, or regret for a mistaken calculation of the balance between possible pains and pleasures.[125]

A compelling spiritual-cum-idealist theory of ethical consciousness awaited its author. At least Rousseau's ideas (producing 'Jacobinism' but mellowing into a 'gentle liberalism'), Burke's 'true philosophical insight', the 'deeper view of life which the contemplative poets [chiefly Wordsworth] originated' and the 'revival of evangelical religion' pointed towards a true philosophy, one of whose purposes was to help orthodox Christianity 'recognize itself ... in the spiritual life of the world.'[126]

Green represented nineteenth-century Positive Philosophy, Utilitarianism and Humean empiricism as parts of the same moment or episode in the history of thought and argued that ascendant forms of social theory were based on wholly misleading descriptions of human thought and moral behaviour.[127] Evolutionism, in his view, did not count as a social theory at all. The significance of Green's anti-positivism and anti-naturalism was recognized by the American John Dewey, who in the early Idealist phase of his career (ca. 1880–94) accepted Green's lesson about the poverty of naturalism:

---

[125] 'Popular Philosophy,'*Works*, iii, p. 121.

[126] 'Popular Philosophy,'*Works*, iii, pp. 117, 120.

[127] 'Locke's formulation of the deliverances of common sense ... is also virtually Spencer's.' Hume's theory of experience and that of the Utilitarians were points along the same trajectory ('Mr. Herbert Spencer and Mr. G. H. Lewes. Their Application of the Doctrine of Evolution to Thought. Part I' [1877], in *Works*, i, pp. 385–7). See also Den Otter, *British Idealism*, chaps. 2–3.

Spencer, in a word, only tells us, taking a longer, more roundabout road than the earlier empiricists followed, using the life of the race instead of that of an individual, that experience is the source of knowledge, while he has a theory of experience which would not allow it to be the source of anything.[128]

Positivist and empiricist theories, extended from the ideas of the Scottish Enlightenment, represented individuals as social atoms bound by or to no unifying consciousness. 'Hedonist' theories of experience resorted to a model of the Self which represented self-seeking behaviour as the ultimate law of being. Utilitarian psychology, whether in its Benthamite or more sophisticated Millian forms, provided rationale for only tentative cooperation among individuals; in offering a very weak theory of mutualism it could do little to serve lasting social purposes, or even explain their existence.[129] Indeed, people were better than Utilitarianism could account for them being. The idea of survival of the fittest, on the other hand, had not been drawn out so as to clarify understanding of morality. Evolutionism as presented by Spencer and G. H. Lewes explained the facts of civilization no more adequately than did Hume.

Green contended that when individuals properly considered the content and consequences of their individuality, which was an expression of their freedom, they achieved moral consciousness; and every individual, from best to worst, was conscious to some degree of ordered or qualified being.[130] Spencer represented human conduct as 'trial and compromise', a conscious and constant balancing in each individual of egotistical and altruistic claims; and the history of civilization as a process of 'conciliation' working towards a higher valuation of altruism.[131] Green did not deny the fact of social evolution in some sense, but he dis-

---

[128] 'The Philosophy of T. H. Green,' *Andover Review*, 9 (1889), p. 343, as quoted in I. M. Greengarten, *Thomas Hill Green and the Development of Liberal-Democratic Thought* (Toronto: Toronto UP, 1981), p. 13.

[129] See in addition to 'Popular Philosophy', 'Hume II,' secs. 51–64; *PE*, secs. 154–170; *LPPO*, sec. 23. Green did concede that Utilitarianism had led to valuable reforms of British society: the Greatest Happiness formula was quasi-democratic in holding one person's pleasure equal to everyone else's; but this did have socially mischievous results (*PE*, sec. 213). On Green's critique of Utilitarianism, see H. Sidgwick, *Lectures on the Ethics of T. H. Green, Mr. Herbert Spencer, and J. Martineau* (London: Macmillan, 1902); Greengarten, *Thomas Hill Green*, chap. 7; and D. Weinstein, 'The New Liberalism and the Rejection of Utilitarianism' in *The New Liberalism*, ed. A. Simhony and D. Weinstein, pp. 159-83.

[130] Book III of *PE*, secs. 199–205 (on the origin of 'social interest' in the individual). Scholars have recognized Green's anti-utilitarian theory of 'unity of self-consciousness' as a distinctive contribution to liberal thought. Richter, *Politics of Conscience*, pp. 170–87; P. Hansen, 'T. H. Green and the Moralization of the Market,' *Canadian Journal of Political and Social Theory*, 1 (1977), pp. 91–117; A. Lawless, 'T. H. Green and the British Liberal Tradition,' *Canadian Journal of Political and Social Theory*, 2 (1978), pp. 142–55; and works by Greengarten and Simhony cited above.

[131] Spencer sketched this process abstractly in many of his writings: e.g. *The Data of Ethics* [1879] (New York: Hurst and Co., n.d.), chaps. 13–14.

played an Aristotelian belief in consciousness of good as a prior condition of morality. It was 'an ultimate fact of human history' that 'out of sympathies of animal origin, through their presence in a self-conscious soul, there arise interests as of a person in persons.' Individuals become 'capable of conceiving and seeking a permanent well-being in which the permanent well-being of others is included.'[132] The development of individuals and societies therefore had a spiritual origin and a spiritual unfolding. As one scholar of English thought has noted,

> The Realists were only interested in the [evolutionary] process as explaining man's development in terms of nature; the Idealists laid emphasis on the supposed end towards which evolution was working, an end which they regarded as spiritual.[133]

Before turning to exposition of Green's theories of experience and morality (Chapter Two) we should have an understanding of the contemporary intellectual and moral climate, the dominant mentality of educated Europeans. Owen Chadwick has described the dominance of naturalism and of empiricist methods in the study of human affairs during the nineteenth century and has linked that story to a historical process, the 'secularization of the European mind'. Secularization, an intellectual phenomenon, was promoted by secularism, a political movement directed against the religious establishment.[134] Science had propelled industrial change since the eighteenth century, and it enabled men of the European innovating classes to impute meaning to the universe unmediated by civil and ecclesiastical authority.[135] When the assumptions and methods of the natural sciences were projected into the realm of human affairs, moral science was born.[136] Hume, Paley, Reid, Condillac, de Tracy, la Metrie, Godwin and Bentham assumed that 'laws' governing the mind and the soul were, in principle, as scrutable as those apparent in the material, phenomenal world. David Hartley (*Observations on Man*, 1749) and James Mill (*Analysis of the Phenomena of the Human Mind*, 1829) had discussed psychology and ethics

[132] *PE* sec. 201.

[133] L. E. Elliot-Binns, *English Thought 1860–1900. The Theological Aspect* (London: Longmans, 1956), p. 71.

[134] Chadwick, *Secularization of the European Mind in the Nineteenth Century*. I have noted in my Introduction some reservations about the 'secularization thesis'. Chadwick gets round many problems by discussing *secularism* as an intellectual and political movement (rather than a tendency of thought) with identifiable actors. He also observes that not all secularists were irreligious: they were hostile above all to the worldly power of clerics and churches.

[135] A. E. Musson, ed., *Science, Technology, and Economic Growth in the Eighteenth Century* (London: Methuen, 1972); and Heyck, *Transformation*, chaps. 3–4.

[136] G. Bryson, *Man and Society: The Scottish Inquiry of the Eighteenth Century* (Princeton, NJ: Princeton UP, 1945); K. Haakonssen, *The Science of a Legislator. The Natural Jurisprudence of David Hume and Adam Smith* (CUP, 1981); *Wealth and Virtue. The Shaping of Political Economy in the Scottish Enlightenment*, ed. I. Hont and M. Ignatieff (CUP, 1983).

as branches of mental chemistry. The phrenologist George Combe (1788–1858) held that human sentiments like affection, acquisitiveness, sympathy and charity originated in distinct compartments of the brain.[137] So pervasive were empiricist, physicalist doctrines by 1829 that Thomas Carlyle complained of the 'mechanical genius of our time,' and of the mechanical derivation of the moral from the physical: 'Not the external and physical alone is now managed by machinery, but the internal and spiritual also.'[138]

Utilitarianism, materialism, positivism and evolutionism approached ethics as a science of causal explanation, underpinned by a 'desire for a simple physical explanation of a complex series of observations' in biological and historical time.[139] As Chadwick has said of Ernst Haeckel, the great German apologist for Darwin, 'he descended from science into his metaphysics.'[140] Echoing Hartley, Erasmus Darwin and James Mill, Haeckel confidently announced, 'We now know that the soul [is] the sum of plasma-movements in the ganglion-cells …'[141] The quip of Jakob Moleschott — 'No thought without phosphorous' — epitomized a typical intellectual stance of the era.[142] Ludwig Büchner's *Force and Matter* went through many editions and translations between 1855 and 1904 and figured as often in ethical as in scientific discussions. Büchner asserted that mind was matter, which could be neither created nor destroyed but only recombined. Frenchmen, Chadwick observes, were surprised by the appearance of Büchner and Moleschott in the country of Schelling and Hegel: 'Accustomed to deride Germans for imagining matter not to exist, they were astonished to find Germans who maintained that mind did not exist.'[143]

In sum, the philosophical and scientific materialism associated with the Enlightenment in France and Britain was firmly rooted in 'mystical' Germany by Green's time. As Green observed in the essay 'Popular

[137] Halévy, *Growth of Philosophic Radicalism*, pp. 7–11, 434–78; Hilton, *Atonement*, pp. 189–202; and R. Cooter, *The Cultural Meaning of Popular Science: Phrenology and the Organization of Consent in Nineteenth-Century Britain* (CUP, 1984).

[138] From 'Signs of the Times' (1829), in *Thomas Carlyle. Selected Writings*, ed. A. Shelston (London: Penguin, 1971), p. 65.

[139] Chadwick, *Secularization*, p. 203. See also J. W. Burrow, *Evolution and Society* (CUP, 1966).

[140] *Secularization*, p. 177. Haeckel was the German T. H. Huxley. His *Natürliche Schöpfungsgeschichte* (1868) was translated into English as *The History of Creation; or, The Development of the Earth and its Inhabitants by the Action of Natural Causes*, trans. E. Ray Lankester (New York: D. Appleton and Co., 1876). Haeckel's subsequent Darwinian works appeared in English translations as *The Evolution of Man* (1879) and *The Riddle of the Universe* (1900).

[141] *Secularization*, p. 178.

[142] *Lehre der Naehrungsmittel* (Erlangen, 1850), quoted in Chadwick, *Secularization*, p. 169.

[143] *Secularization*, pp. 170–3.

Philosophy in its Relation to Life,' 'In Germany itself the people now [ca. 1868] venture to assert a philosophy of their own, and it is not the philosophy of the German philosophers, but of the school of Locke.'[144] Nevertheless, Green, even from the beginning of his career, was habitually identified with 'German thought'. Collingwood suggested in 1939 that such association was really no more than a crude libel: the British Idealists' knowledge of Kant and Hegel helped their philosophical opponents 'to discredit them in the eyes of a public always contemptuous of foreigners.'[145] (Indeed, British Germanophobia grew rapidly in the two decades following Green's death, at the peak of his influence.) Green's study of German authors was sympathetic without being comprehensive or erudite.[146] Pattison, for instance, was better versed in German scholarship and understood it well enough to realize the significance of Green's attempt to replace the 'reigning empirical logic' at Oxford with an anglicized Idealism.[147] Yet in associating Green with scholars who engaged in Hegelian 'flights into the region of hallucination,' Pattison was somewhat dismissive of Green's efforts and expressed scepticism that Hegelianism could be clarified.[148] In this respect Pattison's view of Green's work was similar to Jowett's.

Pattison remarked on a fact of which less learned British thinkers were hardly cognizant: Green's teachings were not really in line with contemporary German thought. J. H. Stirling's *Secret of Hegel* (1865) was well received in Britain, but this reception emphasized the degree to which Hegel's reputation had suffered in his own country.[149] When, in 1844, Benjamin Jowett and Arthur Stanley journeyed to Halle to consult the Hegelian J. E. Erdmann, Hegel was no longer fashionable in Ger-

[144] 'Popular Philosophy,' p. 94.
[145] *Autobiography*, p. 15.
[146] Still, Green's essay on 'The State of Religious Belief among the Jews at the Time of the Coming of Christ' — submitted for the Ellerton theological prize in 1861 — indicates his familiarity with the work of Leopold Zunz, A. F. Gfroerer and J. A. W. Neander, as well as Jowett, John Lightfoot, Richard Laurence and John Keble. 'State of Religious Belief,' in *AW*, pp. 83–104.
[147] Pattison, 'Philosophy at Oxford,' p. 95.
[148] 'Philosophy at Oxford,' pp. 96–7. The complexities of Idealist ('metaphysical') logic, Pattison quipped, 'can only be acquired by time and slow assimilation. It is, as Hegel himself said, like learning to walk upon our heads.' Pattison reviewed here William Wallace's *The Logic of Hegel [Wissenschaft der Logik, translated from the Encyclopaedia of the Philosophical Sciences with Prolegomena by William Wallace]* (Oxford: Clarendon, 1874), as well as Green and Grose's edition of Hume.
[149] As Kirk Willis points out, while Stirling's book was perhaps the single 'most important contribution to the popularization and understanding of Hegelian thought in mid-Victorian Britain ... [,] it did not so much create as encounter a receptive readership.' 'Hegelian Thought in Britain,' p. 100. See also A. P. F. Sell, *Philosophical Idealism and Christian Belief* (New York: St. Martin's, 1995), chap. 1.

many.[150] The historical materialism of Ludwig Feuerbach and Marx (among others), growing out of and away from Hegelianism, was one departure from metaphysical speculation. Marx and Engels proclaimed in the early 1840s, 'Real Humanism has no more dangerous enemy in Germany than spiritualism or speculative idealism which substitutes "self-consciousness" or the "spirit" for the real individual man.'[151]

Few German thinkers after 1848 were interested in going beyond Kant to locate transcendent values or a universal moral ground of political theory. Even during the bloom of German Romanticism and Idealism, an experimental empiricism, whose most gifted proponent was J. F. Herbart (1776–1841), was gaining momentum.[152] In the wake of Herbart, serious philosophers like Edouard Zeller (author of 'On the Significance and Purpose of the Theory of Knowledge', 1862) drew upon Kant to legitimize the claims of philosophy by limiting them.[153] H. Stuart Hughes points to the significance of a '"southwest German philosophy" of a markedly anti-positivist character,' barely visible before the 1890s. Wilhelm Windelband and Heinrich Rickert, who sought to re–establish a transcendental approach to philosophy, inspired Friedrich Meinecke, Ernst Troeltsch and Max Weber, thus shaping twentieth-century practice of history, sociology, anthropology, and even psychology.[154] But these German neo-Kantians were decidedly in the minority, struggling against an intellectual establishment in which philosophy of mind was properly an experimental endeavour with pretensions to the exactness of chemistry, physics and biology.

---

[150] Lewis Campbell, Jowett's first biographer, hinted that Jowett had simply not noticed signs of Hegelianism's decline in Germany (Faber, *Jowett*, pp. 177–83).

[151] Marx and Engels, *The Holy Family*, quoted in S. Avineri, *The Social and Political Thought of Karl Marx* (CUP, 1968), p. 100. On the Left Hegelians, see H. Marcuse, *Reason and Revolution. Hegel and the Rise of Social Theory* (OUP, 1941), Part Two; W. Schuffenhauer, *Feuerbach and der junge Marx* (Berlin: Deutscher Verlag der Wissenschaften, 1965); Sidney Hook, *From Hegel to Marx* (New York: Columbia UP, 1994 [1936]); and J. E. Toews, *Hegelianism* (CUP, 1980).

[152] Along the lines of French materialism (Diderot, Condorcet, de Tracy), Herbart 'conceived the plan of a psychical mechanics, divided into statics and dynamics. To these processes, i.e. the conflict of ideas in the soul, he attempted to apply mathematical calculation through which the resultant intensities of the different ideas could be ascertained.' Merz, *History of European Thought in the Nineteenth Century*, iii, pp. 203–8.

[153] Kloppenberg, *Uncertain Victory*, pp. 55–7; Merz, *European Thought*, iii, pp. 179–91, 210–11. As Richard Rorty observes, 'The "back to Kant" movement of the 1860s was also a "let's get down to work" movement.' Zeller's celebrated essay invited 'those who believe that we can spin all of the sciences out of our own spirit [to] continue on with Hegel, but anyone saner should recognize that the proper task of philosophy (once the notion of the thing-in-itself, and thus the temptations of idealism, are rejected) is to establish the objectivity of the knowledge-claims made in the various empirical disciplines.' R. Rorty, *Philosophy and the Mirror of Nature* (Princeton UP, 1979), pp. 134–5.

[154] H. Stuart Hughes, *Consciousness and Society*, p. 47.

Like the German neo-Kantians, Green believed one of philosophy's tasks to be the testing of empirical science: philosophy should neither swallow up science nor be consumed by it.[155]

By the 1860s, in Britain, Western Europe and North America alike, 'philosophy of mind' overlapped with experimental psychology and focused on the phenomenal.[156] Thus Green's moral philosophy, combining prescriptive and normative aims with an insistence that moral behaviour must refer beyond 'ordinary physical facts', appeared to some 'advanced' contemporaries to be a throwback to an older tradition of ethical inquiry. Where Green appeared innovative to some contemporaries was in his belief in philosophy as an autonomous mode of inquiry and as a profession. If philosophy was not simply a branch of natural science, neither was it a branch of theology; philosophy, as Kantians liked to say, was the queen of the sciences. As Maria Dimova-Cookson has recently argued, Green proposed a method for the investigation of human thought and behaviour that was scientific in privileging rationality and logic. He maintained that the 'natural science moral philosophers' were in fact no more successful in explaining the origins, development and even facts of moral life than were poets, theologians and historians. Human consciousness and its objects, Green held, had to be studied with the same rigour as physical facts, and investigation of consciousness was the proper brief of philosophy.[157]

1.5. THE PROFESSIONALIZATION OF PHILOSOPHY

Henry Sidgwick, in a generous gesture, identified Green as Britain's first professional academic philosopher. Sidgwick's opinion can certainly be questioned: William Hamilton, J. F. Ferrier and Sidgwick himself are among the contenders for that honour. It is a dubious generalization to maintain that philosophers working outside the academy were less 'professional' than academics of the era. Yet there can be no doubt that between the death of Mill (1873) and the publication of G. E. Moore's *Principia Ethica* (1903), the British philosophical profession was transformed, and that Green was partly responsible for the transformation.[158]

---

[155] Kloppenberg suggests that Zeller and others had neutralized Kant. Even professed neo-Kantians like Gustav Fechner and Hermann von Helmholtz 'sacrificed Kant's noumenal realm at the altar of "psycho-physics," the quest for exact measurement of psychological responses to physical stimuli' (*Uncertain Victory*, p. 56).

[156] Kloppenberg, *Uncertain Victory*, chap. 2. Consider Sigmund Freud, whose career began just as Green's ended. Freud studied zoology and physiology, and went on to specialize in neurology before developing psychoanalysis.

[157] Dimova-Cookson, *T. H. Green's Moral and Political Philosophy*, pp. 6-9. 'We find a very similar conclusion in Husserl's critique of the sciences' (p. 9).

[158] These landmarks in historical periodization of philosophy have been suggested by J. B. Schneewind. Bentham, the Mills, Carlyle, Coleridge, Spencer, as well as many

The foregoing discussion of Green's academic career has indicated that while philosophy was taught at Oxford before 1875, a distinct philosophical curriculum was lacking. Most senior dons and many tutors were less interested in intellectual progress than in the conservation of venerated ideas. Nor would contemporary study of philosophy, or even of the history of philosophy, at other English universities be considered sufficiently disciplined by today's standards. J. S. Mill and Spencer, the most famous philosophers before 1875, were not university trained, and teachers of philosophy rarely taught only philosophy. Green helped separate the study of philosophical from that of literary and historical texts; and by creating a philosophy curriculum at Oxford he also established a rationale for trained teachers of philosophy. When Green began his academic career much of the serious writing on philosophical topics was published in journals of opinion devoted to a broad range of ethical, theological and political issues (rarely to 'pure' philosophy). He helped professionalize philosophical writing by encouraging specialized periodicals, such as *Academy* and *Mind*, which were to serve as venues for the results of scholarly research.

Fluctuations in Green's philosophical reputation down to the present have been partly due to varying appreciations of his language, or choice of philosophical idiom. As Collingwood observed, hostility towards the misnamed Oxford Hegelians was founded partly on chauvinism, a prejudice that reinforced positivist claims that metaphysical philosophy was non-science and nonsense. Geoffrey Warnock's dismissal of Green as a maker of resounding phrases is an echo of the conventional philosophical wisdom of the 1950s and '60s, when Melvin Richter felt compelled to apologize for discussing a superannuated thinker.[159] But a philosopher no less *en vogue* than Richard Rorty, without advocating a return to Green's metaphysics, praises his penetrating critique of empiricism and points to meaningful continuity between Green and twentieth–century thinkers like Wilfrid Sellars and J. L. Austin.[160] Metaphysics continues to have its champions because it confronts the ques-

---

other serious philosophical thinkers of the nineteenth century were men of letters, administrators, active politicians, clergy with livings, but not academics. In Scotland, however, philosophy was more clearly academical by this time than in England. The discussion in the following paragraphs of the profession of philosophy in England draws from Schneewind, *Sidgwick's Ethics*, introduction; Heyck, *Transformation*, pp. 174–85; and Collini, *Public Moralists*, chap. 6.

[159] *Politics of Conscience*, pp. 9–12.
[160] Rorty, *Philosophy and the Mirror of Nature*, pp. 139–48; and R. Rorty, *Philosophical Papers, Volume Two* (CUP, 1991), p. 110. A. N. Wilson makes a similar claim about the hidden success of British Idealism. Willard Quine's 'scepticism about modal logic' is of a piece with British Idealism: 'physical facts are all the facts. But about our mode of perceiving facts he [Quine] has pointed out that there is no non-relative fact, no fact which does not relate to another fact.' Wilson, *God's Funeral*, pp. 122–3.

tions that are designated invalid (because unverifiable) by empirical and symbolic philosophies.

1.6. PHILOSOPHY IN THE WORLD: GREEN AND LIBERALISM

Green's teachings figured prominently in professional and academic discussions through the twentieth century, even if his intellectual authority in those circles had declined by the 1930s. By 1930 few of Green's immediate contemporaries were still alive; most of his students and acolytes had reached the end of their working lives and had ceased to exercise much influence in academe, the press, public policy and politics. Printed responses to Green's teachings before about 1920 were relatively unspecialized, since his audience was not limited to the small academic establishment or to the slightly larger community of 'serious' philosophers.[161] During Green's lifetime the social and moral terrain of ethics was constantly shifting, in the sense that no single mode or tradition of moral inquiry commanded the allegiance of the people who conducted such inquiries. Nietzsche's anti–morality, adumbrated in his writings from the late 1880s, was an acute symptom of the loss of consensus. Specialization of knowledge and professionalization had helped render unworkable the ideal of universal knowledge by undermining the positivist myth that the accumulation of facts and inductive truths led to qualitative changes in understanding. Green's teachings, however, were couched in terms comprehensible to a broad, educated public. His statements about ethics, morals and politics were taken seriously by theologians, social and natural scientists, as well as by people active in public life.

Green's impact was due not only to the intrinsic appeal of particular teachings but to the moral weight of his thought, the load of ethical assumptions it was made to bear. People active in British public life, especially before the First World War, had been formed by a pedagogy that emphasized certain relationships between ethical principles and the conduct of private and public life.[162] That is, their moral and intellectual upbringing — shaped by family, school, university, or self–education, or all of these — tended to impress upon them the necessity of self-consciousness about their 'moral bearings', so that discussion of

[161] The following discussion is informed by Heyck, *Transformation*; Annan, *Leslie Stephen*, chaps. 6–10; A. MacIntyre, *Three Rival Versions of Moral Inquiry. Encyclopaedia, Genealogy, and Tradition*, Edinburgh Univ. Gifford Lectures, 1988 (Notre Dame, IN: Notre Dame UP, 1990), chaps. 1–2, 8; and Collini, *Public Moralists*, Parts I, III.

[162] The 1914–18 war is a significant intellectual watershed, not because philosophy in the post-war era was qualitatively different than before 1914 but because of the fashionable conviction (after 1918) that nineteenth-century culture had not only failed to avert catastrophe but had probably caused it.

the ends and means of both individual and common life was itself culturally framed as a kind of moral imperative. Victorian moral theory — despite defences of the principle of self-interest from Bishop Butler to Samuel Smiles — did not yet recognize self-gratification as self-explanatory behaviour; discussions of individualism and liberty were thus somewhat defensive and accompanied by reminders of duty and mutual obligation. Moral philosophy as practiced by Green, J. S. Mill and Herbert Spencer was an enterprise which received due attention from a public considerably wider than the philosophical profession.

It is worth bearing in mind in this regard that Green's intellectual associates were impressed with his engagement with the world, with his attention to practical issues. W. L. Newman recalled, 'His hard abstract studies seemed to prepare him for dealing with practical questions ... '. Henry Nettleship remarked, 'I may say generally here that though he spent most of his life in Oxford, his tone of mind was never what is called academical.' Charles Parker insisted that Green's philosophy was 'no cold barren speculation, but a cherished creed, a help to noblest life.' Robin Collingwood, whose father had been tutored by Bernard Bosanquet, observed that the 'real strength of the [Oxford Idealist] movement was outside Oxford' — and outside academe.[163] Indeed, it was the worldliness of Green's teachings — in contrast to the academic detachment supposedly incumbent upon the serious philosopher — that certain critics used in order to discredit British Idealism. Reflecting on philosophy in the English universities during the half century following Green's death, C. D. Broad cuttingly remarked,

> Even a thoroughly second-rate thinker like T. H. Green, by diffusing a grateful and comforting aroma of ethical 'uplift', has probably made far more undergraduates into prigs than [Henry] Sidgwick will ever make into philosophers.[164]

Still, that some men and women who went forth from the universities to form Britain's governing and culture elites were captivated by Green in their youth does not mean that they remained forever uncritical of his teachings. Take the example of the Radical journalist and sociologist L. T. Hobhouse, who felt the full force of Green's teachings.[165] Although he followed Green closely in his rationale for state action (removing obstacles to the self-development of individuals), Hobhouse came to

---

[163] W. L. Newman, H. Nettleship, C. S. Parker recollections, *GP* 1(b); Collingwood, *Autobiography,* pp. 16–17.

[164] C.D. Broad, *Five Types of Ethical Theory* (London: K. Paul, Trench and Truebner, 1930), p. 144.

[165] Hobhouse became a fellow and tutor at Oxford and composed works on logic, ethics, and politics before turning to full-time journalism in 1897. He wrote leading articles for the *Manchester Guardian,* contributed to *Speaker* and *Nation,* and served as political editor of the *Tribune.* He was professor of sociology at the London School of Economics between 1909 and 1929.

view Idealist abstraction — which he detected in concepts like the 'rational self' (as opposed to the empirical self) — as more a hindrance than an aid to the development of a practical political philosophy.[166] In the decade before 1918 Hobhouse attributed the incoherence of British liberalism in large part to liberal intellectuals' unjustified loyalty to the 'metaphysical' school of Bosanquet, Bradley and Edward Caird.[167] Similarly, Graham Wallas, author of *Human Nature in Politics* (1908) and *The Great Society* (1914), believed that the study of politics must be conducted on a purely empirical basis, and implied that Greenian Idealism, by valourizing both the spiritual and rational capacities of men, could not lead to proper appreciation of the irrational element in politics.[168]

Whether Green's impact on the study of philosophy and on British political debates be judged salutary or merely unfortunate, complex networks of influence extended beyond Oxford's proverbial dreaming spires. One example is the 'University Settlement' movement, effectively beginning in the 1880s with the foundation of Toynbee Hall in London's East End (see Chapter Five below). Between 1880 and 1914 several thousands of privileged men and women lived for short periods among the urban poor to investigate the social conditions at the centre of the world's largest commercial-industrial empire.[169] Few of Green's students took clerical orders, but among those Henry Scott Holland (1847–1918) and Charles Gore (1853–1932) formed the 'Lux Mundi' group of critical theologians in the High Church tradition. 'Lux Mundi' purported 'to put the Catholic faith into its right relation to modern intellectual and moral problems.'[170] These 'Anglo-Catholics' went on to establish the Christian Social Union and sought to buttress Anglican orthodoxy, which had long claimed to reconcile religion to scientific dis-

---

[166] Collini, *Liberalism and Sociology*, chaps. 3–5; Weiler, *The New Liberalism*, pp. 146–7.

[167] S. Collini, 'Hobhouse, Bosanquet and the State: Philosophical Idealism and Political Argument in England, 1880–1918,' *Past and Present*, 72 (1976), pp. 86–111; Collini, *Liberalism and Sociology*; Kloppenberg, *Uncertain Victory*, pp. 305–10; Bowle, *Politics and Opinion*, pp. 275–6, 445–50; W. J. Mander, 'Caird's Developmental Absolutism,' in *Anglo-American Idealism, 1865–1927*, ed. Mander, chap. 3. Hobhouse, in his *Metaphysical Theory of the State*, distinguished between Green's reasoned acceptance of certain Hegelian premises and Bosanquet's crude conflation of the real will of society with the purpose of the state — a distinction lost upon many of Hobhouse's contemporaries.

[168] A. Gamble, 'Wallas, Graham' in *Twentieth-Century Culture*, p. 798; and Wiener, *Between Two Worlds*.

[169] This phenomenon has been discussed most thoroughly by Meacham, *Toynbee Hall and Social Reform*. See also Vincent and Plant, *Philosophy, Politics and Citizenship*, chap. 7; and A. Briggs and A. Macartney, *Toynbee Hall. The First Hundred Years* (London: Routledge and Kegan Paul, 1984).

[170] Named after *Lux Mundi. A Series of Studies in the Religion of the Incarnation* (1889), ed. Charles Gore. 'Lux Mundi,' in *Oxford Dictionary of the Christian Church*, 2nd ed., ed. F. L. Cross and E. A. Livingstone (OUP, 1974), p. 850; Nicholls, *Deity and Domination*, pp. 52-60.

covery (inductive truth). But 'Lux Mundi' was also in accord with heterodox Christians like James Martineau, the Unitarian philosopher and theologian who was a friend of Green. At the time that Green was beginning to systematically reinterpret Christian dogma, Martineau observed, 'the things about which we [theologians] teach are given in perpetuity; but the things to be taught about them are open to revision in every age.'[171]

Green, Martineau and other theologians and clergymen were intellectual forebears of many social reformers active from about 1880 down to the First World War (indeed, during the interwar period as well). They formed a bridge between the English Christian Social movement of the mid-nineteenth century (discussed in Chapter Three below) and the CSU and Toynbee Hall. Although Green was wary of theological dogma and reluctant to align himself with any institutional church, he maintained that religious teachings were essential to ethics and contributed to the best social wisdom of the age. In this sense he belongs to a tradition of humane English churchmanship. In addition to assessing his relation to 'secular' social and political thought, we must consider Green's relation to 'social Christianity'. It is in this context that Green's influence emerges as one of the more fruitful currents of nineteenth- and twentieth-century British social thought — far more authoritative and accessible, indeed, than the tradition of doctrinaire, 'scientific' socialism. Not only 'Lux Mundi' but the economist William Cunningham, Archbishop William Temple (York, 1929–42, and Canterbury, 1942–4), Philip Wicksteed, William Beveridge and other recognized architects of the welfare state (a term coined by Temple) must be understood in relation to Green.[172] If social science — including economics, industrial relations and sociology — was the medium through which these men exerted their influence, their inspiration was the Christian humanitarianism so powerfully articulated by Green. Others, however, have cited Green's practicality and social engagement in order to disqualify him as a philosopher. Lewis Farnell avowed that Green had made him think like a philosopher, but also that the professor was less interested in the profession of philosophy than of philanthropy.[173]

Over the questions of Green's relation to political thought and government policy, there has been more fruitful debate, although the terms of that debate have been framed rather rigidly by A. V. Dicey's *Lectures on the Relation Between Law and Public Opinion in England During the Nine-*

---

[171] 'Theology in Its Relation to Progressive Knowledge' (1865), in *Essays, Philosophical and Theological*, i (New York: Henry Holt, 1875), p. 415.

[172] Discussed in Chapters 5–6 below.

[173] *An Oxonian Looks Back* (London: Hopkinson, 1934), pp. 44–5. Some critics of Green referred to him as 'Bethnal Green', after the East London district settled after 1880 by University-educated philanthropists. Harvie, *Lights*, pp. 200–3.

teenth Century (1905). Although during the 1850s and '60s Green and Dicey were partisan Liberals holding quite similar views about political, economic and social freedom, by the turn of the nineteenth century Dicey bemoaned the shifting of the concept 'liberty' and had become a prominent representative of disaffected Liberals.[174] According to Dicey, under the guise of enabling the greater happiness of the greater number, the British state had justified various instances of 'interference' with the arrangements of private individuals, and simultaneously recognized the rights of groups (e.g. trades unions) to advocate the interests of individuals. The spirit of 'individualism' ca. 1860 had given way to that of 'collectivism'.[175]

Green's ideas about the relation of individuals to the sovereign power — what is held to be his theory of the state — are perhaps the most widely discussed elements of his philosophy. Rodney Barker has bluntly proclaimed that before mobilization for 'total war' in 1914 Britons assumed that states

> were things that foreigners had. In Britain, people were governed, and they argued about how that government should best be conducted and to what ends ... But the state was an alien concept and they got along perfectly well without it.[176]

David Ritchie and John Dewey, however, maintained that Green was the first British thinker since Hobbes to have a theory of the state.[177] Scholars have fitted Green into a Diceyan narrative of decline, featuring the waning of British liberalism and the simultaneous emergence or resurgence of class consciousness and political collectivism. A supposed erosion of liberalism from the late 1880s by socialism and conservatism has been traced by certain observers back to the unsettling influence of Green, particularly his conception of positive liberty and his theory of the state. Many New Liberals did deploy Greenian arguments from the 1880s onward to justify state intervention and to thereby counteract socioeconomic polarization and 'class politics' — the latter being anathema to classical liberals like Mill, Cobden and Bright, and

---

[174] R. S Rait, 'Dicey, Albert Venn' in *Dictionary of National Biography 1922–1930*, fourth supplement, pp. 259–61. Elements of the 'Dicey Thesis' were previewed in his 'The Legal Boundaries of Liberty,' *Fortnightly Review*, n.s. 3 (1868), pp. 1–13. On Dicey's individualism, see J. Stapleton, 'Dicey and His Legacy,' *HPT*, 16 (1995), pp. 234–56.

[175] Or as Ernest Barker observed a decade later, 'While in 1864 [political] orthodoxy meant distrust of the State, and heresy took the form of a belief in paternal government, in 1914 orthodoxy means belief in the State, and heresy takes the form of mild excursions into anarchism.' *Political Thought in England, 1848 to 1914*, p. 23.

[176] Barker, review of J. Meadowcroft, *Conceptualizing the State, Albion*, 29 (1997), p. 142.

[177] See D. G. Ritchie, *The Principles of State Interference: four essays on the political philosophy of Spencer, Mill and Green* (London: S. Sonnenschein, 1891), pp. 130–1; Dewey, *Lectures on Psychological and Political Ethics: 1898*, ed. D. F. Koch (New York: Hafner Press, 1976), p. 234.

indeed to Green himself. Conservatives and laissez-faire liberals could claim that New Liberals had abandoned the principles that had made Britain free and prosperous (e.g. entrepreneurial liberty), while 'socialists' (members of the Fabian Society, the Social Democratic Federation, and later the Labourites) claimed that New Liberals were ambiguous in theory and timid in fact about what kinds of state action empowered individuals and fostered social justice.[178]

Leonard Hobhouse complained that Green and Idealist Liberals could not clearly stipulate what individuals should expect from the state or what obligations on the part of citizens the state should enforce; this deficiency was supposedly a result of Idealist metaphysics. Spencerian Radicalism had the virtue of brutal clarity with regard to central issues: the state existed purely for the narrowly defined protection of the citizen, who could challenge social arrangements he felt to be coercive. (On rather different grounds than Karl Marx, Spencer predicted the extinction of the state as a coercive, external force.) The Greenian view lacked the simplicity and absoluteness of other Radical theories (e.g. Utilitarianism), although state-interventionist Radicals like D. G. Ritchie contended that Green's Idealism provided a superior philosophical foundation for the continuation of Utilitarian political reforms.[179]

On the level of practical politics, many later Victorian Liberals found the ground chosen by the New Liberals to be indefensible. Propertied people viewed the New Liberalism as an actual or potential threat to their interests.[180] Conservatives and classical ('laissez-faire') Liberals were alarmed by legislation like the 1881 Irish Land Act, which established judicial mechanisms for tenant farmers to dispute contracts with landlords. This, critics of the Act contended, contravened the principle of 'freedom of contract'. Such people were irritated by Green's argument in 'Liberal Legislation and Freedom of Contract', which held that freedom of contract had social sanction but was in no way a bilaterally empowering arrangement. Freedom of contract in many cases meant freedom for the landowner, not the tenant; for the urban landlord, not the slum dweller; for the entrepreneur, not the employee. Green clearly

---

[178] M. A. Lawless, 'Liberty and Class Conflict in the Nineteenth-Century British Liberal State: T. H. Green's Concept of Freedom in Relationship to the Development of the Liberal Tradition in Britain' (unpublished doctoral thesis, Univ. of London, 1976); Lawless, 'T. H. Green and the British Liberal Tradition'; Freeden, *The New Liberalism*; Collini, *Liberalism and Sociology*; Greengarten, *Thomas Hill Green*, chaps. 5, 8; Taylor, *Men Versus the State*; J. Meadowcroft, *Conceptualizing the State: Innovation and Dispute in British Political Thought, 1880–1914* (Oxford: Clarendon, 1995).

[179] *The Principles of State Interference*, pp. 142–5. See also, Hansen, 'T. H. Green and the Moralization of the Market'; and Den Otter, *British Idealism*, chap. 3.

[180] A. Offer, *Property and Politics, 1870–1914: Landownership, Law, Ideology and Urban Development in England* (CUP, 1981).

stated that people might have to give up certain liberties in order to enjoy a higher and more comprehensive condition of freedom — a freedom which included such intangible, or at any rate unquantifiable benefits as social harmony. Also working against the New Liberalism was the traditional (not exclusively Liberal) scruple that more government meant more taxes. During the mid-Victorian era the view that cheap government ('Retrenchment' in the Liberal motto 'Peace, Retrenchment, Reform') equals a higher standard of living was as popular among the labouring classes as among the middle and upper classes.[181]

While I do not deny all of Green's purported contributions to the welfare state, I suggest that the 'growth of collectivism' — including the rise of political parties and organizations which rejected certain forms of Victorian individualism — is not the only, or even the most relevant framework in which to consider his ideas. The terms individualism and collectivism were used freely in political discourse from the late 1870s to represent opposing social values. But Green did not believe these terms embodied opposing principles: certain collectivist actions might further a higher individualism.[182] I contend that the innovative nature of Green's ethical and political philosophy had less to do with his view of the state (which was not striking as a reassessment of the concept of the state *per se*) than with his distinctive teleological account of the expansion of the moral ideal. This, I believe, situates Green's thought in the history of Victorian moral and political philosophy differently from previous accounts and in a manner that reveals his relationship to popular liberalism.

1.7. ACADEMIC RADICALISM

Other scholars have been less interested in the 'validity' of Green's philosophy as a basis of political theory than in the social significance of his praxis, identifying Green as a prototype of the modern 'academic radical'. Other university-trained Radicals made important contributions to intellectual life, and some of these were more socially and politically visible than Green. Yet Oxford dons like Dicey, Bryce, George Brodrick and James Thorold Rogers were less academical, being defined more by careers in journalism, law or national politics than by their formal teaching.[183] Certainly it would be missing an important dimension not to con-

[181] E. F. Biagini, 'Popular Liberals, Gladstonian Finance, and the Debate on Taxation, 1860–1874,' in *Currents of Radicalism*, ed. Baigini, pp. 134–62.

[182] H. Perkin, 'Individualism and Collectivism in Nineteenth-Century Britain: A False Antithesis,' in *The Structured Crowd*, chap. 4; Taylor, *Men Versus the State*, introduction; and M. Carter, 'Ball, Bosanquet and the Legacy of Green,' *HPT*, 20 (1999), pp. 674–94.

[183] On academic Radicalism, see Richter, *Politics of Conscience*, chaps. 10–11; R. Terrill, *R. H. Tawney and His Times* (Harvard UP, 1973), pp. 175–81; Collini, *Liberalism and Soci-*

sider Green's life outside the study and the lecture hall, and the present investigation treats these extra-academic activities differently than have previous studies. Green's youthful radicalism did not wear off. As his professional and academic duties grew during the 1870s there was no diminution of his political and public involvements. The culmination of his formal political life was simultaneous with his professional success. Two years before his appointment to the Whyte's Professorship he was elected to the Oxford Town Council, sitting as a householder for the North Ward, not as a member of the University.

Among his social and political activities, Green's involvement in the temperance movement deserves special mention here because of the way it has been slighted by some commentators on Green's philosophy and political theory (discussed in 4.5 below). Many scholars have noted his temperance activism in passing, and some with an implicit sense of embarrassment or withheld censure. Brian Harrison and Peter Nicholson, however, have shown how Green's preoccupation with drunkenness was consistent with his philosophical interest in political virtue.[184] Green had been shaken by his brother's alcoholism and actively promoted temperance among Oxford undergraduates from the later 1860s.[185] After 1872 he extended his efforts to uphold sobriety in the community and became a noted national figure in a movement for 'purity in elections'. It is not incidental that the Drink Question occupied the centre of Green's famous 1881 speech 'Liberal Legislation and Freedom of Contract'. (The speech was published in *Alliance News*, a leading temperance newspaper of the period, and was subsequently distributed by the United Kingdom Alliance in pamphlet form.) Green was convinced that drink corroded political virtue as thoroughly as paternalism, social dependency and poverty. 'Liberal Legislation' not only presents Green's view of modern freedom but also exhibits the scars of his personal battles for responsible liberty.

John Prest remarks that of all major nineteenth-century philosophers, Green appears to have been most aware of the political potential unleashed by the strengthening of local (urban) government during the 1840s and '50s.[186] Green was an important theorist of democratic local-

---

ology, pp. 55–7; Meacham, *Toynbee Hall,* chap. 1; Inglis, *Radical Earnestness,* chap. 2; and Collini, *Public Moralists,* pp. 224–7.

[184] Harrison, *Drink and the Victorians,* chap. 9; Nicholson, 'T. H. Green and State Action: Liquor Legislation.'

[185] Alcoholic excess was a form of undergraduate indiscipline which brought the prompt intervention of college and University authorities. Green's contemporary A. C. Swinburne was 'gated' on several occasions before being 'rusticated' (sent away for a brief period) and expelled. Green's brother Valentine had a similar experience in the early 1850s.

[186] J. Prest, *Liberty and Locality. Parliament, Permissive Legislation and Ratepayers' Democracies in the Nineteenth Century* (OUP, 1990), p. 197. Green was sympathetic to 'municipal

ism. He believed not only that localities were capable of assuming responsibility for common needs like sanitation and education, but that devolution of state authority to localities would strengthen the moral authority of the state on which sovereignty ultimately depended. Effective local government, he held, shaped the ethical consciousness of individuals by impressing upon them the responsibilities of democratic citizenship. Green believed that the sale of alcohol was one of many matters too important to be left either to the market or to Westminster and Whitehall. As legitimate interference with the 'not very precious liberty of buying and selling alcohol' Green envisaged Local Option with authority to grant and revoke pub licenses, set opening hours, or abolish public houses in a district altogether.[187] He dealt aggressively with the rancorous issue of drink provision and property: pubs operated at the sufferance of the community; licenses were not properly property; publicans had no right to compensation for forfeited licenses. In one of Green's last public speeches he argued that the market value of licensed public houses was artificially increased (an unearned increment) due to specific licensing laws and other state action. Such laws were subject to change at any time and a publican was not entitled to compensation for loss of business, especially if licenses were gradually phased out of circulation. Green likened the publican's dilemma to that of a ribbon manufacturer who derived 'artificial' profit from imposition of a duty on foreign products that was later removed.[188]

Green was a partisan in the Liberal interest and organized Oxford's first regular Liberal Association.[189] He petitioned against the election of the Conservative A. W. Hall, a brewer and popular sportsman, in the scandalous Parliamentary contests in the spring of 1880. Despite his own failing health, Green worked in 1880–1 to revoke the licenses of Oxford publicans — Liberals and Conservatives alike — cited in the official investigation of 'corrupt practices'.[190] Irregularities detected by the commission included personation, bribery and 'treating' (or free

socialism' as promoted by Joseph Chamberlain and his allies in Birmingham during the 1870s. But despite his supposed collectivism Green fits into a radical tradition of 'local liberty', represented, for instance, by Joshua Toulmin Smith in the campaign during the 1830s and '40s against Edwin Chadwick, the Board of Health, and administrative centralization.

[187] 'Liberal Legislation,' in *Harris and Morrow*, p. 212.

[188] See 'Important Conference at Oxford and Great Public Meeting,' *Alliance News*, 11 February 1882, pp. 82–6.

[189] On Green and the Liberal Association, see *OCBBG*, 12 January 1878, pp. 2–3.

[190] C. Alfred Pryce, later mayor of Abingdon, Oxfordshire, recalled, 'I believe it was through his exertions that I was instructed to oppose the renewal of the [liquor] licenses ... Consultation before going into Court took place at Professor Green's home' (Pryce to R. L. Nettleship, 13 April 1888, in *GP* 1[c]). The Oxford city magistrates moved non-renewal of the licenses of the cited publicans. The decision was reversed at the County Quarter Sessions but upheld upon appeal. *Alliance News*, 15

provision of food and alcoholic drink to electors and election workers). In the course of questioning by the corrupt practices commission Green claimed that although he was at no point aware of the existence of facsimile and altered ballots in the May 1880 election (at which Harcourt, the Liberal, was defeated by Hall), he was convinced that other serious irregularities had occurred in April and May and had decided to pursue the matter to the utmost of his power.[191]

Between 1878 and 1882 'Councillor Professor' Green laid the groundwork for the Oxford High School for Boys and for Somerville College, served as a governor of the (Birmingham) King Edward VI Grammar School Foundation, lent moral support to the Oxford University Nonconformists' Union, participated in the affairs of local private schools and charities, gave temperance speeches throughout Oxfordshire and adjoining counties and was heavily involved in Liberal politics. Less vigorous fulfillment of his appointed professional duties and a lighter burden of voluntary work might well have spared longer Green's fragile constitution. The actual cause of Green's death was 'blood poisoning' caused by infected tonsils, but since his mid-thirties he had suffered from congenital heart disease, whose debilitating symptoms confined him to bed for days on end.[192] Like his brother-in-law, the scholar-poet John Addington Symonds, Green had been prone since adolescence to that stereotypical Victorian malady 'nervous exhaustion'. Rest cures in the last years of his life, on the Isle of Wight and at Davos, Switzerland, had some restorative effect, but he did not reduce burdensome activities even when so advised by his doctors.

Yet Green was hardly unique among Victorian public moralists in living the life of the mind while devoting a great deal of time to more practical pursuits. While the received image of Green is of an intellectual animated by a zeal for public service, scholars' accounts of his 'practical' activities have been mainly enumerative and descriptive, rarely addressing in a sustained manner questions of motivation or the ethical assumptions behind his efforts. Some commentators have eagerly cited

May 1880 (pp. 310–11), 29 October 1881 (p. 704); *OCBBG*, 2 October 1880 (8), 9 October 1880 (p. 4).

[191] Green was examined by the Oxford corrupt practices commission on 8 January 1881. *Report of the Commissioners Appointed Under Her Majesty's Royal Sign Mutual into the Existence of Corrupt Practices in the City of Oxford, 1881 [c.–2856] (House of Commons Sessional Papers 1881, vol. 44)*, minutes 899–900. On corruption in the Oxford and other 1880 elections, see W. P. Courtney, 'The Cost of the General Election of 1880,' *Fortnightly Review*, 29 n.s. (1881), pp. 467–87; [unsigned], 'Electoral Reform, Electoral Bribery: the Ballot,' *Westminster Review*, 228 (1881), pp. 212–19.

[192] Geoffrey Thomas cites causes of death (from the official death certificate) as ulcerated tonsils (10 days), pyemia (4 days): *Moral Philosophy of T. H. Green*, p. 56n. One contemporary report mistakenly attributed Green's death to scarlet fever: [unsigned], *Oxford Magazine*, 1, no. 7 (1883), pp. 41-2.

his public services in a manner which, while impressing upon us a sense of Green's personal goodness, leads us to the minimal conclusion that he was a philosopher who led a very busy public life. The making of Green into a martyr to Victorian altruism has been an accompanying feature of many accounts of his philosophy and his contributions to liberalism.[193]

The view of Green as moral exemplar and as an apostle of 'civic religion' is conveyed by Mrs Humphry Ward's novel, *Robert Elsmere* (1888), which sold perhaps half a million copies in Britain and the United States before 1890.[194] Mary Ward was a niece of Matthew Arnold and wife of the Oxford tutor (subsequently journalist) T. H. Ward. She dedicated the novel to Green, who had tutored her during the late 1860s, and to Laura Lyttleton ('Linked in my faith about them ... by the love of God and the service of man'). *Robert Elsmere* included verbatim passages from Green's Balliol lay sermon 'The Witness of God' (1870).[195] Green makes a thinly disguised appearance in the novel as Henry Grey, tutor of 'St Anselm's', Oxford, who helps the protagonist out of his religious crisis. Grey refrains from criticizing Elsmere for resigning his clerical living, instead encouraging him to take up the 'social mission' of Christianity. Elsmere accepts the task of educating the economically brutalized and Godless inhabitants of London's East End (anticipating Mrs Ward's own efforts with University Hall and the Passmore Edwards Settlement).

The lesson which the agnostic Elsmere takes to heart is best expressed in another of Green's lay sermons, 'Address on 2 Corinthians v. 7, "Faith"' (1878):

> You cannot find a verification of the idea of God or duty; you can only make it ... Though the failing heart cries out for evidence, at the worst live on as if there were God and duty, and they will prove themselves to you in your life.[196]

---

[193] Green's obituary notice in the *Liverpool Daily Post* (28 March 1882) pronounced, 'The blade has worn out the scabbard.' Untiring service by the privileged to the less privileged was expected and conventional Victorian behaviour. Collini, *Public Moralists*, chaps. 2–3.

[194] R. Ashton, introduction to Mrs Humphry Ward, *Robert Elsmere* (OUP World's Classics ed., 1987); Peterson, 'Gladstone's Review of *Robert Elsmere*'; Sutherland, *Mrs. Humphry Ward*, chaps. 3–7. On Green and civic religion, see Jenks, 'T. H. Green, the Oxford Philosophy of Duty, and the English Middle Class'; and Vincent and Plant, *Philosophy, Politics and Citizenship*, chaps. 2, 5–7.

[195] 'Address on 1 Corinthians v. 7, 8, "The Witness of God"': *Works*, iii, pp. 230–52; and reprinted with 'Faith' with a preface by Arnold Toynbee (London: Longman, 1883). Quoted in Ward, *Robert Elsmere*, pp. 60, 323, 516.

[196] *Works*, iii, 273; and quoted in R. L. Nettleship, 'Professor T. H. Green. In Memoriam,' p. 859.

Not long after Elsmere's fateful removal to London, Grey dies. Elsmere's health soon breaks down as well. He is persuaded to leave London and the 'New Brotherhood of Christ' he has formed there among self-improving working men, but not soon enough to prevent his dying of fever. He is a martyr. Yet the hero's funeral in Robert Elsmere is not Elsmere's but Grey's. Henry Grey is laid to rest in the 'citizens' cemetery on the western side of the town.' 'All the University was there, all the town was there.' Elsmere and a young don 'walked down Beaumont Street together. The rain came on again, and the long black crowd stretched before them was lashed by the driving gusts.'[197] The report of T. H. Green's funeral in the *Oxford Chronicle* read, 'The rain fell in torrents … The funeral procession extended the whole length of Beaumont Street, and it is estimated that the number of persons at the [Jericho] Cemetery could not have been less than 2000. Upon no such similar occasion within our recollection has there been such a display of popular grief and sympathy.'[198]

The hagiographic tone of Mrs. Ward's novel is consistent with other contemporary appreciations of Green, not only the tributes to Green published by his friends and associates in the decade or so following his death, but the readings of Green's opus performed by successive generations of students of ethical and political theory.[199] Illustrations of Green's personal 'goodness' are not substituted in these accounts for actual analysis of his work, but they are deployed to reinforce our appreciation of his work, both professional and extra-professional.[200] The greater the distance they are from the late Victorian era, the less venerational statements about Green become.[201] C. D. Broad's assessment of Green as a breeder of prigs was in keeping with the 'modernist' rejection of Victorianism. To Lytton Strachey and Virginia Woolf, Victo-

---

[197] *Robert Elsmere*, chap. 44.

[198] OBBG, 30 March 1882, p. 8. See also J. Prest, 'The Death and Funeral of T. H. Green,' *Balliol College Annual Record* (1998), pp. 23–6.

[199] Accounts which preserved the memory of Green as an admirable man include R. L. Nettleship, 'Professor T. H. Green. In Memoriam;' J. Bryce, 'Professor T. H. Green,' *Contemporary Review*, 41 (1882), pp. 877–81; [unsigned], 'The Late Professor of Moral Philosophy,' *Oxford Magazine*, 1 (1883), pp. 57–8; F. C. Conybeare, 'On Professor Green's Political Philosophy,' *National Review*, 13 (1889), pp. 771–87; W. S. Lilly, 'Professor Green,' *Dublin Review*, 22, 3rd ser. (1889), pp. 98–118; F. P. B. Osmaston, 'The Religious Teaching of Thomas Hill Green. Being a Lecture Delivered in Rosslyn Hill Chapel, Hampstead, on the 3rd of February, 1889' (privately printed: copy in Dr Williams's Library, London, no. P.2851).

[200] J. MacCunn, *Six Radical Thinkers* (London: Arnold, 1907); J. H. Muirhead, *The Service of the State. Four Lectures on the Political Teaching of T. H. Green* (London: John Murray, 1908).

[201] Some recent studies maintain the venerational stance: Inglis, *Radical Earnestness*; J. Derry, *The Radical Tradition. Tom Paine to Lloyd George* (London: Macmillan, 1967), p. 267.

rian morality was not so much hypocritical as repressive and damaging to personal authenticity. It is, as James Kloppenberg suggests, because the 'orientation' of post–Greenian culture has changed that some modern readers have difficulty entering into the spirit of his work. Evidence of reorientation might be the typical modern response to Green's sermon on 'Faith': 'live on *as if* there were God and duty ...'. Cold comfort to us — but not, Mrs. Ward would have us believe, to Elsmere. And there is evidence that Green's teachings provided comfort and affirmation to members of a generation which had come to suspect the death of God.

The difficulty we have in identifying or empathizing with the moral purposes that Green's work served should suggest to us how that work's meaning was constructed by his society. Green invited people to perform or desist from certain actions or become certain kinds of people, but receptive audiences made his teachings serve specific functions; his work was put to work by others. Stefan Collini suggests as much in assessing Green's success as a public moralist:

> Green theorized more fully and consistently than anyone else [of his time] the assumptions of the anti-selfish sensibility; it was because these assumptions were so widespread that this philosophy enjoyed the success it did, and not vice versa.[202]

Consideration of Green's life and work must therefore take into account the social construction of meaning. One needs to recognize that beyond Green's intentions, his words and actions took on a certain significance from the surrounding culture; and that as the culture changed, so did the interpretation of Green. It may be claimed that our inability to empathize has lent a beneficial critical force to assessments of Green. I have already suggested that scholars have lost certain insights into Green by emphasizing circumstantial and causal factors at the expense of meaningful relations. Yet they also ignore relations between Green's ideas as expressed in his major writings and his social involvements, or they fail to relate Green's rhetoric and actions to those of his contemporaries. The aim of the present study is to show what ideas — and not only Green's — say about modes of communication and the conditions of discourse, and to indicate how those conditions shaped the formation and reception (or uses) of ideas. At issue are the relationships between discourse and culture, between philosophical and political argument and the public space or culture they occupy.

---

[202] Collini, *Public Moralists*, p. 83.

CHAPTER TWO

Green's View of Self and Society

2.1. INTRODUCTION

The purpose of the present chapter is to illustrate a philosophical basis of Green's opinions, although this is not to imply that all of his definite political, ethical or religious opinions were simply derived from philosophical first principles. If there is a philosophical key to Green's thought it is Kant.[1] Green's earliest theories of the self-conscious subject and the 'moral motive', which anchor his ethical and political philosophy, were indebted to the ideas of Kant. According to Locke and Hume, among others, individuals are capable of empirical knowledge of aspects of the universe which they experience. Hume's scepticism lies in his doubt that men are capable of 'scientific' knowledge, because their senses may limit their ability to discern true relations of cause and effect. Kant argues that we are incapable of knowledge of things prior to our apprehending them as a synthesis of self and object; all knowledge is subjective and synthetic.

Green did not believe Kant had invalidated British empiricism, only discredited some of its claims. He criticized Kant for not being clear about what use should be made — for the purposes of philosophy — of the distinction between what is 'given' to the mind ('things-in-themselves') and what the mind adds to it (conscious experience).[2] Green also took issue with Kant's conception of a Self or subject divided between 'animal' and 'rational' natures because he believed such a con-

---

[1] William Wallace's obituary of Green in *Academy*, 21 (April 1, 1882), pp. 231–2. Wallace followed Green in the Whyte's chair of Moral Philosophy.

[2] Green, 'Lectures on the Philosophy of Kant. I. The "Critique of Pure Reason"' (1875–6), in *Works*, ii, pp. 2–81 (especially secs. 5, 49–60).

ception provided an inadequate basis for a theory of morals.[3] Green's divergence from Kant only became more pronounced over time, although the implications of this divergence for his political thought were not decisive.

I have already suggested that Green's writings cannot be understood properly without considering contextual factors, including personal and social circumstances. Nevertheless, the present chapter is primarily a textual investigation, indicating the extent to which Green's beliefs about moral progress, property relations, education, institutional religion and other matters might be inferred from his conception of Self and society, even in its earliest forms. On the whole, Green was remarkably consistent about the fundamental points of his philosophy and did not substantially modify his arguments, even to clarify perceived ambiguities. When he did restate certain ideas later in life it was in order to demonstrate that his philosophy had not been overtaken by newer theories (or new versions of established theories), such as those of Sidgwick, Spencer and G. H. Lewes.

Of these, Green took Sidgwick's doctrine of Universalistic Hedonism — exposited in *The Methods of Ethics* (1874) — most seriously: the final sections of Book Four of Green's *Prolegomena to Ethics*, based on his Hilary Term 1882 lectures at Oxford, included a lengthy critique of Sidgwick. As indicated in the previous chapter, Green denied that Spencer, Lewes and other evolutionists provided tenable explanations of the facts of human consciousness or of social evolution, and he expressed annoyance at the persistence with which evolutionists maintained the continuity of human consciousness with animal being. In light of the consistency of his views, the exposition of Green's ideas in this chapter will take the form of piecemeal illustration of his basic arguments from various manuscripts and printed texts. Green frequently restated the same arguments, so the technique of exposition here will be to present the best or clearest statements of his ideas regardless of the order in which they appear in his writings or reported statements.[4] Arguments of competing thinkers will be elaborated upon only insofar

---

[3]   'Lectures on the Philosophy of Kant. II. The Metaphysic of Ethics' (1878), in *Works*, ii, pp. 83–155 (especially secs. 70–93, 129).

[4]   As R. L. Nettleship observed, it was Green's 'practice, both as college-tutor and professor, to write out and keep full notes for most of his lectures' ('Preface' to *Works*, ii). Green's lectures form overlapping treatments of philosophical issues, in which the same questions and arguments are picked up, dropped, and picked up again. I have confirmed through my examination of the Green Papers that variances between Green's published texts and his statements as a teacher are not usually significant, except as concerns the order in which philosophical statements were made. A. C. Bradley made clear that he rearranged sections (paragraphs) of the *Prolegomena to Ethics* but made few other changes to Green's substantially complete manuscript (see Bradley's 'Preface').

as necessary to indicate what ideas he was responding to. Similarly, treatment of Green scholarship is here kept to a minimum.

Green's ethico–political philosophy had as its basis a distinctive theory of experience and knowledge, purporting to explain the process whereby the individual acquires knowledge, forms a conception of his personal Good, and behaves morally. In his discussions of human psychology in relation to morality Green produced a theory of personality or character, which forms a link to his theory of politics. Green's ethico-political philosophy can be broken down into the following kinds of explanation: (1) epistemology; (2) the springs of individual action — the 'moral motive' and 'enlightened conscience'; (3) a theory of civil society; and (4) the relation of rights to duties in political society. Matters under the first two headings have been regarded typically as relating to Green's moral philosophy, and matters in the last two categories as part of political philosophy. This distinction is meaningful insofar as Green's most detailed discussions of epistemology and the moral motive — above all, in the critique of Hume and the first two books of the *Prolegomena* — serve to display his ideas about the basis of moral freedom in the individual. Once he establishes this basis Green discusses more directly matters of 'external' relations of individuals: social duties, and society's duties to individuals, and thence to questions of sovereignty, public authority and law. These are the main topics of the *Lectures on the Principles of Political Obligation* and they are considered to some degree in Books Three and Four of the *Prolegomena*. Yet all of Green's philosophy is broadly moral and ethical philosophy. In its political aspects it continues the treatment of the moral motive and the formation of enlightened conscience, demonstrating how both function in social interaction, and indicating how empirical investigations of political and social questions might proceed more productively once the implications of the principle of self-realization and the idea of character are recognized.[5]

The uncertain boundary between Green's ethical philosophy and his political theory has puzzled some modern readers accustomed to political theory in the form of dogmatic pronouncements illustrated by logical proofs, historical examples or social data (broadly defined). Green's philosophy is at times assertive, but it does not advance to matters of

[5]   Geoffrey Thomas comments helpfully on this quality of Green's philosophy in a manner which insulates Green from criticism that his was a philosophy of 'ought' rather than 'is' and that it offers few helpful precepts for action in particular kinds of societies. 'Green's moral philosophy has a practical goal, to demonstrate irrevocably the rationality of moral action to anyone engaged in practical thinking with a view to "self-satisfaction."' This is a long way from the moral preaching criticized by Ayer and Broad.' At the same time, Thomas observes, Green is actually more attentive to particular social conditions of the moral life than are modern moral philosophers, such as Thomas Nagel or Philippa Foot. *Moral Philosophy of T. H. Green*, pp. 365–7.

public policy in the 'programmatic' fashion modern readers take to be the customary mode of political theory. John Rawls has observed that 'For the most part the philosophical tradition ... has assumed that there exists some appropriate perspective from which unanimity on moral questions may be hoped for, at least among rational persons with relatively similar and sufficient information ... Different moral theories arise from different interpretations of this point of view, of what I have called the initial situation.'[6] Like Kant, whose philosophy Rawls modifies and extends, Green is concerned primarily with establishing what the 'initial situation' is.[7]

We are perhaps impatient about having to consider a thinker's ideas about epistemology before we can appreciate his or her practical observations about a society and its politics. But as A. D. Lindsay has remarked, for Green no less than for Aristotle, Locke and Hegel, engaging in political theory raised questions demanding philosophical answers.[8] Green's political theory was not intended only for legislators, or for academic or bureaucratic experts, but for conscientious citizens. As Lindsay observes of the teachings of Green and D. G. Ritchie, 'This idealism does not pretend to relieve men of their responsibilities as citizens, of studying the facts as thoroughly and carefully as they can, and thus acting on what is a reasoned faith.'[9] In the conclusion of *Prolegomena*, Green acknowledges that the minute examination of motives, personal versus shared good, the best use of individual talents, the identification of duty, and so forth, is practically possible only 'for persons who have exceptional opportunity for directing their own pursuits, and who do not need to be in a hurry in their decisions' — people of some wealth and leisure. He says,

> To most people sufficient direction for their pursuits is afforded by claims so well established in conventional morality that they are intuitively recognized, and that a conscience merely responsive to social disapprobation would reproach us for neglecting them. For all of us it is so in regard to a greater part of our lives.[10]

Green assumed that all people who wonder about what they do and should do have a proper, if not an abiding interest in philosophy.

---

[6]   Rawls, *A Theory of Justice*, pp. 263-4.
[7]   Green is more concerned than many modern theorists with presenting an accurate explanation of human action — hence *prolegomena* to ethics, and *principles* of political obligation. R. L. Nettleship understood Green's emphasis on preliminaries; he added the word 'principles' to Green's 'Lectures on Political Obligation.' See C. A. Smith, 'The Individual and Society in T. H. Green's Theory of Virtue,' *HPT*, 2 (1981), pp. 195-6.
[8]   *The Modern Democratic State*, i (OUP, 1955 [1943]), p. 30.
[9]   Lindsay, 'Introduction' (1941) to Green, *Lectures on the Principles of Political Obligation* (London: Longmans, Green and Co., 1955), p. xviii.
[10]   *PE* sec. 382.

2.2. BEING AND KNOWING

Green's theories of being and knowledge had as their basis the belief, held by most philosophical idealists, that people are determining more than they are determined in their thoughts and actions. Consciousness arises in the individual as he experiences objects outside of himself and learns that Self consists of matter.[11] But determination of the Self by matter or forces is qualified by its sense that it is a creating as well as a created entity.[12] This quality of human beings is self-consciousness, which Green does not explicitly deny to other beings or organisms but only claims is incapable of examination in its moral effects. He cautioned psychologist-anthropologists like George Henry Lewes (1817–78) against attempting to settle questions about possible relations 'between the feeling and the thinking consciousness ... by a comparison of man with the "lower animals" ... A knowledge of what human intelligence is must precede any profitable discussion of whether "brutes" have anything in common with it.' We cannot properly speak of self-consciousness or morality in ants because we cannot determine how ants conceive of their behaviour, and it is anthropomorphical to speculate about their motives.[13]

All human beings, as self-conscious, creating subjects, are free to will, to serve their interests and to maximize their Good.[14] They are in com-

[11]   *PE*, Book One, especially chap. 2 ('The Relation of Man, As Intelligence, to the Spiritual Principle in Nature'); and 'Mr. Spencer on the Independence of Matter,' in *Works*, i, pp. 410–41 (first published in the *Contemporary Review*, 31 [March, 1878], pp. 744–69).

[12]   See *PE*, Book One, chap. 3 ('The Freedom of Man as Intelligence'). George Berkeley (1685–1753), Bishop of Cloyne, articulated a 'subjective' or 'mentalist' idealism, according to which physical objects are of the same substance as Mind, all individual minds are manifestations of the mind of God, and matter 'exists' only in and for a unified Mind. Green did refer to 'one divine mind' that 'reproduces itself in the human soul' (*PE*, sec. 180) but did not otherwise adhere to the extreme mentalist view. He insisted instead on the '"propaedeutic" value of the study of Berkeley, which is in brief that it shows the necessity of Kant' (Green's review of *The Works of George Berkeley*, ed. A. C. Fraser [Oxford: Clarendon, 1871], in *Academy*, 3, 40 (1872), pp. 27–8. See also Beck, *Handbook in Social Philosophy*, pp. 88–9 (on Berkeley and idealism).

[13]   'Mr. Lewes' Account of the "Social Medium",' in *Works*, i, p. 474 (sec. 96). The introductory sections of Green's *Prolegomena* were first published as a three-part essay entitled 'Can There Be a Natural Science of Man?' in *Mind*, vii (January, April, July, 1882), pp. 1–29, 161–85, 321–48. Green's answer to the question was negative: although the moralist's 'temptation to treat [moral philosophy]. . . as part of natural science is certainly a strong one ...', and though such inquiry may be 'not only plausible but true so far as it goes', 'he will also be aware that experiment and observation, strictly so called', cannot supply answers to 'the most important questions of human behaviour' and the social habits of mankind (*PE*, sec. 2). See also 'Mr. Lewes' Account of Experience', in *Works*, i, pp. 442–70 (first published in *Contemporary Review*, 32 [July, 1878], pp. 751–72).

[14]   *PE*, Book Two, chap. 1 ('The Freedom of the Will').

mand of their motives. That is to say, motives are not created by conditions in nature apart from the will or by 'natural' phenomena occurring
in the individual — as according to Locke and subsequent 'English psychologists', among whom Green included J. S. Mill and Alexander Bain.
Nor is the Self divided — as Kant would have it — between impulses of
the animal being and those 'free' motives supplied by reason (or the
'rational will').[15] If humans did not have power over their motives it
would be meaningless to speak of free will, and free will, as applied to
the individual's mental and moral constitution, is a 'pleonasm'
(amounting to the construction 'free freedom').[16] Motives, as part of
willing, are distinct from 'natural' impulses in being ordered through
self-consciousness.[17]

Individuals seek to gratify their desires — at least many people would
accept this as an explanation of their behaviour — but Green holds that
what they really do is satisfy a Self.[18] Satisfaction of Self involves not the
unreflective 'animal' gratification of impulses but rational comprehension of the Good *as it appears to the individual*.[19] The individual is self conscious, rather than passive, to the extent that he is aware of a Self
'enduring' beyond the sensations it experiences; the Self orders a series
of sensations. If the Self were merely a sum of sensations and derivative
ideas, the individual would be unable to conceive of himself as existing
independently of a series of desires, and he is often, if not always, conscious of his ability to regulate responses to desires; the desires are
always his.[20] Self-consciousness results in the individual's prioritizing
his desires in order that he may present to himself (at many if not all
times) the *idea* of his Good.[21] It is in this sense, i.e. the individual seeking
a good for himself, that Green understands the individual to be

[15] E.g. *PE*, secs. 66–8, 88–114.
[16] 'On the Different Senses of "Freedom" As Applied to Will and to the Moral Progress
      of Man' (1879), sec. 1.
[17] See 'Different Senses of "Freedom",' secs. 8–10; and *PE*, secs. 30–41. '"No doubt," it
      will be said, "there is a particular sense of the phenomena observable by the inner
      sense — a class called acts of will — which are distinguished from other events that
      take place in nature as being directed by our feeling. But we are not entitled to sup-
      pose that in the case of each man there is really a single agent or power exerted in acts
      of willing, a single basis of these phenomena ..."' (*PE*, sec. 116). To this Green replies
      that we cannot understand the basis of 'acts of willing' other than by identifying a Self
      or self-conscious subject.
[18] 'The objects of a man's various desires form a system, connected by memory and
      anticipation, in which each is qualified by the rest ... The system of a man's desires has
      its bond of union in the single subject, which always carries with it the consciousness
      of objects that have been and may be desired into the consciousness of the object
      which at present is being desired' (*PE*, sec. 128).
[19] *PE*, secs. 171–8.
[20] '[General] Introduction to Hume's *Treatise of Human Nature*' (1874), in *Works*, i, pp.
      259–99; and *PE*, secs. 64, 90 *passim*.
[21] *PE*, Book Three, chap. 1.

self-interested. Self-interested behaviour is wholly consistent with morality when it involves the individual's reflection upon the significance of his pleasures and desires.[22]

Green's theory is thus diametrically opposed to Utilitarian 'hedonist' doctrines which argue that individuals simply equate their Good with their pleasure or seek the Good in pleasure or a sum of pleasures. The *Oxford English Dictionary* defines 'hedonism' as 'The doctrine or theory of ethics in which pleasure is regarded as the chief good, or the proper end of action'; it dates the term to 1856. The word had perhaps enjoyed limited use in philosophical circles a decade before that; it was used by John Wilson (1785–1854), J. S. Mill and Henry Sidgwick as well as Green. John Grote (d. 1866), at Cambridge, used the term 'hedonics' as the 'science of human pleasure' in *Exploratio Philosophica* (vol. 1, 1865), and during the early 1860s he launched the first systematic criticism of Mill's *Utilitarianism*; hence 'hedonism' as a synonym for forms of Utilitarianism in Green's time.[23]

According to Green, Good for the individual is sought neither in pleasure *per se* nor as directed by an external agent (e.g. by civil or ecclesiastical authority). The individual seeks the 'abiding satisfaction of an abiding self.'[24] The hardened 'hedonist' realizes as well as the ascetic that his desires are transitory.[25] We can gratify an impulse or a succession of desires and yet remain unsatisfied. Indeed, the chief evidence for man's non-hedonist, rational and enlightened capacity is that he is conscious of an enduring Self that invents new needs, assesses their significance or importance and modifies its conception of the Good. It is not necessary to follow closely Green's disagreements with the British empiricists and with Kant about the relations of feelings to ideas and of ideas to right reason.[26] It is sufficient to observe that Green held the Self to be structured (in a Kantian sense: prior 'categories' such as time and space impinge upon or qualify our experiences) and that he did not see

---

[22] *GP* 2a: MS 9 ('Four Loose Sheets on Moral Philosophy' — unpublished notes, n.d.).

[23] Thomas De Quincey credited John Wilson, a professor of moral philosophy at Edinburgh, with coining the word 'hedonist' in English. *OED*: s.v.'hedonic', 'hedonism', 'hedonist'; Schneewind, *Sidgwick's Ethics*, pp. 90, 183–6; Hilton, *Age of Atonement*, p. 39.

[24] *PE*, sec. 234. James Seth summarizes a good deal of Green's extrapolation from this 'fact' in simply stating, 'Beneath all stimuli from without and impulses within, what "persists" and demands realization is the rational total self; and in the persistent urgency of its demands is to be found the secret of moral progress, whether of the individual or of the race.' 'The Evolution of Morality,' *Mind*, xiv (1889), p. 49.

[25] *PE*, secs. 156–65.

[26] Green held Locke to be inconsistent in his epistemology: is sensation or the idea of sensation (involving mental action) the beginning of our 'experience'? *GP* (2a: MS 6A) ('Notes for Lectures on Locke, Hume, Kant' — unpublished notes, ca. 1876).

how self-consciousness could be possible for an organism that is simply the product of sensations.[27]

The individual satisfies not mere desires but a more complex 'sense of Self', an idea of a state of being. What the individual engages in in striving rationally towards a more complete and permanent Good, and thus an improved state of being, Green calls self-realization. The realizing Self, in Green's theory, is a teleological concept, and is closely related to 'character' in its common meaning as the tendency toward certain behaviour, a moral habit or predisposition.[28] His inspiration for the idea of self–realisation is clearly Aristotelian: the idea of Self both orders the individual's activity and finds its fulfilment or completion in that activity.[29]

Once again, Green does not deny that the human being is part of nature and can be studied, for certain purposes, as an animal organism. He does not object to certain naturalistic explanations of human behaviour: e.g. a person perceiving danger experiences unconscious nervous processes that trigger responses such as movement of his limbs to confront or flee the perceived danger. Green argues in Chapter One, Book Three of the *Prolegomena* that the individual, upon ordinary reflection on his behaviour, perceives himself as 'self-conscious', 'self-determining' and 'self-objectifying', thereby distinguishing between the '"animal rationale"' and 'that capacity for conceiving a better state of himself.'[30] Examination, then, of animal reflexes and impulses in him cannot supply a convincing explanation of his mental activity and his freedom in action.[31]

The tendency of naturalistic examination of human behaviour, focusing on sensations and responses, is to overdetermine the individual. Green asserts that while every human being, even one more or less completely isolated from human company, arranges his needs and regulates

---

[27] On growth of consciousness, see *PE*, Book One, chap. 2.

[28] 'By character, as that to which moral predicates are ultimately relative, we mean the way in which a man seeks self-satisfaction' ('Lectures on the Philosophy of Kant. II. The Metaphysic of Ethics,' sec. 122). Also: *PE*, secs. 98–108; *LPPO*, sec. 6. Thomas observes that Green uses character in two senses. The first is in the fact that as everyone wills and acts, they have character. The second is that 'To be a person of character, or to be a character, is to be self-determined.' The minimum of character (in the second sense) is to have 'categorical desires', those that serve a conscious and perhaps lasting purpose. (Thomas, *Moral Philosophy of T. H. Green*, pp. 202–3.)

[29] Compare 'The Philosophy of Aristotle' (1866), in *Works*, iii, pp. 81–91 [on thought, idea, and potentiality], with *PE*, secs. 171–9, 186–9.

[30] *PE*, secs. 176–9.

[31] One need not inquire further here as to Green's belief about where the threshold lies in the human organism between innate or automatic responses and those responses that are learned — either through the 'evolutionary' development of species, or through training acquired in the individual's experience in the world and in human society. But see again 'Mr. Lewes' Account of the "Social Medium",' pp. 484–501.

his responses to sensations and 'circumstances', no individual, even one 'bound' in his external relation to other individuals, is a 'slave' to circumstances.[32] However, 'unenlightened' individuals — which is to say, persons not sufficiently conscious of their motives — may claim to be prisoners of circumstances in order to rationalize actions that do not contribute to their abiding Good but merely gratify temporary or non-abiding desires.[33] Green does not mean to diminish the importance of external circumstances to the objects the individual *pursues* in self-realization; he merely wishes to dispose of the claim that such circumstances are forces that directly determine an individual's motives.[34]

If an individual is free to satisfy an idea of the Self, what makes an act of willing good or moral?[35] Do personal and moral goods belong to two separate classes? Few moral philosophers with whom Green was familiar held that the morality of an individual's actions could be separated from their good or ill effects, whether upon the individual or upon others.[36] J. S. Mill, for one, argued in his celebrated treatise *Utilitarianism* (1861–3) that we must agree that 'The morality of the action depends entirely upon the intention — that is, upon what the agent *wills to do*. But the motive, that is, the feeling which makes him will so to do, when it makes no difference in the act, makes none in the morality.' Or as Green rephrases the Utilitarian position, 'Unless an action is done *intentionally*, it is not the subject of moral predicates.'[37] Green argues, in contrast (he

---

[32] Green holds that the term 'freedom' is properly applicable only to the individual's relation to others, i.e. his 'external' relations (such as not being in 'bondage' to another person). Yet in ethical discussion it is unavoidable to speak of freedom as an 'internal' condition relating to will and action — as did St Paul, Hobbes, Locke, Kant and subsequent thinkers ('Different Senses of "Freedom"', secs. 2–3).

[33] Green expresses a version of this view in 'The Force of Circumstances,' in *Works*, iii, pp. 3–10. Originally published in *Undergraduate Papers* (Oxford, 1858; reprint, 1974).

[34] *PE*, sec. 106: 'Whatever [circumstance] conditions the man's possibilities does so through his self-consciousness. The climate in which he lives, the food and drink accessible to him, and other strictly physical circumstances, no doubt make a difference to him; but it is only through the medium of a conception of personal good, only so far as the man out of his relations to them makes to himself certain objects in which he seeks self-satisfaction, that they make a difference to him as a man or moral being. It is only thus that they affect his character and those moral actions which are properly so called as representing a character.'

[35] *PE*, sec. 154: a 'distinction between the good and the bad will ... must lie at the root of every system of Ethics.'

[36] John Plamenatz notes that a meaningful distinction can be drawn between those Utilitarians 'who say that the criterion of morality is objective and those who believe that actions are right or wrong only because they are approved or disapproved by all or most of the persons who contemplate them. Hume belongs clearly to the latter class; Bentham, and those in the intellectual descent from him, to the former.' *Mill's 'Utilitarianism,' Reprinted with a Study of the English Utilitarians* (Oxford: Blackwell, 1949), p. 7.

[37] Quoted in Green, *PE*, sec. 155. Mill acknowledged, however, that 'Questions of ultimate ends [of actions] are not amenable to direct proof.' From 'Utilitarianism' (1871

believes) to Mill and in partial agreement with Kant, that considerations about the morality of willing relate both to the nature of the individual's motive and to the effects of his action: 'It is on the specific difference of the objects willed under the general form of self-satisfaction that the [good or bad] quality of the will must depend.'[38] These 'objects willed' determine the quality of self-realization and also stand in a certain relationship to the 'moral ideal' as expressed in a society. Green's proof of the legitimacy of this principle of evaluation is one of his most distinctive and ingenious contributions to ethical theory, if also one of the most thoroughly criticized.[39]

2.3. THE MORAL MOTIVE AND SELF-REALIZATION

In order to present clearly Green's idea of the moral motive, it may be helpful to state what the moral motive and the Good Will are *not*. The moral motive cannot be seen in the mere satisfaction of desires, unless there is ultimate satisfaction in achieving an idea of a Better Self. Thomas Carlyle famously denounced Jeremy Bentham's 'felicific calculus' as a pig philosophy: it could not, and would not, distinguish between qualities of pleasures, and held that every man was the sole judge of his happiness.[40] Carlyle's friend J. S. Mill admitted that it was 'absurd' that 'the estimation of pleasures should be supposed to depend on quantity alone.'[41] According to Mill, we habitually distinguish our lower pleasures from our higher ones, not only our more lasting pleasures from our transitory ones. He refined the Bethamite felicific calculus to allow, for instance, that individuals perform or desist from actions

---

ed.), in J. S. Mill and Jeremy Bentham, *Utilitarianism and Other Essays*, ed. A. Ryan (London: Penguin, 1987), p. 275.

[38] *PE*, sec. 154.

[39] Sidgwick, 'Green's Ethics;' H. D. Lewis, '"Self–Satisfaction" and the "True Good" in Green's Moral Theory,' *Proceedings of the Aristotelian Society*, 45 (1941–2), pp. 151–82; Milne, *Social Philosophy of English Idealism*, chap. 3; C. Smith, 'Individual and Society in T. H. Green's Theory of Virtue,' pp. 187–201.

[40] Bentham 'says, somewhere in his works, that "quantity of pleasure being equal, push-pin is as good as poetry" ... ' Mill, 'Bentham' (1838), in *Utilitarianism and Other Essays*, pp. 173–4.

[41] 'Utilitarianism,' p. 279. In Chapters Four and Five of *An Introduction to the Principles of Morals and Legislation* (1789), Bentham outlines qualifications of pleasure and pain in the individual, from their intensity to their purity, and categorizes pleasures as 'pleasures of sense', 'pleasures of amity', 'pleasures of the imagination', and so on. The felicific calculus is 'extra-regarding' or social only with respect to pleasures and pains of benevolence and malevolence, for these 'suppose the existence of some pleasure or pain of some other person, to which the pleasure or pain of the person in question has regard ...' (New York: Hafner Publishing Co., 1948, p. 41.)

because they value their reputations.[42] While Green acknowledges Mill as the pre-eminent Utilitarian philosopher, he also attributes to him the 'virtual surrender' of the 'stricter Utilitarian doctrine ... that all desire is for pleasure.'[43]

In a detailed analysis of Utilitarian moral doctrines, Green attempts to lay to rest the misconception that moral agents behave according to the dictates of the felicific calculus.[44] We may understand as our 'Good' something that will satisfy a desire, but the feeling of pleasure obtained in satisfaction of a desire is actually incidental to the idea we form of our Good. There are, in fact, many goods, both personal and social, that would not be obtained if the individual were interested only in obtaining pleasure.[45] The subject of desires always distinguishes himself from them.[46] As for the Utilitarian claim that individuals seek lasting happiness in a hypothetical sum of pleasures, Green argues that no sum of pleasures can be desired at all because we cannot feel a sum of pleasures but can only imagine or anticipate the fulfilment of a series of pleasures, and this is not the same as feeling those pleasures.[47]

Rather than experiencing a succession of pleasures as a sum, or desiring such a sum, what we experience is 'a demand for an abiding satisfaction of an abiding self':

> In a succession of pleasures there can be no such satisfaction, nor in the longest prolongation of the succession any nearer approach to it than in the first pleasure enjoyed. If a man, therefore, under the influence of the spiritual demand described [the conception of an abiding self], were to seek any succession of pleasures as that which would satisfy the demand, he would be under a delusion. Such a delusion may be possible, but we are not to suppose that it takes place because many persons, through a mistaken analysis of their inner experience, affirm that they have no idea of well-being but as a succession of pleasures. The demand for an abiding self-satisfaction has led

---

[42] Alan Ryan remarks upon the similarity between 'Mill's picture of the substantiation of moral rules' and 'Hume's derivation of the "artificial virtues."' *The Philosophy of John Stuart Mill*, 2nd ed. (London: Macmillan, 1987), p. 221.

[43] *PE*, sec. 167. Plamenatz, *Study of the English Utilitarians*, p. 11: 'The utilitarians share with Hobbes a complete indifference to the notion of self-improvement as a thing desirable for its own sake. The single exception is John Stuart Mill ...'

[44] *PE*, Book Three. Green's lengthiest discussion of Mill was his treatment of Mill's logic in lectures delivered at Balliol in 1875: printed as 'The Logic of J. S. Mill,' in *Works*, ii, pp. 195–306. These lectures do not criticize Mill's ethics.

[45] Green cites Aristotle in order to acknowledge that some moral theorists found ways of reconciling virtue (as means to a widely accepted Good) with pleasure: '"Thus the rule that the exercise of virtue is pleasant does not hold of all the virtues, except in so far as the end is attained"' (*Nicomachean Ethics*, III.ix.5[–15].). But Green nevertheless holds that people engage in painful or hazardous actions not because they hope thereby to obtain pleasure but because they have determined beforehand that such activity contributes to a Good that may include pleasure (*PE*, secs. 159–60).

[46] *PE*, sec. 219.

[47] *PE*, sec. 221.

> to an ordering of life in which some permanent provision is made, better or
> worse, for the satisfaction of those interests which are not interests in the pro-
> curing of pleasure, but which may be described most generally as interests in
> the development of our faculties, and in the like development of those for
> whom we care.[48]

Green goes so far as to suggest that Mill unintentionally endorses *his*
account of self-realization, for once we admit, as Mill does, 'that the
attainment of a certain disposition may be an object of desire in itself,
irrespectively of any pleasures that flow from it', we admit to forms of
satisfaction in which desire is actually for a state of being that may
include but is not identical to pleasure.[49]

Another version of the moral ideal or idea of Good Will to which
Green responded, and with which he to a considerable extent agreed,
was Kant's. Green held that aspects of Kant's thought had been badly
misunderstood by British thinkers, who had turned Kant's ideas to purposes to which he would have objected. S. T. Coleridge, Sir William
Hamilton, H. L. Mansel and William Whewell were prominent
'intuitionist' or 'transcendentalist' moralists, who sided more with Kant
than with the Utilitarians in their theories of moral action. 'From Sir William Hamilton,' Green observed,

> English 'culture' absorbed Kant's opposition of *a priori* and empirical truth in
> its most misleading form. [Kant] has come to be taken as the great authority
> for a doctrine which sets 'phenomena and noumena' over against each other
> as two worlds, one knowable, the other unknowable … The really prolific
> element in his system, the view of the 'noumenon,' which he calls the ego, as
> the source of the [mental] categories, and thus at once of the order of phe-
> nomena and of our knowledge of it, and again as itself constituting an intelli-
> gible world of ends freely pursued, is meantime entirely overlooked. It thus
> becomes possible for Professor Mansel to extract from Kant an 'agnostic'
> apology for the acceptance of ecclesiastical dogma, on the ground that our
> necessary ignorance of God, as a noumenon, justifies our belief in miracu-
> lous perturbations of phenomena.[50]

Although Green was anxious to rescue Kantianism from the miscon-
ceptions of these philosophers, he found certain of Kant's ideas to be
fundamentally flawed.[51] He agreed with Kant's view that God was
expressed in the human conscience and in the human capacity for reason, and he also agreed that human beings impose (metaphorically

---

[48]   *PE*, sec. 234.
[49]   *PE*, sec. 170.
[50]   'Review of E. Caird: "The Philosophy of Kant",' in *Works*, iii, pp. 126–37 (first pub-
       lished in *Academy*, September 22, 1877). Quotation from p. 127.
[51]   On the British responses to Kantian thought, see again Green's review of Edward
       Caird's book; also J. S. Mill, 'Whewell on Moral Philosophy' (1852), in *Utilitarianism
       and Other Essays*, ed. Ryan, pp. 228–70; Schneewind, *Sidgwick's Ethics*, chap. 3; Ryan,
       Philosophy of John Stuart Mill, chap. 11; and P. Ferreira, 'Caird on Kant and the Refuta-
       tion of Skepticism,' in *Anglo-American Idealism, 1865–1927*, ed. Mander, chap. 4.

speaking) a 'law' of reason on themselves in the form of an imperative to treat others as ends rather than means to selfish ends. Kant's Categorical Imperative subordinates the individual's pursuit of pleasure to his ful-filment of a universal law.[52] Each individual asks of himself, would I wish the motive underlying my action to stand as a moral rule, govern-ing the actions of other persons in similar circumstances? Does my Good have universal validity, in that sense, and if not, do I not have a duty to abandon that 'Good'?

Green argues that the form in which Kant constitutes the Good Will or moral motive is too rigid and empty to explain the origin of moral activi-ties: the categorical imperative 'finds that this good will is will deter-mined by the idea of duty; not merely a will which conforms to duty, but to which duty is the motive.'[53] This, Green says, would disqualify any individual motive and attempt at self-satisfaction which could not con-form to the golden rule:

> If the law obeyed has any object, this object must have no influence in deter-mining the good will to obey it … What conception can we form of the will to obey it [the moral law], how can we know whether we have such a will or no, or whether any action represents such a will or no, unless the law has some content, unless it enjoins something besides willing obedience to itself, by reference to which that willing obedience may be tested? … Does not the notion of 'duty for duty's sake' … [reduce] itself to a duty to do nothing?[54]

To revert to Green's discussion of the Good Will in *Prolegomena*, he objects to Kant's conception of will and reason as 'separate faculties' united in Good Will and conflicting in Bad Will.[55] Green argues in effect that insofar as a man is self-conscious — by examining his will's corre-spondence to the objects of desire — he is already on the way (so to

[52] Discussed in *Groundwork of the Metaphysic of Morals* (1785) and *Critique of Practical Rea-son* (1788).

[53] 'Kant. II.,' sec. 103. In an unpublished sheaf of notes on moral philosophy, Green observes that Kant ends up dismissing as unfree any action motivated by human sense and feeling. Further, Kant cannot recognize 'desire for pleasure in good of *others* as moral motive … He has no place for anything between selfishness and detachment from all interests' (*GP* 2a: MS 10A ['Kant's Moral Philosophy' and untitled notes on moral philosophy] — Green's emphasis).

[54] 'Kant II,' sec. 110. Elsewhere Green acknowledges the benefits of a universal moral law, assuming we actually adhere to it: 'As Kant puts it, that emotion which on the one side is "Achtung" [respect] for the moral law, on the other is "Verachtung" [disgust] for one's selfish inclinations. Such an emotion may not save a man from many conces-sions to his own weakness, but it will make him refuse with contempt to resort to casu-istry for their justification' (*PE*, sec. 314).

[55] *PE*, sec. 179. 'Kant seems to hold that the will is actually "autonomous," i.e. deter-mined by pure consciousness of what should be, only in the rare acts of the best men. He argues rather for our being conscious of the possibility of such determination, as evidence of an ideal of what the good will is, than for the fact that anyone is actually so determined' ('Different Senses of "Freedom",' sec. 3). Compare to Green's treatment of Kant in *PE*, secs. 192–8.

speak) to morality. A person's desire to achieve an improved state of being is a primary condition of morality, even if 'it must be borne in mind that this same capacity is the condition … no less of the vicious life than of the virtuous.'[56]

In order to explain the 'initiative of all virtuous habit and action', Green refers to an 'eternal principle of self-objectification' and 'the divine self-realising principle.'[57] These notions are less mysterious than they might at first appear. The individual's '"heaven-born" nature' is 'actualised' in a 'union [in him] between the developed will and the developed reason.'[58] The life of an individual conscious of this unity 'has always been called, according to a usage inherited from the Greek fathers of moral philosophy, *a life according to reason*.'[59] When persons seek their Good by seeking to realize their better Selves, Kantians say 'that their will becomes conformable to their reason.' But — says Green — will and reason are not 'separate faculties' but 'alike capacities' united in the same Self: reasonable and unreasonable actions alike are acts of willing; and the will does not exercise one faculty and exclude the other. The person aware of this unity in himself is at least intermittently aware of how he fails to live up to the ideal of a better Self — has failed to uphold a duty to himself. Such discovery is also 'the echo in him of the expression which practical reason has so far given to itself in those institutions, usages, and judgments of society, which contribute to the perfection of life.' Morality finally consists in the individual identifying his good with that of *others*: 'every step forward in the self-realization of the divine principle in man involves a determination of will no less than of reason, not merely a conception of a possible good for man, but the adoption by some man or men of that good as his or theirs.'[60]

Green's moral principle, which would appear to be a refinement of Kant's categorical imperative, suggests a standard of conduct both present in the moral agent and external to him. The content of the Good cannot be exclusively shaped by external rules any more than it can follow from Kant's dictum.[61] If it were true that the morally motivated individual were merely governed by a socially sanctioned notion of right behaviour (and by laws), then his will would be empty and the Self

---

[56] *PE*, sec. 178.
[57] *PE*, secs 177–8.
[58] *PE*, sec. 177.
[59] *PE*, sec. 178: italics mine.
[60] *PE*, sec. 179.
[61] 'Must not … [the] effect of [the Categorical Imperative] be either a dead conformity to the code of customary morality, anywhere and at any time established, without effort to reform or expand it, or else unlimited license in departing from it at the prompting of any impulse which the individual may be pleased to consider a higher law?' (*PE*, sec. 198).

might remain unrealized. As Green states in the lectures 'Different Senses of "Freedom"',

> Unless the actions required of him by 'the divine law, the civil law, and the law of opinion or reputation' (to use Locke's classification) tend to realise his own idea of what should be or is good on the whole, they do not form an object which, as contemplated, he can harmonise with the other objects he seeks to understand, nor, as a practical object, do they form one in the attainment of which he can satisfy himself.[62]

The individual, in behaving morally, is not primarily seeking a good that *others* may present to him as a good. The good sought by the individual must be *for* self/individual, i.e. comprehensible by the individual subject. (Hence an apparent justification for *private* property, as means to individual ends: see discussion at the conclusion of this chapter.) Green makes clear that 'Our ultimate standard of worth is an ideal of personal worth. All other values are relative to values for, of, or in a person.'[63]

But if the individual develops his character by seeking to realize his idea of Self, and if his actions, good or bad, derive from and contribute to his 'ideal of personal worth', from what perspective can we disqualify certain of his motives and actions as non-moral or immoral? Is it by identifying the mischievous effects of the individual's actions? Green answers, yes and no. He holds that just as we can distinguish between impulses and motives, so can moral motives be distinguished from immoral and non-moral ones. Non-moral motives are not invariably bad in themselves (they may even have positive social consequences) but are the ones not ordered through self-consciousness in accordance with an idea of its Good which the Self presents to itself.[64] But if conception of what is truly good originates in the self-conscious individual, who embodies a spiritual and eternal principle, what authority can contradict such conception? Green acknowledges the difficulty of other individuals advising an individual that his conception of his Good is flawed or incorrect, that he does not do what he ought.[65] Since, Green decides, the individual is in theory the person most capable of giving a complete account of his own motives, we may have opportunity to

---

[62] Sec. 24.

[63] *PE*, sec. 184.

[64] *PE*, Book Four, chap. 1 ('The Practical Value of the Moral Ideal'). See also Milne, *Social Philosophy of English Idealism*, chap. 3.

[65] Green cautions against applying the predicates '"ought" and "ought not", otherwise than in reflection upon *our own* acts,' for in so many instances we cannot obtain sufficient knowledge of an agent's motives (*PE*, sec. 293; emphasis mine). Though according to the strict Utilitarian view, such knowledge is unnecessary: 'If two actions, done by different men, are alike in their production of pleasure, they are alike in moral value, though the doer of one act is of virtuous character and the doer of the other is not so' (sec. 294).

question the agent about the quality of his motive, 'and there is nothing
in the nature of the case to prevent a true answer being given to it.' But
this is hardly a practical procedure for 'giving men either truer views of
what in particular they ought to do, or a better disposition to do it.'[66]

A complete conception of the moral ideal is unobtainable; it can only
be achieved in limited form by examination of the self-realizing activities of individuals. But, Green says, the divine 'spirit operative in men'[67]
guiding their morality expresses itself in individuals *as members of a society or nation*:

> It is in fact only so far as we are members of a society, of which we can con-
> ceive the common good as our own, that the ideal [of moral improvement]
> has any practical hold on us at all, and this very membership implies confine-
> ment in our individual realisation of the idea.[68]

Although 'our ultimate standard of worth is an ideal of *personal* worth,'
moral activity 'can only have its being in persons ... specially modified
by the special conditions of their intercourse with each other.'[69]

Because of the social embeddedness of the moral ideal it appears that
we are justified in advising an individual that his conception of personal
Good is incomplete (as many such personal conceptions will be), that it
does not take into consideration various circumstances, including
human relationships, that impinge upon his well-being, and that he has
not composed himself and his actions in a manner that will allow him to
satisfy an abiding Good. A tradesman who cheats his customers in little
ways may claim — to himself, or to others when caught out — that his
actions at least enable him to support his family, thus satisfying a legitimate perception of personal Good. Green would hold that this is soph-
istry; in giving such justification to his actions the tradesman
undermines the moral conditions in which all individuals can further
their own goods.[70] This damage outweighs the good the person
achieves in supporting his family, because if such behaviour became
widespread, it would hamper the abilities of each to achieve his or her
goods. Green appears to believe that the individual, in the course of
social interaction, will become convinced of the truth of this and modify
his behaviour accordingly.

Green's 'solution' to the question of correspondence between Good
Will and moral action is in the end proposed only indirectly. To 'be

[66] *PE*, sec. 296.
[67] *PE*, sec. 193.
[68] *PE*, sec. 183.
[69] *PE*, sec. 184.
[70] See, however, *LPPO*, sec. 224: the principle of buying cheap and selling dear may dis-
      guise a host of 'objectionable transactions,' but in taking commodities from places
      where they are of small value and selling them where they are more highly valued,
      'The trader who profits by the transaction is profiting by what is at the same time a
      contribution to social well-being.'

always fingering one's own motives is a sign rather of an unwholesome preoccupation with self than of the eagerness in disinterested service which helps forward mankind.' Other individuals may do the right thing only by limiting their sphere of moral action: they 'hug their reputation within themselves for acting conscientiously [to the extent] that in difficult situations they will not act at all.'[71] Yet we may often have opportunities to assess individuals' motives in relation to what they perceive as their own good *and* in relation to common 'moral sentiments':

> It is no other than the sense of personal responsibility for making the best of themselves in the family, the tribe, or the state, which must have actuated certain persons, many or few, in order to the establishment and recognition of any moral standards whatever. Given such standards, it is the spirit which at once demands from the individual a loyal conformity to them, and disposes him, upon their suggestion, to construct for himself an ideal of virtue, of personal goodness, higher than they explicitly contain.[72]

Of course, the very existence of political society testifies to the fact that the individual's self-interest may on occasion collide with the interests of others — thus the institution of law, insofar as it serves the common good.[73] Having suggested in the *Prolegomena* how laws arise in the first place — that is, in relation to moral sentiments to which individuals over time contribute in their acts of self-realization — Green does not apply his model of moral remonstration and self-questioning to individual actions that are clearly and simply against the law. In cases where the individual engages in actions that prevent others from discharging their *duties*, which laws or customs uphold, we are fully justified in censuring actions that undermine social order. Laws exist to further goods that are shared or common, and to curb activities that prevent the peaceful enjoyment of goods by all.[74] While 'moral duties' are not enforceable by a sovereign, 'obligations' are, and the latter have been designed to establish conditions under which individuals may fulfil their moral duties.[75]

---

[71] *PE*, sec. 297.
[72] *PE*, sec. 309.
[73] *LPPO*, chap. A (secs. 1–31).
[74] Green states in his introduction to Hume, 'Conformity to law [is] not the moral good but the means to it' ('Hume II,' p. 320). In his discussion of the Good Will and the Moral Ideal in *Prolegomena* (Books Two and Three), Green presents conformity to moral custom and law as a *form* of the moral good, but as neither the source of good nor its invariable result.
[75] *LPPO*, secs. 10–16. The business of the law 'is to maintain certain conditions of life — to see that certain actions are done which are necessary to the maintenance of those conditions, others omitted which would interfere with them. It has nothing to do with the motive of the actions or omissions, on which, however, the moral value of them depends' (sec. 13).

Discussion of Green's theory of morals has already crept into the realm of political philosophy. Green held this to be unavoidable, because even the most degraded political societies and their laws have been instituted in light of moral considerations. The existence of laws reflects socially anchored sentiments: 'establishment of obligations by law or authoritative custom, and the gradual recognition of moral duties, have not been separate processes ... [but] have been related to each other as the outer and the inner side of the same spiritual development.'[76] Green's idea of the social existence of moral sentiments is not entirely at odds with the ideas of David Hume and Adam Smith. To Hume, people are passionate, foolish, and prejudiced, and morals and government depend mainly on their calculating preference for security of social arrangements. In their more rational moments they welcome the safety of government and the censure of common opinion.[77] He wrote in his *Enquiry Concerning the Principles of Morals* that to enlist social support for his interests, a man must 'depart from his private and particular situation ...; he must ... touch a string to which all mankind have an accord or symphony'. Yet, as Hume observed in his *Treatise on Human Nature,*

> Men are not able radically to cure ... that narrowness of soul, which makes them prefer the present to the remote ... All they can do is to change their situation, and render the observance of justice the immediate interest of some particular persons.

Such particular persons included judges, clerics, sovereigns and others constituting public authority and serving as the arbiters of custom.

Green argued that Hume and other eighteenth-century moralists had not demonstrated how and why the individual departed from his 'private and particular situation' to touch that string connecting him to his fellows — even for the instrumental purpose of securing social approval or consent.[78] The moral sense, Green claimed, originated not in the isolated individual, apart from usages and judgments of society, nor was it the product of social censure and forcible conformity. It developed rather from practical reason, through the working of self-realization in individuals as they negotiated the intricacies of common life.

Green was attentive to real instances of 'conflict between private opinion and authority' and discussed circumstances in which individuals were presented with such conflicts and might hope to resolve them. The ancient drama 'Antigone' presented the conflicts of duties and sentiments in terms of the conflicting claims of family and state. Green alluded in the *Prolegomena* to 'the crisis ... through which several Euro-

---

[76] *LPPO*, sec. 251.
[77] Quotations from Hume in Plamenatz, *Study of the English Utilitarians*, pp. 33, 40.
[78] See Green's discussion of Hutcheson, Butler and Hume and their accounts of moral sense in 'Hume II,' secs. 24–60.

pean states have recently passed', by which he probably meant the German *Kulturkampf* of the 1870s, in the course of which the Falk laws and other measures were implemented to ensure the loyalty of Catholic subjects to the state.[79] It was perhaps with British events of the nineteenth century (e.g. radical democratic agitations and Chartism) in mind that Green cited the instance of

> the modern citizen, in his capacity as an official or as a soldier, ... called upon to help in putting down some revolutionary movement which yet presents itself to his innermost conviction as the cause of 'God and the People.'[80]

Interestingly in this connection, Green suggests that the origin of conscience, the inner voice speaking to the perplexed individual, is more social than personal:

> If ... it [conscience] is an expression which the ideal of human good gives to itself in the mind of the man who entertains it; then it too rests on a basis of social authority. No individual can make a conscience for himself. He always needs a society to make it for him. A conscientious 'heresy,' religious or political, always represents some gradually maturing conviction as to social good, already implicitly involved in the ideas on which the accepted rules of conduct rest, though it may conflict with the formulae in which those ideas have been hitherto authoritatively expressed, and may lead to the overthrow of institutions which have previously contributed to their realisation.[81]

Green held that moral action is a result both of mental reflection and of individual conformity to social sentiments, and his position (so stated) was consistent with that of other moralists, ancient and modern. Where Green departed from moral doctrines then ascendant in Britain was in his account of the structure of moral action. His advance on the purely 'formal' model of the Good Will supplied by Kant consists in his proof that even the individual inured to criticism and indifferent to the social consequences of his behaviour, comes, without reference to a categorical imperative, to understand that unreflective or impulsive actions tend not to lead to abiding satisfaction of the Self. This is evidence of man's power of judgment (Kant's *Urteilskraft*) as well as his

---

[79] *PE*, sec. 321. H. Holborn, *A History of Modern Germany, Volume 3: 1840–1945* (Princeton: Princeton UP, 1982 [1969]), pp. 261–4.

[80] *PE*, sec. 321. See Green's letter to his family about the Volunteer Movement, cited in the Introduction above.

[81] *PE*, sec. 321. To Green the reality of conscience appears always to have had a double character. In an undergraduate essay, 'How Far Moral Principles are Probable or Conventional', he writes that our 'assurance of the truth' of conscience stems from our consciousness but also from the 'evidence written on the whole framework of our society and in universal language ... We are conscious of a law within ourselves ... but [sic] as our position as members of a society is also part of our consciousness, the necessary laws of society, in other words principles derived from convention, become identified with principles of which we are conscious in ourselves ... It is by convention that our moral principles expand.' *AW*, pp. 36–7.

prior power of intellectual synthesis.[82] It is an expression of his faculty of reason, not intuition.

An individual resists the temptation of sweets: cake is desirable, but consumption of cake may result in an undesirable physique. The cake-lover who is unconcerned about mere physical appearance (i.e. having no self-originating sense of personal incompleteness and insensitive to social censure) may alter his diet when made conscious that his health may suffer, or that family will share in the suffering. In the first instance, the cake-lover is aware of conflict among his separate desires (good health and enjoyment of sugar); in the second, he is aware of conflict between a narrowly personal good and a good which includes the well-being of others. The moral individual is aware of some structure or order of her desires, and the development of self-consciousness leads to her understanding the social context of self-satisfaction. Green is confident that the individual, in her process of moralization, will discover that when her realization of a Good occurs at the expense of others, her idea of Self must appear to her inadequate. It is not only the case that the 'idea [of a true good] does not admit of the distinction between good for self and good for others.'[83] Because she achieves consciousness of objects of self-satisfaction as a member of a society, the individual adjusts her behaviour to include in greater or lesser measure the interests of others: 'True happiness, as ... [an individual] conceives of it for himself, consists in the realisation of the objects of various interests by which he is possessed — interests of which he is only capable through self-identification with a society.'[84]

In the long run, 'hedonist' behaviour will frustrate the needs of the Self just as surely as it will detract from or not contribute to the common good.[85] Yet — negatively — moral actions are not only those which

---

[82] Philosophers have argued at length as to whether Green actually improved upon Kant's theory of moral behaviour. See T. Irwin, 'Morality and Personality: Kant and Green', and R. Meerbote, 'Commentary [on Irwin]', in *Self and Nature in Kant's Philosophy*, ed. A. W. Wood (Ithaca, NY: Cornell UP, 1984), pp. 31–56, 57–72. I will not pretend to have resolved the questions raised by these essays but I will take up an observation by W. H. Walsh about Kant's treatment of will and reason: 'So far as I know, Kant shows no awareness of the possibility that I might learn something about myself by reflecting on my own behaviour.' Walsh, *Kant's Criticism of Metaphysics* (Chicago: Chicago UP, 1975), p. 185 ['Reason and Metaphysics']. Green clearly includes the capacity of self–reflection, as part of self-realization, in his theory of the moral ideal.

[83] *PE*, sec. 235.

[84] *PE*, sec. 236.

[85] Green's theory of the moral motive may well be as untenable as Kant's, in that it appears to rest upon an insecure faith in other individuals' conformity to the moral law. As Ralf Meerbote comments, 'It may even be true that acting morally maximizes for all agents (as a body) the likelihood of achieving self-satisfactions more persistently and effectively than any other scheme would. These considerations make it reasonable to act morally but do not constitute moral justification of actions.' A high

clearly or intentionally contribute to the common good. The scientist or artist may act to achieve a personal good yet add to the good of society.[86] Although such a person may not regularly think of his activity as contributing to a better state of mankind, his creative action is itself a response to a perception of a lack or insufficiency in the received wisdom of society or in its aesthetic sense. His motive is perhaps more complex than those of average persons who (merely) do their duty; but like theirs, his motive is a conception of self-improvement that includes something larger than himself, or a wider sense of self-improvement. From the twin considerations of motive and result Green also argues for the goodness of actions in spite of personal motives which appear (to others) obscure or even sinister, from all we know of them:

> the more we learn of such a person, for instance, as Napoleon, and of the work which seemed to be his, the more clearly does it appear how what was evil in it arose out of his personal selfishness and that of his contemporaries, while what was good in it was due to higher and purer influences of which he and they were but the medium.[87]

2.4. THE MORAL IDEAL AND THE ETERNAL PRINCIPLE

At many points in his lectures constituting the *Prolegomena*, in 'The Different Senses of "Freedom"' and occasionally in the *Lectures on the Principles of Political Obligation*, Green referred (as in the passage about Napoleon Bonaparte cited above) to a medium through which individual selves find moral direction. In Sections 174–8 of the *Prolegomena* he referred to an 'eternal mind,' a 'self-objectifying principle' and a 'divine principle', using these terms to suggest the presence of a higher rationality in individual activity and social practice — or what he called in Section 178 of the *Prolegomena* 'life according to reason.' In Section 180 Green speaks of 'one divine mind [which] gradually reproduces itself in the human soul.' This 'spiritual endowment' of man 'consists in his consciousness of a potential better state of himself.' This 'spiritual endowment ... has been the *parent* [my emphasis] of the institutions and usages, of the social judgments and aspirations, through which human life has been so far bettered.' Yet no individual merely doing his duty, living entirely according to society's rules and mores, 'can exhibit all

---

degree of compliance to the moral law would be necessary for an individual's choice in moral conduct to lead to a personal benefit, and such consequentialism, given the dictates of self-interest, discourages 'conditions for acceptance of the moral law.' Meerbote, 'Commentary [on Irwin],' pp. 71–2.

[86] 'An artist or man of science who "lives for his work" without troubling himself with philanthropy, is yet not living for an object merely private to himself ...' Since others may benefit from his discoveries his is 'a good for which others are the better' (Green, 'Kant II,' sec. 123).

[87] *PE*, sec. 295.

that the Spirit, working through and in him, properly and potentially is.'[88] The bidding of the 'divine principle' is not exhausted by individuals simply adhering to conventional morality.

Green's suggestion that moral actions of individuals in historical time indicate the presence of an 'eternal principle' (sec. 177) or 'self-objectifying spirit' (sec. 216) in persons is of course reminiscent of Hegel's *Weltgeist* and 'Cunning of Reason.'[89] All revelations or manifestations of the Good occur through and in the actions of individuals, and since we cannot assume the omniscient perspective of God or even acquire a total view of human history, we achieve only a partial picture of the Good, and indeed of the full extent of moral freedom.[90]

With respect to the 'innate', divinely implanted component of the moral ideal, Green's thinking runs parallel to that of Joseph Butler, as well as that of Thomas Reid and nineteenth-century 'intuitionists' responding to Hume's construction of social virtues.[91] These intuitionists held the moral motive and the capacity for right action to be naturally constitutive of human character; as moral sense is intuited, the primary conditions of morality are ingrained in the individual, not socially determined.[92] There is an affinity between these ideas and those of the ancient Stoics, who spoke of the man 'who lives for himself, but only according to the true idea of himself, according to the law of his being, "according to nature" …'.[93] Green was aware of the implications of Stoic doctrines for the progressive unfolding of the moral ideal: they were quasi-democratic in attributing to each (sane, healthy) individual some capacity for moral behaviour — in contrast to earlier Greek moral doctrines which held true morality possible only for (male) citizens of the *polis*, men in a certain political and economic condition.[94]

---

[88] *PE*, sec. 183.

[89] Hegel, *Introduction to 'The Philosophy of History,'* ed. L. Rauch, pp. 21–33. See also (on Napoleon), Green, *LPPO*, secs. 128–30. In a manner more sober than Hegel's Green observes, 'Histories, no doubt, would be much shortened, and would be found much duller, if speculations about the motives (as distinct from *intentions*) of the chief historical agents were omitted … It is clearly quite right to take account, so far as possible, of all the circumstances … But this is a different thing from trying to ascertain the state of character on the part of the agents which the actions represent, and in ignorance of which the full moral nature of the acts is not known' (*PE*, sec. 293). Milne, however, is not correct in concluding that Green disqualifies good effects from bad motives (Milne, *Social Philosophy of English Idealism*, chap. 3, sec. 3).

[90] *PE*, secs. 180–4.

[91] Schneewind, *Sidgwick's Ethics*, chaps. 2–3; D. M. Mackinnon, *A Study in Ethical Theory* (London: A. and C. Black, 1957), chap. 5.

[92] Compare to J. S. Mill: 'the moral feelings are not innate, but acquired, [although] they are not for that reason the less natural' ('Utilitarianism,' p. 302).

[93] 'Different Senses of "Freedom",' sec. 7.

[94] *PE*, Book Three, chap. 5. And see discussion of the history of the Moral Ideal below.

As noted earlier, Green sometimes appears to favour the notion of the social construction of morality over the idea of morality arising from man's inherent capacity of rational self-reflection. In 'Different Senses of "Freedom",' Green equates the Platonic with the Hegelian conception of the true good: the objects through which we legitimately attempt to satisfy our conceptions of the Good are provided or suggested to us by a well ordered society or state.[95] Hegel posited the state as the Temple of Freedom, 'the march of God in the world,' a higher realization of the Spirit than that which could be obtained by separate individuals.[96] St Paul and Christian thinkers equated the good will even more narrowly with the individual's subordination to God and God's law (experienced at first as an external authority), and the thwarting of certain human impulses. Yet Green argues that all of these theories are flawed (or incomplete) in the same ways that Kant's is: they set apart good from bad will, and the Good Will as personal from the objects of self-satisfaction as provided by society, in a manner which makes it difficult to discover what our motives are and how we act upon them.

The more important operative ideas in Green's moral philosophy are the Good Will, the moral ideal and the eternal principle. The latter is the most mysterious. It appears that for Green the conditions of morality are provided by the eternal principle in the following sense: the individual achieves (partial) realization of his divine nature by recognizing an affinity between objects of self-realization suggested to him by his society and a conscience (or what some religious persons describe as an inner voice) which directs his will. This would seem to undermine his claim that the man is a freely willing subject. Sidgwick objected to Green's theory of the Good Will by claiming that it fails to identify a genuinely personal motive for individual activity: if possible forms of the Good and the total potential for Good are in a sense foreordained, in what sense is morality the result of 'free' will?[97] Green recognizes the legitimacy of this question but suggests that its inappropriate expression is due to a misunderstanding of the eternal principle and its relation to the 'free' individual will. (We cannot properly speak of will as other than the individual will or the will of God.)

Green's idea about free will and self-satisfaction in relation to morality is that conformity to the true nature of one's being — even if predetermined in a 'theological' sense or that of the Stoics — does not diminish free will or detract from self-realization. Curbing some

---

[95] Secs. 5–7.
[96] G.W.F. Hegel, *Philosophy of Right*, trans. T. M. Knox (Oxford: Clarendon, 1942), secs. 33, 135, 142–50, 258, 260.
[97] Sidgwick discusses Green's conception of the Good Will among other such conceptions he describes as 'theological' (*Methods of Ethics*, 7th ed., pp. 78–80). See also Schneewind, *Sidgwick's Ethics*, pp. 403–11.

impulses does not thwart free will but trains motives and habits in order to more completely express the will. Here external standards might intervene by suggesting to the individual appropriate objects or actions in which the Self can be satisfied. Green accepts in a qualified form the Greek and Hegelian view of custom and the state, and he adds that one need not be a saint, subordinating the ego to God's law, or a soldier on a suicide mission, identifying his good with the good of the nation or state, to behave morally and lawfully.

In the third book of the *Prolegomena* (Chapter Five) Green argues for the superiority of Christian over ancient ethics, as a way of demonstrating the 'moral progress of man' and in order to suggest the potential for freedom enjoyed by members of modern Western societies in which Christianity has been a dominant influence.[98] (Like Hegel, James Mill, J. S. Mill and Macaulay, Green attributed a special moral status to Christianity: in societies influenced by Christianity history had been driven by struggles over the implications of the core Christian doctrine of the spiritual equality of men — hence limited monarchy, representative government, and so on. Conceptions of Self, morality, and the divine suggested by, for instance, Hinduism, Buddhism and Confucianism are beyond Green's purview.) The ancient Greek conception of virtue defines good as goodness, and in terms of defining the Good as 'well-being constituted by character and action,' the Greek conception of Good as virtuousness represents the very highest standard of morality.[99] But in terms of prescribing or suggesting a full complement of actions through which people may satisfy their moral natures it is inadequate. The Greek idea of virtue and virtues, which all good citizens internalized, encompassed all three parts of Locke's scheme of external morality (divine law, civil law and law of opinion).[100] Greek virtue stipulated certain actions incumbent upon citizens for the maintenance of their freedom. 'The idea of a society of free and law-abiding persons, each his own master yet each his brother's keeper,' Green holds, 'was first definitely formed among the Greeks ...'. But the idea 'was limited in its application to select groups of men ...'.[101] Civic virtue, as reflected for instance in the obligations to serve as juror or to fight the enemies of the state, was not incumbent upon less favoured members of society: slaves and women had duties, but as they were held to be incapable of

---

[98]   *PE*, secs. 278–90.

[99]   *PE*, secs. 278–9.

[100] In the Graeco-Roman world, 'the State would gather to itself the sentiments of which, as it is [today], the Church seems the more natural object' (*PE*, sec. 323). Green's view of Greek religion as providing a guide to morality yet being also a non-institutional 'folk religion' was typical of Romantic Christianity. See B. M. G. Reardon, *Religion in the Age of Romanticism. Studies in Early Nineteenth Century Thought* (CUP, 1985), chaps. 1, 3.

[101] *PE*, sec. 271.

the higher virtues, they were not moral agents. One measure of Christendom's superiority to antiquity is in the modern recognition of slaves and women as moral persons:

> The legal investment of every one with personal rights makes it impossible for one whose mind is open to the claims of others to ignore the wrong of treating a woman as the servant of his pleasures at the cost of her own degradation.[102]

Members of Christian societies, as spiritual equals, have wider opportunities of self-realization than slaves in the Athenian polity; and Christian moral doctrine had the historical effect of abolishing fundamental *legal* inequality of persons. Green skims over other historical developments of the universalizing moral ideal, such as Socratic and early Christian ideas of the moral life and the establishment of the 'Pax Romana'.[103] This view of moral progress resembles Hegel's philosophy of history. Hegel pronounced that in the 'Oriental' world (or worldview), one person — the emperor or prince — is free; in the Greek world, some individuals are free; in Christian society, all are free.[104] As far as modern society is concerned, Green says, father or mother, obedient son, conscientious craftsman, charitable gentlewoman are all examples of individuals (or ideal figures) who shape an idea of Self according to their perception of their interests *and* to socially supplied norms. Their conceptions of the Good may appear less well defined than those of the ancient Greeks, concerned as the latter were with specific traits like self-denial and the endurance of pain, but in fact the modern moral ideal is much more inclusive than the Greek.[105] Green states,

---

[102] *PE*, sec. 267. The passage continues: 'Though the wrong is still habitually done, it is done under the rebuke of conscience to which a Greek of Aristotle's time, with most women about him in slavery, and without even the capacity (to judge from the writings of the philosophers) for an ideal of society in which this should be otherwise, could not have been sensible ... Change [in treatment of women] was itself ... the embodiment of a demand which forms the basis of our moral nature — the demand on the part of the individual for a good which shall be at once his own and the good of others.' Green did not believe, of course, that women in ancient Greece were legal chattel but used the comparison metaphorically to indicate that they were not recognized as legal or moral persons. Women and slaves were contained within *oikoi*, households; citizens acted in the *oikos* and the *polis*. See S. R. L. Clark, 'Aristotle's Woman,' *HPT*, 3 (1982), pp. 171–91.

[103] *PE*, secs. 280, 284–5.

[104] Introduction to 'The Philosophy of History,' ed. Rauch.

[105] Greek moral theory had a distinct 'content', was part of an 'art' of living — but of living in a specific and limiting way. 'The most obvious diff. between Ar.'s [Aristotle's] notion of [*politiki*] and the widest modern notion of moral or social science lies in the *practical* object of the former. It is a discipline in the *art* of making good laws and thro' them a good life. The modern tho' he might expect his "social science" to have good effect on legislation wd. not regard it as having for its direct function to teach art of

'Human brotherhood' had no meaning for them [the Greek philosophers].
They had no adequate notion of the claims in response to which the good will
should be exercised. In respect of the institutions and arrangements of life, of
the social requirements, etc., ... a great range of new experience has come
into being for us which did not exist for them. The soul of human society has
realised its capacities in new ways.[106]

2.5. RIGHTS AND CIVIL SOCIETY

Green argues for the sociability of the Self and for the moral ideal operative in progressive societies recognizing the claims of a variety of persons. His discussions of shared will or common good overlap with
treatment of questions of 'right' or 'rights', because rights are commonly
held to exist in order to enable individuals to articulate their wills and
realize their goods. Green is critical, though, of social contract theories
of rights as formulated by Hobbes and Locke, and of Rousseau's theory
of sovereignty, including the notion of a 'General Will' as a legitimate
instrument of sovereignty.[107]

As regards the state and a 'social contract' on which it is supposedly
based, Green faults Hobbes, Locke and Rousseau for misunderstanding
'natural rights' (as recognizing conditions of pre-social, individual
goods) and positing a 'contract' which individuals enter into in order to
safeguard their (pre-political) rights.[108] The existence of rights begins in
a political society when its members agree that an enforcer of individual
claims is necessary to serve goods that individuals hold (or could hold)
in common — and so social contract theory holds. But it is a misconception to argue that rights serving to protect individual and shared goods
in political society had some prior existence. Rights imply enforcement
of mutual obligation, and they cannot be claimed or acted upon without
a state to enforce them or to force individuals to forbear from certain
actions. Green pronounces 'hopeless' Rousseau's attempt to reconcile
'submission to government' supposedly based on natural rights to the
existence of antecedent natural rights.[109]

Green also attacks the notion of a General Will. For one, will cannot be
independent of motive, and all motives originate in Selves; no aggregate
of wills and Selves, whether all or only partially inclusive, can be properly represented as general. A General Will is likely to prevent *somebody's* enjoyment of a right in a way that would incite the resistance of

legislation, nor wd. he look to legislation as a means of making men good' (*GP* 2a: MS
18 [unpublished notes on Aristotle]).

[106] *PE*, sec. 279.
[107] *LPPO*, chapters C–F.
[108] Green recognizes that Rousseau differed from Locke in denying that political societies are *created* by a social contract. Rather society is 'as itself in the act of its formation
becoming a sovereign and ever after continuing so' (*LPPO*, secs. 64–5).
[109] *LPPO*, sec. 77.

many individuals. As an instrument of sovereignty, General Will is less useful than the idea of a common good. Green makes clear that no valid conception of General Will — as proxy for the 'true' wills of individuals — can be formed without regard to common good that encompasses individual goods.[110] It would be wrong to think, as Rousseau does, that in acting for society, the state is properly assuming the wills of the individual parties to a contract, and Rousseau posits the 'prerogatives of the sovereign people, without any corresponding limitation of the conditions under which an act is to be deemed that of the sovereign people.'[111] Green does concede that in 'federated self-governing communes' — such as Rousseau's native Geneva, the other Swiss cantons, and perhaps in the United Provinces of the Netherlands — the General Will and the 'establishment of a sovereign by social pact' are feasible.[112] But Green argues that 'the whole drift of his doctrine is to show that no sovereign ... ,' whether enlightened prince or assembled nation, 'had any claim on obedience.' 'Even under existing representative systems the conditions are not fulfilled which according to him are necessary to give laws the claim on our obedience which arises from their being an expression of the general will.'[113]

Green also discusses in the *Principles* the procedural considerations of sovereignty offered by John Austin in his *Lectures on Jurisprudence* (1861–3).[114] With these Green is unimpressed. His ultimate opinion of Austin is summarized thus:

> Austinians, having found their sovereign, are apt to regard it as a much more important institution than, if it is to be identified with a determinate person or persons, it really is; they are apt to suppose that the sovereign, with the coercive power (i.e. the power of operating on the fears of the subjects) which it exercises, is the real determinant of the habitual obedience of the people — at any rate of their habitual obedience in respect of those acts and forbearances which are prescribed by law. But ... this is not the case.[115]

No more than Rousseau does Austin give a satisfactory account of how individuals recognize sovereignty or might disobey what they perceive to be unjust authority by appealing to a higher, although perhaps

---

[110] *LPPO*, chapters E–F.
[111] *LPPO*, sec. 69.
[112] *LPPO*, secs. 78–9.
[113] *LPPO*, sec. 79.
[114] *LPPO*, chapter F. Austin (1790–1859) was a Benthamite and the 'founder of English nineteenth-century analytic jurisprudence ... Lord Melbourne is said to have remarked of the *Province of Jurisprudence* [Austin's *magnum opus* published in 1832] that It was thé dullest book he had ever read.' Bowle, *Politics and Opinion in the Nineteenth Century*, pp. 67–8.
[115] *LPPO*, sec. 86.

unsanctioned authority.[116] Or as Green puts it, 'No precise rule, there-fore, can be laid down as to the conditions under which resistance to a despotic government becomes a duty.'[117]

Yet people often construct such justification for resistance, success-fully revolt, and may raise legitimate moral claims in doing so. Green discusses the struggle between the American Union and the Confeder-acy and claims that in this case it is fruitless to argue whether a majority or a minority has a right to resist a sovereign.[118] A greater good may ulti-mately ensue from men of good will taking sides with one sovereign or another, than if right were on one side. His purpose, it seems, is to reveal the fallacies of the Austinian argument that sovereignty can be clearly located in the more perplexing political conflicts people experience. Ultimately, Green says, a rebel must consider whether in resisting gov-ernment he is able to thereby secure a real improvement in existing social arrangements and the moral goods they serve, even if imper-fectly. 'No doubt revolutionists do and must to a great extent "go it blind"' — confident that they are able to usher in a better order.[119] Com-pelling justification of disobedience towards the sovereign power might not arrive until after the fact.[120]

Green proposes a way out of such dilemmas (relating to conflicts of authority with morality and reason) in his discussion of rights. Natural rights had been invoked frequently since the eighteenth century in order to alter the relationship between government and governed, and to protest the legal and other subordination of social groups. Natural rights, according to Green, are not actual rights but useful fictions.[121] Green was critical of Edmund Burke's defences of the unreformed Brit-ish legislature and the monarchy, yet he agreed with Burke's organic

---

[116] In his unpublished notes labelled (by R. L. Nettleship) 'Population. Property. Sover-eignty' (*GP* 2a: MS 19) Green observes: 'Modern idea of "sovereign" is that of supreme might, recognized as having right. Difficulty in consequent theory of sovereignty is to find out where such might actually resides ... Aristotle gives no definition of sover-eignty, merely enumerates certain functions as belonging to it ... The truth is that the question, where sovereignty defined as above, resides, is one that can't be answered unless we are content to say that sovereign is "general will" in R.'s [Rousseau's] [best sense], sc. [namely] not as will of majority at any particular, but as 'Reason' (or con-ception of good) always working in men towards its own realisation.'

[117] *LPPO*, sec. 109.

[118] *LPPO*, secs. 102–4.

[119] *LPPO*, sec. 110.

[120] See V. R. Mehta, 'T. H. Green and the Problem of Political Obligation,' *Indian Political Science Review*, 7 (1973), pp. 115–24.

[121] I am indebted to the excellent treatment of Green's theory of rights by Gerald N. Matross: 'T. H. Green and the Concept of Rights' (PhD diss., University of Kansas, 1972); and Rex Martin, 'Green on Natural Rights in Hobbes, Spinoza and Locke,' in *Philosophy of T. H. Green*, ed. Vincent, pp. 104–26. On natural rights theories in histori-cal perspective, see R. Tuck, *Natural Rights Theories. Their Origin and Development* (CUP, 1979).

view that rights properly so called arise out of the historical experience of a nation (e.g. from custom); a government precipitously calling rights and 'liberties' into being will undermine the social conditions of morality.[122] However, Green was receptive to arguments presenting a theory of natural rights as a basis of political reform. Thomas Paine and subsequent Radical ideologues had demanded both the extension of the 'right' of suffrage to the middle and lower classes and the abolition of institutions which frustrated the interests of 'the people'.[123] (Early nineteenth-century British Radicals typically mixed Paineite natural rights arguments with appeals to an 'ancient constitution' — which had been powerfully restated by Burke.) According to Green, claims for the recognition of natural rights may rest upon morally justified claims or entitlements of individuals arising out of social sentiment, though not yet recognized by the sovereign; and through appeal to natural rights individuals might succeed in obtaining recognition of their claims from government. But securing recognition of rights as means to goods could only occur within the context of a political entity (a city or state) to which people bear allegiance, as representing a good with which they can identify.

Green implies that there is a constant tendency in human nature towards social alienation: people are reluctant to respect the interests and rights of individuals with whom they feel little in common, such as foreign nationals or 'alien' minorities within their own societies. Such alienation may be due not only to chauvinism, provincialism or denial of the humanity of strangers but to appreciation of mutual scepticism. I might be justifiably pessimistic about distant individuals recognizing the moral authority and sovereignty of those institutions which I myself recognize as agents of a common good, and I might thus be little inclined to respect their national institutions or institutions purportedly upholding the interests of a larger conglomerate of individuals (e.g. a 'European Parliament').[124] Green observes,

> It is easy to conceive a better [moral] system than that of the great states of Europe, with their national jealousies, rival armies, and hostile tariffs, but the condition of any better state of things would seem to be the recognition of

---

[122] J. G. A. Pocock, 'Burke and the Ancient Constitution' (1960), in *Politics, Language, and Time. Essays on Political Thought and History* (Chicago: Chicago UP, 1989 [1971]), chap. 6; H. T. Dickinson, *Liberty and Property. Political Ideology in Eighteenth-Century Britain* (London: Weidenfeld and Nicolson, 1977), chap. 8; and J. W. Burrow, *Whigs and Liberals. Continuity and Change in English Political Thought* (Oxford: Clarendon, 1988), chaps. 5–6.

[123] Dickinson, *Liberty and Property*, chaps. 6–7; G. Claeys, 'The French Revolution Debate and British Political Thought,' *HPT*, 11 (1990), pp. 59–80; and J. R. Dinwiddy, *Radicalism and Reform in Britain, 1780–1850* (London: Hambledon, 1992), chaps. 3–4, 6, 9–11.

[124] Conversely, I might recognize the United Nations as an agent of international justice while an Iraqi sees it as a tool of imperialist states.

some single constraining power, which would be even more remote from the active co-operation of the individual citizen than is the sovereign power of the great states at present.[125]

Recognition of rights of nations or nationalities is even more problematic than recognizing rights of citizens or subjects within nations. 'International law' is fragile, and where authority and force are lacking, almost impossible to apply; but it is effective when and where diverse individuals recognize the benefits of transnational authorities, because individuals recognize those entities as analogous to entities of narrower scope. Green no doubt saw this as fact because of contemporary successes, limited as they were, in the application of international law. In satisfying the US government over the 'Alabama' claims in accordance with the findings of an international tribunal at Geneva (1872), the Gladstone Government was not recognizing the Americans' 'right' to compensation for damage indirectly produced by the British state during the American Civil War. Rather, in respecting the judgments of the tribunal — which awarded £3.25 million to the US — Gladstone claimed to be setting an example for states to regulate their claims upon each other without resort to 'force'.[126]

2.6. THE STATE AND POLITICAL REPRESENTATION

Whereas Hobbes and Locke focused on the conditions of original consent to government, Green held a more radical view of the relationship of law and the maintenance of the state to social consent: 'The institution of government is not by contract, but by the act of the sovereign, and this act must be confirmed or repealed periodically.'[127] The collective will of a nation is already an abstraction; a state lacking institutions of popular representation cannot even begin to properly express such an abstraction. Despotic states — Czarist Russia, for example — are only 'by a sort of courtesy' called states, because in them sovereignty is exercised by the despot without providing effective means of registering opinions or wills of the populace.[128]

In order for every member of a state to submit to laws and particular social arrangements (regarding, for instance, the rights of property holders), in order for him to 'regard the work of the state as a whole' as legitimate, the citizen or subject 'must have a share, direct or indirect, by

---

[125] *LPPO*, sec. 119.
[126] The British government allowed the construction in British ports of warships for the Confederate government. The 'Alabama' and other commerce raiders did considerable damage to the Union, for which the post-war US government held Britain accountable. Shannon, *Crisis of Imperialism*, pp. 51–3; Bradley, *The Optimists*, pp. 135–6.
[127] R. L. Nettleship's chapter summary of *LPPO*, Section 72, in *Works*, ii, p. xxxi.
[128] *LPPO*, sec. 132.

himself acting as a member or by voting for the members of supreme or provincial assemblies, in making and maintaining the laws which he obeys.'[129] It is in fact rare for every citizen-subject to regard every action of the state as a true realization of a Good for him, nor is it always desirable for him or for others that he do so.[130] In Green's view, unwavering acceptance of the state as the 'march of the Spirit in the world' (Hegel, *Philosophy of Right*) would be, at worst, a symptom of social pathology, and at best an indication that the members of a state have a severely limited conception of the moral ideal. But through direct and indirect instruments of consent — among the latter Green included vigorous media of public opinion — the subject of laws comes to appreciate his role in the maintenance of goods he shares with others and his contribution to a common purpose of the state. Under these conditions, in which 'the nation [is] organised in the form of a self-governing community,' he will develop a 'passion' for serving the state, 'whether in the way of defending it from external attack, or developing it from within.'[131]

Green believes that some political societies and states are morally superior to others.[132] One measure of this is the degree to which state institutions enjoy the confidence of citizens; individuals across the social spectrum must recognize and accept as good for themselves those things that these institutions claim to promote. Such consensus is but rarely achieved in the day to day workings of government. Still, it 'is the fault of the state if this conception [of a common good maintained by law] fails to make ... a loyal subject, if not an intelligent patriot. It is a sign that the state is not a true state.'[133] Green makes clear that his own state and the makers of its laws are by no means the best possible. He queries, what is it

> but an external necessity ... that compels the ordinary citizen to pay rates and taxes, to serve in the army, to abstain from walking over the squire's fields, snaring hares, or fishing in preserved streams, to pay rent, to respect

---

[129] *LPPO*, sec. 122.
[130] A conception of the general good 'does not float in the air. It must be somebody's conception. Whose conception, then, of the general good is it that these institutions [e.g. artificial rights of property] represent? Not that of most of the people who conform to them, for they do so because they are made to ... ' (*LPPO*, sec. 120). 'The idea of a common good which the state fulfils [sic] has never been the sole influence actuating those who have been agents in the historical process by which states have come to be formed ...' (sec. 121).
[131] *LPPO*, sec. 122. This is one of the few passages in Green's writings in which 'passion' carries overwhelmingly positive connotations. The nation is a community in which moral experience happens, and it is a sign of moral progress for an individual to identify with a national purpose. Yet Green leaves little opening for aggressive nationalism. See D. A. Routh, 'The Philosophy of International Relations: T. H. Green vs. Hegel,' *Politica*, 3 (1938), pp. 223–35.
[132] *PE*, secs. 266–71.
[133] *LPPO*, sec. 121.

those artificial rights of property which only the possessors of them have any obvious interest in maintaining, or even (if he is one of the 'proletariate') to keep his hands off the superfluous wealth of his neighbour, when he has none of his own to lose?[134]

The 'true' state maintains conditions in which the self-realization of the greatest number of individuals is possible and, though perhaps no state could do so consistently, does so with equal regard for all individuals. Green was confident that the evolving British state was abundantly capable of such a task. He took pains to convince his audiences that there were adequate grounds for obedience to the state, making one of his most impassioned statements to this effect in section 114 of the *Lectures*:

> To ask why I am to submit to the power of the state, is to ask why I am to allow my life to be regulated by that complex of institutions without which I literally should not have a life to call my own, nor should be able to ask for a justification of what I am called upon to do. For that I may have a life which I can call my own, I must not only be conscious of myself and of ends which I present to myself as mine; I must be able to reckon on a certain freedom of action and acquisition for the attainment of those ends, and this can only be secured through common recognition of this freedom on the part of each other by members of a society, as being for a common good.

In the well regulated society which Green sought to build, all individuals would possess sufficient power of choice to fulfil their moral beings. As has been indicated in previous chapters, social theorists subsequently resorted to Green's notion of 'positive freedom' to assert the doctrine of the state as an equal enabler.[135] In contrast to the Night Watchman or 'laissez-faire' state, the 'welfare state' actively creates social conditions (through law) to allow something approaching equal opportunities for individuals to achieve certain basic goods. In Green's view, not material comfort in itself, but the moral improvement of individuals, was justification for state action: 'No one can convey a good character to another. Everyone must make his character for himself. All that one man can do to make another better is to remove obstacles, and supply conditions favourable to the formation of a good character.'[136] But a member of a modern commercial society, deprived by poverty of access to basic education, is practically prohibited from achieving a

---

[134] *LPPO*, sec. 120. Compare this to his discussion of iniquitous British laws and economic institutions in 'Liberal Legislation and Freedom of Contract' (1881), in *Harris and Morrow*, pp. 194–212.

[135] Some or all members of a political society discover an imperative for sacrifice or forbearance, and their discovery asserts itself as a positive claim upon them. Such claims are actuated by the moral ideal: they 'arise from that enfranchisement of all men which, though in itself but negative in its nature, carries with it for the responsive conscience a claim on the part of all men to such *positive* help from all men as is needed to make their freedom real' (*PE*, sec. 270: emphasis mine).

[136] *PE*, sec. 332.

better Self. In providing for 'free, compulsory, unsectarian' primary education (this was the goal of the National Education League, 1869–74), the state takes a crucial step towards removing 'obstacles' to a more extensive moralization of otherwise unequal individuals.

Green's reasoning about the state establishing conditions of moralization and self-improvement might be extended indefinitely, as his critics have noted. While Ground Game Laws are instituted for the benefit of propertied individuals, national parks allow the multitude to experience and enjoy natural beauty. Cheap or free musical concerts — via public subsidies — allow large numbers to enjoy music. Green argues that since private and public institutions alike are possible only through protective law, the application of law to a wider maintenance of the common good has at least as strong a justification as the recognition of rights that benefit individuals unequally. Indeed, by creating institutions from which less favoured individuals might truly benefit, the Greenian liberal state encourages greater 'self-identification' of individuals with all institutions it maintains, thereby creating a more orderly, justice-loving and equitable society.[137]

2.7. PROPERTY

Thus far the place of private property in Green's ethico-political theory has been suggested only indirectly. Some of Green's most controversial claims about morality and the 'role of the state' hinge upon his treatment of the institution of private property.[138] Green's clear distinction between material and moral goods has been interpreted in different ways. Some commentators contend that Green's justification of property chiefly as a means to moral ends leaves room for, indeed perhaps recommends, communal property arrangements, at least so far as they promote self-realisation; others fault him for failing to recognize the incompatibility of a free market economy with personal development.[139] I believe that the dichotomies of moral–material and private–communal in Green's ethico-political theory have been exaggerated,

---

[137] E.g. *LPPO*, secs. 119-24.
[138] V. Knapp, 'T. H. Green on the Exorability of Property,' *Agora*, 1 (1969), pp. 57–65; Hansen, 'T. H. Green and the Moralization of the Market;' Lawless, 'T. H. Green and the British Liberal Tradition;' Greengarten, *Thomas Hill Green*; Smith, 'Individual and Society in Green's Theory of Virtue'; J. Morrow, 'Property and Personal Development: an Interpretation of Green's Political Philosophy,' *Politics*, 18 (1983), pp. 84–92.
[139] Craig Smith claims (1) that Green has no clear proof that goods, whether material or moral, can be personal and common at the same time; and (2) that he provides no help for resolution of conflicts over finite material resources. A. Simhony concludes that Green's 'common good discourse' does not break down on these points ('T. H. Green: The Common Good Society', p. 246). Simhony basically affirms the sympathetic view of Green's philosophy as represented by, e.g., G. F. Barbour, 'Green and Sidgwick on the Community of the Good,' *Philosophical Review*, 17 (1908), pp. 149–66.

and that evident inconsistencies in Green's treatment of material and moral goods are not so damaging to his theory as has been supposed. When one is clear about Green's ethical principles, certain difficulties about his political theory appear less significant. True, it is easy to understand why ambiguity in Green's ideas about moral and material goods is of importance to those whose main interest in Green is his relation to a liberal tradition in social theory. In 'classical liberal' thought the freedom of individuals to acquire, maintain and dispose of property is one of the primary, or natural, or human rights, along with life and liberty.[140] To Green as well property was one of the obvious means of self-realization, constituting a cherished right of human beings in various social and historical situations.[141]

In Green's view the right of property is not a 'natural right' but a social institution, an arrangement for securing a universally realizable individual good. Property is, as Hegel pronounced, 'realized Will' and people allow the existence of this means to self-realization with the understanding that the condition of security of this good for themselves is universal recognition of the claim to it.[142] It follows from the fact that people realize their wills differently and to varying degrees (i.e. the fact of unequal talents) 'that property must be unequal.'[143] But in addition to 'negatively' acknowledging others' claims to property, Green says, property holders 'conform to the positive condition of possessing it, viz. labour ...'.[144] Green holds that despite a feudal residue in the British system of landholding and law of bequest and the persistence of artificial commercial monopolies, and despite modern growth in the mass of landless hired labourers, there remain fair opportunities, if not exactly equal circumstances, for property accumulation.[145] 'The increased wealth of one man,' he maintains, 'does not naturally mean the diminished wealth of another.'[146] While 'it is true that the accumulation of capital naturally leads to the employment of large masses of hired labourers ... [,] there is nothing in the nature of the case to keep these

---

[140] See particularly C. B. Macpherson, *The Political Theory of Possessive Individualism. Hobbes to Locke* (OUP, 1962).

[141] The essence of Green's most detailed discussion of property — in Chapter N of *LPPO* — is that property is morally justifiable as a means to a 'free life' (e.g. secs. 215–16). Hansen places Green in the 'possessive individualist camp' ('Moralization of the Market,' p. 113).

[142] *LPPO*, sec. 217. 'When one set of men are secured in the power of getting and keeping the means of realising their will, in such a way that others are practically denied the power,' then property is 'held in a way inconsistent with its idea.' 'In that case it may truly be said that "property is theft"' (*LPPO*, sec. 221).

[143] *LPPO*, sec. 223.

[144] *LPPO*, sec. 221.

[145] *LPPO*, secs. 225–30.

[146] *LPPO*, sec. 226.

labourers ... from being on a small scale capitalists themselves.'[147] It is the feudal residue, 'antecedent circumstances' of accumulation, and not contemporary conditions, that may place limitations on each person's ability to accumulate wealth.[148]

Green implies in his further discussion of property that conditions of bequest and land tenure in Britain (and Ireland) may with propriety be altered — free trade in other commodities having already been effectively realized — in order to ensure wider means to the free life. He further asserts that many holders of large properties, especially in highly populated areas, have neglected their social responsibilities: 'nothing till quite lately was done to give such a [post-feudal] population a chance of bettering itself, when it had been brought together. Their health, housing, and schooling were left unprovided for.'[149] There is an implied suggestion that the social responsibilities of large property-holders may be discharged for them: general services may be provided to the whole population through additional taxation of large properties.[150]

Greengarten is incorrect in concluding that 'Green sees in the capitalist economic system a perfect paradigm for his theory of self-realization [sic].'[151] It is true that Green does not explore the possibility that communal property might better promote the 'free life'. But neither does he hold the individual right of property to be absolute and unconditional. With property comes the owner's moral obligation of fulfilling certain 'social functions', such as employing local labour in the owner's fields or factories; even highly imperfect states recognize these social functions in some form, and the 'well-organized state' already enforces the performance of such duties by 'elicit[ing] ... labour from possessors of inherited wealth' and by taxing large properties to 'make sure of some positive return [to society] for the security which it gives to inherited wealth.'[152] Precisely what 'elicited labour' Green has in mind here is not clear. Justices of the Peace had traditionally been recruited from among

---

[147] *LPPO*, sec. 227.

[148] *Ibid*. 'In fact, as we know, in the well-paid industries of England the better sort of labourers do become capitalists, to the extent of often owning their houses and a good deal of furniture, of having an interest in stores, and of belonging to benefit–societies through which they make provision for the future.' Green discusses contemporary conditions of women's property holding in the subsequent chapter of *LPPO*: Chapter O ('The Right of the State in Regard to the Family').

[149] *LPPO*, sec. 230.

[150] Subsequent Radical-Liberals and socialists — Georgeists, Chamberlainites, Fabians — proposed taxes on the 'unearned increment' of wealth, and the Liberal Governments of 1906–15 levied 'supertaxes' on large incomes. Green's more specific and sweeping reform proposals, above all in 'Liberal Legislation and Freedom of Contract', are discussed in Chapter Five below.

[151] *Thomas Hill Green*, p. 88.

[152] *LPPO*, sec. 224.

country gentlemen, and lords had maintained manorial courts. A factory act of 1833 applying to the British textile industries required mill owners to provide schooling on the premises to juvenile labourers. Though this and some other factory acts remained unenforceable for decades, their introduction into the statutes reflected wide acknowledgment of the 'social functions' of wealth during the era of 'laissez-faire'.[153]

Ultimately Green is doubtful about the wisdom of the state confiscating surplus wealth, which by his definition, like that of J. S. Mill, appears to be an increase in value of property without the owner's 'expenditure of labour and capital.'[154] In principle, the proposal that the state appropriate the 'unearned increment' is 'fair enough in itself,' but the 'relation between earned and unearned increment is so complicated' that appropriation of the latter through taxation would lessen 'the stimulus to the individual to make the most of the land, and thus ultimately ... [lessen] its serviceableness to society.'[155] For example, the urban landlord in an expanding metropolis, when faced with the prospect of taxation of 'natural' property appreciation, might act to maximize his rents, or he might allow the property to deteriorate (or sell it) in order to save on his tax bill.

Green implies that confiscation of added value would outrage property owners to the extent that they would refuse to perform conscientiously their 'social functions.' He recognizes that some already seek to avoid their duties because they are antisocial. He does not directly consider the possibility that under a different system of property relations the individual might use what he possesses differently, with a wider sense of public spirit, such as acquiescing in the application of 'his' wealth by the 'sovereign' to purposes beyond his immediate control and perhaps even inconsistent with his preference. (With regard to the lot of the urban landowner mentioned above, there is a third possibility available in the modern welfare or social-democratic state: confronted

[153] Early British legislation for the management of railways also did not conform to laissez-faire. Railways were organized by the 1840s as stock-holding companies under limited liability. Yet the state reserved the option to purchase those enterprises outright after a fixed period of time and exercised extensive rights to fix fares and to stipulate how localities should be served by rail. R. K. Webb, *Modern England*, 2d ed. (New York: Harper and Row, 1980), pp. 270–1.

[154] *LPPO*, sec. 232. Mill, continuing the Ricardian economists' discussion of land and rent, had established the rectitude of taxing the unearned increment of wealth, i.e., 'natural' appreciation in value. State appropriation of the unearned increment 'would not properly be taking anything from anybody; it would merely be applying an accession of wealth, created by circumstances, to the benefit of society, instead of allowing it to become an unearned appendage to the riches of a particular class.' *Principles of Political Economy*, 1871 edn., edited by D. Winch (London: Penguin, 1970), 169–71. See also H. Holloway, 'Mill and Green on the Modern Welfare State,' *Western Political Quarterly*, 13 (1960), pp. 389–405.

[155] *LPPO*, sec. 232.

with punitive taxation the landowner might use his property for some recognized public purpose in order to enjoy a 'tax shelter'.) It may be argued that under *no* political–economic system does any taxpayer have direct control over his taxes as public expenditure. Yet it is difficult to conclude that the New Liberals from the late 1880s were unduly stretching Greenian doctrine when they asserted views like this one of John Hobson:

> Just as it is essential to the progress of the individual that he shall have some 'property', some material embodiment of his individual activity which he may use for the realisation of his rational ends in life, so the moral life of the community requires public property and public industry for its self-realization, and the fuller the life the larger the sphere of the external activities.[156]

Green endorsed private property and capitalist economic relations because they represented a rational *improvement* upon feudalism and slavery in the moral freedom they promoted. Capitalism, at least in the regulated version he envisioned, reconciled personal freedom with a stable society broadly conforming to principles of justice and equality; whereas slavery was an outrage to men's equal potential for morality and freedom, and feudalism merely institutionalized stability and security of unequal persons at the expense of the moral freedom of less favoured individuals.[157] Yet, as in the moral sphere of ethics, we can never acquire a total view of a 'perfect' economic system, but only recognize — historically and cross-culturally — practices and arrangements that conduce to a better state of society, as measured by the increased opportunities available to the mass of individuals. The strongest argument for capitalism that one can construct from Green's philosophy is that capitalism in its actual, imperfect form represents a morally 'higher' stage of social development than systems preceding it in history — but not a *telos* of social development.

As we shall see in Chapters Five and Six, observers of British society after 1880 found room in Green's theory of moralization and social development for considerable modification of property relations. As Avital Simhony observes, Green's criticism of misuse of property and persons by capitalists (whether great or small) rests upon his theory of personality, of how moral personhood is achieved and how it shapes and is shaped by society. From Green's discussion of the moral ideal in Book Three of *Prolegomena*, Simhony concludes that in Green's philosophy,

> Reciprocal recognition by all of everyone's personhood is an essential part of one being a person. This is why one cannot achieve self-realization [sic], according to Green, if others are exploited. The individual who treats others

[156] Hobson, quoted in Freeden, *The New Liberalism*, p. 46.
[157] *LPPO*, secs. 218, 225, 229–31.

as means only cannot himself or herself exist consistently as an end or a free agent.[158]

According to Green, the True Good never 'admits of competition,'[159] and this obtains in the following sense: my realizing myself via acquisition of a particular good cannot be morally justified when it clearly prevents another from pursuing the same good. (On the other hand, my success or failure in acquiring a good under circumstances of 'free' competition cannot impugn the justice or moral quality of the system.)

Green asserts that it is possible and necessary for individuals to acquire states of goodness (i.e. being) via material and non-material satisfactions accessible to all of us. To this it might be objected that even if one person's wealth does *not* depend on another's lack of it, self-realizing actions of some persons may effectively close off choices to others. Not all of us can become the same kind of capitalist. Henry George and other quasi–socialists had by the late 1870s revived early modern, 'mercantilist' claims that wealth was static: in any given state of the economy and at any particular point in time, some people having more necessarily meant that others had less. Even classical liberals opposing socialism in all forms admitted that economic crisis from the mid-1870s — in the form of stagnating land values and de-acceleration of wage increases, combined with a secular decline in the prices of basic commodities — raised the spectre of serious social instability.[160]

Though Green was interested in the problems of unequal deserts and poverty in the midst of plenty, he approached them more as moral than as economic problems. Following Green's ethical principles, it is possible to identify the irresponsible capitalist as an 'unenlightened' hedonist, unaware of True Self and True Good. A trader on the stock market plays a positive social role in transferring capital from situations where it does little to produce wealth to others where it may be employed more profitably. But he who loves the game of buying and selling unrelated to an abiding good is no better than an inebriate or a gambler relieving his 'itch': living for the moment and enjoying a constant succession of plea-

---

[158] 'Idealist Organicism: Beyond Holism and Individualism,' p. 525. 'Thus, ontological mutual interdependence generates and justifies ethical mutual interdependence' (*ibid.*).

[159] *PE*, sec. 235.

[160] On these developments, see Lynd, *England in the Eighteen-Eighties*, chaps. 4–5; Shannon, *Crisis of Imperialism*, pp. 208–14; Offer, *Property and Politics*; and Gertrude Himmelfarb, *Poverty and Compassion. The Moral Imagination of the Late Victorians* (New York: Vintage-Random, 1992), chaps. 17–18, 20. A convenient source of contributions to public debates over these questions is provided by M. Taylor, ed., *Herbert Spencer and the Limits of the State. The Late Nineteenth-Century Debate Between Liberalism and Collectivism* (Bristol: Thoemmes Press, 1996).

sures blots out any sober and moral consideration of means and ends.[161] It should be clear from Green's moral theory why he was put off by claims like that of Bernard Mandeville — that 'private vice equals public virtue' — and why he disagreed with Adam Smith's theory of self-interest and commercial balance — i.e. that the free market harmonizes private pursuits of interest into shared good.[162]

2.8. DUTY, VIRTUE, FREEDOM

Implicit criticism of materialism, at least in those persons who possess ample leisure and security, is revealed in Green's many statements about the individual's duties to society. Many of Green's interpreters, during his own time and subsequently, have identified his most useful contribution to ethics and politics as his 'philosophy of duty'.[163] Certainly, this view can be constructed from Green's many statements about forbearance from pleasure, benevolence, adherence to social sentiment and obedience to conscience. The moral individual's perception of his duties toward particular others — such as family and neighbours — and his more abstract recognition of his personhood as 'created' by society should lead to positive social action on his part (e.g. to relieve the poor). In his often quoted statement in *Prolegomena* sec. 183 — 'Each has primarily to fulfil the duties of his station' — Green's interpreters have found another moral imperative: not only are we to make the best of ourselves but ameliorative actions (or missions) are incumbent on all of us according to our talents and means.[164] Greengarten, among others, amplifies this message by reading it against section 381 of *Prolegomena*, in which Green suggests that where the state of a society or of mankind

---

[161] It is tantamount to the 'wild beast in man' not yielding 'obedience to the rational will' (*LPPO*, sec. 217). Here Green has clearly not thrown off the yoke of Kant.

[162] On these doctrines, see N. McKendrick, 'The Consumer Revolution of Eighteenth-Century England' in *The Birth of Consumer Society*, ed. McKendrick, J. Brewer, J. H. Plumb (London: Hutchinson, 1983), pp. 9–33; Hont and Ignatieff, eds., *Wealth and Virtue*; and J.G.A. Pocock, *Virtue, Commerce, and History: essays on political thought and history, chiefly in the eighteenth century* (CUP, 1985), chap. 6 ('The Mobility of Property and the Rise of Eighteenth–Century Sociology').

[163] Conybeare, 'On Professor Green's Political Philosophy;' Richter, 'Intellectual and Class Alienation'; Hoover, 'Liberalism and the Idealist Philosophy of Thomas Hill Green'; Jenks, 'T. H. Green, the Oxford Philosophy of Duty and the English Middle Class'; Vincent and Plant, *Philosophy, Politics and Citizenship*; and Meacham, *Toynbee Hall and Social Reform*, pp. 14–23.

[164] This view of self-realization being directed (almost intuitively) toward social duty was expressed even more strongly by F. H. Bradley and related by him to a theory of social organism (in *Ethical Studies*, 1876). My self-realization is 'concrete', not arbitrary. I need look no farther than my 'station' in life to know who I am and what I must do. See R. Wollheim, *F. H. Bradley* (London: Penguin, 1959); Milne, *Social Philosophy of English Idealism*, chaps. 2, 5; and Nicholson, *Political Philosophy of the British Idealists*, Study I, especially secs. 6–7.

is painfully imperfect, our more self-indulgent and self-regarding activities are offences against the moral ideal.[165] Much more may and will be said about the imperative nature of social service in Green's philosophy. But I will conclude the present treatment of Green's philosophy by emphasizing the anti-materialist bias of his political thought. The person endowed with material wealth appears to be under a greater obligation than the less fortunate to make some positive and social use of himself. When he does not do so he disregards both his social constitution — the way in which his personhood has been formed by other persons and his specific relation to them[166] — and the social conditions which allow him to have *material* things to call his own.

Men and women of 'enlightened conscience' are not confused when asked to identify their duties because these become apparent to them as they realize their own 'ideas of perfection.'[167] As has been shown, Green's conscience is not a transcendent and mysterious entity. Conscience does not float in the air but is found in persons, whose exercise of it is influenced by their social circumstances. Although the implications of Green's reference to an 'eternal principle' require elaboration (see Chapter Three), conscience stands in indistinct relation to the spiritual as external, while its relation to individual consciousness is clear. Revelations of conscience — as Green's specifically religious statements indicate — may occur in individuals during states of heightened awareness. But such occasions are not separate from rationality: the means to self-knowledge and awareness of social duties is reason.

Nineteenth-century liberals were preoccupied with the rule of reason, and with justifying individual and collective action through reference to right reason. Green thus aided the development of liberal thought at a critical historical juncture by demonstrating the 'rationality' already implicit in men's actions. (Indeed, with rather different political emphasis, this was one of Hegel's accomplishments as well.) The eighteenth-century Scottish scientists of society had done the same in attempting to reveal the rationality of self-interest in commercial relations. Like them, Green was concerned with the maximization of freedom and the restriction of 'license'. Green's theory of moral formation suggests that development of individual character leads to improvement of society. The society experiencing moral advancement will in

[165] 'In some Italian principality of the last century, for instance, with its civil life crushed out and its moral energies debased, excellence in music could hardly be accounted of actual and present value at all … Under such conditions much occupation with music might imply indifference to claims of the human soul which must be satisfied in order to the attainment of a life in which the value of music could be actualised.' See also Greengarten, *Thomas Hill Green*, pp. 41–9.
[166] *PE*, sec. 234.
[167] *PE*, Book Four, chaps. 1–2.

turn be more sensitive to a variety of moral claims actuated by character development.

Such a theory of character as Green's was not in itself politically partisan.[168] Yet nineteenth-century liberals were particularly enamoured of an idea of character connected to a faith in individuality as rational self-development. The conservative Edmund Burke argued that national experience and customs were essential determinants of character — a view with which Hegel, J. S. Mill and Green sympathized. (For some implications of agreement between Mill and Green on this matter, see discussion in 5.3–5.4 below.) Burke was not averse to the Scottish Enlighteners' view that commercial expansion produced 'new' virtues and new types of character, but he believed that men were sadly limited in their capacity for self-improvement, especially when excited by abstract claims to rights.[169] The 'Utopian Socialist' Robert Owen proclaimed that our characters are formed *for* us, not by us. We have little power to act against our 'circumstances', and we are less able to conceive of Good when our influences are evil.[170] Here Owen's Enlightenment optimism about producing superior character through careful control of external influences was balanced by more pessimistic currents, including the ideas of Rousseau and William Godwin.

John Burrow, among other historians, has demonstrated how 'character' in nineteenth-century liberal thought successfully supplanted 'virtue' as a prime social and political value.[171] Indeed, character and virtue were both of particular significance to Victorian Liberal moralists like J. S. Mill and Green.[172] As an attribute of personality character was perhaps the most important factor in the individual's attempt to realize the 'free life', yet pursuit of character as vigorously self-interested activity had to be balanced by consciousness of the good of society, a consciousness modulated by the notion of 'virtue' and actuated by the practice of

---

[168] Consider, for instance, an 'aesthetic' perspective on liberty and self-development, as traced from Wilhelm von Humboldt to J. S. Mill to Oscar Wilde, which privileged personal multi-facetedness (*Vielseitigkeit*) and social *variety* of character. These thinkers were less set than Green on particular 'model-characters' and each of them upheld different political systems as providing the best conditions for self-development (*Bildung*). See U. Vogel, 'Liberty is Beautiful: Von Humboldt's Gift to Liberalism,' *HPT*, 3 (1982), pp. 77–101; Burrow, *Whigs and Liberals*, chap. 4; and G. N. Izenberg, *Impossible Individuality. Romanticism, Revolution, and the Origins of Modern Selfhood, 1787–1802* (Princeton, NJ: Princeton UP, 1992).

[169] N. K. O'Sullivan, *Conservatism* (New York: St. Martin's, 1976), especially chap. 4.

[170] 'A New View of Society' (1813–16), in *'A New View of Society' and Other Writings*, ed. G. Claeys (London: Penguin, 1991), pp. 1–92.

[171] *Whigs and Liberals*.

[172] S. Collini, 'The Idea of "Character" in Victorian Political Thought,' *Transactions of the Royal Historical Society*, ser. V, 35 (1985), pp. 29–50; and Collini, *Public Moralists*, Part One, chaps. 2–3.

virtue as social duty.[173] (In the *polis* and later republics, the latter included the citizen's duty to bear arms in defence of the state, serve as legislator and juror, and so forth.) As indicated by Green's statements above about political rights and social practice, he was skeptical about the ability of morality and virtue to survive in a society stratified by privilege. In contrast to ancient republican thinkers who connected virtue to an undemocratic political order, Green held the *res publica* to be very nearly co-extensive with the entire society of adult males. (As we shall see in Chapter Six below, he was sensitive to the moral and social necessity of women's political activity as well.)

Green's philosophy was quintessentially liberal in its reliance on a notion of character, but 'character' carrying the moral imperatives of ancient republican virtue. From his philosophy one can easily adduce positive statements about what character is and how it is formed; about how character development is promoted or frustrated in different kinds of society; and about what social and political actions may be necessary (on the part of individuals and society) for optimum development of the 'free', self-determining personality. Social interaction is a constant testing of freedom and of character. Only through 'possession' of character can an individual withstand the rigours of this interaction and actually form a conception of positive freedom:

> a positive power or capacity of doing or enjoying something worth doing or enjoying, and that, too, something that we do or enjoy in common with others ... The mere removal of compulsion, the mere enabling a man to do as he likes, is in itself no contribution to true freedom.[174]

An even lengthier and more detailed exposition of Green's philosophy than that presented here could not forestall substantial criticisms of that philosophy. For instance, while his theory of Self and society distinguishes between moral and dutiful behaviour, it does not delineate how, or in what circumstances, society or state may promote morality by imposing duties. Indeed, it is difficult to imagine how a moral ideal, in the Greenian sense, would operate in society, given Green's expressed reservations about social censure as a spur to ethical behaviour in the individual. If we are really the best judges of our own motives, as the 'individualist' Green maintains, what legitimacy can we

[173] See especially Pocock, *The Machiavellian Moment*, on the idea of virtue between the Renaissance and the era of the American and French revolutions. Illuminating observations about republican virtue after 1789 are to be found in B. Semmel, *John Stuart Mill and the Pursuit of Virtue* (New Haven, CT: Yale UP, 1984); B. J. Smith, *Politics and Remembrance* (Princeton, NJ: Princeton UP, 1985); P. Pettit, *Republicanism: A Theory of Freedom and Government* (Oxford: Clarendon, 1997); and Q. Skinner, *Liberty Before Liberalism* (CUP, 1998).

[174] 'Liberal Legislation and Freedom of Contract', in *Harris and Morrow*, p. 199. That Green appears to allow character as a 'possession' does not imply that it is a quality apart from the 'Self'.

recognize in 'opinion' conflicting with our own, much less in the authoritative, coercive acts of society? Yet it is hardly fair to condemn Green's theory of the moral ideal on the grounds that he holds law and the imposition of duties by society and the state necessary to safeguard conditions of morality, and that law may sometimes require us to act contrary to our real preferences; every political theory short of anarchism relies on a well-organized state to serve, directly or indirectly, the goods of individuals. Green was interested in demonstrating the morality of every-day behaviour and in proving the efficacy of character. In these terms, Green's philosophy was highly effective as a defence of the interests of a humane liberal polity, even if people armed with Greenian principles were unable to avert collisions of 'individualism', diminish the attraction of countering ideologies or discourage behaviour hostile to liberal order.

CHAPTER THREE

Rational Religion, 'Sittlichkeit' and the Christed Self

3.1. INTRODUCTION

Exposition of Green's theory of the self and the social has revealed his use of metaphysical ideas and concepts, namely the 'eternal consciousness' and the 'spiritual principle'. While it has been indicated in the preceding chapter what roles these play in Green's philosophy, it remains to be seen how these ideas and concepts relate to Green's more explicitly *religious* statements and what meanings his religious expressions and statements about religion impart to his thought as a whole. Sidgwick specifically criticized Green's 'theological' derivation of a theory of motive. In *Hegelianism and Personality*, Andrew Seth criticized both Green and Fichte for positing but never clearly distinguishing between an 'empirical' and a 'transcendental' self. Of Green's theory of personality and moral development Seth asked, 'What is meant in such a relation [as self-consciousness] by the divine Self, and what by the human self? Here Green seems to fail us.'[1] A. J. Balfour similarly complained that the eternal consciousness suddenly appeared, as a *deus ex machina*, to supply a missing explanatory element in Green's account of the development of the moral sense.[2] Philosophers of subsequent generations

---

[1]   Andrew Seth, *Hegelianism and Personality* (Edinburgh and London: William Blackwood, 1887), pp. 4 (quotation), 58–9, 62–3.

[2]   See A. J. Balfour, 'Green's Metaphysics of Knowledge,' *Mind*, 9 (1884), pp. 73–92; and Balfour, 'A Criticism of Current Idealistic Theories,' *Mind*, 2 n.s. (1893), pp. 28–40. F. H. Bradley, initially the most Hegelian of the British Idealists, came to disown metaphysics as 'the finding of bad reasons for what we believe upon instinct' (*Appearance and Reality*, 1st ed. 1893). His use of 'instinct' instead of 'faith' is revealing. See Nicholson, *Political Philosophy of the British Idealists*, Study I, Conclusion.

lambasted the British Idealists generally for their dependence on entities whose existence cannot be empirically demonstrated but must
instead be taken on faith. The Idealists' metaphysical and theological
language, they argued, indicated a faulty understanding of philosophical first principles. Harold Prichard — as we have seen — regarded
Green's metaphysical idiom as a symptom of the disease his philosophical proofs purported to cure.

This 'anti-metaphysical' view, however, no longer dominates assessments of Green's thought. Scholars in recent years have argued that
Green's theological expressions retain explanatory power and make his
philosophy both distinctive and compelling. David Boucher and
Andrew Vincent remark, with apparent approval, that 'Religion was
viewed by the Idealists, in general, as an inextricable part of the process
of self-realisation.' Mark Francis and John Morrow observe a further
distinction between Green and F. H. Bradley: 'While Bradley thought of
religion as part of ideal morality, Green regarded it as fundamental to
both morality and politics.'[3] Leslie Armour argues that 'Green's ethics is
based on the notion that the proper end of finite selves or con-
sciousnesses is to realise their potential in sharing in the eternal consciousness'; that this 'metaphysic provides a necessary foundation for
his moral and political theories'; and that although this metaphysic is
not susceptible to logical proof (as Green himself concedes in *Prolegomena to Ethics*, sec. 174), it can explain the process by which individuals
realize the good.[4]

Some thirty years before these positive assessments of Green's religious philosophy, Melvin Richter, in *The Politics of Conscience: T. H.
Green and His Age*, and Jean Pucelle, in *La nature et l'esprit dans la
philosophie de T. H. Green*, shook Green studies out of their then mori-
bund condition by carefully re-examining relations between Green's
philosophical and religious ideas.[5] Theirs was a line of inquiry that had
been ignored by many philosophers or dismissed as infertile during the
middle third of the twentieth century. Richter's study was particularly
significant given the anti-metaphysical bias of contemporary (i.e.
1950s–'60s) Anglo-American philosophy — specifically, the linguistic-
analytical school which pronounces much traditional ethical vocabulary to be 'emotive' or 'prescriptive', not 'descriptive' and 'factual'. To

---

[3]   Boucher and Vincent, *British Idealism and Political Theory*, p. 9; Francis and Morrow,
       History of English Political Thought in the Nineteenth Century, p. 272.
[4]   'Green's Idealism and the Metaphysic of Ethics' (paper read to the conference 'T. H.
       Green and Contemporary Philosophy', Harris Manchester College, Oxford, 4 Sep-
       tember 2002), pp. 1–3, 9–11, 16–17 (quotations p. 1).
[5]   J. Pucelle, *La nature et l'esprit dans la philosophie de T. H. Green*, 2 vols. (Louvain: Éditions
       Nauwelaerts, 1960–5). This included a transcript of Green's 1860 Ellerton Theological
       Essay. A still earlier noteworthy study of Green as theologian is Montagné, *Un Radical
       Religieux en Angleterre au XXIXe Siècle ou la Philosophie de Thomas Hill Green*.

thinkers of the linguistic-analytical school 'ethical statements are clearly not descriptive but prescriptive, and hence they function as imperatives or commendations.' The proper task of the political or social philosopher is thus to distinguish between descriptive statements (about sovereignty, rights, etc.) and prescriptive ones. According to this approach, metaphysical language in ethics and politics cannot help us understand why individuals and societies function in certain ways ('factual relationships'). However, we may find valuable the exposure of 'emotivism' and ideology through analysis of ethical statements.[6]

Despite his positive interest in Green's religious statements, Richter helped perpetuate the anti–metaphysical bias by maintaining that Green's theological language could be reduced to secular ethico-political ideas or concepts. Richter cited evidence of Green's intention to produce such a reduction or translation and he concluded that Green's ultimate view of religion was that 'everything significant in traditional Christianity can be better put by Idealism.'[7] I. M. Greengarten pronounced, in response to Richter, that it is wrong to take Green's political thought as 'an aspect of a theology.'[8] Even more recently Geoffrey Thomas has contended that theological formulae and expressions are not instrumental to Green's ethical theory, and therefore should not be used to discredit it. Thomas observes that 'Green does not attempt anything like the derivation of rules, precepts, and judgements from a [metaphysical] principle of morality. He offers an ethics not of principles and rules but of character and of what I shall term "moral presumptions."'[9] Maria Dimova-Cookson suggests that Green posits an eternal consciousness in order to explain how aspects of our individual experiences are universal or mutually comprehensible, but she concludes that a universal consciousness is not necessary to explain the functioning of moral agency in the individual.[10] Greengarten, again, regards Green's religion as an opiate — of the intellectuals as well as the people. He concedes that Green's religion 'made him more sensitive to certain problems of his time'; but Green's approval of charity and his sentimental approach to poverty is supposed to alert us to the fact that one of the 'fundamental aims' of his religion 'was to justify the industrial-

---

[6]   Beck, *Handbook in Social Philosophy*, pp. 160–71. Beck cites such exemplary works of the logical positivist school as Hare, *The Language of Morals*, Laslett, ed., *Philosophy, Politics and Society*, and Weldon, *The Vocabulary of Politics*. See also Q. Smith, *Ethical and Religious Thought in Analytic Philosophy of Language* (New Haven, CT: Yale UP, 1998).
[7]   Richter, *Politics of Conscience*, p. 103.
[8]   Greengarten, *Thomas Hill Green*, p. 7.
[9]   Thomas continues: 'The notion of God as a model of the moral self can simply be jettisoned for any work which it does in Green's ethics.' *Moral Philosophy of T. H. Green*, pp. 156–7.
[10] *T. H. Green's Moral and Political Philosophy: A Phenomenological Perspective*, pp. 65-70.

capitalist basis' of Victorian society.[11] From this Marxist perspective, Green's metaphysical and religious statements are not worthy of serious consideration; they serve simply as rationalizations of bourgeois economic and political interests.

Andrew Vincent, Alan Sell, Raymond Plant, Mark Bevir and A. N. Wilson, among others, have remarked on Green's religious language in the way of identifying the social purposes of his philosophy: British Idealism reflected its creators' religious concerns and served as a 'surrogate faith' for those unwilling to accept either orthodox Christianity (with its claims about the strict veracity of Biblical narrative) or the death of God.[12] It was clearly the metaphysical, even theological aspect of Green's teachings that interested some members of his audiences, and in order to understand the social meanings of Green's life and work we must consider the basis for the sympathy or antipathy of his listeners to his religious pronouncements. Sell emphasizes the emotional commitment of Green and other British Idealists to preserving Christian faith, implicitly accepting the notion that Green inferred ethical and social principles from an understanding of the Absolute; but he (Sell) concludes that Idealist reformulations of Christian doctrines ultimately precipitated the decline of Christianity.[13] Vincent argues, in something of a rebuke to Richter, that Green had no intention of transcending Christianity or distilling from it a universal ethic or *Soziallehre*: to Green 'the Christed self and metaphysical eternal subject are, *at the same moment*, the true common good of the citizen and the principle of individual moral agency.'[14] In insisting on this Vincent means presumably to distinguish Green from modern liberal philosophers like John Rawls. Many modern liberals are hostile to religion and metaphysics, perceiving them as sources of false authority and causes of social divisiveness. Others concede that faith and communal spirit may sometimes foster positive social purposes, and they then speculate about how religion might become civic and socially inclusive (i.e. transcend religious communities). Vincent maintains that Green had a genuinely metaphysical interest in religion, rather than an instrumentally political one.

In an essay on Green's religious thought Bernard Reardon describes its 'general tenor' as 'evidently Hegelian', and in so doing he generally disputes its originality. What Reardon says of J. S. Mill's *Three Essays on Religion* (published in 1874) he implicitly extends to Green: 'what [Mill] offers the believer ... is pretty cold comfort, although his appreciation of "the prophet of Nazareth" is unstinted if hardly very imaginative.'

---

[11]　Greengarten, *Thomas Hill Green*, p. 7.

[12]　The term 'surrogate faith' was introduced by Richter. See discussion and footnotes in the Introduction above, pp. 5–7.

[13]　Sell, *Philosophical Idealism and Christian Belief*, pp. 5–6.

[14]　Boucher and Vincent, *British Idealism and Political Theory*, p. 50 (my emphasis).

Reardon's low estimation of Green's contribution to religious thought derives from a consideration of the sources of Green's thought which is limited to examination of the German 'Higher Criticism.'[15] This, as we shall see, is to take a narrow view of Green's thought and to assume that the 'Hegelian' element is decisive and all explanatory. Moreover, Reardon's dismissal begs the question of significance. Thinkers can be highly regarded in their time and broadly influential without being particularly original. In this light, one might consider Green's contemporary James Martineau (1805–1900), Unitarian divine and philosopher.[16] About Martineau the author and critic R. H. Hutton wrote,

> We doubt whether the historian of English thought of our time will credit Martineau with any distinct modification of the theological and philosophical opinions of this age. It was something that went below opinion; it was a revelation of spiritual power and character.[17]

Many scholars similarly emphasize Green's consonance with his age, conceding that he engaged in his way with the leading religious and ethical questions, but their narrow treatments of his religious opinions are not linked to the development of his philosophy and can scarcely explain the basis of its significance.

Should Green be understood as a secularizer in philosophy or as a religious moralist? What are we to make of his approach to ethico-political problems and his resort to Christian explanation? Raymond Plant contends that Hegel, Green and other ideologists of 'Bourgeois-Christian Society' (a term used by Lucio Coletti) sought '"the reconciliation of two worlds"': the 'narrative of Jesus as the Incarnate Lord [was] to be transformed into a philosophical doctrine about the indwelling of God in the whole of humanity ...'.[18] But why did Green retain reli-

---

[15] Quotations from Reardon, 'T. H. Green as a Theologian,' pp. 42, 40. See also R. Vernon, 'J. S. Mill and the Religion of Humanity' in *Religion, Secularization and Political Thought*, ed. J. E. Crimmins (London: Routledge, 1989), pp. 167–82; and B.M.G. Reardon, *From Coleridge to Gore: A Century of Religious Thought in Britain* (London: Longmans, 1971), chap. 10 (on Higher Criticism and Hegelianism).

[16] Martineau's biographer, James Drummond, claims that Martineau 'knew Prof. T. H. Green well, and loved him much' (*Life and Letters of James Martineau*, vol. ii (New York: Dodd, Mead, 1902), pp. 359–60). Although no correspondence between Green and Martineau is to be found in the main collections of their papers, the two were well acquainted, having met, Peter Nicholson suggests, through Jowett. *AW*, p. 422n; and communication to the author (DL) by Ms Margaret Sarosi, Manchester College, Oxford (24 November 1992).

[17] Quoted in Merz, *A History of European Thought in the Nineteenth Century*, iv, p. 376n. In fact, Martineau had a large contemporary following and his impact on British theology continued into the twentieth century through the work of Andrew Seth Pringle-Pattison, A. E. Taylor, and C. B. Upton. See Sell, *Philosophical Idealism and Christian Belief*, chaps. 5–6.

[18] Plant, *Politics, Theology and History*, pp. 132–3. The phrase in single quotations is from Coletti, *Marxism and Hegel*.

gious terms and symbols, and, indeed, affirm their uses, if Christianity's ethical content was to be transformed into philosophy? (Hegel, in contrast, generally avoided religious language after the 1790s.) What meaning are we to give Green's validation of specific religious practices and encouragement of religious persons and agencies — not only in the matters of their worship but in their educational, social service and political activities?

Scholars interested in Green's theology have expressed little interest in his political activities (or have simply asserted that the former impelled the latter), while those interested in Green's political theory have generally paid little attention to his religion — except, in some cases, to indicate that his condemnation of various forms of religious discrimination was consistent with his insistence on equal moral personhood. What is lacking to greater or lesser degree in most treatments of Green's thought is careful analysis of the sources of his religion, and of 'family resemblances' and resonances in Green's ethical and political language with contemporary and historical vocabularies of Christianity. It is argued in this chapter that Green retained certain elements of religious explanation because of their intellectual and spiritual efficacy. He believed that some religious ideas, concepts and symbols *worked*, in his own time and historically, to explain the basis of moral life and to sustain ethical progress. In this way Green differed from the German rationalizers following Kant, many of whom deployed secular language and terminology for religious ends. Not only the 'purely' philosophical aspect but the religious content and tone of Green's teachings must be accounted for in assessing his impact on British society and beyond. In relation to my claim that Green's metaphysical and religious expressions need to be taken seriously, I attempt to demonstrate here that Green's references in the *Prolegomena* and his other 'philosophical' writings to the 'eternal consciousness', the 'self-objectifying principle' and so forth (statements examined in the previous chapter) become more concrete — and that the range of meanings they suggest becomes more clear — when these are read against certain of Green's less frequently cited writings, particularly 'Christian Dogma' (ca. 1860–3) and the 'Four Lectures on the English Revolution' (1867).

3.2. RELIGION, REASON AND ROMANTICISM

I have thus far indicated the centrality of religion to Green's work by suggesting that his model of moral formation owes something to religious categories of explanation and by revealing his claim that Christian societies afforded special opportunities for an individual's moral development. Green can be situated within a tradition of 'rational religion'.[19] For while modern observers perceive Green's metaphysic as oddly archaic, many contemporaries regarded his thought as daringly rationalist, unorthodox and erosive of revealed religion.[20] Green demonstrated in the *Prolegomena* that Christianity marked an epoch in human history by imparting new content to the Moral Ideal. Yet neither the *Prolegomena* nor the *Lectures on the Principles of Political Obligation* appeared to demonstrate a permanent linkage between Christianity and moral progress (i.e. neither claimed that Christian principles will necessarily guide future moral and social development). Nevertheless, Green suggested particular relationships between reason and conscience and he endorsed a rational approach to Christianity that had emerged in Europe during the ages of Enlightenment and Romanticism. Rational religion was neither a British invention nor a project confined to the nineteenth century.[21] As far as Green was concerned, British contributions to natural theology since the eighteenth century (e.g. the theology of William Paley) had been superseded by German efforts to explicate the moral foundation of true religion. Green was appreciative not of 'British thought' or 'German thought' in themselves. Rather, he regarded the wider Protestant Reformation as a critical episode in the advancement — he supposed — of moral freedom; and he viewed innovations of the Enlightenment and Romanticism as contributions to the development of a humanistic, rational theology.

Kant (1724–1804) and J. G. Fichte (1762–1814) were major contributors to rational theology, respected by some and criticized by many ortho-

---

[19] The term was in common use in Green's time and in ways consistent with Green's religious philosophy. E.g. Goldwin Smith, *Rational Religion, and the Rationalistic Objections of the Bampton Lectures for 1858* (Oxford: J. L. Wheeler, 1861); C. B. Upton, *Lectures on the Bases of Religious Belief* [Hibbert Lectures, 1893] (London: Williams and Norgate, 1894): Lecture V, subtitled 'Culture and Rational Religion'. Smith (1823–1910) was Regius Professor of Modern History at Oxford, 1858–66. *Rational Religion* was a response to H. L. Mansel: 'I say of those [Mansel's] doctrines, in the words of Clark, that '"if we argue upon them consistently, we must finally recur to absolute Atheism"' ('Preface,' p. ix).

[20] R. L. Nettleship notes that 'the distinction of orthodox and heterodox, with all its attendant babel [sic] of controversy, had but little interest for him … ' ('Memoir,' p. c). Green largely accepted the 'estrangement from christian society' that was the consequence of his idiosyncratic religious position (p. cvi). Yet he actively sought out people of diverse religious beliefs.

[21] On the British tradition or style of thought that can be called rational religion or rational theology, see Elliott-Binns, *English Thought 1860–1900*; U. C. Knoepflmacher, *Religious Humanism and the Victorian Novel* (Princeton, NJ: Princeton UP, 1965); Owen Chadwick, *The Victorian Church*, 2 vols. (London: A. and C. Black, 1966–70); Reardon, *From Coleridge to Gore*; Haakonssen, ed., *Enlightenment and Religion: Rational Dissent in Eighteenth-Century Britain*; R. K. Webb, 'The Limits of Religious Liberty: Theology and Criticism in Nineteenth Century England' in *Freedom and Religion in the Nineteenth Century*, ed. R. Helmstadter (Palo Alto, CA: Stanford UP, 1997), chap. 4.

dox theologians for their efforts to use philosophy to shed light on the meaning and functions of religious thought and practice. The deployment of Reason against Authority was of course a central feature of the Enlightenment movement, threatening civil as well as ecclesiastical leadership. Thus Kant's treatise *Religion Within the Limits of Reason Alone* (1793) offended the Prussian king, Friedrich Wilhelm II. Fichte went even further than Kant, whom he viewed as his master and chief rival, in attempting to reformulate Christian dogmas as guides to moral action (*A Critique of All Revelation*, 1792).[22] Kant and Fichte helped precipitate an upheaval of German theology and philosophy that registered strongly in Britain as well between about 1820 and 1860. The rational-critical approach engendered by Kant and Fichte had manifold consequences; among these was a revolutionary Christology that found expression not only in technical works of theology but in the widely read 'lives' of Jesus by David Friedrich Strauss (1835) and Ernest Renan (1863). (The young George Eliot published an English translation of Strauss's *Das Leben Jesu*, acquainting a wider British public with 'German' rationalism.) Renan 'saw in Jesus the greatest genius and inspired transformer of human society,' but not a being to whom 'supernatural facts' had occurred or through whose sacrifice human beings should expect supernatural transformation.[23] Three years after the appearance of Renan's *Life of Jesus* the Cambridge historian J. R. Seeley published (anonymously) *Ecce Homo*, emphasizing the humanity of Jesus, glossing over the question of miracles and focusing on the moral value of Christ's teachings.

To orthodox believers, rationalist, philosophical and historical approaches to Christianity led directly to atheism, yet these approaches were experimented with everywhere in the Western world from the seventeenth century on. For the purposes of the present investigation 'rational religion' can be defined as religion that sought to resolve the 'problem' of the mystical and miraculous aspects of religion, mainly by considering the relation of revealed religion to inductive truths about man and the universe; that emphasized the moral utility and social value of Christianity; and that applied religious insights to the examination of new and enduring problems of society. Not all such rationalizing efforts can be understood as contributions to a secularization project and the intentions of rational religionists must be considered as care-

---

[22] The literature on Kant and his German successors in relation to theology is too massive to be listed here. See in particular W. Weischedel, *Der Gott der Philosophen* (Darmstadt: Wissenschaftliche Buchgesellschaft, 1983); and A. Denker, 'Kant und Fichte: Kann die Religion vernuenftig sein?,' *Fichte-Studien*, 8 (1995), pp. 1–13.

[23] Chadwick, *Secularization of the European Mind*, pp. 211–20. *The Life of Jesus* 'was the most famous book written in France during the nineteenth century, and until about 1900 its author [1823–92] was the most famous of French writers' (p. 219).

fully as the apparent consequences of their efforts. Indeed, rational religionists professed to preserve the essence of Christianity, and to this end they tried to accommodate inductive knowledge instead of ignoring it. From inductive knowledge and philosophy they attempted to form conclusions not only about the meaning of Christian doctrine but about the spiritual yearnings of individuals and about institutional and social values.

As many scholars have demonstrated, the 'conflict between science and religion' in Britain during the nineteenth century has been overstated. Many theologians and ordinary men of the cloth — like the educated British public generally — demonstrated positive interest in developments and 'discoveries' in the natural sciences.[24] However, they held that theories of man and nature based upon inductive knowledge (e.g. evolutionism) had not in fact invalidated Christian explanation. Some of them were disturbed by attacks on hitherto fundamental Christian doctrines, but others regarded the discarding of untenable dogmas and the advance of the inductive method as parts of a widely affirmative project — strengthening rather than weakening their religion. Some doctrines, they believed, were compatible with the progress of the mind. Even so ferocious a 'bishop-eating' evolutionist as Thomas Huxley 'express[ed] guarded approval for old-fashioned Calvinism':

> The doctrines of predestination; of original sin; of the innate depravity of man and the evil fate of the greater part of the race ... appear to me to be vastly nearer the truth than the 'liberal' popular illusions that babies are born good and that the example of a corrupt society is responsible for their failure to remain so ...[25]

For all the theological innovation of Archdeacon William Paley (1743–1805), author of the celebrated *Evidences of Christianity* (1794) and *Natural Theology* (1802), his purposes were overwhelmingly conservative and little different from those of the medieval Scholastics. To proponents of 'natural religion', natural philosophy and moral philosophy

[24] B. Willey, *Nineteenth Century Studies. Coleridge to Matthew Arnold* (New York: Columbia UP, 1949), especially chaps. 2, 8; N. Annan, 'Science, Religion, and the Critical Mind,' in *1859: Entering an Age of Crisis*, ed. Appleman *et al.*, pp. 31–50; W. F. Cannon, 'The Problem of Miracles in the 1830s,' *VS*, 4 (1960), pp. 5–32; Cannon, 'Scientists and Broad Churchmen: An Early Victorian Network,' *JBS*, 4 (1964), pp. 65–88; J. Morrell and A. Thackray, *Gentlemen of Science: Early Years of the British Association for the Advancement of Science* (Oxford: Clarendon, 1981); and R. Yeo, 'Science and Intellectual Authority in Mid Nineteenth-Century Britain: Robert Chambers and *Vestiges of the Natural History of Creation*' in *Energy and Entropy. Science and Culture in Victorian Britain*, ed. P. Brantlinger (Bloomington, IN: Indiana UP, 1989), pp. 1–27.

[25] 'An Apologetic Irenicon,' *Fortnightly Review*, n.s. LVIII (1892), p. 569, quoted in Irvine, *Apes, Angels, and Victorians*, p. 326. The characterization of Huxley is Irvine's.

were complementary ventures in explaining God's Creation.[26] Many clerics down to the middle of the nineteenth century were apparently less disturbed by the destructive work of natural science than by theological controversies — over the meaning of atonement, or of the incarnation — that did not originate in specifically scientific disputes. Rather, it was theological dispute which carried over, in substance and in tone, into the moralistic social sciences, such as political economy and psychology.[27]

The nineteenth century witnessed significant restatements and reformulations of Christian doctrines: these included atonement, asserting 'man's reconciliation with God through the sacrificial death of Christ'; the incarnation, asserting simultaneously the personality and the divinity of Jesus, and the human and historical conditions of his life; and Divine immanence, focusing on the continuing presence of the divine in human history and the conditions of moral life.[28] Reformed (mainly Protestant) theologians were conscious of a need to make Christianity, if not necessarily more rational, more relevant to believers in an age of challenges to faith by natural science and humanistic philosophy. Although people throughout the ages have been intrigued by the 'mystery of the person of Jesus', nineteenth-century thinkers perceived this as a problem in a way that would have struck eighteenth-century rationalists — whether deists or orthodox Christians — as quite odd.[29]

As we shall see, Green's attempts to resolve these and other theological problems were themselves responses to a crisis of rationalism — the fact that rationalist approaches to religion were leading people into collision with what they believed intuitively and emotionally. For instance,

---

[26] Evidences of Christianity 'traced to most people's satisfaction the hand of the Creator in every work of Nature' (Burrow, *Evolution and Society*, p. 133) and defined virtue as '"doing good to mankind in obedience to the will of God, and for the sake of everlasting salvation"' (quoted in D. C. Somervell, *English Thought in the Nineteenth Century* (London: Methuen, 1929), p. 19). Some nineteenth-century commentators described Bentham, the father of Utilitarianism, as 'Paley minus Hell-fire' (Somervell, *English Thought*, p. 44).

[27] Hilton, *Age of Atonement*, chaps. 2–4.

[28] For these definitions, which are admittedly schematic and do not do justice to wide variations in doctrine, I am indebted to D. M. Ballie, *God Was In Christ. An Essay on Incarnation and Atonement* (New York: Scribner's, 1948); F. L. Cross, ed., *Oxford Dictionary of the Christian Church*, 2d ed. (OUP, 1974), pp. 104–5, 696–7 ('Atonement', 'Incarnation'); and B. A. Gerrish, *Tradition and the Modern World. Reformed Theology in the Nineteenth Century* (Chicago: Chicago UP, 1978).

[29] Many *philosophes* attacked the basis of the churches' interpretations of miracles, but to many Enlighteners Christianity was not — or need not be — mysterious. Belief in an 'original cause of all things' (Voltaire) was not contrary to reason, nor was a certain understanding of and appreciation for Jesus Christ equivalent to superstition and mysticism. On the pervasiveness of 'sensibility', private emotion and mysticism in the eighteenth century, see H. M. Jones, *Revolution and Romanticism* (Cambridge, MA: Harvard UP, 1974), chap. 4.

the modern attitude towards sin (or the individual's sense of sin) was already emerging in Green's time. Modernists increasingly regarded preoccupation with sinfulness as irrational and neurotic (just as would many psychologists today); its immediate *meaning* was the individual's maladjustment to reality. Fichte is supposed to have said that he had no time for penitence — implying that atonement was a matter of reconciliation with Self, not God.[30] Yet many who reflected on these matters discovered that it was as difficult to do without God as to accept orthodox Christianity.

D. M. Ballie offered a rebuke to 'modernism' in remarking, 'There is a modern inability to understand the sense of sin and especially the meaning and the need of divine forgiveness.'[31] What is implied in this statement is that individuals who find freedom in shedding a sense of sin (and belief in the Christian atonement) also find themselves inexplicably lonely and disoriented. Ballie attempted to formulate a christology in opposition to the historically oriented theological schools arising during the nineteenth century — schools which, as we shall see, had a significant impact on Green. Ballie addressed the fact that Western thought since the nineteenth century has tended to empty conflict in the individual and society of divine meaning. Green was conscious of this sea-change of thought and attempted to reclaim divine meaning for the experience of persons and societies by locating their places in a divine order. According to one summation of Green's theology,

> He held that the analysis of consciousness proved that reality was an organic whole … ; that the evidence of art, morality, and religion all pointed to the spiritual nature of reality; that God … was realized in each individual person; and that, since personality alone gave meaning to the evolutionary process, the permanence and immortality of the individual were assured.[32]

While this view of religion places 'salvation' in a rather different light than that of orthodox Christianity, it gives transcendent meaning to the lives of individuals. In the sense that he allowed sin and immortality, as well as moral growth, Green was theologically modern without being a modernist.

Discussion in previous chapters of the intellectual climate of Green's era has identified the currents of rationalism, materialism, critical realism and evolutionism. But his was still an age of Romanticism, and Romantic tendencies were as evident in religious thought as in historical study and the arts. Religious Romanticism was a *continuation* of the Enlightenment project in its attempt to reconcile religious faith with the demands of reason. Where religious Romanticism departed from the

---

[30] H. R. Mackintosh, *Types of Modern Theology: Schleiermacher to Barth* (London: Nisbet and Co., 1937), p. 232.

[31] Ballie, *God Was In Christ*, p. 161.

[32] Cross, ed., *Oxford Dictionary of the Christian Church*, s.v. 'Green, Thomas Hill'.

Enlightenment was in its treatment of feeling and subjective experience.[33] We have seen already how Green sought to resolve questions
about the derivation of our beliefs and conscious actions from our feelings and to clarify how our sensations relate to our attempts at self-
realization. Green regarded these issues as central to religion as well.
While the present discussion delineates the rational character of Green's
religion, it in no way suggests that he dismissed the emotional and subjectivist aspects of Christianity. Green's philosophical idealism stipulated that self-conscious subjects impose order on the universe; it is only
through consciousness that the universe appears to us as given. Similarly, his Romantic interpretation of Christianity located the truth of
revealed religion not in the dictates of religious authority, presented as
objective and external, but in the experience of individual believers and
in religious fellowship.

It is difficult to construe a single and continuous tradition of British
rational religion. Part of the difficulty has to do with periodization and
typology: definitions of Enlightenment, Romanticism and Naturalism-
Critical Realism tend to obscure continuities in religious thought. A survey of British rational religion would properly include thinkers as
divergent as Paley and Jowett, both of whom believed in forms of progressive revelation.[34] In any case, Green's religious ideas resonate with
indigenous ideas and sentiments as well as 'foreign' ones. The sources
of Green's religion included English 'Puritanism' and its descendant
forms of Protestantism; the evangelical movement precipitated during
the eighteenth century by John and Charles Wesley and George
Whitefield; European Romantic transcendentalism arising later in the
eighteenth century; English Christian Socialism as articulated by F. D.
Maurice (1805–72) and others; and the Broad Church or liberal Anglican
movement nurtured in the Ancient Universities from the 1830s. All of
the religious traditions, influences and informing contexts under
discussion here carried with them social assumptions, beliefs about
individuals as members of social and political as well as religious communities.

It is deceptively easy to characterize Green's Christianity as unorthodox, approaching theism. Moreover, his theological statements often
blended with political and social criticism in such a way that it is difficult to isolate his criticisms of doctrine from those of institutions.

---

[33] See Reardon, *Religion in the Age of Romanticism*, chap. 1.
[34] The natural theology tradition of Paley has been seen as a prerequisite of Darwinism,
        although in contrast to Malthus' emphasis on struggle, Paley saw harmony in natural
        evolution. P. J. Bowler, 'Malthus, Darwin, and the Concept of Struggle,' *Journal of the
        History of Ideas*, 37 (1976), pp. 631–50; and Hilton, *Age of Atonement*, pp. 73–91. Peter
        Hinchliff contends that Jowett never really understood Darwin but reserved decisive
        judgment on the question of human evolution in the Darwinian sense. *Jowett and the
        Christian Religion*, pp. 186–91.

Although Green did make strident statements against the Church of England as a political institution, for most of his life he was neither a defender nor attacker of the Anglican communion. What got him into the most difficulty in orthodox circles was his use of the language of the Higher Criticism. Not only Anglicans but non-Anglican Protestants were startled by his apparently German theology. R. F. Horton (1855–1934), a Fellow of New College and the first Nonconformist examiner in Divinity at Oxford University (a small scandal erupted over his appointment in 1881), criticized the Christianity of Jowett and Green as 'too philosophical and ethical.' Although Horton was supported in his appointment by the Broad Church party, he was not comfortable with its theology. He recalled,

> I attended Thomas Hill Green's lectures on Kant, and came into close personal contact with him. Never can I forget his expression when one day he found that I had a real and vivid faith in Christ. His own faith was philosophical and ethical; but Christ, as a Person, had been dissolved by criticism. 'You are very fortunate' was his brief, intense comment.[35]

Green spoke of human spiritual needs being 'rather met by the sympathies of a society breathing the christian [sic] spirit than by the propositions of an anthropomorphic theology.'[36] Indeed, Green's religion tended towards radical immanentism, locating human history and human life as the site of divine revelation. According to John Theodore Merz, 'the Hegelian view,' adhered to by Green and D. F. Strauss,

> looked upon [the process of personification of the immanent spirit] as the gradual manifestation in time and history of the Divine Mind, which was there from the beginning and only hidden from the human observer. From this point of view the highest form of human life and thought is not an analogue of the flower in which the life of the plant is consummated and eventually consumed; it is more like the mind of a poet or an artist which manifests itself to the world in its creations, but does not exhaust itself in them.[37]

Does Green's acceptance of an immanentist view suggest that he believed orthodox Christianity to be a 'creed outworn', to be superseded by some religion of humanity, as Comte had proposed, or by critical philosophy? This chapter will demonstrate that this was not the case, and that whatever objections Green raised against dogma and religious formulae, he did not fear the dissolution of the Christian spirit. A medieval Scholastic dictum pronounced philosophy the handmaid of religion. Some nineteenth-century Christians objected to the inversion of

[35]   Horton must have heard Green's lectures at some point before his final Greats examination (in 1878). R. F. Horton, *An Autobiography* (London: Allen and Unwin, 1917), pp. 43, 57–8. See also Mark D. Johnson, *The Dissolution of Dissent, 1850–1918* (New York: Garland, 1987), pp. 180–1.

[36]   Quoted in Nettleship, 'Memoir,' p. cv.

[37]   Merz, *History of European Thought in the Nineteenth Century*, iv, pp. 174–5.

this relationship and feared that speculative and critical philosophers were doing away with religion altogether. John Henry Newman and the Oxford Tractarians contended that 'liberalism' and the free intellect eroded spiritual authority, without which no religion or morality were possible.[38] If this is so, and if Green was partly responsible for this erosion, it is still clear that he did not wish to replace Christianity with something else. He held that religion might be clarified by philosophy but that it was nonetheless unassailable as a means to salvation and moral perfection.

Thus Green believed in the Christian incarnation, the meaning of which was effectively conveyed by the Fourth Gospel of the New Testament (the book of John). Jesus of Nazareth was not a phantom or celestial substance appearing to men at a moment in history (Docetism). Nor was He a personification of God, sent among humans as a moral exemplar and a model for 'becoming' — as held by the gnostics. As Green remarks in a lecture on the Incarnation, 'The prevalence of either of ... [these interpretations] would have prevented christianity from becoming what it has actually, in its best form, become, a *means through which unphilosophical men* have come to think of and worship God under the attributes of *perfect moral life.*'[39] If there is condescension here, it is of a generous and realistic kind which takes people as they are and affirms many of the traditional purposes of religion.

3.3. GREEN'S RELIGIOUS INHERITANCE

Some of the influences on Green's religious thought were direct and personal. Green's relation to Jowett, one of the most radical Broad Churchmen of the era, has already been noted. Richter, Craig Jenks and others have asserted that Green's religious views were shaped by his evangelical upbringing and family relation to evangelical thinkers. They argue that under the influence of Maurice and Jowett, Green gradually moved out from underneath the moral load of this evangelical inheritance.[40] In support of this view they cite Green's expressed wish to eschew 'any conventional use of theological language' and to 'repro-

---

[38] The rejoinder of theological liberals was that Newman and company were both ignorant and anti-intellectual. Mark Pattison, who began as an evangelical, became a Tractarian, and died an atheist, recalled in his memoir, 'A. P. Stanley once said to me, "How different the fortunes of the Church of England might have been if Newman had been able to read German." That puts the matter in a nut-shell; Newman assumed and adorned the narrow basis on which Laud had stood 200 years before. All the grand development of human reason, from Aristotle down to Hegel, was a sealed book to him.' *Memoirs*, p. 210.

[39] Green, 'Extract from Lecture on the Fourth Gospel. Incarnation' [no date], *Works*, iii, p. 214 (my emphasis).

[40] See Richter, 'T. H. Green and His Audience'; Jenks, 'T. H. Green, the Oxford Philosophy of Duty'; Montagné, *Un Radical Religieux en Angleterre*; and V. R. Mehta, 'The Ori-

duce with as much exactness as modern phraseology admits of . . . the essence of St. Paul's belief in Christ.'[41] In his 1879 essay 'On the Different Senses of "Freedom"' and in his printed lay sermons 'The Witness of God' (1870) and 'Faith' (1878) Green discussed in detail Paul's epistles. Indeed, one gets the impression from reading Green's sermons and religious addresses that the essential core of Christianity was for him encompassed in the thought, or perhaps rather in the experience, of Paul.[42]

The extent to which Green actually distanced himself from evangelicalism and other conventional modes of Christian thought is considered below. Jowett thought that he saw Green doing this, and his respect for the attempt to impart the ethical message of Christianity was tempered by his belief in Green's reprehensible eccentricity.[43] In any case, the 'evangelical inheritance' of Green, F. H. Bradley, Sidgwick, Leslie Stephen and other intellectually prominent scions of evangelical families has been oversimplified; as suggested in Chapter One above, reference to evangelicalism, assuming it to be the unified source of beliefs and attitudes, cannot by itself explain the style or content of Green's religion.[44] Accounts of Victorian intellectuals and public figures are frequently encumbered by lengthy descriptions of their family connections, and these have led sometimes to sweeping conclusions about the relationship of greatness to mediocrity among Britain's 'intellectual aristocracy'.[45] Genealogy nevertheless reveals some useful facts about T. H. Green and his formative influences.

Green's mother died when he was an infant, and until the age of fourteen he was constantly in the company of his father, Valentine Green, the rector of Birkin with Haddlesey, in Yorkshire. (T. H. Green was the younger of Valentine's two sons through his first marriage to the eldest

gins of English Idealism in Relation to Oxford,' *Journal of the History of Philosophy*, 13 (1975), pp. 177–87.

[41]   Green, 'Witness of God' (1870), *Works*, iii, p. 235 (cited in Hinchliff, *Benjamin Jowett*, p. 161).

[42]   For all the value to historical Christianity of Matthew's report of Jesus' sermon on the Mount, we 'would do well to ask … , what christianity would have been without the teaching of St. Paul …' ('Christian Dogma,' *Works*, iii, p. 165). This essay is discussed at length below.

[43]   See Jowett's remark to Florence Nightingale (1872), quoted in my Introduction. Jowett tried to force his friends and students into a certain mould and often interpreted their independence as signs of arrogance or unworthiness. Yet he was sympathetic towards some of his more rebellious pupils, like Swinburne and Gerard Manley Hopkins.

[44]   W. L. Newman, a Fellow of Balliol, observed of Green, 'Like many other earnest men, he came from an Evangelical household' (from a letter to Charlotte Green, 27 November 1882, in CBG copy-book, pp. 1–19, *GP* 1[b]).

[45]   See N. G. Annan, 'The Intellectual Aristocracy' in *Studies in Social History. A Tribute to G. M. Trevelyan*, ed. J. H. Plumb (London: Longmans, 1955), chap. 8; and Parry, 'The State of Victorian Political History.'

daughter of E. T. Vaughan. Valentine Green produced two daughters from a second marriage.) Raised in a clerical household, T. H. Green must have heard and read many hundreds of sermons and religious treatises before he reached Oxford. As Richter observes, religion would have presented to him many 'forced options' (as William James characterized them in his famous 1902 study *The Varieties of Religious Experience*) and 'traditional answers to the all-important questions of "What shall we do and how shall we live?"'[46] Valentine Green, son of a Leicestershire landed gentleman of the same name, was by all indications a modest man who owed his preferment as rector of Birkin to his first wife's brother.[47] He appears not to have published any sermons or even left journals or letters from which we might compare his religious views — or, indeed, his opinions about other matters — to those of T. H. Green. At any rate, the son remembered his father as a gentle man and at no point revealed evidence of any great disagreements or struggles between them.[48]

T. H. Green was related to other clerical figures of greater fame and intellectual stature. These included his maternal grandfather, Edward Thomas Vaughan, Sr. (1772–1829), and his uncles Charles John Vaughan (1816–97) and David James Vaughan (1825–1905), all of whom were fellows of Trinity College, Cambridge.[49] E. T. Vaughan was vicar of All Saints and St Martin's, Leicester, and a noted figure in the Evangelical Party of the early nineteenth century. His son Charles was also vicar of St Martin's before appointment in 1844 to the headmastership of Harrow.[50] David Vaughan succeeded E. T. Vaughan, Jr., as vicar of St

---

[46] Richter, 'T. H. Green and His Audience,' p. 450.

[47] R. L. Nettleship, 'Memoir,' p. xi. After obtaining his BA in 1822 at St John's, Cambridge, Valentine Green was ordained deacon at Lincoln, 1823, and priest, 1824. He served as curate at Aylestone, Leics., 1823–6, and in other junior clerical positions before assuming the rectorship of Birkin with Haddlesey, Yorkshire, on 31 July, 1835, which he held until his death on 2 December, 1873. *Alumni Cantabrigienses, 1752–1900*, iii (Cambridge, 1922) and *Index Ecclesiasticus, 1800–1840* (Oxford: Parker and Co., 1890).

[48] Upon Valentine Green's death, Thomas Hill wrote that his father 'was not only father and mother to me in one, but also the most genial of companions, and every object here [in Birkin] brings him back to me with all his brightness and tenderness.' THG to A. C. Bradley, letter of 6 December 1873, in *GP* 1(a).

[49] The latter two are noted in the *DNB*.

[50] C. J. Vaughan was toppled from the headmastership in 1859 by a homosexual scandal involving (indirectly) John Addington Symonds, of which T. H. Green later obtained some knowledge. Vaughan was in effect blackmailed by Symonds' father, a wealthy Bristol physician, and John Conington, the Oxford classicist, into refusing promotion in the Church. This involved delicate negotiations with A. P. Stanley and other prominent clerics. Vaughan nevertheless ended his life as Dean of Llandaff (1879–97). *The Memoirs of John Addington Symonds*, edited with introduction by P. Grosskurth (London: Hutchinson, 1984), chap. 5 and pp. 110–16.

Martin's; he is best known as a Broad Church theologian and activist in the 'Christian Socialist' circle of F. D. Maurice.[51]

E. T. Vaughan, Sr., was an outspoken representative of Calvinism within the Establishment during the 1810s and '20s.[52] He believed that the evangelical revival had mischievously tended toward Arminianism, a doctrine of universal salvation which denied predestination or any efficacious covenant of grace. He held further that the ascendant 'moderate' evangelicals — above all, John Venn, William Wilberforce and others associated with the 'Clapham Sect' — had encouraged a foolishly optimistic view of God's inclination to control good and evil in the world. Vaughan simultaneously faulted the Claphamites for adhering to a doctrine close to deism: i.e. that the divine order was predetermined or fixed; that divine intervention was implausible; and that human intervention in the name of divine will was futile. Vaughan believed in the spiritual invincibility of the chosen ones and in the redemptive sacrifice of Christ for *every* person: it was imperative that every person understand that Christ was sacrificed as his substitute, not vicariously for his benefit, and denial of this meant everlasting damnation for the sinner.

Edward Vaughan's theological opinions had certain social implications. Boyd Hilton associates Vaughan with 'extreme' evangelicals, such as Edward Irving (1792–1834) and Henry Drummond (1786–1860). Irving, Drummond and other 'pre-millenialists' believed not only in the possibility of God's intervention in the world *before* the millenium but that God intervened specially and particularly, rather than regularly and generally, in order to encourage or chastise individuals and nations.[53] Vaughan, like Lord Shaftesbury, acknowledged the *inscrutability* of Providence as much as the righteousness of His ways. But rather than inclining them towards fatalism and acceptance of a corrupt society, this interpretation of salvation and Providence convinced men like Vaughan and Shaftesbury that 'those whom it had pleased God to place in positions of worldly influence should exercise a ... measure of control

[51] On Maurice and Christian Socialism, see especially Norman, *Victorian Christian Socialists*; and T. R. Sansom, 'From God to Man? F. D. Maurice and Changing Ideas of God and Man' in *Religion, Secularization, and Political Thought*, ed. Crimmins, pp. 153–66.

[52] There is no biography of Vaughan. Hilton discusses Vaughan's views expressed in his printed sermons. *Age of Atonement*, pp. 17, 286–8.

[53] Hilton, like the evangelicals who are the subjects of his study, employs the metaphors 'lawful' and 'arbitrary' in the familiar manner of the seventeenth and eighteenth centuries. The God of Enlightenment rationalists was the creator of mechanisms — e.g. gravitational force — which performed regularly and predictably without need for special intervention. A moderate evangelical like William Wilberforce shared something with the deists Matthew Tyndal, Voltaire and Thomas Paine: God's presence to men was in his laws, not in arbitrary interventions like miracles. *Age of Atonement*, pp. 10–16.

over society.'[54] Hence the social paternalism of Shaftesbury and others, more often Tories than Whigs, as evidenced by their promotion of Factory Acts and other social legislation from the 1820s and '30s; and their antipathy towards the Claphamites, who held that God 'does not often meddle with his own mechanism, so man should not meddle either.'[55]

None of the foregoing suggests that T. H. Green was influenced directly in his theological or other opinions by his grandfather. The latter was a Tory and a Calvinist while the former was an advanced Liberal in both politics and religion. Still, it is significant that neither man placed undue significance on the laws of political economy, substituting Adam Smith's 'invisible hand' of commercial relations for 'Christian duty' or social responsibility. Vaughan and Green both criticized Britons' indifference to the material poverty of their fellows and they dismissed the facile view that poverty revealed the divine will. While there is no question of an intellectual-spiritual bequest of E. T. Vaughan, Sr., to T. H. Green, there is evidence of meaningful connection between Green and his uncle David James Vaughan.[56]

Vaughan was the sixth and youngest of Edward Vaughan's sons, and he came of age when the evangelical disputes about Providence and human catastrophe had been resolved, according to Hilton, in favour of the moderate, laissez-faire evangelicals. While a Fellow of Trinity College, Cambridge (1850–8), D. J. Vaughan did pastoral work in London and Leicester. He was presented in 1860 to the living of St Martin's, a clerical office that had been in effect the property of the Vaughan family. During the 1850s his view of the status and function of the Anglican Church changed almost as radically as was possible for a cleric who remained within the Establishment. Vaughan's early Anglicanism reflected the catholic spirit of the Oxford Tractarians; he believed in the Anglican Church's complete continuity with 'that infant Society, which heard Jesus himself say, "This do in remembrance of me!"' But Vaughan was greatly impressed by the controversial theory of Atonement expressed by John MacLeod Campbell (1800–72), who was deposed by the Church of Scotland for heresy in 1831. The Kirk upheld the Calvinist view that Christ died not for all but for the elect, while Campbell argued

[54]   Hilton, *Age of Atonement*, p. 16. On Shaftesbury's religious beliefs and tone, see J. L. and B. Hammond, *Lord Shaftesbury*, 2nd ed. (London: Constable, 1923).

[55]   Hilton, *Age of Atonement*, p. 16. Other studies have emphasized the social and political reformism of the Clapham Sect: E. M. Howse, *Saints in Politics. The 'Clapham Sect' and the Growth of Freedom* (London: Allen and Unwin, 1971 [1952]); F. K. Brown, *Fathers of the Victorians. The Age of Wilberforce* (CUP, 1961).

[56]   The following is based on the entry for Vaughan in the *DNB*; A. J. Allaway, 'David James Vaughan. Liberal Churchman and Educationist,' *Transactions of the Leicestershire Historical and Archeological Society*, 33 (1957), pp. 45–58; and B. Lancaster, *Radicalism, Cooperation and Socialism: Leicester Working-Class Politics, 1860–1906* (Leicester: Leicester UP, 1987).

that salvation was possible for all through acceptance of God's grace: 'he deliberately reached after fresh slogans of grace,' since orthodox 'phrases for conveying the unconditional gospel had lost their power to persuade.'[57]

David Vaughan, like Campbell, Maurice, Jowett and other liberal theologians, repudiated the strict 'penal theory' of Atonement, according to which Christ bore the sins of all and all were therefore in a state of permanent spiritual debt. Rather, he suggested that the sacrifice of Christ compelled believers not to 'self-denial, but [to] surrendering their own wills to that of the loving God.'[58] The merciful Christ depicted by Vaughan and other liberals was a paradigm of character and a promoter of religious and social transformation, if not of revolution. David Vaughan realized that the Establishment did not have a monopoly on religious wisdom and came to the conclusion that in keeping with the English national character the national clergy must tolerate diversity of belief and practice ('Multitudinism').[59] He came to advocate disestablishment of the Irish Church, the Anglican communion in Ireland adhered to by about one-tenth of the population. Vaughan was also in the thick of educational controversy. As vicar of St Martin's, Leicester (1860–93), he was *ex officio* chairman of the managing committee of the parish schools. After 1870 he opposed nonsectarian teaching in the Board Schools (which had been recommended by the Nonconformist-dominated National Education League) because he feared that removal of credal religious instruction would weaken morality.

F. B. Westcott (1825–1901) and J. Llewelyn Davies (1826–1916) were Vaughan's close associates. Through Davies, Vaughan made acquaintance with Maurice, the preeminent Christian Socialist and (as R. K. Webb observes) 'most profound' Broad Churchman of the century.[60] Vaughan thus belonged to a growing body of liberal Churchmen who impatiently dismissed the factionalism of High and Low Church, Establishment and Dissent, and he tried to get around dogmatic controversy by emphasizing the life of Christian fellowship over religious formulae. Significantly, these Christian Socialists took a more than casual interest

---

[57] Vaughan dedicated his book *Christian Evidences and the Bible* (1865) to Campbell. Gerrish, *Tradition and the Modern World*, chap. 3 (quotation from p. 78); and Hilton, *Age of Atonement*, pp. 286–8.

[58] These are not Vaughan's words but Boyd Hilton's paraphrase of the view of John Llewelyn Davies, an ally of Vaughan. See Hilton's discussion of Davies, Wilfred Richmond, and Charles and David Vaughan (*Age of Atonement*, pp. 329–36); also, Cross, ed., *Oxford Dictionary of the Christian 'Church*, s.v. 'Atonement'.

[59] Allaway, 'David James Vaughan,' p. 48.

[60] Webb, *Modern England*, p. 407. The *Life of Frederick Denison Maurice*, 2 vols. (New York: Scribner's, 1884), by his son J. F. Maurice, contains excerpts from four of Maurice's letters to D. J. Vaughan, indicating the former's appreciation of the latter's sermons and pastoral work.

in the temporal (economic, social, political) conditions in which Christians had to live.[61] In 1855 Vaughan was appointed a curate of St Mark's, Whitechapel, where he came into contact with the new London Working Men's College directed by Maurice and John Ludlow, whose purpose was to re-Christianize labouring men, improve their minds and foster economic cooperation.

The Christian Socialists of the mid-nineteenth century believed that the intellectual and moral elevation of the working classes was a necessary concomitant of religious revivalism. Though they emphasized moral improvement, these men were concerned that moralized working men enjoy their fair share of national prosperity. They perceived a connection between the 'irreligion' of Chartists and other radical workingmen and their opposition to the emerging commercial-industrial order. Though not as authoritarian as Carlyle, who bemoaned anarchy in *Signs of the Times* (1829) and *Chartism* (1839), the Christian Socialists argued that politically aware intellectuals should help reclaim artisans and labourers for Christ. In 1860, David Vaughan founded a Working Men's College in Leicester on the London model.

Green and his 'Uncle David' were separated in age by eleven years. (David was Edward Vaughan's son by his second marriage, and he was thus the *half* brother of Green's mother). Green's elder brother, Valentine Green, Jr., was a troubled youth, melancholy and prone to excessive drinking, and the Green family continued to be consumed with worry about Valentine in his adulthood. The impression given by Tom's correspondence during adolescence and young adulthood is that he was the better adjusted and more responsible of the brothers. As has been noted, Tom tried to rescue Valentine from drunkenness and other irregularities.[62] Given Valentine's inadequacy as role model, it is tempting to imagine David Vaughan as Tom Green's surrogate elder brother — that is, as the person Tom looked up to as younger to elder brother. Charlotte Green's notes indicate that Green was on very good terms with his Uncle David while at Rugby (1850–5) and during his first decade at Oxford (1855–65). It was almost certainly with Vaughan's encourage-

---

[61] P. N. Backstrom, Jr., 'The Practical Side of Christian Socialism in Victorian Britain,' *VS*, 6 (1963), pp. 305–24.

[62] Valentine Jr. appears to have been an alcoholic from his early twenties. He matriculated at Oriel College and at Merton College, Oxford, before being 'sent down' in 1854; he went to Cambridge and was promptly expelled from Magdalene College. Thomas Green's letters from this time reveal that he and his father were 'overwhelmed with care' over the younger Valentine's 'misfortune'. The two brothers shared rooms in St. John Street, Oxford, for a period in 1861–2, but after 1862 there is no mention of Valentine in his brother's letters. Two letters of THG to David Hanbury, March 1854 and May 1854: *GP* 1(a); *Alumni Oxoniensis; Alumni Cantabrigiensis*.

ment that Green read Maurice's celebrated theological essays in 1854.[63] He was at Leicester with his uncle in January, 1861, and it was perhaps through his uncle that he was introduced to Maurice in April of that year.

If Green was not a participant in the Leicester Working Men's College, he was nevertheless well aware of his uncle's work. It is possible that Green's idea (ca. 1865–6) to leave Balliol in order to teach at Owens College, Manchester, was inspired by his Uncle David. Although Green did not in the end leave Oxford for Manchester, his doing so would have been consistent with Christian Socialist ideas about useful work with urban labouring men. As we shall see, Green applied this idea to other venues, especially Oxford, where there had been talk in the 1850s and '60s of establishing a Working Men's college.[64]

T. H. Green's formative religious influences were evangelical, Christian Socialist and (so far as it can be separated from Christian Socialism) Broad Church. He felt something of the Broad Church spirit at Rugby school, which he entered in 1850. Though Rugby's most famous headmaster, Thomas Arnold, had died in 1842, the 'muscular Christianity' preached by Dr Arnold and popularized by Thomas Hughes (author of *Tom Brown's School Days*), Charles Kingsley and Arthur Stanley was a trademark of that institution by Green's time.[65] 'Rugbeian' ideals were in fact not unique to the place; other schools and schoolmasters had contributed to them since the 1830s and many educators transplanted the ideals to new institutions.

The Muscular Christianity of the reformed 'public' schools was essentially anti-theological in that it dispensed with many religious formulae and dogmas that were morally confusing and socially divisive. Muscular Christianity presented itself as common-sense Christianity. It taught practical morality and exhorted boys and men to go forth and be active in the world, to defend their beliefs yet to be tolerant of unpopular ideas. And it counselled persistence in social as well as personal tasks: work with men as you find them as well as how you would have them.[66] Green disliked Rugby — this is clear from his contemporary correspondence — and it was only some years after his leaving that his feelings

[63] CBG notes; and THG letter to D. Hanbury, September, 1854 (in *GP* 1a).

[64] Letter of THG to David Hanbury (undated: probably 1856) in *GP* 1(a); and Harvie, *Lights of Liberalism*, pp. 144–51.

[65] Newsome, *Godliness and Good Learning*; and Briggs, *Victorian People*, chap. 6. Kingsley was a Christian Socialist novelist; Stanley was Arnold's biographer and a close associate of Jowett, appointed Dean of Westminster in 1864.

[66] Peter Gay, 'The Manliness of Christ' in *Religion and Irreligion in Victorian Society. Essays in Honor of R. K. Webb*, ed. R. W. Davis and R. J. Helmstadter (New York: Routledge, 1992), pp. 102–16. *The Manliness of Christ* was published in 1879 by Thomas Hughes.

softened.[67] Perhaps the chief elements of 'Arnoldian' religion picked up by Green were its social activism and emphasis on fellowship. Though I discuss the 'German' and 'liberal Oxford' influences on Green's religion below, it must be remembered that Green's first exposure to theological innovation and religious liberalism occurred in his adolescence.

3.4. 'GERMAN' INNOVATIONS AND GREEN'S THEOLOGY

Green was heavily influenced by the general sensibility of Romanticism as well as by specifically Romantic ideas. He appreciated Wordsworth, Walter Scott and Coleridge for their literary qualities and believed the Romantics represented an advance in the 'moral sense' of British culture.[68] He illustrated philosophical points in his lectures by referring to Wordsworth and Walter Scott.[69] The influence of Thomas Carlyle is evident in the tone of some of Green's early writings, and contemporaries remarked on this as well as on Green's cultural patriotism in his appreciation of British writers. Green gained some insights into German Romanticism generally and philosophical Idealism specifically through his youthful reading of Coleridge and Carlyle — the writers commonly cited as the chief spokesmen for German thought in Britain during the first half of the nineteenth century. In the summer of 1861, Green studied Hegel with some intensity, and this first enthusiastic engagement with German Idealism provided some of his motivation for travelling in Germany the following summer.[70]

The 'Romantic' religion of the German Idealists — especially Schelling, Hegel and Schleiermacher — had a major impact on British theology after the 1820s. J. H. Newman, Edward Pusey and other

---

[67] Green's personal dislike for the headmaster, E. M. Goulburn (who moved from moderate evangelicalism to High Churchmanship and became Dean of Norwich), was scarcely concealed. Shortly after going up to Oxford Green wrote to Andrew Fairbairn and expressed his low opinion of Oxford men recently arrived from Rugby and his concern that Rugby would continue to decline 'while the Dr. [EMG] is there' (letter to Fairbairn, [Oct.?] 1855, in *GP* 1a). Green testified to the intellectual apathy of Rugbeians and also to the mania for organized games that was to pervade the public schools by the 1860s. Green's letters to David Hanbury ([Nov.?] 1853, Dec. 1853, [May?] 1854). Green gave thousands of pounds to educational institutions but nothing to Rugby.

[68] 'Popular Philosophy in its Relation to Life,' *Works*, iii, pp. 92–125. See also 'An Estimate of the Value and Influence of Works of Fiction in Modern Times': Green's 1862 Chancellor's English Prize essay, reprinted in *Works*, iii, pp. 20–45.

[69] He cites the case of 'Jennie Deans', a character from Walter Scott's *The Heart of Mid-Lothian* (1818), to illustrate 'perplexity of conscience': *PE*, secs. 314–15, 321.

[70] On Green's reading of Hegel, see Wempe, *Beyond Equality*, pp. 22–3. On Green's trip to Germany between July and September, 1862, see the cited memoirs of Symonds, James Bryce and Dicey. Early in 1863 Green is reflecting nostalgically on his 1862 travels and tells David Hanbury, 'Possibly I may establish myself in Germany for some time' (*GP* 1a: letter to Hanbury, 26 January 1863).

Tractarian Churchmen were critical of German scholarship, while liberals appropriated it (not all of it of a Romantic character) for their own purposes.[71] As Bernard Reardon observes, many religious Romantics wished to objectify and systematize Christianity by treating it 'as a historical and social phenomenon.'[72] Eighteenth-century apologetics — represented in England by Paley, for instance — presented Christian beliefs 'in the guise of pseudo-scientific propositions.' Romantics perceived that apologetics had shaped up badly against Enlightenment developments in philosophy and science, and held that Christianity had to be reformulated 'to safeguard ethical freedom against a system of "nature" subject to the fixed patterns of uniform law.'[73]

Systematic theologians in Germany and elsewhere believed that a critical, more scientific theology might shore up the crumbling basis for Christian belief by disposing of dogmatic accretions and dangerous myths that made orthodoxy appear both anachronistic and ridiculous in the light of reason. Friedrich Schleiermacher (1768–1834), for instance, was positively concerned with dogmatics. In the Romantic mode, he privileged individual spiritual experience while asserting that, because divine revelation became 'historical' in Christ, and because a Church bore witness to the events of Christ's life, it is through the Church and its doctrines that believers know the events. But doctrines and dogmas are historical products, and to the historian of dogma falls the responsibility of chronicling their development, including their perversion.[74] Schleiermacher wrote to F. H. Jacobi in 1818,

> The Bible is the original interpretation of the Christian feeling, and for this very reason so firmly established that we ought not to attempt more than further to understand and develop it. This right of development, however, I, as a Protestant theologian, will allow no one to defraud me of …[75]

Dogmatics and *Dogmengeschichte* were pursued by generations of theologians according to the historical and critical principles laid down by Schleiermacher. A rationalist approach to Christianity was reconciled with the Romantic celebration of spiritual feeling. One danger perceived in this course by many orthodox theologians was that the history

---

[71] Ward, *Victorian Oxford*, chap. 7.

[72] Reardon, *Religion in the Age of Romanticism*, p. vii.

[73] Reardon, *Religion in the Age of Romanticism* , p. viii. 'Apologetics' — the science of 'the argumentative defence of Christianity' — dates to 1733 (*OED*). It was, in the eyes of many Romantics, a symptom of the disease.

[74] Gerrish, *Tradition and the Modern World*, pp. 42–6. Schleiermacher was connected to the Romantic movement in part through his friendship with the poet and critic Friedrich Schlegel. His most famous work was the *Glaubenslehre* (1821–2: *Christian Belief Presented in its Connection with the Principles of the Lutheran Church*), which remained one of the most respected works of Protestant theology in the nineteenth century.

[75] Letter of 30 March 1818, quoted in Gerrish, *Tradition and the Modern World*, p. 44.

of Christian doctrine became the history of human religious thought, so that one arrived at Ludwig Feuerbach's heretical definition of religion '"as the relation of Man to himself, i.e., to his own Being, but as if it were another Being."'[76] Orthodox Christians feared the subjectivity or relativism of Romantic 'rationalism', which made dogmas and religious formulae irrelevant and thereby dissolved authority.

The aspect of Romantic religion Reardon calls subjectivist consisted in its appeal to the emotions and feelings of individual believers. The Romantics perceived a need to render Christianity more authentic to individuals' subjective experience: 'its primary "objectivities", the content of an alleged divine revelation, [needed to be] interpreted with reference to the psychological needs and moral aspirations of the believer himself.'[77] 'Left' Hegelians were skeptical that Christian doctrines and institutions actually served such moral aspirations. Feuerbach argued that the only genuine meaning religion could have was that projected onto it by individual subjects; its 'objective' purpose was control of the masses by elites.[78] Green too was interested in the subjectivist aspect of religion in relation to natural and social objectivities; he wished to historicize Christianity but also to protect it from excessive rationalism.

Although it may appear misplaced to devote so much space here to German religious thought, it is justifiable on many grounds. Given Green's Idealism and his demonstrated enthusiasm for German thought, we might wonder about the impact on him of German Romanticism and German Protestant theology. Further, Green's religious and intellectual experience followed a pattern quite similar to that of some of the German *Frühromantiker*, whose religious upbringings jarred with Enlightenment rationalism. As we have seen in an earlier chapter, Green criticized the 'moral sense' of the Enlightenment and specifically attributed the growth of religious and social understanding in his age to the influences of Romantic art (especially poetry) and the 'enthusiastic' varieties of eighteenth-century religion. Therefore, a thorough account of Green's religious work should include a treatment of the specifically

---

[76] Merz, *History of European Thought in the Nineteenth Century*, iii, pp. 160–75 (Feuerbach, *The Essence of Christianity*, quoted p. 174).

[77] Thus Reardon cites Coleridge: '"I more than fear the prevailing taste for books of Natural Theology, Physio-Theology, Demonstrations of God from Nature, Evidences of Christianity, and the like. Evidences of Christianity! I am weary of the word. Make a man feel the want of it; rouse him if you can, to the self-knowledge of the need of it; and you may safely trust to its own Evidence"' (*Religion in the Age of Romanticism*, p. 9).

[78] Marcuse, *Reason and Revolution. Hegel and the Rise of Social Theory*, Part Two, chap. 1; K. E. Bockmuehl, *Leiblichkeit und Gesellschaft: Studien zur Religionskritik und Anthropologie im Fruehwerk von Ludwig Feuerbach und Karl Marx* (Goettingen: Vandenhoeck und Ruprecht, 1961); Schuffenhauer, *Feuerbach und der junge Marx*; S. Avineri, *Hegel's Theory of the Modern State* (CUP, 1972), chap. 5.

religious and spiritual currents that formed Schleiermacher, Hegel, F. C. Baur and other thinkers whose ideas Green found worthy of attention.

Many studies of Romantic art, religion and philosophy emphasize the revolutionary character of the Romantic project.[79] So too did the evangelical revival in Britain ca. 1740–1840 represent the revolt of 'enthusiasm' against latitudinarian, reasonable religion; in the value it put on feeling evangelicalism threatened the careful theological and ecclesiastical compromises achieved since the Restoration and the Glorious Revolution.[80] In their religion as well as their art, Romantics yearned to escape from what Hegel called 'the Unhappy Consciousness' and to throw off the dead hand of the past.[81] It would be misleading, however, to suggest that European Romantics were satisfied simply with discarding dead dogmas and freeing religion from the bonds of authority, or that all of them advocated an individualistic Christianity.[82]

Continuities between neo-classicism or Enlightenment and Romanticism are difficult to ignore, but the hallmark of Romanticism was a confidence in individual imagination and 'genius' and a consequent diminishment of formalism. Not all expressions of genius were personal; genius might be manifested in folkways, in tradition and in history.[83] Indeed, to some Romantics, true freedom was to be found in tradition. J. G. Herder, 'Novalis' (Friedrich von Hardenberg) and the French Catholic François René Chateaubriand emphasized the spiritual, political and 'aesthetic' unity of pre-Reformation Europe as a model for post-revolutionary society. Novalis (1772–1801) proclaimed in 1799 that

[79] Marcuse, *Reason and Revolution*, Introduction; H. S. Reiss, ed., *The Political Thought of the German Romantics, 1793–1815* (New York: Macmillan, 1955), Introduction; J. Ritter, *Hegel und die französische Revolution* (Frankfurt: Suhrkamp, 1965 [1957]); E. D. Hirsch, Jr., *Wordsworth and Schelling: A Typological Study of Romanticism* (New Haven, CT: Yale UP, 1960); G. A. Kelly, *Idealism, Politics and History. Sources of Hegelian Thought* (CUP, 1969); M. H. Abrams, *Natural Supernaturalism: Tradition and Revolution in Romantic Literature* (New York: W. W. Norton, 1971); Jones, *Revolution and Romanticism*; Toews, *Hegelianism: the Path Toward Dialectical Humanism, 1805–1841*; D. Punter, *Blake, Hegel and Dialectic* (Amsterdam: Rodopi B.V., 1982); and Izenberg, *Impossible Individuality*.

[80] I. R. Christie, *Wars and Revolutions. Britain, 1760–1815* (Cambridge, MA: Harvard UP, 1982), pp. 33–9; R. B. Barlow, *Citizenship and Conscience. A Study in the Theory and Practice of Religious Toleration in England during the 18th Century* (Philadelphia, PA: Pennsylvania UP, 1962); M. Watts, *The Dissenters: Reformation to French Revolution* (Oxford: Clarendon, 1978); and G. Rupp, *Religion in England, 1688–1791* (OUP, 1986).

[81] Thus the proto-Romantic Friedrich Schiller: 'To which religion do I subscribe? None of those you present to me! — And why not? Because of religion!' Hegel discussed the Unhappy Consciousness in his great work published in 1807, *Phenomenology of Spirit*, trans. A. V. Miller (Oxford: OUP, 1977), sections 206–30 ('Freedom of Self-Consciousness').

[82] See Izenberg on Romantic individuality and its clashes with 'individualism' (*Impossible Individuality*, intro.).

[83] Reiss, *Political Thought of the German Romantics*, Introduction.

> Christendom will arise from the sacred heart of a venerable European Coun-
> cil, and the business of religious awakening will be performed according to
> an all-embracing Divine plan. No one will then be able to protest further
> against Christian and secular compulsion, for the essence of the Church will
> be true freedom, and all necessary reforms will be carried out under its guid-
> ance as peaceful and formal processes of the state.[84]

It is important to acknowledge the extent to which the *Frühromantiker*
were positively formed by historical religion; their 'religious turns' cannot simply be understood as reactions to the disappointments of the
Enlightenment and the French Revolution.[85] Hegel and Schleiermacher,
for instance, oscillated between criticism of religious orthodoxy and
acceptance of it as part of the unalterable fabric of society. Friedrich
Schlegel, though he carried his Romantic celebration of *Volksreligion* to
defence of Catholic principles, upheld a view similar to that of Hegel
and Green: 'The first stirring of the ethical [*Sittlichkeit*] is opposition to
positive legality and conventional righteousness, and a boundless sensitivity of Spirit [*Geist*].'[86] (As has been demonstrated in the previous
chapter, Green too believed that *Geist* operated in individuals and their
surrounding society.) Criticism of orthodoxy could lead the believer to a
more heart-felt and stronger faith. It is worth remarking that the attacks
by some Romantics on orthodoxy were consistent with major currents
of the Reformed or Protestant tradition. Schiller, Schelling, Novalis,
Schleiermacher and Hegel, among others, were deeply influenced by
eighteenth-century Pietism, just as Green was shaped by his English
Protestant 'inheritance', including Puritanism, the sects of the English
Civil War, Old Dissent and the evangelical 'revival' precipitated by John
Wesley.[87]

Laurence Dickey, in his detailed study of the Protestant cultural contexts of Hegel's thought, demonstrates the influence of Protestant Pietism in the Hegelian formation of a *Sittlichkeitsreligion* (ethical religion).
Dickey characterizes Pietism as a movement of people aspiring to
achieve a Second Reformation against the solidification of Reformed

---

[84] Novalis, 'Christendom or Europe,' quoted in Reiss, *Political Thought of the German Romantics*, p. 141.

[85] A classic account of Romantic alienation and reaction is provided by Abrams, *Natural Supernaturalism*.

[86] Quoted in Reardon, *Religion in the Age of Romanticism*, p. 27.

[87] Old Dissent refers to Protestant sectaries excluded from the Establishment during the seventeenth and eighteenth centuries or 'voluntarily' holding themselves aloof from it: Quakers, Unitarians, the English Presbyterians, Congregationals, and Baptists, among others. A study brilliantly bringing together the currents of enthusiasm, quietism and pietism (and not only in the Protestant tradition) is R. A. Knox, *Enthusiasm. A Chapter in the History of Religion* (OUP, 1961).

Church orthodoxy.[88] Like Methodism in England, Pietism anticipated Romanticism in privileging the immediate emotional experience and intuition of Christian believers over the truth of doctrines passed down to the laity by the clergy. Pietists in Swabia and elsewhere advocated a retreat from theological (hence, sacerdotal and liturgical) 'formalism and rigidity' and urged the faithful to practice Christian piety through religious observance and the performance of good works.[89] (Faith versus works remained one of the salient issues of Reformed Church controversy following Martin Luther's protests in the sixteenth century.) Philipp Jakob Spener (1635–1705), 'the father of German Pietism', decried the confessional politics of the German princes while simultaneously believing in the eventual moral regeneration of society through the efforts of princes, preachers and laity.

Dickey and historians of German Protestantism argue that Pietism's object was not merely the spiritual salvation of the community but harmonious social relations between religious communities as well as within them. *Praxis pietatis* was to have civil as well as religious consequences.[90] Theology and religious knowledge were not trusted as means to spiritual and social regeneration.[91] Rather, through *Sittlichkeit*, the practice of life with attention to Christian moral and social duties, citizens and subjects would substantiate Christian teachings and realize the moral life. Pietism, then, represented (in the minds of the Pietists themselves, at least) an especially pure expression of early Christian ideals: a Godly people constituting themselves as a social and political community through a shared religious spirit.

However, by focusing on Spenerian Pietism, Dickey emphasizes the conservative moral and civic functions ('social control' features) of German Reformed Church institutions; in some ways he diminishes the 'enthusiastic' aspects of German Protestantism during the seventeenth and eighteenth centuries.[92] He makes no mention of the more radical and

---

[88] Pietism was a movement of Protestants since the seventeenth century 'to challenge the religiopolitical orthodoxy *of their own Reformation*' (Dickey, *Hegel*, p. 60). The movement spanned both sectarian Protestantism and the (Lutheran) Reformed church, corresponding roughly to Dissent and Establishment in Britain. (In 1817, the two Protestant 'families' were officially united in the Prussian territories.) A. W. McCardle, *Friedrich Schiller and Swabian Pietism* (New York: Peter Lang, 1986), chap. 1; F. E. Stoeffler, 'Pietism', in *Encyclopedia of Religion*, xi, ed. M. Eliade (New York: Macmillan, 1987), pp. 324–6.

[89] Dickey, *Hegel*, p. 61.

[90] H. Holborn, *A History of Modern Germany. Volume 2: 1648–1840* (Princeton, NJ: Princeton UP, 1982), pp. 137–46; McCardle, *Friedrich Schiller*, pp. 10–18; and Stoeffler, 'Pietism'.

[91] Dickey remarks, rather inaccurately, 'None of the leading spokesmen of German Pietism was a systematic theologian' (*Hegel*, p. 70).

[92] Hartmut Lehmann too stresses the conservative or non-progressive nature of Württemberg Pietism, which, he suggests, was suited to small-scale agriculturalists,

'primitive' varieties of Pietism that stood in lineage to Anabaptism and the mysticism of Jakob Boehme (Böhme, 1575–1624). One such form of Pietism was that represented by Count Nikolaus Ludwig von Zinzendorf (1700–60) of Saxony, who gave protection on his family estate to Protestant refugees from Moravia and Bohemia and supported 'Moravian' congregations in Britain and North America. Although the count never intended to establish the Moravian Brethren (or *Unitas Fratrum*) as a sect or separate communion, the 'Moravians' were distinguished from other German Protestants by their experiments in communal living (such as those at the Zinzendorf estate at Herrnhut, Saxony, and at Bethlehem, Pennsylvania) and also by their religious enthusiasm.[93] Zinzendorf asserted that 'Religion can be grasped without the conclusions of reason … '; and that 'Religion must be a matter which is able to be grasped through experience alone without any concepts …'.[94]

If Pietism generally represented a second Reformation, the Moravian movement was a sort of reformation within a reformation; Moravian Pietism became reconciled with Protestant orthodoxy at a later date than did Spenerism.[95] Pietism's reconciliation with the Protestant establishment was hastened by the spread of the Enlightenment in Germany after 1700: the ascendancy of the rationalist philosophies of Leibnitz and Wolff in the German universities forced the Pietist movements into alignment with their establishment antagonists.[96] By the late eighteenth century, according to Brian Gerrish, the seminary at the University of Halle, which had been organized according to Pietist principles by A. H.

tradesmen, and professionals uninterested in the 'capitalist' virtues identified by Max Weber: 'Since they hoped for the return of Christ, spending time to make money was almost a waste of time in their eyes, and was, at best, neither harmful nor helpful' (pp. 97–8). '"Community" and "Work"' As Concepts of Religious Thought in Eighteenth-Century Württemberg Pietism' in *Protestant Evangelicalism: Britain, Ireland, Germany and America, c.1750–c.1950. Essays in Honour of W. R. Ward* [Studies in Church History. Subsidia: 7], ed. K. Robbins (Oxford: Blackwell, 1990), pp. 79–98. See also W. R. Ward, 'Zinzendorf and Money,' *Studies in Church History*, 24 (1987), pp. 283–305.

[93] Knox, *Enthusiasm*, chap. 17. Penelope Fitzgerald's novel *The Blue Flower* (New York: Houghton Mifflin, 1995), treating the life of Novalis, imaginatively explores Moravian life. Novalis spent part of his childhood in the Moravian colony at Neudietendorf, Saxony.

[94] From 'Thoughts for the Learned and Yet God-Willed Students of Truth' (1732), in *Pietists. Selected Writings*, ed. P. C. Erb (New York: Paulist Press, 1983), p. 291.

[95] Other forms of Pietism had been institutionalized in Swabia and in Halle (annexed to Brandenburg-Prussia in 1680). The Swabian clergy were represented in parliamentary assemblies, and the *Kirchenrat* exercised considerable political power in administering Church property. When Karl Alexander, a Catholic, became Duke of Württemberg in 1733, authority over the Lutheran Church devolved upon his Privy Council, which included Pietists. Stoeffler, 'Pietism'; McCardle, *Schiller and Swabian Pietism*, pp. 12–15; and Dickey, *Hegel*, pp. 10–11, 33–7, 111–37.

[96] Stoeffler, 'Pietism'.

Francke, was 'the home, not of pietism, but of rationalism.' Halle theology attempted to balance rationalism in religion with the 'deliberate cultivation of penitential agonies,' while the Moravian Brethren were moved by a 'joyful sense of communion with the ever-present Lord.'[97] Although it was neutralized by the religious establishment in the German states, Pietism accounted for certain enthusiastic, egalitarian and social revolutionary tendencies in popular Protestantism and German social thought after 1750.[98]

The significance of Pietism for discussion of Green, religion and Idealism is two-fold. First, Pietism ran counter to the Enlightenment emphasis on reason by cultivating emotions and inward experience, and it was a critical ingredient of a general 'evangelical revival' in Western Europe and North America which lasted into Green's era. Second, it was a formative influence on the German *Sturm und Drang*, German Romanticism and Idealism. Moravian congregations quickly spread with eighteenth-century German emigration. John Wesley came into contact with German Pietists in North America and England (1733–9), and to their heart-felt style of worship and emphasis on religious fellowship he attributed his own spiritual awakening. Wesley translated selections from Zinzendorf's *Herrnhut Gesangbuch* and published them in his *Hymns and Sacred Poems* (1739). Significantly, E. P. Thompson identifies the Moravian Brethren, recognized by Act of Parliament in 1749, as 'cousins' to the English 'Ranters' of the seventeenth century — that is, to antinomian and 'revolutionary' sectaries who refused to be 'bound' by ecclesiastical and civil authority.[99]

German Pietism may thus have reinforced British currents of religio-civic nonconformity and social activism. Thompson charges John and Charles Wesley with neutralizing the radical social and political tone of Pietism. By exaggerating the 'necrophily and perverse imagery which is the least pleasant side of the Moravian tradition' the Wesleys reduced a social religion concerned with penitence, charity and equality, to a life-denying creed and an outlet for 'emotional onanism'.

---

[97] Gerrish, *Tradition and the Modern World*, p. 17.

[98] 'Contacts with English nonconformists, probably established by Swabian emigrants to the New World, brought into existence Baptist congregations [in the German states after 1800] which upheld their belief against the State church and government and defended it as the true meaning of Scripture.' Holborn, *History of Modern Germany. 1648–1840*, p. 495. See also H. Lehmann, 'Pietistic Millenarianism in Late Eighteenth–Century Germany' in *The Transformation of Political Culture. England and Germany in the Late Eighteenth Century*, ed. E. Hellmuth (London: German Historical Institute, 1990), chap. 13.

[99] E. P. Thompson, *Making of the English Working Class* (New York: Vintage, 1966 [1963]), p. 40. On the Ranters and other revolutionary sects, see N. Cohn, *The Pursuit of the Millennium*, revised and expanded ed. (OUP, 1970), chaps. 8–9; and C. Hill, 'Antinomianism in Seventeenth-Century England,' in *Collected Essays of Christopher Hill* (Amherst, MA: UP Mass., 1986), essay ten.

Some Methodists perverted the emotional content of Pietism to con-struct 'a religion hostile to intellectual enquiry and to artistic values ...' 'Here was a cult of "Love" which feared love's effective expression, either as sexual love or in any social form which might irritate relations with Authority.'[100] Whether or not Thompson's view is justified, it is true that like German Pietism, early Methodism emphasized *Gefühl* and intuition to a degree disquieting to the religio-political establishment; the evangelical revival precipitated by the Wesley brothers and Whitefield whipped up passions reminiscent of those of the English Civil War.[101]

Scholars have traced certain utopian and revolutionary aspects of German Romanticism to the Pietist upbringings of Romantics and Ide-alists. Schelling and Hegel, for instance, embarked on theological study at the Tübingen *Stift*, at a time when Pietist teachings were ascendant, and Schleiermacher was educated among the Moravian Brethren at Gnadenfrei and at Halle University. These Idealists saw themselves as good Protestants and as upholders of Christianity against clericalism and atheism. They had little sympathy for what Schleiermacher (in 1799) called the 'cultured despisers of religion' and could not accept the Voltairean view of 'the infamous thing' as the destroyer of the human spirit and the arm of worldly tyranny. Yet, at least in their young adult-hood, they found orthodox Protestantism stifling and they objected to the authoritarianism of the evangelical and established Reformed churches. Their intolerance of ecclesiastism paralleled their discontent with political authority.[102]

In the view of the German Romantic-Idealists, both the excessive rationalism of the Enlightenment and narrow Protestant orthodoxy ignored the individual's 'subjective' relationship to the divine. It was no doubt their Pietist upbringing that taught them that while one task of religion was to ensure salvation, another was to promote morality so as to shape the totality of the individual in his earthly and civil existence. In reacting against religious establishments which had assimilated Pietist doctrines, the German Romantics heeded, perhaps less rather than

[100] Thompson, *English Working Class*, pp. 40–1, 370–1. See also Donald Davie's criticism of this 'puritanical' interpretation: *A Gathered Church. The Literature of the English Dissent-ing Interest, 1700–1930* (OUP, 1978), pp. 45–7. Considerable controversy continues to attach to historical and sociological interpretations of Methodism: was it, in its Wes-leyan, Arminian forms, a religion promising the meek the inheritance of the earth, or was it a quietist movement because of its largely self-imposed isolation from temporal matters? E. Halévy, *England in 1815*, 2nd ed. (London: E. Benn, 1949), Part 3, chap. 1; V. Kiernan, 'Evangelicalism and the French Revolution,' *Past and Present*, 1 (1952), pp. 44–56; B. Semmel, *The Methodist Revolution* (New York: Basic, 1973); and D. Hempton, *Methodism and Politics in British Society 1750–1850* (Palo Alto, CA: Stanford UP, 1984).

[101] Knox, *Enthusiasm*, chaps. 18, 21; and F. C. Gill, *The Romantic Movement and Methodism. A Study of English Romanticism and the Evangelical Revival* (London: Epworth, 1954).

[102] Toews, *Hegelianism*, chap. 2.

more consciously, the original German Pietist impulses. The pioneering Pietists had objected to the Lutheran clergy's claim to religious and civil leadership on the basis of superior knowledge acquired through reason and study. Following the Pietists, Romantic-Idealists disputed the efficacy of *Verstand* because, by discounting the passions and feelings, it offered incomplete means of comprehending the complexity of human experience.[103] In their efforts to comprehend the relations between individuals, nature and God, Schelling and Hegel believed they were pursuing reason and science beyond the constraints built into them, as it were, by the Enlightenment's mechanical conceptions of man and the universe. Much the same can be said for Wordsworth, Coleridge, Carlyle and T. H. Green.

There is no evidence that Green had specific knowledge of German Pietism, although he was probably aware of the Moravian underpinnings of John Wesley's spiritual awakening during the 1730s. However, in his chief historical study of English religion and politics, the 'Four Lectures on the English Revolution' (1866–7), Green referred to the 'family likeness' between radical German Protestantism and the doctrines of Sir Henry Vane the Younger (1613–62), who was executed upon the Restoration as the most dangerous living regicide. Green viewed Vane as the chief seventeenth-century representative of the 'evangelical conscience'.[104] In the same context Green noted the continuing influence of the Society of Friends (Quakers) and other sectaries in England, who, like the German Pietists, had been receptive to Boehme's teachings and, in some cases, those of Vane.[105]

Green did not offer a scientific-historical argument in the 1867 lectures about influence and historic continuity. Rather, he made observa-

---

[103] In the Pietist mode of religious experience 'an accident, illness, dream, or the reading of a particular biblical verse ... ' could lead to 'certainty of redemption.' Through 'exact examination of his emotions, thoughts and actions ...' the Christian could 'ascertain his relationship to God. It was this attitude which led to the profusion of works of self-confession and self-observation in eighteenth century German literature.' Friedrich Schiller's Karl Moor and Luise Millerin 'reflect the Pietist origins of this tradition.' McCardle, *Schiller and Swabian Pietism*, pp. 11–12.

[104] 'The English Commonwealth. Lecture I,' in *Works*, iii, pp. 294–5. Lectures originally delivered to the Edinburgh Philosophical Institute in January 1867; ms. notes in *GP* 3. The lectures were referred to in the Edinburgh press as 'The English Commonwealth and the Protectorate' and as printed in *Works*, Volume Three bear the page heading 'The English Commonwealth.' Scholars have commonly referred to these as the 'Four Lectures on the English Revolution'. See *AW*, p. 405n.

[105] Boehme's esoteric teachings are almost impossible to summarize, but he held that God the Father held the 'germs' of both good and evil and that man 'can avoid hell by uniting himself to Christ by faith.' The English 'Behmenists' merged with the Quakers. 'Boehme has exercised a far-reaching influence, especially in Germany and the English–speaking countries ... In England he was a source of inspiration to P. Sterry, the Cambridge Platonists, to the 17th–18th cent. "Philadelphia Society," and to W. Law' (Cross, ed., *Oxford Dictionary of the Christian Church*, pp. 182–3).

tions about what Ronald Knox calls the 'almost normal concomitants of enthusiasm' among the Anabaptists, Quakers, Ranters, Wesleyans, etc.: heeding the 'inner light', communal witnessing of 'convincements' and the physical signs of spiritual inspiration ('being taken with the Power').[106] Green focused on the forms of religious and civil organization encouraged by belief in the in-dwelling spirit. English Protestant sectaries since the Elizabethan era were opposed to the instruments of religious conformity and a 'magisterial' ecclesiastical polity; the sectaries of the English Civil War held free faith and voluntary spiritual fellowship to be the basis of a just civil order and government.[107] Many affirmed the value of what Spener in Germany called *ecclesiolae* 'little churches' and free assemblies of 'brethren' modelled on those that kept faith alive during the first centuries of the Christian era.

According to Green, the popularity in England during the seventeenth century of non-coercive, decentralized and at times anarchical Christianity was indicative of the 'higher enthusiasm' that had transformed English moral and spiritual life and 'belonged to the universal spiritual force which as ecstasy, mysticism, quietism, philosophy, is in permanent collision with the carnal interests of the world ...':

> 'The people of England,' he [Vane] said again, 'have been long asleep. I doubt they will be hungry when they awake.' They have slept, we may say, another two hundred years. If they should yet awake and be hungry, they will find their food in the ideas which, with much blindness and weakness, he vainly offered them, cleared and ripened by a philosophy of which he did not dream.[108]

The 'higher enthusiasm' of radical sectaries had been temporarily subdued upon the Stuart Restoration but had never died out and had taken shape as a new, more powerful philosophy. While scholars have made much of Green's reference in his closing statement in the English Revolution lectures to Idealism, it has escaped notice as Green's endorsement of free religion and pluralism: true religiosity and moral freedom are maintained by a pervasive Christian spirit, not by the observances and laws of a national church.[109] Furthermore, Green's reference to 'the universal spiritual force ...' surviving political upheavals

---

[106] Knox, *Enthusiasm*, p. 150.

[107] H. N. Brailsford, *The Levellers and the English Revolution* (London: Cresset, 1961); M. Walzer, *The Revolution of the Saints* (Cambridge, MA: Harvard UP, 1965). The case for the tolerant attitude of Puritans and non-Establishment Protestants and their commitment to religious pluralism has been convincingly restated by John Coffey, 'Puritanism and Liberty Revisited: the Case for Toleration in the English Revolution,' *HJ*, 41 (1998), pp. 961–85.

[108] 'The English Commonwealth. Lecture IV,' p. 364. Here 'carnal interests' clearly imply political authority. The statement below is cited from the same page.

[109] Paul Harris and John Morrow point out the significance of Green's reference, as did R. L. Nettleship in his 'Memoir'. *Harris and Morrow*, p. 351, n.32.

does not imply an endorsement of 'quietism' but signals his belief that the liberal spirit in religion, whether quietist or activist, 'has since been the great spring of political life in England.'[110] Marxist historians especially have commented on the resurfacing of English Civil War antinomianism and revolutionism in British popular radicalism and socialism after the French Revolution. Thus Christopher Hill remarks that ideas like those of Gerrard Winstanley the Digger and John Milton do not 'get totally forgotten: men were discussing Winstanley's writings in a Welsh valley in the seventeen-nineties ...'.[111]

There are obvious resemblances between the sentiments Green displayed in his English Commonwealth lectures and some of the radical theological and ecclesiastical principles endorsed by Christian Socialists and Broad Churchmen of his own time. Furthermore, Green's understanding of tensions between the personal and institutional aspects of Western Christianity had strong affinities with the beliefs of German Romantic-Idealists, which tended toward a kind of radical subjectivism. The 'inwardness' and 'subjectivism' in German Protestant culture, according to Dickey, engendered opposite habits which have since characterized German culture and politics: 'submission to outer political authority' and 'a strong, antiauthoritarian, civil impulse.'[112] In the 'English Revolution', according to Green, spiritual subjectivism supported an idea of spiritual *equality*; and spirituality was not merely inward and personal but secured and articulated through participation in religious affairs and civil life. To those contemporaries of Cromwell animated by a heightened religious sense, the line separating spiritual and social-political equality was a porous one. Like many German Romantics, including the younger Hegel, Green held that the idea of non-magisterial religious polity best served individual quests for grace and had advanced human freedom.

3.5. LIBERAL THEOLOGY AND THE HISTORY OF DOGMA

In the 'Four Lectures on the English Revolution' Green discussed religious ideas in relation to social and political history. In other writings he dealt more directly with theology and its philosophical implications. It

---

[110] 'English Commonwealth. Lecture IV,' p. 364. John Morrow has recently observed how the philosopher William Godwin (d. 1836) anticipated Green's interpretation of the English Commonwealth. I think, however, that there can be no question of Godwin's direct influence on Green in this respect. John Morrow, ed., 'Introduction,' *History of the Commonwealth of England [1824–28]: William Godwin* (Bristol: Thoemmes Press, 2003), pp. xxx–xxxi.

[111] Winstanley, who advocated social and sexual equality and the abolition of private property, opined that '"No man shall be troubled for his judgment or practice in the things of his God"' (Hill, 'God and the English Revolution' [based on a 1984 lecture], in *Collected Essays. Volume Two*, p. 339).

[112] Dickey, *Hegel*, p. 9.

should be noted at this juncture that Green had had little exposure to systematic theology before his arrival at Oxford. At Rugby he had followed theological controversies, such as the furore surrounding Maurice's repudiation (in *Theological Essays*) of doctrines which held the punishment of sinners to be everlasting.[113] Green's religious thought during his undergraduate years was informed in a broad way by Jowett. Jowett, like Maurice and D. J. Vaughan, took issue with the doctrine of everlasting punishment. In his 1855 study of Paul's Epistles, Jowett rejected the orthodox interpretation of the redemptive sacrifice of Jesus Christ, substituting for it the notion that Christ's victory over death suggested the death of sin in all believers who followed Christ's example. Regardless of any credence we might or might not give to the events of Christ's life and death as history, the poetic expression of the Gospels compelled belief in the intersection of the human and the divine.[114] Finally, Jowett advocated (in his contribution to *Essays and Reviews*, 1860) reading the New Testament 'like any other book,' which was widely taken as an endorsement of the application of 'German' historical and philological methods to scriptural interpretation.[115] Green's approach to New Testament studies and the history of Christianity was shaped by Jowett, but from the early 1860s Green was reading independent of Jowett and testing his own ideas.

A notebook of Green's (in his papers at Balliol College) covering the period ca. 1865–70 contains a list of books he lent and borrowed, and it provides important clues to his intellectual interests and influences.[116] The list includes works of Renan, Claude Bernard and Thierry, and of various Swiss and German historians, philologists, philosophers and theologians. Noteworthy here are D. F. Strauss (*Das Leben Jesu* and *Dogmengeschichte*), Schwegler (*Das hochapostolische Zeitalter*) and 'Baur' (F. C. Baur, 1792–1860). To the entry 'Baur' is appended the note 'vol. 1 lent to Jowett'. This is undoubtedly the *Geschichte der christlichen Kirche*, published posthumously in 1863, the translation of which Green embarked upon in the 1860s.

Henry Nettleship recalls that Green was engrossed ca. 1862–3 in 'Tübingen School' theology and critical history (represented principally by Strauss and Strauss's teacher, Baur). Nettleship reveals that around

---

[113] On Maurice, see Sampson, 'The Limits of Religious Thought.'
[114] Jowett, *The Epistles of St. Paul to the Thessalonians, Galatians and Romans: with Critical Notes and Dissertations*, 2 vols (London, 1855; 2nd ed., 1859). Green cited this commentary in his 1861 essay submitted for the Ellerton Theology prize (printed in *AW*, pp. 83–104). He particularly appreciated Jowett's account of how Jewish religious doctrine had been Hellenized and 'changed into a system of philosophy' (*AW*, p. 90).
[115] Faber, *Jowett*, chap. 11; Hinchliff, *Jowett and the Christian Religion*, pp. 72–90.
[116] In *GP* 1(c): labelled 'Notebook of School Inspection' because it contains at the beginning questions and information relating to Green's schools inspection tours in 1865–6. It also contains details of Green's Balliol tutorial assignments before 1870.

this time Green, under the influence of Schwegler, arrived at the conclusion that the fourth Gospel was non-apostolic and that it represented 'the most advanced stage of New Testament thought.'[117] 'John', to a much greater extent than other Gospelists, had added interpretation and symbolization to his account of the life of Christ. Many theological liberals utilized the gospel of John and the letters of Paul as the chief evidence for their interpretation of the meaning of the Christ events — namely, that the death and resurrection of Jesus were events not only in Him but events for and in Christian believers since the time of the apostles.

There is nothing uniquely Protestant or modern in the view of 'death to sin' in Christ and in the awakened believer, but Jowett was among the chief British critics of a literal view of the efficacy of the incarnation (one event, with consequences for everybody), upholding instead a theory of spiritual process in humanity and history.[118] Many liberals of this sort were eager to demonstrate the mischievous effects of Christian dogmas — that is, the obstacles they presented to Christian faith. Peter Hinchliff usefully notes that Jowett was less tolerant of dogma and dogmatists than were Schleiermacher, Strauss and Baur: Jowett's greatest interest was in God's presence in Christ, not in the Church that claimed continuity with the gospelists.[119]

R. L. Nettleship remarks on Green's claim that Baur was 'nearly the most instructive writer I ever met with.'[120] In the *Geschichte der christlichen Kirche*, Baur outlined the evolution of the Christian spirit in Idealist fashion, and located the '"ideal" form of the "philosophical" Christ' (Nettleship's words again) in Protestant theology. Like Hegel and other Idealists, Baur presented Christianity as a momentous and *continuing* discovery, with ethical and political, as well as religious

---

[117] Nettleship recollection: *GP* 1(b), pp. 23–65 in CBG copy–book.

[118] Compare to a modern centrist position between reliance on a strictly 'historical' account of the person Jesus — supposing this can be accomplished — and dependence on a New Testament 'portrait of Christ' (as suggested by Karl Barth or Paul Tillich). No one should seriously dispute that a person called Jesus existed, and a believer can view the doctrine of incarnation in connection with an event; the doctrine of incarnation 'specifies the locus in human existence where God's defining revelation and presence are to be found.' The 'formal significance' of the doctrine is that it provides 'a kind of metaphysical pointer to the place in human history where we must look for the answer … ' to our question about 'the *content* of our conception of God.' 'In this man [Jesus] God is present to us' — but not only there. G. D. Kaufman, *Systematic Theology: A Historicist Perspective* (New York: Scribner's, 1968), pp. 184–9.

[119] Hinchliff, *Jowett*, pp. 86–91. Jowett 'could not … conceive of the Church as the medium through which Christ was communicated to the believer' (p. 88). Henry Nettleship reports Professor Bernays of Breslau (whom he met) describing Jowett as 'Schleiermacher anglisiert' (Nettleship to James Bryce, 29 April 1865: Bodleian, MSS. Bryce 110, fols. 11–14).

[120] 'Memoir,' pp. xxxvii–xxxviii.

implications. According to Baur and many British liberal theologians influenced by the Higher Criticism, the incarnation of the divine in Jesus of Nazareth was an occurrence of world-historical importance, and this not simply because God the Father had sacrificed his Son in order to set men free. Rather, Christ's life and death provided an example of ethical living which would transform individuals in their earthly as well as their spiritual existence: the 'death' of the 'carnal' man in the spiritual process of sanctification, the emptying of the self and individual's recognition of the risen Christ within him, and his participation (emotionally and intellectually) in the 'wisdom of God' — all these movements of the spirit described by Paul prepared the believer to live out the moral idea of Christ in his own life.

Green's reading of Baur appears to have convinced him that Christianity was above all a social religion following a historical teleology. Christianity's world-historical mission was to transform human beings' earthly existence. Or as in Richard Nettleship's paraphrase of Green (paraphrasing Baur), 'the incarnation is not completed, the truth which Jesus proclaimed is not fully revealed, until the whole of mankind and the whole of nature become a perfect vehicle for the life which lived in him.'[121] Green's philosophical view of Jesus of Nazareth is similar not only to Baur's but to the view taken by contemporary Unitarians like James Martineau and Charles Upton.[122] Indeed, the doctrine denying 'the objective efficacy of the Cross and looking [sic] upon the death of Christ as primarily an example to his followers' appears to have been first articulated by the Socinians (the name given to Unitarians in the seventeenth century).[123] Similar views were elaborated by F. D. Maurice, who had been raised as a Unitarian, and by Jowett, although neither renounced entirely belief in the supernatural being of Christ.[124]

---

[121] 'Memoir,' pp. xxxix.
[122] C. B. Upton (1831–1920) was trained under J. J. Tayler and James Martineau at the nominally Unitarian Manchester New College, where he himself taught philosophy and theology. In the preface to his Hibbert Lectures (*Lectures on the Bases of Religious Belief*) he states, 'I feel utterly unable to accept that system [Absolute Idealism] as a whole, [though] I am well aware that I owe much to the writings of T. H. Green and of the gifted brothers [John and Edward] Caird ...' (p. ix). Yet the philosophical Christianity Upton upholds in the lectures is very close to Green's: 'the Incarnation ... most completely manifested in the personality and teachings of Jesus of Nazareth, is by no means peculiar to him, but is, in its essence, the intrinsic property and highest privilege of all rational souls' (p. viii).
[123] Cross, ed., *Oxford Dictionary of the Christian Church*, s.v. 'Atonement.'
[124] On Mauricean theology see Sansom, 'From God to Man?' Goldwin Smith complained that Mansel had injured Jowett in his Bampton lectures 'by the association of his name with those of Socinus, [Joseph] Priestley, Fichte, and other writers most odious to the Church' (*Rational Religion*, p. viii). Priestley (1733–1804) was an English Unitarian and natural philosopher.

From the perspective of English orthodoxy, the tendency of liberal theologians to throw into question the divinity of Christ smacked of Unitarianism. Indeed, James Martineau, the most intellectually daring and influential Unitarian thinker of the nineteenth century, was criticized by orthodox Anglicans and Dissenters for his Germanizing bent; he was denied a professorial chair at King's College, London in the 1860s because of orthodox protest. Martineau combatted materialism and pantheism in a manner derived from Schleiermacher and the Aristotelianism of Adolf Trendelenburg.[125] Charges of Green's heresy and infidelity may have been based on perceptions of his sympathy with Martineau. Some contemporaries only vaguely familiar with Green's work mistakenly took him to be crypto-Unitarian, just as Jowett was criticized for sympathies which more conservative Anglican clergy associated with unitarianism.[126]

Central to Green's theological endeavour was the reinterpretation of the miraculous and figurative elements of Christian writings. However, he rejected some tendencies of the Higher Criticism as misconceived and mischievous. For instance, he denied that the 'rational' and 'dogmatic' aspects of Christian doctrine could be conveniently separated. Christians had to view both kinds of expression of religious truth in a different light by appreciating the symbolic, metaphorical and analogical qualities of the entire body of Christian teachings. Green wished to render Christian faith less vulnerable to the assaults of scientific and historical criticism, yet also to demonstrate that the uses of the Christian tradition were different to a philosophical and scientific age than to a theological one. Green's essay 'Christian Dogma', delivered to the 'Old Mortality' Society some time between 1858 and 1860, previews his mature view of how Christianity was to be rationalized and philosophized.[127]

---

[125] The similarities between Martineau's and Green's view of religion and ethics were noted by a German scholar, Friedrich Jodl, who included Martineau with Green and F. H. Bradley in the school of 'Neo-Idealists'. F. Jodl, *Geschichte der Ethik als philosophische Wissenschaft*, ii (Stuttgart: J. G. Cotta, 1912), p. 533 and *passim*; and Merz, *History of European Thought in the Nineteenth Century*, iv, p. 374 and *passim*.

[126] In 1861 Green confessed to favouring a kind of 'modified unitarianism', but in the same year he criticized a bill before Parliament to abolish clerical subscription to articles of faith (R. L. Nettleship, 'Memoir,' pp. xxxv–xxxvi). Although Green was appreciative of the preaching of various 'Low Church' and Dissenting clergy, there is no evidence of his wishing to convert to Unitarianism.

[127] 'Christian Dogma' (25 pp. ms. in *GP* 4a), printed in *Works*, iii, pp. 161–85: undated essay written for the Old Mortality Society, to which Green was elected in 1858. Edmund Gosse reports in his *Life of Swinburne* (1917) that when Green delivered the essay on dogma to the Old Mortality he noticed Swinburne wearing an 'expression compounded of unutterable ennui and naif astonishment' (quoted in Thomas, *Swinburne*, p. 37). Swinburne cannot have heard the essay later than the spring of 1860 (when he was expelled from the University). It is likely, however, that the manuscript

In 'Christian Dogma' Green argues that it was necessary for the Church Fathers (i.e. institutionalized Christianity) to construct dogmatic representations of the spiritual intuitions of Christ's original followers. The problem with this kind of substitution, however, is that formulation of dogma — bypassing the spiritual process in the individual, in effect — cannot reproduce in individual Christians the spiritual experience and the yearning for a moral life which had produced Christianity in the first place. Because dogma is 'not regarded by the [individual] subject as in any sense its own product, but as something offered to it by an unknown God,' it cannot sustain faith and true religiosity. Dogmatists, in trying to shape the ways in which believers apprehend Christian truths, render faith and life in the Christian spirit more rather than less difficult.[128] Green made a similar observation about the poverty of dogma is his 1870 sermon 'The Witness of God':

> The original intuition of the crucified and risen one ... [,] depending, as it seems to have done, on peculiar personal and historical conditions, could never be reproduced in its native form and force. It had to be translated into other terms ... In this altered state it constantly required new supports of the understanding, and suggested new deductions, which have gradually constituted the theology of the church ... Dogmatic theology is quite other than the christian [sic] life, quite other than the practical idea on which that life rests.[129]

The tendency opposite to adherence to dogmas, according to Green, was reliance on a purely subjective 'inward light' or unthinking 'free' faith. This had its own pitfalls. The undisciplined faith which rejects the 'law' in favour of the individual's 'primary intuition' or apprehension of Christ — the faith of Luther, Elizabethan Puritans, radical sectaries of the English Civil War and the Pietists — 'recognized in the truths of revelation the highest utterances of the reason that is in every man ...'.[130] Free faith 'will not fix the relations which the various doctrines are to hold to the individual.'[131] It is this refusal to 'formulate' or be 'bound' to specific content that undermines positive Christianity and allows its relapse into dogma. Dogma presents a greater danger than intuition

---

in *GP* 4a is a later, improved version of the essay Swinburne heard read to the Old Mortality.

[128] 'Christian Dogma,' p. 176.

[129] 'Witness of God,' in *Works*, iii, pp. 237–8. This view is reminiscent of Schleiermacher's: doctrine is at best an aid to religious *feeling* and should be developed with this service in mind.

[130] 'Christian Dogma,' p. 182. Elizabethan and Stuart Puritans did not necessarily advocate 'freedom' and individualism in scriptural interpretation, but they defied the attempts of the ecclesiastical establishment to limit the conditions and frequency of clerical preaching. In the essay on dogma, as elsewhere, Green apparently conflated the Quaker ideal of 'waiting' for the utterance of the Spirit in individual believers with the Puritan resistance to ordinance.

[131] 'Christian Dogma,' p. 182.

and the free intellect to the survival of the Christian spirit. But dogma cannot be cut away from the body of Christianity like dead tissue: 'it must be transformed into a philosophy.'[132]

Green observes that human beings, in order to mediate their finite 'consciousness of union with an infinite God,' must participate in the Christian mystery both through intuition and as reasoned, *shared* principle.[133] While religious ordinance refuses to acknowledge individuals' intuitions as movements of the Spirit, radical subjectivism 'rests on the notion that intuition is the sole or ultimate activity of the spirit, that the immediate experience of the christian [sic] can remain such, and not strive to reflect itself in definite ideas.'[134] Here is the crucial link between religion and philosophy: vital religion requires an at least partial transcendence of the spiritual intuition to its *idea*. 'To the modern philosopher the idea itself is the reality.'[135] The idea cannot replace the intuition but is its complement and justification, as it transcends intuition's 'sensuous limitations.'[136] The 'idea becomes more concrete as the intuition becomes more abstract. God has died and been buried, and risen again, and realised himself in all the particularities of a moral life.'[137] The 'first characteristic [of dogma], as an intuition become abstract, must vanish, that it may be assimilated by the reason as an idea.'[138] The idea or principle apprehended by philosophy is that Christ's death and resurrection is to Christians their death to sin and their awakening to God's grace.[139]

There is in Green's treatment of dogma here a self-conscious defence of German critical principles and a 'metaphysical' tone of which Jowett, for one, disapproved.[140] The story of Jowett's persecution at the hands of Edward Pusey and Samuel Wilberforce after 1860, in connection with *Essays and Reviews*, has been alluded to in an earlier chapter. Jowett had done much to irritate Oxford theological conservatives. In his revised Pauline commentaries (1859) Jowett argued that theologians since

---

[132] *Ibid·*
[133] *Ibid.*, p. 179.
[134] *Ibid.*, p. 182.
[135] *Ibid.*
[136] *Ibid.*, p. 183.
[137] *Ibid.*, p. 184.
[138] *Ibid.*, p. 182.
[139] Compare to 'Witness of God': 'If Christ died for all, all died in him ... He constitutes in us a new intellectual consciousness, which transforms the will, and is the source of a new moral life' (*Works*, iii, p. 233). To say that Christ as God 'is an idea, or form of intellectual consciousness ... is the very reverse of reducing him to an impotent abstraction' (p. 235).
[140] A. M. Fairbairn, Congregationalist theologian, remarked on the basis of Jowett's opposition to the systematizing efforts of Green and Edward Caird (Jowett's successor as Master of Balliol). Jowett's appreciation of Scripture and Classical texts was 'personal', 'intuitive' and 'literary' and he disliked 'systematic thinking in whatever field.' Fairbairn, 'Oxford and Jowett,' *Contemporary Review*, 71 (1897), pp. 829–51.

Luther had erred in defining 'faith as faith in the blood ... [and] the death of Christ' — which St Paul had never done — and he 'described the conventional explanation of the atonement as revolting to men's moral feelings.'[141]

In the conclusion of his essay on dogma Green jabbed at 'the children of them that stoned the prophets' — an apparent reference to Jowett's opponents — and claimed that through

> the gradual development of the thinking spirit it [the Christian life] rises to a more adequate conception of itself. It is this elaboration of its speculative side which brings it into new relations with the intelligible world, and it is this which orthodox dogmatists denounce.[142]

Green offered here a spirited defence of the reviled Jowett. It is likely that criticism at Oxford from the 1860s of Green's politics, religion and philosophy stemmed in part from his association with Jowett.[143]

We have encountered already claims that one of Green's philosophical goals was to translate Christian ideas and doctrines into purely ethical principles, to empty the Christian religion — which he regarded as the most mature and complete of the world's religions — of its *rationally* untenable contents. Although Green never took holy orders, as a college administrator he was responsible for the moral and religious care of Balliol undergraduates. Two 'lay sermons', 'The Witness of God' (1870) and 'Faith' (1878), were privately printed and were subsequently included by Richard Nettleship in Green's collected works (Volume Three) with other fragments on religion.[144] Shortly after the publication of 'Faith', Green wrote an apologetic letter to James Legge (1815-97), Oxford's first professor of Chinese and an evangelical Congregationalist. Perhaps rattled by charges of infidelity from Oxford conservatives, Green assured Legge that his Balliol addresses were

> not written with a view to altering the beliefs of those who accept the miraculous narration of the Gospel, but to save those who, like myself, are unable to do so from being shaken in their moral and religious convictions.[145]

[141] Hinchliff, *Jowett*, pp. 61–3.

[142] 'Christian Dogma,' pp. 184–5.

[143] When in 1865 Green applied for a position on the Taunton education commission, 'He was a good deal surprised to learn through Dr. Temple, who was one of the commissioners and obtained the place for him, that his appointment caused some alarm to other members of the commission; they had heard that he was "an extreme man, an ultra-radical in politics, an ultra-liberal in religious opinions"' (R. L. Nettleship, 'Memoir,' p. xlv). Temple's introduction to Green would have been through Jowett, who would not at *that* time have criticized Green.

[144] On the uses of Green's lay sermons, see Nettleship, 'Memoir,' p. xcii. The two sermons mentioned were also published by Longmans and Co. in 1883, with an unfinished preface by Arnold Toynbee.

[145] THG to Legge, 29 April [1878]: Bodleian MS.Top.Oxon.c.528, fols. 123–4. The circumstances alluded to by the letter lead me to believe that the discourse referred to is

In these two published sermons, as in his other religious writings, Green was at pains to claim the practical inseparability of philosophy and religion: the former was the 'reasoned intellectual expression of the effort' contained in the latter. Despite his criticisms of religious 'ordinance', Green did not underestimate the value of Christian rites and other tangible aspects of religion. He made many more or less direct statements about the efficacy of Christian rites. In 'The Witness of God,' delivered to Balliol students taking of holy communion, Green assured his audience that

> The christian [sic] ordinances are at hand for our refreshment, and if we are wise we shall not neglect them. We cannot afford to individualise ourselves even in respect of outward symbols ... We shall not value such expression the less, because to us it is only an expression.[146]

Green admitted, then, that while many religious expressions might be philosophized, the value of Christian symbols was embedded in their sensuous forms and to tamper with them was to undermine them as aids to faith. Or as Richter concludes from his reading of 'Faith', creeds and religious formulae should be reasonable, because they are used by men to convince other men. In contrast, 'prayers are not meant to be heard by men' but by God. Nor is it imperative that worshippers understand rites and rituals but rather that through them they feel God's presence.[147]

Green was ambivalent and perhaps opportunistic about *creeds*. He pledged conformity to the Thirty-Nine Articles upon taking his Balliol fellowship (1860) and around the same time he opposed the abolition of clerical subscription. But only a few years later he opposed creedal conformity in the universities because he believed that creeds presented unnecessary intellectual obstacles to earnest people who agreed with the broad purposes of Christian institutions. With rites in principle he had fewer problems. As Green admitted to his student Henry Scott Holland in 1872, 'From orthodox Christianity, as expressed in prayer, and in the ordinances of Protestant worship, I feel no alienation, while I could not subscribe to one of the creeds.'[148]

Both Idealist philosophy and rational Christianity sought to define the boundaries of intuition and sense perception, on the one hand, and authority, on the other. Because Green privileged the idea over the sensuous experience (by itself and separate from its comprehension in thought) as the means to God and the moral ideal, he was biased against styles of religious belief he regarded as sensuous and unmanly. In this

---

'Faith' (delivered late in 1877 or early in 1878). I accept Peter Nicholson's dating of the letter (*AW*, p. 466n).

[146] 'Witness of God,' p. 251.
[147] *Politics of Conscience*, pp. 116–17.
[148] Quoted by Richter, *Politics of Conscience*, p. 117.

he was not alone: a Public Worship Act was passed in 1874 to discourage Anglo-Catholic (or High Church) ritualism. Although Green steered clear of heresy hunting he was known to criticize the 'Catholic' extremes of sacramentalism and sacerdotalism. This perhaps reflected a residual evangelical and patriotic horror of Popery.[149] Henry Nettleship remarked that his friend Green was not 'so free from prejudice in this instance as might have been expected from a man of his power and culture.'[150] Green also pointed to misinterpretations of the symbolism of Christ's Atonement perpetrated by strict evangelicals. Yet he conceded that symbols and rituals undoubtedly served the intuitive requirements of belief. While insistence on the sacramental power of the clergy was to strengthen the authority principle in a manner antagonistic to free faith, Christianity altogether stripped of rites and socially shared symbols would not fulfil the subjective requirements of belief.

Green believed that the deity of all Christians — trinitarians, unitarians, evangelicals, quietists, and so on — is an eternal consciousness. In Green's view, the conception of eternal consciousness or Spirit is what all Christians hold in common, regardless of their disagreements over the nature of Christ, the efficacy of His death and resurrection, and so on. Green's conception of an eternal consciousness is similar but not identical to the Hegelian Absolute Spirit. Like Hegel's *Geist*, Green's eternal consciousness, eternal mind, or self-objectifying principle can be detected through analysis of the self-realization of individual, determinate persons; and because it operates in individuals it is also a presence registered in human history. Like Hegel, Green identified the metaphysical with a higher rationality. For Green this was embodied in the particularities of social life and in individual conscience. Hegel, however, saw this higher rationality as fixed in the state, as the temple of freedom.[151] Green remarked on this claim that 'Hegel's account of freedom as realised in the state does not seem to correspond to the facts of

---

[149] On the 1874 Act, see Webb, *Modern England*, 2nd ed., p. 406; and, on popular anti-Popery, W. Arnstein, *Protestant versus Catholic in Mid-Victorian England. Mr. Newdigate and the Nuns* (Columbia, MO: UP Missouri, 1982). Shaftesbury and the Archbishop of Canterbury (Tait) were the ecclesiastical movers of the 1874 bill passed by Disraeli. The controversy over ritualism reached its peak towards the end of the century, and those defending variety in religious practice included Green's students, the Anglo-Catholics Charles Gore and Scott Holland.

[150] Nettleship notes Green's antipathy towards Catholicism and ritualist Anglicanism, with its incense, sumptuous clerical vestments, eastward orientation of the altar, etc. Green championed plain Protestantism as being 'less fettered by historical tradition and a particular external organization and discipline.' Yet he was 'never unkind to the popular presentation' of doctrines of God and immortality. Nettleship recollection in *GP* 1(b).

[151] Hegel, *Philosophy of Right*, especially secs. 257–360.

society as it is, or even as, under the unalterable conditions of human nature, it ever could be ... '.[152]

We have seen in this chapter (3.1) that Geoffrey Thomas denies that Green really intends to posit God as a model of the moral self. In fact, Green does refer to the eternal consciousness as the complete embodiment of the moral idea (or moral ideal) which finite moral beings might approach, if never achieve:

> There is a conception to which every one who thinks about himself as a moral agent almost instinctively finds himself resorting, the conception variously expressed as that of the 'better,' the 'higher,' the 'true' self. This conception, I believe, points the way to that true interpretation of our moral nature, *which is also the only source of a true theology.*[153]

Green's view of God and consciousness parallels that of F. D. Maurice. Maurice wrote in a letter to Green's uncle David Vaughan that

> Revelation must be the discovery of God to a creature formed to know Him and be like Him, revelation therefore to the reason and conscience of men, a revelation of the Will that is every moment acting on his will ... I ask for a demonstration of the Spirit with power to my spirit.[154]

We look to Christ and the church for signs of God, we look to the movements of the Spirit in the world, and not least of all we look to the true revelations of our being and our nature. Over these points a variety of Victorian Christians could find themselves in agreement. Thus it is not surprising that the Methodist preacher, social reformer and journalist Hugh Price Hughes (1847–1902), hearing Green's Oxford lectures in 1880 or 1881, approved of Green's representation of the rational will as the law of our being (which is also God within us): he took Green's view as a restatement of 'the good old Methodist doctrine of entire sanctification'.[155]

There were, of course, important differences between Green's philosophical Christianity and popular evangelicalism, but this does not mean that they led in opposite directions. No less than Establishment theologians, Nonconformists were unsettled by 'German' Biblical criticism; some came to terms with it. Richard Helmstadter claims that by the 1880s 'No sophisticated Nonconformist searched the Bible anymore for texts that would prove Christ died for all men and that all who truly

---

[152] Green, 'Different Senses of "Freedom",' sec. 6.

[153] 'The Word Is Nigh Thee,' *Works*, iii, p. 223 (my emphasis). See also *PE*, secs. 180, 185–9.

[154] From a letter to D. J. Vaughan, 22 November 1865, in J. F. Maurice, *Life of F. D. Maurice*, ii, pp. 509–11. Compare to Green in the sermon 'Faith': 'In the higher forms of the christian [sic] religion the spirit of man has reached that stage ... in which the consciousness of God is a consciousness of him, no longer as an outward power, but as one with itself, as reconciled and indwelling ... It is the God in you which strives for communication with God' (*Works*, iii, pp. 270, 273).

[155] Quoted in D. P. Hughes, *Life of Hugh Price Hughes* (London: Hodder and Stoughton, 1904), p. 134.

believed in Him would win everlasting peace.'[156] But most Nonconformist preachers and laity in Green's time were not 'sophisticated', as
Matthew Arnold (1822–88) and other Broad Churchmen frequently
remarked, and the evangelical revival lasted longer among Nonconformists than among Anglicans. Nonconformist evangelicalism was
alive and well in Green's time. The Biblical literalist and inspirationist
C. H. Spurgeon (1834–92), preached 'to probably the largest congregation in Protestant Christendom' in South London's Metropolitan Taber-
nacle.[157] During the 1870s, the American revivalists Moody and Sankey
made triumphant tours of Britain reminiscent of those of John Wesley
and George Whitefield more than a century before.

Though Green did not centre the experience of salvation on the person of Christ to the extent that most contemporary evangelicals did, his
view of salvation as self-perfection conveyed something of traditional
Protestant, evangelical 'enthusiasm'. While considerable numbers of
evangelicals by ca. 1865 (both Anglicans and Nonconformists) had
rejected the doctrine that a covenant of grace was necessary for man's
salvation, they nevertheless held that being a Christian meant above all
having faith in Christ. Green expanded on the evangelical idea of salvation: salvation was not to be thought of as the Christian's being (pas-
sively) 'brought to Christ' through symbolic acts like holy communion;
rather, as Maurice stated, God is discovered *by and in* creatures 'formed
to know Him and be like Him.' Green believed that the impulse toward
self-perfection is the divine aspect of our being. Though he may have
been brought to this view through unorthodox means (including the
Higher Criticism), many orthodox Christians agreed with Green's religious and ethical conclusions.

3.6. GREEN'S 'FOUR LECTURES ON THE
ENGLISH REVOLUTION' (1867)

The movement of the spirit was to be seen not only in man's nature but
also in history. Green detected processes of religious and philosophical
evolution, and he believed that spiritual expression had been tending
towards more complete forms — forms that more adequately corresponded to man's nature as a thinking and feeling being. Idealist philosophy represented a critical moment in this historical evolution because
it provided intellectual tools with which Christian believers might reconcile their discovery of new truths (e.g. in natural science) with their
religious inheritance. The germ of this intellectual revolution, according

---

[156] 'The Nonconformist Conscience', p. 161. For evidence of the growing 'sophistication'
of the Nonconformist ministry during the second half of the nineteenth century, see
K. D. Brown, *A Social History of the Nonconformist Ministry in England and Wales
1800–1930* (Oxford: Clarendon, 1988).

[157] Davie, *A Gathered Church*, p. 88.

to Green, was to be found in the history of the sixteenth and seventeenth centuries. There is reason to revisit here Green's 'Four Lectures on the English Revolution'.

Green regarded the English Commonwealth — the history of which he described as 'an old love of mine' — as an illustration of the march of *Geist* or world-spirit, and a true revolution in religion, philosophy and politics.[158] The lectures were first delivered to the Edinburgh Philosophical Institute in January, 1867, at which time Green was interested in a professorship at Edinburgh University. The 'Four Lectures' are Green's most serious contribution to historical scholarship. Later historians, most of a Whiggish tendency, found merit in them. Richard Nettleship entrusted C. H. Firth, who became Regius Professor of Modern History at Oxford (1904–25) but who was at the time (1885) a tutor at Pembroke College, with revising Green's lectures for publication.[159] Here Green's interpretation of 'Puritanism' and 'Independency' clearly reflected evangelical principles: individual communion with God and the cultivation of the Spirit were the essence of the Puritan movement.[160] He interpreted the Puritan episode in English history, culminating in the establishment of the Commonwealth, as a flawed experiment in government through the agency of what nineteenth-century evangelicals called the self that is Christed. Spiritual and social regeneration were to be achieved through the voluntary collaboration of individuals who felt the Christ rising within them. As John Coffey has remarked, the 'radical tolerationist argument' of the seventeenth century, articulated by Henry Vane, Milton and others Green admired, 'pointed to many of the key elements of modern political liberalism ...' — including social cooperation and 'respect for individual conscience.'[161] 'The hotter sort of

---

[158] R. L. Nettleship, 'Memoir,' p. lviii. Alberto de Sanctis has drawn attention to the importance of these lectures in 'T. H. Green and the "Force of Circumstances": Can Uncommon Individuality Be Consistent with Democracy?' (paper for the Political Studies Association-UK, 50th Annual Conference, 10–13 April 2000, London).

[159] See Nettleship's 'Preface' to *Works*, iii. In terms of scholarly refinement, the lectures fall somewhere between the popular histories of Carlyle, J. Franck Bright, and J. R. Green, and the more academic work of C. H. Firth and S. R. Gardiner.

[160] In Green's time Congregational chapels and seminaries were often called 'Independent' (e.g. Lancashire Independent College), as were some Baptist institutions; some are so called today. Some Congregationals at the end of the nineteenth century wished to join other Dissenters as a 'Free Church' and some of their chapels were so named. 'Free Church' Presbyterians (e.g. Campbell) in nineteenth-century Scotland had abandoned Calvinism.

[161] 'Puritan tolerationists ... incessantly appealed to humane sentiments against the "cruelty" of religious coercion ... The gulf between puritanism and nineteenth-century nonconformity was not always as wide as some historians have suggested' (Coffey, 'Puritanism and Liberty Revisited,' pp. 984–5). Among the 'Puritan tolerationists' Coffey includes John Goodwin (an Independent), Roger Williams, and Vane the younger.

Protestants, by virtue of their primitivist zeal, had reached some remarkably liberal conclusions.'[162]

Entrenched in Green's unusually favourable view of Independency was a critique of Anglicanism both past and present. The so-called Whig theory of history emerging during the eighteenth century represented the Stuart monarchy as an obstacle to the organic or constitutional growth of English freedom.[163] Green, among others, emphasized the tyranny of clergy over laity and the clergy's adherence to privilege and 'ordinance', encouraged notoriously by Archbishop Laud (1573–1645). In Anglican ordinance prior to the English Civil War, and in the 'Clarendon Code' upon the Stuart Restoration, Green identified a principle antithetical to religious truth, intellectual freedom and political liberty; and he saw in Puritanism principles conducive to religious and political freedom. Green's contemporary A. M. Fairbairn offered a similar view:

> I do not say … that the Whig was a duplicate of the Puritan revolution, but I not only say that the one made the other possible, but also that the Whig was the victory of principles, though in a very imperfect form, which the Puritan had affirmed and made good.[164]

So adamant was Green in the belief that the opponents of Charles I were on the side of general right that he was willing to offer excuses for some of the extreme measures of Cromwell and the militant republicans. The 'levelling' army animated by religious and political enthusiasm was not the complement but the antithesis of the 'watching, waiting Spirit' represented by The Protector.[165] The two cancelled each other in the political short term, allowing the Stuart Restoration with limited political liberty and a somewhat less strict ecclesiastical settlement. But the quiet-

---

[162] *Ibid.* Godwin was a modern Radical who appreciated these qualities. Morrow notes that 'Godwin's stress on the intellectual and moral heroism of the English Republicans found an echo [in] … T. H. Green.' Morrow, 'Introduction,' *History of the Commonwealth of England: William Godwin*, p. xxxi.

[163] A classic expression of the Whig view was William Stubbs' *Constitutional History of England* (1873–8). Burrow ventures that, insofar as Stubbs viewed 'constitutionalism' as an organic principle in English history, his 'underlying metaphysic [was] Hegelian.' J. W. Burrow, *A Liberal Descent. Victorian Historians and the English Past* (CUP, 1981), p. 147.

[164] A. M. Fairbairn, 'The Puritan in History,' *The Speaker*, 28 November 1896, pp. 568–70 (a review of S. R. Gardiner's Ford Lectures on Cromwell). Quotation p. 570. Fairbairn continued: '… Where the Whig revolution failed most completely was where the Puritan was most in earnest − in the matter of the Church. From that failure we all suffer to-day' (p. 570). Whigs had failed to accept the logic of Church disestablishment. See also, T. Lang, *The Victorians and the Stuart Heritage* (CUP, 1995), chaps. 3–5.

[165] 'The army [after 1647] … was the real constituency of the republican government. It contained dangerous elements over which parliament had not the least control, and which might at any time overturn the parliamentary system' ('English Commonwealth. Lecture III,' p. 337). 'The fact [of the mutinies of 1649] … is unique because the army was unique, being not a mercenary machine, or even an embodiment of patriotic impulse, but an armed organisation of opinion' (p. 340).

ism of Diggers and Quakers, while politically ineffective, produced a lasting 'protest against the plausibilities of the world' and 'supplied [sic] a constant spring of unconventional beneficence to English life.'[166]

Green suggested that while the Cromwellian revolution could not be re-enacted, Puritan principles might be applied to modern life. More than a decade after he delivered the English Revolution lectures, Green opined that in forms of voluntary and egalitarian 'Christian fellowship ... the moralising functions grow as those of the magistrate diminish,' and the number of individuals 'whom society awakens to interests in objects contributory to human perfection tends to increase.'[167] The Puritan version of *Sittlichkeit* (to use an Idealist term designating 'ethical life') depended on the special ethical predisposition of the Godly and it fed off religious enthusiasm. The Puritan conscience which had awakened England to the idea of liberty during the seventeenth century continued into Green's own era as the 'evangelical conscience'.

Green represented Henry Vane the Younger, the Civil War martyr, as the embodiment of the 'evangelical conscience':

> the stage in which the human spirit, perfectly conformed to Christ's death and resurrection, crucified to outward desire and ordinance, holds intercourse 'high, intuitive and comprehensive' with the divine.[168]

The 'natural conscience', a lower 'stage' in the 'conscience of man,' was akin to the natural law ideas Green located in the ancient Stoics: it 'was the light of those who, having not the law, were by nature a law unto themselves.'[169] The 'legal conscience', the antithesis of the natural conscience, 'belongs to the champions of the covenant of grace [Presbyterians] as much as to their [Anglican] adversaries. It represents the stage in which the christian clings to rule, letter, and privilege.'[170] In the third, synthetic stage Green called evangelical conscience, individual obedience to the divine voice within (the inward light) comprehends or sublimates external law.

Individuals in whom an 'inward light' is kindled are free, and they are impelled by conscience to contribute to the awakening of their fellows and to work for the improvement of society. Rationality and freedom are entwined in the morally awakened individual. It is rational for us to

[166] 'English Commonwealth. Lecture III,' p. 341.
[167] Green, 'Different Senses of "Freedom",' sec. 5. Puritans and Dissenters of an earlier period offered the same sort of arguments for voluntarism and free religious association. See James Jones, *A plea for liberty of conscience: grounded upon the Holy Word, and the royal word of the King: containing twelve weighty reasons against the prosecuting of Protestant dissenters* (London: printed by George Larkin ..., 1684); and D. Defoe, *The Present State of the Parties in Great Britain, particularly an enquiry into the State of the Dissenters in England and the Presbyterians in Scotland* (London: J. Barker, 1712).
[168] 'English Commonwealth. Lecture I,' pp. 294–5.
[169] *Ibid.* Compare to 'Different Senses of "Freedom",' secs. 2, 7.
[170] 'English Commonwealth. Lecture I,' p. 295.

recognize in each of our fellows an equal moral capacity (i.e. potential for bad or good), and it is through encouraging this capacity (self-realization) in others that we help attain our own freedom. Only those individuals who are rational are free, and only rational individuals can create a society in which moral claims can be recognized and reconciled.[171]

Green put his interpretation of Puritanism and Independency to the service of Idealist philosophy and suggested that a Puritan moment awaited its fulfilment. In the ideal religious-political community toward which the Puritans and other Protestant sectaries were striving, external ordinance could eventually be rendered less necessary, if not dispensed with altogether. The principles of Independency, as understood by Green, suggest the Hegelian notion of *Sittlichkeit*, in which is found 'the reconciliation of the mere externality of law and the mere inwardness of morality.'[172] Some Christians, including the Christian Socialists of Green's youth, maintained that the infusion into all members of society of the Christian spirit would mitigate the coercive character of Church and State.

Melvin Richter notes Green's pride in his family relationship (on his paternal side) to Cromwell, and he correctly claims that 'Green saw in [the Liberal Party] and in Philosophical Idealism the fulfilment and correction of Puritanism.'[173] In the English Revolution lectures Green offers historical illustrations of the movements of conscience, subjective religiosity and the spirit of fellowship, and provides an analysis of these as philosophical principles that complements his more abstract observations in the *Prolegomena* and other writings. Yet Richter appears to regard Green's treatment of Puritanism in the 1867 lectures more as a matter of sentimental attraction than as an important analysis of the civil-political consequences of religious faith. Richter thereby diminishes and others ignore the significance of Green's advocacy of contemporary Dissent and Dissenting principles.

---

[171] *Ibid.*, pp. 295–6. Superimposing St. Paul on Kant, Green argues that the recognition of other wills as similar in nature to one's own makes the individual the 'author' of the laws he obeys ('Different Senses of "Freedom",' secs 2–4).

[172] Barker, *Political Thought in England 1848–1914*, p. 27. De Sanctis observes, 'Green pointed out that the main weakness of German thought stemmed from its inability to realize that the reality of Church and State could not correspond to any spiritual idea.' In contrast to the Lutheran Reformation, the English Revolution 'centered itself upon ... the right to freedom of conscience towards both Church and State' ('T. H. Green and the "Force of Circumstances",' p. 6).

[173] *Politics of Conscience*, p. 41.

3.7. MODERN PURITANS AND THE DISSIDENCE
OF DISSENT

Green's view of Puritanism and Independency past and present was highly partisan — and unusual for a son of the Establishment. At the time that Green was representing Puritanism and other forms of anti-establishment Protestantism as the harbingers of modern English freedom, another theological liberal, the poet and critic Matthew Arnold, was deploring the Puritan residue of English culture and the influence of Nonconformity on English liberalism.[174] Like Arnold, Green used the term Puritan imprecisely. He included among Puritans many 'evangelical' Protestant sects of his time as well as 'quietists', like the Quakers. While this may suggest a disregard for historical accuracy, Green was less interested in precise taxonomy than in exposing a basic dichotomy of religious style and spirit.[175] Dissenters of his time also differentiated rather crudely between religion that respected 'conscience' (theirs) and the Establishment communion, which (they claimed) did not.

Green's approving representation of Puritan principles mirrored many features of historical and contemporary Dissenting propaganda. He argued along the lines of Robert Vaughan, William Mitchell Fawcett, Robert William Dale and other Nonconformist controversialists of his time that the 'inward light' and 'religious republicanism' were gifts of Dissent to modern British society and culture.[176] Green believed that religious republicanism embodied in congregational polity had been more conducive to the movement of the spirit than Catholicism, whose valuation of the authority principle had been carried over into the Establishment (the Church of England) and Presbyterianism. Moreover, Green implied that just as the congregational polity and style of worship during the seventeenth century had been conducive to a progressive

---

[174] Arnold's *Culture and Anarchy* began to appear serially in 1867 and was published as a single work in 1869. On Arnold's critique of culture, see especially R. Williams, *Culture and Society: 1780–1950*, revised edition (New York: Columbia UP, 1983 [orig. 1958]), chap. 6.

[175] On problems of taxonomy and genealogy of ideas and religious sects during the sixteenth and seventeenth centuries, see C. Hill, 'History and Denominational History' (1967), in *Collected Essays. Volume Two*, essay one.

[176] R. Vaughan, *Congregationalism: or, the Polity of Independent Churches* (London: Jackson and Walford, 1842); *Religious Republicanism: Six Essays on Congregationalism*, ed. W. M. Fawcett (London: Longmans, Green, 1869); R. W. Dale, 'Congregationalism,' *British Quarterly Review*, 73 (1881), pp. 1–12, 265–88. Robert Vaughan (1795–1868) was a historian and a professor at University College, London, and at Lancashire Independent College. He edited the *British Quarterly Review* between 1845 and 1865 and made it one of the most respected (i.e., moderate) journals of Dissenting opinion (s.v., *DNB*). William Mitchell Fawcett was a London barrister (*Religious Republicanism*, contents page). Dale is discussed in the next chapter. Timothy Lang discusses some of these propagandists (although not Green) and their interpretations of the seventeenth century in *Victorians and the Stuart Heritage*, chap. 3.

spirit, it might prove more effective in maintaining a harmonious and just *civil* order in his own era than would a comprehensive and 'magisterial' state church; a 'Free Church' polity could satisfy the practical *need* for moral order while accommodating liberal social and economic arrangements.

Green's optimism was not without foundation. First, many Dissenting chapels were self-governing congregations electing their pastors. Second, while wealthy Dissenters might dominate the affairs of their congregations, they lacked the *legal* coercive power of lay patrons of Anglican parishes (e.g. gentry who controlled the livings of vicars). As nineteenth-century Dissenters habitually observed, the Church of England was effectively ruled by bishops and made spiritually unnecessary distinctions between clergy and laity. Such distinctions faded to nullity in some Dissenting congregations, the chief claim of the Dissenting minister to superiority over his flock being his superior learning (which in many cases was not obvious). Methodist ministers were often selected by official bodies, but many were less hampered by ecclesiastical and lay control than were the Anglican clergy.[177]

It is significant that as late as 1881, when certain legal advantages of the Church of England had been removed, along with many civil disabilities of Dissenters, Green was recommending the 'congregationalization' of the Church.[178] Disestablishment of the Church of England was politically untenable: while 'much is to be said for it,' every clergyman in some 15,000 parishes with a family to support would regard it 'as a personal wrong.' And disestablishment would further polarize dispute between the 'catholicizing' and 'evangelical' wings of the Anglican communion: 'Whichever prevails' in retaining the 'fabrics of the episcopalian sect,' the 'result will be lamentable.' Disestablishment 'would make [the] clergyman of the future either a mere priest or a mere preacher, instead of [a] leader in useful social work, and in the administration of such public business as is not directly administered by [the] state, as he now often is.'

Still, there was 'a want of congregational life in [the] Church', especially in rural districts where there had been an 'extinction of communal life for all purposes, secular as well' and where the 'people have no

---

[177] See again Vaughan, *Congregationalism*; Fawcett, *Religious Republics*; R. W. Dale, 'The Nonconformists,' *Daily Telegraph*, 25 December 1873, pp. 5–6; and Brown, *Social History of the Nonconformist Ministry*. On squire and parson in the Church of England, see Owen Chadwick's dual biography, *Victorian Miniature* (CUP, 1991 [orig. 1960]).

[178] 'Notes for a Speech on Church Reform at Merton. Wed. Dec. 7? 1881': CBG copy in GP 1(c). These notes, with a report of the speech from the *Oxford Chronicle* (10 December 1881, p. 8), are printed in *AW*, pp. 376-9. The Irish Church had been disestablished in 1869, most Oxford and Cambridge fellowships were freed from credal subscription in 1871, and laws prohibiting the burial of Dissenters in Churchyards with non–Anglican rites were abolished in 1880.

share, direct or indirect in appointment of clergy, and are not associated with him in conduct either of worship, or of school, or of relief of sick and poor.' In many urban districts the 'practical efficiency of clergy' is low. In a *congregationalized* church worshippers would play some part in selecting pastors and in influencing the mode of worship, while bishops would continue to ensure the quality of ordinands and would see that 'a certain elastic uniformity was maintained in order of worship.'[179] A national 'Congregational Council' might retain a veto function over local decisions. Green concludes that the 'success of any such plan manifestly depends on [the] possibility of restoring congregational life in the parishes. Perhaps too late: but begin with trying to do this.'

Green clearly believed that a salutary liberalization of British religion might be effected through a form of 'Puritanization', and that Puritan-radical Protestant experiments conducted since the seventeenth century suggested civil as well as spiritual benefits. Green's recommendations for church reform are remarkable not so much for their practical value, which is debatable, but for their acceptance of the virtues of congregational polity and religious pluralism proclaimed by Dissenters themselves. In *Culture and Anarchy* (1869), Matthew Arnold ridiculed his Protestant contemporaries who held as a badge of honour their continuity with Puritanism and the Reformation.[180] The true legacy of Puritanism to modern England, Arnold said, was the narrowness of the Dissenting world-view, the 'Philistinism' and 'Hebraism' of Dissenters that made them hostile to 'culture', to the state and to many plans for systematic improvement of society.

Some Victorian Dissenters, however, were well aware that their communal feeling and the character of their organizations represented the worst as well as the best aspects of English polity and society. As William Mitchell Fawcett observed, 'Novelists who hold up to ridicule the Congregational Salem may find similar food for their humour in our

---

[179] 'Declarations of opinion not to be required at ordination' (Green, 'Notes on Church Reform'). There is a marginal note reading 'How define congregation?' Green, like other church reformers, was apparently uncertain about the governing role of casual attendants. T. M. Herbert, minister of the Independent Church at Cheadle in 1869, claimed that Congregationals did not believe in an 'outward rite' as a condition of membership in a Christian community, but observed that some attendants at worship were still excluded from the closer (e.g. administrative) deliberations of the congregation. 'There remains outside each Congregational Church a body of persons who join statedly in its worship, larger in general than the church itself, and called, by a name misleading to strangers, the congregation.' Herbert, 'The External Relations of Congregationalism,' in *Religious Republicanism*, ed. Fawcett, pp. 61–7.

[180] In 1862 English Dissenters celebrated the two hundredth anniversary of the ejection of several hundred Church of England ministers from their livings for refusal to conform to the rubric of the Book of Common Prayer. In 1872 there were numerous commemorations in England of the St Bartholomew's Day Massacre, the slaughter in 1572 of 20,000 French Protestants.

town-councils, boards of guardians, and wherever indeed the small shop-keeping classes rule.'[181] Both Green and Matthew Arnold recognized that the Dissenting interest had defined the character of Victorian liberalism. Yet Matthew Arnold interpreted the 'Dissidence of Dissent' as a crippling malady of British culture, while Green saw Dissenting congregations as vehicles for a progressive bourgeois republicanism.[182]

Arnold saw in the 'Dissidence of Dissent' men at war with the Greek ideals of self-perfection and self-government. Green saw the Greek and Dissenting spirits as complementary. Arnold proclaimed in the chapter 'Hebraism and Hellenism' in *Culture and Anarchy*,

> As Hellenism speaks of thinking clearly, seeing things in their essence and beauty, as a grand and precious feat for man to achieve, so Hebraism speaks of becoming conscious of sin, or awakening to a sense of sin, as a feat of this kind ... As one passes and repasses from Hellenism to Hebraism, from Plato to St. Paul, one feels inclined to rub one's eyes and ask oneself whether man is indeed a gentle and simple being, showing traces of a noble and divine nature; or an unhappy chained captive, labouring with groanings that cannot be uttered to free himself from the body of this death.[183]

Arnold saw the quest for sanctification as self-torture, and as incompatible with moral beauty. In his lectures 'On the Different Senses of "Freedom"', Green presented Hellenism and the spiritual journey of Saul of Tarsus as discrete but related moments of human consciousness, which in their synthesis reaffirmed the traditional meaning of Atonement as reconciliation. Some routes to grace and moral certainty lead inevitably to communion with that which is most beautiful.

To Puritans the instrument of piety, morality and social duty is the Christed Self, and the individual's quest for sanctification was above all a journey of feeling (not reason). Yet religion served to awaken the individual to the reason within him, and intuition and feeling might work in conjunction with reason. Richard Greaves has argued that Puritan epistemology, for all its appeal to Spirit or intuition, did not always emphasize a *divergence* between Reason and Spirit. Some politically, theologically and intellectually conservative Puritans (including Presbyterians) insisted on retaining reason as the ultimate test of inspi-

---

[181] Fawcett, 'Congregational Polity,' in *Religious Republicanism*, ed. Fawcett, p. 56.

[182] The motto of the *Nonconformist*, the newspaper edited by Edward Miall, was 'The Dissidence of Dissent and the Protestantism of the Protestant religion!' Clyde Binfield remarks, 'Theirs [Dissenters'] was above all a culture based on committed chapel membership and voluntary zeal. Its traditions are prouder than Arnold was able to understand in his high-minded, but remarkably crude, idealisation of culture.' 'Hebrews Hellenized? English Evangelical Nonconformity and Culture, 1840–1940' in *A History of Religion in Britain: Practice and Belief from Pre-Roman Times to the Present*, ed. W. J. Sheils (Oxford: Clarendon, 1994), pp. 322–45.

[183] *Culture and Anarchy*, edited and with introduction by J. Dover Wilson (CUP, 1960), pp. 135–6.

ration.[184] As the Puritan divine and Baconian philosopher Richard Baxter (1615–91) claimed,

> the Spirit and reason are not to be ... disjoined, much less opposed. As reason sufficeth not without the Spirit, being dark and asleep; so the Spirit worketh not on the will but by reason.[185]

It should be noted that while Baxter's conception of will is somewhat different from Green's, Green would otherwise have agreed with Baxter's formula.[186]

Green's religio-philosophical view of conscience includes a social principle. While all Christian traditions have been concerned with the salvation of the individual, they also reveal beliefs about the relationships of God to His children, of the righteous to the unredeemed, and of religious bodies or communities to wider society (whether conceived of as the nation, Christian civilization or humanity). We have seen how the Christian Socialists retreated from doctrinal controversy and emphasized the moral and ethical lessons of Christianity. Christians in complex commercial societies could learn simple and practical lessons from the example of the Nazarene.[187] Certain forms of catholic Protestantism and evangelicalism proposed a congruity of religious values and social mores, of piety and morality, and of religious and secular law — in other words, theocracy.[188] But Green embraced the weaker or 'freer' forms of these traditions, endorsing toleration and the movements of individual conscience against the authority principle expressed, in different eras, by Archbishop Laud, J. H. Newman and other 'children of those who stoned the prophets.'[189]

---

[184] R.L. Greaves, *The Puritan Revolution and Educational Thought. Background for Reform* (New Brunswick, NJ: Rutgers UP, 1969), chaps. 4, 6.

[185] Quoted *ibid.*, p. 115.

[186] Green cited the *Reliquiae Baxterianae* (1696) in his English Revolution lectures. Richard Baxter was a Presbyterian and an opponent of the radical Independents and other sectaries. It is possible that Green was aware of Baxter's view of spirit and reason and recognized it as an innovation of the English Revolution and an anticipation of Idealist theories. *Harris and Morrow*, pp. 348–51 (notes to their edition of Green's 'Four Lectures'). On Baxter, see also B. Willey, *The Seventeenth Century Background* (London: Chatto and Windus, 1934), pp. 72–5; and W. Lamont, *Richard Baxter and the Millennium* (London: Croom Helm, 1979).

[187] Richter, *Politics of Conscience*, p. 42. J. S. Mill valued Christianity as well: Vernon, 'J. S. Mill and the Religion of Humanity'; Britton, 'John Stuart Mill on Christianity;' and S. V. LaSelva, '"A Single Truth": Mill on Harm, Paternalism and Good Samaritanism,' *Political Studies*, 36 (1988), pp. 486–96.

[188] The Church of England and Scottish Presbyterianism in the reign of Charles I, and contemporary European Calvinism were all 'catholic' in the sense that they claimed continuity with the true Apostolic church. The conviction of continuity is exactly what the Tractarians in Green's time feared had been lost to their church.

[189] 'Charles [I] and Laud alike represented that jesuitical conscience (if I may be allowed the expression) which is fatal to true loyalty ... Such a conscience ... dare not look into

3.8. RELIGION, MORALITY, COMMUNITY:
IDEALISM VS. ARNOLDISM

Green was concerned with the nature of Belief, and with the effects (as it were) of Belief on the individual. He was also convinced that spirituality could be experienced and sustained *communally*, through fellowship, and that the established church of his time was, by and large, less successful in promoting fellowship than were the 'free' churches. People needed to participate in religious life as a corporate experience and a shared principle, and from religious activity they would learn to govern themselves and others. Green's view of religion and civil society resembled Hegel's notion of the 'positivity of the Christian religion.' In Hegel's view Christian positivity was revealed by the ways in which the state had co-opted organic religion (including the spiritual, moral, and aesthetic yearnings of the *Volk*) in order to ensure civil order, morality and national purpose. In 'The Positivity of the Christian Religion' (ca. 1795) criticizing institutional Christianity, Hegel suggested that the church (by which he meant the German state churches: e.g. in Prussia, Lutheranism) had lost sight of the civil purposes of religion:

> the aim and essence of all true religion, our religion included, is human morality, and … all the more detailed doctrines of Christianity, all means of propagating them, and all its obligations (whether obligations to believe or obligations to perform actions in themselves otherwise arbitrary) have their worth and their sanctity appraised according to their close or distant connection with that aim.[190]

As we have seen, Bernard Reardon regards Green as a *theological* epigone of Hegel, but his and similar assessments obscure the important differences between Green and Hegel in their understandings of the ideal relationship of Church and State. Hegel came to believe that the State had supplanted the Church in the all-important matter of tutoring morality; that the state, having absorbed this religious function, was entitled to mould the church according to its own (civil) requirements; and that the subject's attitude toward the state religion must be one of

---

the law of liberty, or conceive of the operation of God except in a system of prescribed institutions, about which no questions are asked, and in the maintenance of which cruelty becomes mercy and falsehood truth' ('English Commonwealth. Lecture I,' pp. 287–8). On the question of Puritanism and its enemies in relation to toleration, see W. Lamont, *Puritanism and Historical Controversy* (Montreal: McGill-Queen's UP, 1996).

[190] Hegel, 'The Positivity of the Christian Religion,' p. 68. Hegel here equates positivity with ecclesiastical regulation and restrictions on the human spirit. Ancient Greek religion was a folk religion without institutions to burden the human conscience and humans' attempts to obtain moral beauty. Jesus of Nazareth's spiritual journey had also been 'free', and he ran into conflict with static Jewish law. But 'Christianity', like Judaism, took on a positive and binding form. See also Kroner's introduction to the above (pp. 1–66), and Reardon, 'T. H. Green as a Theologian.'

all-or-nothing.[191] Green, however, believed in the constant reformation of the church from within and without. He could not agree with Hegel that the ethical content of religion could be fixed by and in the state.

During the German Wars of Liberation (1806–13) Hegel adopted the view that the German states, in order to prevent domination by revolutionary France, had to adopt French principles of law, organization and discipline. By such means a uniform and energizing German morality could be implanted through state control of religious and educational matters. 'Right' Hegelians saw in the state a unified source of morality (*Sittlichkeit*), including religious teaching. Because civil institutions and law had been formed by religious principles, and because (in the German states) the church had been in effect absorbed by the state, religious morality had been transformed into civil morality, supposedly effecting the ethical, spiritual and aesthetic unity sought by Novalis. Not only German conservatives but many political liberals accepted this view. J. G. Droysen (1808–84), a liberal parliamentarian, called the Prussian bureaucracy 'the most noble spiritual force in the Fatherland.'[192] As James Sheehan remarks,

> The principal reason why many liberals were willing to acknowledge the state's power in educational affairs was their belief that it was a necessary ally against other, even more dangerous influences at work in German life, such as the Catholic church, whose hold over its members had to be broken before an enlightened public could emerge.[193]

Some German Idealists argued that *Sittlichkeit* could be sustained through the ethical and educational activities of a special class in society, which conservative Idealists identified with the state bureaucracy. Hegel discussed the identity and functions of a 'first' or 'universal' class in *System of Ethical Life* (1802).[194] Hegel's first class was 'free' — a group of individuals exempt from physical labour and the degrading competition of the market who would exemplify the process of self-realization for other members of society. As described in his *System of Ethical Life*, Hegel's 'first class' was to have a special social identity without special political authority: 'The first class is clear, mirror-bright identity, the spirit [*Geist*] of the other classes.'[195] (Hegel's idea of a universal, representative class reappeared, of course, in his glorification of the civil ser-

---

[191] Avineri, *Hegel's Theory of the Modern State*, chaps. 2–3, 9; C. Taylor, *Hegel and Modern Society* (CUP, 1979); and Toews, *Hegelianism*, Part Two.
[192] Quoted by J. Sheehan, *German Liberalism in the Nineteenth Century* (Chicago: Chicago UP, 1978), p. 40.
[193] *Ibid.*, p. 41.
[194] Dickey, *Hegel*, pp. 231–77.
[195] Hegel quoted by Dickey, *Hegel*, p. 276.

vice in the *Philosophy of Right*: the *Volk* 'is that part of the State which does not know what it wants … '.)[196]

Samuel Coleridge, the most brilliant Germanizer of early nineteenth-century Britain, introduced the idea of a 'clerisy' in *On the Constitution of the Church and State* (1830), referring to a corps of teachers within a reformed and rejuvenated Church of England which would be responsible for the spiritual and ethical development of the nation.[197] Because the religious 'powers that be' in Britain were a 'mere mirror' of an unreformed state (Coleridge was writing shortly after Catholic Emancipation and before the parliamentary reforms of 1832), this clerisy would have to be composed of men neither associated with a corrupt establishment nor 'alienated' from society.[198] They would correct both aristocracy and democracy. While Coleridge was concerned with liberation, he was equally concerned with authority and order (as was Carlyle); he cannot be characterized as an egalitarian. Like other Romantics, Coleridge brought traditional Christian concerns about 'salvation' and moral perfectibility into the modern age by considering the consequences of the rise of commercial society.[199]

For all his supposed authoritarianism, Hegel was perhaps more sensitive than Coleridge to the consequences of social functionalism, the division of labour and 'alienation'. Hegel was confident that neither his clerisy would become indifferent to the producers nor the producers antagonistic to the clerisy. Yet if Hegel's idea of a 'universal class' was not realized in the German bureaucracy and *Bildungsbürgertum*, neither did Britain witness the success of a Coleridgean clerisy.[200] British society did not allow the development of a reactionary intelligentsia or an unequivocally progressive one.[201] Green adopted neither Hegel's idea of a universal class nor Coleridge's idea of a clerisy, yet he developed similar ideas about morality and social values and the means by which the Moral Ideal might be advanced. Green had not read Hegel's 'Positivity of the Christian Religion' (the essay was not published until

[196] *Philosophy of Right*, trans. Knox, secs. 205, 303 (quotation).

[197] Knights, *The Idea of the Clerisy in the Nineteenth Century*.

[198] *Ibid.*, pp. 3–15. See *On the Constitution of the Church and State* (London: J. M. Dent, 1972), chaps. 8–9 and the section entitled 'Idea of the Christian Church'.

[199] J. S. Mill, 'Coleridge' (1840), in *Utilitarianism and Other Essays*, ed. A. Ryan (London: Penguin, 1987), pp. 177–226. See also Morrow, *Coleridge's Political Thought*.

[200] It has been argued that the German intelligentsia's acceptance of dependence on the state bureaucracy and subordination to the aristocratic ruling class, combined with its voluntary isolation from popular politics even before the 1848 revolutions, resulted in an alignment with or co-optation by 'reaction'. F. Stern, *The Politics of Cultural Despair: a Study in the Rise of the Germanic Ideology* (Berkeley: California UP, 1961); and F. Ringer, *The Decline of the German Mandarins. The German Academic Community, 1890–1933* (Cambridge, MA: MIT UP, 1969).

[201] See the conclusion of Raymond Williams, *Culture and Society: 1780–1950*, which remains a masterful explanation of the conditions of cultural leadership in Britain.

1907) and he was probably unacquainted with the *System of Ethical Life*; yet his understanding of Christianity in relation to *Sittlichkeit* and of the state's capacity for encouraging or corrupting the moral sense was distinctly Hegelian. Green had certainly read Hegel's *Philosophy of Right*. Paul Harris and John Morrow have suggested that Green's understanding of the impact on morality of commercial values owed something to Coleridge's *Lay Sermons* (1816–17) as well as the aforementioned *Constitution of Church and State*.[202] Green subsequently took a rather more sympathetic view of the entrepreneurial middle classes than did Coleridge. Green was less alarmed by the rise of commercial society than were Hegel and Coleridge, and he saw bourgeois democracy as inextricably linked to the development of the Moral Ideal. In a sense Green brought forward the ideas of Hegel and Coleridge about the ameliorative role of the intelligentsia, adapting them to an age of bourgeois politics.

Christopher Harvie, in *The Lights of Liberalism*, includes T. H. Green among a sort of clerisy constituted by young men at Oxford and Cambridge between 1860 and 1886 (most of whom, not incidentally, had evangelical upbringings). These men were committed to simultaneous reform of Church and State as conditions for the establishment of a just and moral society in the face of the clashes of liberal capitalism and the vicissitudes of democratic politics. This clerisy did not assume the forms suggested by Hegel and Coleridge, or even that of Matthew Arnold, who had such high hopes for the 'lights of Liberalism' as a corrective force in British culture and politics.[203] Explanation of why these intellectuals were supposedly so ineffective is beyond the scope of the present study, but it is significant that Arnold saw their failure in their reluctance "'to work inwardly upon the predominant force in our politics — the great middle class — and to cure its spirit.'"[204]

Significantly, Harvie presents an image of Green as a self-fashioned and self-conscious 'plain' man of the people, 'recall[ing] Wesley on circuit, a secular Wesley whose gospel was the spiritual fulfilment of individuals in the cooperative effort of a political commonwealth.'[205] As much as this image may seem garish or sentimental, Harvie conveys

[202] *Harris and Morrow*, pp. 361–2 (editorial notes)

[203] Arnold wrote of the 'lights of Liberalism' in 1886: 'The great Parliamentary machine has gone creaking and grinding on … and there one sees them [University men] now, helping to grind — all of them zealous, all of them intelligent, some of them brilliant and leading. What has been ground, what has been produced with their help? Really, very much the same sort of thing which was produced without it?' ('The Nadir of Liberalism,' in *Nineteenth Century*, quoted in Harvie, *Lights*, p. 9).

[204] Quoted in *Lights*, p. 9. One of the Liberal lights in the House of Commons, James Bryce, remarked to the historian E. A. Freeman that Arnold was a babbler who should leave politics and religion alone (Bryce to Freeman, 18 February 1887: Bodleian MSS. Bryce 9, fols. 263–5).

[205] *Lights*, p. 23. By describing Green as a self-fashioned and self-conscious plain man I mean that he (as Harvie agrees) had a habit of identifying with 'the people' in a way

here something essential about Green's inspiration and purpose. In analysing in 1886 the failures of mid-Victorian Liberal intellectuals, Arnold described precisely the mission Green *did* accept — that of 'curing the spirit' of the middling classes. While historians commonly regard the era of Gladstone, Disraeli, Rosebery and Salisbury as that of the first flowering of 'mass politics', no less was it one of middle-class ascendancy. Indeed, the struggle for dominance between Conservative and Liberal parties following the Second Reform Act (1867) depended less on rallying the lower classes to the banner of party than on winning the hearts and minds of the middle orders. As H. J. Hanham has observed, middle-class Nonconformists after mid century formed 'the largest, most active, and most high-principled section of the Liberal Party ...'.[206] The ideas and practices of Victorian Nonconformity revealed to Green both the malady and the cure of the British spirit; and in the Liberal Party that Nonconformists did so much to animate between 1830 and 1914 Green saw the future of Britain.

Discussion of T. H. Green and Matthew Arnold and their beliefs about English Nonconformity in their own time has led us some distance from our original consideration of the metaphysical aspect of Green's philosophy. However, this chapter has attempted to demonstrate that Green's 'eternal consciousness' or 'spiritual principle' was a 'self-objectifying principle' (*LPPO*, secs. 175-7) that could be seen in the self-realizing behaviour of individuals. It was simultaneously a presence registered in or revealed by the historical process, in what Hegel called the movement of the Spirit. In Green's view, *Geist* in the sense of a growing consciousness of freedom—experienced both individually and collectively — had brought Christian civilization, and British society in particular, to its current juncture. It was his belief too that people within his own society who had achieved a significant degree of self-actualization included those with spiritual insights, sharing a sense of religious duty; and that such people were specially placed to direct the course of the national future.

---

that denied his privileged origins and social position. Green's nephew, John St Loe Strachey (1860–1927), reported a story about Green as young Oxford fellow: on a trip home to Yorkshire Green was chided by a farmer that he resembled not an Oxford don but a cattle drover (St Loe Strachey and J. A. Symonds recollections in *GP* 1c).

[206] Hanham, *Elections and Party Management. Politics in the Time of Disraeli and Gladstone,* quoted in N. J. Richards, 'British Nonconformity and the Liberal Party 1868–1906,' *Journal of Religious History,* 9 (1977), p. 387.

CHAPTER FOUR

Religious Principles and Social Change

As far as he had been an observer of English life, he should say Congregationalism was an essential element in what he might call the higher life, especially of English towns. He always felt sure, when he came amongst Congregationalists, that he should meet men who appreciated the true nature of political freedom ... Among Congregationalists he found the questions involving the essential principles of political justice were sure to be understood.[1]

4.1. INTRODUCTION

The preceding chapter has considered Green's metaphysics, indicated some sources of his religious views and suggested how his understanding of religion undergirded his political ethics. The present chapter explores some connections between the religious and the social and political dimensions of Victorian Liberalism. The main purposes here are to clarify T. H. Green's understanding of the mission of the Liberal Party and to demonstrate the connection in the minds of Green and many contemporary Liberals between religious principles and social goals. I discuss in the following pages aspects of Green's political life in order to draw attention to his unusually sympathetic and cordial relations with Protestant Nonconformists. I attempt thereby to demonstrate that Green's Liberal partisanship rested upon an understanding of Liberal 'belief' quite similar to that of the Nonconformist Liberals whose

[1] T. H. Green, 'Congregationalism, 27 May 1880': speech as reported in the Oxford Chronicle (29 May 1880, p. 8), reprinted in *AW*, p. 368. The speech was occasioned by the laying of the foundation stone of a Congregational chapel and school in Cowley Road, Oxford.

religious and civil demands he supported. The chapter begins with a discussion of the condition of English Nonconformity and of Nonconformist political activism from about 1830, with attention to the political and cultural dynamic of the 'Church–Chapel' (i.e. Established Church–Dissenting Protestantism) divide. The chapter then turns to Green's practical, reformist activities that brought him into contact with Nonconformists from the early 1860s: the struggle for a national system of elementary education, the reform of 'middle-class' schools, the temperance movement and the campaign for religious equality in the Ancient Universities.

Green's religious beliefs were bound up with his theory of moral freedom and informed his understanding of culture and politics. His acceptance of many principles of liberal theology and his commitment to religious liberty made him vulnerable to charges of infidelity and agnosticism. Like J. S. Mill, Green regarded 'freedom of conscience' as a concomitant of individuality, and both philosophers expressed scepticism that morality and social order could be *imposed* on a complex commercial society. Green believed that social harmony and the wider enjoyment of freedom could only emerge from a state of society in which individuals of varying opinions and talents, and enjoying different degrees of material security, saw that they had a stake in evolving social organization and in the maintenance of civil institutions. This kind of consciousness could not develop in the absence of freedom of conscience — a spiritual aspect of security of personhood — and where expression of personality was permitted for some individuals and restricted in others. Religious liberty was therefore a necessary condition of social order and of progress.

Concern for religious liberty had been one of the defining characteristics of British Whiggism as well as of the broader (including Continental and American) liberal tradition. Foregoing discussions have already noted the strong correspondence between Green's youthful Radicalism and contemporary currents of liberal Protestantism, as well as the Christian Social movement of mid century, with its *rejection* of key elements of orthodox (liberal) political economy. British Liberalism became increasingly polarized towards the end of Green's life between a laissez-faire faction and a growing segment of the party advocating 'state intervention'. Yet one plank of the Liberal platform that provided coherence to Liberal political identity throughout the nineteenth century was the commitment to religious liberty. To be sure, Liberals who pushed this demand to great lengths found themselves increasingly consigned to the 'faddist' fringe after about 1885, but commitment to the principle remained a touchstone of Liberal identity. Moreover (as shall be demonstrated in Chapter Five below), religious conviction fostered an approach to social questions that registered strongly in British politics into the twentieth century.

A revealing instance of Green's liberality with regard to freedom of conscience and spiritual expression was his attitude toward the 'Bradlaugh Case'. Charles Bradlaugh, a professed atheist and advocate of contraception, was elected four times (1880–5) as a Liberal to represent the Parliamentary borough of Northampton but was denied a seat in the Commons (until 1886) for refusing to take an oath of religious faith. While Green found it regrettable that the electors of Northampton should repeatedly choose such a representative he believed that Bradlaugh should be allowed his seat in the Commons. He had no real sympathy with Bradlaugh's militant atheism, but like other Liberals and Radicals Green denied the authority of Parliament to dictate matters of faith. Thus the precise reason for his espousal of Bradlaugh's cause was his conviction that the *vox populi* trumped legislative authority.[2]

His apparent tolerance for atheism and his occasional statements about transcendence of historical religion aside, Green was far less interested in yielding a *new* religion — as proposed by, for instance, the Comtists, the Ethical Socialists, or (later) the Labour Church — than in harnessing actually existing religious sentiment for moral and social purposes.[3] The present chapter underlines a point made in earlier chapters about interpretation of innovative and traditional aspects of Green's thought: in focusing on Green's conscious attempts to correct prevailing moral and social doctrines, scholars obscure continuities between his ethics and the beliefs and assumptions held by a wider British public.

As has been demonstrated in Chapter Two, Green believed in a stage-like progress of the moral ideal; that some societies and their institutions were morally superior to others; and that some individuals, institutions and organizations represented a truer conception of the

---

[2]   *GP* 1(c): 'Notes for a speech given at a North Ward Liberal Association meeting on Tuesday, March 7, 1882' — Green's last public address. That only nine Liberal MPs opposed Gladstone's Affirmation bill (1882) — to allow parliamentarians to substitute an affirmation for an oath — is not an indication of Liberals' agnosticism but rather that most regarded Parliament as a political, not a Christian assembly. See Walter L. Arnstein, *The Bradlaugh Case. Atheism, Sex, and Politics among the Late Victorians* (OUP, 1965); E. Royle, *Radicals, Secularists and Republicans. Popular Freethought in Britain, 1866–1915* (Manchester: Manchester UP, 1980); Bradley, *The Optimists*, pp. 97–8; and F. A. d'Arcy, 'Charles Bradlaugh and the English Republican Movement, 1868–1878,' *HJ*, 25 (1982), pp. 367–83.

[3]   See K. S. Inglis, *Churches and the Working Classes in Victorian England* (London: Routledge, 1963), pp. 218ff. (on the Labour Church); Wright, *The Religion of Humanity*; and I. D. MacKillop, *The British Ethical Societies* (CUP, 1986). E. Belfort Bax remarks on the tensions between religion and secularism in British Radicalism and socialism down to 1918: see *Reminiscences and Reflexions of a Mid and Late Victorian* (New York: A. M. Kelley, 1967 [orig. 1918]).

moral ideal than others, were embodiments of our social inclinations (as opposed to our selfish and socially antagonistic impulses), and thus deserved the attention and the obedience of rational people. Philosophical Idealists detected an evolution of human culture — in some societies — toward the more complete and comprehensive articulation of humans' capacities for reason. Like Kant, Green believed that while social struggle is as much a part of humans' (biological) nature as the instincts of benevolence and cooperation, our 'nature' and our history reveal our improving collective capacity for social harmony. It was therefore realistic to imagine a state of 'perpetual peace' as a goal of human history.[4] Green was perhaps more optimistic than Kant in his conviction that religious teaching grounded in a proper understanding of human nature could offset what Kant called (in *Religion Within the Limits of Reason Alone*) the 'radical evil in human nature'.

Green's interest in radical Protestantism in the European past parallelled his interest in forms of modern Christianity. He clearly preferred non-magisterial Protestantism as that which expressed most completely the spirit that refuses to be bound, an inchoate yearning for moral perfection in the individual and in society. Yet Green was by no means unique in recognizing (or perhaps rather, asserting) that 'Puritan' principles had penetrated the British national consciousness. To Matthew Arnold, Nonconformity appeared as one of those unruly forces, such as the working-class element in British politics, that presented obstacles to an enlightened liberal order. In relation to national education, Arnold's abiding interest, the Dissidence of Dissent represented not 'principle', but do-nothing-ism.[5] Green, in contrast, believed that Puritanism had had an ameliorative effect on modern society. He displayed this conviction by proclaiming the virtues of contemporary Dissent — as indicated by the quotation at the head of this chapter — and by cooperating with high-minded Dissenters in the pursuit of various causes and by encouraging their constructive engagement with social problems.

Green's celebrated defence of positive liberty or freedom must be understood in relation to his view of Dissent and Puritan principles. Although Green's doctrine of positive liberty has been commonly taken as a rationale for 'state interference', 'grandmotherly government' and

---

[4]   On Kant's views of sociability, morality, and historical development, see A. W. Wood, 'Unsocial Sociability: the Anthropological Basis of Kantian Ethics,' *Philosophical Topics*, 19 (1991), pp. 325–51; P. Nicholson, 'Kant, Revolutions and History' in *Essays on Kant's Political Philosophy*, ed. H. L. Williams (Chicago: Chicago UP, 1992), pp. 249–68; and P. Kleingeld, 'Kant, History, and the Idea of Moral Development,' *History of Philosophy Quarterly*, 16 (1999), pp. 59–80.

[5]   See F. G. Walcott, *The Origins of 'Culture and Anarchy'. Matthew Arnold and Popular Education in England* (Toronto: Toronto UP, 1970), especially chap. 4; and P. Honan, *Matthew Arnold. A Life* (Cambridge, MA: Harvard UP, 1983), chaps. 14–15.

'constructionism', he justified state action in terms of removing obstacles to individual self-realization. Like earlier generations of reformers and liberals, Green believed that one side of moral, social and political reform was destructive or negative: individuals had to be freed of restraints from certain actions. The denial of recognition of full personhood and personality to some classes or categories of individuals (e.g. slaves) hampered the development of the moral ideal within societies. This was true whether inequality was based on fixed legal (or socially assigned) distinctions among persons or on negotiated ('free') social interaction — inequality resulting from 'contract' instead of inherited status.[6]

In 'Liberal Legislation and Freedom of Contract' (1881), Green reviewed for his audience various government interferences in private affairs and contractual relations, which were demonstrably in the best interests of individuals and society. Factory acts restricting the conditions of employment of women and children, as well as legislation intended to secure better urban sanitation, had been implemented during the early and middle years of the nineteenth century, when 'laissez-faire' economic and political doctrines emerged as the conventional wisdom of the British governing classes. Such interferences, occurring in a 'laissez-faire' political climate, indicated an explicit acknowledgment by the governing classes that less favoured individuals — Green referred to them as 'the suffering classes' — were not practically able to remove themselves from physically and morally deleterious conditions of work and habitation.[7] Compulsory education (see discussion below) had finally, or nearly, been achieved with the 1870 Education Act due to widespread recognition that

> Without a command of certain elementary arts and knowledge, the individual in modern society is as effectually crippled as by the loss of a limb or broken constitution. He is not free to develop his faculties … [I]t is as certainly

[6]   In *Ancient Law* (1861) and subsequent writings, Henry Maine identified as a chief characteristic of 'progressive' societies the establishment of social identity and status through individual acts of 'contract'. In ancient 'Aryan' society, as among the ancient Celts and in modern India, it was inherited status which determined the individual's rights, duties and career in life. In Western states developing under the influence of Greek civilization and Roman law individuals had been enabled through legal devices to move somewhat beyond fixed social custom and to make 'voluntary adjustments' in their social and economic interactions. See C. Brinton, *English Political Thought in the Nineteenth Century* (Cambridge, MA: Harvard UP, 1949), pp. 266–81; and Burrow, *Evolution and Society*, chap. 5.

[7]   Green also remarks that a legal and moral argument can be made against labour contracts under which, by mutual agreement, labour is sold 'under conditions which make it impossible for the person selling it ever to become a free contributor to social good in any form … [, as] when a man bargains to work under conditions fatal to health, e.g. in an unventilated factory' ('Liberal Legislation,' in *Harris and Morrow*, p. 201).

within the province of the state to prevent children from growing up in that
kind of ignorance which practically excludes them from a free career in life,
as it is within its province to require that sort of building and drainage necessary for public health.[8]

This sort of basic freedom *from* external restrictions on self-realization
was the condition for wider, socially enjoyed 'freedom', and a state of
society in which individuals framed moral justifications for their own
actions, and created an imperative to contribute directly or indirectly to
the good of others.

Green believed that Dissenters' struggles for religious liberty and
social parity with the Anglican Establishment constituted a *collective*
struggle for social and political inclusion, and that their exclusion from
participation in many aspects of British life was incompatible with recognized principles of justice and social order.[9] We have seen in the preceding chapter how Green objected to religious regulation. In his view,
the restrictions on Dissenting worship and on Dissenters' civic and
social participation amounted to something like caste-laws, and their
survival was a reproach to the industrious, just and liberal spirit in British society. Although Green romanticized the struggles of Dissent, he
also recognized the positive and constructive consequences of their
efforts, both historically and in his own time.

4.2. LIBERALISM AND THE DISSENTING EXPERIENCE

Dissenters not only asserted themselves in their sectarian 'interest' but
played a part disproportionate to their numbers in Britain during the
1830s, '40s and '50s in agitations for Complete Suffrage, 'free trade',
administrative reform, anti-militarism and primary education — campaigns which had done much to define the political identity and agenda
of the parliamentary Liberal Party, formally constituted in 1859. Complete suffragism and anti-militarism after 1838 were broadly plebeian
movements, rather than autonomously working-class in character.
Many Radical leaders were bourgeois 'free-thinkers' or Dissenters (and
almost without exception advocated Church disestablishment). John
Bright, the leader of Parliamentary Radicalism from the 1850s, was a
Quaker, as was Joseph Sturge, a leader of the Peace Society. Henry Vincent, an influential complete suffragist from the working class, established a Chartist Church at Bath. In many cases, plebeian Radicalism

[8]   *Ibid.*
[9]   Julia Stapleton has recently commented on the significance for modern British politi-
      cal thought of Green's Radical vision of inclusiveness: 'Political Thought, Elites and
      the State in Modern Britain,' *HJ*, 42 (1999), p. 253. On religious emancipation in the lib-
      eral world-view, see S. Wendehorst, 'Emancipation as Path to National Integration' in
      *The Emancipation of Catholics, Jews and Protestants: Minorities and the Nation-State in
      Nineteenth Century Europe*, ed. R. Liedtke and S. Wendehorst (Manchester: Manches-
      ter UP, 1999), chap. 10.

and reformism were justified in religious or quasi-religious terms.[10] While few of these agitations were of distinctly sectarian character, Dissenters were impelled toward political involvement by what might be called their religious instincts. The struggle for repeal of the Corn Laws (directed by the Anti-Corn Law League, 1838–46), which would result in the 'Big Loaf' for the common people instead of an artificially enriched land-owning elite, seemed simply consistent with God's purpose, as Dissenters saw it.[11]

The mid-Victorian vision of Britain as a constitutional and democratic monarchy, committed to international 'free trade' and to 'moral suasion' in world politics was not only a fundamentally Liberal one, but one with which Dissenters habitually identified, and which they contrasted to a corrupt order upheld by the Established Church. Church and aristocracy had been favourite targets of Radical ideologists since the time of Thomas Paine, Joseph Priestley and William Godwin, and the English commercial classes found common ground with plebeian radicals in placing responsibility for inefficiency and injustice at the feet of the establishment.[12] The importance of this critique of the Established Church should not be underestimated in assessing the composition of British reformism into the nineteenth century.[13] Indeed, the 'ideology' of popular Protestantism since the Glorious Revolution, emphasizing Protestant unity and the abolition of the connection between the state

[10] See R. G. Cowherd, *The Politics of English Dissent* (New York: New York UP, 1956); A. Tyrrell, *Joseph Sturge and the Moral Radical Party in Early Victorian Britain* (London: Croom Helm, 1987); and M. C. Finn, *After Chartism. Class and Nation in English Radical Politics, 1848–1874* (CUP, 1993). On these phenomena in relation to party formation, see N. Gash, *Politics in the Age of Peel. A Study in the Technique of Parliamentary Representation 1830–1850* (New York: Norton, 1971 (orig. 1953)); Vincent, *Formation of the British Liberal Party*; and Parry, *Rise and Fall of Liberal Government*.

[11] On the Nonconformist currents of liberal 'revolutionism' since ca. 1830, see F. R. Salter, 'Political Nonconformity in the Eighteen-Thirties,' *Transactions of the Royal Historical Society*, 5th series, no. 3 (1953), pp. 125–43; C. Binfield, 'Thomas Binney and Congregationalism's "Special Mission",' *Transactions of the Congregational Historical Society*, 21 (1971), pp. 1–10; and Binfield, *So Down to Prayers: Studies in English Nonconformity, 1780–1920* (London: J. M. Dent, 1977), chaps. 4–5.

[12] See A. Lincoln, *Some Political and Social Ideas of English Dissent, 1763–1800* (CUP, 1938); J. C. D. Clark, *English Society 1688–1832. Ideology, Social Structure and Political Practice During the Ancien Regime* (CUP, 1985), Parts 4–5; and M. Fitzpatrick, 'Heretical Religion and Radical Political Ideas in Late Eighteenth-Century England' in *The Transformation of Political Culture. England and Germany in the Late Eighteenth Century*, ed. E. Hellmuth (OUP, 1990), pp. 339–73. Before 1789 at least as many English Dissenters inclined to social and political conservatism as to Radicalism. It required the injection of 'French' republican ideas, and government censure of heterodoxy ca. 1790–8, to produce a clear alignment of Dissent with Radicalism. See C. B. Cone, *The English Jacobins. Reformers in Late Eighteenth-Century England* (New York: Scribner's, 1968), chaps. 1–2.

[13] This has been argued in different ways by Clark, *English Society 1688–1832*; and Vernon, *Politics and the People*, especially chap. 8.

and a particular church, became a dominant feature of Radical rhetoric. It is true that some Radicals and populists — William Cobbett, for instance — represented the Church of England as the true protector of the liberties and rights of Englishmen, the embodiment of Englishness. But with increasing frequency after the accession of George III, popular Radicalism pitted a non-exclusive, activist Christianity against a complacent Anglicanism which protected the interests of an elite. As late as the 1860s and '70s — witness the public uproar over the case of the 'Tichborne claimant' — there was a strong connection in the popular imagination between anti-aristocratic and anti-Anglican sentiment.[14]

In his study of the formation of the Liberal Party, John Vincent has remarked on a 'Christian dimension of Liberalism' and its particular strength in provincial manufacturing towns. The manufacturers who made Britain the workshop of the world in the mid-nineteenth century — the 'men who made the North what it is' (or was) — along with the preachers, journalists and opinion-shapers who propagated their views, 'took orthodox, traditional Christianity as the conscious expression of their modernity and their sense of belonging to a revolutionary elite for a newer and better civilization.'[15] The 'traditional' Christians Vincent mentions in elaborating upon this statement are mainly Dissenters, Christians whose particular faith was often unsophisticated and austere, and whose membership in an 'elect' reminded them that they were chosen by God but also rejected by the temporal powers.[16] Thus, in pointing to the 'Christian element in Liberal politics', Vincent identifies as essential not Christian sentiment generally but the Dissenting Protestantism whose adherents were at a distance from 'metropolitan "good society"', that is, from the world of Trollope, Thackeray, and Bagehot.'[17]

---

[14] Arthur Orton, a butcher's son, claimed to be Roger Tichborne, heir to a wealthy estate. He was aided in his deception by Lady Tichborne. The case was tried in 1871 and 1874, resulting in Orton's indictment for perjury and his counsel being disbarred. Yet Orton was widely regarded as a victim of aristocratic snobbery and vindictiveness, and his counsel, Dr. Kenealy, was elected MP for Stoke-on-Trent in 1875. Rumours circulated that Orton-Tichborne's legal case had been sabotaged by Jesuits — an interesting intrusion of contemporary anxiety about 'foreign' Anglo-Catholic ritualism. Public interest in the case 'led many anxious Liberals to doubt the capacity of the working classes for sustained intelligent interest in serious public affairs' (Shannon, *Crisis of Imperialism*, p. 497). See R. McWilliam, 'Radicalism and Popular Culture: the Tichborne Case and the Politics of "Fair Play", 1867–1886' in *Currents of Radicalism*, ed. Biagini and Reid, chap. 3.

[15] Vincent, *Formation of the British Liberal Party*, p. xxx.

[16] Thus Vincent cites George Eliot's recollections 'of the quaint and homely religion of her youth "which ran in families"', and remarks on the self-conscious snobbery of chapel-going, and predominantly Liberal Leeds families like the Baineses, Talbots, Pyes, and Condors (*ibid.*, pp. xxxi–xxxii).

[17] *Ibid.*, pp. xxxi–xxxiii.

In contemporary Liberalism and Dissent Green saw evidence of a two-fold mission of destruction and reconstruction: to eliminate obstacles to equality and free cooperation, and to build institutions and practices which would strengthen the better aspects of human nature. He assumed that once Dissenters' religious, civil and social disabilities had been removed, their zeal for improvement could be channelled into wider ameliorative action. Green took seriously the 'Christian element in Liberal politics' and appreciated its Dissenting flavour, setting himself apart, in some respects, from 'good society'. Matthew Arnold viewed Dissenters as sanctimonious and morally blighted by worship of commercial values, impervious to 'sweetness and light' and cherishing a legacy of discrimination which belied their gradual integration into polite society.

Arnold exaggerated the opposition of Anglican and Dissenting mentalities, but he was correct in detecting a significant polarity in Victorian culture and politics based not upon consciousness of class but upon religious consciousness. Donald Davie's analysis of a literature of the English Dissenting Interest and his identification of a Dissenting sensibility since the time of Daniel Defoe and Isaac Watts complement studies in social and political history which demonstrate that Church and Chapel marked a fundamental rift in social identity and sentiment down to the early twentieth century.[18] Ernest Barker observed in 1942 that 'the general relations, the general balance, and the general interaction of Anglicanism and Nonconformity have been a cardinal factor in English life and development for over three centuries.'[19] And G. M. Trevelyan remarked that 'the continuity of the two parties in English politics [during the nineteenth century] was largely due to the two-party system in religious observance, popularly known as Church and Chapel.'[20] Roman Catholics and Jews were of course not included among either Establishment or Dissent. Perhaps three-quarters of Roman Catholics in England ca. 1851 were Irish immigrants, and many of these were too poor to qualify for the pre-1867 parliamentary franchise. Under these circumstances the Catholic Vote was not yet a major factor in English national politics. Jews were a very small minority in England before the 1880s; they had been politically 'emancipated' in the first half of the century but they never aligned themselves clearly with a single political party. *Wesleyan* Methodists did not habitually include themselves with

---

[18] 'Distinguished individuals from the ranks of Dissent have indeed enriched our culture in every generation since 1700, but Dissent as such, as a corporate force in our society, can at a certain point be shown *to have ceased to do so*' (*A Gathered Church*, p. 3) Davie vaguely locates this point at ca. 1900.

[19] *Britain and the British People*, quoted in Davie, *A Gathered Church*, p. 2.

[20] *An Autobiography* (1949), quoted in Davie, *A Gathered Church*, p. 2.

'Dissent', as John Wesley was an ordained Anglican clergyman who never declared his separation from the Church.

If anything, the split between Establishment and Dissent assumed an even greater significance in the Welsh, Scottish and Ulster 'national' experiences. For instance, as Binfield observes, Nonconformists in Wales were always in the majority and 'what was most vital about them was expressed in the Welsh language, and therefore a different culture.' Scotland's Established Church 'was firmly within the Reformed Tradition' — which the Church of England was not — and 'those who dissented from it included Episcopalians'.[21] Although the non-English dimensions of the Establishment–Dissent polarity cannot be discussed here, recent scholarly attention to the schism runs parallel to reassessment of the place of class consciousness in Victorian society. Confessional identity was as great a factor in British society during the eighteenth and nineteenth centuries as consciousness of class and, as just indicated, formed a basis of social (including regional, national and ethnic) identity.[22]

The alignment between Liberalism and Dissent in Green's time was the product of many cultural and political circumstances. Central to the Dissenting experience — or to the collective historical memory of English Nonconformity — was the 1662 'Uniformity Act' (14 Car. II, c. 4): 'An Act for the uniformity of public prayers and administration of sacraments and other rites and ceremonies.' Clergy refusing to 'declare … unfeigned assent and consent' to 'all and every thing' in the Book of Common Prayer were threatened with ejection from their benefices and denied all promotion.[23] The Corporations Act of 1661 and the Test Act of 1673 disqualified Nonconformists from holding municipal office and Crown appointments (although some Dissenters continued to hold political offices through the practice of 'occasional conformity'). Because many Dissenters, like Anglicans, feared a Jacobite reversion to 'Romanism', they supported the Hanoverian dynasty and the Whig fac-

[21]   Binfield, *So Down to Prayers*, p. xi. See also K. Robbins, *Nineteenth-Century Britain. England, Scotland, and Wales: the Making of a Nation* (OUP, 1988), chaps. 1–3; Harvie, 'Gladstonianism, the Provinces, and Popular Political Culture, 1860–1906;' Biagini, *Liberty, Retrenchment and Reform*, introduction and chap. 6; D. Hempton, *Religion and Political Culture in Britain and Ireland. From the Glorious Revolution to the Decline of Empire* (CUP, 1996), chaps. 3–5.

[22]   L. Davidoff and C. Hall, *Family Fortunes. Men and Women of the English Middle Class, 1780–1850* (Chicago: Chicago UP, 1987), Part One; *Religion in Victorian England*, ed. G. Parsons (Manchester UP, 1988); L. Colley, *Britons. Forging the Nation 1707–1837* (New Haven: Yale UP, 1992), chaps. 1, 3–4, 8; Hempton, *Religion and Political Culture*. E. P. Thompson has demonstrated that religious factors (e.g. the 'ideology' of the 'free-born Englishman') were by no means incidental to the emergence of a plebeian or working-class consciousness (see *Making of the English Working Class*).

[23]   J. P. Kenyon, *The Stuart Constitution, 1603–1688. Documents and Commentary* (CUP, 1969), pp. 378–82.

tion at Court and in Parliament as the best guarantee of religious and political liberty.

Education was an area in which Dissenters faced discrimination and (see discussion 4.3–4.4 below) mass mobilizations of Dissenters against real or perceived injustices of this sort continued into the twentieth century. The ancient universities had been purged of Puritans and other heterodox after 1660 and Dissenters were effectively prevented from taking degrees there until the mid-nineteenth century. Yet this was of little concern to them before about 1830. The better 'Dissenting academies' — such as Daventry, Hackney, Hoxton and Warrington — produced distinguished theologians and scientists, and many Dissenters must have agreed with Adam Smith that Oxford and Cambridge were 'sanctuaries in which exploded systems and obsolete prejudices found shelter and protection, after they had been hunted out of every other corner of the world.'[24]

Restoration measures to contain religious 'enthusiasm', such as the 1665 Five-Mile Act (banning unlicensed preachers within five miles of a city or town), were less onerous and probably did little to hamper Dissenting worship. More significant than punitive regulation were the facts that 'Nonconformist fission constantly produced its own dissidents' (in the words of Roy Porter) and wealthy Dissenters, as prosperous subjects with reputations to make or uphold, felt social pressure to convert to the Establishment. Between 1700 and 1740 the number of English Dissenters may have declined by as much as forty percent, before rising again in the evangelical movement that grew out of Methodism.[25]

Despite quietism and the temptations of conversion, many Dissenters insisted upon their fundamental identity as persecuted Christians. The Protestant Dissenting Deputies were formed in 1732 to secure repeal of the Test and Corporations Acts, and down to the repeal of the acts in 1828 the Dissenting Deputies constituted the most 'respectable' Dissenting pressure-group.[26] But the improving situation of non-Anglicans was at least equally the work of Daniel O'Connell and the Catholic Association. The strenuous efforts of this mass organization of

---

[24] Smith quoted in I. Woloch, *Eighteenth-Century Europe. Tradition and Progress, 1715–1789* (New York: Norton, 1982), p. 203. On the Academies, see Roy Porter, *English Society in the Eighteenth Century* (London: Penguin, 1982), pp. 98, 179–80. The University of London was founded in 1828 by Dissenters and radicals as a 'nonsectarian' college. Although University College London joined with the Anglican King's College in 1836, the new University of London had a less sectarian character than both Ancient Universities.

[25] Porter, *English Society*, pp. 195–200.

[26] Helmstadter, 'The Nonconformist Conscience,' pp. 144–5. On Dissenters and the repeal campaign, see R. W. Davis, *Dissent in Politics, 1780–1830: The Political Life of William Smith, M.P.* (London: Epworth, 1971).

political pressure resulted not only in Catholic Emancipation (1829) but also in a more open field for non-Anglicans throughout the United Kingdom.[27]

Following the Parliamentary Reform Act of 1832 and its 'postscript' — the 1835 Municipal Corporations Act — Dissenters were able to gain political influence commensurate with their economic status.[28] Yet due to developments in the mobilization of public opinion, such as the agitation for the abolition of slavery (from the 1780s), and in the wake of both class-conscious and class-cooperative workingmen's associations and 'Political Unions' which claimed to be the engines of political reform, the Dissenting Interest, like other traditional elements in English politics, was forced to improve upon techniques of organization and 'pressure' which it had pioneered.[29] Reform had the effect of raising the ambitions and determination of disenfranchised artisans (increasing numbers of whom were not independent entrepreneurs) and the 'proletariat'. The Dissenting Deputies after 1832 were gradually overshadowed, if never entirely eclipsed, by organizations with markedly populist orientations.

The fact that English Dissenters in Green's time sometimes disagreed with Parliamentary Liberals and Liberal intellectuals over policy matters does not gainsay the truth of the widespread contemporary identification of the Liberal Party as the Dissenting party. The post-1815 Whigs had fashioned their party as the party of peaceful 'reform' and political change consistent with constitutionalism, and the Whig principles of religious liberty and civil inclusion were carried into the early Liberal Party.[30] Although some prominent spokesmen for Liberalism, such as Mill and John Morley, were 'freethinkers', most British Liberals were not secularists of the militant Continental type, who placed themselves in the tradition of Voltaire and other opponents of institutional reli-

---

[27] G. I. T. Machin, *The Catholic Question in English Politics, 1820–1830* (Oxford: Clarendon, 1964). R. F. Foster takes into account recent Irish studies of Catholic Emancipation (*Modern Ireland, 1600–1972* (London: Penguin, 1989), pp. 289–302).

[28] The 1835 Act was passed by parliamentary Radicals with the support of Nonconformists at large. It abolished 'closed' town councils (from which Dissenters had been effectively excluded) and opened new possibilities for local government. Boards of Guardians (of the Poor) also became sites of denominational and other social conflict. G. Finlayson, 'The Politics of Municipal Reform, 1835,' *EHR*, 81 (1966), pp. 673–92.

[29] On abolitionism, see D. B. Davis, *The Problem of Slavery in the Age of Revolution* (Ithaca, NY: Cornell UP, 1975), especially chaps. 2, 8–9. On the political unions and extra-parliamentary pressure, see C. Flick, *The Birmingham Political Union and the Movement for Reform in Britain, 1830–1839* (Hamden, CT: Archon, 1978); Tyrrell, *Joseph Sturge*; N. Lopatin, *Political Unions, Popular Politics and the Great Reform Act of 1832* (New York: Macmillan/St Martin's, 1999).

[30] R. Brent, *Liberal Anglican Politics: Whiggery, Religion and Reform, 1830–1841* (Oxford: Clarendon, 1987); Burrow, *Whigs and Liberals*; I. Newbould, *Whiggery and Reform, 1830–1841: the Politics of Government* (Palo Alto, CA: Stanford UP, 1991).

gion.[31] While British Liberalism had to make room for atheists and free-thinkers, in the interests of freedom, it was never defined as an anti-religious movement. The struggles of Dissent for parity with the Establishment ca. 1828–1906 never formed the basis of a separate political movement.[32] There was little reason for a 'Free Church' party because many Dissenting causes were taken up into a general movement for reform led by Whigs, Liberals and Radicals. Victorian Dissenters identified more freely with the Liberal than with the Conservative party.[33]

If a single political figure can be held responsible for Dissent's alignment with the Liberal Party during the mid- and late-Victorian period, it was William Ewart Gladstone.[34] Gladstone cleverly appealed to the cultural and political ambitions of Dissenting leaders, not hesitating to flatter them for their piety and their ability to manage opinion. Thus, at Mr Newman Hall's on 15 November 1864, Gladstone met with Dr Robert Vaughan (the Congregationalist historian and man of letters) 'and a party of Dissenting Ministers,' who 'behaved extremely well' to him.[35] Yet Gladstone's courtship of Dissent from the mid-1860s, like Green's sympathy with Dissent, implied the existence of a functioning Christian moralism with a strong Dissenting flavour, susceptible to political mobilization or management. The Dissenting tail did in many instances wag the Liberal dog. As Eugenio Biagini has pointed out, the Gladstonian Liberal agenda remained 'to a large extent the *political* projection of the Dissenting experience ...'.[36]

It was significant for the Liberal Party that the mid-Victorian 'Dissenting experience' was 'shockingly middle class' (but reaching down to the ranks of artisans): 'all but 8.6 percent of [Dissent's] strength came from that 67 percent of [English] society which fitted between the profes-

[31] P. A. Bertocci, 'Positivism, French Republicanism, and the Politics of Religion, 1843–1883,' *Third Republic. Troisième Republique*, 2 (1976), pp. 182–227.

[32] In 1902 the Conservative Government passed a (secondary) Education Act making denominational schools (the majority of which were run by Anglicans and Roman Catholics) eligible for direct subsidies from local rates. The Liberal Government formed in 1906 failed to resolve the problem to the satisfaction of its Nonconformist supporters. See especially Koss, *Nonconformity in Modern British Politics*, chaps. 3–5.

[33] Even after the religious reforms of the last third of the nineteenth century (e.g. disestablishment of the Irish Church) there were 'insuperable obstacles to a Nonconformist affiliation with the Tories, who defended sectarian education, scorned temperance reform, and were thoroughly identified as the champions of a corrupt and irrelevant Anglicanism' (Koss, *Nonconformity*, p. 16).

[34] 'It fell almost entirely to Mr. Gladstone to attract the forces of religious revival behind an accommodating but unredeemed party not connatural with its supporters' (Vincent, *Formation of the British Liberal Party*, p. xxxvi).

[35] *The Gladstone Diaries*, vi (1861–8), ed. Matthew, p. 313. Such a cordial meeting between a delegation of Dissenters and Peel or Palmerston is scarcely imaginable.

[36] *Liberty, Retrenchment, and Reform*, p. 16.

sional classes and the unskilled ...'.[37] Quakers and Unitarians formed the aristocracy of Dissent: many were professionals and owners or managers of sizable economic enterprises, and the first Dissenters raised to the peerage were Unitarians. Most Methodists and Primitive Baptists were drawn from the lower and lower-middle classes, while other Baptists and Congregationals were predominantly shopkeepers, small-scale entrepreneurs, and professionals. Congregationals appear to have achieved 'respectability' through economic advance at a more rapid rate than Baptists and Methodists.[38] Dissenting Protestantism may have reflected in various ways the middle-class relationship to the means and mode of production, or served as a 'rationalization' of bourgeois economic interests.[39] At any rate, the Dissenting interest down to the late Victorian period was rarely opposed to the interests of the middle classes.

Liberalism fared best between 1850 and 1914, electorally and as a 'moral' force, in the north and west of England and on the 'Celtic Fringe' — that is, in precisely those regions where Old Dissent and Methodism commanded the largest followings.[40] Metropolitan Liberal leaders were often irritated by their provincial allies and resisted the notion that the Party was somehow beholden to the Dissenting Interest.[41] While most Dissenters largely accepted the position of an interest or pressure group which should properly defer to the Liberal national agenda, others advocated a separate political identity and the principle of opportunistic alignment with the Liberals, in the manner of the Irish nationalists and Liberal 'labourism' (the Lib–Labs) since the 1860s.[42] When a writer in the *British Weekly* proclaimed in 1909, 'We do not know what the Liberal Party is, if it is not a Nonconformist party,' he meant that the Liberal

[37] A. D. Gilbert, *Religion and Society in Industrial England. Church, Chapel, and Social Change, 1870–1914* (London: Longman, 1976), cited in Binfield, *So Down to Prayers*, p. 9.

[38] D. W. Bebbington, *The Nonconformist Conscience. Chapel and Politics, 1870–1914* (London: Allen and Unwin, 1982), chap. 1. On the pronounced middle-class character of nineteenth-century Congregationalism, see Binfield, 'Thomas Binney and Congregationalism's "Special Mission"', pp. 1–10.

[39] R. H. Tawney took up the question of correlation between Protestantism and capitalism (discussed by Weber, Troeltsch and others) in his 1922 Holland Memorial Lectures: *Religion and the Rise of Capitalism* (Gloucester, MA: P. Smith, 1962; reprint of the 1937 ed.). See also J. E. Bradley, *Religion, Revolution, and English Radicalism: Nonconformity in Eighteenth Century Politics and Society* (CUP, 1990).

[40] In addition to Vincent (*Formation of the British Liberal Party*, pp. xxxviii–xlvi), see e.g. H. McLeod, 'Religion in Nineteenth–Century Britain' [review essay], *JBS*, 38 (1999), pp. 385–91.

[41] Discussion in the following two paragraphs is based significantly on Parry, *Democracy and Religion*, and Parry, *Rise and Fall of Liberal Government*.

[42] See H. J. Hanham, *Elections and Party Management. Politics in the Time of Disraeli and Gladstone*, revised ed. (Hassocks, Sussex: Harvester, 1978), pp. 117–24.

Party ignored the support of Nonconformists at its own peril.[43] But there was an inescapable corollary, which was, that when the Dissenting Interest was left in the lurch by the Liberal Party, Dissenters had no other viable political force to which they could turn.

While nation-wide factors have thus far been adduced to demonstrate the relation of denominationalism to political partisanship, this cultural–political dynamic (and its import for Victorian politics) is rendered especially clear through examination of local politics. Religious controversy at the local level often submerged or disguised nascent social and economic conflicts, allowing the development of mass political parties that regularly transcended 'sectional' interests such as those of region or social class.[44] For instance, in Birmingham, the centre of the Midlands 'Hardware District', Dissenters assumed leading roles among Liberals and Radicals from ca. 1815, fashioning Liberal-Radicalism against Tory-Anglican and 'aristocratic' exclusionism.[45] Birmingham Radicals established political unity across lines of occupation and social class by exploiting local memory of *sectarian* inequality, as distinct from socioeconomic inequality. Dissenters and the working classes were able to neutralize Conservative influence in local institutions, and Birmingham became the headquarters of Radical organizations of national significance, such as the National Education League and the National Liberal Federation.

As a result, Birmingham Churchmen by the 1870s and '80s were in the unusual position of feeling that they — rather than Dissenters — were

[43] 'Nonconformity and Politics by a Nonconformist Minister' (unattributed), quoted in Bradley, *The Optimists*, p. 99. Richard Helmstadter describes the *British Weekly*, edited by W. R. Nicholl between 1886 and 1923, as 'the preeminent newspaper of Nonconformity' and an organ of opinion no Liberal politician could safely ignore ('The Nonconformist Conscience,' p. 137).

[44] J. Garrard, 'The History of Local Political Power — Some Suggestions for Further Analysis,' *Political Studies*, 25 (1977), pp. 252–69; J. Seed, 'Theologies of Power: Unitarianism and the Social Relations of Religious Discourse, 1800–50' in *Class, Power and Social Structure in British Nineteenth-Century Towns*, ed. R. J. Morris (Leicester: Leicester UP, 1986), pp. 107–56; G. Barnsby, *Birmingham Working People. A History of the Labour Movement in Birmingham, 1650–1914* (Birmingham: Printing Co-Partnership, 1989), chaps. 4–7 (on anti–Anglicanism and secularism).

[45] On the centrality of Dissenting–Anglican conflict to the political development of Victorian Birmingham, see A. Briggs, *History of Birmingham: Volume II, Borough and City, 1865–1938* (OUP, 1952); E. P. Hennock, *Fit and Proper Persons. Ideal and Reality in Nineteenth-Century Urban Government* (London: Arnold, 1973); D. Smith, *Conflict and Compromise: Class Formation in English Society, 1830–1914. A Comparative Study of Birmingham and Sheffield* (London: Routledge and Kegan Paul, 1982), and D. Leighton, 'Municipal Progress, Democracy and Radical Identity in Birmingham, 1838–1886,' *Midland History*, 25 (2000), pp. 115–42.

second-class citizens.[46] Having vanquished 'reactionary' elements in their community, Birmingham Dissenters were able to harness a 'civic gospel' to class-cooperative, Liberal political organizations. They achieved impressive results in 'social reform' under the mayoralty (1873–6) of the Unitarian Joseph Chamberlain and determined thereafter the agenda of the Radical wing of the national Liberal Party. As a leading municipal gospelist, the Congregational minister Robert William Dale (1829–95) proclaimed, 'Medicine and not the gospel alone is necessary to improve the homes of the poor.'[47] Early Victorian campaigns in Birmingham for 'freedom of conscience' and wider social access to political institutions evolved into a progressive reform agenda which dissolved boundaries between private and public institutions and justified substantial state intervention through appeal to civic duty and Christian social justice.

Yet as Matthew Arnold complained, Political Dissent down to the 1880s tended to mobilize itself negatively, against the state and hegemonic institutions. 'The most important political organization of the [Victorian] Nonconformist community' was the Anti-State Church Association, later named the Liberation Society; and the movement to disestablish the Church of England was the most sustained and well-orchestrated national campaign for religious liberty and freedom of conscience in Victorian Britain.[48] Edward Miall, a Congregational minister in Leicester, was the undisputed leader of the disestablishment movement. He left his pastorate in 1843 to found the Anti-State Church Association and its official press organ, the *Nonconformist*, and between 1852 and 1874 served as the chief Parliamentary spokesman for dises-

[46] Hennock (cited above) compares Birmingham to Leeds local politics, and Smith discusses denominational politics in Birmingham and Sheffield. See also P. T. Phillips, *The Sectarian Spirit: Sectarianism, Society, and Politics in Victorian Cotton Towns* (Toronto: Toronto UP, 1982); and J. Seed, 'Unitarianism, Political Economy and the Antimonies of Liberal Culture in Manchester, 1830–50,' *Social History*, 7 (1982), pp. 1–25.

[47] From *Laws of Christ for Common Life* (1893), quoted in J. Kenyon, 'R. W. Dale and Christian Worldliness' in *The View from the Pulpit. Victorian Ministers and Society*, ed. P. T. Phillips (Toronto: Macmillan of Canada, 1978), p. 205. On the Birmingham civic gospel see especially A. Briggs, *Victorian Cities* (Berkeley: UP California, 1993 [orig. 1965]), chap. 5. On Birmingham leaders, especially Joseph Chamberlain, and national Radicalism, see Emy, *Liberals, Radicals and Social Politics*.

[48] Helmstadter, 'The Nonconformist Conscience,' pp. 150–1. See also S. M. Ingham, 'The Disestablishment Movement in England, 1868–74,' *Journal of Religious History*, 3 (1964), pp. 38–60; A. R. Vogeler, 'Disestablishmentarianism: the Liberationist Crusade Against the Church of England, 1868–1886' (doctoral thesis, Columbia University, 1973); D. M. Thompson, 'The Liberation Society 1844–1868' in *Pressure From Without in Early Victorian England*, ed. P. Hollis (New York: St. Martin's, 1974), pp. 210–38; Bebbington, *The Nonconformist Conscience*, chap. 2; and T. Larsen, *Friends of Religious Equality. Nonconformist Politics in Mid-Victorian England* (Woodbridge, Suffolk: Boydell and Brewer, 1999).

tablishment. He mobilized Political Dissent to help secure disestablish-ment of the Irish Church (i.e. the Anglican Church in Ireland) in 1869. But though disestablishment of the Church of England continued to be debated in Parliament, it was (politically) a lost cause after the early 1870s.[49]

4.3. ANGLICANS, DISSENTERS AND EDUCATION, 1833–1870

'Disestablishmentarianism' overlapped with Dissenters' concerns about elementary education, so that a struggle to institutionalize reli-gious pluralism became conflated with struggles to impose the correct religious and moral character on educational instruction.[50] Signifi-cantly, the immediate reason for Miall's establishing the Anti-State Church Association was Dissenters' dissatisfaction with government plans to subsidize elementary education. Other European states during the nineteenth century witnessed bitter social and religious conflict over primary education.[51] Yet in much of northern Europe — namely the German states, the Low Countries and Scandinavia — there was some degree of public agreement over the conditions of primary education or, in the absence of this, a political-bureaucratic elite committed to com-pulsory primary education.[52] (Prussia, for instance, had a general *Schulreglement* in 1745.) The British public, however, was not united over educational policy, and Parliament did not dare impose a compre-hensive, and therefore expensive elementary education system.[53]

T. H. Green's ideas for the reform of primary and secondary educa-tion were far reaching, although the harmony between his ideas and those of Christian social gospelists has not received sufficient atten-

---

[49] Compulsory Church rates were abolished in England in 1869. Disestablishment of the Church in Wales was finally carried through Parliament in 1914 (and suspended upon the outbreak of the war). See I. Machin, 'Disestablishment and Democracy, c. 1840–1930' in *Citizenship and Community. Liberals, Radicals and Collective Identities in the British Isles*, ed. E. F. Biagini (CUP, 1996), pp. 120–48.

[50] G. F. A. Best, 'The Religious Difficulties of National Education in England, 1800–70,' *Cambridge Historical Journal*, 12 (1956), pp. 155–73.

[51] See e.g. T. Zeldin, ed., *Conflicts in French Society. Anticlericalism, Education and Morals in the Nineteenth Century* (London: Allen and Unwin, 1970).

[52] R. Gildea, *Barricades and Borders. Europe 1800–1914*, 2nd ed. (OUP, 1996), pp. 238–41.

[53] The account below of English primary education is derived from F. Adams, *History of the Elementary School Contest in England* (London: Chapman and Hall, 1882); H. B. Binns, *A Century of Education, Being the Centenary History of the British and Foreign School Society, 1808–1908* (London: J. M. Dent, 1908); E. C. Mack, *Public Schools and Brit-ish Opinion Since 1860* (New York: Columbia UP, 1941); Walcott, *Origins of 'Culture and Anarchy'*; W. P. McCann, 'Trade Unionists, Artisans and the 1870 Education Act,' *Brit-ish Journal of Education Studies*, 18 (1970), pp. 134–50; H. G. Hebranck, 'Manchester and the Struggle for Nondenominational Education 1847–1870' (doct. thesis, Univ. of Minnesota, 1976); Smith, *Conflict and Compromise*, chaps. 5, 8; and P. Hollis, *Ladies Elect. Women in English Local Government 1865–1914* (Oxford: Clarendon, 1987).

tion.[54] Nowhere is Green's combination of idealism and practicality more apparent than in his treatment of basic education. He had been appointed in 1865 an assistant to a governmental Schools Inquiry Commission, the 'Taunton Commission', whose findings were published in 1868.[55] Green had clear aims, realistic expectations and a deep appreciation of the positions of socially and politically marginalized groups — Dissenters, *petite bourgeois* tradesmen, artisans and labourers. In the course of his inspections Green compiled information about the social background and religious affiliation of pupils: e.g. 'How many go to University?', 'Religious teaching?', 'Went Dissenting school?', 'Difference in social status between boys in 2 depts. [Classical and business-oriented]?' He also felt the suspicion and even resentment of schoolmasters and parents at his inspections.[56]

Green was too perceptive an observer of society to preach (*pace* Arnold) the efficacy of 'sweetness and light.'[57] While he was conscious of the cultural narrowness of the commercial and labouring classes, Green did not ignore the political circumstances that had fostered their insularity. He sought out the most broad minded among them and won their respect by his unpatronizing manner and willingness to see their point of view.[58] Instead of attempting, in Coleridgean or Arnoldian fashion, to mould English educational practice into conformity with an abstract conception of an educated society, Green gave serious consideration to the historical development of English education — an approach which led him to weigh the expectations and demands of social groups.

[54] Treatments of Green's educational reform activities include Lynn, 'Thomas Hill Green and His Involvement in Victorian Education', which is inaccurate on some points of fact, and Gordon and White, *Philosophers as Educational Reformers. The Influence of Idealism on British Educational Thought and Practice.* The latter considers ideas of Green and other Idealists about the moral goals of primary, secondary, university and adult education in terms of their larger political vision. See also J. Marler, *History of the Oxford Boys' High School* (undated typescript held in the Oxford Central Library: shelf number OXFO 373 High b); and Williams, 'Arthur Acland, Tom Ellis and Welsh Education: A Study in the Politics of Idealism.'

[55] Matthew Arnold had inspected European schools as Assistant Commissioner for the 'Newcastle Commission' in 1859 as well as British schools for the 'Taunton Commission.' Green reported mainly on endowed and proprietary schools in the Midlands. These included private academies as well as grammar schools maintained through endowments.

[56] Green, 'Notebook of School inspection:' *GP* 1(c).

[57] For an insightful modern critique of Arnold's educational ideals, see G. Graff, 'Arnold, Reason, and Common Culture,' a commentary appended to *Culture and Anarchy,* ed. S. Lipman, pp. 186–201.

[58] As testified to by R. W. Dale and A. R. Vardy (headmaster of the King Edward VI Grammar School, Birmingham, 1872–1900) at Green's burial service. *OCBBG,* 20 May 1882: reportage of memorials at Green's funeral; and letter of Vardy to R. L. Nettleship, 17 Sept. 1882, in *GP* 1(b).

The point at which Green became involved in campaigns for national education coincides with the beginning of a period of empirical verifiability with regard to 'public opinion'. With the easing of press restrictions after 1836 and the abolition of the 'newspaper stamp' (duty) in 1855, artisan– and working–class Britons were able to register their opinions in the rational fashion recommended by members of the elite and educated classes. Not only government commissions, Parliamentary debates and the elite press but the mass press from this time offer representative insights into national opinion about education.[59] English (private) 'public' schools, and grammar school foundations (most of which had been established with gifts from monarchs or the Church) catered to only a small section of the British population before the 1860s. The 'voluntary' sector included denominational schools, 'dame schools' and the 'ragged schools' established on a wide scale in large towns and cities by Christian philanthropists since the 1820s. A handful of enlightened manufacturers, like the socialist Robert Owen, had set up schools for their juvenile workers. Factory Acts in 1802, 1819 and 1833 made provision for education of juveniles employed in some sectors of the manufacturing economy, though these acts were scarcely enforceable, given the very small number of professional school and factory inspectors.

The rudiments of a system of state-managed elementary education were established in 1833. In that year Parliament made available £20,000 for the building and upkeep of denominational schools, which was to be distributed through the National Society for Educating the Poor in the Principles of the Established Church, and, to Dissenting schools, through the British and Foreign School Society.[60] Increasing annual grants were made to denominational schools and in 1839 a permanent position was created in the Privy Council for an educational advisor. In 1843 Sir James Graham introduced a factory bill to expand provision of education, which was to be effectively managed by the Established Church. There was immediate uproar among Dissenters about religious tyranny, and even typically apolitical Wesleyan Methodists joined in the agitation against the Graham Act specifically and 'state assistance' for education generally.

[59] Habermas, in *Strukturwandel der Öffentlichkeit*, has argued that 'public opinion' was a creation of the late eighteenth century, but there are many indications that this formation did not become fully visible in England until the 1820s and '30s. See Bradley, *The Optimists*, pp. 30–5; and D. Vincent, *Literacy and Popular Culture. England 1750–1914* (CUP, 1989), chap. 7 (on the effects of repeal of the 'knowledge taxes' on working-class literacy and the formation of 'opinion').

[60] The initial grant amounted to one-twentieth of the Prussian educational budget of that year (J. Murphy, *Church, State and Schools in Britain 1800–1970* [1971], cited in Binfield, *So Down to Prayers*, p. 80). In the same year Parliament voted £20 million to compensate West Indian planters for the abolition of slavery.

For the next twenty-five years Anglicans and Dissenters debated the propriety of state support of education and how 'freedom of conscience' could be reconciled with the fact of state educational aid falling disproportionately to Anglican-controlled schools. State aid for Anglican schools appeared even more socially iniquitous given the fact that, according to the 1851 national census of religious worship, nearly as many Sunday worshippers attended Dissenting and Roman Catholic as Anglican services.[61] Dissenters were divided amongst each other on the question of state subsidies. Some influential Dissenters upheld the voluntary principle as the only 'just' means of educational provision, while many Dissenting school committees and managers accepted state subsidies.[62]

The Lancashire Public School Association (1847–50), one of whose founding members was Jacob Bright (MP for Manchester, 1867–74, 1876–85), advocated a completely nondenominational system to be financed from local rates. One controversial point was the claim that unsectarian moral instruction could be provided for children by simple reading of Scripture, without 'interpretation'. The Manchester and Salford Committee on Education (1851–5) added a 'conscience clause' to their plan for denominational, but rate-aided, instruction: parents objecting to the character of religious instruction in the schools could have their children excused from the hours of religious instruction. In 1853 Lord John Russell discussed the possibility of an 'education rate' assessed on borough householders to be distributed among existing denominational schools, but this provoked Parliamentary and popular opposition about the formulae and means of distribution.

By the 1860s it was no longer possible to ignore the fact that educational voluntarism had utterly failed to provide sufficient quantity or quality of instruction to children of the working and lower-middle classes.[63] The statistics for 1869 show 1.3 million English children attending primary schools receiving state aid, while one million

---

[61] 3,773,474 Anglican attendees versus 3,153,490 Protestant Nonconformists and 305,393 Roman Catholics. Figures cited in Hanham, *Elections and Party Management*, p. 117n.

[62] Edward Baines, Sr., the Congregational proprietor-editor of the *Leeds Mercury*, declared in 1850 that 'in plain fact, the philosophy of national education is that of communism … it is based on an entire distrust of individual energy and a hatred of free competition: and it rushes with Robert Owen and Louis Blanc into a forced co-operative society of the entire nation' (quoted in Binfield, *So Down to Prayers*, p. 87). Baines, Jr., continued to defend the voluntary principle in the pages of the *Leeds Mercury* until the mid-1860s, when it was clear to most observers of English education that the principle was failing in practice. *So Down to Prayers*, pp. 89–90.

[63] By the mid-1860s influential spokesmen for the working classes were of the opinion that restrictions on juvenile employment and better educational provision were necessary to avert 'the destruction of childhood' and to diminish 'the misery of the working classes'. Statistics were produced to show that wages of juveniles *and* adults were

attended schools without any state support (or effective oversight) and two million children attended no school, except perhaps Sunday Schools.[64] An Educational Bill Committee was established in Parliament in 1866 and initially proceeded with a refined version of the 1853 Russell plan to collect a rate to supplement the activities of existing schools. In 1869 the Committee agreed upon a mixed system of local rating and central government aid: existing denominational schools would continue to collect government grants upon adherence to a conscience clause; in addition, new undenominational schools would receive support from government grants and through local rating. The latter were to be undenominational in the sense that specifically doctrinal religious instruction would occur only outside regular instruction, so that children of different denominations could easily absent themselves from objectionable religious teaching.

The immediate reason for this bold course of policy, which resulted in the 1870 Education Act creating a new network of 'Board Schools', was government recognition of the inadequacy of the voluntary system, but this was due largely to effective lobbying by new pressure groups. The most of important of these was the Birmingham Education Society founded in 1867, whose leaders included the Unitarian hardware entrepreneur Joseph Chamberlain (1836–1914) and R. W. Dale, and out of which grew the National Education League (1869–74). Many BES members were simultaneously involved in the 'civic gospel' movement discussed above, and both the BES and the NEL took on a general social reformist tone, whereas earlier Dissenting organizations concerned with national education appeared to have been motivated by narrowly sectarian interests. The BES/NEL cut the Gordian Knot of sectarian controversy, opting for 'free' (rate-aided), compulsory and secular elementary education, administered directly by local, elective bodies. The latter were initially to support one-third of the cost of new schools, with the remaining two-thirds, mainly for buildings, to be provided by the central government.

The Birmingham educationists enjoyed comparatively good relations with local working-class and artisan Radicals and heeded the complaints of their leaders that children of the lower classes had been untouched by education (and were in fact driving down the price of local labour, to the detriment of lower-class families). Dale and George Dawson (Dissenting minister of the Church of the Saviour) had cooper-

---

lowest in localities with low school attendance: a direct result of child labour was *poorer* working–class families. See 'The Children's Employment Commission,' *The Beehive. A Journal of General Intelligence, Advocating Industrial Interests*, 27 January 1866, p 4 Also *The Beehive*, 3 February 1866, p. 4; 10 February 1866, p. 4; 17 February 1866, p. 4; 10 March 1866, p. 4.

[64] Figures cited in Shannon, *Crisis of Imperialism*, p. 87.

ated with the Reform League, including former Chartists, to secure an expanded Parliamentary franchise and championed other popular causes.[65] They were also — crucially — able to enlist the support of moderate Anglicans to open the King Edward VI Grammar School Foundation to Dissenters, satisfying a key Dissenting grievance as well as effectively extending middle-class educational provision. By 1867–8 Birmingham Liberal progressives had effectively neutralized Conservative and Anglican influence in the town council and other local institutions through the Liberal Association or 'Caucus' (1865). The pressure which the BES/NEL was able to bring to bear on Parliament ca. 1868–70 was a direct result of Dissenters' populist outreach. The confidence of the NEL during the 1870s in its own power and in the utility of local control of 'public' education and other services was built upon the early successes of Birmingham Dissenters.

The Education Act of 1870, piloted through Parliament by W. E. Forster (a Quaker turned Anglican), set up elective, rate-collecting School Boards to complement, not replace, the voluntary sector. The act irritated some Dissenters with its twenty-fifth clause that partially circumvented the Cowper–Temple amendment (abolishing denominational formularies in moral instruction): local authorities would pay the fees of poor children, such as those in Poor Houses, to attend schools in which doctrinal instruction was likely to be conducted by Anglican teachers. In such cases, which were far from rare, it seemed that 'freedom of conscience' could be violated.[66] Dale, who had met with Gladstone and other Cabinet members to discuss education proposals, claimed to have been betrayed by the Parliamentary leadership's compromise with Anglican elements.[67] Gladstone had proclaimed in Parliament, 'How essential it is to proceed in this measure not by endeavouring to give effect to any abstract and inflexible opinion, but to allow conflicting considerations to meet and equitably to modify one another.'[68] Dale was one of the organizers of a Central Nonconformist

---

[65] Both men were instrumental in the election of John Bright, the preeminent Radical of the mid–Victorian period, as Birmingham's Liberal MP in 1859. See McCann, 'Trade Unionists, Artisans, and the 1870 Education Act;' and Smith, *Conflict and Compromise*, chaps. 3–6.

[66] Bebbington notes that 'in 1872 *only* forty-three school boards chose to send any very poor children to Church schools' (*Nonconformist Conscience*, pp. 129–30, my emphasis). This was a significant fraction of existing School Boards. See G. Sutherland, *Policy-Making in Elementary Education, 1870–1895* (OUP, 1973).

[67] R. W. Dale, 'The Nonconformists and the Education Policy of the Government,' *Contemporary Review*, 22 (1873), pp. 641–62. See also A. W. W. Dale, *Life of R. W. Dale of Birmingham*, 4th ed. (London: Hodder and Stoughton, 1899), chap. 12.

[68] *Hansard*, ccii [1870], p. 275, quoted in Hebranck, 'Struggle for Nondenominational Education,' p. 130. Gladstone wrote to John Bright (25 November 1871), 'I hope that a little time will bring the Dissenters to clear and decided views, not only on Clause 25

Committee (Birmingham), which like the Manchester Nonconformist Association was set up to protest misapplication of the 1870 Act.[69]

While National Education Leaguers believed that priority should be given to providing education to as many children as possible, they found it impossible to ignore the Establishment's distinct advantages in elementary education and believed that the Church might abuse its superior position. In the wake of the 1870 Act many religious persons joined School Boards — not in order to set up new undenominational schools but to stall such efforts and thereby preserve denominational control of local education. It was usually Anglicans, and occasionally Roman Catholics, who claimed that existing voluntary schools were sufficient for local needs.[70] Leaguers protested that the post-1870 education system continued to give generous subsidies to denominational teacher training colleges, thereby undercutting secular education.[71] The NEL led by Chamberlain continued to complain about discriminatory provisions of the Education Act and many members either gave half-hearted support to the act or, like their Establishment adversaries, stalled its implementation (e.g. by pledging to resist payment of School rates). League members thus incurred the blame of many Liberals for the Liberal Party's subsequent electoral defeat in 1874.[72]

However, the dust kicked up by Dale, Miall, Chamberlain and others about the inadequacies of the educational system they helped shape has tended to obscure the fact that the 1870 Act helped equalize the posi-

---

(for the matter cannot be dealt with piecemeal), but on the whole subject, so that we may know with what materials we have to deal.' *Correspondence on Church and Religion*, ii, ed. Lathbury, pp. 142–3.

[69] See R. W. Dale, *The Politics of Nonconformity* (Manchester Nonconformist Association, 1871); J. G. Rogers, *Why Ought Not the State to Give Religious Education. An Argument Addressed to Nonconformists* (London: Jas. Clarke and Co., 1872); *Education Act Amendment Bill. Speeches of Mr. Henry Richard, M.P., Delivered in the House of Commons, July 17 and July 30, 1873* (reprinted by M.N.A. [1873]). These pamphlets are bound together with others relating to religious and educational issues in a volume in the Mansfield College Library, Oxford (shelf number: 5257D [Gallery]).

[70] By 1873 the Manchester School Board had not built a single Board School. Oxford still had no Board Schools in 1881 but had an industrial day school subsidized by local rates. Patricia Hollis provides a comprehensive account of School Board struggles in London and provincial English towns down to 1903 (*Ladies Elect*, chaps. 2–3).

[71] Indeed, Oxford Liberals complained of such provisions while the Forster bill was still being debated. See 'National Education,' *OCBBG*, 29 January 1870, p. 8.

[72] T. W. Reid, *Life of the Rt. Hon. W. E. Forster*, i (New York: A. M. Kelley, 1970 [orig. 1888]), chaps. 12–13; W. H. G. Armytage, 'The 1870 Education Act,' *British Journal of Educational Studies*, 18 (1970), pp. 121–33; M. R. Temmel, 'Liberal versus Liberal, 1874: W. F. Forster, Bradford and Education,' *HJ*, 18 (1975), pp. 611–22; P. Auspos, 'Radicalism, Pressure Groups, and Party Politics: from the National Education League to the National Liberal Federation,' *JBS*, 20 (1980), pp. 184–204.

tions of religious parties.[73] In comparatively few cases were School Boards dominated for extended periods by members of a single religious (or secular) party, and Boards were equally free to fight for public revenue. The resulting mixed system of elementary education largely satisfied demands for 'freedom of conscience'. In many urban areas after 1870, Dissenters, Roman Catholics and working-class elements were able to gain access to the educational authorities, and they accepted the rules of engagement. Education was made compulsory in 1880, much working-class resistance to the withdrawal of children from economic enterprise having dissipated. The nominal student fees ('school pence') paid directly to Board Schools were abolished in 1891. (It had been widely accepted that nominal fees were a means of safeguarding the dignity and respectability of poor parents and their children.) By 1900 about six thousand Board Schools educated more than two million English children, and fourteen thousand denominational schools educated two and a half million.[74]

4.4. GREEN AND THE IDEA OF NATIONAL EDUCATION

Green was of course well aware of the import of denominational and class struggle for national education. His brief as an assistant to the Taunton Commission in 1865–6 was the inspection of endowed and proprietary schools operating largely through private means, not factory schools or those institutions receiving substantial state grants. He found little to praise in the schools he visited in market towns and villages of the middle of England but he was impressed by the activities of Birmingham educational progressives. It appears that the successes of the latter gave him a falsely optimistic view of the ease with which progressive reforms could be realized through elective local government backed by pressure-groups. Whereas Matthew Arnold and Robert Lowe (1811–92) held that education should be protected from politics by placing its management in the hands of 'disinterested' bureaucrats, Green believed that some ill effects of educational politicization could

---

[73] These were among the organizers and main speakers at a Central Conference of Non-conformists, held in Manchester, 23–25 January 1872. Although disestablishment, marriage and burial bills, and religious inequality in the Ancient Universities were among the topics discussed, the conference appears to have been one long complaint about the defects of elementary education. *Authorized Report of Proceedings* (Manchester: A. Ireland and Co., 1872): Mansfield College Library shelf number 5232T [Gallery].

[74] Shannon, *Crisis of Imperialism*, p. 91. See also Sutherland, *Policy-Making in Elementary Education*. Total central government expenditure for primary education in England, Scotland and Wales rose from £1.1 million in 1872 to £3.8 million in 1886. School Board (i.e. local) rates for England and Wales totalled £71,185 in 1871–2 and £1,990,163 in 1883–4. *Statistical Abstract for the U.K. in Each of the Last Fifteen Years, from 1871 to 1886* (London: HMSO, 1886), pp. 38, 193.

be avoided through *greater* local control.[75] Unscrupulous politicians might make local education boards the sites of religious and social struggle, but, on the whole, education would be improved if the communities in which it was dispensed held a larger stake in its governance.

When Green joined the Oxford School Board in 1874 he endorsed the NEL platform of national, 'free' and unsectarian primary education. Leaguers were in a minority on the first Oxford School Board (1871), and on the 1874 and 1880 Boards of which Green was a member.[76] Like other Oxford Liberals, Green was annoyed by the obstructive tactics of Oxford Conservatives. Although some Anglicans, such as W. V. Harcourt (Oxford's Liberal MP elected in 1868), were committed to providing more and better primary schools under Church auspices, many local Churchmen stalled attempts to make the Board system work.[77] Professor George Rolleston maintained in a letter to the *Oxford Chronicle* that common (free, public and secular) schooling had increased the incidence of criminality in the United States![78]

On the eve of the first School Board election in Oxford, the NEL candidates 'Messrs. Hughes, Castle, Hawkins, and Reid emphatically declare[d] themselves to be in favour not only of Bible reading but Bible teaching in rate-aided schools; and under the question of rate, their maxim is "efficiency, with economy."'[79] NEL members fiercely contradicted arguments of Oxford Anglicans that unsectarian education would promote 'irreligion' and immorality, and that existing facilities were adequate, but Liberals were clearly on the defensive in trying to

---

[75] Lowe, 'Conservative Liberal', sat in Commons 1852–80, before being raised to the peerage as Viscount Sherbrooke. He served as Chancellor of the Exchequer, 1868–73, and Home Secretary, 1873–4. He was the Education Member on the Privy Council, 1859–64, where he advocated cautious reform. Although he opposed Parliamentary reform, he conceded even before passage of the 1867 Reform Act that franchise extension made it imperative for 'our future masters to learn their letters.'

[76] Strictly speaking, Green was appointed rather than elected in 1874. The formula of composition of the Oxford Board was three representatives of the University, three of the Church and three members elected at large. Green was an elected member of the 1880 Board.

[77] Harcourt's opinion that the Oxford Diocesan Board of Education 'will largely direct their attention to the religious training of schoolmasters ...' in order to continue the 'essential' role of the national Church in education is referred to in 'The Elementary Education Act,' *OCBBG*, 19 November 1870, p. 7. For Liberal claims of Tory obstructionism, see 'Oxford School Board' [editorial], *OCBBG*, 14 January 1871, p. 5; 'School Board Election,' 4 February 1871, p. 5; letter from R. S. Hawkins [one of the defeated Liberal candidates for the Board], 4 Feb. 1871, p. 5 ('the bugbear of rates has been fluttered in your eyes ...'); 4 March 1871, p. 7 (on alleged Tory 'Dodges' and irregularities at the Board election); 'Three Years' Work of the School Board' [editorial], 17 January 1874, p. 5.

[78] *OCBBG*, 29 January 1871, p. 2.

[79] 'The School Board Election,' *OCBBG*, 28 January 1871, p. 5. Presumably they meant by 'Bible teaching' religious instruction outside regular hours of instruction.

influence local opinion. Green himself, alarmed by the Tory walk-over in the 1874 General Election, took a grave view of Tory obstruction on the School Board. He was one of the Board members complaining of the frequent absences of fellow Board member G. H. Morrell, member of a prominent Tory family of brewers.[80] In fact, the Oxford School Board was during its early years an educational authority without schools; during Green's tenure on the Board the members were reduced to begging for unused rooms in Church schools and to subsidizing childrens' fees to denominational institutions. The sole success of the OSB was the establishment in 1877 of an industrial day school, one of the first of its kind in England, supported partially by Board rates.[81]

In sum, Green's efforts to improve public primary education in his home town were baffled by the Anglican establishment. However, he was more effective in other areas of elementary and secondary education. He played a significant role in the restructuring of a major educational foundation, the King Edward VI Grammar School, Birmingham — initially (1865–6) as a schools inquiry assistant commissioner and subsequently (1878–82) as the Teachers' Representative on the Board of Governors.[82] Green's ideal of a 'ladder of learning' owed something to Jowett but he was more practical than his teacher in concerning himself with the details of implementation.[83] Just as he came to agree with Birmingham progressives (specifically, the NEL) over measures of public primary education, Green was also impressed by the efforts of the 'Birmingham School' to improve secondary education and extend its provision to less privileged classes of society.

[80] See 'Hazy Morality at the School Board' and 'Oxford School Board': *OCBBG*, 12 December 1874, pp. 5, 8.

[81] Hollis, *Ladies Elect*, pp. 149–50. The initiative for the project came from Miss Eleanor Smith, elected to the 1871 Board as an 'independent' candidate. See discussion in this chapter and 6.6. below.

[82] T. W. Hutton, *King Edward's School Birmingham, 1552–1952* (Oxford: Blackwell, 1952), chaps. 8, 13. In his Taunton Commission report concerning the KES Green recommended reducing the number of nominated pupils and increasing the number of students admitted through competitive examination. See *PP* Reports from Commissioners: 1867–8. Schools Inquiry [3966–VII, XI, XV]. These are the three 'Taunton Commission' volumes containing Green's reports on schools he inspected in April–June 1865 and May 1866. The first named (3966-VII) includes the 'Special Report on Birmingham Free School, and Gen. Report on the Counties of Stafford and Warwick, by T. H. Green, Esq.,' pp. 91–145. The second volume includes Green's report on schools in Buckinghamshire and Northamptonshire, and the third, his report on Leicestershire schools.

[83] See J. M. Prest, ed., *Jowett's Correspondence on Education With Earl Russell in 1867. A Supplement to the Balliol College Record* (Oxford: Oxonian Press, 1965); W. G. Addison, 'Academic Reform at Balliol, 1854–1882: T. H. Green and Benjamin Jowett,' *Church Quarterly Review*, 153 (1952), pp. 89–98; and D. Allsobrook, *Schools for the Shires. The Reform of Middle-Class Education in Mid-Victorian England* (Manchester: Manchester UP, 1986).

Like the Birmingham School, Green believed that although the mixed educational system of voluntary and state schools had its defects, it could nevertheless serve the principle of meritocratic promotion. A sturdy ladder of learning could be built by having Board Schools feed qualified pupils into the reformed grammar schools. Green's 'Special Report on Birmingham Free School' lent force to Birmingham progressives' efforts to open that hitherto closed foundation.[84] Green enjoyed cordial relations with the school's headmaster in the mid-1860s, the Rev. Charles Evans, an Old Edwardian who cooperated with Birmingham Dissenters to make the KES Board of Governors a better mirror of local society and opinion.[85] Indeed, Green's subsequent success in establishing a grammar school in Oxford was based on his experience in the reform of the Birmingham King Edward School.

Jowett and others since the 1850s had aimed at creating a more socially heterogeneous elite through meritocratic promotion in education. Green himself spoke of rendering obsolete the phrase 'education of a gentleman.'[86] No more than Jowett did Green wish to fuse together all types of education to serve a single social purpose, but he did hope to establish a system in which, through different curricula, children would be prepared for different kinds of useful social work; education should not perpetuate distinctions of social class but rather diminish them. The mushrooming of new institutions aping the old public schools testified to the social aspirations of the rising commercial classes, and Green complained that many new boarding schools advertised prestige while being deficient in educational substance; such schools did much to promote snobbery yet did little to provide education that could be described as either practical or 'gentlemanly'.

[84] By an Act of Parliament in 1883, eight of twenty-one of the school's Governors were appointed by the Birmingham town council, and these Council members (many of them political allies of Chamberlain and Dale) led efforts to direct Board School pupils into the eight lower schools and two High Schools of the Foundation.

[85] Green had been in Evans' House when the latter was an assistant master at Rugby. Hutton describes Evans' crucial role from 1862 in placating the Dissenters, who were the main force behind the Free Grammar School Association founded in 1864 (*King Edward's School Birmingham*, pp. 47–53). Green reported to the Taunton Commission: 'The Board [of Governors of KES] has fairly represented the upper or more select section of society in Birmingham so far as this section is politically Conservative and attached to the Established Church. It has been necessarily careless or contemptuous of local politics. To belong to it has been a certain social distinction. Social and political distinction have not coincided and hence the Board has been an object of public animosity, irrespectively of the manner in which it has exercised its functions' (quoted Hutton, *King Edward's School Birmingham*, p. 49).

[86] Green hoped to see a time when the phrase 'education of a gentleman' would 'have lost its meaning': 'The Work to Be Done by the Oxford High School for Boys' [1881], in *Works*, iii, pp. 456–76. Also indicative of his democratizing intentions are his lectures 'On the Grading of Secondary Schools' [1877] and 'The Elementary School System of England' [1878], both reprinted in *Works*, iii.

Meanwhile, many grammar schools, lacking the *cachet* of Harrow or Clifton, were nevertheless staffed by talented men of substantial learning. Speaking in 1877 to a Birmingham audience, Green observed that many of the 'new boarding schools, charging from 60l. to 120l. a year', and designated by successive education commissions as of the 'first grade', took in boys who would be better served by cheaper day schools 'ticketed as "second grade"' (for no other reason than that they had historically served children of non-gentlemen).[87] Green believed that the new model grammar foundations could offer at less expense — and even with superior results — the kind of education provided by lesser public schools.

There was certainly need and demand for day secondary schools that both provided practical knowledge (e.g. modern languages, statistical mathematics and accounting techniques) and fostered the 'higher' mental and aesthetic cultivation supposedly achieved through study of Greek and Latin. Growing numbers of 'new professionals' — such as engineers, bureaucrats and schoolmasters — wanted utilitarian, pre-professional education for their sons while simultaneously recognizing the value of higher culture.[88] It was with the King Edward's School in mind that Green opined, 'probably the nonconformist ministers and the masters of public elementary schools form [a] most definite nucleus of the unsatisfied instinct after learning that I speak of ...' Through 'a good system of secondary schools in their native town ...' boys

> would have the opportunity of entering that sort of intellectual aristocracy, which there is some ground for saying can only be found at our universities, and might be under the eye and influence, if not under the direct teaching, of a high-minded scholar or man of science.[89]

Here Green's efforts were tied to his interest in 'continuing' education and university extension. Green had been appointed in December 1866 a Local Examination Delegate by Oxford University, i.e. an examiner of 'boys who are not intended to enter the University' but who, by distinguishing themselves in the examinations, might be 'induced' to enter Oxford University — or one of the new civic colleges (such as those in Manchester, Leeds and Liverpool, joined together in 1880 as Victoria University).[90]

---

[87] 'Grading of Secondary Schools,' pp. 402–3. Delivered to the Birmingham Teachers' Association and first published in *The Journal of Education*, May, 1877.

[88] Reader, *Professional Men*; Perkin, *The Rise of Professional Society*, chaps. 3–4.

[89] 'Grading of Secondary Schools,' p. 409.

[90] Bodleian MS.Top.Oxon.d.517 notes Green's local examinership. On the system of local examinations, see *[Oxford] Student's Handbook*, p. 187. This was extended in 1873–4 to girls and women. On the post-1851 civic universities in relation to the Oxbridge system of university extension, see S. V. Barnes, 'England's Civic Universi-

We have seen in Chapter One that Green considered teaching outside Oxford and was particularly attracted to the idea of teaching in an industrial-commercial city not properly served by Oxbridge. At the time of Green's school inspections Birmingham had no university but had a technical (and adult education) institute, the Birmingham and Midland Institute. Green proposed employing two Grammar School masters, one of literature and modern history and one of natural science, to lecture three evenings a week to adult audiences at the Birmingham and Midland Institute.[91] In Green's view, the preparation of men for the universities was only one of the purposes of the grammar schools. Since the majority of grammar school pupils were destined for business careers, and were not likely to stay in the higher school for more than a few years, Green cautioned that 'care should be taken to make sure of some real knowledge of mathematics and one modern language being acquired within that period.'[92]

1874–5 marked the effective beginning of a movement to provide better secondary education for boys and girls in Oxford.[93] When Green was elected in 1876 to the Oxford Town Council, he made it known that one of his main goals was the improvement of secondary education. He became the prime mover behind the Oxford Boys' High School, which opened in 1881 as a day-school supported by pupil fees, private donations and local endowments.[94] The High School was specifically com-

ties and the Triumph of the Oxbridge Ideal,' *History of Education Quarterly*, 36 (1996), pp. 271–305.

[91] 'Notebook of School inspection', *GP* 1(c), last twenty pages. One-fifth of each lecturer's salary would be paid by the BMI and four-fifths by the Grammar School. Green publicly supported University Extension to Birmingham in 1878: speech reported in *Birmingham Daily Gazette*, 27 Sept. 1878, reprinted in *AW*, pp. 328–30. R. Waterhouse, *The Birmingham and Midland Institute 1854–1954* (Birmingham: Birmingham Mail, 1954). The Mason College of Science opened in 1880, rendering Green's scheme rather irrelevant. In 1892 Mason College absorbed the medical faculty of the Queen's Hospital. A 'massively-endowed' University of Birmingham, 'inspired by the examples of Edinburgh and Glasgow,' was established in 1900 (Smith, *Conflict and Compromise*, pp. 215–19).

[92] 'Grading of Secondary Schools,' p. 411.

[93] See *OCBBG*: 'Oxford Public High School' [editorial], 27 June 1874, p. 5; 'The Proposed Grammar School,' 4 July 1874, p. 8; 'The Freemen and the Education Scheme,' 29 August 1874, p. 5; 'Proposed High School for Girls,' 6 February 1875, p. 6; 'The Proposed High School for Girls,' 6 March 1875, p. 5; 'The Freeman and Nixon's School,' 31 July 1875, p. 5; 'Oxford High School for Boys,' 2 February 1878, p. 7; [editorial], 16 February 1878, pp. 4–5; [editorial], 17 April 1880, p. 5, and 'Oxford High School for Boys' (p. 8); 'Opening of the Oxford High School for Boys,' 17 September 1881, p. 8. Green bought shares, in 1875, in the Girls' Public Day School, Ltd.: receipts are in *GP* 1(d), box 2.

[94] 'City of Oxford Council Minute Book, 1876 to 1882' (Oxfordshire County Record Office, no. C.5.3). Minutes directly concerning the Boys' High School are on pp. 112, 141, 154, 168ff., 175, 183, 187, 212, 216, 265, 273ff., 278, 296, 423, 458, 474, 478, 485. Also

mitted by statute to educating the sons of freemen of the city because it absorbed the endowments of earlier Oxford institutions, chiefly Nixon's School and the Blue Coat School.[95] Following Green's recommendation, the High School also provided a large number of scholarships for academically qualified boys regardless of status.[96]

Like KES Birmingham and other superior grammar schools, the OBHS provided both Classical and 'modern' curricula (along lines similar to those of the German *Realschulen*), and some flexibility was retained in passing students between the business-oriented and university preparatory programmes. One of the better known graduates of the High School was T. E. Lawrence, who won a classics scholarship to Magdalen College, Oxford, and achieved fame as 'Lawrence of Arabia'. Green and his wife, who were childless, personally contributed more than £1000 to the High School in the form of scholarships, and at Green's memorial service about £550 were immediately subscribed for additional OBHS scholarships.[97]

One measure of Green's success as a reformer of English secondary education is the fact that schools like the KES Birmingham and the Oxford Boys' High School were widely popular in Britain well into the twentieth century, highly prized as instruments of upward social mobility.[98] Only during the 1950s and '60s did 'comprehensivization' of secondary schools receive serious support at the highest level of govern-

---

'Oxford High School, 1879–1884. Letter Book' (OCRO, no. Q.4.13): containing copies of letters acknowledging receipt of donations from Charlotte B. Green (5 April 1883) and Miss E. Green (17 Highfield St., Leicester: 20 April 1883, 21 January 1884).

[95] Green served on the Oxford Council's committee of Nixon's School from November 1876 and again from 1879: see 'City of Oxford Council Minute Book, 1876–79' [OCRO: no. B.4.13]: 23 November 1876; and 'City of Oxford Council Minute Book, 1876–82' [C.5.3]: 12 November 1879.

[96] The Council resolved, on 5 November 1877, that the High School should offer fifty scholarships, each tenable for three years, and that thirty of them were to be reserved for boys from public elementary schools, entrants examined according to the Sixth Standard of the Education Code. Entrance was to be offered resident boys 'without regard to the Religious belief of parents or their Social positions.' 'City of Oxford Council Minute Book, 1876–79': 5 November 1877 [Green's report on behalf of Grammar School and Nixon's School Committee].

[97] See 'Memorial to Professor Green,' *OCBBG*, 20 May 1882, p. 7. The list of financial donors to the O.B.H.S. between 1880 and 1884, though dominated by Oxford dons (as would be expected), is very nearly a 'Who's Who' list of Britain's liberal intelligentsia.

[98] On permeation of the elite by state and grammar school graduates, see H. Perkin, 'Who Runs Britain? Elites in British Society Since 1800' (1978), in *The Structured Crowd*, chap. 9. The Labour Party's education Ministers between 1945 and 1951, Ellen Wilkinson and George Tomlinson, were working-class products of the grammar schools, and they accepted the 'tripartite division of secondary schools' (state/grammar/'public') enshrined in the Butler Education Act of 1944. 'Educational egalitarianism,' Kenneth Morgan concludes, 'was hardly on Labour's agenda' in the immediate post-WWII period. *The People's Peace. British History 1945–1989* (OUP, 1990), pp. 40–1.

ment.[99] By any contemporary measure, however, Green was an educational progressive, valuing merit over status. It should also be emphasized that the Oxford and Birmingham grammar schools demonstrated the practicality of Greenian principles, as these efforts satisfied, on the one hand, the concerns of educationists for intellectual quality, and, on the other, the interests of local communities in the socially equitable management of educational provision.

4.5. TEMPERANCE

Another popular cause with which Green identified was restriction of Drink, and his interest in this again links him conceptually and politically with the Dissenting element of mid- and late-Victorian Liberalism. While temperance was not a Dissenting cause *per se*, it appealed widely to Nonconformists, who comprised a large portion of the membership and the leadership of Victorian temperance and prohibitionist organizations.[100] As Richard Helmstadter observes, 'It is not surprising that Nonconformists who valued sturdy independence, thrift, self-motivated effort, and success should come to regard drink as a device of the devil.' Personal proclamations of abstinence from liquor became as important a feature of Chapel life as proclamations of religious conversion.[101] This is not to deny that Churchmen were active in the temperance movement or to assert that temperance was somehow a particular Dissenting concern. But Green's temperance activism revealed a preoccupation with social and political 'purity' that was also a distinctive feature of the Dissenting concern with the evils of drink.

It was said that the fastest way out of Manchester for its labouring inhabitants was through a bottle, and this was no less true in Oxford, which ranked second only to Cambridge among English urban areas in density of public houses and taverns.[102] National per capita consumption of beer and ale was nearly three times greater in 1875 than in 1960, consumption of spirits four times greater.[103] Like other temperance 'mil-

---

[99] Anthony Crosland, Secretary of State for Education and Science in 1965, confided in private that 'If it's the last thing I do, I'm going to destroy every fucking grammar school in England and Wales and Northern Ireland' (quoted in Morgan, *People's Peace*, p. 248). The Oxford Boys' High School was closed in 1966.

[100] 'Of a sample of 273 teetotal leaders during the period 1833–72, all but 41 turned out to have been Nonconformists' (Bebbington, *The Nonconformist Conscience*, p. 46).

[101] Indeed, foreswearing strong drink was one of those evidences of respectability and right-thinking attached to inclusion among the closer circles of the chapel. Helmstadter, 'The Nonconformist Conscience,' p. 156.

[102] Oxford had one public house per 110 inhabitants. See J. Chamberlain, 'Municipal Public Houses,' *Fortnightly Review*, n.s. 22 (1877), pp. 147–59. (Chamberlain's plan for community control of pubs was similar to Green's ideas.)

[103] G. F. A. Best, *Mid-Victorian Britain 1851–75* (London: Fontana, 1979), pp. 240, 333 n. 34. See also Harrison, *Drink and the Victorians*; and A. E. Dingle, *The Campaign for Prohibi-*

itants', Green doubted that attempts to reform individual drunkards through moral suasion were sufficient to combat a 'social' evil — that is, an individual pathology that injured other more or less innocent persons. He thought it naive to regard widespread drunkenness as the accumulation of individual lapses of personal responsibility. As he observed in 'Liberal Legislation and Freedom of Contract',

> We know that, however decently carried on, the excessive drinking of one man means an injury to others in health, purse, and capability, to which no limits can be placed. Drunkenness in the head of a family means, as a rule, the impoverishment and degradation of all members of the family; and the presence of a drinkshop at the corner of a street means, as a rule, the drunkenness of a certain number of heads of family in that street. Remove the drinkshops, and, as the experience of many happy communities sufficiently shows, you almost, perhaps in time altogether, remove the drunkenness ... It is a poor sophistry to tell us that it is moral cowardice to seek to remove by law [viz., a licensing act] a temptation which every one ought to be able to resist for himself. It is not the part of a considerate self-reliance to remain in presence of a temptation merely for the sake of being tempted.[104]

Green made a direct attempt at amelioration through counterattraction, by opening a temperance coffee-house in St Clements, Oxford, in 1875.[105] His own avoidance of alcohol was due to a number of factors: drink, like consumption of rich food, made him ill; intemperance seemed to him a distasteful indulgence; and his family had been anguished by his brother's alcoholism. Even social drinking made him uncomfortable. But more than that, his teetotalism after 1872, as we shall see, was clearly a matter of principle and a symbol of political commitment.[106]

It is impossible to ascertain the extent to which, if at all, Green appreciated habitual drunkenness as an illness, but he clearly viewed it as a conscious refusal to face or live up to one's responsibilities.[107] Intemperance was thus a moral shortcoming with social and political overtones.

tion in Victorian England: the United Kingdom Alliance, 1872–1895 (London: Croom Helm, 1980).

[104] *Works*, iii, pp. 384, 386. Lecture delivered 18 January 1881 at the Leicester Temperance Hall, and printed in *Alliance News*, 29 January 1881.

[105] Green owned shares in the Oxford Café Company (share receipt dated 27 June 1877 in business correspondence with C. D. Cave: *GP* 1[a]). *GP* 1(d), Box 1, contains a tenancy agreement for the premises at 96 High Street.

[106] As Dean at Balliol Green must have been well acquainted with student drunkenness as a disciplinary problem, and with the sometimes deadly consequences of alcohol. He was present in 1870 at an inquest relating to the drowning of James Greg, Exhibitioner of Balliol, in the Thames. The *Oxford Chronicle* report of the incident hints at inebriation as a contributing factor: 'Melancholy Suicide in Port Meadow,' 28 May 1870, p. 7.

[107] Harrison notes that the word 'alcoholism' came into use 'only about 1860', although 'dipsomania' was in medical usage in 1843 (*OED*). He claims that something approaching the current understanding of alcoholism (i.e. as a disease of 'chemical

Male drunkards — Green scarcely ever noted female drunkenness — ignored their familial obligations, and were thus both unmanly and a social burden. Artisans and 'respectable' working people had internalized this belief to some extent and many proletarian political organizations from the 1820s harped on the evils of drink. The ideal of the sober and provident working man was not simply imposed upon British society by elites. Responsible drinking and abstinence were elements of working-class (male) self-fashioning since at least the 1830s.[108]

While public drunkenness was one of those habits that had fallen into almost universal disrepute after ca. 1820, the persistence of intemperance, public and private, was especially problematic to Victorian liberalism. Like other chaotic practices and institutions, alcohol abuse appeared contrary to the rational order which reformers and Radicals since the eighteenth century had aspired to. Furthermore, as a form of self-imposed slavery and indiscipline, wasteful drinking represented an internalization of 'Tory' social dependency. To be besotted was, in some sense, to ignore one's potential for self-improvement and to succumb to fatalism. Green apparently regarded such fatalism among the lower classes as tantamount to accepting socioeconomic stratification as inescapable and permanent. Running counter to the ideal of self-improvement in 'working–class culture', however, was the acceptance of drinking as one of the manly attributes; the creation by some working men of teetotalism as an alternative masculine ideal during the last third of the nineteenth century had not solved the Drink Problem. Bourgeois moralists like Green saw much room for improvement.

With the expansion of electoral politics (locally as well as nationally) since the 1830s there was more reason for reformers to identify the plentitude of pubs as an unnatural and artificial impediment to the discharge of personal and political responsibilities. Demands for prohibition of intoxicating drink, or at least stricter licensing of pubs, swelled into a powerful movement by the 1850s. Various organizations, many with clerical support and leadership, coalesced around prohibitionism. One of the most effective organizations — as measured by vigour of propaganda and by official 'presence' in government — was the nonsectarian United Kingdom Alliance [UKA] for the Total and Immediate Legislative Suppression of the Traffic in Intoxicating Liquors as Beverages (1853). The Alliance was modelled on the Anti–Corn Law League

---

dependency') emerged in Britain and North America by the 1870s (*Drink and the Victorians*, pp. 20–22).

[108] See especially B. Harrison, 'Teetotal Chartism,' *History*, 58 (1973), pp. 193–203; W. Seccombe, 'Patriarchy Stabilized: the Construction of the Male Breadwinner Wage Norm in Nineteenth Century Britain,' *Social History*, 11 (1986), pp. 53–76; F. M. L. Thompson, *The Rise of Respectable Society. A Social History of Victorian Britain, 1830–1900* (London: Fontana, 1988), pp. 319–23.

and the Anti-State Church Association; it had central and regional offices, held frequent national and local conferences, and had a newspaper, *Alliance News*. Its leader and representative in Parliament was Sir Wilfred Lawson, an evangelical Anglican who enjoyed the respect of many Dissenters. Green joined the Alliance in 1872 and was appointed as one of its vice-presidents in 1878.[109] The Alliance had some impact upon legislation, such as H. A. Bruce's licensing act of 1872, although, predictably, its members were dissatisfied with the slow progress of the law and the ready availability of drink.

In 1874, Green chaired the Electoral Committee of Oxford's predominantly Liberal 'temperance electors'.[110] Although two Liberals, W. V. Harcourt and Edward Cardwell, were returned in the February election, Cardwell was elevated to the Lords, necessitating another run-off. A Conservative, A. W. Hall, defeated the Liberal J. D. Lewis in the March election, and Liberals fared badly in other English elections.[111] Gladstone complained that the electors, and Liberal hopes, had been 'borne down in a torrent of gin and beer.'[112] Charles Fyffe recalled Green's dismay at the Liberal defeat, noting that Green attributed it in part to the indiscipline of working-class electors.[113] After 1874 Green attended and gave addresses to many temperance meetings.[114] Indeed, he closed 'Liberal Legislation and Freedom of Contract' by asking the

---

[109] Green was elected president of the Oxford Band of Hope and Temperance Union in 1876. He was also elected treasurer of the Oxford Diocesan Branch of the Church of England Temperance Society, which caused him some embarrassment since he saw himself as a rather loose Churchman. See Green's obituary in *Alliance News*, 1 April 1882, p. 193.

[110] 'Meeting of Temperance Electors,' *OCBBG*, 31 January 1874, p. 5.

[111] Some Oxford temperance electors followed the instruction of the UKA to abstain from voting for candidates who had not supported the 1872 Permissive Bill. Green, however, did vote for Cardwell (Sec. State for War, 1868–74) and Harcourt (Solicitor General, 1873–4). Green had upbraided the latter in 1873 for his reluctance to support a liquor licensing bill being discussed in Parliament. Harcourt's letters to Green (8 January 1873, 20 January 1873) in *GP* 1(a); THG letter to Harcourt (?10 January 1873): Bodleian MSS. Harcourt, dep. 246, fols. 69–70.

[112] W. E. Gladstone to his brother Robertson (6 February 1874), quoted in Magnus, *Gladstone*, p. 228. Upon his resignation Gladstone also confided to the Queen that the 1874 General Election was the most devastating verdict on a Government's policies in modern times.

[113] Green spoke of the 'ridiculous political action' of the new electors and 'dwelt with great disappointment on the use made by the workmen of their half holidays and their shorter hours' — too many of which were spent in pubs (Fyffe recollection in *GP* 1b).

[114] E.g. on 18 January 1878 he spoke about temperance at the Oxford Workmen's Hall (*AN*, 26 Jan. 1878, p. 62). On 18 March 1879 he spoke at the Oxfordshire Band of Hope conference in Chipping Norton (*AN*, 12 Apr. 1879, pp. 230–2). On 12 December of that year he presided over a temperance meeting at the Oxford Liberal Hall (*AN*, 3 Jan. 1880, p. 11). Green's speech to the U.K. Alliance in Oxford on 1 February 1882 is a masterful statement of the principles of 'Local Option' in temperance legislation and an

'citizens of England', who 'now make its law ... to put a restraint on themselves in the matter of strong drink,' perhaps even to give up 'the not very precious liberty of buying and selling alcohol, in order that they may become more free to exercise the faculties and improve the talents which God has given them.'[115]

Helmstadter makes some significant observations about Dissenters' involvement in the temperance movement. Temperance activism marked the turn of Dissent towards 'social reform', as opposed to purely religious or political reform. Yet temperance reform never received the support of Dissent as a *whole* because the dominant temperance organizations came to embrace the conviction that state action, rather than individual conscience, provided the solution to the Drink Problem.[116] This interventionist mentality sat uncomfortably with 'laissez-faire' Liberals and with Dissenters (like Baines Sr.), who through the 1880s generally identified government and state regulation as the cause of their disadvantaged position as a community. Green's temperance activity, of course, was not a direct indication of sympathy with Political Dissent, but like the many Dissenters who joined the Alliance or denominational organizations, he was concerned with the purity of the community. In its obituary of Green, the *Daily News*, a mouthpiece for both Nonconformity and 'Manchester School' Liberalism, implied the common understanding of Green and Dissenters of drunkenness as a *political* disorder:

> Bribery and treating were in his eyes not subjects for grave public condemnation and amused secret tolerance, but accursed things, which would, if condoned, eat away the morality of the community which practiced or permitted them.[117]

Green was no prude in detecting a sinister 'drink interest' at work in Oxford and the nation, for brewers and publicans were stalwarts of the Conservative party and opponents of state interference.[118] His temperance enthusiasm has evoked some scholarly sneers about his paternal-

---

important source for understanding his theory of direct local democracy ('Important Conference at Oxford and Great Public Meeting,' *AN*, 11 Feb. 1882, pp. 82–6).

[115] 'Liberal Legislation,' *Harris and Morrow*, p. 212.

[116] Helmstadter, 'The Nonconformist Conscience,' pp. 155–7.

[117] Undated press clipping contained in a scrapbook of obituaries and reviews of Green's writings: *GP* 1(d) — box 2. Oxford Liberals filed a complaint against 'corrupt practices' in the 1880 Parliamentary elections at Oxford, including unusually high and irregular campaign expenditures and frequent 'treating' of electors and campaign workers at pubs.

[118] Green agreed with temperance activists who identified the Drink Interest with local and national licensed victuallers' associations and other organizations with a 'corporate sense opposed to the nation'. See 'Special Conference at Oxford,' *AN*, 1 May 1880, pp. 278–9 (including transcript of Green's remarks). His stance was also politically expedient: the local Conservative party was headed by brewers.

ism — as if he failed to comprehend the alienating nature of 'class society', intentionally ignored the pressures of poverty and trampled on individual freedom.[119] The view of temperance legislation as class discriminatory state action — for it is true that in gentlemen's clubs drink flowed day and night — is different from the philosophical charge that Green is inconsistent in his view of satisfaction of desire in relation to the common good. Is drinking bad because individuals impaired by alcohol detract from 'the common good' or is it an irrelevant pleasure because it is not a virtue and not conducive to 'moral personality'?[120] Geoffrey Thomas says little about Green's temperance enthusiasm but implies that Green deplored drunkenness because alcoholic satisfaction was transitory and could not achieve 'an abiding satisfaction of an abiding self.'[121] But this observation does not directly address the *political* issue of control of a pleasure-inducing substance because of its abuse by a minority.

Green had remonstrated with the Solicitor General, Harcourt, in early 1873, about the latter's reluctance to support stricter licensing laws:

> How can it hold right to interfere with a man's freedom by directly compelling him to send his child to school, yet wrong to interfere with it by indirectly preventing him from drinking himself and his family to rags?[122]

While Green may have been guilty of bourgeois do-good-ism, he should be absolved of the charge of legislating virtue or 'forcing people to be free'. In fact, he held that individuals in immediate face-to-face interaction were the best judges of the common good. People in communities should be enabled to determine, through local government (based on a household franchise) and 'permissive legislation', the availability of intoxicating drink.[123]

4.6. GREEN AND DISSENT AT OXFORD

We have seen how Green's view of educational reform was influenced by his perception of denominational and other social inequality. He was admired by Dissenters for his services to education because his efforts to promote sectarian harmony indicated his genuine concern for freedom of conscience. Green's public lecture 'The Work to Be Done by the New

---

[119] Clarke, *Liberals and Social Democrats*, p. 15; Greengarten, *Thomas Hill Green*, pp. 90–2, chap. 8.

[120] See J. P. Plamenatz, *Consent, Freedom and Political Obligation* (OUP, 1938), chaps. 3–4.

[121] *Moral Philosophy of T. H. Green*, pp. 168–80.

[122] Letter to W. V. Harcourt (cited n.111 above).

[123] Nicholson, 'T. H. Green and State Action: Liquor Legislation,' pp. 79–82, 93–5. John Prest observes that Green was more attentive to 'self-government in a local community' than were J. S. Mill or Spencer. Mill was 'too obsessed with individuals to pay much attention to localities', while in Spencer's view even local authority was a trespasser on individual freedom. Prest, *Liberty and Locality*, pp. 197–8.

Oxford High School,' delivered early in 1882, was dedicated to Joseph Richardson, headmaster of the Oxford Wesleyan School.[124] The invitation to lecture was made by Hugh Price Hughes (1847–1902), the Methodist preacher and journalist who later (during the public controversy over the divorce suit involving Parnell, the Irish nationalist leader) coined the term 'Nonconformist Conscience'.[125] Green was committed to religious and social equality at Oxford University even before many Dissenters devoted serious attention to such issues.[126] As we have seen (1.2, 3.4–3.5 above), Green went on record early in his academic career against creedal subscription for fellowships and most collegiate and university offices. Moreover, he objected not only to the pretensions of the Establishment to spiritual monopoly but to the Church's overbearing social and political presence at Oxford, a presence related to its economic power. Speaking before the Oxford Reform League in 1867, Green found an opportunity to complain not only of the restrictive Parliamentary franchise but of the 'protected and exclusive system' of English higher education whose 'artificial' expense was based upon 'the unequally distributed endowments — of the established church.' In the late 1860s he was the effective manager of Balliol Hall, a non-collegiate institution for 'unattached students', established so that less privileged students could avoid some of the expense of college residence.[127]

Perhaps no public effort of Green's indicated his neo-Puritanism more directly than his encouragement, during the last years of his life, of the Oxford University Nonconformists' Union, which was the germ of Mansfield College, the first non-Anglican college at Oxford.[128] Following the University reforms of 1854 Nonconformists were allowed to take up residence in Oxford colleges without formal creedal subscription and to take degrees; after 1871, most fellowships were opened to non-Anglicans. Athough Green welcomed these reforms, he was concerned about what he perceived to be the weakened religious tone of Oxford and the absence of true religious fellowship and community.[129] He was especially concerned about the religious alienation of Dissent-

[124] Noted by R. L. Nettleship, 'Preface' to THG, *Works*, iii.

[125] King, 'Hugh Price Hughes and the British "Social Gospel",' pp. 69–70.

[126] Thus John Bright opined in a letter to Green (19 March 1861) that the Dissenting community was on the whole rather apathetic about the matter of religious tests at Oxford. K. Robbins, *John Bright* (London: Routledge and Kegan Paul, 1979), p. 173.

[127] See R. L. Nettleship, 'Memoir,' pp. cvii, cx–cxi (quoting Oxford Reform League speech: Green's 'first appearance on a political platform').

[128] W. T. Pennar Davies, *Mansfield College: Its History, Aims and Achievements* (privately printed, 1947); D. Leighton, 'T. H. Green and the Social Aspects of Evangelicalism,' unpublished paper delivered to members of the Middle Common Room of Mansfield College, 30 May 1991; and E. Kaye, *Mansfield College, Oxford. Its Origin, History, and Significance* (OUP, 1996).

[129] In October 1875 Green still showed leanings toward evangelicalism and Dissent. He wrote to his wife, 'Last night I worshipped at St. Ebbes [Low Church], where Mr.

ers. Green must have become acquainted with R. W. Dale, the Congregational leader in Birmingham, when he was employed by the Taunton Commission in 1865–6. In 1880 or 1881 Green advised Dale,

> The opening of the national Universities to Nonconformists has been, in my judgment, an injury rather than a help to Nonconformity. You are sending up here, year after year, the sons of your best and wealthiest families: they are often altogether uninfluenced by the services of the Church which they find here, and they not only drift away from Nonconformity — they drift away and lose all faith: and you are bound as soon as you have secured the opening of the Universities for your sons to follow them when you send them here, in order to defend and maintain their religious life and faith.[130]

On 10 May 1881, sixteen Nonconformist undergraduates, graduates and fellows of Oxford colleges met in the rooms of R. F. Horton, a Congregational fellow of New College, to discuss the prospects of a Nonconformists' association.[131] These included J. E. Legge of Queen's, J. King of Trinity, and T. E. Ellis of New; most were 'Independents', although other Dissenters and Anglicans attended subsequent meetings. James Bryce, Regius Professor of Civil Law (1870–93), was offered the presidency of the organization.[132] James Legge, the Professor of Chinese and a devout Congregationalist, and Green were offered vice-presidencies. On 27 January 1882 the Union clarified its intentions:

> This Society has been formed to remove the feeling of isolation, which Nonconformists in the University experience, especially upon coming up as freshmen, to bring about intercourse among them, to discuss questions connected with Nonconformity, and to promote religious equality.[133]

Although Green was titular vice-president of the Nonconformists' Union, he was frequently ill during the autumn of 1881 and the winter of

French took the service — He preached a better sermon than one can hear from any of the Town clergy. I should be rather inclined to go there in Vacations' (letter quoted in CBG recollections, GP 1[d]; original letter missing).

[130] Quoted in Pennar Davies, *Mansfield College*, pp. 9–10; and in A. W. W. Dale, *Life of R. W. Dale*, p. 496. The original letter no longer exists; it may have been destroyed with the bulk of Dale's personal papers (personal communication from Dr Mark D. Johnson, 4 April 1990).

[131] Minute Book of the Oxford University Nonconformists' Union [1881–6]: Mansfield College Library, cupboard 23.

[132] Bryce's ancestors were Lowland Scots and Ulstermen. His paternal grandfather was a Presbyterian pastor in Co. Antrim. Bryce himself grew up in Belfast. Since he had trouble with religious conformity at Oxford (in 1857), it is not surprising that Bryce became a propagandist for a Nonconformist college. See J. Bryce and A. M. Fairbairn, 'Nonconformity and the Universities: the Free Churches and a Theological Faculty,' *British Quarterly Review* (April, 1884), pp. 372–98.

[133] OUNU Minute Book, pp. 10–11. The featured speaker was W. J. Ashley, BA of Balliol, who spoke on 'The Church and the Social Question.' Ashley became a distinguished economic historian (see 6.2. below). For testimony to the feeling of isolation, see F. Tillyard, 'The Oxford Nonconformists' Union 1883–1886,' *Congregational Quarterly*, 25 (1947), pp. 133–7.

1881–2, and otherwise engaged in town council duties and the Oxford high school project; he never attended a meeting of the Union.

At a meeting in Horton's rooms following Green's death, Professor Legge 'gave some interesting remarks about his connection with him' (which were unfortunately unrecorded) and moved an expression of sympathy to Charlotte Green.[134] Horton read a paper on the principles and probable effects of disestablishment, whereupon W. J. Ashley of Balliol 'urged that the difficulties and dangers of disestablishment should make us look for an alternative.' W. R. D. Adkins, also of Balliol (and later a Liberal MP), asserted that religion 'should address itself to the inward mind and not the outward formality'; and S. Wadsworth (Balliol) reiterated that there was a need for 'a national religion [presumably expressed through the Church of England] as well as a[n] inward spiritual religion'. Green would have been pleased with the thoughtful and measured tones of the discussion and reassured by subsequent meetings of the Union, in which 'social reform' under religious auspices was a frequent topic.

The further steps toward the establishment of Mansfield College in 1889 cannot be followed here, but it should be noted that a distinctive Nonconformist presence at Oxbridge was an irresistible temptation to those committed to religious equality and the logic of 'disestablishmentarianism'. The official opening of Mansfield was a gala event and among early visitors was Mr Gladstone.[135] The college, though initially restricted to educating men with certificates from theological colleges or university degrees, or simultaneously enrolled as undergraduates at other Oxford colleges, paved the way for other Nonconformist colleges at Oxford and Cambridge over the next fifty years.[136] That Victorian Dissenters regarded Mansfield as their return to the bastion of the Establishment — countering the Restoration 'purge' of Puritans from Oxford — and as the symbol of their arrival in respectable society, is indicated by the generosity of financial support from England's leading Noncon-

---

[134] OUNU Minute Book, p. 17.
[135] Visitors Book, 1889–1909, entry for 6 February 1890: Mansfield College Library, cupboard 24.
[136] The Unitarian James Martineau met with Mansfield's first Principal, A. W. Fairbairn, in 1888 to discuss the relocation of Manchester New College from London to Oxford. Drummond, *Life and Letters of Martineau*, ii (New York: Dodd, Mead, 1902), p. 147. Mansfield initially had no voting representative on the governing councils of Oxford University. It admitted regular undergraduates after the Second World War and was promoted to 'permanent private hall' in 1955. In 1995 it was granted a royal charter and full collegiate status. E. Kaye, *Mansfield College, Oxford*. On Mansfield and the life of the University, see W. B. Selbie, 'Fifty Years at Oxford,' *Congregational Quarterly*, 14 (1936), pp. 282–90.

formist families.[137] Mansfield College was made possible by the same Dissenting families that had financed the Anti-Corn Law League, the Liberation Society and the United Kingdom Alliance.

Though Mansfield lacked the prestige of other Oxford colleges, Mansfield men distinguished themselves in intellectual, social and political work, becoming the 'lights' of Nonconformity. Yet the question arises as to whether Mansfield College, indirectly a product of Green's preference for and Arnold's aversion to Puritanism, was really what was needed, either for Oxford or for Nonconformity. As Clyde Binfield, Stephen Koss, Mark Johnson and others have pointed out, the Dissenting Interest — based on a sense of distinctive communal identity — effectively dissolved during the quarter century before the Great War; and this despite the fact that Dissenters, like the aforementioned Hugh Price Hughes and Dr John Clifford, became powerful arbiters of public opinion. Koss observes that 'in late Victorian and Edwardian times, Nonconformists were elected to Parliament as the avowed auxiliaries of their denominational authorities, and often with their indispensable support.'[138] But ca. 1910 'the [Nonconformist] giants of the pulpit' had already been overshadowed by Nonconformist MPs and other public figures, and after 1918 many pulpit politicians 'invited embarrassment and even ridicule by presupposing the survival of traditional loyalties.'[139] Many distinctly Dissenting political goals of the mid-Victorian period had been achieved by 1914 (disestablishment of the Church in Wales was agreed to in that year) and few new ones had been invented.[140]

4.7. THE NONCONFORMIST SOCIAL CONSCIENCE

The 'dissolution of Dissent', and the bearing of the facts of its demise on Green's insights about Puritanism, Nonconformity and Liberalism, will be picked up again in Chapter Six. Green's letter to R. W. Dale, drawing attention to the absence of a Dissenting moral and spiritual tone at

[137] Of the £50,000 raised for Mansfield by 1890, more than £6,000 'came from a group of Manchester textile families, Armitages, Haworths, Rigbys and Lees ...'. Nearly £5,000 was subscribed by the 'Spicer–Unwin connexion (chiefly London)', and £1,600 by the 'Samuel Morley connexion'. Binfield, *So Down to Prayers*, p. 167 and n. (from the chapter 'The Shores of Philistia').

[138] *Nonconformity in Modern British Politics*, p. 224. Thus in 1906 a total of 185 Nonconformist candidates were elected to Parliament, 157 of them as Liberals and 20 as Labour members (p. 228).

[139] *Ibid.*, p. 224.

[140] See *ibid.*, chaps. 8–10. Two free-thinkers in the Liberal Cabinet, John Morley and J. H. Burns, resigned upon Britain's declaration of war in 1914, but delegates to a March 1918 meeting of the National Free Church Council could not decide if they were militarists or pacifists (p. 141). Also, Binfield, *So Down To Prayers*, chap. 9 ('"No Quest, No Conquest"').

Oxford, implied that the *presence* of such would improve both Oxford and the nation. It may be that Nonconformity's convergence with the Establishment in the later years of the nineteenth century was actually a disguised form of co-optation; Dissenters' quests for influence and respectability had consequences they did not foresee, and one result of their social and political success was a dulling of the radical edge of the 'Dissenting Interest'.[141]

Yet while the heroic age of Political Dissent appears to have ended almost as soon as Dissenters had become conscious of it, many Dissenters from the 1870s maintained an activist stance by channelling their spiritual enthusiasm into social reform. As Beatrice Potter (later Webb) put it in 1884, members of the governing classes, Dissenters included, were changing the object of their devotion from God to man.[142] Thomas Hill Green had proclaimed a few years earlier that 'a verification of the idea of God' was not to be found but rather *made*, and many who listened to him made their faith through commitment to social service. Charles Gore, Henry Scott Holland and others at Oxford under Green's influence went on to publish the 'Lux Mundi' essays in 1889, discussing Idealism, evolutionism and other expressions of 'rationalism' so repugnant to the successors of J. H. Newman and John Keble. They also founded a Christian Social Union — from the conviction that the Church had largely ignored economic and social evils.[143] The late Victorian flowering of Anglican Christian Socialism — as well as related Church ventures like the Guild of St Matthew — would seem to indicate a more radical and progressive consciousness among the representatives of the religious Establishment than among Dissenters.[144] Yet it can be argued that the *theological* innovations of Churchmen in this period — the intellectual impressiveness of their attempts to reconcile, in doctrines, traditional theological priorities with new 'demands' of the world — have overshadowed the fact of contemporary Dissenters internalizing the new social turn (discussed in the next chapter).

---

[141] Martin Wiener has made many interesting points about cultural co-optation — for instance, in arguing that the British 'decline of the industrial spirit' was due in part to the manufacturing-commercial classes, including many Dissenters, sending their boys to the English public schools, where they were taught to value Greek and despise metallurgical chemistry. M. Wiener, *English Culture and the Decline of the Industrial Spirit, 1850–1980* (CUP, 1981).

[142] From *My Apprenticeship* (1926), cited in Himmelfarb, *Poverty and Compassion*, p. 4. Beatrice's father, though an Anglican convert, had a north-country, Unitarian, Radical background.

[143] Richter, *Politics of Conscience*, pp. 122–30.

[144] For the social progressiveness of the later Victorian Church, see Jones,*The Christian Socialist Revival;* Norman,*The Victorian Christian Socialists,* and Matt Carter, *T. H. Green and the Development of Ethical Socialism* (Exeter: Imprint Academic, 2003) especially chaps. 2, 4.

The social turn of Dissent from the 1880s may indeed have been more widely felt than Anglican social activism, and it had important consequences for British society and polity down to 1914. As the Fabian and historian R. C. K. Ensor observed sixty years ago, around 1900 'the labour and socialist movement poached extensively on [the Chapels'] preserves.'[145] While this phenomenon may have indicated the political maturation of the British working classes, or the secularization of British society, it pointed to other political-cultural realities as well. Ensor remarks that the 'Pleasant Sunday Afternoon' (PSA) ca. 1900 — entertainment or instruction in church following regular worship, 'secular in character' — had become a characteristic Dissenting practice; and

> while few conservative politicians were invited to speak at P.S.A.s and many liberals were not either, a leading socialist might spend practically every Sunday afternoon in them ... One way and another the rising labour movement owed an immense debt to nonconformity [sic]. The fund of unselfish idealism which sustained the early I.L.P., came mostly from this source ... Broadly *it was due to non-conformity that socialism in England never acquired the anti-religious bias prevailing on the Continent.*[146]

Ensor's claims, offered as little more than anecdotal remarks about 'mental and social aspects' of late Victorian and Edwardian Britain, do not make an argument for the 'religious' (much less specifically Nonconformist) nature of British socialism. At least as significant as religion in the late Victorian-Edwardian socialist formation (or revival) were currents of free-thought, atheism and 'science'. Yet British socialism was one aspect of a new social outlook from the 1880s, characterized by humanitarianism and spiritual concern, which many Nonconformists came to share. Green's philosophy, arguing for the social constitution of the Self in a manner at odds with prevailing liberal theory, helped create this new outlook. In allying himself with contemporary 'Puritans', Green promoted approaches to social facts and problems that were simultaneously traditional and progressive. In becoming a tutor, as it were, to both the Nonconformist Conscience and revived Christian Socialism, Green served as an arbiter of cooperation among progressive elements in British politics and culture, many of whom aligned themselves with Gladstonian Liberalism and Radicalism, and many subsequently with socialism, in order to expand the agenda of 'reform'.

---

[145] R. C. K. Ensor, *England 1870–1914* (Oxford: Clarendon, 1936), p. 528.

[146] *Ibid* ., pp. 528–9 (my emphasis). An offshoot of the PSA was the interdenominational but strongly Congregationalist 'Brotherhood Movement', enrolling at one point 300,000 men and described by Binfield as 'a socialism without Socialism'. Binfield, *So Down to Prayers*, pp. 211–12. (ILP: Independent Labour Party, founded 1892–3.)

CHAPTER FIVE

The Social Gospel and Radicalism, 1870–1900

5.1. INTRODUCTION

Many historians have remarked on T. H. Green's philosophy in relation to a 'social turn' in 'the moral imagination of the late Victorians.'[1] While the 1867 and 1884 Reform Acts signalled the democratization of British politics, there ensued from the late 1870s a process described by Gertrude Himmelfarb as the democratization of compassion. An aspect of this that was characteristically Greenian in its combination of meliorism and moral cultivation was the 'University Settlement' movement, involving initially men educated at the Ancient Universities. The recognized beginning of the University Settlement movement is 1884, when Toynbee Hall was established in Whitechapel (East London). Within a decade Toynbee Hall had inspired dozens of imitations, from London to New York and Toronto.[2] The hall was named after Arnold Toynbee

---

[1]   Himmelfarb, *Poverty and Compassion*, introduction. See also Lynd, *England in the Eighteen-Eighties*; A. B. Ulam, *Philosophical Foundations of English Socialism* (Cambridge, MA: Harvard UP, 1951); Richter, *Politics of Conscience*, chaps. 9–11; Meacham, *Toynbee Hall and Social Reform*.

[2]   Church of England clergy established a settlement house in Manchester in 1877 to enable middle-class philanthropists to live among the poor. Toynbee Hall impressed observers in France (Clemenceau) and Germany, and it had a great influence on American ethical socialists (Dr Stanford Coit, Howard D. Bliss, the American Ethical Society) and progressive reformers (Jane Addams, Ellen Starr). W. Picht, *Toynbee Hall and the English Settlement Movement* (London: G. Bell, 1914); Lynd, *England in the Eighteen-Eighties*, pp. 319–25; L. E. Nettleship, 'William Fremantle, Samuel Barnett and the Broad Church Origins of Toynbee Hall,' *Journal of Ecclesiastical History*, 33 (1982), pp. 564–79; A. Kadish, *Apostle Arnold: The Life and Death of Arnold Toynbee* (Durham, NC: Duke UP, 1986); Meacham, *Toynbee Hall*, pp. 24–34.

(1852–83), the Oxford economist and student of Green who had served as assistant to Canon Samuel Barnett in the parish of St Jude's. The hall represented a culmination of the work of Samuel and Henrietta Barnett, who had been active in the Charity Organisation Society (founded 1869); and the organizational foundations of the settlement were laid by Sidney Ball (1857–1918), a tutor of St John's College, Oxford, and by Green's friend James Bryce (then an MP for Tower Hamlets).

Canon Barnett was thoroughly Broad Church in his sympathies and attitudes and there were few doctrinal or political hindrances to cooperation between the Barnetts and the ecumenical or quasi-Christian ethicists common at Oxbridge by the late 1870s. Indeed, it is significant that Green's student Henry Scott Holland founded Oxford House in 1884 with many of the same purposes as Toynbee Hall, but with a distinctly High Church and less vaguely 'ethical' flavour. Holland and other Anglo-Catholics who came to found the Christian Social Union in 1889 were philosophical and political radicals, but they were loath to give ground to Dissent and infidelity. The Guild of St Matthew as well, founded by Rev. Stewart Headlam (curate of Bethnal Green) in 1877, had a High Church tone. (The CSU and the Guild shared many members.) Guild members, who numbered no more than a few hundred, were self-conscious revivers of the Christian Socialism of Maurice and Kingsley: they sought 'to justify God to the people' and 'to promote the study of Political and Social questions in light of the Incarnation.'[3]

There were important theological and political differences among the social reformers of the period ca. 1875–95. They differed also in some of their objectives. It is remarkable, however, that so many involved in the social turn approached social, economic and political issues from a Greenian perspective. Some self-proclaimed socialist atheists proved willing to cooperate with social reforming Christians, and vice versa. Some 'socialist' reformers protested rather too loudly about the flaws of Green's philosophy and the bourgeois consciousness of moral obligation. Sidney and Beatrice Webb opposed the conception of charity shared by many members of the COS, and they found bourgeois philanthropy as arrogant as it was inefficient. Yet their interpolations of moral development out of the conception of the social organism had a ring that was not only Spencerian and Darwinian but Greenian. They remarked in *Problems of Modern Industry* (1902):

> It is of comparatively little importance, in the long run, that individuals
> should develop life to the utmost, if the life of the community in which we

---

[3]   Lynd, *England in the Eighteen-Eighties*, pp. 314–26. Headlam was an early member of the Fabian Society. In 1906 the Guild issued an official congratulation to the thirty newly elected Labour MPs. The CSU grew beyond its High Church origins, representing a wide spectrum of theological opinion by 1900. It was also larger than the Guild, numbering some 2,600 members by 1897.

live is not thereby served … A society is something more than the sum of its members; … a social organism has a life and health distinguishable from those of its individual atoms.[4]

As for the University Settlers specifically, many of them down to 1914 were thoroughly familiar with Green's teachings; they were overwhelmingly (before 1900) men who had gone up to Oxford and Cambridge when Green's academic influence was at its zenith. They shared a conception of responsible citizenship and expressed an enthusiasm for voluntarism and a confidence in moral suasion.[5] They were proud bearers of Green's intellectual and moral 'legacy': libraries and common rooms at Toynbee Hall, the Passmore Edwards Settlement (in Bloomsbury), and Mansfield House (in Canning Town) were named after him. The object of the present discussion is to reveal the ideological underpinnings of an apparently new social ethos from the 1880s, and to indicate how Green's ideas reinforced other prevailing beliefs encouraging an activist society and polity.

5.2. THE SOCIAL TURN OF THE 1880s

The social turn, beginning about 1875, reflected widening acknowledgement that 'self-help', philanthropy and the pragmatic enactment of industrial and social legislation had failed to improve the living and working conditions of large numbers of Britons — not only women and children but men, who had not previously been identified (by Britain's elites, at any rate) as a social category in need of special protection.[6] Victorian public moralists, legislators, charity workers, bureaucrats and experts had offered various explanations of and responses to

---

[4] *Problems of Modern Industry*, p. 250, cited in Meacham,*Toynbee Hall*, p. 93. D. G. Ritchie, Sidney Ball, Samuel Alexander and C. R. Buxton were expressing many of the same sentiments in the 1880s. Collini, *Liberalism and Sociology*, pp. 160-70.

[5] Of the one hundred and two residents of Toynbee Hall between 1884 and 1900, at least fifty-two men came from Oxford, with the largest contingent from Balliol. At least twenty-seven came from Cambridge. Meacham, *Toynbee Hall*, p. 44. University Hall, established in 1890 by Mrs Humphry Ward, was no exception to the pattern of homosociality, but its governing committee included Frances Power Cobbe and the Dowager Countess Russell. Sutherland, *Mrs. Humphry Ward*, pp. 217-21. 'By 1914 women outnumbered men as settlement residents … ' (Anderson, 'The Feminism of T. H. Green: A Late Victorian Success Story?,' p. 687.)

[6] Such legislative interferences as had occurred before 1875 — e.g., factory acts, the Poor Law Amendment Act, the Forster Education Act, public health measures — were implemented with the understanding that they would not compromise self-reliance and individual freedom, the principles enshrined in Samuel Smiles's widely popular book *Self-Help* (1859). A. Fox, *History and Heritage: The Social Origins of the British Industrial Relations System* (London: Allen and Unwin, 1985), chap. 4.

entrenched poverty.[7] However, there was a significant shift in interpretations of such problems during the later Victorian period.

A major feature of the social turn was a belief in the authority of empirical social science, an acceptance of incontrovertible data of poverty and deprivation. But to empirical demonstration was added the moral insistence that individual degradation, whether due to individual or 'structural' (social) causes, was intolerable; deprivation was to be regarded not as a challenge to character but as a social pathology weakening moral and immoral alike.[8] An official register of the social turn was the marked increase in 'social and industrial' legislation after 1875, including the 1875 Artisans' Dwelling Act, providing for slum clearance and rebuilding with public funds, and employers' liability acts, stipulating terms of compensation for industrial accidents. The 1881 Irish Land Act, while not industrial, represented a curbing of entrepreneurial liberty: it guaranteed 'fixity of tenure' for tenant farmers, 'fair rents', and 'free sale' of land (i.e. abolition of fees to landlords upon exchange of leases and titles). The 1894 death duties Act taxed large estates of all kinds for the specific purpose of financing other schemes, not all of them 'social'. The 1911 National Insurance Act, compensating workers in the event of illness or unemployment, was a logical extension of rather than a revolutionary departure from this legislation.[9]

'Advanced [or New] Liberals' and 'socialists' celebrated legislative interferences in the relations of individuals as contributions to communal freedom and social stability. Not all of these were Liberal measures, and indeed they offended the sensibilities of 'laissez-faire' liberals, significant numbers of whom were transferring their allegiance from the Liberal to the Conservative party.[10] Some public moralists denied that collective assistance and state 'interferences' were necessary to help already 'free' citizens make the best of themselves — or make them-

[7] Early in the century Cobbett, Carlyle and others had discussed 'the condition of England' — specifically, the coexistence of poverty and prosperity — in terms critical of laissez-faire liberalism. On the Tory–Radical side, Benjamin Disraeli (in *Sybil, or the Two Nations*, 1845) had stated the problem of 'the two nations', rich and poor.

[8] On the centrality of the notion of 'character' to changing conceptions of society, see once again Collini, 'The Idea of "Character" in Victorian Political Thought.'

[9] Ensor, *England 1870–1914*, pp. 217–18, 445–6, 519–20; also B. B. Gilbert, *The Evolution of National Insurance in Great Britain. The Origins of the Welfare State* (London: M. Joseph, 1966).

[10] Note how the 1894 death duties, promoted by the Liberal W. V. Harcourt and the Liberal-Imperialist Alfred Milner, neatly contravened the principle of 'free sale' in the 1881 Irish Land Act. The 1881 act was intended to undercut the resentment of tenant farmers at having to pay a quasi-feudal tribute to their landlords upon transfer of a lease. The 1894 act, on the other hand, reflected belief that an inheritance tax upon transfers of large property was a matter of social justice. Such measures pushed wealthy Liberals into the Conservative party. See Offer, *Property and Politics*.

selves better according to their own lights, which was the same thing.[11] Others accepted certain state interferences as necessary to safeguard the moral freedom of individuals, and they justified these measures as extensions of 'constitutional' principles.

According to the Fabian Sidney Webb, the social turn of the last quarter of the nineteenth century marked the departure from 'Gladstonian Liberalism' which '"thinks in individuals"' and the discovery by 'the ordinary man ... [of] a new category ... The opening of the twentieth century finds us all, to the dismay of the old-fashioned individualist, "thinking in communities".'[12] Late Victorian Britons remained subjects of a constitutional monarchy, but the more frequent invocation of citizenship indicated a widening of the conception of social duty to include not only fulfilment of legal obligations but the realization of what Green called positive liberty: performing in one's life those actions 'worth doing' to advance the Moral Ideal, instead of pursuing narrowly self-regarding interests.

5.3. TWO CONCEPTS OF LIBERTY?

In his famous 1958 lecture 'Two Concepts of Liberty', Isaiah Berlin implied the illiberal and un-English character of Green's idea of liberty. It was neither.[13] Berlin represented J. S. Mill as the leading proponent of 'negative liberty', or freedom *from* restraint by others (citing above all Mill's 1859 essay *On Liberty*). This evaluation was rather myopic, for as Graeme Duncan and Richard Bellamy, among others, have pointed out, Mill was very sensitive to the ways in which liberty was qualified by other goods. He was concerned about abuses of liberty and the flights of popular opinion into error and was not averse to experts guiding political deliberations.[14] In *On Liberty*, Mill remarked on the emptiness and aimlessness of many individual pursuits of freedom; and by strongly

[11] There is a huge body of literature on Victorian 'individualism' and contemporary debate about the justice and practicality of state interference. Some significant contributions include W. C. Lubenow, *Politics of Government Growth: Early Victorian Attitudes Toward State Intervention, 1833–1848* (Newton Abbot: David and Charles, 1971); Bristow, 'The Liberty and Property Defence League and Individualism'; D. Roberts, *Paternalism in Early Victorian England* (New Brunswick, NJ: Rutgers UP, 1979); Taylor, *Men Versus the State*.

[12] In *Nineteenth Century*, 100 (September 1901), p. 369, quoted in Bradley, *The Optimists*, p. 236.

[13] *Four Essays on Liberty* (OUP, 1969), pp. 118–72. On the context and reception of Berlin's lecture, see Noel Annan's 'Foreword' to *Isaiah Berlin. The Proper Study of Mankind. An Anthology of Essays*, ed. H. Hardy and R. Hausheer (New York: Farrar, Straus and Giroux, 1998), p. ix; and R. Bellamy, *Rethinking Liberalism* (London: Pinter, 2000), chap 2 ('J. S. Mill, T. H. Green and Isaiah Berlin on the Nature of Liberty and Liberalism' [1992]).

[14] G. Duncan, *Marx and Mill: Two Views of Social Conflict and Social Harmony* (CUP, 1973), chap. 8; Bellamy, *Rethinking Liberalism*, chap. 2.

emphasizing, in *Considerations on Representative Government* (1865), a 'principle of participation' and a 'principle of competence' as criteria for the 'goodness of government', he affirmed the role of government and educated social sentiment in forming conceptions of 'the ends of life'.[15] These and other of Mill's statements counter the view of him as a proponent of merely formal freedom and qualify the supposedly fundamental differences between Mill and Green.

An important point of continuity between Mill and Green was the belief that individual expressions of freedom were trained by social sentiment and shaped by 'national spirit'. Mill's critique of Benthamism indicated his dissatisfaction with the idea that meaningful realizations of individual freedom could arise *outside* a social context. Mill as much as Green held that Benthamism was an impoverished philosophy; it could account neither for our understanding of freedom nor our expanding consciousness of the good. Bentham lacked experience of the world. Taking no regard of national character, he saw a world consisting of individuals and collectivities, to which there corresponded individual and collective interests. Mill wrote in his essay 'Bentham':

> Bentham's theory of life ... will enable a society which has attained a certain state of spiritual development, and the maintenance of which in that state is otherwise provided for, to prescribe rules by which it may protect its material interests. It will do nothing (except sometimes as an instrument in the hands of a higher doctrine) for the spiritual interests of society; nor does it suffice of itself even for the material interests ... A philosophy of laws and institutions, not founded on a philosophy of national character, is an absurdity ... All he can do is but to indicate means by which, in any given state of the national mind, the material interests of society can be protected; saving the question, of which others must judge, whether the use of those means would have, on the national character, any injurious influence.[16]

Green insisted that 'there can be nothing in a nation however exalted its mission, or in a society however perfectly organised, which is not in the persons composing the nation or the society.'[17] What is often emphasized about this passage from the *Prolegomena* is Green's 'ideal of *personal* worth' (italics in original), as opposed to an imputed 'national spirit and will', as posited by Rousseau and Hegel. Indeed, Green goes on to caution readers against equating national spirit with 'a series of phenomena of a particular kind' or with God.[18] Yet we may correctly understand national spirit to refer to practices, usages and institutions

[15] D. F. Thompson, *John Stuart Mill and Representative Government* (Princeton, NJ: Princeton UP, 1976); Berlin, 'John Stuart Mill and the Ends of Life [1959],' in *Four Essays on Liberty*, pp. 173–206.
[16] 'Bentham' [1838], as printed in [Mill and Bentham,] *'Utilitarianism' and Other Essays*, ed. A. Ryan, p. 157.
[17] *PE*, sec. 184.
[18] *Ibid.*

of people resulting from 'the special conditions of their intercourse with each other':

> The degree of perfection, of realisation of their possibilities, attained by these persons is the measure of the fulfilment which the idea of the human spirit attains in the particular national spirit.[19]

Both Green and Mill held that societies were more than mere congeries of individuals and agreed that in order to understand members of societies *as individuals* we must know something about the character of their shared culture and their common past. Moreover, both Mill and Green implied that understanding of national spirit offered important clues about the potentialities of individuals within societies — that is, their capabilities and *expectations* with regard to individual and social goals. While this insight in its abstract aspect might appear unobjectionable, even banal, it bears repeating here that an idea of liberty, as human possibility conditioned and given form by social practice, and being grounded at least potentially in a notion of a shared or common good, was neither illiberal nor at odds with the main currents of British social thought in the nineteenth century.

The historian J. A. Froude (1818–94) approached the idea of positive liberty, liberty as a capacity given content and shape only by something else. John Burrow describes Froude's idea of liberty as a 'Platonic-Christian conception, mediated probably by Carlyle: freedom consisted in the right ordering of one's life, obedience to the dictates of the moral law — even submission to a moral superior.'[20] Charles Kingsley, the Christian Socialist, advanced similar ideas of liberty and responsibility in his novel *Alton Locke, Tailor and Poet* (1850): false freedom leaves a man free to do as he likes, while true freedom is where a man is free to do what he *ought*, and the Bible provides practical guidelines to how individuals should use their God-given freedom.[21] Green's view of liberty and license was similar in many points to the views of Froude and Kingsley, and these notions had considerable popular purchase. That is, the idea of liberty with *content*, given shape by other 'goods', even if denounced as erroneous by some philosophers, was nevertheless validated by many popular doctrines.

Given the consistency of Greenian positive liberty with other contemporary ideas, it reveals a certain academic complacency and insularity to insist (as Berlin and John Plamenatz do) on the logical inconsistency

---

[19] *Ibid.*
[20] Burrow, *A Liberal Descent*, p. 237. Notions of positive liberty were shared by many members of the Whig historical school in the nineteenth century.
[21] *Alton Locke, 1876 edition* (p. xxxiii), cited in Brinton, *English Political Thought in the Nineteenth Century*, p. 124. Also Williams, *Culture and Society*, pp. 100–2.

of positive liberty.[22] If one examines 'thought' in the manner of Stefan Collini (indeed, in the manner of Green himself) — that is, with attention to the ways in which 'political theory' and 'political argument' are 'parasitic upon' popular 'habits of response and evaluation' — it is clear how cultural and social events during the second half of the nineteenth century were preparing a fertile soil for Green's ideas of 'ordered' self-realization and social responsibility.[23]

5.4. THE SOCIAL TURN AND 'ORGANIC REFORM'

It is relevant to note at this point some ideological and partisan trends within the historical literature pertaining to the period ca. 1875–1914 because of the different ways in which the Social Turn has been represented.[24] Gertrude Himmelfarb insists upon a sort of panicked headlong rush of British society from 1875 towards collectivism and 'welfarism', a process hastened by the Great Depression, two world wars and the loss of the empire, and halted only with the successes of Thatcherism during the 1980s. Marxists, in contrast, have distinguished revolutionary from social accommodationist tendencies in the history of the welfare state, and for them the 1880s mark a watershed, for it was at this point that a politically conscious working class divided between reformism (represented to some degree by all 'established' political movements) and revolutionary socialism, although the principles of the latter were only partly incorporated in 'independent labourism'. According to this view, elites — including a labour elite — were the main beneficiaries of a reformism, or reform policies, antithetical to the real interests of the majority.

Historians in recent years, however, have devoted serious attention to continuities between late and early nineteenth-century 'radicalisms'.[25] Scholars of this new wave emphasize the limited social

---

[22] John Plamenatz dismisses Green's theory as 'false' and ignores contemporary consensus as to its instrumentality. *Consent, Freedom and Political Obligation*, especially chap. 3. Peter Nicholson notes the ubiquity of Green's 'real freedom': *Political Philosophy of the British Idealists*, p. 127 and notes 28, 29.

[23] Collini, *Public Moralists*, pp. 4-5 (discussed in Chapter One above). Green discussed in his 1862 prize essay, 'An Estimate of the Value and Influence of Works of Fiction in Modern Times', the didactic uses of poetry, tragedy and modern fiction, and their relation to 'philosophy' (in *Works*, iii, pp. 20-45). He implied here that to acquire a true picture of 'thought' in commercial society it is necessary to examine popular and mass culture (e.g. the novel) as well as elite culture.

[24] Two particularly relevant examinations of ideology and historiography are E. J. Hobsbawn, 'Labour History and Ideology,' *Journal of Social History*, 7 (1974), pp. 371–81; and M. Taylor, 'The Beginnings of Modern British Social History?,' *History Workshop Journal*, 43 (1997), pp. 155–76.

[25] A pioneering example of this approach is B. Harrison and P. Hollis, 'Chartism, Liberalism and the Life of Robert Lowery,' *EHR*, 82 (1967), pp. 503–35. See also Finn, *After*

appeal of Marxist socialism in Britain, and they maintain that the labouring population, far from being hoodwinked into following political courses opposed to its best interests, maintained a strong sense of historical mission in its political activities. This was fed not by 'class identity' (or at least not consistently) but by a collective memory of the Englishman's birthright, a 'populist' doctrine placing the common people within the nation, not outside the trajectory of national political development.

According to Gareth Stedman Jones, many Marxist social historians in their heyday of the 1960s, '70s and '80s shared (often unwittingly) with Michel Foucault a 'vision of "governmentality"' which regards public discourse as a mere tool of social groups asserting the interest of one or another group at the expense of others. Stedman Jones contends that political authorities or 'dominant' classes do not control 'interpretation of utterances and actions'; hegemonic discourses still 'provide the most powerful means through which the weak are occasionally enabled to combine together and defeat the strong.'[26] As Hugh Cunningham has argued, even 'patriotism' in some forms embodied positive and popular aspects of social cohesion and national progress; it was not simply an ideology constructed by elites to trick the working class into sacrificing itself in imperialist wars.[27]

Patrick Joyce, James Vernon, Dror Wahrman and others have indicated the ways in which 'constitutionalism', 'Chartism', 'socialism' and other liberationist languages were constructed from organic ideas and shared evaluative language available to the humble as well as the powerful. Discourses of 'social science' in Britain from the 1830s gained currency during the 1870s and '80s, just as Idealism began to supplant Utilitarianism from 1875 as a preferred mode of discussing individual and common good. Despite their origins in academic and professional circles, neither 'social science' nor 'Idealism' can be understood as an elite discourse, for neither was constructed in a social vacuum or at a remove from common perceptions of social problems. While these discourses may have been more esoteric than the language of 'constitutionalism', they lent themselves to contestation and political

---

Chartism; M. Taylor, *The Decline of British Radicalism, 1847–1860* (OUP, 1995); and Biagini, ed., *Citizenship and Community*.

[26] Gareth Stedman Jones, 'The Determinist Fix: Some Obstacles to the Further Development of the Linguistic Approach to History in the 1990s,' *History Workshop Journal*, 42 (1996), pp. 19–35.

[27] H. Cunningham, 'The Language of Patriotism, 1750–1914,' *History Workshop Journal*, 12 (1981), pp. 8–33.

deployment because they often occurred 'around some kind of language of popular democracy and radical humanism.'[28]

Elite advocates of social reform in the late Victorian and Edwardian periods, as well as those citizens who were assumed to benefit especially from new social policy measures — the 'demoralized' members of the working classes — made use of readily accessible languages in order to help define new social purposes and political policies. No single one of these languages, and no single political tradition, can account for a new view of society. However, in their ultimate concern for the moralization of society (not only of the poor), many of the most influential advocates of social legislation down to 1914 adhered to a social vision informed by Christian humanism and Gladstonian Liberalism. These languages or views of society carried great authority and had considerable social purchase, and Greenian philosophy reformulated rather than supplanted these 'moral' languages.

Green noted in 'Liberal Legislation and Freedom of Contract' that 'our modern legislation ... with reference to labour, and education, and health ... ,' mostly implemented since the Second Reform Act, had been justified pragmatically, without much special pleading on the basis of new-fangled philosophies:

> [it was] justified on the ground that it is the business of the state, not indeed directly to promote moral goodness, for that, from the very nature of moral goodness, it cannot do, but to maintain the conditions without which a free exercise of the human faculties is impossible.[29]

Like A. V. Dicey, Green maintained that Philosophic Radicalism or utilitarian doctrines had assumed special importance in reform discussions since the 1830s.[30] Yet utilitarians had been able to agree with Christian moralists, political economists and practical politicians about a variety of policy measures, even if their discussions did not amount to a single, ideologically consistent discourse of reform. Green did not believe that a more comprehensive view of citizenship and reciprocal obligation — Sidney Webb's 'thinking in communities' — had begun to take hold without social and ideological struggle, but his account of social evolution resembled what has been called the Whig Idea of History.

---

[28] Robert Gray does not specifically discuss social science and Idealism but he uses this last quoted phrase to emphasize that social movements 'are constructed as alliances ... in which different languages of mobilization have to be articulated together ...'. 'The Deconstructing of the English Working Class [review article],' *Social History*, 11 (1986), p. 373.

[29] 'Liberal Legislation,' in *Harris and Morrow*, p. 202.

[30] 'There is no doubt that the theory of an ideal good, consisting in the greatest happiness of the greatest number, as the end by reference to which the claim of all laws and powers and rules of action on our obedience is to be tested, has tended to improve human conduct and character' (*PE*, sec. 331).

Green's statements about British politics and society suggested that the nineteenth-century progress of law and opinion, as chronicled by Dicey and others, could be explained and accepted as part of the evolution of the British constitution. In this way, certain theories of social progress became non-ideological; which is to say, the idea of social progress was taken not as Liberal or Conservative, Spencerian or Comtean, Christian or secularist, but was regarded simply as the impetus behind modern British life. Indeed, there are meaningful parallels between the growth of an ethos of (domestic) social concern and the rise of imperialist sentiment, or rather, between the ways in which these developments were rationalized. In *The Expansion of England* (1883), the historian J. R. Seeley characterized the expansion of the British empire during the nineteenth century as occurring in 'a fit of absence of mind' — not as the result of consistent imperial policy but in response to a series of separate foreign policy challenges and reflecting the spread of a sense of 'civilizing' mission.[31] Within the vast literature on British social policy ca. 1870–1914 there remains a tendency — informed by the Whig idea of history — to minimize the ideological significance of the Social Turn by representing it as the natural or organic manifestation of social sentiment in a prosperous, free society.[32]

Green's manner of seeking a sanction for new political courses in the national character generally, and in specific tendencies such as the Puritan principle, resembled the Whiggish pattern of argument from constitutional principles and the notion of 'organic' development.[33] Although historians of political and social thought have tended to identify the 'law of organic development' as central to social Darwinism, and have indicated how such was deployed (e.g. by Herbert Spencer) in order to reinforce laissez–faire liberalism, Liberals and Radicals of the 'interventionist' school also relied on organicist arguments.[34] Setting aside for the

[31] Shannon implies such a parallel: see *Crisis of Imperialism*, pp. 33–6, 144–5. Shannon notes that while Green and many other Radical-Liberals of the 1870s and early 1880s were 'Little Englanders', the logic of moral suasion in international relations drew many Liberals, such as Chamberlain and Charles Dilke, to the banner of Empire. See also Ensor, *England 1870–1914*, p. 227 and note.

[32] See Stapleton, 'Dicey and His Legacy,'; and Stapleton, 'Political Thought, Elites, and the State in Modern Britain'. José Harris discusses intellectual innovations of the era, emphasizing the relation of 'progressivist' ideology to organic social growth: 'Political Thought and the Welfare State'.

[33] On the idea of organic development in relation to moral-political argument, see especially Burrow, *Evolution and Society*; Burrow, *Whigs and Liberals*; J. P. Von Arx, *Progress and Pessimism: Religion, Politics, and History in Late Nineteenth-Century Britain* (Cambridge, MA: Harvard UP, 1985); and Collini, *Public Moralists*, chap. 7.

[34] Mark Francis has shown how Spencer utilized social organicism to justify extreme laissez-faire-ism only towards the end of his life (from the 1880s). 'Herbert Spencer and the Myth of Laissez-Faire,' *Journal of the History of Ideas*, 39/2 (1978), pp. 317–28.

moment Spencerian evolutionism, Conservative organicism (à la Burke) and the development of constitutionalist doctrines by Tory Radicals to legitimize (or to limit) social reform, Victorian Whigs and Liberals commonly justified political change by reference to opinion and social sentiment. Whig historians, from Macaulay and Hallam to Froude and Seeley, illustrated the tendencies or principles of 'national character'. They relied not on social statistics, in the manner of the modern social scientist, nor merely on examination of a relatively narrow body of sources, such as documents of state or Church and statements of authorities. Like members of German historical schools, Whig historians examined folk-ways, myths, legal practices and other cultural practices as evidences of national mind or national character.[35]

Victorian political commentators applying organic and constitutionalist arguments often spoke of opinion (or cited it), but this was less the product of empirical investigation than a creative process of locating the leading ideas or principles of groups, institutions and societies. Social sentiment in this Whiggish sense could be registered not only in opinions consciously and consistently expressed but in the right reason revealed in the ways people led their lives.[36] To revert again to Mill's discussion of Bentham, he criticized Bentham's Philosophic Radical view of life as 'wholly empirical, and the empiricism of one who has had little experience.' But if we are to take Mill's statements in the essay on Bentham as indicating Mill's own view of what 'opinions' signify, his idea is different from the notion of deriving 'organic principles of society' from *select* opinions and expressions. Mill speaks of the 'opinion of mankind' as a sum or 'average of the conclusions of all minds, stripped indeed of their choicest and most recondite thoughts, but freed from their twists and partialities.'[37]

Yet despite his effort to put social science on an empirical foundation, Mill was more in line with Whiggish contemporaries than with Utilitarians in his proposal that 'opinion of society' be understood as an *average* of a *sum* or selection of opinions. For many public moralists and social observers from the early nineteenth century the court of appeal for polit-

See also D. A. Stack, 'The First Darwinian Left: Radical and Socialist Responses to Darwin, 1859–1914,' *HPT*, 21 (2000), pp. 682–710.

[35] Savigny, Pauli, the Grimm brothers, Gierke and other German scholars can be said to have promoted the historical rather than the scientific study of society and culture. F. A. Wolf represented 'Homer' as a series of anonymous bards and D. F. Strauss explained the development of the New Testament in reference to the 'collective mythopoeic faculty' of the peoples of the Mediterranean and Asia Minor. It may be that the habits of anthropological examination as well as the interest in racial past — so pronounced in the work of Kemble, Maine and Maitland — derived from Germanic paradigms. Burrow, *A Liberal Descent*, pp. 119–25.

[36] On opinion in this sense, see especially Burrow, *Whigs and Liberals*, chaps. 2–3.

[37] Mill, 'Bentham,' in Ryan, ed., *Utilitarianism and Other Essays*, pp. 146, 150.

ical ethics and legislative policy was not an idea of divine order, nor was it to be found only in the evidence of the empirical process. The independent judgment of political leaders might be inadequate, as the opinion of the majority might also prove to be. Despite his validation of representative government Green too was sceptical about public opinion as a dependable guide to political conduct and policy. In addition to heeding the institutions of popular consent, governing authorities could locate the best wisdom of society in 'organic principles'. When Green discussed freedom and political conditions that could diminish or enhance people's moral capacities, and when faced with the realization that people sometimes misused liberty and were confused about the uses of government, he invoked the authority of organic principles.

In this light it is relevant to examine the exchange of letters in 1873 between Green and Harcourt, the latter at the time a Liberal MP and soon to be Solicitor-General, in which each man stated his view of 'organic reform'.[38] Their exchange of views provides insight into how Liberals decided on the correctness of political actions, and their disagreements are particularly revealing given the fact that Harcourt subsequently moved from the 'laissez-faire' towards the 'constructionist' wing of the Liberal party. The aforementioned death duties act of 1894, which alarmed Gladstone, was moved through the House of Commons by Harcourt. Yet by this time Harcourt no longer perceived a disjunction between judicious constructionist legislation and the spirit of reform that had buttressed laissez-faire-ism. Harcourt proclaimed in 1889, 'We [Liberals] are all Socialists now', yet four years later he still claimed to support the Gladstonian policy of retrenchment: 'I believe the Prime Minister and myself are the last representatives of the vanished creed [economy].'[39]

In speeches delivered in Oxford in December 1872, Harcourt went on record in opposition to restrictions on the liquor trade beyond those enforced by the unpopular Licensing Act of that year (see discussion in Chapter Four). Green responded to these pronouncements in a letter to the *Oxford Chronicle* and in an exasperated private letter to Harcourt.[40] Green criticized Harcourt's inconsistent view of liberty and charged him with giving aid and comfort to the 'pot-house' party (i.e. Conservatives and anti-temperance Liberals). Harcourt in turn made clear that Green's view of moral correction and giving shape to liberty through

[38] Three letters in *GP* 1(a). (1) Harcourt to Green (8 Jan. 1873); (2) Green to Harcourt (undated draft, but letter sent to Harcourt [Jan. 1873] is in Harcourt Papers, Bodleian, dep. 246, fols. 69–70); (3) Harcourt to Green (20 Jan. 1873). Letter (2) printed in *AW*, pp. 448–53.

[39] Quoted in Bradley, *The Optimists*, pp. 237, 251. Green himself noted Harcourt's new willingness to countenance legislative interference in 'Liberal Legislation' (as printed in *Harris and Morrow*, p. 202).

[40] *OCBBG*, 4 January 1873; reprinted in *AW*, pp. 217–19.

stricter licensing of pubs was supported neither by 'Mr. Bright and Mr. Mill' nor by 'the general body of the Liberal Party.'

H. A. Bruce, the Home Secretary, had sponsored in 1871 a bill calling for reduction of the hours of operation of public houses, reduction of the number of pub licences issued in any community according to a ratio of population, and a 'veto' of grants of licences by two-thirds (originally only three-fifths) of a community's ratepayers. The 1872 Licensing Act was passed minus the first and third of these provisions.[41] Weak as the Bruce bill was, Liberals refused to support more comprehensive restrictions on 'free trade' in intoxicating drink. Harcourt was correct in telling Green that such restriction was politically insupportable: if the Drink Question were to be made a 'touchstone' it would 'destroy the Liberal Party.' Conservatives eagerly exploited Liberal disunity over temperance. Ensor claims that 'From midsummer 1871 till the dissolution of [Parliament in] 1874 nearly every public-house in the United Kingdom was an active committee-room for the conservative party.'[42]

Green regretted the failure of Bruce's original 1871 bill because he believed Bruce's proposals had dealt systematically and fairly with the main issues and in accordance with popular sentiment.[43] First, it was a regulationist bill and not a prohibitionist one, so objections about tyranny were misplaced: it would not have denied the poor man his daily pint of ale.[44] Moreover, Bruce's 'Local Option' or local veto upheld democratic principles. Although borough and county magistrates would continue as licensing authorities, once a certain number of licences had been issued, a poll of three-fifths of local ratepayers could veto further licensing. A tax on licences would have supported a special inspectorate, which Green was confident would have withdrawn many licences from circulation.[45]

---

[41] Harrison, *Drink and the Victorians*, chap. 12. That Gladstone could not get himself interested in temperance and liquor legislation boded ill for Bruce's efforts.

[42] *England 1870–1914*, p. 21.

[43] In 1880 Green was still expounding the benefits of the 1871 local option bill and recommending it as a model for further legislation: see *Alliance News*, 1 May 1880, pp. 278–9 ('Special Conference at Oxford' [24 April]).

[44] Bruce himself became a temperance advocate but had not been a temperance enthusiast. As M.P. for Merthyr Tydfil (South Wales), 1857–68, he had resisted demands from some constituents for a 'Permissive Bill' (local prohibition). Such legislation would be unfair to the poor, and he insisted that the 'improved intelligence and morality of the people' was the only true 'remedy' for intemperance. He opposed the 'Gothenburg Scheme' of reform, supported by S. G. Rathbone and (later) Joseph Chamberlain, which would have placed power of licensing in the hands of borough councils. Harrison, *Drink and the Victorians*, p. 263.

[45] The number of beerhouse 'on–licences' declined during the 1870s and per capita consumption of beer, wine and spirits fell after 1877. Harrison, *Drink and the Victorians*, p. 278.

Despite some support for 'Sunday Closing' from Nonconformists and numbers of working men, most proposed restrictions on the drink trade were unpopular. Yet effective liquor licensing was in Green's view a necessary and justified 'organic reform'. He wrote to Harcourt in January of 1873 that

> it is properly the right [lined out: within the province] of the State to prevent a certain commodity being sold in a certain way ... when it can be shown that such traffic imposes a heavy burden on the public in the shape of crime and pauperism.

A two-thirds vote of the community in favour of indirect restriction on drinking, which would be easily obtained in many localities, would significantly reduce both individual misery and the communal burden of drinking. Green observed, 'That the law cannot make men good — that its business is to set them free to make themselves good — I quite agree. The question is how these truisms are to be applied' (letter cited above).

On the issue of drink, regulation had occurred since the 1830s in the form of limits on pub operating hours (e.g. 1830 Beerhouse Act, 1854 Sunday Beer Act). Further regulation was already being demanded in hundreds of communities across the nation, and Green was confident that popularly sanctioned restrictions would have been secured if not for the clumsiness of the United Kingdom Alliance and the confusion of other Liberals in 1871–2. In the meantime, Green continued in the same letter to Harcourt,

> It is idle to say that education and more comfortable habits will check the vice in time. The education of the families of the sober has no effect on the families of the drunken. Unless the vice is checked by a dead lift of the national conscience, education and comfortable habits are impossible in those very families which are to be saved from drunkenness by them.

Green rarely entertained illusions about a 'dead lift of the national conscience,' much less a sudden turn of opinion in favour of his proposals. The behaviour of politicians, electors, non-electors and publicans in the 1874 and 1880–1 Parliamentary elections at Oxford showed Green and other temperance advocates the power of beer and balderdash, and the deplorable state of the 'conscience' of the working class.[46] The whole campaign of A. W. Hall in the spring of 1880, Green stated, was 'one of the most disgraceful pieces of political agitation he could recollect.'[47]

---

[46] As mentioned in the previous chapter, Green was bitterly disappointed by the 1874 General Election. 'Temperance Propaganda was the first necessity ... unless this was done, legislation on land, etc. would help them [the working classes] little.' Yet Green believed that the labour aristocracy had already elected teetotalism, had accepted it 'as the rule of life.' C. A. Fyffe recollection in *GP* 1(b): from Charlotte Green's copy-book, pp. 115–39.

[47] The electors of Oxford would be foolish to 'reject a first-rate statesman [Harcourt] for a second-rate brewer [Hall].' The Liberal James Thorold Rogers added his protest:

Such political irregularities occurring in Green's own neighbourhood weakened his faith in mass politics, but his theory of responsible citizenship did not require legislation to follow the vagaries of electoral democracy. He lectured Harcourt in 1873 that 'constructive Liberals' both in and out of Parliament would pursue 'organic social reforms', whether or not they had a mandate in public opinion, and with an eye to justice and rectitude rather than expediency.

Harcourt, however, appears to have deliberately misunderstood Green's definition of 'organic social reforms':

> If they mean Reforms based upon a violation of the organic framework of English Society I am not and never have been the advocate of Reforms so understood. I do not believe such principles to have ever been the principles of the leaders and the general body of the Liberal Party nor do I believe them to be so now.[48]

Green responded by stating that organic reforms included compulsory education (already secured in 1870), reform of land law and the law of 'settlement' of property, 'the inspection of dwelling houses, [and] the compulsory provision of them in certain cases ...', and 'the compulsory reservation of a certain number of allotments.' He continued:

> All these measures, tho' it may be fairly said that in the long run and on the whole they are essential to individual liberty, should be excluded by the mere 'laissez faire' application of the doctrine that government has only to provide for the protection of persons and property ... Tho' how you can do so consistently with the principle of individual liberty, on the strength of which you denounce interference with the drink traffic, I do not understand.[49]

Another instance of how Green advocated state interferences or restrictions on 'license' in the face of divided public opinion concerned the Contagious Diseases Acts (1864, 1866, 1869), 'introduced as exceptional legislation to control the spread of venereal disease among enlisted men in garrison towns and ports.'[50] As Walkowitz has demonstrated, the campaign to repeal the CD Acts (successful in 1886) brought together feminists, Nonconformists, labouring men and various public

---

'Did Mr. Hall appeal to their [electors'] reason? He appealed through his bungs and through his taps ...'. From a report on two of Green's public speeches in April 1880, in *Alliance News*, 15 May 1880, pp. 310–11 ('The Oxford Election').

[48] *GP* 1(a): Harcourt to Green, 8 January 1873 (response to Green's letter to *OCBBG* cited above).

[49] Green to Harcourt, [January] 1873 (in *GP* 1a). My transcription of the letter differs slightly from that of Peter Nicholson: see *AW*, p. 352.

[50] J. Walkowitz, *Prostitution and Victorian Society. Women, Class, and the State* (CUP, 1980), pp. 1–2. The acts enabled special constables in 'subjected districts' to apprehend suspected 'common prostitutes', have them examined by physicians, and have them interned in the venereal wards of hospitals for up to nine months. These measures were not applied to their customers, whether servicemen or civilians, and the women refusing to comply with the acts could be brought before the magistrates.

moralists. Some Repealers believed that the Acts gave sanction to immoral conduct (prostitution was not in itself illegal before 1885), while others — mainly working-class men and women — resented the official identification of common prostitutes, given the fact that an indeterminate number of lower-class women resorted to casual prostitution as a way of getting by.[51] In other words, many labouring people opposed the CD Acts because the Acts appeared to classify lower-class women as a Social Problem.

Green was not among the active 'Repealers' nor among the proponents of the CD Acts, but he did go on record in favour of the Acts as justified public health measures, although they were not applied to the town in which he lived. In a letter to the *Oxford Chronicle* Green protested the Acts being made a political football by the supporters of the Conservative A. W. Hall.[52] Green's letter could be explained away as evidence merely of his animus towards Hall and Oxford Conservatives who, as we have seen, stalled other 'organic reforms' Green supported. Indeed, a great deal of political expediency is revealed in Green's letter, but the fact that he went on record in favour of the CD Acts is interesting. Hall's supporters had represented their man as an opponent of the Acts and his Liberal challenger, J. D. Lewis, as their champion. Green noted that he did not write as 'an advocate of these Acts, but merely to protest against a good cause being damaged and a good man discredited by a false statement of their nature.'

In Green's view, Lewis was far more likely to hit at the evils of prostitution in his support for the continuation of Lord Cardwell's Army reforms than Hall was likely to do in opposing the same. Among defenders of the CD Acts

> may be those who think too lightly of one form of immorality, as among their opponents are certainly those who think too lightly of another ... [Mr Lewis] is not in favour of their extension, but being personally connected with one of the garrison towns where they are in force, he holds, like others of the best men there, that under the peculiar conditions of those towns, they are at present the only means of checking a terrible physical evil, which affects the innocent as well as the guilty ...[53]

---

[51] Walkowitz cites evidence that the vast majority of prostitutes interned under the CD Acts were daughters of unskilled and semiskilled workingmen, and the majority of these women had worked as general servants, laundresses, street vendors, and at other low-skilled, low-waged jobs. *Prostitution*, pp. 15–16.

[52] *OCBBG*, 14 March 1874, p. 8.

[53] The letter continues: 'Doubtless the physical evil rests on a moral one — and against that moral evil many of the defenders of the Acts in question fight quite as earnestly as their opponents, but no one has shown that we are more likely to be rid of the moral evil for neglecting the physical ... The main cause of the peculiarly vicious state of our garrison-towns is to be found in our military system, which having coaxed men into the Army from the loosest part of the population, keeps them during a long period of

Green concluded his letter by appealing to defenders of 'domestic purity' to support Lewis instead of Hall: 'If through their ill-judged interference he [Hall] is returned, there will be much joy in the public-houses, but much sorrow in houses where domestic purity is held dear.'

Green's hostility towards Hall and the 'pot-house party' provided a large part of the motivation for his protest, but he exhorted his audience to see the whole man — and thereby to recognize Lewis as the true advocate of necessary moral and physical reforms. This letter, like his other statements about contemporary controversies, indicated Green's interest in constructive reforms — in which moral and material concerns are seen as intertwined. It also indicated his tendency to seek ethical sanction for such reforms not only in the popular will (as expressed in majority opinion) but in supposedly higher sentiments or right reason visible in organic society, including social sentiments and practices expressive of national character. 'Domestic purity' was an ideal transcending social classes in mid-Victorian Britain.[54] Hence the real issue for Green was to decide on the best means for the protection and encouragement of common ideals. In deciding upon such Green was attentive to opinion — arguably in a more responsive manner than those who were preoccupied with manipulating public opinion, or those who relied on the abstract Greatest Happiness Principle as a guide to social policy.

Green and most contemporary Radical-Liberals remained comfortably within the Liberal fold in holding that a liberal society, for all its defects, was creating and safeguarding circumstances favourable to self-realization and cooperation. As has been indicated in previous chapters, many critics of Green have charged him with inconsistency or confusion: is it freedom that Green wishes to maximize, or something else? Liberals of the present day as well have been criticized for inconsistency in their view of equality and freedom as criteria of social justice, confusing equality of means ('opportunities') with equality of ends (e.g. incomes, living conditions).[55] Some self-professed egalitarians assume the naturalness of individuals' self-seeking behaviour without

---

[54] On Victorian ideas of sexual purity, chastity, etc., see in particular F. Barret-Ducrocq, *Love in the Time of Victoria*, translated by J. Howe (London: Penguin, 1992).

[55] Amartya Sen does not discuss Green is his study *Inequality Reexamined* (Delhi: OUP, 1995). However, his discussion of Rawls, Ronald Dworkin, Thomas Nagel, Thomas Scanlon, Robert Nozick and other contributors to modern debates over freedom and inequality indicates that modern liberal thinkers, like Green before them, display inconsistencies in their views of what human capacities and goods are to be equalized. The main question we need to ask in our ethico-political speculations is 'Equality of What?': opportunities, incomes, entitlements (access to goods and institutions), social capacities, or whatever else we judge to be measures of our freedom.

acknowledging (1) the fact of unequal access to goods — the very unequal initial positions of individuals engaged in self-realization; and (2) that the unequal results of competition might perpetuate existing inequalities or establish new, equally invidious ones. It has been argued (by Henry Sidgwick, John Plamenatz, Geoffrey Warnock and others) that Green never seriously confronted these problems or offered a way out of them. Nevertheless, a distinctive feature of Green's ethico–political thought was his recognition that public authority might intervene in private relations so as to help individuals define 'stations' in which they could realize their goals and perform their duties. Part of the work of liberalism, or of liberal government, was to address structural inequalities so that individuals might effectively occupy those stations. As Robert Beck paraphrases the British Idealist Bernard Bosanquet, 'Neither more nor less government is the basic issue ... ; the basic issue is to have the best government.'[56]

To Green, organic principles could justify new applications of public authority. In his view new applications of civil authority and conceptions of The Good were already suggested by prevailing conceptions of public right. Further, individuals can and do achieve ideas of what they ought to do beyond the norms supplied by their immediate surroundings and wider society.[57] For instance, 'conscience' suggests a guide to conduct by predisposing the individual to treat humanely even persons whom his society has taught him to ignore or despise. The 'eternal principle', or the spiritual process at work in individuals and human history, may be a source from which new conceptions of the good are derived. The individual may conceive of goods not widely recognized by his society. He then experiences an imperative to work towards the wider moralization of society by making the best of himself, and by making contributions (intellectual, artistic, material) conducing towards a state of culture and society in which others are enabled to make the best of themselves. A democracy allowed such other-regarding behaviour and popular conceptions of justice, trained by religious sentiment, encouraged it.

5.5. GREEN, CHRISTIAN MELIORISM AND 'SOCIALISM'

Green's theory of the organic location of conceptions of freedom and of the social constitution of individual goods impressed many of his contemporaries as novel. Sidney Webb claimed that 'thinking in communities' marked a break from mid-Victorian orthodoxies, particularly Gladstonian Liberalism. Others too detected in late Victorian philan-

---

[56] *Handbook in Social Philosophy*, p. 97. See also J. Morrow, 'Private Property, Liberal Subjects, and the State' in *The New Liberalism*, ed. Simhony and Weinstein, chap. 4
[57] *PE*, sec. 185.

thropic initiatives and legislative-bureaucratic activity a certain departure from earlier treatments of social questions and commented upon the economic, social and political changes which had produced it. L. A. Atherley-Jones maintained in 1889 that with Gladstone, Liberalism's political Titan, lay

> The responsibility to devise and formulate those reforms by which, without violence to persons or shock to the principles of public morality, there may be compassed for our people a wider diffusion of physical comfort, and thus a loftier standard of national morality. This is the new Liberalism.[58]

Some critics of 'constructionism' argued that fear of social disorder and revolutionism had led members of the governing class to pander irresponsibly to the working classes and, even more reprehensibly, to push social 'radicalism' into courses which 'the people' had no natural inclination to follow.[59]

In addition to those who regarded social radicalism as dangerous were social reformers advocating Greenian measures for reasons quite different from Green's. Considerations of social justice and an altruistic interest in maximizing freedom drove some reform efforts, but these were mixed with pragmatic concern for 'national efficiency', in light of increasing commercial and military rivalry among the Great Powers (including, by the later 1880s, the United States).[60] Members of the 'Fabian Society' (founded 1883), some other Socialists (e.g. H. M. Hyndman and the Social Democratic Federation) were either unimpressed by Idealist social theory or hostile to efforts which apparently stemmed from bourgeois largesse and guilty conscience, and religious sentiment, because such efforts were subjective and unscientific.

Yet most of these reformers and radicals active ca. 1880–1914 responded to questions raised by Green about social responsibility and citizenship, and many of them took Green's ethical philosophy into account in their examinations of the social problems of industrial

---

[58] L. A. Atherley-Jones, 'The New Liberalism'; *Nineteenth Century*, 26 (1889), p. 192. See also G. W. E. Russell, 'The New Liberalism: A Response,' *Nineteenth Century*, 26 (1889), pp. 492–9; J. Guinness Rogers, 'The Middle Class and the New Liberalism,' *Nineteenth Century*, 26 (1889), pp. 710–20.

[59] W. H. Mallock, 'Radicalism and the People,' *National Review*, 1 (1883), pp. 101–11; and Mallock, 'The Radicalism of the Market Place,' *National Review*, 1 (1883), pp. 507–30. Mallock identified Joseph Chamberlain, the *Pall Mall Gazette* and the *Spectator* as drivers of an irresponsible Radicalism, whose object was to set the masses against monarchy and aristocracy in order to safeguard 'middle-class' Radicals' property and interests.

[60] See especially G. E. Searle, *The Quest for National Efficiency: A Study in British Politics and Political Thought, 1899–1914* (Berkeley: California UP, 1971); Fox, *History and Heritage*, chaps. 4–6; A. M. MacBriar, *An Edwardian Mixed Doubles: The Bosanquets Versus the Webbs: A Study in British Social Policy* (Oxford: Clarendon, 1987); and C. Shaw, 'Eliminating the Yahoo: Eugenics, Social Darwinism and Five Fabians,' *HPT*, 8 (1987), pp. 521–44.

democracy, even if, ultimately, to reject it.[61] To repeat the observations of Collini and den Otter, the Greenian approach was persuasive to so many social reformers because it coincided with a wider contemporary search for a new 'foundation for community'. Green's philosophy was regarded with particular interest between 1880 and 1914 because it offered an appealing reformulation of some prevailing ideas, ideas whose efficacy had been severely tested by social and economic pressures from 1875. Reformers in the Greenian mould were concerned about protecting individuals from depersonalizing economic and social forces. They deplored uniformity and mediocrity as much as physical misery. On the whole they were less concerned with establishing some 'social minimum' (of income or living standards) than in bringing deprived individuals under better moral influences and restoring a sense of collective purpose and civic identity.[62]

Poverty was perhaps less pervasive and acute in 1880 than in 1830, but paradoxically more visible. As mentioned above, there had emerged a new conviction in the authority of social data (empirical social science), but this did not in itself lead to a rediscovery of poverty or a new consciousness of inequality.[63] Early Victorians had been assiduous collectors of social statistics, but the most compelling social studies had not been empirical. Henry Mayhew's exposé *London Labour and the London Poor* (1851–62) offered pseudo-scientific confirmation of the social descriptions of Dickens or Kingsley.[64] A pamphlet by the Congregational minister Andrew Mearns, *The Bitter Cry of Outcast London* (1883), is frequently cited in social policy studies as signalling the begin-

[61] Pelling, *Origins of the Labour Party 1880–1900*; S. Pierson, *Marxism and the Origins of British Socialism. The Struggle for a New Consciousness* (Ithaca: Cornell UP, 1973); Terrill, *R. H. Tawney and His Times*; J. Harris, *William Beveridge. A Biography* (Oxford: Clarendon, 1977); A. Vincent, 'The New Liberalism and Citizenship,' in *The New Liberalism*, ed. Simhony and Weinstein, chap. 9.

[62] G. Gaus, 'Bosanquet's Communitarian Defense of Economic Individualism,' in *The New Liberalism*, ed. Simhony and Weinstein, chap. 6; Carter, *T. H. Green and the Development of Ethical Socialism*, chap. 3.

[63] For the view that there was no radical departure in the 1880s from early and mid-Victorian attitudes towards poverty, see E. P. Hennock, 'Poverty and Social Theory in England: The Experience of the Eighteen-Eighties,' *Social History*, 1 (1976), pp. 67–91. Later Victorians were as sentimental (or tough-minded?) about the poor as their predecessors.

[64] Pseudo-scientific because Mayhew presented a typology of poverty and the poor: e.g. the blameless poor versus 'those that will not work' (a subtitle of the fourth volume). Friedrich Engels' *The Condition of the Working Class in England in 1844*, presenting the urban working classes as victims of capitalism, did not appear in English translation until 1887, and it was published in the United States. The novels of Dickens, Disraeli, George Eliot and Elizabeth Gaskell encouraged readers to draw certain conclusions about the responsibilities of rich and poor. On authorial intention and the reception of major social novels, see C. Gallagher, *The Industrial Reformation of English Fiction, 1832–1867* (Chicago UP, 1985).

ning of a social turn. Yet *The Bitter Cry* contained few social data that would have surprised philanthropists or readers of government reports earlier in the century. Mearns' insistence that Britons were not 'doing a thousandth part of what needs to be done, a hundredth part of what could be done by the Church of Christ ...' to stem 'THIS TERRIBLE FLOOD OF SIN AND MISERY' was an echo of the social injunction made at mid century by Christian Socialists and charity organizers.[65] According to one eminent historian of the period, *The Bitter Cry* inspired a flood of social investigations of a 'scientific' — rather than 'subjective, anecdotal and impressionistic' — nature.[66]

However, the divergence between sentimental and scientific arguments in the social turn of the 1880s has been overstated by both defenders and attackers of welfarism. Even practitioners of the 'dismal science' (economics) ca. 1880–1914 framed their statistical and scientific studies of society in moral terms.[67] As we have seen in Chapter One, Alfred Marshall appreciated Green's moral approach to social questions. This should encourage us to examine seriously the claim that a certain 'metaphysical' outlook fostered empirical social investigation, not vice versa. Even a proud empiricist like Beatrice Webb embarked upon social scientific investigation and practical social work from moral and religious conviction.[68] This was true also of men and women with meaningful connections to Green: Arnold Toynbee, Henry Scott Holland and Charles Gore, Bernard Bosanquet (active in the Charity Organisation Society after 1881), Mrs Humphry Ward, Hugh Price Hughes and Percy Alden.[69]

Henry Pelling, in *Origins of the Labour Party*, mentions Green's teachings in relation to the rise of a '"socialistic" and humanitarian ... and collectivist outlook,' yet he asserts that this 'was so widespread and so vague that it cannot be said to have had any special significance in the development of the Labour Party.' Pelling claims that '[Green's] work was not read either by members of the working class, who could not have understood it, or by the active middle-class Socialists, who rarely proceeded further into philosophical speculation than was required to

---

[65] Quoted from *The Bitter Cry of Outcast London*, ed. A. S. Wohl (Leicester: Leicester UP, 1970), pp. 55–6.

[66] J. F. C. Harrison, *Late Victorian Britain, 1875–1901* (London: Fontana, 1990), p. 186.

[67] See Himmelfarb's discussion in *Poverty and Compassion*, chaps. 1–2, 7.

[68] D. E. Nord, *The Apprenticeship of Beatrice Webb* (Ithaca, NY: Cornell UP, 1985), chaps. 5–6.

[69] In addition to the aforementioned studies by Himmelfarb, Lynd, Meacham and Picht, see Rowland, 'Some Free Church Pioneers of Social Reform'; Inglis, 'English Nonconformity and Social Reform, 1880–1900'; S. Rowbotham, 'The Call to University Extension Teaching 1873–1900,' *University of Birmingham Historical Journal*, 12 (1969), pp. 57–71.

appreciate the ethics of Comte or Spencer.'[70] This gives a misleading and inaccurate impression about Green and the growth of a 'collectivist outlook'. Many middle-class 'Socialists' active from the '80s had gravitated toward socialism from advanced Liberalism and Radicalism and many were well acquainted with Green's teachings. The 'Fellowship of the New Life', established in London the year after Green's death, discussed the ideas of Kant and Green; some of its members later became involved with the Fabian Society, the SDF and the Independent Labour Party.[71] D. G. Ritchie (1853-1903) had been Green's student and creatively expounded his teacher's ideas. Ritchie remained close to members of the Fabian Society but was reluctant to be included among its official membership. Similarly, Belfort Bax, friend of Hyndman and William Morris, had read Green. Although he attacked 'Hegelianism' in an obscure pamphlet entitled *The Problem of Reality*, in other essays (e.g. 'The Religion of Socialism'), Bax offered a 'history of the development of the Socialistic idea' in which the democratic element of 'socialism', with a Greenian emphasis on free choice and fellowship, appears foremost.[72]

As for working-class opinion, it seems unlikely that many working-class leaders of the1880s had read Green or heard much about him, excepting perhaps the 'self-improving' types Green addressed at temperance or education meetings in Oxford and Birmingham.[73] Yet we should not assume that working-class people would only have understood and appreciated Green by reading *Prolegomena to Ethics* or the *Lectures on the Principles of Political Obligation*. There is at least some anecdotal evidence that working-class men had encountered Green's ideas in a somewhat diluted form. When Mrs Ward visited Toynbee Hall in 1889 she was struck by the fact that in the library *'Robert Elsmere* had been read to pieces, and in a workmen's club which had just been started several ideas had been taken from the "New Brotherhood".'[74] It

---

[70] Pelling, *Origins*, p. 11.

[71] See Pierson, *Marxism and the Origins of British Socialism*, pp. 107–12, 220–1. The 'New Brotherhood' established by Robert Elsmere in the eponymous novel by Mrs Humphry Ward appears to be an artisan-class version of the 'Progressive Association' (founded 1882) and the 'Fellowship of the New Life'.

[72] Bax's 'The Religion of Socialism' was very much, in fact, in the vein of Ritchie's *The Principles of State Interference* (1891), which was published in the same 'Social Science Series' by Swan Sonnenschein & Co. Bax was hostile towards Engels' mono-causal explanation of social change by economic factors. Bax, *Reminiscences and Reflexions*, pp. 48–57, 66–7, 157–62. I believe that Mark Bevir contradicts much of his own analysis when he disputes that Bax can be 'assimilated' to 'the intellectual movement represented by [George] Eliot, Green, and [Beatrice] Webb.' 'Ernest Belfort Bax: Marxist, Idealist, and Positivist,' *Journal of the History of Ideas*, 54 (1993), p. 128.

[73] For instance, see the report of Green's 25 September 1878 lecture on University Extension in the *Birmingham Daily Gazette*, reprinted in *AW*, pp. 328-30.

[74] From Janet Trevelyan's *Life of Mrs. Humphry Ward* (London, 1923), p. 79, quoted in Sutherland, *Mrs Humphry Ward*, p. 218.

should also be remembered that relatively few labouring men and women were exposed to doctrinaire, 'scientific' socialism before the beginning of the twentieth century; and that many were influenced by 'ethical' socialism. Mark Bevir and Matt Carter have recently commented upon the Greenian stamp of the Ethical Socialist and Labour Church movements down to the First World War: to working-class leaders and their middle-class allies, labour representation and redistributive economics were the means to creating a society breathing the spirit of fraternity and justice.[75]

David Blaazer has argued that Green deeply influenced generations of British 'progressives' — Liberals, Labourites and socialists — active down to the 1930s. In this connection Blaazer discusses Ritchie, J. H. Muirhead (1857–1940), John Hobson (1858–1940), Leonard Hobhouse, Sidney Ball, H. N. Brailsford (1873–1958), and even Harold Laski (1893–1950). Many of these progressives had been at Oxford or were otherwise placed to be influenced by Green's teachings, although some were removed from Green by one or two generations. Brailsford, for example, came from a Nonconformist background and became a student of Green's friend Edward Caird at Glasgow University. (Caird taught at Glasgow before succeeding Jowett as Master of Balliol.) Making a career of Radical journalism, Brailsford promoted the League of Nations, trumpeted the Bolshevik Revolution in 1917 (although his enthusiasm waned by the early 1920s) and championed Indian independence by the early 1930s.[76] This is not to deny that many Socialists and progressives from 1885 — Hobhouse and Hobson come to mind on this point — had reservations about aspects of Green's teachings, but few were ignorant of or uninterested in them. Green's influence on political debates was scarcely vague, nor was his impact greatest on tepid reformers hostile to labour representation or modification of property rights, as Pelling's account would suggest.

Mention has already been made in previous chapters of specifically philosophical (or logical) critiques of Green's thought. Some observers discounting (as distinct from deploring) the Greenian element in British social and political thought in the late nineteenth and early twentieth centuries do so for plausible reasons. There is one sort of argument concerning ideology and doctrine which bears mention here that might be called the classical Left Labour view. According to this true socialism entails complete repudiation of liberal political economy, Liberal (or, for

[75] Bevir, 'Welfarism, Socialism, and Religion'; Bevir, 'The Labour Church Movement, 1891–1902,' *JBS*, 38 (1999), pp. 217–45; Carter, *T. H. Green and the Development of Ethical Socialism*, chaps. 4–6.

[76] D. Blaazer, *The Popular Front and the Progressive Tradition. Socialists, Liberals, and the Quest for Unity, 1884–1939* (CUP, 1992). See also F. M. Leventhal, *The Last Dissenter: H. N. Brailsford and His World* (Oxford: Clarendon, 1985).

that matter, Conservative) reformism and sentimental meliorism; a socialist policy must be grounded in a purely 'scientific' (i.e. Marxist) doctrine. Yet, as is well known, Marxism took hold rather late in Britain, despite the fact that Marx had spent most of his adult life in London, and made little impact on 'working-class thought' before 1917. In the later nineteenth century, labourist ideology emphasized the political representation of the labour interest but did not preclude cooperation with progressive middle-class elements. Labourism, as distinct from the (Marxist) Social Democratic Federation and like advanced Liberalism, drew eclectically from elite teachings and popular sentiment, from 'scientific' literature, the ideas and expressions of 'progressive' Christianity (including revived Christian Socialism) and popular constitutionalism.[77] The latter especially reinforced popular beliefs about obligation and entitlement, so that many British working people during the last third of the nineteenth century held strong opinions about the rectitude of their participation in public affairs and about (economic) distributive justice. Working-class belief in a '"moral economy" of free trade' included recognition of the 'right' to a stake in productive enterprise.[78]

Pelling is correct in describing the 'collectivist outlook' ca. 1890 as 'vague'. It was also politically multivalent, susceptible to mobilization by various partisan interests. Popular radicalism could and did find political expression in varieties of scientific socialism, in Tory Radicalism, in advanced Liberalism and in a general labourism aligning itself opportunely with established political parties. There was, however, a striking correspondence between these populisms and Green's insights about self-development, social justice and communal freedom. There were similarities of language as well, in emphasis, tone and appeal that must be held as important as differences in terminology. There was a language of populism that sometimes transcended partisan vocabularies.[79] James Keir Hardie (1856-1915), the Scottish miners' leader who founded the Independent Labour Party in 1892, explained in 1896,

> I am a Socialist because Socialism means fraternity founded on Justice, and the fact that in order to secure this certain economic changes are necessary is a mere incident in our great human crusade. My protest is against economics being considered the whole of socialism or even the vital part of it.[80]

[77] On science and the Left, see Stack, 'The First Darwinian Left'. On the remarkable pliancy of constitutionalism, see J. Vernon, ed., *Re-Reading the Constitution. New Narratives in the Political History of England's Long Nineteenth Century* (CUP, 1996).

[78] See especially E. F. Biagini, ed., *Citizenship and Community*, chaps. 6–9.

[79] Patrick Joyce remarks on Brightian populism that 'As with Gladstonisation [sic] it involved being invited to share with and through the orator a sense of communion, with God but also with history' (*Democratic Subjects*, p. 101).

[80] Quoted in K. O. Morgan, *Keir Hardie, Radical and Socialist* (London. Weidenfeld and Nicolson, 1975), p. 207. See also F. Reid, 'Keir Hardie's Conversion to Socialism' in

This proclamation certainly carries overtones of John Ruskin, William Morris and other 'aesthetic' socialists but also of Green, Sidney Ball, R. B. Haldane (1856–1928), Henry Jones (1852–1922) and the quasi–religious discourse central to Gladstonianism and advanced Liberal–ism.[81]

Once again, the specifically religious resonances of Keir Hardie's language of social transformation are significant. Nearly a decade before becoming secretary of the Scottish Miners' Federation (in 1886), Hardie had regularly preached to a schismatic and evangelical Free Church in Cumnock, Ayrshire. The style of rhetoric Hardie deployed as a labour organizer from the 1880s, and in his ILP campaign from 1892, was both emotionally genuine and carefully trained, and members of his audiences were as susceptible to it as they were to the speeches of Gladstone, 'The Grand Old Man', or of John Bright. Sam Hobson, who was Hardie's secretary during the ILP agitation, observed that Hardie and other ILP speakers 'always spoke of the appeal to the heart; their speeches were a blend of religion and sentiment … '.[82] Why should this approach have been so much more effective in mobilizing people than careful, logical argument and scientific ideology?:

> I soon realized that the I.L.P. had appeared at a moment in time when Yorkshire Nonconformity was in a process of disruption … The I.L.P. accordingly set out to capture the soul of Nonconformity and Yorkshire was the battle ground.[83]

Although late Victorian labourism and Socialism confronted harsh economic and social realities, the emotional currents sustaining them were the same as those feeding the social turn of the 1880s, influencing primarily the British middle classes. Because the Social Turn was a sentimental and moral one, caution must be exercised in explaining the origin of a new social service ethic and a new climate of expectations (among both middle and labouring classes) on the basis of strictly economic factors. In terms of standard indexes like wages, prices, rents, profits and returns assessed to the income tax, the whole period 1870–86 was one of economic advance (albeit not as marked as during the previous two decades), with obvious improvement in the national standard

---

Essays in Labour History, 1886–1923, ed. A. Briggs and J. Saville (Hamden, CT: Archon, 1971), chap. 2.

[81] W. Morris, 'Art Under Plutocracy' (1883 lecture), reprinted in *Political Writings of William Morris,* ed. A. L. Morton (London: Lawrence and Wishart, 1973), pp. 57–85; R. B. Haldane, 'The New Liberalism,' *Progressive Review,* 1 (1896), pp. 133–43; S. Ball, 'The Socialist Ideal,' *Economic Review,* 9 (1899), pp. 425–49; H. Jones, 'The Corruption of the Citizenship of the Working Man,' *Hibbert Journal,* 10 (1911), pp. 155–78.

[82] From Hobson's 1938 memoir, *Pilgrims to the Left,* p. 40, quoted in Pierson, *Marxism and the Origins of British Socialism,* pp. 201-2.

[83] *Ibid.*

of living.[84] But there were social consequences of change in the structure of the national economy that gave reason for pause. Like the rest of the industrializing world, Britain suffered an economic depression beginning in 1873, from which it recovered only towards the end of the decade.[85] The real wages of industrial labourers increased due in large part to a secular decline (on a global scale) in commodities prices, including prices of foodstuffs; this same development resulted in a decline in value of agricultural land and in the wages of agricultural labourers. While the decline of the English peasantry had been a topic of national discussion since the eighteenth century, from the 1870s Britons were more acutely aware of the rise of industry and commerce at the expense of agriculture.

Although the labouring week was actually shortened for many workers, increasing industrial competition threw more workers into irregular and sweated employment; less skilled workers were forced into the margins of poverty.[86] In addition to hyper-competition in industry and the decline of British agriculture, Ensor identifies two other significant 'economic' developments during the last quarter of the nineteenth century that had a major impact on British social relations. One was the rise of the limited liability company. In industry,

> Patriarchalism disappeared. The owner-entrepreneur disappeared also. Property passed to shareholders concerned only for dividends; control was exercised on the shareholders' behalf by boards of directors, nominally elected by them, but in fact mainly co-opted ... and devoid of any specialized understanding of the firm or even of the industry.[87]

Workplace relations were greatly altered in many industries ca. 1870–85, due in part to the rise of salaried managers who had little 'paternal' feeling for employees. In the coal industry, particularly in newer enterprises in South Wales, large firms with impersonal relations between masters and men were already the rule. In great ports much labour had long been 'casual' and the handling trades were notorious for their uneasy relations between employers and employed. Thus it is not surprising that the 1889 strike of the London dockers, to secure a minimum hourly wage (the 'docker's tanner', or sixpence), was one of

[84] Ensor, *England 1870–1914*, chap. 4; W. W. Rostow, *British Economy of the Nineteenth Century* (OUP, 1948), chaps. 3–4.
[85] The Depression of 1873–7 was felt most acutely in banking, stocks, and private and government bonds. British industrial prices fluctuated throughout the period, with increased industrial competition and downward pressure on wages into the mid 1880s.
[86] T. Matsumura, *The Labour Aristocracy Revisited. The Victorian Flint Glass Makers, 1850–1880* (Manchester UP, 1983); J. A. Smiechen, *Sweated Industries and Sweated Labor. The London Clothing Trades, 1860–1914* (Urbana, IL: Illinois UP, 1984).
[87] Ensor, *England 1870–1914*, p. 113. See also P. L. Payne, *British Entrepreneurship in the Nineteenth Century* (London: Macmillan, 1974).

the most bitterly memorable of the century. Many social investigators as well as labour leaders traced social unrest not to poverty *per se* but to changes in the quality of relations between employers and employed.[88]

A second development heightening social tensions during the 1880s and drawing attention to poverty amidst plenty was 'the rise into visible prominence of a rentier class', a development of course related to changes in entrepreneurship and investment.[89] Investors in the East India Company ca. 1750 as well as purchasers of railway stocks a century later could be described as 'rentières', but 'rentier' as a loan–word from French dates only to 1881 (*OED*). Radical-Liberals especially around this time focused on absentee landownership and the existence of 'artificial' restrictions on the exchange of land as the source of significant social problems. As we have seen already (Chapter Two), in Green's view it was 'feudalism', not capitalism, that was the source of much social injustice of his time.

The urban aspect of rentiership must also be considered in assessing the grounds for social tensions after 1875 and in tracing new interpretations of social problems, including the 'discovery' of relative deprivation and widening perceptions of the declining quality of social relations. As Judith Walkowitz has pointed out about London, the increasing presence in urban space of the rentier class and the new men of officialdom (government workers as well as the managers of banks, insurance companies, and the like) and their uses of leisure, produced new social tensions between the *haute bourgeoisie* and workers in the provisioning and service trades, such as shopgirls and seamstresses.[90] There were also tensions between elite men and middle-class male defenders of early-Victorian moral rectitude and the work ethic. Although laissez-faire capitalism had progressively dissolved traditional moral scruples about 'freedom' in getting and spending, by the 1870s the rentier-class libertine (an idle man-about-town, not necessarily an aristocrat) was the object of both working-class and 'Puritanical' middle-class opprobrium. Campaigns of the 1860s, '70s and '80s for 'social purity', as well as the more specific hysteria about the Jack the Ripper murders (1888–9), gave evidence of widespread anxiety about the

---

[88] Lynd, *England in the Eighteen-Eighties*, chap. 7; Pelling, *Origins of the Labour Party*, chap. 5.

[89] Ensor, *England 1870–1914*, p. 114. See also W. D. Rubinstein, *Men of Property: The Very Wealthy in Britain Since the Industrial Revolution* (London: Croom Helm, 1987); and Perkin, *Rise of Professional Society*, chaps. 1–4.

[90] Public moralists and social reformers of the 1880s, such as the 'New Journalist' W. T. Stead, identified the pathologies of 'male pests' and 'fast women'. The latter were often assumed to be prostitutes or were otherwise identified as bad influences on working–class women. Walkowitz, *City of Dreadful Delight*, chaps. 3–4. See also, on problems of female 'emancipation' ca. 1885, R. Brandon, *The New Women and the Old Men. Love, Sex and the Woman Question* (New York: W. W. Norton, 1990).

mixing of social classes in urban space and the sexual predations of men of the leisured classes. New patterns of consuming, spending and leisure from the mid-nineteenth century were often discussed in terms of social pathologies — as illnesses apparently arising from unequal prosperity — and such problems occupied reformers almost as much as more conventional questions about urban sanitation and overcrowding.[91]

The aforementioned developments are relevant to the present discussion because beliefs about the enjoyment of wealth (as a form of liberty) so often informed discussions of social responsibility. J. S. Mill and other economists elaborating upon the 'socialistic' implications of a labour theory of value already drew a moral distinction between earned and unearned wealth, and they proposed measures such as land law reform — to facilitate the natural or market-driven redistribution of land — and progressive taxation.[92] The American radical Henry George, author of *Progress and Poverty* (1879), had a considerable impact on British social thought in such respects; he suggested that the unearned increase in the value of land be appropriated through taxation in order to slow the growth of large estates. British Georgeists applied such ideas to the problem of declining peasant proprietorship in Ireland.[93] Even before George's appearance on the scene the Radical-Liberal John Bright had been sympathetic to this kind of state interference: 'The great evil of Ireland is this, that the Irish people, the Irish nation, are dispossessed of the soil.'[94] Thus not only agricultural unionists (like Joseph Arch) but the chief spokesmen for laissez-faire Liberalism agreed upon the efficacy of state interference in breaking up large landed estates — or at least halt-

[91] Greater London grew from 3.3 millions in 1861 to 6.6 millions in 1901, with more than two-thirds of the increase occurring outside the metropolitan centre. Certain inner urban districts were virtually emptied of their wealthier inhabitants. Social segregation marked not only the large cities but holiday towns like Eastbourne and Bournemouth. G. S. Jones, *Outcast London: A Study in the Relationship Between Classes in Victorian Society* (Oxford: Clarendon, 1971); Harrison, *Late Victorian Britain*, chap. 4; Thompson, *The Rise of Respectable Society*, pp. 256, 290–1.

[92] C. J. Holmes, 'Laissez-faire in Theory and Practice, Britain 1800–75,' *Journal of European Economony History*, 5 (1976), pp. 671–88; J. W. Mason, 'Political Economy and the Response to Socialism in Britain, 1870–1914,' *HJ*, 23 (1980), pp. 565–87; G. Claeys, 'Justice, Independence, and Industrial Democracy: The Development of J. S. Mill's Views on Socialism,' *Journal of Politics*, 49 (1987), pp. 122–47; J. Plowright, 'Political Economy and Christian Polity: the Influence of Henry George in England Reassessed,' *VS*, 30 (1987), pp. 235–52.

[93] Green voiced his approval of the Irish Land Act of 1881 in 'Liberal Legislation and Freedom of Contract'. See also the contribution of Green's fellow Oxford Liberal, George C. Brodrick: *English Land and English Landlords* (New York: Augustus M. Kelley, 1968; orig. 1881); and, on popular movements, N. Scotland, 'The National Agricultural Labourers' Union and the Demand for a Stake in the Soil, 1872–1896' in Biagini, ed., *Citizenship and Community*, chap. 6.

[94] *The Times*, 31 Oct. 1866, p. 12, quoted in Bradley, *The Optimists*, p. 203.

ing their growth — in order to realize the Smithian principles of free trade.

Although members of the late Victorian middle and upper classes complained about the licentiousness of the labouring population and the growth of 'class feeling', there were quite frequent instances of agreement between middle-class and working-class Britons about social pathology, in light of which the rentier class and the 'irresponsible' wealthy were identified, as much as the demoralized poor, as problematic and antisocial elements. Elite and middle-class spectators of rioting in London's West End in 1886 and the strikes of the London Match Girls and East End dockers in 1889 were alarmed by the violence of 'King Mob' in their midst, and by the apparent arrival at group consciousness of the classes constituting the economic 'residuum'. Yet many educated and prosperous people responded to industrial disturbances with sympathy, and employers demonstrated a willingness to negotiate fair measures of wage compensation even in defiance of the reigning economic doctrines.[95]

Purely empirical (e.g. economic) observations about the 'condition of the working classes' were informed, after as well as before 1880, by moral observations and critiques. Philanthropists and social reformers of the 1880s were as leery as the proponents of the New Poor Law (1834) had been about 'indiscriminate' charity and 'poor relief' delivered without expectation of behavioural reform on the part of individuals. The Charity Organisation Society was founded in 1869 and was highly influential until the beginning of the next century. Like Henry Mayhew, its members insisted on a distinction between the deserving and the undeserving poor. During the 1890s reformers continued to recognize a sociological hierarchy more moral than economic: the categories of the poor (e.g. the thriftless, the workless, and the worthless) referred more to the absence or presence of a 'work ethic' among the impoverished than to their material condition.[96]

Yet clearly waning by the late 1870s and '80s was the belief that the poor are always with us, a belief grounded in the Calvinist dogmas that

---

[95] 'Classical political economy' (*pace* T. R. Malthus, David Ricardo) held that the 'wages-fund' could not sustain wage rates when the average rate of profit was falling. Yet many employers did not cut wages during the 1873–6 downturn. The 'demand for labour, as for other commodities, was maintained ... The employers, one by one, "found it prudent" to restore the former wage' (Rostow, *British Economy*, pp. 95–6). On conflict and consensus in industrial policy ca. 1850–90 see Fox, *History and Heritage*, chaps. 4–5.

[96] Lynd overplays the political acceptance of 'new norms, new criteria of social values, new conceptions of freedom' (*England in the Eighteen-Eighties*, p. 17). Himmelfarb observes that the COS maintained an interest in the moral improvement of the poor which — she claims — was ignored by socialists and most welfarists after 1900 (*Poverty and Compassion*, chap. 13).

poverty is the result of someone's (not always the pauper's) moral transgressions and that the poor are a reminder of Original Sin.[97] This shift in popular religious attitudes certainly contributed to the rise of social sympathy. More precisely, it strengthened the view that duty to God was in fact duty to Man; and it fed the conviction that charity was not enough to moralize the poor — that structured assistance, rational policies and legislative 'interferences' could enable the poor to make the best of themselves. Whether one examines the statements of conservative or Radical social reformers from the 1870s, one encounters scepticism about the efficacy of mere philanthropy. The historian and cleric J. R. Green (1837–83), who was a friend of John Ruskin and an early member of the Barnetts' circle, 'despised the "relief" by which the middle classes squared their consciences with annual £5 notes, coal, and soup ... The middle classes must themselves work and — more importantly — reside among the poor if they wanted to help the poor.'[98] Private doles did little to dispel, in either givers or recipients of charity, the spirit of atomistic individualism which Christian reformers perceived as an affront to Godly order.

Not only were large numbers of social reformers during the 1880s and '90s convinced that poverty was eradicable, given sufficient political will, but they agreed that the factors of insufficient wages and 'unemployment' had to be considered in addition to 'individual' causes, the moral failings of individuals such as idleness, lack of initiative, or thriftlessness. Himmelfarb contends that only after 1900 did the term unemployment connote 'an impersonal condition resulting from impersonal causes' — that is, a systemic or structural problem which could not be attributed to individual poor or unemployed, as William Beveridge made clear in his famous 1909 book *Unemployment: A Problem of Industry*.[99] Even by the 1880s, however, there was significant agreement among active philanthropists that many individual cases of poverty resulted from 'impersonal causes'.

Of course, there remained equally significant disagreements between Liberals and Conservatives, between labourites and Liberal reformers, and between Radical (or Socialist) revolutionists and reformers, over

---

[97] Hilton, *Age of Atonement*, chaps. 8-9; and Hilton, 'The Role of Providence in Evangelical Social Thought' in *History, Society and the Churches. Essays in Honor of Owen Chadwick*, ed. D. Beales and G. Best (CUP, 1985), p. 215ff.

[98] Sutherland, *Mrs Humphry Ward*, p. 215.

[99] The economist Alfred Marshall had used phrases like 'irregularity of employment' and 'out of employment' in the late 1880s as objective or non-judgmental descriptions of socioeconomic facts. John Hobson used the term unemployment in essays appearing during the 1890s. Only after the turn of the century, however, says Himmelfarb, did the term suggest 'an impersonal condition resulting from impersonal causes. In the new usage it was the condition that was problematic, not the individuals afflicted by it.' Himmelfarb, *Poverty and Compassion*, chap. 3, and p. 41 (quotation).

the causes of and remedies for poverty and material inequality.[100] But what was significant here is that elite reformers of the 1880s and '90s largely accepted the charge that the governing classes had failed the poor and the labouring population by ignoring their humanity and by reifying the laws of political economy. As Arnold Toynbee confided to a working-class audience in 1883, 'We have neglected you; instead of justice we have offered you charity, and instead of sympathy we have offered you hard and unreal advice.'[101] Hugh Price Hughes exposed the futility of the belief that slum dwellers were as capable of self-improvement as more comfortable Britons: 'How do you expect virtue and morality from people living in one room?'[102]

Religious and quasi-religious humanitarianism, emphasizing reciprocal social obligations and the moral regeneration of society, was one of the strongest impulses behind the social turn.[103] The members of the Christian Social Union attempted to assert the right relation of social scientific data to practical ethics and the art of government, just as, under T. H. Green's tutelage, they tried to set inductive knowledge in right relation to religious truth. Scott Holland, who went on to become a Canon of St Paul's, editor of *Commonwealth* and chief spokesman of the CSU, urged the Church of England to take responsibility for the social and economic realities of the age.[104]

The response of a Christian nation to poverty in the midst of plenty, Holland said, should be based on a properly Christian economics:

> When our economy is caught in a tangle, we fly off to our morality. When our morality lands us in a social problem, we take refuge in some naked economic law ... [Economic science must succeed] in being ethical, without ceasing to be scientific.[105]

While Dr Temple, Bishop of London, 'was actively hostile to the [dock] workers' during the 1889 London strikes, CSU clergymen in East London offered meeting rooms in several parish churches to the dockers.[106] Another leading member of the CSU, Bishop Westcott (of Durham),

---

[100] Mason, 'Political Economy and the Response to Socialism'; and J. Breuilly, 'Liberalism or Social Democracy: A Comparison of British and German Labour Politics, c. 1850–75,' *European History Quarterly*, 15 (1985), pp. 3–42.

[101] '"Progress and Poverty": A Criticism of Mr. Henry George' (1883), quoted in Meacham, *Toynbee Hall and Social Reform*, p. 16.

[102] H. P. Hughes, *Social Christianity: Sermons delivered in St. James's Hall, London, by Hugh Price Hughes* (London: Hodder and Stoughton, 1889), p. 14.

[103] L. E. Nettleship strongly emphasizes settlement and charity workers' 'unpolitical' sense of the mission of the Church ('William Freemantle, Samuel Barnett and the Broad Church Origins of Toynbee Hall').

[104] Lynd, *England in the Eighteen-Eighties*, chap. 8; d'A. Jones, *The Christian Socialist Revival*; Carter, *T. H. Green and the Development of Ethical Socialism*, chap. 4.

[105] From Holland's preface to *Economic Morals* (1890), quoted in S. Paget, ed., *Henry Scott Holland. Memoir and Letters* (London: J. Murray, 1921), pp. 172–3.

[106] Lynd, *England in the Eighteen-Eighties*, p. 326.

stated as one object of the Union '"to make clergy-men read Blue Books."'[107]

5.6. RADICALISM AND MORAL FERVOUR: THE GLADSTONIAN IMPULSE

Christian meliorism from the 1880s took many theological and political as well as organizational forms. Anglican Christian Socialism was theologically coherent but not all of its adherents followed the same political path. The CSU purported to represent the social mission of the true church independent of party considerations. Yet many Christian reformers after 1875 aligned themselves with advanced Liberalism or with 'Socialism'. Indeed, the CSU by the later 1890s was less distinctly Anglo-Catholic ('High Church') and more an alliance of socially engaged Churchmen of diverse theological views willing to ally with 'secular', purely political organizations. Two leading Anglo-Catholic reformers, Holland and Charles Gore, remained supporters of the Liberal Party, identifying it as the most practical vehicle for their 'socialist' ends.[108] Toynbee, too, had little difficulty in reconciling his Christian humanitarianism with Liberal partisanship. H. P. Hughes was also strongly committed to Liberalism and turned his pulpit into a political platform. In 1890 he assumed the mantle of the 'Nonconformist Conscience' in condemning Parnell's adultery and urging Liberal leaders to exercise moral suasion over the Irish nationalists. His urge to combat 'immorality' in the form of prostitution turned easily into campaigns to elevate the poor by improving their material condition through philanthropy and state action.[109]

Crucial factors in the alignment of Social Reform with Liberalism (and thence to 'Socialism') during the period ca. 1870–1900 were the per-

---

[107] From 'The Ground of Our Appeal' (1908), quoted in Lynd, *England in the Eighteen-Eighties*, p. 326. In Westcott's view, expressions of religious good will towards men were useless unless delivered from a position of awareness of social and economic facts. He was a friend of the economist Alfred Marshall. Westcott delivered addresses during the 1890s deploring individualism. In 1890 he intervened in a coal strike. *England in the Eighteen-Eighties*, pp. 323–6.

[108] Holland was appointed to his canonry by Gladstone, he met with Gladstone on many occasions between 1878 and 1893, and he corresponded with Gladstone's daughter Mary for forty years. Holland was not dismayed by Gladstone's utter disregard for both socialism and a separate labour interest, and he believed that the Liberals could be drawn away from their hectoring of the Church (e.g. Disestablishment, campaigns against High Church ritualism). He believed the enemy of the working man and of true Liberalism was 'the Nonconformist capitalist'. Carter, *T. H. Green and the Development of Ethical Socialism*, chap. 4.

[109] King, 'Hugh Price Hughes and the British "Social Gospel"'; Helmstadter, 'The Nonconformist Conscience,' pp. 165–71; Bebbington, *Nonconformist Conscience*, chap. 3.

sonality of Gladstone and the political style of Gladstonianism.[110] It was the moral seriousness and enthusiasm of 'The People's William' that rallied both 'the masses' and members of the elites to the Liberal banner, despite the emergence of counter-attractions. Of course Liberals were not alone in taking an interest in social reform and national uplift in the era of mass politics following 1867.[111] Conservatives (who were in power for twelve of the twenty years between 1875 and 1895) could point to a respectable tradition, going at least as far back as Robert Peel, of social accommodation and conciliation. No less than the Liberals, modern Conservatives like Lord Randolph Churchill endeavoured to blunt class and sectional interests by pushing a programme of national unity, which included limited industrial and public health legislation. Yet the most gifted late Victorian reformer in the Conservative interest was Joseph Chamberlain, who entered Parliament in 1876 as a Liberal-Radical but broke with the Liberal leadership over the Irish Home Rule question in 1886.[112] In terms of domestic legislation, 'Liberal Unionism' was a new label for constructionist Radicalism. Before his break with Liberal Home Rulers Chamberlain appealed widely to advanced Liberals with his 'Unauthorized Programme' (1885), so named in order to emphasize the reluctance of the Liberal party leadership to champion its main principles.[113]

Chamberlain asserted in 1892 that 'Almost all the legislation dealing with labour questions has been initiated by Tory statesmen ... and it is therefore historically inaccurate to represent the Tory party as opposed to socialistic legislation.'[114] The Lib-Lab MP Alexander McDonald claimed in 1879 that 'the Conservative party had done more for the

---

[110] See especially Hilton, *Age of Atonement*, chap. 9.

[111] On Conservative reformism, see W. J. Wilkinson, *Tory Democracy* (New York: Octagon Books, 1980 [orig. 1925]); J. Cornford, 'The Transformation of Conservatism in the Late Nineteenth Century,' *VS*, 7 (1963), pp. 35–66; P. Smith, *Disraelian Democracy and Social Reform* (London: Routledge, 1967); Shannon, *Crisis of Imperialism*, chap. 5; R. Blake, *The Conservative Party from Peel to Thatcher* (London: Methuen, 1985), chaps. 4–5.

[112] Before 1885–6, no more than ten Radicals in the Commons voted for Irish Home Rule; in 1886, 131 Radicals (as identified by T. W. Heyck) voted for and thirty-two against Home Rule. Radical Unionist MPs 1886–92 numbered twenty, including *all* seven MPs from the Birmingham-West Midlands Division and four sitting for Scottish constituencies. T. W. Heyck, *The Dimensions of British Radicalism. The Case of Ireland 1874–95* (Urbana, IL: UP Illinois, 1974), pp. 25, 253, 255.

[113] He championed legislation along the lines of the 'municipal socialist' measures he had pushed forward as mayor of Birmingham, 1873–6. See E. Gulley, *Joseph Chamberlain and English Social Politics* (New York: Columbia UP, 1926); A. Hooper, 'From liberal-Radicalism to Conservative corporatism: the pursuit of "Radical business" in "Tory livery". Joseph Chamberlain, Birmingham, and British Politics, 1870–1930' in *Victorian Liberalism*, ed. R. Bellamy (London: Routledge, 1990), pp. 193–212.

[114] From the *Annual Register, 1892*, quoted in Wilkinson, *Tory Democracy*, p. 160. The Artisans' Dwelling Act of 1875, the Mines' Regulation Act, and two Workmen's Compen-

working classes in five years than the Liberals had in twenty.'[115] After 1880 Liberal and Conservative politicians competed to appease organized labour and to emphasize their social reform commitments.[116] Twenty Liberal-Unionist MPs of 1886–92 cooperated with a handful of true Conservative MPs in promoting social reform measures. Yet these MPs opposed not only Irish Home Rule but many other constitutional reform proposals then popular in the country, such as limitations on the power of the Lords; whereas during the same period no fewer than 159 Liberal-Radical MPs pushed constitutional and social reforms.[117]

While some Liberal social reform measures were resisted by the Whigs, between 1874 and the 1890s the Liberal Parliamentary leadership was more balanced than that of the Conservative Party, so that on the whole Liberals were less hostile than Conservatives towards social reform. Charles Dilke (1843–1911), Arthur Acland (1847–1926) and James Bryce were among the influential younger Liberals advocating sweeping reform; Hartington (1833–1908), 'the greatest Whig chieftain of his times' (according to Richard Shannon), applied the brake to this. A group of peers including Granville (1815–91), Kimberley (1826–1902), Ripon (1827–1909), and Rosebery (1847–1929) steered a middle course: they tempered the extremes of Gladstone's moral politics — by going slowly with measures to 'save' Ireland, or to protect Bulgarian and Armenian Christians from Turkish persecution — while respecting one side of Gladstonianism, fiscal orthodoxy and political pragmatism.[118]

Most of the vaunted 'Tory' social and industrial measures of the period 1874–99 would not have been passed without Liberal-Radical support. The Third Reform Act, extending suffrage to male agricultural labourers, was largely a Liberal measure, though like the 1867 Reform Act it was actually passed into law under a Conservative Government. The Local Government Act of 1894, setting up democratically elected parish councils (which could include women), was a Liberal measure. The Chancellor of the Exchequer, Harcourt, and the chairman of the Inland Revenue Board, Alfred Milner (who had studied at Balliol in Green's time), were the chief promoters of the aforementioned death

---

sation Acts (stipulating terms of compensation for industrial accidents) were Tory measures.

[115] *Staffordshire Sentinel* (18 January 1879), quoted in Wilkinson, *Tory Radicalism*, p. 162.

[116] D. Powell, 'The Liberal Ministries and Labour, 1893–1895,' *History*, 68 (1983), pp. 408–26.

[117] Three-quarters of the latter voted in favour of land redistribution in Scotland and Ireland, disestablishment of the Church of Wales and the Church of Scotland, the reduction of Royal grants, abolition of the hereditary principles of the House of Lords and the payment of MPs (one of the demands of the 1838 'People's Charter'). Heyck, *Dimensions of British Radicalism*, chap. 1, and pp. 255 63.

[118] Shannon, *Crisis of Imperialism*, chaps. 8, 10; Parry, *Rise and Fall of Liberal Government*, chaps. 11–12.

duties act (1894). This was not the first such measure, but as Ensor observes, Milner 'had established a great new direct tax; comparable to the income-tax, yet quite independent of it, and capable like it of being augmented automatically. . .'[119] If an Employers' Liability bill was killed in the House of Lords in the same year, it was due to the undeniable partisanship of that august body, not lack of skill and enthusiasm on the part of Milner's fellow Balliolite, Herbert Asquith, and other Liberal-Radical sponsors of the bill.[120]

Despite Sidney Webb's demurral, the widest 'ideological' basis of social reform in Britain down to 1895 was the moral crusading impulse of Gladstonianism and the Gladstonian ideals of spiritual commitment and moral consensus. It was natural for Atherley-Jones (quoted in the preceding section) to identify Gladstone as the unquestioned leader of the New Liberalism. Liberalism from the late 1860s owed much to Gladstone's faith in the moral capacities of the nation at large and to the manner in which he referred political questions to the country. Gladstone appealed directly to the 'common people' on important questions in domestic and foreign policy. This was apparent during the national agitation in 1876 against Turkish persecution of Bulgarian Christians, and again during Gladstone's electoral campaign of 1879–80, when he decried the expansionist policies of Russia, Turkey and the Disraeli Government and lectured the British population on the morality of collective security arrangements (embodying principles of international law). Yet even with regard to domestic, 'constructionist' legislation, Radicals and New Liberals as well as their critics viewed Gladstone as the leader of change. Acton wrote to Gladstone's daughter Mary in 1885, 'I quite agree with Chamberlain that there is latent socialism in the Gladstonian philosophy.'[121]

Gladstonians attempted to placate the Dissenting 'section' of the Liberal party and they rallied a wide segment of popular opinion around the principles of Peace, Retrenchment and Reform. Liberals received considerable political credit for suffrage expansion and improved relations between industrialists and trades unions. 'Lib-Lab' MPs complained about the inadequate representation of the working class in Liberal party machinery (e.g. the Liberal Associations, the National Liberal Federation). Despite very limited success before 1895 in securing 'labour representation' via the Liberal Party, many labouring men

[119] Ensor, *England 1870–1914*, p. 217. A death duty, the immediate purpose of which was to finance naval building without increasing the income tax, had been passed by the moderate Conservative G. J. Goschen in 1889. Milner's measure was more clearly ideological, stemming from a commitment to social reform. Interestingly, Ensor attributes Milner's frame of mind to his German heritage and upbringing.

[120] Ensor, *England 1870–1914*, pp. 213–14.

[121] Letter of 11 November 1885, quoted in Fasnacht, *Acton's Political Philosophy*, p. 18.

remained loyal to Liberalism.[122] Gladstonianism encouraged social reform despite Gladstone's own opposition to systematic state intervention. Gladstone and John Bright did not personally favour a large number of state interferences; both men were criticized by labouring men for their opposition to factory acts and to extension of the rights of trades organizations.[123] Gladstone regarded trade unionists as 'faddists', on a par with 'militant' Nonconformists and temperance enthusiasts.[124] However, it was under the mantle of Gladstone that there arose Liberal Parliamentarians more sympathetic to sectional interests, among them W. P. Adam (Chief Whip from 1873), T. E. Ellis (Chief Whip, 1894–9), a chief promoter of Welsh interests, and Alfred Illingworth, a Nonconformist industrialist who maintained ties with labour leaders. All of these took a page out of Gladstone's book in making moral appeals to Liberals at large and in taking them seriously as contributors, to some degree, to the party agenda.

In its selective application of constructionist principles the Liberal party lost the allegiance of laissez-faire-ists during the 1880s, but the party retained the loyalty of Nonconformity.[125] Hamer observes that Gladstone

> became a hero for so many Nonconformists because of his style of leadership and stress on the moral factor in politics … [He] created an important bridge and led Nonconformist faddists often to make much greater allowances for him than they were prepared to make for his colleagues.[126]

---

[122] See G. Howell, 'The Caucus System and the Liberal Party,' *New Quarterly Magazine*, 10 (1878), pp. 579–90. Henry Broadhurst cooperated with James Bryce and William Morris to establish a short-lived National Liberal League in 1879. F. M. Leventhal, *Respectable Radical. George Howell and Victorian Working-Class Politics* (Harvard UP, 1971), pp. 198–201. The Independent Labour Party of 1893 was not very successful as an electoral machine.

[123] Barker, *Gladstone and Radicalism*; Bradley, *The Optimists*, pp. 210–16, 245–52. On working-class criticism of Bright's opposition to factory legislation, see e.g. 'Mr. Bright and the Factory Acts,' *Beehive*, 28 July 1865, p. 4; and 'New Labour Bill. Birmingham and Staffordshire District,' *Beehive*, 3 Feb. 1866, pp. 4–5. This criticism was particularly significant given the facts that Birmingham was Bright's Parliamentary constituency and that the West Midlands were known for 'harmony' in industrial relations. But Bright and Gladstone retained their status as 'plain men of the people' and popular heroes. Joyce, *Democratic Subjects*, chap. 11.

[124] David Hamer observes, Gladstone 'was very remote from them [faddists] and their world … He disliked them very much, because he felt that they selfishly placed the satisfaction of their own special demands above considerations of the common interest.' D. A. Hamer, *The Politics of Electoral Pressure. A Study in the History of Victorian Reform Agitations* (Hassocks, Sussex: Harvester, 1977), pp. 6–7.

[125] Alfred Illingworth and H. P. Hughes helped carry the bulk of Political Nonconformity towards Home Rule. Despite misgivings in 1886, Hughes pronounced in 1888 (in the *Christian Weekly*), 'Home Rule is to me one form of the Golden Rule.' Bebbington, *Nonconformist Conscience*, chap. 5 (Hughes quoted on page 84).

[126] Hamer, *Politics of Electoral Pressure*, p. 7.

Rosebery (Liberal PM, 1894–5) offended Liberal 'Puritans' with his Turf activities: his horses Ladas and Sir Visto won the Derby in successive years. Meanwhile, Hartington had a sense of 'evangelical purpose' and sometimes sided with Nonconformists on religious and educational matters, but he was too aristocratic to be a Nonconformist favourite.[127] As Peter Clarke points out, when Gladstone was deserted by elite politicians and intellectuals from the later 1870s because of his erratic flights into demagogy (and indeed into almost messianic delusions), he simultaneously consolidated his status as 'The Ayatollah of Victorian Christianity'.[128]

Gladstone, writes Christopher Harvie, 'was the man whose portrait stared down from millions of artisan parlour walls …'.[129] Historians have adduced many reasons for the continuing loyalty of the British working classes to the party of Gladstone. These reasons or speculations cannot be profitably discussed here except to state that the working population may have 'gone' for Gladstone simply because, like Dissent, it was habituated to following 'moral' leaders. Plebeian Radicals earlier in the nineteenth century, such as Feargus O'Connor, Arthur O'Neill and J. R. Stephens, believed that while political authority came from the people, those representing the people's will were permitted to bring errant individuals into line with correct sentiments, values and policies.[130] Gladstone and other Liberal leaders from 1860 benefited from habits of popular obedience. There appears to have been a religious dimension to this. According to Eugenio Biagini, the prevailing ethos of plebeian Radicals and reformers in the north of England and on the 'Celtic fringe' was one of democratic communitarianism regulated through the 'Puritan self-policing community.'[131] (Recall Sam Hobson's

---

[127] Parry, *Democracy and Religion*, pp. 67, 148, 412.

[128] Clarke, 'Gladstone: The Politics of Moral Populism' (1991), quoted in Joyce, *Democratic Subjects*, p. 217.

[129] Even the socialist leader of the Scottish miners, Bob Smillie, recognized the 'Grand Old Man' as the greatest politician he had ever met. Harvie, 'Gladstonianism, the Provinces, and Popular Political Culture, 1860–1906', p. 153.

[130] O'Connor ('the Lion of the North'), Stephens, and Arthur O'Neill (only the latter can be described as a Liberal–Radical) emphasized democratic communitarianism and did so in Biblical terms. See J. Epstein, *The Lion of Freedom: Feargus O'Connor and the Chartist Movement, 1832–1842* (London: Macmillan, 1982). On the use of religious language by Stephens and others in 'the aesthetic framing of the social', see Joyce, *Democratic Subjects*, chaps. 14, 17. On O'Neill and his Chartist Church, see Barnsby, *Birmingham Working People*, chaps. 4–6.

[131] *Liberty, Retrenchment and Reform*, pp. 175–7. In contrast, the Radical ethos of London and the south of England was libertarian-democratic, emphasizing 'science and education' (self–help) as means for advancing the condition of the working class and the nation with it. Mechanics Institutes for adult education were popular and to some extent successful since the 1820s in London and the south, while Owenism and the consumer co-operative movement, which challenged the individualist emphasis of

observations about the 1892–3 successes of the ILP in Yorkshire.) Significantly, support for Gladstonianism through the 1890s was comparatively weak in the south, where the strength of Dissent was also dispersed, and comparatively strong and constant in the north.

Members of the working classes were interested in political representation by their own but were also willing to submit to rightly constituted authority. Liberal political economy constituted a non-traditional set of ideas, more often at odds with than in line with popular conceptions of justice.[132] But Liberal leaders, both nationally and locally, were able to tap into the traditional sense of justice by flattering the people for its morality and wisdom. Gladstone and metropolitan ideologists were impressed by the dignified and 'moral' action of the common people during the 1860s: Lancashire textile workers responded sympathetically to the 'just' cause of the American Union, although the blockade of the Confederate states (and resulting cotton famine) meant widespread unemployment in some British industries.[133] Clarke, Joyce, Harvie and others have argued that the cult of Gladstone developed in tandem with the cult of the common man, and the 'narrative of providence came to the aid of the narrative of progress' — progress being realized through the infallible leader (Gladstone) cheered on by a moralized people.[134]

T. H. Green agreed with Gladstone's moral vision in many of its aspects. For example, Gladstone was notably less inclined to apply British military force than were Conservative leaders, preferring diplomacy and conciliation. As we have seen, Green was an anti-militarist, believing that Britain enjoyed a moral authority that it could and should exercise peacefully in international politics. He was one of the conveners of the 1876 Eastern Question Conference, demanding that England protect Bulgarian Christians from their Turkish persecutors.[135] While Glad-

---

orthodox political economy, made inroads (beginning in the 1830s) mainly in Lancashire, the West Riding of Yorkshire and the Midlands.

[132] Tory paternalist factory owners who offered work to entire working-class families and clans, sponsored factory picnics and day-trips, and so on, were often more successful in directing working-class political allegiances than Liberal employers who, wedded to classical political economy, appeared indifferent to the employment and living conditions of factory hands. See P. Joyce, *Work, Society and Politics: the Culture of the Factory in Later Victorian England* (New Brunswick, NJ: Rutgers UP, 1980); N. Kirk, *The Growth of Working Class Reformism in Mid-Victorian England* (Urbana: Illinois UP, 1985); Vernon, *Politics and the People*.

[133] Admiring middle-class Liberals like R. W. Dale raised subscriptions 1862–4 for the relief of the Lancashire cotton operatives. A. W. W. Dale, *Life of R. W. Dale*, chaps. 8, 11. University Liberals too saw the cotton famine as evidence of the wisdom of the people, while Liberal leaders in Parliament continued to criticize Gladstone for bowing to the ignorant masses. Bradley, *The Optimists*, pp. 153–5; Parry, *Democracy and Religion*, pp. 442–6.

[134] Joyce, *Democratic Subjects*, p. 217.

[135] Shannon, *Gladstone and the Bulgarian Agitation 1876*, pp. 202–21.

stone was an astute *Realpolitiker*, he expressed idealism in foreign policy. In his 'Second' Midlothian speech (26 November 1879) Gladstone asked listeners (women among them) to consider the consequences of Conservative 'Forward Policy', particularly the invasion of Afghanistan:

> Those hill tribes had committed no real offence against us. We, in the pursuit of our political objects, chose to establish military positions in their country. If they resisted, would not you have done the same? And when, going forth from their villages they had resisted, what you find is this, that those who went forth were slain, and that the villages were burned ... The meaning of the burning of the villages is, that the women and children were driven forth to perish in the snows of winter.[136]

Should 'the name of England, under no political necessity, but for a war as frivolous as ever was waged in the name of man ... be associated with consequences such as these?'

Green's criticism of the 1874–80 Conservative Government was less sentimental. Rather, Green remarked on the waste of national expenditure (the country was '£50 million poorer' than when Gladstone left office) and the cravenness of a Government 'wantonly and needlessly' pursuing grand imperial policy from Africa to Asia without having 'the courage to ask the English people to pay for it': the Afghan War was charged instead 'to "the mild Hindoo".'[137] He remarked also on Disraeli's duplicity in making on 9 November 1876 a 'speech full of defiance against Russia,' 'with a declaration of the Czar in his pocket, desiring the friendly cooperation of England' in dealing with the Turks.

Green's nephew, John St Loe Strachey (1860–1927), who was to become an influential national journalist, recalled Green waxing into a satirical mood, humorously imitating Gladstone's speech and mannerisms when he was preparing a welcome address to Gladstone (January 1878) on behalf of the Oxford Liberal Association.[138] By all indications, Green held the mission of Liberalism separate from the personality of Gladstone: the source of Gladstone's popularity was the sense of moral purpose and righteousness which Gladstone and Bright — but not only they — had harnessed for political purposes. The zeal for improvement demonstrated by social reformers after 1880 was not created by Gladstone. Yet Guinness Rogers, Atherley-Jones and other commentators on the New Liberalism believed that the new militancy in voluntarism and legislation exemplified both the logic and the spirit of Gladstonianism.

---

[136] *Midlothian Speeches 1879*, with an introduction by M. R. D. Foot (Leicester: Leicester UP, 1971), p. 92.

[137] 'Notes of a Speech at Abingdon Liberal Meeting [1880]': CBG copy in *GP* 1.

[138] 1882 recollection in *GP* 1(b): Charlotte Green's copy-book, pp. 103–13. An account of the speeches to and by Gladstone is in the *Oxford Chronicle*, 2 Feb. 1878, special supplement.

Insofar as they wore the clothing of Christian justice, social reform measures attracted support from people with political or non-political commitments. The Greenian 'religion of citizenship' enabled reformers to advocate political action while appearing to be above the fray of party politics.[139] Social reform was a class-relative duty only in the sense that more favoured individuals were under a sharper discipline to contribute to the moral advance of society. Individuals who did not do so, as Green argued in *Prolegomena to Ethics*, would feel a sense of inadequacy or incompleteness. The same sense of incompleteness was expressed as a need for religious devotion. Artistic and scientific endeavours were personal and individual devotions that contributed to a wider good. When given shape in forms of religious fellowship, the 'spiritual impulse' in man would apply itself to the wider needs of the civil community. Through service to society, men and women produced their justification of God and faith.

Practical Christianity entailed devotion to principles and encouraged useful action in the world. Mid-Victorian Christian Socialists believed that by comprehending within the Church all sincerely religious people, they would make the Church 'what it was meant to be': '"a society for the purpose of making men like Christ — earth like heaven — the kingdoms of the world the Kingdom of Christ."'[140] Maurice, Thomas Hughes and other Christian Socialists were social evangelicals, holding that

> the Kingdom must encompass nothing less than the whole of God's creation, and religion cannot stand aloof; it must therefore concern itself intimately with the fate of all mankind and with the condition of the secular world in which men are forced to live.[141]

The Evangelical Revival, preceding but overlapping with Christian Socialism, had reinforced rather than weakened doctrines of paternalism and obligation. As Melvin Richter argues, for a William Wilberforce or a Lord Shaftesbury, the agitation against slavery or for factory acts was simply an extension of the individual's concern for the spiritual well-being of his brethren. Interference with individual property rights 'seemed, like evangelising, to follow from the assertion that religion

---

[139] Jenks, 'T. H. Green, the Oxford Philosophy of Duty and the English Middle Class'; Nettleship, 'William Freemantle, Samuel Barnett and the Broad Church Origins of Social Reform.'

[140] The phrase in double quotations is from A. P. Stanley's life and correspondence of Thomas Arnold, quoted in Richter, *Politics of Conscience*, p. 50. See also H. De B. Gibbons, *English Social Reformers* (London: Methuen and Co., 1892), pp. 155–80, and Norman, *Victorian Christian Socialists*.

[141] d'A. Jones, *The Christian Socialist Revival*, p. 12.

alone regenerates. And if regeneration is the only road to salvation, then he who has been saved is obliged to save his neighbour.'[142]

The Christian Socialist revival of the late 1870s indicated that the evangelical impulse had not been overwhelmed by laissez-faire liberalism. Whether in the form of Anglo-Catholic social reclamation or in Green's theory of citizenship the Social Gospel was a reproach to atomistic individualism. Canon Barnett's critique of Victorian charity rested on the claim that in ensuring that individuals reap the benefits of their efforts, his fellow citizens had lost sight of the more important mission of salvation and amelioration.[143] The principle of social concern evident in the Charity Organisation Society, the Christian Social Union and the University Settlements was not activated by a misconceived 'generosity' but by an interest in spiritual regeneration, both individual and social. Toynbee's sense of his class and the social order it promoted having 'failed' the poor thus had a hidden theological origin.

5.7. THE DISSENTERS AND CHRISTIAN SOCIALISM

While Dale, Chamberlain and H. P. Hughes participated in the turn towards social evangelicalism, many Protestant Nonconformists were less disposed to do so. Dissenters were able to justify service to their religious communities (the 'Visible Saints', the persecuted), but it was difficult for them to contemplate extending this service ideal to society as a whole. Those engaged with the 'Liberation Society' at mid-century had little faith that social improvement could be realized through the mechanisms of the state. Some evangelicals and many Dissenters conflated the State with the entirety of sinful, temporal life; most rejected the attachment of religious polity to state because they held that the state as such bore no relation to the idea of divine order.

Those Dissenters who were most tardy in embracing the social turn were frequently those who were uncertain about their relation to the state Church, and thus to the temporal order — namely, the Methodist sects. The fact that Methodists were active participants in many movements throughout the nineteenth century to empower 'the people' and the dispossessed does not gainsay the social conservatism of most of

---

[142] *Politics of Conscience,* p. 21. Laurence Dickey observes that 'Protestant civil piety' was antithetical to complacency. In the civil pietistic mood or frame of mind it became increasingly difficult to maintain that salvation is a wholly personal and asocial matter or conversely, that society has no obligation toward suffering and imperfect individuals. Dickey, *Hegel,* pp. 7–12.

[143] Barnett's motto was 'Fear not to sow because of the birds.' He was concerned by what modern economists call the free-rider problem but he did not allow it to blot out other considerations of individual or social good. Lynd, *England in the Eighteen-Eighties,* p. 321.

their preachers.[144] As is well known, notable labour leaders throughout the Victorian period began their public lives as Methodist lay preachers; however, many Wesleyan Methodists were, in the tradition of John Wesley himself, anti-revolutionary, not tolerant of sin and injustice, but willing to render unto Caesar what was Caesar's.

As we have seen, many Dissenters were won over to systematic schemes of social regulation and state interference — not only with respect to elementary education and the Drink Problem, but to residential overcrowding, industrial arbitration and sweated labour. Dale and Hugh Price Hughes were outstanding examples of non-Anglicans turning passionately to questions about 'man's duty to man.'[145] Although it is possible in the case of the Broad Church movement and Anglican Christian Socialism to trace ideals of social commitment to theological development, it is more difficult to do so in the case of the Nonconformist sects.[146] Few social activist Dissenters of the period were as theoretically advanced as their Anglican clerical counterparts — that is to say, as adept in grounding social policy in a theology. Yet Stanley Pierson identifies Congregationalism from the 1880s as 'a major source of inspiration for popular Socialism': 'Men and women of Congregational background would play key roles in developing an idiom which made the new social creed congenial to important sections of the working classes.'[147]

As we have seen in Chapter Four, if the Unitarian Joseph Chamberlain was the commander-in-chief of Birmingham Radicalism, Dale led the big battalions of Congregationalists and Independents to champion interferences of local authority in the name of the common good ('gas-and-water socialism') and to advocate ambitious political reforms as measures strengthening 'national life'. Dale's attempts to extend elementary education to poor children and bring clean water to Birmingham and the Black Country stemmed from a general social concern — based on a perception of physical misery and waste of life and energy — as well as confessional interest. A. M. Fairbairn (1838–1912), though less active as a pastoral leader and clerical politician than as a theologian and

[144] See E. Halévy, *The Birth of Methodism in England*, trans. B. Semmel (Chicago: Chicago UP, 1971); R. F. Wearmouth, *Methodism and the Struggle of the Working Classes, 1850–1950* (Leicester: Leicester UP, 1954); Semmel, *The Methodist Revolution*; Hempton, *Methodism and Politics in British Society, 1750–1850*.

[145] See J. M. Davidson, *Eminent English Liberals In and Out of Parliament* (Freeport, NY: Books for Libraries Press, 1972 [orig. 1880]) — on Dale, Spurgeon, Moncure Conway. Also: R. F. Horton, 'Robert William Dale,' *Contemporary Review*, 75 (1899), pp. 34–44; Kenyon, 'R. W. Dale and Christian Worldliness'; King, 'Hugh Price Hughes and the British "Social Gospel"'.

[146] See Reardon, *From Coleridge to Gore*, chap. 5; Pierson, *Marxism and the Origins of British Socialism*, pp. 12–21; and Webb, 'The Limits of Religious Liberty.'

[147] *Marxism and the Origins of British Socialism*, pp. 17–21. Quotation p. 17.

scholar, had taken an interest in social and economic questions while head of Airedale Independent (i.e. Congregational) College in Bradford, and he was acutely aware of the potential for working-class alienation from (too) solidly middle-class congregations.[148] His student J. W. Dixon became a full-fledged socialist in the 1880s, whether because of Fairbairn or in spite of him is not clear.

In the cases of Hughes and R. F. Horton it is easy to trace the particular influence of T. H. Green on both their philosophical and social views.[149] According to his daughter, Hughes called Green 'the most splendid Christian that I ever met.'[150] Hughes took up the social reform crusade as editor of the *Methodist Times* from 1885, and indeed in a Greenian spirit: Christians, he pronounced in 1889, had been 'selfishly individualistic'. While other Methodists denounced constructionist legislation, Hughes viewed the controversy over the Contagious Diseases Acts as an opportunity to launch an assault on White Slavery and related vice.[151] Bebbington observes that Hughes not only sought repeal of the Acts but encouraged 'preventive and reclamatory work in which the powers of the state and of municipal authorities could be invoked'; this would include inspection of dwellings and measures to prevent overcrowding. He 'directly repudiated "a laisser faire policy"' and rejected local veto in liquor licensing in favour of the more interventionary Gothenburg system favoured by Chamberlain.[152] It is unfortunate that Hughes is more readily recalled as the blow-hard moralist who helped topple Charles Stewart Parnell in 1890 as the leader of the Irish Nationalists (by hectoring him in print as a known adulterer repugnant to the 'Nonconformist Conscience'), than as a dogged social reformer convinced of the connections between vice, poverty, misery and 'laissez-faire'.[153]

Not only the Methodist Hughes but Robert Horton and other Congregationalists (including Mearns, of *Bitter Cry* fame) joined with the Christian Social Union in support of strikers in London and elsewhere in 1889, and in championing industrial arbitration. A leading man of the

---

[148] See A. M. Fairbairn, *Religion in History and in Modern Life. Together with an Essay on the Church and the Working Classes* (New York: Herrick and Co., [1893]), pp. 1–62 ('The Church and the Working Classes').

[149] Horton emphasized his closeness to Professor Green. He developed a friendship with a Norwegian Congregationalist, Knut Kvikne, who married Emily Green, T. H. Green's sister. Horton, *An Autobiography*, p. 76.

[150] D. P. Hughes, *Life of Hugh Price Hughes*, p. 134.

[151] Bebbington, *Nonconformist Conscience*, pp. 38–42.

[152] Letter to J. Chamberlain, 30 April 1891 (criticizing legislators' persistent deference to laissez–faire principles), cited in Bebbington, *Nonconformist Conscience*, p. 42; also Hughes' promotion of the Gothenburg system in the *British Weekly* (1894), cited in *Nonconformist Conscience*, p. 49.

[153] Ensor, *England 1870-1914*, pp. 183–5 and Appendix B.

Congregational Union, Albert Spicer (who also managed the financing of Mansfield College), assisted in the formation in 1891 of a Social Questions Committee, which among other things stated its opposition to sweated labour. Horton sided with striking coal miners in 1891 and supported the eight-hour working day for men, to which even some Lib-Lab leaders (like Henry Broadhurst) were opposed.[154] As pastor of the comfortably middle-class Lyndhurst Road chapel, Hampstead (founded 1884), Horton promoted domestic and foreign missionary activities, formed a Social Reform League (1889), and started an adult school, Lyndhurst Hall, in neighbouring Kentish Town.[155]

In Chapter Three was noted Horton's discomfort with Oxford Broad Church criticism and the teachings of Jowett and Green especially. However, he confessed to experiencing 'an exhilarating emancipation' from dogma and Biblical literalism through the Higher Criticism and Christian immanentism, although he suffered under charges of heterodoxy upon publication of his book *Inspiration and the Bible* (1888).[156] Horton always suspected that the disapproval of some of his suburban flock stemmed not only from his theological heterodoxy but his advocacy of social causes. Of the Lyndhurst Hall project he commented, 'However little this passionate desire to help Labour and the Democracy accomplished, it operated powerfully enough in alienating the rich from the Church.' Although Horton, in his autobiography, did not draw a direct connection between his theological-intellectual development and his interest in social reform, it is clear that he, like Hughes and Arnold Toynbee, found in social service a proof of God and faith. Like Hughes, and Dale in Birmingham some twenty years earlier, Horton was frequently irritated by suburban smugness and he believed that the Lyndhurst Hall settlement would teach his parishioners social understanding and sympathy. Horton recalled approvingly a speech by Hughes upon the opening of a new town hall in Hampstead (1884): 'He told us that the people of Hampstead were going to Kentish Town to save Kentish Town, but knowing the perils of a suburban Church, he said that it was really Kentish Town that would save Hampstead.'[157]

---

[154] Bebbington, *Nonconformist Conscience*, pp. 54–5.

[155] Horton, *An Autobiography*, pp. 64–83. He claimed that the Lyndhurst Chapel people during his pastorate gave about £50,000 and thirty missionaries to the London Missionary Society. Horton was a fellow of New College, Oxford, and a member of the Nonconformists' Union. His friends included A. M. Fairbairn, Bryce, James Legge, Herbert Asquith, and H. P. Hughes; all these men encouraged Horton's move to London in 1884, believing he would be more effective as a socially engaged clergyman than as a don.

[156] *Autobiography*, pp. 82–93.

[157] *Autobiography*, p. 66.

5.8. GREEN AND THE UNSECTARIAN
SOCIAL SERVICE IDEAL

Hughes, Horton and Scott Holland were sensitive to the criticism of those they ministered to and they sometimes felt themselves to be hampered in their social activism by their clerical office. As Richter has observed, many Oxford men who engaged in social service after 1870, including those who participated in university settlements, decided against taking holy orders because they experienced religious doubt; and even those without such doubts came to feel that taking holy orders would create a sort of barrier between themselves and the people they elected to 'serve'.[158] Holland was perhaps exceptional in not feeling such separation. Upon his nomination as Canon of St Paul's in 1884 he wrote to Charlotte Green: '*He* [THG] would have been very glad of this, I think. It will, I trust, take me nearer to work that he would hold dear, among the working-men of that great city.'[159] T. H. Green was already by the late 1870s a kind of hero to socially sensitive Oxbridge men, as he engaged in social and political work in a 'religious' spirit; he preached a Social Gospel without being a clergyman and without exhibiting partiality towards any particular denomination.[160]

Although some University Settlers and charity workers were supported by churches as curates or chaplains, most were unpaid. This does not mean that they were altruists. They did not wish to exhaust themselves in the work required to manage a parish (as 'Robert Elsmere' did in Mrs Ward's novel) but at the same time they believed that quasi-pastoral apprenticeship within a university settlement — in which living specimens of the working classes were more often visitors than residents — would be useful preparation for political, bureaucratic or journalistic careers.[161] The settlements, as 'colonies' of self-training social workers, were attempts to extend the social reach of the Ancient Universities and to broaden their functions. Herbert Asquith described Barnett's parish and Toynbee Hall as 'a research laboratory for social reformers.'[162] The settlers owed much to Green's teachings about

---

[158] Richter, *Politics of Conscience*, chaps. 10–11. One of the last of the clerical reformers in the mid-Victorian Christian Socialist mode was J. R. Green, author of the very popular *Short History of the English People*. Like T. H. Green, he was regarded by many contemporaries as a martyr to the cause of social service. He was one of the models for 'Robert Elsmere'. Sutherland, *Mrs Humphry Ward*, pp. 84, 115.

[159] Letter (undated) in Paget ed., *Henry Scott Holland: Memoir and Letters*, p. 113 (emphasis in original).

[160] Jenks, 'T. H. Green, the Oxford Philosophy of Duty'; Inglis, *Radical Earnestness*, chap. 2.

[161] Meacham, *Toynbee Hall*, chaps. 2–3.

[162] Quoted in Lynd, *England in the Eighteen-Eighties*, p. 321. Asquith was on friendly terms with many religiously-inspired social reformers (Holland, Horton), but his own commitment to reform was only vaguely spiritual. He had converted from Congregation-

responsible citizenship, especially as some of them professed to be interested in learning from urban dwellers as well as about urban industrial conditions. Settlers wanted to moralize the poor, to realize their own and others' best selves; but like the University Liberals of Green's generation they were also interested in establishing for themselves a new social identity between 'the classes' and 'the masses', as (paradoxically) *disinterested* experts and advisors. The appreciation of distance was a 'scientific' element of the Social Turn.

Many early apologists and architects of the welfare state participated in the University Settlement movement. William Beveridge (1879–1963) was a settlement resident in 1903–4.[163] Although a life-long Liberal, he participated in labourite and socialist study groups, and in his famous 1942 White Paper Beveridge sketched the plan of state assistance 'from cradle to grave' that shaped Labour policy after 1945. The economic historian R. H. Tawney (1880–1962) was a settlement resident during 1903–6 and 1908–13. He became a socialist and a driving force behind the Workers' Educational Association. Tawney's own experience as a settler appears to have sharpened his (negative) sense of class privilege. At a meeting ca. 1909 about the organization of the WEA someone remarked, 'Of course we should have them [middle-class students], just like any other class; God made the middle classes.' Tawney rejoined, 'Are you sure?'[164] Philip Wicksteed, Unitarian minister of Little Portland Street Chapel, who debated Bernard Shaw and Graham Wallas about Marxian economics during the 1880s, was warden of University Hall from 1890. Although all of these activists advocated systematic state intervention to address structural defects of economy and society, they also agreed with the moral suasionist aims of the settlement movement.[165]

Congregationalists established their settlement, Mansfield House, at 89–93 Barking Road, Canning Town, in 1890 — while Mansfield College was still under construction in Oxford. The first Warden of Mansfield

alism in his youth to a rather complacent Anglicanism. R. Jenkins, *Asquith. Portrait of a Man and an Era* (New York: Chilmark Press, 1964), chaps. 2–3.

[163] While at Balliol in 1899, Beveridge 'wrote his mother that he "would like to do something" for the hall, "but I seem incapable of teaching anything that is wanted except perhaps swimming"' (quoted in Meacham, *Toynbee Hall*, p. 133).

[164] In 1914, he enlisted in the army and refused an officer's commission. At a military hospital in Oxford in 1916, Bishop Gore was astonished to find Sergeant Tawney recuperating in the enlisted men's ward. Terrill, *R. H. Tawney and His Times*, pp. 44 (quotation), 48–52. See also L. Goldman, *Dons and Workers: Oxford and Adult Education since 1850* (Oxford: Clarendon, 1995).

[165] Wicksteed became a socialist. He was replaced as warden of the Passmore Edwards Settlement (the refoundation of University Hall) by R. G. Tatton, a Fellow of Balliol and a Liberal. Pelling, *Origins of the Labour Party*, pp. 132–44; Meacham, *Toynbee Hall*, chaps. 6–7; Sutherland, *Mrs. Humphry Ward*, p. 223; Carter, *T. H. Green and the Development of Ethical Socialism*, chap. 6.

House was Percy Alden (1865–1944), who as a boy had met Green and Toynbee, had gone up to Balliol the year after Green's death, and joined the Nonconformists' Union.[166] Alden later served on the London School Board and the West Ham Borough Council, then as Radical MP (Tottenham, 1906–18) and Labour MP (S. Tottenham, 1923–4); he was knighted in 1933. Although he was perhaps not of the same intellectual calibre as Beveridge and Tawney, Alden wrote pamphlets on social questions, including 'The Unemployed — A National Question'. Like Toynbee Hall, Mansfield House presented university men from Nonconformist backgrounds (although others were not excluded) with the opportunity to shed their sense of class isolation and to become aware of their own class privilege. Tawney, when preparing the publisher George Unwin's collected papers in 1927, perceived that the mood of Mansfield House, where Unwin had lived in 1898, was of self-criticism, or rather of criticism of one's class, and that settlers believed they were there to fulfil their social obligations by building bridges to the lower classes.[167]

While the value to working–class neighbourhoods of the boys' and girls' clubs, guest lectures and musical evenings conducted by the settlement houses can be questioned, university settlers were acutely aware of benefits to themselves. Beveridge wrote in 1904, 'No man can really be a good citizen who goes through life in a watertight compartment of his own class ... Toynbee Hall provides therefore a sort of general culture in political and social views.'[168] Settlers were themselves conscious of dilettantism and naiveté, and members of the SDF and the Fabian Society ridiculed voluntary social service by members of the British elites as egotistical and guilt-ridden, the dying gasp of Christian philanthropy and social Liberalism. The ideal of 'Only connect' (applied disastrously by the Schlegel sisters in E. M. Forster's novel *Howards End*, 1910), of becoming humanized through engagement with the lower classes, was fine and good, but university settlers, charity workers and social gospelists also had the privilege of disconnecting. The socialist George Lansbury (1859–1940) opined,

> The one solid achievement of Toynbee Hall, and the most important result of
> the mixing policy of the Barnetts, has been the filling up of the bureaucracy of

[166] Envelope marked 'Mansfield House' in the Mansfield College Library, Oxford, cupboard 2: including posters, press clippings, personal notes by Alden and Will Reason, and an article from *The Quintinian* (November 1892): 'Social and Educational Centres of the Metropolis'. Alden met Arnold Toynbee 'in the house of Professor Green' (ca. 1880–81). P. Alden, 'Arnold Toynbee,' *Mansfield House Magazine*, 1 (1894), p. 49.

[167] Unwin 'glorified' T. H. Green. He said of the working-class men he encountered at Mansfield House, 'In their aspirations lies the future of England, if it is to have any. The future of Christianity lies with them too' (quoted from a letter of Unwin to his wife in 1901). Meacham, *Toynbee Hall*, pp. 156–7, 170–1 (quotation).

[168] Quoted in Meacham, *Toynbee Hall*, p. 145.

government and administration with men and women who went to East London full of enthusiasm and zeal for the welfare of the masses, and discovered the advancement of their own interests and the interests of the poor were best served by leaving East London to stew in its own juice while they became members of Parliament, cabinet ministers and civil servants.[169]

Beveridge and Tawney were no less critical than Lansbury of the philanthropic impulse; they often alluded to the sense of social distance that would not be dispelled by university settlements and other forms of middle-class social outreach. They were aware that not all middle-class settlers were willing to engage the poor as social equals, and that familiarity with working-class life gained through social service did not invariably breed mutual admiration or respect. Mrs Humphry Ward was sceptical of the capacity of the working classes for rational thought and action; she combined a tremendous faith in self-help with a disposition towards authoritarianism and top-down solutions to social and political problems.[170]

T. H. Green's theory of active citizenship and social service was at once a symptom of and an antidote to social alienation. It held special attraction for men and women in comfortable circumstances who were not only sensitive to 'physical evils' surrounding them but who perceived a decline in the quality of social relations. Many British social reformers from the late 1870s were committed to social dialogue and interaction as moral processes 'spiritualizing' the privileged as well as the poor. Gladstonian Liberalism had helped form the ethical climate of the social turn in the 1880s by insisting on the basic soundness of popular morals and deploying the language of popular constitutionalism. Gladstone's idea of The People as hero drew the populace to Liberalism, while the successes of his populism encouraged some liberal intellectuals to believe that they could effectively mediate between the classes and the masses, correcting the errors of both, and regenerate the nation.

The Webbs and many other early Fabians had reservations about democracy and labour representation. Their theory of 'permeation' entailed the gradual transformation of Britain from above by tutoring the educated classes in their ideas about economy and society and by putting right-minded people into positions of political and administrative responsibility. Fabians did not deny the need for a mass socialist party, but neither were they convinced that mobilizing the masses was

---

[169] From Lansbury, *My Life* (1928), quoted Meacham, *Toynbee Hall*, pp. 123–4.
[170] Many Toynbee Hall members championed causes to which Mrs Ward was unsympathetic or hostile: Irish Home Rule, women's suffrage, the rights of the Boers in the 1899–1902 South African war. Sutherland, *Mrs Humphry Ward*, pp. 197, 217, 266–7, 310–11.

the most effective *immediate* strategy for ushering in a 'socialist' order.[171] Green was sometimes disturbed by the manipulations of popular politics; hence his great interest in diminishing forces that warped popular reason (e.g. Drink).[172] He believed political democracy to be an end in itself, but he also imagined that the best wisdom of society would be channelled into productive political action by invoking the principles of organic society. Green believed that change occurred in individual persons and that social transformation had to proceed from — as well as result in — a spirit of fellowship. Neither collective action (from below) nor administrative measures of an enlightened elite — whether Hegelian 'universal class' or Coleridgean 'clerisy' — could be effective in absence of this.

Green's influence on British social policy during the three decades before the First World War was considerable because his ideas had effects on the most influential people, from Cabinet members and civil servants to settlement workers and social investigators. At least as much as the ideas of the Fabians, Green's teachings permeated the educated British public. It is difficult to determine the size of Green's popular audience, and hence the social depth of his impact, but a plebeian autodidact reading Green's *Lectures on the Principles of Political Obligation* in the 1890s was sure to have been a Radical in politics. In 1865 J. S. Mill had identified optimism and faith in the future as attributes distinguishing the Liberal from the Conservative: 'A Liberal is he who looks forward for his principles of government, a Tory looks backward.'[173] Green looked towards the past ('organic principles') as well as forward for principles of government and he was confident that people from all social classes would embrace those principles. His idiom proved attractive to people seeking to reconcile individuality and social responsibility. Many intellectuals and practical reformers believed that Green's theory of self-realization provided collective as well as individual benefits; as much as his ideas, they cherished Green's memory and example. Even as some of them came to dismiss voluntarism as inadequate to deal with modern social and industrial problems, their philanthropic activities, policy contributions and legislative achievements showed that Green's faith in social improvement through self-perfection and moral suasion was not exhausted in his time.

[171] Permeation and the adoption by Radicals of socialist ideas would point out the contradictions of the existing political system: e.g. wealthy Radicals advocating piecemeal social reforms. See H. Bland, 'The Outlook,' in *Fabian Essays in Socialism*, ed. G. B. Shaw (New York: Dolphin Books, n.d. [orig. 1889]), Essay Eight.
[172] Although he does not mention Green specifically, Paolo Pombeni comments on the anxieties of like-minded Liberals about the dynamics of democracy. 'Starting in Reason, Ending in Passion. Bryce, Lowell, Ostrogorski and the Problem of Democracy,' *HJ*, 37 (1994), pp. 319–41.
[173] *Morning Star*, 6 July 1865, quoted in Bradley, *The Optimists*, p. 47.

CHAPTER SIX

Green and Political Memory

6.1. RIGHT AND LEFT GREENIANS

Green's reputation as a philosopher, political theorist and social activist has waxed and waned. While the present study has noted how some of Green's contemporaries and later commentators faulted him for logical inconsistencies or philosophical ambiguities, it is also clear that many observers idolized or denigrated him for reasons having less to do with his philosophy than with his specific political recommendations. Still others lauded or criticized Green's example as a socially engaged intellectual. The main object of this chapter is to locate Green's place in the political memory of liberalism by analysing the political and cultural meanings of his 'legacy'.

Many Greenians down to the Second World War were philosophical liberals or liberals in spirit. These could be found among the supporters of the post-1906 Liberal Party as well as among dissidents who distanced themselves from official Liberalism because they believed its leaders had abandoned its moral priorities. (1906 was a watershed because the 'Liberal Landslide' in the General Election, achieved with the cooperation of Labour, enabled a united left to push through such radical measures as old age pensions and unemployment insurance.) Disenchanted Liberals of the Right included Green's friends from the 'Old Mortality', James Bryce and A. V. Dicey, as well as Mrs Ward, who by the turn of the century had come to deplore collectivism and fear the Labour movement.[1]

---

[1] Bryce wrote to Dicey (3 July 1911): 'Don't you think that the whole problem of Democratic government as we regarded it when we wrote those essays in 1866–7 has been fundamentally changed by the coming of the Labour movement into politics? … We used to complain of class legislation by landowners. Now we have it by working men;

Greenians were to be found also among Radical-Liberals who moved towards socialism, such as Percy Alden, William Beveridge, Lord Haldane, Leonard Hobhouse, H. W. Massingham and William Temple; and among those who, like the 'Independent' city councillor and MP Eleanor Rathbone, eschewed political labels. All of these radicals may be properly regarded as pioneers of the Welfare State, a term coined by William Temple, the social activist Bishop of Manchester (1921–9) who ended his clerical career as Archbishop of Canterbury.[2] (His father, Frederick Temple, had also been the chief prelate of the Church of England some thirty years after appointing Green to the Taunton schools commission.) William Temple was a contemporary of Beveridge and R. H. Tawney at Balliol, and like them he became active in the Workers' Educational Association. He joined the Labour Party at the end of the First World War. It is not incidental that Temple took a leading role as well in the World Council of Churches. Haldane, a Hegelian philosopher, had been Secretary for War and Lord Chancellor in the (Liberal) Asquith Government and occupied a Labour seat after 1918.[3] Massingham edited the *Daily Chronicle* and the *Nation*. Although he resigned from the Fabian Society in 1893, due to its break with official Liberalism, he remained sympathetic to socialists and labourites.[4] Eleanor Rathbone (1872–1946) was a graduate of Somerville Hall, an institution which Green had been instrumental in establishing, and she became an active social reformer around the turn of the century. As an Independent town councillor in Liverpool (from 1909) and an Independent MP (holding a University Seat, 1929–45), she worked for protection of casual labourers and for family endowment; the Family Allowance Act of 1945 was passed as the result of her decades of effort. Rathbone was a model 'lady' social activist and politician of the kind Green had encouraged in his work for women's education and local government (see discussion in this chapter below).[5] Many of these liberals in spirit invoked Green's moral authority and even regarded themselves as executors of Green's moral legacy.

---

and it looks like pressing harder and longer.' Bodleian Library, Bryce MSS. 4, fols. 42–3.

[2]   Nicholls, *Deity and Domination*, pp. 44–52, 66–81; J. Kent, *William Temple: Church, State and Society in Britain, 1880-1950* (CUP, 1992).

[3]   A. F. Havighurst, *Britain in Transition. The Twentieth Century*, 4th ed. (Chicago: UP Chicago, 1985), p. 157 and *passim*; Blaazer, *The Popular Front and the Progressive Tradition*, pp. 52–4.

[4]   A. F. Havighurst, *Radical Journalist: H. W. Massingham (1860-1924)* (CUP, 1974); Collini, *Liberalism and Sociology*, pp. 74–5.

[5]   Hollis, *Ladies Elect*, pp. 397, 408 and *passim*; S. Pedersen, 'Eleanor Rathbone (1872–1946): the Victorian Family Under the Daughter's Eye' in S. Pedersen and P. Mandler, eds., *After the Victorians: Private Conscience and Public Duty in Modern Britain* (London: Routledge, 1994), chap. 4.

Because Greenians represented a wide spectrum of British political attitudes ca. 1918 Green's political legacy cannot be defined simplistically in terms of policies or programmes, but it is relevant to summarize here his priorities. While Green was a vigorous opponent of social privilege — in the sense of an individual's favoured access to hegemonic institutions, owing to wealth, social position or religious creed — his interest in economic democracy remained subordinate to his political goals. He believed the rights and duties of citizenship applied to all able members of society. Green had some direct acquaintance with labour organization. When he addressed an 1872 meeting of the National Agricultural Labourers' Union Green agreed that 'the only way to obtain what they wanted was by combined action.'[6] By 1881 he firmly pronounced that prevailing forms of 'free contract' were often, and to many, but 'an instrument of disguised oppression.'[7] However, Green did not understand a labour 'interest' as corresponding to that of a Marxian proletariat. He used the term 'proletariate' in the *Lectures on the Principles of Political Obligation* and from this we might infer that he had at least a notional understanding of Marx's ideas.[8]

H. M. Hyndman, founder of the Social Democratic Federation, had discussed Marx's theory of surplus value in *England For All* (1881), and Green's associates William Wallace and Arnold Toynbee commented on aspects of Marx's work around the same time.[9] Yet Wallace and Toynbee disagreed with Marx's analysis of class struggle and economic exploitation and there is nothing in Green's writings or speeches to suggest that he was any more in agreement with Marxist theory than they. 'Scientific socialism' scarcely existed in Britain at the time of Marx's death in 1883. (The International Workingmen's Association had nearly perished in England during the 1870s.) Hyndman's original Democratic Federation (whence sprang the Social Democratic Federation) espoused social revolution instead of reform. Yet the postulates of the SDF struck even other 'socialists' of the 1880s and early '90s, such as the Fabians, as odd and impractical.[10] It seems therefore unfair to fault Green (as Greengarten, Lawless and others have done) for not having subscribed to Marxian economics or social theory in the early 1880s.

Indeed, there was some gap between Green's view of the 'suffering classes' and the viewpoint shared by many labour leaders of the 1880s and '90s. The latter certainly shared Green's interest in elementary edu-

---

[6]   From speech on 23 October 1872, reported in *Oxford Chronicle*, printed in *AW*, p. 239.
[7]   'Liberal Legislation,' in *Harris and Morrow*, pp. 208-9.
[8]   *LPPO*, secs. 225-9.
[9]   Toynbee, *Lectures on the Industrial Revolution in England*, pp. 31n, 109, 113; W. Wallace, *Lectures and Essays on Natural Theology and Ethics* ... (Oxford: Clarendon, 1898), pp. 412-18. I am grateful to John Morrow for these specific page references.
[10] Lynd, *England in the Eighteen-Eighties*, chap. 10.

cation and university extension lectures. Yet few of them regarded temperance as the cure for the maladies of the working class, even if they were sensible to the evils of drink. Green's support of other sectional causes, namely those of Dissenters and women, was consistent with the egalitarian tendency of liberalism. Although 'women's rights' scarcely registered on the agenda of the Parliamentary Liberal party before 1910, there existed by the 1870s a clique of advanced Liberals devoted to women's emancipation who could not simply be dismissed as faddists. Green was concerned that members of marginalized social groups achieve access to the institutions of civil society so that they would more readily identify with the common good. In large part because he emphasized principles of inclusion and participation Green came to exemplify a new type of hero for middle-class emulation: not a political leader (born to power or self made), not a prophet, not a sage, but a practical thinker. Green was a convenient role model for intellectuals who sought simultaneously to improve society and to assert their social authority in an age of mass politics and collectivism.

British political debate evolved in such a way after Green's death as to make his definite policy recommendations and general political outlook appear rather conservative. Indeed, Andrew Vincent and Raymond Plant have suggested that, just as Hegel scholars speak of *Linkshegelianer* and *Rechtshegelianer*, there is reason to distinguish between Left and Right Greenians ca. 1890–1914.[11] Matt Carter has recently argued that the distinction is a misleading, if not wholly false one. He contends that Sidney Ball, the Fabian don who claimed to be both a Socialist and a Liberal, and Bernard Bosanquet, who upheld strict economic 'individualism', could equally claim to be true to Green's principles and priorities. Whether Liberals or not, those claiming to represent Green's legacy were attentive both to 'character' in self-realization and to the force of 'circumstances' (social or economic conditions) limiting individual opportunities.[12] However, political commentators and actors after 1882 eagerly mined Green's teachings for their 'socialistic' or 'individualistic' implications, and many of them purported to speak for the partisan Left or Right in doing so. There is reason to acknowledge a distinction between Left and Right Greenians, although it is equally clear that the distinction does not, in many individual cases, translate simply into socialist or left liberal versus conservative.

It is fair to characterize Bernard Bosanquet's political recommendations as conservative in the context of their time, particularly after 1900. Bosanquet was not only an influential Idealist philosopher but also a leading member (after 1881) of the Charity Organisation Society, an

---

[11] See *Philosophy, Politics and Citizenship*.
[12] 'Ball, Bosanquet and the Legacy of T. H. Green.'

association dedicated to the scientific study and application of charity. His half brother Charles had been the first secretary of the COS and Bernard's wife, Helen, became also a key figure in the association. Bernard Bosanquet emphasized not state intervention but 'citizenship': a proper understanding of citizenship, with its correlative virtues, duties and obligations, implied a philosophy of social voluntarism rather than one of 'grandmotherly government'. Bosanquet also gave emphasis to Green's validation of private property as a means of self-realization, whereas many other Idealist (and non-Idealist) Radicals focused attention on the social uses and misuses of individual property.[13] His endorsement of responsible individualism combined with his expressions of concern about excessive state action tended by 1900 to locate Bosanquet as a Conservative in all but name. Yet Conservatives were far from displaying unanimity on these principles and some were just as inclined as advanced Liberals and socialists to 'think in communities'.

6.2. RADICAL CONSERVATIVES

Some late Victorian and Edwardian acolytes of Green were proud to identify themselves with Conservatism and Unionism. Laissez-faire Liberals deserted to the Conservative party from the 1880s because they saw the Liberal Party as forsaking individualism, yet individualism was only one strand of Conservatism as it moved into the twentieth century. Conservatives had been traditional defenders of community and nation, and many were more receptive than classical liberals to a philosophy of socially qualified or socially inscribed individual being. There is reason to characterize as Greenian certain Unionist and Conservative intellectuals active politically after 1886 who advocated not traditional paternalism but producer cooperation (in industry as well as agriculture) and economic protectionism (e.g. Tariff Reform). Joseph Chamberlain's 1894 programme of 'Social reform in a Conservative spirit' had a powerful impact on Conservative-Unionist thought. Chamberlainism was as symptomatic of Sidney Webb's 'thinking in communities' as Radical-Liberal measures (e.g. Asquith's failed 1893 Employers' Liability Bill) or Webb's own advocacy (while chairman of

---

[13] Bosanquet said more about the state than did Green, but his state idea was a decidedly conservative one: private property was the pillar of society. B. Bosanquet, 'The State and the Individual,' *Mind*, n.s. 28 (1919), pp. 75–8. When Hobhouse identified British Idealism as a force of 'bed-rock conservatism', he had mainly Bosanquet in mind — and he effectively exempted Green of the charge. J. Morrow, 'Liberalism and British Idealist Political Philosophy: A Reassessment,' *HPT*, 5 (1984), pp. 91–108. See also Nicholson, *Political Philosophy of the British Idealists*, pp. 198–9, 228, Carter, 'Ball, Bosanquet and the Legacy of T. H. Green,' pp. 675, 681–5; Gaus, 'Bosanquet's Communitarian Defense of Economic Individualism.'

the London County Council Technical Education Board) of universal, compulsory education into adulthood.[14]

In representing Green as a thinker in the liberal tradition scholars have underestimated his influence (and that of Arnold Toynbee) on Conservatism, particularly in its 'organicist' and 'corporatist' aspects. Indeed, students of philosophy and political theory have tended to assume that Green, as a partisan Liberal, appealed exclusively to liberals. Historians of British politics and political movements, however, have helped assemble a different picture of Green. In a recent study of the Conservative party in the three decades before the First World War Ewen Green has named among 'the house intellectuals of the Edwardian Conservative Party' the historical economists W. A. S. Hewins, W. J. Ashley and William Cunningham.[15] Hewins moved within the orbit of Toynbee, while Ashley and Cunningham had been directly exposed to Green's teachings and acknowledged their importance. A graduate of Wolverhampton Grammar School, Hewins went up to Pembroke College, Oxford, and read history (he was a contemporary of Leonard Hobhouse). He participated in University Extension and, like the University Settlers, 'wished to bring about an improved social order and direct our activities to an end great enough to give them dignity and meaning.'[16] Hewins helped organize the London School of Economics and was its first Director. In 1903 he was invited by Joseph Chamberlain to serve as Secretary of the Tariff Reform League (a lost cause that split the pre-1914 Conservative Party). He remained a Tariff Reformer through the 1920s and was a leading player in the Unionist Business Committee. Hewins was undersecretary at the Colonial Office in the Lloyd George Coalition Government and published his memoirs in 1929 as *The Apologia of an Imperialist*.[17]

William Ashley too was a Chamberlainite, heading the commerce school at the new University of Birmingham (1900).[18] Ashley had very

---

[14] Richard Shannon discusses Unionist-Conservative social and economic thought after 1886 in *Crisis of Imperialism* (see pp. 298–306), and at greater length in *The Age of Salisbury, 1881–1902: Unionism and Empire* (London/New York: Longman, 1996). See also Hooper, 'From Liberal-Radicalism to Conservative Corporatism;' and P. Marsh, 'Backward versus Radical Conservatives [review essay],' *JBS*, 38 (1999), pp. 261–6.

[15] E. H. H. Green, *The Crisis of Conservatism: The Politics, Economics and Ideology of the British Conservative Party, 1880–1914* (London: Routledge, 1995), p. 183.

[16] Hewins, *Apologia*, i, p. 15, quoted in Collini, *Liberalism and Sociology*, p. 166n.

[17] To my knowledge there is no published biography of Hewins, but see D. Butler and A. Sloman, *British Political Facts, 1900–1975*, 4th ed. (New York: St. Martin's, 1975), pp. 10, 99; and the guide to the Hewins Manuscripts (Ref. MS 74) in the University of Sheffield Library (www.shef.ac.uk/library/special/hewins.html).

[18] On the academic careers of Ashley and Cunningham, see Soffer, *Discipline and Power*, pp. 57–62, 228–9n. Collini notes Ashley's friendship with David Ritchie and their shared belief in parallel evolution of society and morality (*Liberalism and Sociology*, pp.

likely heard Green's lectures at Oxford. He was a student of Toynbee's at Balliol, graduating with history honours in 1881, and winning a fellowship at Lincoln College in 1885, the same year in which his innovative book *Introduction to English Economic History and Theory* was published. A friend of D. G. Ritchie, Ashley had been a member of the Oxford University Nonconformists' Union, a promoter of denominational cooperation and an advocate of 'social outreach' from the Universities (see Chapter Four above). Ashley was instrumental in transplanting the Green-Toynbee service ethos to the Empire: while teaching in the Department of Political Economy of the University of Toronto during the late 1880s he helped establish a University Settlement.[19]

Cunningham, a fellow and chaplain of Trinity, Cambridge, was slightly older than Hewins and Ashley. His *Growth of English Industry and Commerce* appeared in 1882 and he lectured in economic history at Cambridge from the 1880s. Cunningham became Archdeacon of Ely. Richard Shannon describes him as 'a disciple of T. H. Green, [arguing] historically the case for a managed rather than a laissez-faire economy.'[20] The attribution of discipleship is supported by Cunningham's admiring references to Green in *The Common Weal. Six Lectures on Political Philosophy*.[21] Like Shannon, Ewen Green remarks on the influence of T. H. Green on both Cunningham and H. S. Foxwell, and concludes that the Green-Toynbee school of 'Oxford Collectivism' had powerful repercussions for Conservative economic and industrial policy down to 1914.[22]

The case of a lesser-known Radical Conservative of this period illustrates the extent of Green's teachings and their hold on the generations reaching maturity between 1875 and 1900. Arthur Boutwood (1864–1924), a civil servant attached to the Charity Commission, believed that T. H. Green's true legacy was a progressive Conservatism. Boutwood complained to the second Viscount Halifax early in 1910 that the Conservatives under the leadership of A. J. Balfour had become 'a party of mere negation, living upon the fear of threatened interests and unwillingly following (and occasionally blunderingly destructing) that great democratic movement which it could not guide.'[23] 'It is many a long

---

162–3, 166).See also S. Burke, *Seeking the Highest Good: Social Service and Gender at the University of Toronto, 1888–1937* (Toronto: Toronto UP, 1996), chaps. 1–2.

[19]   S. Burke, *Seeking the Highest Good*, chaps. 1–2.
[20]   *Crisis of Imperialism*, p. 211.
[21]   Cambridge UP, 1917.
[22]   *Crisis of Conservatism*, pp. 179–80. See also D. J. Dutton, 'The Unionist Party and Social Policy 1906–1914,' *HJ*, 24 (1981), pp. 871–84.
[23]   Letter dated 19 January 1910: Hickleton Papers, A4.270 V, Borthwick Institute, University of York. I am grateful to Dr Derek Blakeley for a transcript of this letter. Ewen Green does not mention this letter but does discuss Boutwood's few published papers

year since Conservatism had a thinker,' he pronounced, but Conservatism correctly interpreted was 'a reasoned and spiritual doctrine of progress':

> T. H. Green's work needs to be done over again — as he himself saw. If it were done over again, the result would be a magnanimous Imperialistic conservatism genuinely alternative to Socialism, and not a Liberalism inclining to Socialism.

Thus Green's legacy was politically malleable. His widow mused to James Bryce in 1903, 'I always feel he would be now what is called a Little Englander. How I should like to know what he would say about the Education bills [i.e. 1902 Education Act].'[24] Green died before the full flowering of British High Imperialism — and before the split within the Liberal party over Irish Home Rule, the resurgence of the independent labour movement and the great constitutional crises over the House of Lords (1909-11). We can only speculate about how he would have responded to these and other developments at home and abroad. The foregoing biographical sketches merely indicate that people who valued Green's ideas followed political paths quite different from the one his widow and other intimates imagined he would have taken. His nephew John St Loe Strachey, for instance, appears to have admired him and to have learned from him, but also to have taken contrary positions on most political questions.[25] Strachey was sent to live with his Uncle Tom and Aunt Charlotte while preparing for university (1877-8). He read history at Balliol and took his BA in the year of Green's death. Already a leading political journalist by the turn of the century, Strachey was a staunch imperialist, yet neither a Chamberlainite nor an Asquithite 'social imperialist'. While opposing Irish Home Rule, Strachey also opposed Tariff Reform. Holding 'individualistic views on social questions' (*DNB*), in 1908 he published *The Problems and Perils of Socialism*.

Mrs Humphry Ward (1851-1920), one of the most financially successful English novelists of the late Victorian-Edwardian era, was a Greenian theological liberal but a political conservative. Mary Augusta Arnold Ward had flourished under the attention of Jowett, T. H. Green

---

in *Ideologies of Conservatism. Conservative Political Ideas in the Twentieth Century* (OUP, 2002), Chapter 2.

[24]   Letter of Charlotte B. Green to James Bryce, 26 April 1903: Bodleian Library, MSS. Bryce 73, fols. 4–5.

[25]   Strachey, *The Adventure of Living: A Subjective Autobiography (1860-1922)* (London: Hodder and Stoughton, 1922), chaps. 10 (discussing his time at Oxford), 12, 24, 26–7; s.v. *DNB*, 4th supplement (1922–1930). The Green Papers contain Strachey's recollection of his uncle (*GP* 1b).

and the historian J. R. Green during the 1870s and '80s.[26] With Tom and
Charlotte Green she had pushed for systematic educational opportunities for women at Oxford and subsequently became involved in larger
social and political issues. Mary believed her intellectual work and
social outreach activities fulfilled Green's legacy, but she became an
imperialist and staunch anti-suffragist and was appalled by labour politics.[27] One of her reasons for founding the Passmore Edwards Settlement only a few years after establishing University Hall was that 'her'
first settlers 'did not want to be "students" and reconstruct Christianity.
They wanted to reconstruct London.'[28] In her suspicion of the masses,
Mary Ward resembled more closely her uncle, Matthew Arnold, than
her spiritual tutor, Green.[29] Still, as John Sutherland observes, to the end
she appears to have been conscious of Green's moral authority. Her 'last
public intervention' (1919–20) was to arrange a collective letter to *The
Times* protesting an Enabling Bill that would have made participation in
Holy Communion a 'necessary test' of Anglican faith. The 'plea for a lib-
eralized Anglicanism' was part and parcel of the 'idiosyncratic Christian humanism' Ward had imbibed from Green — and defended in her
1881 pamphlet *Unbelief and Sin*.[30] But for her sex, Mary Ward would
count as a member of the 'clerisy' discussed by Harvie in *The Lights of
Liberalism*.

6.3. INTELLECTUALS IN POLITICS AND THE IDEA OF CHARACTER

Green's ideas were regarded with respect not only by mild 'collectivists'
of the 1880s and '90s but by those after 1910 who welcomed a fundamental transformation of British society through communal ownership and
the elimination of class privilege. Leonard Hobhouse, who began his

[26] See Mrs Humphry Ward, *A Writer's Recollections* (London: W. Collins, 1918), especially pp. 132–70.

[27] So outraged were the Somerville College people at Mary Ward's anti-suffragism that
they broke off relations with her in 1909. Sutherland, *Mrs. Humphry Ward*, chaps. 18,
25, 28, and p. 306.

[28] At Marchmont Hall, set up by disaffected University Hall colonists, 'there was no
preaching [sic] and there was no middle-class atmosphere' to make working-class
people 'feel out of place.' Mothers brought their children with them and at evening
gatherings 'over classless tobacco and tea the residents could jaw endlessly about
Marxist theory with actual labouring men.' Sutherland, *Mrs. Humphry Ward*, p. 220
and *passim*.

[29] Green wrote to Mary's husband, T. H. Ward, 'Your wife is the only lady I have known
who has a rational enthusiasm for politics …' (Bodleian Library, MS. Eng. Lett. e.118,
fols. 150–1: letter of 16 September 1881). Had Green lived to witness Mary's later political conduct, he would have perhaps regretted this evaluation.

[30] Sutherland, *Mrs. Humphry Ward*, pp. 62–3, 373. On the circumstances behind 'Unbelief and Sin' and Green's response to the pamphlet, see Ward, *A Writer's Recollections*,
pp. 167–70.

working life as a Liberal but later gave qualified support to the Labour Party, found lasting value in Green's philosophy. Stefan Collini observes that Hobhouse's theory of society, expressed most cogently in his 1913 book *Development and Purpose*, 'rested upon a teleological conception of reality which was heavily Idealist in origin'; Hobhouse was sympathetic to religion as a source of individual and social meaning; and, like Green, he tended 'generally to concentrate on the potential for [social] harmony at the expense of analysing the actuality of conflict.'[31] Hobhouse saw that liberalism had evolved since Green's time and that politicians who adhered to a set of policy recommendations that would have been acceptable to Gladstone, Rosebery or Henry Campbell-Bannerman (the Liberal Premiers down to 1908) were out of touch with the demands of the age. As noted above, Hobhouse believed that Bernard Bosanquet had been untrue to Green both philosophically and politically. Bosanquet on the one hand had committed the error of attributing a will and personality to the State; on the other, like laissez-faire Liberals and Conservatives, he represented private property as the foundation of order and social progress. Hobhouse remarked in a 1924 letter to C. P. Scott, editor of the *Manchester Guardian*, that 'essential Liberalism' and 'Good Liberals' could be found in all political parties and factions save the Conservative.[32]

Other intellectuals on the Left — such as Beveridge, Tawney, A. D. Lindsay and William Temple — approved of Green's democratic priorities. Greenian 'citizenship' at least approached social and political questions in the right spirit. But liberal and socialist intellectuals may have been even more impressed by Green's example as an activist. His academic radicalism defined an important place for the intellectual in an age of mass politics, increasing social specialization and bureaucratization. This middle-class role model, of course, had not been constructed by Green alone but he gave it an attractive shape. Political notables at the time Green began his professional life were of course recognized for their scholarly activities. Gladstone published serious works in Church history and was respected for his Homeric studies. Not only Green's peers Bryce and Dicey, but intellectuals Mill, Morley, Thorold Rogers, Brodrick and Henry Fawcett brought scholarly and technical expertise to bear in their discharge of public duties. Ian Bradley remarks on how the Liberal Party of the period 1865–1915

---

[31] Collini, *Liberalism and Sociology*, p. 241. See also D. Weinstein, 'The New Liberalism of L. T. Hobhouse and the Reenvisioning of Nineteenth-Century Utilitarianism,' *Journal of the History of Ideas*, 57 (1996), pp. 487–507.

[32] From a letter dated 7 November 1924, quoted in Collini, *Liberalism and Sociology*, p. 247.

was able to secure the active services of several of the leading thinkers and writers of the time in a way that would be impossible today because of the pressures of political life and the specialization of academic life.[33]

As Christopher Harvie suggests, the attractiveness of public life combined with the ability of male British intellectuals (as gentlemen) to move within the highest circles of political power drew Green's generation of university-trained intellectuals away from merely academic life; they would neither be content with the status of apolitical 'dons', comfortably free from the obligations of public life, nor protect Academe from the political complications of social change.[34] A minor but instructive illustration of this development is the *Undergraduate Papers* privately printed in 1858 by Green and his friends in the 'Old Mortality'.[35] The epigram on the frontispiece of *Undergraduate Papers* reads 'Gladly would we learn, and gladly teach,' and it succinctly describes not only the attitude of the 'Lights of Liberalism' to the world within and outside the university but the viewpoint of successive generations of activist intellectuals.[36]

Green came to represent a kind of outsider's insider who resisted the temptation to employ political influence at the price of independent thinking, speaking and acting.[37] He was fitted into this role by others because he exemplified 'character', an idea central to liberalism. Green's fellow University Liberals had already formed an elevated conception of their own role in society, but his conception of self and society, or of

[33] *The Optimists*, p. 35.
[34] *Lights of Liberalism*, chaps. 1–2. Some of the University Liberals were never properly at home in academe. During his last weeks as Ambassador to the US, James Bryce wrote to A. V. Dicey (24 March 1913), 'What you say about the living permanently in any University is perfectly true. Though tempted to take up dwelling there, first after I had got my Fellowship and secondly after being appointed to the Regius chair I had a kind of instinct that it was not the best place in which to keep up energy or to be abreast of the general movements of the world' (Bodleian, MSS. Bryce 4, fols. 57–62). Prior to his ambassadorship Bryce had been Chancellor of the Duchy of Lancaster, chairman of a royal commission on secondary education and Chief Secretary for Ireland.
[35] *Undergraduate Papers. [An Oxford Journal Conducted by A. C. Swinburne, John Nichol, T. H. Green, and Others]* (New York: Scholar's Facsimiles and Reprints, 1974).
[36] Bodleian, MSS. Bryce 2, fols. 156–7: letter of A. V. Dicey to Mrs James Bryce, 1 May 1893. 'I look with great satisfaction on the fact that the Old Mortality, to which James and I belonged, though we have not done quite as brilliantly in the world as we expected, has never had any reason to be ashamed of its members, and considering we were utterly without connection, to have produced one Cabinet Minister [Bryce], and I think six Professors[,] who perhaps in the aggregate may be taken as equivalent to the one C.M.[,] is not bad. Oh, I forget, we have also the best on the whole of living English poets.'
[37] Inglis, *Radical Earnestness*, chap. 2. R. L. Nettleship notes in his 'Memoir' of Green that the Councillor Professor was approached by Oxford Liberals to stand for Parliament. Green refused, doubting his physical stamina, but one suspects he also entertained doubts about his temperament for such office.

self *in* society, powerfully reinforced their sense of mission. Green represented service to the state as an important form of service to society and he strongly implied that people who chose to serve in such a way had attained a high stage of consciousness. Yet every individual could serve society according to his or her 'station' in life. Even when denied active political rights (e.g. the ballot), a citizen could perform social duties and pursue legitimate conceptions of the good as shaped by the wisdom of civil society and trained by conscience.

James Meadowcroft observes that by the 1880s 'the state emerged as a theoretical category of liberal self-identity in a way that it did not for either conservatism or socialism.'[38] It would be perhaps more accurate to say that the idea of citizenship functioned more centrally in (new) liberalism than in mainstream conservatism or socialism.[39] Yet Green's philosophy, while offering a compelling account of citizenship and clarifying the 'province' of the state, did not lend itself rigidly to a single partisan identity. What liberals — not only Liberals, but moderate socialists and Radical Conservatives as well — down to the Second World War found most valuable in Green's teachings were not specific political policies but an approach to social questions that prioritized an idea of character, grounded in the metaphysic of self-realization.

Green not only reasserted the importance of character to a democratic society in which vast social and economic forces appeared to minimize the significance of individual action; Green *had* character. Some people were less impressed by Green's theories than by his *praxis*, which they regarded as a demonstration of his character. Dorothea Hughes observed of her father, the Dissenting journalist and public moralist Hugh Price Hughes, 'His particular regard for Professor Green lay in his character, I imagine, more than in his ideas.'[40] More recently, John Derry has compared Green and J. S. Mill in a manner revealing the persistence of the idea of character. 'T. H. Green,' he writes,

> adapted Hegelian idealism to English conditions, justifying the state on idealist grounds, yet attempting to ensure the virtues of choice, spontaneity and participation. Mill never achieved anything as impressive or coherent ...

[38] *Conceptualizing the State*, p. 58. J. H. Muirhead titled his book on Green's teachings *The Service of the State*.

[39] Vincent, 'The New Liberalism and Citizenship.'

[40] *Life of Hugh Price Hughes*, p. 136. Mark D. Johnson has pointed out to me that some Dissenters habitually paid tribute to Green as a way of bragging (personal communication: 4 April 1990). Hughes attended Green's lectures but he claimed (or his daughter did) that Green 'called upon him shortly after his arrival [in Oxford].' 'Young Turks' like Hughes and Horton who were out of sympathy — politically as much as intellectually — with the leaders of their denominations must have derived intellectual and social security from acquaintance with an Establishment figure (albeit a heretical one) like Green. But they idealized his 'character' for much the same reasons as other Liberals.

Again, while Green was active in local politics in Oxford, giving practical effect to his ideals, Mill's attitude was curiously mixed.[41]

Derry's evaluation is hardly fair to Mill, who was attentive to freedom, choice and individuality. Moreover, Mill's public life was at least as impressive as Green's: he worked for many years at India House, occupied a Parliamentary seat for Westminster (albeit briefly), and courageously supported such unpopular causes as contraception, women's rights and representative government in the colonies. But Derry is as captivated by Green's practicality and social engagement as were Green's contemporaries, who remarked on his 'spirit of earnestness and simplicity of purpose,' his sense of philosophy not as 'cold and barren speculation, but a cherished creed, a help to noblest life,' his 'rigour, humour, health of soul, and gentleness combined with rough masculine force.'[42] It was precisely 'health of soul' that Mill sometimes believed he lacked, as he testified in his famous *Autobiography*; and he engaged public issues in an abstract and intellectual manner.

Henry Nettleship remarked approvingly that Green's 'tone of mind was never what is called academical,' and in doing so he implied certain contrasts. Arthur Hugh Clough, a Balliol poet who died young and to whom Green was occasionally compared, was a gifted dreamer; Green was a doer.[43] Jowett was famous for his hubris, reserve and elitism; Green sought out people of intelligence and energy regardless of their social status.[44] Mark Pattison was a misanthrope. His erudition led him to a position of absolute skepticism: he had encountered every possible idea but could recommend none.[45] Green's learning, in contrast, reinforced intuitive beliefs, and he grasped philosophy as an aid to life, not a retreat from it. The personal attributes that Green's contemporaries found admirable in him were signs of character, and to many Victorians the 'contents of character' were more important than contents of minds.

To Victorians, to be a person of character was to be self–motivated, and to be sensitive to social mores but also willing to go against the

---

[41] *The Radical Tradition*, p. 267.

[42] From the recollections by A. R. Vardy, C. S. Parker, and J. A. Symonds, in *GP* 1(b). Dicey and Sidgwick, in contrast, recalled the young Green (ca. 1853–63) as carrying an air of tired superiority; and Green had a reluctance to 'enter into things' (*GP* 1b).

[43] H. Nettleship recollection: *GP* 1(b).

[44] There is a Balliol rhyme cited in many studies of Jowett: 'Here I go, my name is Jowett. There is no knowledge but I know it. What I don't know isn't knowledge. I am the Master of this college.' He reflected at the age of sixty–one or sixty–two, 'I seem to have had great power in thinking and dealing privately with persons, but no power in public or society.' Quoted in Faber, *Jowett*, p. 404.

[45] This impression is borne out in Mrs Ward's *Robert Elsmere*. Pattison was the model for 'Squire Wendover', the private scholar and landowner who is indifferent to the welfare of his tenants and whose arguing with Elsmere precipitates the latter's crisis of faith.

grain.[46] Not only did Green, Leslie Stephen, Henry Sidgwick and others live under a heavy sense of moral duty but they found in the discovery of their own characters a firm ethical foundation when other certainties of Victorian life collapsed around them. Even as they shook loose certain moral imperatives (above all, the 'evangelical' battle for personal salvation), these men remained in the grip of a religious sense of everyman's 'calling' in society. The ordinary individual achieved a sense of his or her own character through discovery of personal talents, limitations and duties, which was itself possible only through social engagement. Even in the case of the religious ascetic, artist or cloistered scholar, discovery of character occurred through exploration of consciousness transcending the personal.[47]

Character discovery, as understood by Victorian liberals, was manly in the sense that it involved hardship, facing unpleasant truths or duties (toward oneself or others); character development was antithetical to comfort and complacency. Correlatives of character were independence, discipline, fortitude, virtue. 'Virtue' was its own reward and might go unrecognized. *Virtu* during the Renaissance was literally that which defined a man. Virtues (e.g. the martial virtues) were correlative to male social and civic duties, yet a man and citizen performed such duties for their own sake, not because he profited from them but because they defined him. Edmund Burke was in the 'civic humanist tradition' in reasoning that virtues were more important than laws, for where order was possible with the latter, there could be no morality without the former.[48]

It is no exaggeration to state that the civic humanist/Renaissance conception of virtue had been reduced, in Victorian Britain, to the ideal of character. The idealization of character formed an ethical bedrock of British Liberalism, in part because the correlative values of character were precisely those that (supposedly) brought economic success.[49] But the values surrounding character — or the possession of which indicated character — more generally enabled the individual to find his way

[46] Stefan Collini's writings on the Victorian conception of character and John Burrow's on liberal (and essentially Romantic) 'individuality' have been noted in Chapters One and Two above. Also, Joyce, *Democratic Subjects*, pp. 98-103.

[47] Goethe, in *Dichtung und Wahrheit*, described the work of the poet as connecting the world inside him to the world outside of him. On manliness and Victorian self-fashioning, see T. L. Broughton, *Men of Letters, Writing Lives: Masculinity and Literary Autobiography in the Late Victorian Period* (London/New York: Routledge, 1999).

[48] Skinner, *Foundations of Modern Political Thought. Volume I*, chap. 4; Semmel, *John Stuart Mill and the Pursuit of Virtue*; Pocock, 'Virtues, Rights, and Manners,' in *Virtue, Commerce, and History*, chap. 2.

[49] Briggs, 'Samuel Smiles and the Gospel of Work,' in *Victorian People*, chap. 5.

in the world, to seek but not to yield.[50] Character in this sense was quintessentially masculine, imperative to men, and a sort of moral glue of liberalism. John Vincent reminds us that 'The great moral ideal of liberalism was manliness, the rejection of the various forms of patronage, from soup and blankets upward, which had formerly been the normal part of the greatest number.'[51] Circumstances and personal obstacles were to be surmounted and trials of circumstance showed the individual what he was made of. Yet this was not the sport of heroes; self–realization and the training of personal character were part of the moral process experienced by all people.

The Victorian idea of character was part of the mental furniture of political progressives in the age of Green, socialists as well as Liberals. Green's theory of the self in society provided only equivocal endorsement of the Smilesean ideal of self-reliance. Green softened the cult of character by exposing the bad faith involved in the belief that self–help was equally effective for all individuals, or that it could be effectively exercised by individuals surrounded by deleterious influences. In this he was by no means out of line with the Fabians, one of whose stated goals was 'The cultivation of a perfect character in each and all.'[52] He would have agreed with a socialist of the 1890s who observed that 'individualist economists' feared socialism because they believed it would 'deteriorate character', while socialists believed that 'under individualism character is deteriorating.'[53]

6.4. CHARITY, VOLUNTARISM, STATE ACTION

A difficulty, in theory at least, for the appropriation of Green by full fledged socialists was the fact that he offered no explicit argument for collective ownership (such as nationalization of economic enterprise); nor did he recommend state assistance to individuals through pensions or direct income supplements. His skepticism about redistributive measures — for this was how John Hobson, Sidney Webb and others registered Green's position — echoed earlier Victorian Liberal cautions about sapping individual initiative and energy. State appropriation of

---

[50] Green himself suggested something along these lines in his Old Mortality essay (published in 1858) entitled 'The Force of Circumstances' (*Works*, iii, pp. 3–10). Like Thomas Hughes or Charles Kingsley, Green believed that invoking circumstances as obstacles to personal action was often a form of moral laziness. Not all people can surmount circumstances (Green specifically mentions 'laws of political economy' on page 9) and the laws of their being, but then again no individual is free from outward circumstances. The good man in a free society is 'slave' only to Him 'whose service is perfect freedom' (p. 9).

[51] *Formation of the British Liberal Party*, p. xxviii.

[52] E. R. Pease, *History of the Fabian Society* (1916), p. 32, quoted in Collini, *Public Moralists*, p. 93.

[53] *Encyclopaedia of Social Reform* (1898), p. 895, quoted in Collini, *Public Moralists*, p. 93.

the 'unearned increment' might discourage private investment and defeat the idea of property. On the other hand, 'friendly' and building societies, consumer co-operatives, postal savings banks (Gladstone passed the legislation for the latter in 1861) and other financial institutions available to the working classes were useful. First, these encouraged thrift. Second, they revealed the very practical value of fellowship and cooperation and demonstrated to the working class its potential to improve its collective condition through peaceful means.

Green lent himself to liberalism in his emphasis on 'intermediate' institutions of civil society as aids to moralization. He assumed that such moralization was encouraged through wider property ownership. Green supported in a modest way co-operative initiatives to provide land allotments and low-cost homes: he held shares in the Oxford Cottage Improvement Company.[54] Radicals with whom Green was on close terms, James Thorold Rogers and George John Shaw Lefevre, took the lead in establishing a National Liberal Land Company, Ltd. (1881), 'with a view of assisting in promoting, through joint-stock enterprise, a practical reform of the existing land system, and of realising the legitimate profits which, as is well known, result from the operation of all properly managed land companies.' The objects of the company included purchase and development of freeholds and resale of land in small parcels; abolition of prohibitory taxes upon exchange of land; 'simplification and registration of all titles'; 'and the enabling of members of all classes of the community to reside in their own freehold houses.' Such ventures were not intended as substitutes for direct legislative action; in part they represented Radicals' frustration with the tardiness of other Liberals in pushing social reform.[55]

Green emphasized the power of the state, both national and local, to attack directly harmful environmental conditions — e.g. decrepit and unsanitary housing, drink shops surrounding the slum-dweller — and to provide basic needs, such as elementary education, without which individuals were incapable of helping themselves. The residue of feudalism was effectively defeating attempts at self-improvement. Even

---

[54] *GP* 1(a) contains Green's shares in the Oxford Cottage Improvement Co., Ltd. (dated 27 March 1879).

[55] Advertisement in *AN*, 2 April 1881, p. 223. Similar projects of the time included the Land Nationalisation Society, the Free Land League, the English Land Restoration League and the Allotments and Small Holdings Association. *Liberal and Radical Yearbook 1887*; Offer, *Property and Politics*; and M. Chase, 'Out of Radicalism: the Mid–Victorian Freehold Land Movement,' *EHR*, 106 (1991), pp. 319–45. Thorold Rogers (Liberal MP, 1880–6) had been professor of political economy at Oxford; active in local and national politics, he had spoken on platforms with Green since the mid-1860s. He was involved also in temperance propaganda and women's education. Shaw Lefevre was a member of Liberal Governments from 1868 and was elevated to the peerage in 1906. He supported schemes for the higher education of women.

where land was not withdrawn from cultivation, throwing peasants into the urban proletariat, rural tenants and lease-holders, especially in Ireland, were cheated of the value of improvements they made to the land they worked. The 1881 Irish Land Act as well as the Allotments Extension Act and Settled Land Act of 1882 were consistent with those organic reforms Green recommended to Harcourt in 1873. The Corrupt Practices Act of 1883 — which among other things held campaign managers to account for spending on elections — was passed in no small part due to the fuss Green had raised about 'treating', bogus spending and malfeasance in the 1880–1 elections at Oxford. From the Greenian point of view, all of these reforms were 'organic', but negative rather than constructionist: they facilitated the proper working of *existing* institutions rather than adding complicated new instruments of improvement.

Green's revision of 'self-help' distinguished him from laissez-faire Liberals; he never regarded self-help as sufficient for the purposes of either self-realization or the 'moral development' of society. Philanthropy was also problematic. Charity Organisation Society members opposed regular or general doles because these did not provide for the moral supervision of their recipients. Green, who contributed to the COS, was also concerned with the moral activation of the charity–givers.[56] He held the charitable impulse to be, psychologically, self–regarding; it stemmed from recognition that an imperfect state of society was also an imperfect state of self. Mechanical distribution of charity, without social engagement, did little to activate the conscience of the charity–giver. When charity took the form of distribution of a few pence or shillings to any hard-luck case who came into immediate view (securing temporary relief from bad conscience), the self-realization of the charity–giver had effectively ended, not begun. Philanthropy should promote the self-realization of the philanthropist as well as serve the moral and material improvement of the poor.

Socialists such as Sidney and Beatrice Webb believed that philanthropy was ineffective because too often it did not attack the roots of deprivation. Yet the contrast of views between them and the proponents of discriminate charity has been overstated. Late Victorian and Edwardian proponents of state intervention had the same moral goals in mind as more conservative reformers. Opposition to doles and other forms of state assistance had been a feature of liberal thought since the early nineteenth century and remained a characteristic attitude of early twentieth-century anti-socialist liberals. (Thirty-five percent of Poor Law expendi-

---

[56] Canon Barnett believed that a dole, whether delivered privately or through the state, had equal power to improve or degrade a person. He did support old-age pensions. Meacham, *Toynbee Hall*, pp. 69–78, 111–15; Himmelfarb, *Poverty and Compassion*, p. 187ff.

ture in England and Wales, of gross £8 million a year, 1876–80 was still going to 'outdoor-relief', the provision of which the reformers of the 1830s had deplored.)[57] The Webbs expressed their irritation with this view in their 1909 minority report to the Poor Law Commission: the tedious moralism of the majority reporters underscored their refusal to recognize the extent of structural poverty, preserved by entrenched inequality and an unregulated labour market.[58] The Webbs believed that resistance to redistributive measures and to progressive taxation was the outmoded moralistic legacy of the 1834 poor law, which threw the infirm and able bodied together in workhouses, and depressed wages by subsidizing the most poorly remunerated labour. They took the logic of the 'New' Poor Law even further. 'Why, asked the Webbs, should it be left to the masters of the workhouses to give a free education to the pauper children when all children now had in principle the right to a free education?' And why should the unemployed be left to compete inefficiently in the regular labour market when instead they could be given 'special relief work' and re-educated for regular employment in a trade?[59]

Yet it cannot be fairly claimed, as Gertrude Himmelfarb does, that the Webbs and other socialists had lost sight of the 'characters' of the poor. Many non-revolutionary socialists — as indeed the majority of socialists undoubtedly were — upheld Green's priorities. Remedies of structural problems would only lead to lasting solutions when they left room for individual initiative. This regard for initiative, self-improvement and character is obvious in the measures promoted by advanced Liberals, such as Herbert Asquith, Winston Churchill and David Lloyd George, who with the support of organized labour pressed forward the sweeping social legislation of 1906–14. The legislation securing old age pensions and unemployment insurance required substantial contributions from individual workers, not only for the purpose of financing these schemes without crippling taxation but in order to maintain a visible component of self-help.[60] Liberals who advocated caution in social and industrial reform, such as the Idealist Henry Jones, echoed the older warnings against grandmotherly government. Jones feared the 'corruption of citizenship' as a consequence of workers becoming accustomed to the state, or to trade unions, doing for them what they should do for

---

[57] Best, *Mid-Victorian Britain*, p. 161.
[58] E. Halévy, *The Rule of Democracy*, 2nd ed. (London: E. Benn, 1961), pp. 244–63; A. Vincent, 'The Poor Law Reports of 1909 and the Social Theory of the Charity Organisation Society,' *VS*, 27 (1984), pp. 343–63; Himmelfarb, *Poverty and Compassion*, chaps. 21, 23, and epilogue.
[59] Halévy, *Rule of Democracy*, pp. 258–9.
[60] Gilbert, *Evolution of National Insurance*; R. J. Scally, *The Origins of the Lloyd George Coalition. The Politics of Social-Imperialism, 1900–1918* (Princeton, NJ: Princeton UP, 1975).

themselves.[61] Such warnings, indeed, were true to the legacy of Green, but so too were such socialist projects as the Guild of St Matthew and the Labour Church movement, focusing on fraternity, fellowship and spiritual life.[62]

While Green's view of welfare appears more congruent with mid-Victorian attitudes than with the ideology of the modern welfare state, it is possible to construct from Green's philosophy an argument for judicious state assistance, due to his very flexible view of the application of public authority. The claim that property is a social right was to him a truism: the question was not *whether* there existed social rights that the state should properly safeguard to avert collisions of individual will, but *how* such conceptions of the social should be articulated. Security of property in all its mechanisms presumes some fundamental, if not always outwardly expressed, social consent to the idea of property and its uses. When property was used improperly, in ways 'inconsistent with its idea', it was 'within the province of the state' to secure social and economic adjustments promoting more equitable enjoyment of recognized goods.

Whether or not Green deserves to be identified as the father of the New Liberalism in Britain, his idea of the democratic state as a vehicle of moral improvement provided, for half a century, an inspiration for advanced Liberalism and socialism.[63] His influence was strongly felt in middle-class Radical and socialist circles, among the sort of people who went for Fabianism, University Settlement and the Workers' Educational Association. Indeed, as Matt Carter has demonstrated, men like Sidney Ball, Edward Caird and D. G. Ritchie, who in their philosophy and ethics were perhaps closer to Green than to F. H. Bradley and Bosanquet, sympathized with and participated in socialist or labour organizations while cooperating with and even identifying themselves as Liberals.[64] H. N. Brailsford, who had come under the tutelage of Edward Caird at Glasgow in the early 1890s, has been characterized by Fred Leventhal as 'The Last Dissenter'. Like the eminent Victorian Nonconformist Edward Miall, who upheld the Dissidence of Dissent, Brailsford believed strongly in conscience and the individual's right of free expression. Brailsford fiercely championed the rights of individuals and of subordinate social groups while advocating causes that struck some socialists and labourites as excessively radical. Having founded a

---

[61] 'The Corruption of the Citizenship of the Working Man.'
[62] A characteristic contemporary expression of this is Stewart Headlam, *Christian Social-ism*, Fabian Society Tract 42 (London, 1892). See also Bevir, 'Labour Church Move-ment'; Bevir, 'Welfarism, Socialism and Religion'; Inglis, *Churches and the Working Classes*; Pierson, *Marxism and the Origins of British Socialism*, pp. 226–45; Carter, *T. H. Green and the Development of Ethical Socialism*, chap. 4.
[63] Clarke, *Liberals and Social Democrats*; Weiler, *The New Liberalism*.
[64] *T. H. Green and the Development of Ethical Socialism*, chaps. 3, 5.

Fabian club in Glasgow in 1896, he broke with the Fabians in 1899 over
their refusal to condemn the war instigated by the British in South
Africa (and he sided with the predominantly Liberal 'Pro-Boers').
Brailsford welcomed the Bolshevik revolution but from the mid-1920s
he was more outspoken than many fellow members of the ILP in criticizing the Bolsheviks' persecution of their opponents. He engaged in
polemics with theoreticians of the Communist Party of Great Britain,
such as R. P. Dutt.[65] Among Green's students, David Ritchie was perhaps the staunchest advocate of state interference yet was also a political
democrat. Ritchie had sympathized with the early Fabians and he disliked the class nature of the ILP. He believed the Fabians had been
wrong (in 1893) to cut themselves loose from Liberalism. His letter of
resignation to the Fabians' secretary, Edward Pease, is worth quoting at
length:

> If the Society is to adopt the practical policy of the SDF and to become a soci-
> ety for the propagation of Keir Hardies, I do not care to be connected with
> it … I had hoped that, with an official fling at official Liberalism — to please
> the gallery — the Society intended to continue with its useful work of perme-
> ating Liberalism with Socialism … and on the other hand its no less useful
> work of turning useless or mischievous intransigent Socialists into practical
> Socialist Radicals.[66]

Although Leonard Hobhouse displayed some concern for deteriora-
tion of character through excessive state action, he advocated 'collectivism' during the 1890s and was not fearful of Labour after 1900.[67] Like
Ritchie, Hobhouse viewed socialism as compatible with Liberalism and
Radicalism. He remarked to C. P. Scott in 1924 that 'Labour in office —
has on the whole represented essential Liberalism … *better* than the
organized party since C-B's [Campbell-Bannerman's] death.' The distinction between the 'Labour man who does not want to go whole hog
on nationalization … and the Liberal who wants social progress … is
obsolete.' Only 'traditions and class distinctions kept many good Liberals outside Labour.'[68] Left Liberals after 1914 supported nationalization
of some industries (coal mining was taken under state control in 1915 in

---

[65]   Leventhal, *The Last Dissenter: H. N. Brailsford and His World*; Blaazer,*Popular Front and
        the Progressive Tradition*, pp. 131-42.

[66]   Letter to E. R. Pease, 31 October 1893, as quoted in Blaazer, *Popular Front and the Pro-
        gressive Tradition*, p. 53. Sidney Webb and Bernard Shaw had stated the Fabian posi-
        tion in 'To Your Tents, Oh Israel', published in *Fortnightly Review*, n.s. 54 (1893), pp.
        569–89. H. W. Massingham resigned from the Fabian Society for reasons similar to
        Ritchie's.

[67]   Hobhouse believed legislation and state action could promote conditions for
        self-realization: see 'The Ethical Basis of Collectivism,'*International Journal of Ethics*, 8
        (1898), pp. 137-56.

[68]   Hobhouse to Scott, 7 November 1924, quoted in Collini, *Liberalism and Sociology*,
        p. 247.

the name of wartime efficiency), extensive residential building, the League of Nations and collective security. British progressives were involved in some contradictions with regard to foreign policy during the 1920s and '30s: while they were sympathetic to Indian demands for self-government, some also accepted the Mandate System of the League of Nations, bringing 'Iraqis', 'Jordanians' and others under British tutelage.[69] Many of those theorists of international relations upholding the freedoms of nationalities, including non-European nationalities, echoed Green's own opinions, and some sought justification for their views in his philosophy.

6.5. RIGHTS OF NATIONS AND ANTI-IMPERIALISM

Many late Victorian progressives, including the Liberal H. H. Asquith and some founding members of the Fabian Society (including Sidney Webb), either advocated British territorial expansion or argued that social peace and reform at home were inextricably linked with the fate of the Empire.[70] Yet contemporary anti-militarism and anti-imperialism, as expressed for instance by the 'Pro-Boers' (1899-1902), were consistent with Green's 'Little England-ism' and his hope that the inhabitants of the Empire should live together under 'one system of equal law'.[71] Green's beliefs during his undergraduate years about British rule in India — recall that he went up to Oxford only two years before the great Indian 'Mutiny' — were recognizably evangelical and Benthamite. He expressed agreement with evangelicals that Britain had a duty to 'civilize' the Indian subcontinent; but given the impracticality of converting Indians to Christianity as a 'vital spiritual religion', it was imperative that Indian policy be 'a practical embodiment of the civil and religious principles we profess', including 'the maintenance of toleration and of equality in personal rights.'[72] Like Benthamite reformers of the time, Green appears to have assumed that legal and social changes could be imposed upon Indians without their explicit consent — in effect, for their own good. To the extent that Green accepted the 'White Man's Burden' he can be counted an imperialist. There is no doubt that

[69]   Havighurst, *Britain in Transition*, p. 165; M. Freeden, *Liberalism Divided: A Study in British Political Thought, 1914-1939* (Oxford: Clarendon, 1986), chaps. 2, 4–6, 9. Tawney took a particular interest in Republican China during the 1920s and '30s. Terrill, *R. H. Tawney*, pp. 67–71.

[70]   See especially Searle, *National Efficiency*; and Shaw, 'Eliminating the Yahoo'.

[71]   Green commented about one system of law in remarks about unrest in Ireland. 'Notes for a speech given at the North Ward Liberal Association meeting on Tuesday March 7, 1882': *GP* 1(c).

[72]   'British Rule and Policy in India,' undergraduate essay in undated notebook, *GP* 2(b); printed in *AW*, pp. 22–4. On British liberalism and India, see E. Stokes, *The English Utilitarians and India* (Oxford: Clarendon, 1959); and U. S. Mehta, *Liberalism and Empire: India in British Liberal Thought* (Chicago: UP Chicago, 1999).

he was convinced of the moral superiority of British society over at least non-European societies.

Yet Green echoed the anti-imperialism of the early and mid-Victorian era, the era of Cobden and Bright, when he warned in an 1880 speech to the Abingdon Liberal Association that imperial expansion was unnecessary and thoroughly counterproductive due to the expenses that would have to be charged to the home and colonial governments. He condemned the 1879 military expeditions in South Africa and Afghanistan and stated that 'The only lasting defence of the Indian Empire is the contentment of the Indian people.' 'Unjust exaction' of taxes is what threatens British interests there, next to which 'Russian aggression is nothing.'[73] Green had no imperial idea, only a theory of individual states representing their own ideas in the world.[74] He could not have approved of the strident imperialism of the rising Balliolites of his time, Alfred Milner (High Commissioner of the Cape Colony, 1897–1905) and George Curzon (Indian Viceroy, 1899–1905).[75]

Although it is counterfactual to speculate very far about Green's attitude towards non-European nationalism, he regarded national self-determination as an aspect of self-realisation.[76] No system of rule could be stable and effective if the majority of subjects could not identify with the general purposes of the state; and such was the case when *morally responsible* colonial subjects were barred from the exercise of most governmental and civic functions. It is not difficult to imagine Green supporting C. P. Ilbert's Criminal Jurisdiction bill of 1883, devised to enable Indian magistrates to preside over trials of Europeans. (Ilbert was nearly an exact contemporary of Green and also a Fellow of Balliol.) The act was never implemented due to fierce opposition in 1883–4 from Anglo-Indians, who were generally hostile to the outlook of the Liberal viceroy, Lord Ripon.[77] The Ilbert bill's objectives were partly practical,

---

[73] 'Notes of a Speech at Abingdon Liberal Meeting [1880]': *GP* 1(c). In 1882 he observed that there was 'No great magnanimity in using our strength to crush a population of Dutch farmers [in the Transvaal], of whom [there are] not so many thousands as millions in England.' 'Notes for a speech given at the North Ward Liberal Association meeting on Tuesday March 7, 1882': *GP* 1(c).

[74] Routh, 'Philosophy of International Relations: T. H. Green versus Hegel,' pp. 223–35; D. Boucher, 'British Idealist International Theory,' *Bulletin of the Hegel Society of Great Britain*, 31 (Spring 1995), pp. 73–89.

[75] On the imperial idea at Oxford, see Symonds, *Oxford and Empire. The Last Lost Cause?*

[76] Like his friends in the 'Old Mortality', Green was a fan of Mazzini. There were distinct similarities between Mazzini's ideas about individuality and nationality and Green's views. See I. McMenamin, '"Self-Choosing" and "Right Acting" in the Nationalism of Giuseppe Mazzini,' *History of European Ideas*, 23 (1997), pp. 221–34; J. Gibbins, 'Liberalism, Nationalism and the English Idealists,' *History of European Ideas*, 15 (1992), pp. 491–7.

[77] The controversy and protests in India over the Ilbert bill led directly to the formation of the Indian National Congress. See F. Pollock's obituary of Ilbert in *Proceedings of the*

to reduce the administrative burden on British officials. More fundamentally, the bill revealed the willingness of Liberal imperial statesmen
to fulfil the ideal of 'Indianization' that Macaulay had proposed in the
1830s — that is, to put Indian administration in the hands of men English in every respect but colour and blood. The ethical assumptions
behind the Ilbert bill were certainly shared by Green: namely, that Indians who had acquired Western educations and appreciated Western
values had reached a stage of moral development enabling them to be
co-rulers with Europeans.

Green complained in 1880 that high-handed military action, popular
jingoism and the paternalism and racial prejudice of Englishmen (and
women) abroad had led to the 'alienation of people who ought to be our
friends.'[78] His attack on the Conservatives' 'Forward Policy' might easily be dismissed as political partisanship, pure and simple. Yet this and
Green's other statements about British foreign and imperial policy and
international relations form a link between liberal internationalism of
the first half of the nineteenth century and the outlook shared by many
Liberal and Labour 'Progressives' during the first decades of the twentieth century. Liberal internationalists after 1900 emphasized not only
humanitarianism, implying Britons' paternal obligation to those people
they identified as backward, but a principle of participation. John
Morley, the Liberal Secretary for India in 1908–9, expressed doubt that
India could ever be suited to Western parliamentary democracy; but the
Morley-Minto reforms at least involved the Indianization of local and
provincial councils. Not the least significant of the differences between
Liberal imperialism of this era and the enlightened despotism practiced
by Lord Curzon (and advocated by Conservative imperialists) was the
emphasis of the former on participation of the governed in their own
government — even though British colonial officials in India, Africa and
the Caribbean through the 1930s habitually found reason to constrain
native self government.

One genuinely progressive and Greenian exposition of international
relations theory was that expressed by Henry Hetherington and John
Muirhead during the First World War. In *Social Purpose: A Contribution
to a Philosophy of Civic Society*, these Idealists reiterated the Mazzinian
claim that the individual's 'membership of a national state' tutors him
or her in 'obligation to the wider whole of Humanity.'[79] They cited
Green to support the claim that 'it is by the smaller and closer groups

British Academy, vol. 11 (1924–25), pp. 441–5; and S. Wolpert, *A New History of India*,
2nd ed. (OUP, 1982), pp. 208–15, 256–60.

[78]   Quotation from Green's 1880 Abingdon speech (cited above). His laying all moral
failures in foreign and imperial policy at the feet of the Tories let Liberals off the hook.

[79]   H. W. Hetherington and J. H. Muirhead, *Social Purpose: A Contribution to a Philosophy
of Civic Society* (London: Allen and Unwin, 1922 [1918]), p. 265.

that we are led to feel our kinship with the whole [of humanity]'; and they insisted that 'the principle of Nationality is not the highest principle of political obligation.'[80] Like Green, Hetherington and Muirhead maintained that national and international governance rested on a 'genuine community of will': the latter is impossible to find or achieve when any group of people (e.g. nation) senses that it is 'compelled into an unnatural or artificial unity with those to whom it is alien in feeling.'[81] Alienation may arise around a collective sense of 'unsatisfied national ambition'; a sense of community of will, in contrast, may develop when a nationality group within a multinational state is satisfied in administering its own church or religion, is allowed a system of local or regional government, or is guaranteed the use of national language in education and administration.[82] This theory allowed for wide interpretation of international relations and colonial policy, yet it grounded the idea of nationality in relation to rights in a Greenian manner.[83]

6.6. GREEN AND THE RIGHTS OF WOMEN

Green features in the political memory of liberalism again as a champion of 'women's liberation'. His efforts to improve education for girls and women have been mentioned in previous chapters, as has his personal support for lady intellectuals like Mary Ward. To some present–day equality feminists, he ranks as 'a late Victorian success story.'[84] How this can be so requires some explanation, for Green's vision of women's emancipation had its limits. For instance, he does not appear to have given active support to female Parliamentary suffrage, which many contemporary advanced Liberals and Radicals also were reluctant to embrace. Moreover, his statements in *Lectures on the Principles of Political Obligation* and in other instances suggest that he held to a version of the classic 'separate spheres' argument: woman's ideal place was in the household, although she might with propriety engage in philanthropy or intervene in the public sphere (politics) in matters concerning

---

[80]   *Ibid.*, pp. 265, 264.

[81]   *Ibid.*, p. 263.

[82]   *Ibid.*, pp. 263–4.

[83]   For another illustration of British Idealist thought applied to colonial policy, see M. P. Cowen and R. W. Shenton, 'British Neo-Hegelianism and Official Colonial Practice in Africa: the Oluwa Land Case of 1921,' *Journal of Imperial and Commonwealth History*, 22 (1994), pp. 217-50.

[84]   Anderson, 'The Feminism of T. H. Green.' Marian Sawer argues that Green's critique of liberal contractarianism and promotion of 'social liberalism' served important feminist aims — and perhaps more directly in Australia than in Britain itself. 'Reclaiming the State: Feminism, Liberalism and Social Liberalism,' *Australian Journal of Politics and History*, 40 [special issue] (1994), pp. 159–72; and 'The Ethical State: Social Liberalism and the Critique of Contract,' *Australian Historical Studies*, 114 (2000), pp. 67–90.

the well-being of women and children (e.g. factory and school inspection, poor relief).[85]

In examining Green's view of gender relations, it is relevant to consider also the view of J. S. Mill, which many continue to regard as the paradigmatic liberal position. In his celebrated 1869 essay *The Subjection of Women*, Mill attempted to establish the idea of gender equality as an inescapable corollary of liberalism's quest for equality of persons under the law. Liberal theory justifies equality of opportunity for equal moral agents, and historically this has led to demands for fair access to institutions which are recognized as means to expression of personhood and individuality. There are indications that Green recognized the force of such arguments, as articulated not only by J. S. Mill and his wife Harriet Taylor, but by mid-Victorian liberals such as Millicent Garrett Fawcett (wife of Henry Fawcett, Cambridge political economist and Liberal Cabinet member), Jacob Bright (who, with Mill, introduced bills into Parliament for women's suffrage) and Frances Power Cobbe. That Green's feminism reveals its limitations when measured against modern expectations should not blind us to the fact that Green was more progressive than many contemporaries in his view of gender relations. Many otherwise liberal men and women during the nineteenth century braked short of Mill's insistence on the identical nature of male and female intellectual, and hence moral, capacities. Cobbe, for instance, advocated women's suffrage but maintained that 'women and men had different natures and that women's most fundamental duties were maternal and domestic.'[86] Scholars aware of the social context of Green's beliefs about gender — Olive Anderson, Brian Harrison, Gillian Sutherland and Marian Sawer, among others — find exemplary his statement of a liberal case for women's emancipation.

However, other scholars suggest that Green's theory of self-realization was consciously or unconsciously gendered. Jeannie Morefield has recently argued that Green and the New Liberals looked

[85] The following discussion draws upon B. Harrison, *Separate Spheres: The Opposition to Women's Suffrage in Britain* (New York: Holmes and Meier, 1978); S. M. Okin, *Women in Western Political Thought* (Princeton, NJ: Princeton UP, 1979); D. David, *Intellectual Women and Victorian Patriarchy. Harriet Martineau, Elizabeth Barrett Browning, George Eliot* (Ithaca, NY: Cornell UP, 1987); Davidoff and Hall, *Family Fortunes*; M. L. Shanley, *Feminism, Marriage, and the Law in Victorian England, 1850–1895* (London: I. B. Tauris, 1989); M. Pugh, 'The Limits of Liberalism: Liberals and Women's Suffrage, 1867–1914' in Biagini, ed., *Citizenship and Community*, pp. 45–65; and T. Akkerman, 'Liberalism and Feminism in Late Nineteenth-Century Britain' in *Perspectives on Feminist Political Thought in European History*, ed. T. Akkerman and S. Stuurman (London/New York: Routledge, 1998), pp. 168-85.

[86] Shanley, *Feminism, Marriage, and the Law*, p. 18. This had been the view of Mary Wollstonecraft in the 1790s, though she believed many flaws of English womanhood were the product of nurture. *A Vindication of the Rights of Woman [with J. S. Mill's 'The Subjection of Women']* (London: J. M. Dent, 1992), chaps. 2–4, 12.

toward the 'pre-liberal and pre-idealist' patriarchal family in order 'to fill the void left by liberalism's incapacity to speak of social responsibility': a particular, conservative idea of the family was implicated in the community conception of Green, Bosanquet, Ritchie and Hobhouse (among others).[87] Given the indications that Green implied the (pre-political) existence of female family *duties*, and given his apparent reluctance to support the most radical demands of the time for women's political participation, Morefield's claim merits attention. She observes, for instance, that Ritchie, Muirhead and the Bosanquets (but not Green) identified the participation of married women in paid economic enterprise as a factor in social degeneracy and national decline.[88] (So, indeed, did non-Idealist socialists like the Fabians.) Yet Morefield concedes that Bernard Bosanquet 'and most new liberals' advocated better women's education and political and property rights for women equal to those of men. Ultimately, it is impossible to sustain Morefield's argument about Green's patriarchalism and the structural defects of Greenian liberalism with respect to gender. Neither Green nor other Idealist New Liberals recognized sexual differences of mind (as did eighteenth-century moralists such as Rousseau). No more than John Stuart Mill did Green accept the argument of different moral-political statuses of men and women based on their divergent 'natures'. Whatever their gender prejudices and beliefs about the ideal family (implying the greater obligation of women to serve as family caretakers), Green and many Idealist New Liberals consistently argued for closing gaps between male and female educational, economic and political opportunities.

Green can be said to have widened the scope of liberalism with regard to gender by feminizing the cult of character. He indicated ways in which character and self-realization were incumbent upon women, who were being allowed new opportunities for moral development — above all, through property ownership, improved education and limited participation in government. Green's actual opinions with regard to these issues were logically inferred from his theory of self-realization. Men needed to have property in order to realize their personhood, a stake in the making and enforcement of laws, and basic intellectual skills in order to make their way in a commercial society. Women denied access to significant means of self-development (including paid employment) and contribution to the common good could not be expected to view civil society and the state as expressions of *their* will, and as institutions safeguarding their personhood. Green approved of contemporary efforts to expand women's legal rights and he actively promoted girls' and women's education because he believed social har-

---

[87] 'Hegelian Organicism, British New Liberalism and the Return of the Family State,'*HPT*, 23 (2002), pp. 141–70. Quoted words from p. 170.

[88] *Ibid.*, pp. 166–8.

mony and lasting stability to be impossible under conditions of gender inequality.

In *Lectures on the Principles of Political Obligation* (Chapter O: 'The right of the state in regard to the family') Green gave expression to the morality of *more* equitable — if not identical — rights and duties of men and women. He implicitly rejected the idea of coverture — i.e. that the married couple formed 'one person', whose interests and rights were represented by the husband — which had been a fundament of British law. Like Hegel, Green acknowledged that the family was an institution of civil society, to which there were corresponding family rights. But while he upheld the 'moral purposes' of the family Green also acknowledged the facts of multiple persons within the marriage bond and possibly diverging interests of persons within the family.[89] Before 1857 the sole legal ground for divorce in Britain was ecclesiastical annulment by private act of Parliament. Even after the 1857 Divorce Act, the 1858 Matrimonial Causes Amendment Act and the 1878 Matrimonial Causes Act, a divorce initiated by a wife was problematic (she had to prove her husband's 'adultery in combination with incest, bigamy, or extreme physical cruelty'), and custody of the children customarily went to the husband.[90] Green argued for free divorce by either man or wife upon such demonstrable minimal cause as adultery, for an unwilling union tended to undermine the moral purposes served by the institutions of marriage and family. Yet he argued against adultery being regarded as a crime, an offence requiring prosecution by the state, independent of the desire of the injuring or injured parties. He opined:

> Though rights, in the strict sense, undoubtedly arise out of marriage, though marriage thus has its strictly legal aspect, it is undesirable that this legal aspect should become prominent. It may suffer in respect of its higher moral purposes, if the element of force appears too strongly in the maintenance of the rights to which it gives rise.[91]

---

[89] As Avineri points out, 'What stands out in Hegel's treatment of the family is his insistence that it is not a contract' (*Hegel's Theory of the Modern State*, p. 139). Hegel wrote in *Philosophy of Right* (sec. 163) that while marriage begins as a contract, it transcends 'the standpoint from which persons are self-subsisting units.' Green, in contrast, focuses on marital duties and obligations in a more contractual manner. Just as a 'free' contract between labourer and employer loses its moral justification if the rewards and disadvantages accruing to one party of the contract are vastly unequal to those of the opposite party, so marriage loses its rationale if there is much more freedom in it for one party than for the other. In Green's view, the conjugal pair is not a self but a moral alliance of two selves seeking realization. The family is not a moral person. On the other hand, Green was critical of the principle of allowing divorce on the grounds of *mere* 'incompatibility' (*LPPO*, sec. 245).

[90] Quotation from Shanley, *Feminism, Marriage, and the Law*, p. 138.

[91] *LPPO*, sec. 244. Further: 'the rights that arise out of marriage are not of a kind which can in their essence be protected by associating penal terror with their violation, as the rights of life and property can be ... They are claims which cannot be met without a

As for property, since Green recognized men and women as persons with equal capacities for morality, he agreed with the rationale behind the Married Women's Property Acts of 1870 and 1882. Prior to these a woman's property became her husband's upon marriage, as did income and assets she acquired while married. Working-class husbands and wives did not have access to legal machinery which would have enabled them to make complex assessments of individual property, but middle-class Britons did, and the aforementioned property legislation gave encouragement to professional women, who, at least in the strictly legal sense, were no longer forced to choose between economic independence and matrimony.[92] Since the franchise depended up to the First World War on the possession of at least some property, the expansion of women's property rights prepared the groundwork for women's suffrage.

Green did support women's suffrage in *local* government. This was undoubtedly a reflection of his belief that women's political participation would increase their self-identification with the state and public work. In a postscript to the 1867 Reform Act granting Parliamentary suffrage to male urban householders, some propertied women were included in the municipal franchise after 1869. This provision was extended in 1870–1 to School Boards. Married women, widows and 'spinsters' not only elected local authorities but were themselves elected to such bodies.[93] By 1880 seventy-one women were members of School Boards in England and Wales.[94] Green showed staunch support for Miss Eleanor Smith, the sister of Professor Henry Smith (a Fellow of Balliol), in her attempt to win a seat on the Oxford School Board.[95]

The late Victorian laws for female enfranchisement in parish and borough-level elections (and from 1894 in county council elections)

---

certain disposition on the part of the person upon whom the claim rests, and that disposition cannot be enforced.'

[92] Olive Anderson has recently shown that legal separation (as an alternative to divorce) was common in Britain after 1850 and was resorted to by women at all social levels. It had a certain emancipatory effect in enabling women's financial security. 'State, Civil Society and Separation in Victorian Marriage,' *Past and Present*, 163 (1999), pp. 161-201.

[93] Patricia Hollis estimates that, in 1871, for every three married women in England over the age of twenty there were two spinsters and widows. P. Hollis, ed., *Women in Public, 1850-1900: Documents of the Victorian Women's Movement* (London: Allen and Unwin, 1979), p. 32.

[94] There were isolated cases of women elected to Boards of Guardians (of the Poor) going back to the 1830s, and female Guardians were common by the late 1880s. By 1903, five hundred women had been elected to School Boards, and women sat on nearly every urban Board and on dozens of rural ones. Hollis, *Ladies Elect*, chaps. 2–4, and Appendix B.

[95] [Notice of School Board election], *OCBBG*, 17 January 1874, p. 4; 'Oxford School Board,' *OCBBG*, 28 February 1874, p. 7. See also Hollis (*Ladies Elect*, pp. 132, 138–50) on Eleanor Smith and her support from and for Oxford Liberals.

restricted direct political participation to widows and spinsters — that is, to those women not contained within a patriarchal household. (Miss Smith was identified as a spinster in the Oxford press.) Married women remained in effect hostage to the idea of coverture until after the First World War: as members of households they were represented by their husbands in Parliamentary elections. If unmarried and outside a patri-archal household, they were not directly represented at all. Green does not appear to have made statements — in public or in private — in sup-port of or in opposition to the Parliamentary enfranchisement of women, but his disapproval of *national* suffrage for women might be inferred from Charlotte Green's views. She was among the signatories to 'An Appeal Against Female Suffrage,' headed by Mrs Humphry Ward in 1889.[96] Yet the logic of Green's own statements (above all in the *Prolegomena*, Book III) about individuals, moral development and the life of the community implicitly recommended significant political participation for women. Charlotte Green departed from her anti-suffragism of 1889. In light of the support given women's Parliamentary suffrage *before* 1914 by Gore, Holland, Ritchie, Muirhead, the Bosanquets and others (but not Mrs Ward), it is likely that T. H. Green too would have gone in this direction.

One of the main claims for Green's feminism concerns his advocacy of higher education for women.[97] He supported efforts to improve girls' secondary education (at least for the middle classes) in the 1870s. Such improvements, he held, would not upset the balance of the sexes but would render women better able to perform existing and anticipated social functions; some women would desire to and might be required by circumstances to earn a living; and educated mothers would be better able to educate their children.[98] In Green's time the University of Lon-don was already allowing women to attend lectures and take degrees. In 1869, women were allowed to hear some Cambridge University lec-tures. Green's acquaintance Anne Clough headed Newnham College,

---

[96] In *Nineteenth Century*, 25 (June 1889), pp. 781–8. Signatories included Lady Randolph Churchill, Miss Beatrice Potter [later Webb], Mrs H. H. Asquith, Mrs Leslie Stephen and Mrs Matthew Arnold. In a subsequent statement (*Nineteenth Century*, 26, p. 357) the same ladies opined that female suffrage 'would be a measure distasteful to the great majority of the women of the country — unnecessary — and mischievous both to themselves and to the State.'

[97] See discussion in Chapter One above and sources cited there.

[98] See his speech at the opening of the Wyggeston Girls School, Leicester, 18 June 1878, as reported by the *Leicester Chronicle and Leicester Mercury*, 22 June 1878, reprinted in *AW*, pp. 322-8. Canon D. J. Vaughan was one of the school's founders. The speech clearly indicates the extent and limit of Green's feminism. Interestingly, Green pre-dicted that well educated mothers would help produce, in their sons, 'a higher type of character developed among us — a character not less manly, but more gentle and sympathetic and religious than they found in our present race of young men ...' (p. 327).

Cambridge, in 1871, and the residential Girton College for women was relocated to Cambridge in 1872. In 1873–4 Green had helped sponsor a course of lectures for women at Oxford (outside the collegiate system and without participation in university examinations), whose beneficiaries included Charlotte Green and Mary Ward.

In June, 1878, Green became Secretary Pro Tempore of the Association for Promoting the Higher Education of Women in Oxford. In addition to the Greens and Mrs Ward early APHEW members included Mr and Mrs Henry Nettleship, A. V. Harcourt (Christ Church), P. Percival (Trinity), G. G. Bradley (University College) and F. H. Peters (University). Although the Oxford colleges *as* institutions remained aloof from the project, by late 1878 the heads of Balliol, Queen's, University, Jesus, Keble and Hertford Colleges had subscribed funds, along with more than fifty other dons and private citizens, including Scott Holland, Charles Gore, A. H. D. Acland, F. H. Bradley and Bosanquet.[99] By early 1879 there were sufficient funds to begin a residential ladies' college, *in* if not of Oxford.

On February 15, 1879, the Association announced that it would select a Lady Principal to supervise the resident ladies (aged seventeen and older) of Somerville Hall. 'Care will be taken in the conduct of it [the hall] that members of different religious denominations are placed on the same footing. The life of the student will be modelled on that of an English family.'[100] Opening of the hall was delayed by religious squabbles. Those sponsors insisting on Church of England affiliation broke away to establish Lady Margaret Hall. Somerville Hall opened late in 1879. Green actively promoted the hall in 1879–80, even appealing for funds on his visits to Birmingham as Teachers' Representative on the King Edward VI School Board of Governors. He wrote to a Mr Martineau in Birmingham:

> I should quite hope that in the future Birmingham will be able to provide the highest education for its daughters without sending them elsewhere. And as a rule it is no doubt better that young women should stay at home till they marry. But there will probably always be some, either having a special turn for study or intending to become teachers, for whom the opportunities which Oxford affords both in the way of instruction and continuous reading would be a great advantage … [Somerville Hall would] secure to them a quiet, healthy, economical, and at the same time refined, way of living.[101]

---

[99] Many of the same donated to the Oxford Boys' High School, and later to the University settlement houses.

[100] From a circular dated February 1879, cited in Lynn, 'Green and His Involvement in Victorian Education,' Appendix 13.

[101] Letter to 'Mr. Martineau', 22 November [1880], cited in Lynn, 'Green and His Involvement in Victorian Education,' Appendix 11. I have not seen the original of this letter. Peter Nicholson has identified the addressee as Thomas Martineau (1828-93), solicitor and Birmingham Town Councillor, and a nephew of James Martineau. A meeting

Green here, as presumably on other occasions, emphasized the safe 'domestic' atmosphere of the proposed ladies' college — just as dons and tutors of men's colleges were supposedly standing *in loco parentis*. If he was not as adamant in support of women's higher education (for example, by advocating the award of university degrees to women) as he was of elementary education and temperance, it was perhaps because his political experience had taught him caution. Henry Nettleship claimed that he and Green were agreed upon the theory of women's education but not on political strategy: Green was more inclined to ease into the flow of public opinion in the matter of women's education than to directly challenge it.[102] In any case, women's higher education in Oxford was scarcely equal to that of men. Before the First World War women were restricted in the lectures they could attend, they were not able to sit for all examinations and they could not take degrees. But this changed in time and many women (witness Mary Ward) were able to benefit even from the informal lecturing schemes of the early 1870s. Green played an important role in the effective beginnings of women's education at Oxbridge. As with the cases of Dissenters and self-improving labourers, Green was sensitive to social prejudice and lack of opportunity thwarting female intelligence and ability. 'Organic principles', to Green's mind, did not invariably counsel conservatism in the academy any more than they did in society at large.

6.7. GREEN AS PHILO-DISSENTER

This study has illustrated Green's services to Dissent and cited significant instances of Dissenters returning his respect. Christopher Harvie's characterization of Green as a secular Wesley on circuit (discussed in 3.8 above) is reminiscent of the contemporary perception of Green as a philo-Dissenter. Theologically, there remained a wide gulf between liberal, nominally Anglican Protestants like Green, and the bulk of Nonconformists ca. 1880; the latter, even if they were not Biblical literalists, were alarmed by the humanization of Christ and other doctrines radically recasting Christian belief. Yet Green lent weight to the struggles for religious freedom and denominational equality. Further, we have seen how he approved of the Puritan tradition and regarded the idea of the 'inner light' as a discovery of the English national consciousness. Henry Nettleship claimed in the recollection of Green he provided for Mrs Green and R. L. Nettleship that one of Green's enthusiasms was to 'bring the young dissenting preachers to Oxford and turn them into Hegelians.' Yet Green recognized (and demonstrated in his 1867 lec-

---

concerning Somerville Hall took place in Birmingham on 25 November 1880 and was reported in the local press. See *AW*, pp. 473–4.

[102] Recollection, *GP* 1(b).

tures on the English Revolution) that Dissenting theology already contained a theory of self-realization and socially qualified being, although
contemporary Nonconformists might hardly know it. In church polity,
Green admired the Dissenting model of the self-governing congregation and he believed its wider adoption would invigorate British Christianity.

Green affirmed many political and social demands of the Dissenting
Interest. During the 1850s and '60s he and other Oxbridge Liberals had
identified denominational inequality as a grave defect within the academy, which the universities would have to remedy if they were to set a
proper example for the nation they purported to serve. Bryce reminded
his friend Albert Dicey in 1913 of how liberty of conscience and intellectual freedom, and not 'the misfortunes of the poor', had assumed priority in the imaginations of the 'Old Mortality' and other University
Liberals: 'This may have been partly because religion formed the framework of life and thought more largely than it does today — or at least
because the other world seemed nearer and more certain.'[103] 'Disestablishment and the relations of Church and State generally', the Tests
Question and 'the deliverance of the University from clericalism and its
popularization' were as important as support for 'struggling nationalities' and 'Political Liberalism' (i.e. suffrage extension).

While Bryce and Green, as well as the Oxford historians Goldwin
Smith and Edward Augustus Freeman, had opposed the 'clerical party'
in the universities since the 1850s, they were by no means in agreement
with the Liberal Matthew Arnold. Green and Bryce were sought out by
Oxford Nonconformists during the 1870s and '80s; both found Arnold's
deep prejudice against Dissent obnoxious and counterproductive. Yet
neither they nor their Nonconformist friends, such as Robert William
Dale, could easily dismiss Arnold's criticism of Dissenting 'Philistinism'. The friends of religious equality ca. 1870 believed that improved
education and a broadening of Dissenting culture would help bridge
the Church–Chapel divide, which Augustine Birrell likened (albeit
looking back from 1937) to 'Offa's dyke ... broad, deep, and practically
impassible, cutting clean through social life.'[104]

Some Dissenters ca. 1870 conceded that Dissenting narrowness had to
do with the fact that relatively few of them, even their ministers, had
received gentlemanly educations. R. W. Dale, the Congregational pastor of Carr's Lane Chapel, Birmingham, was deeply impressed by the

[103] Bodleian Library, MSS. Bryce 4, fols. 57–62: letter dated 14 November 1913.
[104] From *Things Past Redress*, quoted in Koss, *Nonconformity in Modern British Politics*,
p. 15. In the eighth century AD King Offa of Mercia had built an earthwork to separate
'Saxon England' from the Welsh lands. Birrell was son of a Baptist minister and one of
the rising Liberal politicians of the 1890s. He became President of the Board of Education in 1906 and succeeded Bryce (in 1907) as Chief Secretary for Ireland.

Arnoldian conception of culture, Arnold's criticism of narrowly utilitarian values and his advocacy of 'Hellenist' ideals. Even before the
appearance of *Culture and Anarchy*, Dale had advocated, if not precisely
the Nonconformists' 'return' to the Ancient Universities (from which
they had been expelled upon the Stuart Restoration), then the improvement of higher education for Nonconformist ministers.[105] Kenneth
Brown's study of the Nonconformist ministry reveals that during the
period 1860–89, only a small minority of Wesleyan Methodist, Baptist
and Congregationalist ministers held the BA (usually from London
University or the Scottish universities), but a majority of them had spent
at least two years at an academy, theological college or university.[106] In
1869 William Mitchell Fawcett observed approvingly that two-thirds of
Independent ministers listed in the *Congregational Yearbook* of 1867 had
at least attended a seminary or university, sometimes both, and that
more than half of the remaining third had received advanced private
training under other ministers.[107]

By the 1870s Dissenters at Oxford and Cambridge had distinguished
themselves in competition for scholarships and fellowships. Green,
however, maintained that they lacked a moral and spiritual presence at
Oxford. Dr Edwin Hatch, Vice-Principal of St Mary's Hall, Oxford, and
a Bampton Lecturer (1880), argued in 1885 that a Nonconformist college
at Oxford was needed to give Nonconformity 'a literary education'.
Nonconformity's 'intellectual influence is not at all adequate to its real
intellectual force. It is out of touch with elements of society which it
might, if it would, control.' Hatch was confident that a blending of Nonconformity and Establishment in Oxford would increase the 'vitality' of
English religion.[108]

Green had movingly addressed himself to R. W. Dale ca. 1880 (see 4.6
above) about the alienation of young Dissenters at Oxford from the faith
of their fathers. Yet Dale was, according to his son and biographer, 'dubious' about the utility of a Nonconformist faculty or college at Oxford

---

[105] 'Our Theological Colleges,' *Eclectic Review* (January, 1859), pp. 87–106. Dale's son
(and biographer) went to Cambridge.
[106] *A Social History of the Nonconformist Ministry*, pp. 57–84. Only six percent of Baptist
ministers held university *degrees*, including honorary degrees, and only three percent
of Wesleyan Methodist preachers had equivalent qualifications. Nearly seventeen
percent of Congregational ministers had these qualifications. As early as the 1840s
many students at Highbury, Stepney, and Airedale (Independent training colleges)
were enrolled concurrently at London University. Brown does not include statistics
for Unitarians or Presbyterians, who generally belonged to a higher social stratum
than other Old Dissenters and Methodists and were better educated.
[107] 'Congregational Polity,' in *Religious Republics*, ed. Fawcett, p. 33.
[108] News clipping from *Methodist Times* (? June 1885), in a volume marked 'Building
Fund: Circulars, Papers, Progress Reports, etc.': Mansfield College Library, cupboard
24.

and a 'late convert' to the plan for Mansfield College.[109] Dale became the political engineer of the project in 1885 only after Andrew Martin Fairbairn, principal of Airedale Independent College, Bradford, and D. W. Simon, head of Spring Hill (Congregational) College, Birmingham, were pledged to a Nonconformist return to the stronghold of Anglicanism.[110] Mansfield's founders spared no pain and expense to make the institution a physical replica of the other Oxford colleges. Building commenced in 1887 according to the design of Basil Champneys, who had remodelled collegiate buildings in Oxford and Cambridge and was responsible for the remarkable John Rylands Library in Manchester. Clyde Binfield describes Mansfield as

> a Nonconformist *tour-de-force*[,] beating Oxford at its own game, exquisite in its library and chapel, sufficiently ponderous in its dining-hall and common rooms, its full-blooded Collegiate Gothic reflecting here the Reformation of Edward VI, there the Reformation of John Wycliffe, but nowhere the Reformation of Henry VIII, a morning star for causes which Oxford would not be allowed to lose.[111]

The Dissenters were fastidious in selecting a college principal of sufficient scholarly standing and social respectability to withstand the snobbish scrutiny of the dons. They succeeded admirably in this with A. M. Fairbairn, an esteemed theologian and church historian. Fairbairn had won a moral philosophy prize at Edinburgh University but never took a degree there. He studied in Berlin in 1865 at the feet of Dorner, a disciple of Hegel and Schleiermacher. While a pastor at Bathgate (1860–72), Fairbairn accumulated a library of more than two thousand volumes, including many on Indian, Chinese and Semitic religions.[112] James Bryce believed Fairbairn to be the right man, perhaps the only one, for directing the foundation of a Free Church college at Oxford: 'Lord Acton, the most learned Englishman then living, once said to me that he doubted if there was anyone in the university whose learning equalled Fairbairn's.'[113]

As suggested in Chapter Four above, Hatch, Green and others were somewhat mistaken in their predictions about the cultural mainstreaming of Dissent: religious liberation had social consequences

---

[109] A. W. W. Dale, *Life of R. W. Dale*, p. 497.

[110] Congregationalists considered using some of the endowments of Spring Hill College for an Oxford college, but the legal sticking point concerned the use of those endowments for new purposes. The Charity Commissioners agreed on 17 September 1885 to the transfer of some Spring Hill funds to 'Mansfield College', provided a new endowment and a separate building fund were raised. Pennar Davies, *Mansfield College*, pp. 10–12.

[111] *So Down to Prayers*, p. 166.

[112] W. B. Selbie, *Life of Andrew Martin Fairbairn* (London: Hodder and Stoughton, 1914), pp. 4–40.

[113] Bryce quoted in Selbie, *Life of Fairbairn*, pp. 182–3.

unforeseen by its proponents. In attempting to join the main currents of British intellectual life, Dissenters undercut their political as well as cultural strength. There is scant evidence that Dissenters' acquisition of liberal and gentlemanly culture changed the balance between the Establishment and Dissent or increased the vitality of English religion — least of all, English Dissenting religion.[114] R. F. Horton, W. B. Selbie and other Oxbridge graduates led efforts to unite the Dissenting churches in a 'Free Church.' After the Great War this project was continued, indeed effectively supplanted, by plans for ecumenical Christianity and a World Council of Churches, whose advocates included Dissenters as well as Anglicans.[115] As demonstrated in the preceding chapter, Dissenters participated in the late Victorian 'social turn' and Dissenting ministers helped establish the twentieth-century pattern of the English clergyman as practical economist, sociologist and social worker.[116]

The upward educational and social mobility of Dissenters, facilitated by such institutions as Mansfield College, appear to have been factors in the 'dissolution of Dissent'. In the days when Nonconformist clergy were not counted as gentlemen in polite society, they were nevertheless accorded some respect by outsiders due to their influence over their co-religionists. To the tradesmen and artisans and their families who constituted the majority of his congregation, the Dissenting minister of 1850, with his certificate from a theological college and year or more of learning picked up at London or Glasgow University, appeared to be an enlightened and well-informed man, perhaps even too comfortable with novel ideas.[117]

---

[114] See Binfield, *So Down to Prayers*, especially chap. 9 ('No Quest, No Conquest'); Davie, *A Gathered Church*; and Johnson, *The Dissolution of Dissent*.

[115] Bebbington, *Nonconformist Conscience*, chap. 4. An Anglican champion of the ecumenical movement was William Temple.

[116] The movement of social Christianity provided many opportunities for interdenominational cooperation. A typical project was the 1924 Birmingham interdenominational conference on 'Politics, Economics, and Citizenship', chaired by the Bishop of Manchester, which 'undertook … to establish "a norm of Christian thought and action for the further working out of a Christian order"' (quoted in Havighurst, *Britain in Transition*, pp. 157–8).

[117] Dale, though he renounced clerical costume and even the title of Reverend, believed firmly in a 'learned ministry' because of the intellectual challenges to faith which the minister would have to help his congregation get over. But the minister also had to possess a spiritual and moral authority 'that could not be claimed by any layman.' So had been the Nonconformist ideal since the seventeenth century. As widely influential as John Milton had been as a Christian poet, the depth of his influence could not equal that of Richard Baxter as a pastor in Kidderminster. Kenyon, 'R. W. Dale and Christian Worldliness,' pp. 190–2 (the anecdote about Milton and Baxter is quoted from Dale's *Essays and Addresses*, 3rd ed. (1901), p. 57).

When Dr Hatch predicted that Nonconformity's acquisition of 'a literary education' would polish its roughness and increase its influence on national life, he assumed that the clergy would be the chief agents of such improvement. Many middle-class Dissenters entering the major secondary schools and universities after 1860 sought qualification not as preachers but as lawyers and other professionals;[118] and the pious Dissenters of 1850 who eschewed reading novels, card playing and going to the theatre gave way to the more cultivated Dissenters of the 1880s.[119] The fact that Nonconformist ministers after 1880 were sometimes *no better* educated and no more cultivated than their lay co-religionists must have played some part in the decline of 'pulpit politics' and of the 'Nonconformist Conscience'.

The foregoing discussion is not intended to suggest that the establishment of Mansfield College, directly affecting only small numbers of Dissenters, was the culmination and exhaustion of Political Dissent. Rather it reiterates that the *cultural dynamic* of Church-versus-Chapel, about which Matthew Arnold and T. H. Green held such divergent views, determined the political character and direction of both Dissent and Liberalism. Nonconformists had constituted a powerful pressure group on (or within) the Victorian Liberal Party because their conviction in a 'special mission' was based on a sense of grievance and injustice; as traditional outsiders they believed themselves to be in some sense the natural allies of the excluded and oppressed. As Victorian Dissenters gained access to hegemonic and national institutions, and helped mould some of those institutions in their own image, many lost their distinctive communal ethos and identity, their sense of a special faith that 'ran in families' and lent them strength in a wicked world. Those who continued to insist on a traditional separateness appeared increasingly ridiculous and reactionary.

Few of the major Dissenting politicians from the later Victorian period chose to identify with a particular religious denomination in their political lives, or to espouse religion as a source of their social and political commitments. Herbert Asquith joined in with Nonconformist opposition to the (Conservative) Education Bill of 1902, which threat-

---

[118] Joseph Chamberlain, a Unitarian, sent his sons Austen and Neville to Rugby. Few ambitious Unitarians would have done this ca. 1840. Austen went on to Cambridge and Neville to business college in Birmingham.

[119] Two significant cultural developments since the 1870 Education Act were the *general* rise of British literacy, so that working-class Britons became more familiar with the mysterious workings of elite politics and even with such esoteric subjects as political economy, and the 'gentrification' of the Philistine middle classes through secondary schooling (sometimes at decidedly inferior public schools) and the serious periodical press. See Vincent, *Literacy and Popular Culture*, chaps. 7–8; and Bax, *Reminiscences and Reflexions*, pp. 11–19, chap. 3 (providing anecdotal evidence of the growth of later Victorian middle-class enlightenment).

ened to overturn the 'rule' of no local rate support for denominational schools, but he otherwise held aloof from religious controversy. When Lloyd George came to head the Coalition Government in December 1916, the *Christian World* proclaimed him the first Nonconformist prime minister. But as Stephen Koss observes, Lloyd George's Dissenting activism, central to his political identity during the 1890s, by 1914 did not go much beyond 'sanctimonious reference to his Welsh chapel or to his beloved Uncle Lloyd.' Three Unionist Cabinet members in 1916, Bonar Law, F. E. Smith and Austen Chamberlain, came from Dissenting backgrounds, as did nearly a dozen Liberal and Labour members of the Government. Their Nonconformity made little difference to their political conduct.[120] Mrs Asquith was reported by the Tory *Morning Post* (28 August 1923) as bemoaning the demise of the Nonconformist conscience: 'At one time the Nonconformist Conscience was the backbone of the country, but the men I know who claim to have it to–day are maidenly, mulish, and misled.'[121] In one of his predictions, at least, about the relationship between politics and Dissent, Green was correct. In his last public speech, commenting on the Bradlaugh controversy, Green observed, 'If ever the Liberal Party lost the religious spirit which has hitherto animated its most vigorous members, it would be a bad lookout for the Liberal Party.'[122]

* * *

The Liberal Party was successful in channelling religious enthusiasm into politics during its Gladstonian heyday (1865–93) but was significantly less effective in this after 1900. Yet some of the moral enthusiasm that had animated Gladstonian Liberals, including Green himself, since the 1860s permeated Radical-Liberalism and 'socialism' from the 1880s. This was not mere coincidence, as both the 'old' Liberals and later Victorian Radicals, taking their cue from Green, responded to the same ethico-political ideas, operated within the perimeters of a common moral vocabulary and were susceptible to many of the same sentiments. Like the Dissenters ridiculed by Matthew Arnold, many advanced Liberals and socialists believed they fought not for the material and political interests of a social group but for the soul of a nation and collective spiritual ends. Few public figures of the age had done more than T. H. Green to impart this particular moral tone to British social politics. While the formation of Liberalism, socialism and Christianity dissolved

---

[120] Jenkins, *Asquith*, chap. 1, and pp. 134–6; Koss, *Nonconformity*, pp. 135–40 (quotation p. 140).
[121] Quoted in Koss, *Nonconformity*, p 167.
[122] 'Notes for a speech given at the North Ward Liberal Association meeting on Tuesday March 7, 1882': *GP* 1(c).

as an effective *political* force after the First World War, its characteristic forms of argument were reiterated in political discourse for many decades thereafter. Green's teachings were a locus for such argument, and persons of different political and ideological persuasions referred to them. Green's philosophy had a considerable impact for a time on professional circles, such as those of academic philosophers or civil servants, but more significant than that was the wider diffusion of a Greenian sensibility throughout British society.

EPILOGUE

Green, Social Philosophy and the Question of Belief

Green's public life as well as his professional writings indicated to his contemporaries and successors how intellectuals could shape individual and institutional activity for the good of society; his life was conspicuous in its instrumentality. James Kloppenberg notes affinities in this way between Green, Max Weber and John Dewey.[1] All of them were pragmatists in the sense that they believed in the instrumentality of truth; truth was valid not (or at least not only) in the abstract but to the extent that it aided society in its interpretation of the past and in the solution of present and future problems. The debate over individualism and collectivism and 'the idea of the state' preoccupied British Idealists and their opponents between the 1880s and 1940s. There are similar arguments in political philosophy today. What are the 'limits' of the individual's rights *vis-à-vis* the community? What are the limits of the community's right to protect itself from individuals or to impose a certain character on them? How are we to determine how the community (*qua* state) might regulate social interactions and shape individual conduct so that each can realize his or her potential? Green remains a 'political classic', as relevant to modern ethical discussions as Aristotle, Kant, J. S. Mill or John Rawls.[2]

---

[1] *Uncertain Victory*, chap. 2, section 3.
[2] This is claimed by Richard Hudelson: see *Modern Political Philosophy*, chaps. 5, 7, 9.

Yet Green was different from us. He represents a critical point or moment not only in the development of liberalism but in the wider history of Western thought. What Max Weber and other social scientists have described as the secularization process was well under way in Green's time. Many of Green's ideas do not strike us today as traditional, in the sense that the ideas of Augustine, Aquinas or Bishop Butler are so recognized. Nor do they seem wholly modern, and the sticking point turns out to be Green's treatment of religion and its constituting categories. Green did little to formulate a cultural science of religion, in the manner of Wilhelm Dilthey, Emile Durkheim or William James, or to found a religious sociology, like Weber, Ernst Troeltsch or Tawney.[3] There is some justice in observing that, in contrast to Kant and Fichte a few generations before him, or Martin Heidegger and Karl Loewith a generation or two after him, Green did not engage directly enough a fundamental ontological question, How does God come into Philosophy?[4] Yet if Green did not offer a Germanic onto-theology, he nevertheless displayed original and significant insights about the functions of religion, including its roles in forming morality and political ideology.

Green is perhaps the last major thinker in the Liberal Tradition to assert the positive value of religion to individual and social development. 'Christian principles' and Christian statements of moral truths were not anachronisms to him, efficacious only for a time. Green understood religious truths as organic principles, since it was evident that people of his time and place — modern Britons, but modern Westerners as well — used them or recurred to them in their everyday ethical and political deliberations. To Green, God resided not only in Christ but in the universe and in the world people made for themselves. The germ of real spirituality — that which enabled Christians to change themselves and others — was located in the individual experient.

William James elaborated on one facet of this idea, eschewing both the mathematical logic of Bertrand Russell and Hegelian Idealism (both of which reduced 'concrete realities' to abstractions), in his book *The Varieties of Religious Experience, A Study in Human Nature* (1902).[5] James

---

[3]   On these thinkers and their study of religion in 'traditional' and 'modern' societies, see Hughes, *Consciousness and Society*, chaps. 6, 8; and on Weber in particular, see F. Ringer, *Max Weber's Methodology: the Unification of the Cultural and Social Sciences* (Cambridge, MA: Harvard UP, 1997).

[4]   On German thinkers' engagement with or evasion of the question, see A. Denker, 'Kant und Fichte: Kann die Religion vernuenftig sein?', and Weischedel, *Der Gott der Philosophen*.

[5]   Kloppenberg, *Uncertain Victory*, pp. 57–8, 96–114, 189–95. Kloppenberg observes that James 'was saddened by the prospect that the delightful serendipity distinguishing our experience of life from our experience of logic might be banished from the world of philosophical discourse by analytic philosophers' (p. 101). Dewey as well dismissed 'analytic realism' as '"land[ing] philosophy in a formalism like unto scholasti-

argued that the religious person, through introspection and devotion (prayer), might achieve self-understanding; and in thus composing himself he might discover emotional-spiritual resources enabling him to better understand his duties and more effectively perform them. Although Green would have viewed James's empirical method (i.e. the attempt to demonstrate religious insight empirically) as futile, he would not otherwise have objected to the argument that prayer is effective: whether devotional or propitiative, prayer connects the believer to the divine by helping him comprehend his relation to the world of concrete realities.[6]

If Green was not modern in his attitude toward Belief, neither was he traditional. Green was a heretic to some contemporaries in stepping back from Christianity as dogma, or as literal, unchanging truth. Other theologians of his time were still engaged in a quest for catholicity, searching for proof that theirs was the 'true' Church: A. M. Fairbairn and the 'Lux Mundi' group were as preoccupied with this as J. H. Newman, John Keble and Gladstone had been during the 1830s and '40s. In contrast, Green adopted the 'liberal' and 'German' view that Christian formulae and institutions were essentially social adaptations, manifesting national character, the 'genius' of different peoples, or the moral discoveries of social groups, and he held that such usages were valuable (and organic) to the extent that they supported life in the Christian spirit.

Nineteenth-century Positivists, like Voltaire and the Enlightenment thinkers before them, repudiated sectarianism. Moreover, they represented religion generally as an atavism and an irrelevance: the theological age, or moment, of civilization had been succeeded by a philosophical one, which was itself in the process of being replaced by a scientific or 'positive' era. Natural scientific investigators increasingly refused to apply metaphysical categories to explain what was apparently within nature. It was in response to the rising current of positivism and naturalism, parallelled in popular 'free-thought', that Green asserted the lasting relevance of religion as a perspective or viewpoint that encompassed more than the science of his time. Green agreed with Giuseppe Mazzini:

> Man is one being: you cannot cut him in two and expect him to agree with you on the principles that are to regulate the social order, when he differs

---

cism"' (from *Essays in Experimental Logic*, quoted in Kloppenberg, *Uncertain Victory*, p. 101).

[6]   As John Dewey put it, religion is 'whatever introduces genuine perspective into the piecemeal and shifting episodes of existence.' Kloppenberg, *Uncertain Victory*, p. 39.

from you on the question of his origins, his destiny and the laws governing his life on earth.[7]

Green was reticent about the origin of species and had no tolerance for theories that were silent about the origin or goals of social development. In his view, Spencer's leap from biological to social evolution was soul-less, and evolutionary doctrines were better able to account for our competitive and anti-social inclinations than for our cooperative impulses. The latter could only be explained by our rational and intuitive capacities (not biological or physical instincts) tutored by some consciousness existing both within and beyond individual persons. There could indeed be a 'natural science of man', but this did not necessitate making nature the measure of human beings, individually or collectively. Green's philosophical theology offered a means of relocating Man in relation to both God and Nature. As late as 1902, A. M. Fairbairn stated the anti-naturalistic viewpoint in terms and language closely resembling Green's:

> The code of ethics which he [man] makes for himself out of himself distinguishes him from every other merely natural being; and it signifies that it is by transcending nature that he becomes himself ... Since man as active will and immanent law transcends nature, he cannot be measured by it.[8]

In Chapter One above was noted James Kloppenberg's skepticism that Green could be widely regarded today as a relevant philosopher, because of the changed ethical 'orientation' of modern (Western) culture. Andrew Vincent observes that 'The problem for the contemporary reader of Green is that the language of the "protestant state" and "Christian citizen" appears remote and anachronistic.'[9] In this sense the Greenian moment has passed. Spiritual concerns and an idea of divine purpose no longer appear to be paramount, or even incidental to the deliberations of most political thinkers and political elites, although these remain important to some members of the wider populations of Western nations. Kloppenberg clearly understands modern culture as a synonym for secular, pluralist democracy; he sees the 'tolerant', liberal citizen as the receptor of the modern sensibility.

Yet this view is surely too simple, in the sense that certain social philosophies remain compelling to large numbers of people because of rather than in spite of their religious inspiration or spiritual tone. Theology retains an instrumental rationality: people lead 'secular' lives, observing conventions of civility and engaging in complex transactions despite wide ideological differences, yet they remain susceptible to reli-

---

[7]   Mazzini quoted in G. Salvemini, *Mazzini*, trans. I. M. Rawson (Palo Alto, CA: Stanford UP, 1957 [orig. 1905]), p. 63.

[8]   A. M. Fairbairn, *The Philosophy of the Christian Religion* (London: Macmillan, 1902), pp. 90–1. He cites here the Stoics and Kant but not Green.

[9]   Boucher and Vincent, *British Idealism and Political Theory*, p. 50.

gious explanations of how things work or how they should be. This is clearly the case when and where 'tradition' (as social structures and the ideas justifying them) is perceived as being undermined by universalizing forces with a Western face (e.g. 'globalization'). To the extent that traditional (or neo-traditional) religions validate cherished ideas and activities not yet eliminated, co-opted or efficiently marketed by outsiders, they serve as mobilizing points for activists purporting to defend national or communal authenticity and freedom. Thus tradition and fetishized religious values animate political culture in ways that dismay or confound the stubbornly secular liberal.

The destructive and dehumanizing aspects of pseudo-religious political theology are all too obvious these days in the Balkans, much of the Arab and Islamic world and on the Indian subcontinent; in a somewhat quieter, smug form, political theology continues to shape opinion in the West. In the liberal worldview, however, sectarian violence easily impeaches religious politics: Protestant marchers asserting their 'civil rights' each July in Ulster, militant 'defenders of Islam' active from the West Bank to the Philippines and beyond, Christian fundamentalists picketing abortion clinics in the US — all would appear to prove that religious 'conviction' is antithetical to civil harmony and human dignity. Still, it would be naive to associate religious bases of social identity and politics unequivocally with barbarism and fanaticism (existing only in the margins of Western society, the West before 1700, and the non-Western world today), or to represent them as fundamentally hostile to democracy or humanism.[10] Even in the homelands of secular liberalism, some philosophers and social theorists express the idea that religion and 'belief', if not always by themselves forming the basis of a viable social or civic philosophy, animate liberalism by counteracting anomie, alienation and irresponsible individualism.[11] As the historian David Hollinger has pointed out, the viewpoint of unselfconscious secularism makes it difficult to understand fully the histories even of lib-

---

[10] On 'civilization', religion and popular morals in southeastern Europe down to the present, see the insightful and concise statements of Mark Mazower in *The Balkans: A Short History* (New York: Modern Library, 2000), pp. 54–76 and Epilogue ('On Violence'). On India, see T. B. Hanson, *The Saffron Wave: Democracy and Hindu Nationalism in Modern India* (Princeton, NJ: Princeton UP, 1999); and A. Nandy, 'Telling the Story of Communal Conflicts in South Asia,' *Ethnic and Racial Studies*, 25 (2002), pp. 1–19. The latter two qualify the view that strong religious identification leads only to social dysfunction and conflict.

[11] D. B. Forrester, *Christian Justice and Public Policy* (CUP, 1997); M. A. Razavi and D. Ambuel, eds. *Philosophy, Religion and the Question of Intolerance* (Albany, NY: SUNY Press, 1997); Paul J. Weithman, ed., *Religion and Contemporary Liberalism* (Notre Dame, IN: Notre Dame UP, 1997); A. T. Peperzak, *Reason in Faith: On the Relevance of Christian Spirituality for Philosophy* (Mahway, NJ: Paulist Press, 1999); R. Audi, *Religious Commitment and Secular Reason* (CUP, 2000); C. J. Eberle, *Religious Conviction in Liberal Politics* (CUP, 2002). These are only a few recent examples of such argument.

eral democracies that, mercifully, have been relatively free from sectarian violence.[12]

Perhaps the chief legacy of the Liberal Tradition in the West down to the present is a deep rooted skepticism about having things done for rather than by people. This is apparent in the 'centrism' of the US Democratic party since the 1980s, the 'New Labour' in Britain, and of course the new Conservatism of Margaret Thatcher and others which was largely responsible for Labour's right turn. John Vincent's statements about Victorian Liberal manliness quoted on more than one occasion in this book evoke some of Thatcher's pronouncements during the 1980s: substitute 'conservatism' for 'liberalism' as connoting the rejection of dependency. Not only was Mrs Thatcher's political style 'masculine' in the mode of mid–Victorian Liberalism but her idealization of 'Victorian virtues' came straight out of Smiles's *Self-Help*. Collini maintains that Mrs Thatcher's disingenuous invocation of self-help and other Victorian virtues shows that the character ideal 'had long since ceased to occupy a genuinely animating and central role' in political argument.[13]

Collini's judgment, if it has any practical value, is surely premature. The deployment of the character ideal since the 1980s by conservative American ideologues like William Bennett, Francis Fukuyama and Dinesh D'Souza, as well as by successful politicians of the Left in Britain, indicates the centrality of the idea of character to liberalism. 'Welfare liberalism', now everywhere on the defensive, represents social justice as a tangible goal, requiring redistribution of wealth beyond what the free market is capable of doing — indeed, perhaps in direct opposition to the distribution of wealth produced by 'market forces', whether in national economies or on a global scale. Yet even liberal proponents of social justice regard redistributive economics and — analogously — legally enforced 'equal opportunity' in education or employment not as ultimate goals but rather as the means of individual empowerment. Not the resulting material condition of individuals but their 'fairer' opportunity to make something of themselves is seen as the end of policy. Conservatives, on the other hand, insist that state interventions intended to achieve equality penalize those who have already made the most of their opportunities. Neither redistributive liberalism (weakly articulated by the fragmented Left) nor conservative liberalism (represented by US Republicans and British Conservatives) presumes that society has a right or duty to impose a specific character upon individuals, although (paradoxically) it is often conservative liberals who recommend state action to promote moral uniformity, or at least similarity in

---

[12] See D. A. Hollinger, 'The "Secularization" Question and the United States in the Twentieth Century,' *Church History*, 70 (2001), pp. 132–43 (and the literature cited therein).

[13] *Public Moralists*, p. 118.

individual characters.[14] While discussions of 'values' and 'character' in the post-communist era appear to be the prerogative of the political Right and Centre, Green's teachings continue to serve as a kind of philosophical wedge by which not only ethical but spiritual issues may be reintroduced into political debate and public life. It may be that the legacy of Green is maintained by those who, while eschewing the traditional labels of Right and Left, consider the moral consequences of materialism and unrestrained consumption of goods and resources. Green's observations about self-realization and the acquisition of property in the *Prolegomena* certainly counsel against 'hedonism' and recommend attention to the social relationships which impinge upon our conceptions of material wealth as an end in itself. Green's ideas can also lend force to humanistic religion, suggesting that individuals cannot find their own salvation or spiritual fulfilment without parallel regard for the condition of other people. This humanistic but anti-individualistic tendency continues in the view that spiritual institutions have a primary responsibility in humanitarian aid and social amelioration.

There is also a Greenian resonance in the conviction that if we would be true to our nature we must use our science with a proper understanding of our relation to the natural world. The latter attitude rests on the insight — shared by religious persons from Francis of Assisi to Wordsworth — that humans are not alone in creation and that the myth of our 'species superiority' may be our undoing. Green might have agreed that our anthropocentrism is one of our limitations but one to be transcended. To him, as to thinkers of the Christian tradition, humans' attempts to understand the natural world to which they belong reveal a 'longing for reconciliation' with God. Indeed, it is that longing that shows people their location in the order of things.[15] Green's first biographer, R. L. Nettleship, paraphrased him thus:

> The consciousness of one reality and one perfection, which is the consciousness of God, is the source alike of science and of religion, of understanding and of love; in both God communicates himself to us, in both we attain partial freedom from our limitations and come to our true selves.[16]

Nettleship's characterization of the Greenian project indicates why Green's ideas were particularly attractive to the first post-Darwinian generation. It also suggests that ethical progressivism may require a 'traditional' metaphysical foundation if it is to be compelling and truly responsive to the needs of the present.

[14] Thus Christian conservatives in the US who support special tax credits to encourage traditional marriage. Likewise their efforts to have 'Creationism' taught and Christianity observed (e.g. through prayer) in the public schools, or to 'encourage' prayer at school sporting events.

[15] 'Faith,' *Works*, iii, p. 264.

[16] 'Memoir,' p. xcix.

Selected Bibliography

I
MANUSCRIPTS AND UNPUBLISHED PRIMARY SOURCES

A. Papers of T. H. Green [GP] at Balliol College, Oxford
Manuscript materials cited according to the categorization of the Balliol librarians, as modified by Geoffrey Thomas. See G. Thomas, *The Moral Philosophy of T. H. Green* (Oxford: Clarendon, 1987), Bibliography.

    (1) Biographical Material (a–d).
    (2) Philosophy: (a) Numbered MSS, (b) Unnumbered MSS.
    (3) History: (a) MSS, (b) Annotated Books.
    (4) Religion: (a) MSS, (b) Translation of F. C. Baur, *Geschichte der christlichen Kirche*, 1863 [two manuscripts, first marked 'Fragment of an Essay on Christianity', second marked 'T. H. Green'], (c) Books.

B. Manuscripts in Other Collections
Department of Western Manuscripts, Bodleian Library, Oxford

    MSS. Bryce, deps. 2, 4, 9, 73, 110. Letters to and from James Bryce, dated 1865–1913.
    MSS. Harcourt, deps. 8, 246. Letters to and from William Vernon Harcourt, dated 1873–80.
    MSS. Eng. Lett. d. 81
    MSS. Eng. Lett. e. 76
    MSS. Eng. Lett. e. 118
    MSS. Top. Oxon. c. 528
    MSS. Top. Oxon. d. 517

Borthwick Institute, University of York, England: Hickleton Papers. A4.270 V.
Letter of Arthur Boutwood to 2nd Viscount Halifax, 19 January 1910.

Mansfield College [Library], Oxford, England.
Early Circulars, Papers, Invitations etc. [ca. 1885–90]. Cupboard 24.
'Fairbairn, A. M.' [marked envelope]. Cupboard 23.
'Mansfield House' [marked envelope]. Cupboard 2.
Minute Book of the Oxford University Nonconformists' Union, 1881–6. Cupboard
   23.
Visitors Book, 1889–1909. Cupboard 24.

II
GREEN'S PUBLISHED WRITINGS AND LETTERS; REPORTED SPEECHES

[United Kingdom] *Alliance News*, 1876–82. [Reported speeches of THG].
Collected Writings of T. H. Green. Volume Five: Additional Writings, edited with
   introduction by Peter Nicholson. Bristol: Thoemmes Press, 1997.
Contemporary Review, 1877–8, 1881–2. [All reprinted in *Works*, ed. R. L. Nettleship]
'Hedonism and the Ultimate Good,' *Mind*, 2 (1877), pp. 266–9.
Lectures on the Principles of Political Obligation and Other Writings., ed. P. Harris and
   J. Morrow. CUP, 1986.
Oxford Chronicle and Berkshire and Buckinghamshire Gazette, 1867–82. [Reports of public
   meetings, and of speeches by THG]
Political Theory of T. H. Green, ed. with an introduction by J. R. Rodman. New York:
   Appleton-Century-Crofts, 1964.
Prolegomena to Ethics, ed. A. C. Bradley. Oxford: Clarendon, 1883.
Review of *The Works of George Berkeley*, ed. A. C. Fraser (Oxford: Clarendon, 1871), in
   Academy 3, no. 40 (January 15, 1872), pp. 27–8.
Thomas Hill Green's Hume and Locke, ed. with an introduction by R. M. Lemos. New
   York: Thomas Y. Crowell, 1968.
Works of T. H. Green, 3 vols., ed. R. L. Nettleship. London: Longmans, Green, and Co.,
   1885–8.

III
PARLIAMENTARY PAPERS AND PUBLIC DOCUMENTS

Oxfordshire County Record Office. Copies of Oxford City Council minutes, 1876–82
   [B.4].
O.C.R.O. Oxford City Council records, 1876–82: Minute books and books of
   documents and records [C.5.3].
O.C.R.O. 'Oxford High School, 1879–84. Letter Book' [Q.4.13].
U.K. Parliament. 'Minutes of Evidence Taken Before the University of Oxford
   Commissioners, 1877. Reports from Commissioners, Inspectors, and Others [c.
   2868].' *Sessional Papers* (Commons), *1881*, Vol. 56.
U.K. Parliament. *Parliamentary Papers. Education – General, 1867–8* [c. 3966 – III, IV,
   VII, XI, XIV, XV]. Reports from Commissioners: 1867–8 (Schools Inquiry), Vol. 8.
U.K. Parliament. 'Royal Commission on Oxford Election (inquiry into the existence of
   corrupt practices): 1880. Report and Minutes of Evidence [c. 2856–56i].' *Sessional
   Papers* (Commons), *1881*, Vol. 44.

IV
SOURCES ORIGINALLY PRINTED BEFORE 1914

Abbott, Evelyn, and L. Campbell. *Life and Letters of Benjamin Jowett, M.A. Master of Balliol College, Oxford.* 2 vols. London: J. Murray, 1897.

Adams, F. *History of the Elementary School Contest in England.* London: Chapman and Hall, 1882.

Alden, Percy. 'Arnold Toynbee,' *Mansfield House Magazine*, 1 (1894), pp. 48–50.

Alliance News, 1 April 1882, p. 193. Unsigned obituary of T. H. Green.

Alumni Oxonienses, 1715–1886. Oxford: Privately printed, 1888.

'An Appeal Against Female Suffrage,' *Nineteenth Century*, 25 (1889), pp. 781–8.

Arnold, Matthew. *Culture and Anarchy [1869]*, ed. with an introduction by J. Dover Wilson. CUP, 1960.

—, *Culture and Anarchy*, ed. S. Lipman with commentaries by M. Cowling, G. Graff and others. New Haven, CT: Yale UP, 1994.

Athenaeum, no. 2840, 1 April 1882, p. 414. Unsigned obituary of THG.

Atherley-Jones, L. A. 'The New Liberalism,' *Nineteenth Century*, 26 (1889), pp. 186–93.

Balfour, A. J. 'A Criticism of Current Idealistic Theories,' *Mind*, 2 n.s. (1893), pp. 28–40.

—, 'Green's Metaphysics of Knowledge,' *Mind*, 9 (1884), pp. 73–92.

Ball, Sidney. 'Socialism and Individualism: A Challenge and an Eirenicon,' *Economic Review*, 7 (1897), pp. 490–520.

—, 'The Socialist Ideal,' *Economic Review*, 9 (1899), pp. 425–49.

Barbour, G. F. 'Green and Sidgwick on the Community of the Good,' *Philosophical Review*, 17 (1908), pp. 149–66.

Bentham, Jeremy. *An Introduction to the Principles of Morals and Legislation [1789]*, with an introduction by L. J. Lafleur. New York: Hafner, 1948.

Binns, H. B. *A Century of Education, Being the Centenary History of the British and Foreign School Society, 1808–1908.* London: J. M. Dent, 1908.

Bland, H. 'The Outlook' in *Fabian Essays in Socialism*, ed. George Bernard Shaw. London, 1889; reprint, Garden City, NY: Dolphin-Doubleday, n.d.

Bosanquet, Bernard, ed. *Aspects of the Social Problem, by Various Writers.* London: Macmillan, 1895.

—, *The Civilization of Christendom, and Other Studies.* London: Swan Sonnenschein and Co., 1893.

—, *The Philosophical Theory of the State.* London: Macmillan, 1899.

Bosanquet, Helen. *The Family.* New York: Macmillan, 1906.

Bradley, A. C., ed. *Philosophical Remains of Richard Lewis Nettleship.* London: Macmillan, 1901.

Bradley, F. H. *Appearance and Reality. A Metaphysical Essay*, 2nd ed. London: Swan Sonnenschein and Co., 1902.

—, *Ethical Studies.* London: Henry S. King & Co., 1876.

Brodrick, George C. *English Land and English Landlords.* London: Cassell, Petter, Galpin and Co., 1881; reprint, New York: Augustus M. Kelley, 1968.

Brown, J. Baldwin. 'The English Church and the Dissenters,' *Contemporary Review*, 16 (1871), pp. 298–320.

Bryce, James, and A. M. Fairbairn. 'Nonconformity and the Universities: the Free Churches and a Theological Faculty,' *British Quarterly Review* (1884), pp. 372–98.

Bryce, James. 'Professor T. H. Green,' *Contemporary Review*, 41 (1882), pp. 877–81.

—, *Studies in Contemporary Biography.* London: Macmillan, 1903.

Burke, Edmund. *Reflections on the Revolution in France [1790]*. Garden City, NY: Anchor-Doubleday, 1973.

Campell, Lewis. *The Nationalisation of the Old English Universities.* London: Chapman and Hall, 1901.

Carlyle, Thomas. *Selected Writings [1828–81]*, ed. with an introduction by A. Shelston. London: Penguin, 1971.

Chamberlain, Joseph. 'Municipal Public Houses,' *Fortnightly Review*, n.s. 22 (1877), pp. 147–59.

—, 'Old Age Pensions,' *Fortnightly Review*, 3rd ser. 18 (1893), pp. 721–39.

Chubb, Percival. 'The Significance of Thomas Hill Green's Philosophical and Religious Teaching,' *Journal of Speculative Philosophy*, 22 (1888), pp. 1–21.

Coleridge, Samuel Taylor. *On the Constitution of the Church and State* [1830], edited with an introduction by J. Barrell. London: J. M. Dent, 1972.

Conybeare, F. C. 'On Professor Green's Political Philosophy,' *National Review*, 13 (1889), pp. 771–87.

Courtney, W. P. 'The Cost of the General Election of 1880,' *Fortnightly Review*, 29 n.s. (1881), pp. 467–87.

Crosskey, H. W. 'National Education: Practical Aims for the Guidance of Liberal Policy,' *Macmillan's Magazine*, 35 (1876-7), pp. 139–46.

Dale, A. W. W. *Life of R. W. Dale, of Birmingham, By His Son*, 4th ed. London: Hodder and Stoughton, 1899.

Dale, R. W. 'Anglicanism and Romanism,' *British Quarterly Review*, 43 (1866), pp. 281–338.

—, 'Congregationalism,' *British Quarterly Review*, 73 (January–April 1881), pp. 1–12, 265–88.

—, 'The Liberal Party and Home Rule,' *Contemporary Review*, 51 (1887), pp. 773–88.

—, 'M. Gambetta: Positivism and Christianity,' *Contemporary Review*, 43 (1883), pp. 476–97.

—, 'The Nonconformists,' *Daily Telegraph*, 25 December 1873, pp. 5–6.

—, 'The Nonconformists and the Educational Policy of the Government,' *Contemporary Review*, 22 (1873), pp. 641–62.

—, 'Our Theological Colleges,' *Eclectic Review* (January 1859), pp. 87–106.

—, *The Politics of Nonconformity*. Manchester: Manchester Nonconformist Association, 1871.

Davidson, J. M. *Eminent English Liberals In and Out of Parliament*. London, 1880; reprint, Freeport, NY: Books for Libraries Press, 1972.

Defoe, Daniel. *The Present State of the Parties in Great Britain …* London: J. Barker, 1712.

Dewey, John. *Early Works, 1882–1898. Volume 3*. Carbondale, IL: Southern Illinois UP, 1972: 'Green's Theory of the Moral Motive' (1892); 'The Philosophy of T. H. Green' (1889); 'Self-Realization as the Moral Ideal' (1893).

Dicey, A. V. 'The Legal Boundaries of Liberty,' *Fortnightly Review*, 3 n.s. (1868), pp. 1–13.

—, *Lectures on the Relation Between Law and Public Opinion in England During the Nineteenth Century*. London: Macmillan, 1905.

Drummond, J., and C. B. Upton, eds. *Life and Letters of James Martineau*. 2 vols. London: J. Nisbet, 1902.

'Electoral Reform, Electoral Bribery: the Ballot' [unsigned], *Westminster Review*, 228 (1881), pp. 212–19.

[Fabian Society.] 'To Your Tents, Oh Israel,' *Fortnightly Review*, n.s. 54 (1893), pp. 569–89.

Fairbairn, Andrew Martin. 'David Friedrich Strauss,' *Contemporary Review*, 27 (1876), pp. 950–77.

—, 'Genesis of the Puritan Ideal,' *Contemporary Review*, 48 (1888), pp. 695–723.

—, 'Oxford and Jowett,' *Contemporary Review*, 74 (1897), pp. 829–51.

—, *The Philosophy of the Christian Religion*. London: Macmillan, 1902.

—, 'The Philosophy of Religion: Historical and Critical,' *Contemporary Review*, 41 (April, June 1882), pp. 583–97, 963–80.

—, 'The Puritan in History,' *The Speaker*, 28 November 1896, pp. 568–70.

—, 'Reason and Religion,' *Contemporary Review*, 45 (1885), pp. 842–61.

—, *Religion in History and in Modern Life. Together with an Essay on the Church and the Working Classes*. New York: Herrick and Co., n.d. [1893].

Fawcett, Henry. 'On the exclusion of those who are not members of the established church from fellowships and other privileges of the English universities,' *Macmillan's Magazine*, 3 (1860–1), pp. 411–16.

Fawcett, William Mitchell, ed. *Religious Republicanism: Six Essays on Congregationalism*. London: Longmans, Green and Co., 1869.

Fichte, Johann Gottlieb. *Attempt at a Critique of All Revelation* [*Versuch einer Kritik aller Offenbarung*, 1792], translated, with an introduction, by Garrett Green. CUP, 1978.

—, *Early Philosophical Writings*, translated and edited by Daniel Breazeale. Ithaca: Cornell UP, 1988.

Freeman, E. A. *Disestablishment and Disendowment*. London: Macmillan, 1874.

—, 'Owens College and Mr. Lowe,' *Macmillan's Magazine*, 35 (1876–7), pp. 407–16.

General Conference of Nonconformists, held in Manchester, January 23rd, 24th, and 25th 1872. Authorised Report of Proceedings. Manchester: Alexander Ireland and Co., 1872.

Gibbons, H. de B. *English Social Reformers*. London: Methuen and Co., 1892.

Gladstone, W. E. *Correspondence on Church and State of W. E. Gladstone*. Ed. D. C. Lathbury. 2 vols. London: Macmillan, 1910.

—, *Midlothian Speeches 1879*, with an introduction by M. R. D. Foot. Leicester: Leicester UP, 1971.

—, '"Robert Elsmere" and the Battle of Belief,' *Nineteenth Century*, 23 (1888), pp. 766–88.

Gore, Charles. *Christianity and Socialism*. Christian Social Union Pamphlet 24. London: n.d.

—, ed. *Lux Mundi. A Series of Studies in the Religion of the Incarnation*. London: John Murray, 1890 [1889].

Haeckel, E. *The History of Creation; or, the Development of the Earth and its Inhabitants by the Action of Natural Causes*, trans. E. Ray Lancaster. New York: D. Appleton and Co., 1876 [translation of *Natuerliche Schoepfungsgeschichte*, 1868].

Haldane, R. B. 'The New Liberalism,' *Progressive Review*, 1 (1896), pp. 133–43.

Hamilton, Sir William. 'Universities of England — Oxford,' *Edinburgh Review*, 5 (June, 1831), reprinted in *Reform and Intellectual Debate in Victorian England*, ed. Barbara Dennis and David Skilton. London: Croom Helm, 1987.

Headlam, Stewart D. *Christian Socialism*. Fabian Society Tract 42. London: 1892.

—, *The Socialist's Church*. London: George Allen, 1907.

Hegel, G. W. F. *Early Theological Writings* [*1795–1809*], trans. T. M. Knox, with an introduction by R. Kroner. Philadelphia: Pennsylvania UP, 1971.

—, *Hegel's Philosophy of Mind. Being Part Three of the Encyclopaedia of the Philosophical Sciences* [*1830*], trans. W. Wallace. Oxford: Clarendon, 1894; reprint, Oxford: Clarendon, 1971.

—, *Introduction to 'The Philosophy of History', with an Appendix from 'The Philosophy of Right'*, trans. L. Rauch [from an 1840 compilation]. Indianapolis, IN: Hackett, 1988.

—, *Phenomenology of Spirit* [*1807*], trans. A. V. Miller. OUP, 1977.

—, *Philosophy of Right* [*1821*], trans. T. M. Knox. Oxford: Clarendon, 1942.

Hobhouse, Leonard T. 'The Ethical Basis of Collectivism,' *International Journal of Ethics*, 8 (1898), pp. 137–56.

—, *Social Evolution and Political Theory*. New York: Columbia UP, 1911.

Horton, R. F. 'Robert William Dale,' *Contemporary Review*, 75 (1899), pp. 34–44.

Howell, George. 'The Caucus System and the Liberal Party,' *New Quarterly Magazine*, 10 (1878), pp. 579–90.

Hughes, Dorothea Price. *Life of Hugh Price Hughes*. London: Hodder and Stoughton, 1904.

Hughes, Hugh Price. *Social Christianity. Sermons delivered in St. James's Hall, London, by Hugh Price Hughes, M.A.* London: Hodder and Stoughton, 1889.

Hughes, Thomas. 'National Education: More Practical Aims for the Guidance of Liberal Policy,' *Macmillan's Magazine*, 35 (1876–7), pp. 230–8.

Hume, David. *An Enquiry Concerning the Principles of Morals [1777]*. Chicago: Open Court, 1930.

Huxley, T. H. 'Natural Rights and Political Rights,' *Nineteenth Century*, 27 (1890), pp. 173–95.

—, *Science and Education. Essays*. London, 1893; reprint, New York: D. Appleton, 1899.

Index Ecclesiasticus, 1800–1840, ed. J. Foster. Oxford: Parker and Co., 1890.

Inquirer, 1 April 1882, p. 207. Unsigned obituary of T. H. Green.

Inquirer, 16 March 1895, p. 1. Unsigned obituary of R. W. Dale.

Inquirer, 14 January 1899, pp. 19–20. Unsigned review of *Life of R. W. Dale*, by A. W. W. Dale.

[Jamaica Committee.] *Facts and Documents Relating to the Alleged Rebellion in Jamaica, and the Measures of Repression: Including Notes of the Trial of Mr. Gordon*. London: Privately printed, 1866.

James, William. 'On Some Hegelianisms,' *Mind*, 7 (1882), pp. 186–208.

—, *The Varieties of Religious Experience: A Study of Human Nature*. New York: Random House, 1929 [1902].

Jodl, Friedrich. *Geschichte der Ethik als philosophische Wissenschaft*. 2 vols. Stuttgart: J. G. Cotta, 1912.

Jones, Henry. 'The Corruption of the Citizenship of the Working Man,' *Hibbert Journal*, 10 (1911–12), pp. 155–78.

Jones, James. *A Plea for Liberty of Conscience …* London: George Larkin, 1684.

Jowett, Benjamin. *The Epistles of St. Paul to the Thessalonians, Galatians, and Romans: with Critical Notes and Dissertations*. 2 vols. 2nd ed. London, 1859.

Kant, Immanuel. *Critique of Pure Reason [1781]*, trans. F. Max Müller. 2 vols. London: Macmillan, 1881; reprint, Garden City, NY: Doubleday-Dolphin, 1961.

—, *Kant's Political Writings [1784–98]*, trans. H. B. Nisbet, with an Introduction and notes by H. S. Reiss. CUP, 1970.

'The Late Professor Green' [unsigned], *The Spectator*, 54 (1 April 1882), pp. 417–18.

'The Late Professor of Moral Philosophy' [unsigned], *Oxford Magazine*, 1 (1883), pp. 57–8.

Liberal and Radical Yearbook 1887. London: Privately printed, 1887.

Lilly, W. S. *First Principles in Politics*. London: John Murray, 1899.

—, '"Our Great Philosopher",' *Contemporary Review*, 55 (1889), pp. 752–70.

—, 'Primitive Christianity,' *Nineteenth Century*, 44 (1898), pp. 502–20.

—, 'Professor Green,' *Dublin Review*, 3d ser., 22 (1889), pp. 98–118.

'A Lost Leader. In Memoriam T. H. Green,' *Macmillan's Magazine*, 46 (1882), p. 87.

MacCunn, John. *Six Radical Thinkers*. London: Arnold, 1907.

Mallock, W. H. 'Radicalism and The People,' *National Review*, 1 (1883), pp. 101–11.

—, 'The Radicalism of the Market-Place,' *National Review*, 1 (1883), pp. 507–30.

Manchester Nonconformist Association. Pamphlets issued 1871–4. Manchester: Alexander Ireland and Co., 1871–4. [From a bound volume held in the Library, Mansfield College, Oxford: shelf number 5257D—Gallery.]

Martineau, James. *Essays, Philosophical and Theological*. 2 vols. New York: Henry Holt, 1875.

—, *Types of Ethical Theory*, 3rd ed. 2 vols. Oxford: Clarendon, 1898.

Maurice, J. F., ed. *The Life of Frederick Denison Maurice, chiefly told in his own letters*. 2 vols. New York: Scribner's, 1884.

Mearns, Andrew. *The Bitter Cry of Outcast London*. London, 1883; reprint, edited by A. S. Wohl, Leicester: Leicester UP, 1970.

Merz, John Theodore. *A History of European Thought in the Nineteenth Century. Vols. 3–4.* Edinburgh: W. Blackwood, 1912; reprint, Gloucester, MA: Peter Smith, 1976.

Mill, J. S. *Autobiography*. London, 1873; reprint, OUP, 1924.

—, *On Liberty [1859]*, ed. with an introduction by G. Himmelfarb. London: Penguin, 1982.

—, *Principles of Political Economy [1871 ed.]*, ed. D. Winch. London: Penguin, 1970.

—, *'Utilitarianism' and Other Essays*, ed. A Ryan. London: Penguin, 1987.

Mind, 8 (1882), pp. 457–9. Unsigned obituary of T. H. Green.

Morris, William. *Political Writings of William Morris [1877–94]*, ed. with an introduction by A. L. Morton. London: Lawrence and Wishart, 1973.

—, and E. Belfort Bax. *Socialism: Its Growth and Outcome*. London: S. Sonnenschein, 1893.

Muirhead, John Henry, ed. *Nine Famous Birmingham Men*. Birmingham: Cornish Bros., 1909.

—, *The Service of the State: Four Lectures on the Political Teaching of T. H. Green*. London: J. Murray, 1908.

Nettleship, R. L. 'Memoir' in *Works of T. H. Green*, vol. iii, ed. Nettleship. London: Longmans, Green and Co., 1888.

—, 'Professor T. H. Green. In Memoriam,' *Contemporary Review*, 41 (1882), pp. 857–77.

Newman, W. L. 'The Land Laws' in *Questions for a Reformed Parliament*. London: Macmillan, 1867.

'Notes and News' [unsigned], *Oxford Magazine*, 1 (1883), pp. 41–2.

Osmaston., F. P. B. 'The Religious Teaching of Thomas Hill Green. Being a Lecture Delivered in Rosslyn Hill Chapel, Hampstead, on the 3rd of February, 1889'. Privately printed, 1889 (Dr Williams' Library: P.2851).

Owen, Robert. *'A New View of Society' and Other Writings [1813–49]*, ed. with an introduction by G. Claeys. London: Penguin, 1991.

Pattison, Mark. *Memoirs*. London: Macmillan, 1885; reprint, Fontwell, Sussex: Centaur, 1969.

—, 'Philosophy at Oxford,' *Mind*, 1 (1876), pp. 82–97.

Pfleiderer, Otto. *The Development of Theology in Germany Since Kant, and its Progress in Great Britain Since 1825*, translated by J. Frederick Smith. London: Swan Sonnenschein, 1890.

Picht, Werner. *Toynbee Hall and the English Settlement Movement*. London: G. Bell, 1914.

[Pringle-Pattison] Andrew Seth, and R. B. Haldane, eds. *Essays in Philosophical Criticism*. London: Longmans, Green and Co., 1883.

[Pringle-Pattison] Andrew Seth. *Hegelianism and Personality*. Edinburgh and London: William Blackwood, 1887.

Rae, W. F. 'Political Clubs and Party Organization,' *Nineteenth Century*, n.s. 3 (1878), pp. 908–32.

Rashdall, Hastings. *Philosophy and Religion*. London: Duckworth, 1911.

'Reform of King Edward's School. Deputation to the Governors [A report of an interview between deputations from the Town Council and the Grammar School Association and the Governors of King Edward's School]'. Birmingham: Privately printed, 1865.

Reid, T. Wemyss. *Life of the Rt. Hon. W. E. Forster*, with an introduction by V. E. Chancellor. London: Chapman and Hall, 1888; reprint, New York: Augustus Kelley, 1970.

[Richard, Henry.] *Education Act Amendment Bill. Speeches of Mr Henry Richard, M.P., Delivered in the House of Commons, July 17 and July 30, 1873*. Manchester: Manchester Nonconformist Association [1873].

Ritchie, David G. *Darwinism and Politics*. London: S. Sonnenschein and Co., 1891 [1889].

—, *The Principles of State Interference: four essays on the political philosophy of Spencer, Mill and Green*. London: S. Sonnenschein, 1891.

Rogers, J. Guinness. 'The Middle Class and the New Liberalism,' *Nineteenth Century*, 26 (1889), pp. 710–20.

—, 'Mr. Gladstone and the Nonconformists,' *Nineteenth Century*, 44 (1898), pp. 30–45.

—, 'Political Dissent,' *Fortnightly Review*, 22 (1877), pp. 811–26.

—, *Why Ought Not the State to Give Religious Education. An Argument Addressed to Nonconformists*. London: Jas. Clarke and Co., 1872.

Rousseau, Jean–Jacques. *The Basic Political Writings [1750–62]*, trans. D. A. Cress with an introduction by P. Gay. Indianapolis, IN: Hackett, 1987.

Rugby School Register, ed. A. T. Michell. 3 vols. Rugby: Privately printed, 1901–4.

Russell, G. W. E. 'The New Liberalism: A Response,' *Nineteenth Century*, 26 (1889), pp. 492–9.

Salvemini, G. *Mazzini*, trans. I. M. Rawson. Palo Alto, CA: Stanford UP, 1957 [1905].

Samuel, Herbert. *Liberalism*. London: Grant Richard, 1902.

Selbie, W. B. *Life of Andrew Martin Fairbairn*. London: Hodder and Stoughton, 1914.

Seth, Andrew: *See* Pringle-Pattison, Andrew Seth.

Seth, James. 'The Evolution of Morality,' *Mind*, 14 (1889), pp. 27–49.

Shaw Lefevre, George John. 'Economic Law and English Land-ownership,' *Fortnightly Review*, n.s. 21 (1877), pp. 32–53.

Sidgwick, Henry. 'Bentham and Benthamism in Politics and Ethics,' *Fortnightly Review*, 21 n.s. (1877), pp. 627–52.

—, 'Green's Ethics,' *Mind*, 9 (1884), pp. 169–87.

—, 'Hedonism and the Ultimate Good,' *Mind*, 2 (1877), pp. 27–38.

—, *Lectures on the Ethics of T. H. Green, Mr. Herbert Spencer, and James Martineau*. London: Macmillan, 1902.

—, *The Methods of Ethics*, 7th ed. London: Macmillan, 1907; reprint, with Foreword by John Rawls, Indianapolis, IN: Hackett, 1981.

Smiles, Samuel. *Self–Help [1866 ed.]*, with an introduction by Asa Briggs. London: J. Murray, 1958.

Smith, Goldwin. *Rational Religion, and the Rationalistic Objections of the Bampton Lectures for 1858*. Oxford: J. Wheeler, 1861.

Sorley, W. R. 'The Method of a Metaphysic of Ethics,' *Philosophical Review*, 14 (1905), pp. 521–34.

Spencer, Herbert. *The Data of Ethics*. New York: Hurst and Co., n.d.

—, 'Professor Green's Explanation,' *Contemporary Review*, 39 (1881), pp. 305–11.

'Statement of the Present Educational Work of the Foundation, as compared with provisions of the new scheme for the management of the [King Edward VI] school, etc.' Birmingham: Privately printed, 1878.

Statements of Christian Doctrine, Extracted from the Writings of B. Jowett. Oxford: J. H. and James Parker, 1861.

Statistical Abstract for the United Kingdom In Each of the Last Fifteen Years from 1871 to 1885. London: HMSO, 1886.

The Student's Handbook to the University and Colleges of Oxford, 6th ed. Oxford: Clarendon, 1881.

The Times, 27 March 1882, p. 6: unsigned notice, death of T. H. Green.

The Times, 28 March 1882, p. 10; 30 March 1882, p. 5: unsigned reports on funeral of T. H. Green.

Toynbee, Arnold. *Lectures on the Industrial Revolution in England*. London: Longman's Green and Co., 1884.

Undergraduate Papers. An Oxford Journal (1857–58) conducted by A. C. Swinburne, John Nichol, T. H. Green, and Others. London, 1858; reprint, New York: Scholar's Facsimiles and Reprints, 1974.

Upton, C. B. *Lectures on the Bases of Religious Belief. Delivered in Oxford and London In April and May, 1893.* London: Williams and Norgate, 1894.

—, 'Theological Aspects of the Philosophy of T. H. Green,' *The New World*, 1 (1892), pp. 139–57.

Vaughan, D. J. 'Scottish Influence upon English Theological Thought,' *Contemporary Review*, 32 (1878), pp. 457–73.

Vaughan, Robert. *Congregationalism: or, the Polity of Independent Churches.* London: Jackson and Walford, 1842.

Wallace, William. *Lectures and Essays on Natural Theology and Ethics, by William Wallace... edited with a Biographical Introduction, by Edward Caird.* Oxford: Clarendon, 1898.

—, [obituary of T. H. Green], *Academy*, 21 (1 April 1882), pp. 231–2.

'The Want of Leaders in Oxford' [unsigned], *Oxford Magazine*, 1 (1883), pp. 45–6.

Ward, Mrs. Humphry [Mary Ward]. *Robert Elsmere [1888],* with an introduction by R. Ashton. OUP, 1987.

Wollstonecraft, M. *A Vindication of the Rights of Woman [1792]* [with J. S. Mill's *The Subjection of Woman*]. London: J. M. Dent, 1992.

V
OTHER PRINTED SOURCES SINCE 1914

Abbagnana, Nicola. *Il nuovo idealismo inglese e americano.* Naples: Società Anonima, 1927.

Abrams, M. H. *Natural Supernaturalism: Tradition and Revolution in Romantic Literature.* New York: Norton, 1971.

Acton, 1st Lord [John Dalberg]. *Essays in the Liberal Interpretation of History: Selected Papers by Lord Acton.* ed. W. H. McNeill. Chicago: UP Chicago, 1967.

Adams, Pauline. *Somerville for Women. An Oxford College, 1879–1993.* OUP, 1996.

Addison, W. G. 'Academic Reform at Balliol 1854–1882 — T. H. Green and Benjamin Jowett,' *Church Quarterly Review*, 153 (1952), pp. 89–98.

Akkerman, Tjitske. 'Liberalism and Feminism in Late Nineteenth Century Britain' in *Perspectives on Feminist Political Thought in European History*, ed. Akkerman and S. Stuurman. London: Routledge, 1998.

Allaway, A. J. 'David James Vaughan. Liberal Churchman and Educationalist,' *Transactions of the Leicestershire Archaeological and Historical Society*, 33 (1957), pp. 45–58.

Allen, R. T. 'Idealism, Theism and Education: Some Footnotes to Gordon and White,' *Journal of the Philosophy of Education*, 21 (1987), pp. 283–6.

—, 'Self–Realization, Religion and Contradiction in *Ethical Studies*,' *Idealist Studies*, 4 (1974), pp. 276–85.

Allett, John. *The New Liberalism: the Political Thought of J. A. Hobson.* Toronto: Toronto UP, 1981.

Allsobrook, D. *Schools for the Shires. The Reform of Middle–Class Education in Mid–Victorian England.* Manchester: Manchester UP, 1986.

Altholz, Josef L. *The Religious Press in Britain, 1760–1900.* Westport, CT: Greenwood, 1989.

Alumni Cantabrigienses, 1752–1900. Cambridge: Privately printed, 1923.

Anderson, O. 'The Feminism of T. H. Green: a Late Victorian Success Story?,' *HPT*, 12 (1991), pp. 671–94.

—, 'State, Civil Society and Separation in Victorian Marriage,' *Past and Present*, 163 (1999), pp. 161–201.

Annan, Noel. 'The Intellectual Aristocracy' in *Studies in Social History. A Tribute to G.M. Trevelyan*, ed. J. H. Plumb. London: Longmans, Green and Co., 1955.

—, *Leslie Stephen. The Godless Victorian*, revised ed. Chicago: UP Chicago, 1984.

—, 'Science, Religion, and the Critical Mind' in *1859: Entering an Age of Crisis*, ed. Phillip Appleman, W. A. Madden, and M. Wolff. Bloomington, IN: Indiana UP, 1959.

Appleman, Philip, W. A. Madden, and M. Wolff, eds. *1859: Entering an Age of Crisis*. Bloomington, IN: Indiana UP, 1959.

d'Arcy, Fergus A. 'Charles Bradlaugh and the English Republican Movement, 1868–1878,' *HJ*, 25 (1982), pp. 367–83.

Armytage, W. H. G. 'The 1870 Education Act,' *British Journal of Educational Studies*, 18 (1970), pp. 121–33.

Arnstein, Walter L. *The Bradlaugh Case. Atheism, Sex, and Politics among the Late Victorians*. OUP, 1965; reprint, Columbia, MO: UP Missouri, 1983.

—, *Protestant versus Catholic in Mid–Victorian England. Mr. Newdigate and the Nuns*. Columbia, MO: UP Missouri, 1982.

Asquith, H. H. *Memories and Reflections: 1852–1927*. 2 vols. Boston: Little, Brown, 1928.

—, *Some Aspects of the Victorian Age*. The Romanes Lecture 1918. Oxford: Clarendon, 1918.

Atsuko, Hirai. 'Self–Realization and the Common Good: T. H. Green in Meiji Ethical Thought,' *Journal of Japanese Studies*, 5 (1979), pp. 107–36.

Audi, Robert. *Religious Commitment and Secular Reason*. CUP, 2000.

Auspos, Patricia. 'Radicalism, Pressure Groups, and Party Politics: from the National Education League to the National Liberal Federation,' *JBS*, 20 (1980), pp. 184–204.

Avineri, Shlomo. *Hegel's Theory of the Modern State*. CUP, 1972.

—, *The Social and Political Thought of Karl Marx*. CUP, 1968.

Ayer, Alfred Jules. *Language, Truth and Logic*, 2nd ed. New York: Dover, 1952.

Backstrom, P. N., Jr. 'The Practical Side of Christian Socialism in Victorian England,' *Victorian Studies*, 6 (1963), pp. 305–24.

Bailey, Victor. 'English Prisons, Penal Culture, and the Abatement of Imprisonment, 1895–1922,' *JBS*, 36 (1997), pp. 285–324.

Baillie, D. M. *God Was In Christ. An Essay on Incarnation and Atonement*. New York: Scribner's, 1948.

Barker, Ernest. *Political Thought in England, 1848 to 1914*, 2nd ed. OUP, 1928; reprint, Westport, CT: Greenwood, 1980.

Barker, Michael. *Gladstone and Radicalism: the Reconstruction of Liberal Policy in Britain, 1885–94*. Hassocks, Sussex: Harvester, 1975.

Barker, Rodney. Review of *Conceptualizing the State*, by J. Meadowcroft, *Albion*, 29 (1997), p. 142.

Barlow, R. B. *Citizenship and Conscience. A Study in the Theory and Practice of Religious Toleration in England During the Eighteenth Century*. Philadelphia: UP Pennsylvania, 1962.

Barnes, S. V. 'England's Civic Universities and the Triumph of the Oxbridge Ideal,' *History of Education Quarterly*, 36 (1996), pp. 271–305.

Barnsby, George. *Birmingham Working People. A History of the Labour Movement in Birmingham 1650–1914*. Birmingham: Birmingham Printing Co–Partnership, 1989.

Baron, Hans. 'Calvinist Republicanism and its Historical Roots,' *Church History*, 8 (1959), pp. 30–42.

Barret–Ducrocq, Françoise. *Love in the Time of Victoria*, trans. J. Howe. London: Penguin, 1992.

Barth, Karl. *Protestant Theology in the Nineteenth Century: its Background and History.* London: S. C. M. Press, 1972 [translation of *Die protestantische Theologie im 19. Jahrhundert*, 1947].

Bax, Ernest Belfort. *Reminiscences and Reflexions of a Mid and Late Victorian.* London: Allen and Unwin, 1918; reprint, New York: Augustus M. Kelley, 1967.

Bebbington, D. W. *Evangelicalism in Modern Britain: A History from the 1730s to the 1980s.* London: Unwin Hyman, 1989.

—, *The Nonconformist Conscience: Chapel and Politics, 1870–1914.* London: Allen and Unwin, 1982.

Beck, Robert N. *Handbook in Social Philosophy.* New York: Macmillan, 1979.

Behrman, Cynthia Fansler. 'The Annual Blister: A Sidelight on Victorian Social and Parliamentary History,' *Victorian Studies*, 11 (1968), pp. 483–502.

Belchem, J. C. 'Republicanism, Popular Constitutionalism and the Radical Platform in Early Nineteenth-Century England,' *Social History*, 6 (1981), pp. 1–32.

Bellamy, Richard. 'A Green Revolution? Idealism, Liberalism and the Welfare State,' *Bulletin of the Hegel Society of Great Britain*, 10 (1984), pp. 34–9.

—, 'Hegel and Liberalism,' *History of European Ideas*, 8 (1987), pp. 693–708.

—, *Liberalism and Modern Society: A Historical Argument.* Oxford: Polity, 1992.

—, *Rethinking Liberalism.* London: Pinter, 2000.

Bentley, Michael. *The Climax of Liberal Politics: British Liberalism in Theory and Practice, 1868–1918.* London: Arnold, 1987.

—, *Politics Without Democracy 1815–1914.* London: Fontana, 1984.

Berlin, Isaiah. *Four Essays on Liberty.* OUP, 1969.

—, *The Proper Study of Mankind. An Anthology of Essays*, ed. H. Hardy and R. Hausheer, with an introduction by Hausheer and a foreword by N. Annan. New York: Farrar, Straus and Giroux, 1998.

Berry, Christopher J. 'From Hume to Hegel: the Case of the Social Contract,' *Journal of the History of Ideas*, 38 (1977), pp. 691–703.

—, *Hume, Hegel and Human Nature.* The Hague: Nijhoff, 1982.

Bertocci, Philip A. 'Positivism, French Republicanism, and the Politics of Religion, 1848–1883,' *Third Republic*, 2 (1976), pp. 182–227.

Best, Geoffrey F. A. *Mid–Victorian Britain 1851–75.* London: Weidenfeld and Nicolson, 1971; reprint, London: Fontana, 1979.

—, 'The Religious Difficulties of National Education in England, 1800–70,' *Cambridge Historical Journal*, 12 (1956), pp. 155–73.

Beveridge, W. H. *Voluntary Action.* London: Allen and Unwin, 1948.

Bevir, Mark. 'Begriffsgeschichte [review article],' *History and Theory*, 39 (2000), pp. 273–84.

—, 'Ernest Belfort Bax: Marxist, Idealist, and Positivist,' *Journal of the History of Ideas*, 54 (1993), pp. 119–35.

—, 'The Errors of Linguistic Contextualism,' *History and Theory*, 31 (1992), pp. 276–98.

—, 'The Labour Church Movement, 1891–1902,' *JBS*, 38 (1999), pp. 217–45.

—, 'Mind and Method in the History of Ideas,' *History and Theory*, 36 (1997), pp. 167–89.

—, 'Review Article: English Political Thought in the Nineteenth Century,' *HPT*, 17 (1996), pp. 114–27.

—, 'Welfarism, Socialism and Religion: On T. H. Green and Others,' *Review of Politics*, 55 (1993), pp. 639–61.

Biagini, Eugenio F. *Liberty, Retrenchment and Reform. Popular Liberalism in the Age of Gladstone, 1860–1880.* CUP, 1992.

—, 'Popular Liberals, Gladstonian Finance, and the Debate on Taxation, 1860–1874' in *Currents of Radicalism. Popular Radicalism, Organized Labour, and Party Politics in Britain, 1850–1914*, ed. E. F. Biagini and A. J. Reid. CUP, 1991.

—, and A. J. Reid, eds. *Currents of Radicalism. Popular Radicalism, Organized Labour, and Party Politics in Britain, 1850–1914.* CUP, 1991.

Bill, E. G. W. *University Reform in Nineteenth Century Oxford: A Study of Henry Halford Vaughan, 1811–1885.* OUP, 1973.

Binfield, Clyde. 'Hebrews Hellenised? English Evangelical Nonconformity and Culture, 1840–1940' in *A History of Religion in Britain: Practice and Belief from Pre-Roman Times to the Present,* ed. W. J. Sheils. Oxford: Clarendon, 1994.

—, *So Down to Prayers: Studies in English Nonconformity, 1780–1920.* London: J. M. Dent, 1977.

—, 'Thomas Binney and Congregationalism's "Special Mission",' *Transactions of the Congregational Historical Society,* 21 (1971), pp. 1–10.

Blaazer, David. *The Popular Front and the Progressive Tradition. Socialists, Liberals, and the Quest for Unity, 1884–1939 .* CUP, 1992.

Blake, Robert. *The Conservative Party from Peel to Thatcher.* London: Methuen, 1985.

Bockmühl, Klaus Erich. *Leiblichkeit und Gesellschaft: Studien zur Religionskritik und Anthropologie im Fruehwerk von Ludwig Feuerbach und Karl Marx.* Goettingen: Vandenhoeck und Ruprecht, 1961.

Bosanquet, Bernard. *Social and International Ideals, Being Studies in Patriotism.* London: Macmillan, 1917.

—, 'The State and the Individual,' *Mind,* n.s. 28 (1919), pp. 75–8.

Boucher, David. 'British Idealism and the Just Society' in *Social Justice from Hume to Walzer,* ed. Boucher and P. Kelly. London: Routledge, 1998.

—, 'British Idealist International Theory,' *Bulletin of the Hegel Society of Great Britain,* no. 31 (Spring, 1995), pp. 73–89.

—, ed. *The British Idealists.* CUP, 1997.

—, and A. Vincent. *British Idealism and Political Theory.* Edinburgh: Edinburgh UP, 2000.

—, 'Histories of Political Thought in the Post-Methodological Age,' *HPT,* 14 (1993), pp. 301–16.

Bowle, John. *Politics and Opinion in the Nineteenth Century. An Historical Introduction.* London: Jonathan Cape, 1954.

Bowler, P. J. 'Malthus, Darwin and the Concept of Struggle,' *Journal of the History of Ideas,* 37 (1976), pp. 631–50.

Bradley, Ian. *The Optimists. Themes and Personalities in Victorian Liberalism.* London: Faber and Faber, 1980.

Bradley, J. 'Hegel in Britain,' *Heythrop Journal,* 20 (1979), pp. 1–24, 163–82.

Bradley, James E. *Religion, Revolution, and English Radicalism: Nonconformity in Eighteenth Century Politics and Society.* CUP, 1990.

Brailsford, H. N. *The Levellers and the English Revolution.* London: Cresset, 1961.

Brandon, Ruth. *The New Women and the Old Men. Love, Sex and the Woman Question.* New York: Norton, 1990.

Brazill, William. *The Young Hegelians.* New Haven, CT: Yale UP, 1970.

Brent, Richard. *Liberal Anglican Politics: Whiggery, Religion and Reform, 1830–1841.* Oxford: Clarendon, 1987.

Brett, G. S. 'Green, Thomas Hill' in *Encyclopaedia of Religion and Ethics,* ed. J. Hastings. New York: Scribner's, 1920.

Breuilly, John. 'Liberalism or Social Democracy?: A Comparative Study of British and German Labour Politics, c. 1850–75,' *European History Quarterly,* 15 (1985), pp. 3–42.

Briggs, Asa. *History of Birmingham: Volume II, Borough and City, 1865–1938.* London: OUP, 1952.

—, *Victorian Cities.* London, 1965; reprint, Berkeley, CA: California UP, 1993.

—, *Victorian People. A Reassessment of Persons and Themes 1851–1967.* Revised ed. Chicago: UP Chicago, 1970.

—, and Anne Macartney. *Toynbee Hall. The First Hundred Years.* London: Routledge Kegan Paul, 1984.

Brilioth, Y. T. *Three Lectures on Evangelicalism and the Oxford Movement.* Oxford: Clarendon, 1934.

Brinton, Crane. *English Political Thought in the Nineteenth Century,* revised ed. Cambridge, MA: Harvard UP, 1949.

Bristow, E. J. 'The Liberty and Property Defence League and Individualism,' *HJ*, 18 (1975), pp. 761–89.

Britton, K. W. 'John Stuart Mill on Christianity' in *James and John Stuart Mill: Papers of the Centenary Conference*, ed. J. M. Robson and M. Laine. Toronto: Toronto UP, 1976.

Broad, C. D. *Five Types of Ethical Theory.* London: K. Paul, Trench, and Truebner, 1930.

Brock, M. G., and M. C. Curthoys, eds. *The History of the University of Oxford. Volume VI: Nineteenth-Century Oxford, Part 1.* Oxford: Clarendon, 1997.

—, eds. *The History of the University of Oxford. Volume VII: Nineteenth-Century Oxford, Part 2.* Oxford: Clarendon, 2000.

Broughton, Trev Lynn. *Men of Letters, Writing Lives: Masculinity and Literary Autobiography in the Late Victorian Period.* London: Routledge, 1999.

Brown, Alan Willard. *The Metaphysical Society: Victorian Minds in Crisis, 1869–1880.* New York: Columbia UP, 1947.

Brown, Daniel. *Hopkins' Idealism: Philosophy, Physics, Poetry.* Oxford: Clarendon, 1997.

Brown, Ford K. *Fathers of the Victorians. The Age of Wilberforce.* CUP, 1961.

Brown, Kenneth D. *A Social History of the Nonconformist Ministry in England and Wales, 1800–1930.* Oxford: Clarendon, 1988.

Bruce, Steve, ed. *Religion and Modernization. Sociologists and Historians Debate the Secularization Thesis.* Oxford: Clarendon, 1992.

Bryson, Gladys. *Man and Society: the Scottish Inquiry of the Eighteenth Century.* Princeton, NJ: Princeton UP, 1945.

Budd, Susan. *Varieties of Unbelief. Atheists and Agnostics in English Society, 1850–1960.* New York: Holmes and Meier, 1977.

Burke, Kenneth. *A Grammar of Motives.* Berkeley and Los Angeles, CA: UP California, 1969.

Burke, Sara Z. *Seeking the Highest Good: Social Service and Gender at the University of Toronto, 1888–1937.* Toronto: Toronto UP, 1996.

Burrow, John W. *Evolution and Society. A Study in Victorian Social Theory.* CUP, 1966.

—, *A Liberal Descent: Victorian Historians and the English Past.* CUP, 1981.

—, *Whigs and Liberals: Continuity and Change in English Political Thought.* OUP, 1988.

Butler, David, and A. Sloman. *British Political Facts, 1900–1974,* 4th ed. New York: St Martin's, 1975.

Cacoullos, Ann C. *Thomas Hill Green: Philosopher of Rights.* New York: Twayne, 1974.

Cannon, W. F. 'The Problem of Miracles in the 1830s,' *VS*, 4 (1960), pp. 5–32.

—, 'Scientists and Broad Churchmen: An Early Victorian Network,' *JBS*, 4 (1964), pp. 65–88.

Carritt, E. F. *Morals and Politics: Theories of Their Relation from Hobbes and Spinoza to Marx and Bosanquet.* OUP, 1935.

Carter, Matt. 'Ball, Bosanquet and the Legacy of T. H. Green,' *HPT*, 22 (1999), pp. 674–94.

—, *T. H. Green and the Development of Ethical Socialism* (Exeter: Imprint Academic, 2003; read in manuscript).

Chadwick, Owen. *The Secularization of the European Mind in the Nineteenth Century.* CUP, 1975.

—, *The Victorian Church.* 2 vols. London: A. and C. Black, 1966–70.

—, *Victorian Miniature*. London: Hodder and Stoughton, 1960; reprint, CUP, 1991.

Chapman, Richard A. 'Thomas Hill Green (1836–1882),' *Review of Politics*, 27 (1965), pp. 516–31.

Chase, Malcolm. 'Out of Radicalism: the Mid–Victorian Freehold Land Movement,' *EHR*, 106 (1991), pp. 319–45.

Chrétiene, Maurice, ed. *Le nouveau liberalisme anglais*. Paris: Economica, 1999.

Christie, I. R. *Wars and Revolutions. Britain, 1760–1815*. Cambridge, MA: Harvard UP, 1982.

Claeys, Gregory. 'The French Revolution Debate and British Political Thought,' *HPT*, 11 (1990), pp. 59–80.

—, 'Justice, Independence, and Industrial Democracy: The Development of J. S. Mill's Views on Socialism,' *Journal of Politics*, 49 (1987), pp. 122–47.

Clark, Albert C. 'F. C. Conybeare,' *Proceedings of the British Academy*, 11 (1924–25), pp. 469–74.

Clark, J. C. D. *English Society, 1688–1832. Ideology, Social Structure and Political Practice During the Ancien Regime*. CUP, 1985.

Clark, Steven R. L. 'Aristotle's Woman,' *HPT*, 3 (1982), pp. 177–91.

Clarke, Peter. *Liberals and Social Democrats*. CUP, 1978.

Cockshut, A. O. *The Unbelievers: English Agnostic Thought, 1840–1890*. New York: New York UP, 1966.

Coffey, John. 'Puritanism and Liberty Revisited: the Case for Toleration in the English Revolution,' *HJ*, 41 (1998), pp. 961–85.

Cohn, Norman. *The Pursuit of the Millennium*, revised ed. OUP, 1970.

Colaiaco, James A. *James Fitzjames Stephen and the Crisis of Victorian Thought*. New York: St Martin's, 1983.

Colley, Linda. *Britons: Forging the Nation, 1707–1837*. New Haven, CT: Yale UP, 1992.

Collingwood, R. G. *An Autobiography*. OUP, 1939.

Collini, Stefan. 'Hobhouse, Bosanquet and the State: Philosophical Idealism and Political Argument in England 1880–1918,' *Past and Present*, 72 (1976), pp. 86–111.

—, 'The Idea of "Character" in Victorian Political Thought,' *Transactions of the Royal Historical Society*, 5th series 35 (1985), pp. 29–50.

—, *Liberalism and Sociology: L. T. Hobhouse and Political Argument in England, 1880–1914*. CUP, 1979.

—, 'Political Theory and the "Science of Society" in Victorian Britain,' *HJ*, 23 (1980), pp. 203–31.

—, *Public Moralists. Political Thought and Intellectual Life in Britain 1850–1930*. OUP, 1991.

Cone, Carl B. *The English Jacobins. Reformers in Late Eighteenth–Century England*. New York: Scribner's, 1968.

Cook, Chris. *A Short History of the Liberal Party 1900–1976*. New York: St Martin's, 1976.

Cooter, Roger. *The Cultural Meaning of Popular Science: Phrenology and the Organization of Consent in Nineteenth–Century Britain*. CUP, 1984.

Coppa, Frank J. 'The Religious Basis of Mazzini's Thought,' *Journal of Church and State*, 12 (1970), pp. 237–53.

Cornford, J. 'The Transformation of Conservatism in the Late Nineteenth Century,' *Victorian Studies*, 7 (1963), pp. 35–66.

Cosgrove, Richard A. *The Rule of Law: Albert Venn Dicey, Victorian Jurist*. London: Macmillan, 1980.

Cowen, M. P., and R. W. Shenton. 'British Neo-Hegelian Idealism and Official Colonial Practice in Africa: the Oluwa Land Case of 1921,' *Journal of Imperial and Commonwealth History*, 22 (1994), pp. 217–50.

Cowherd, Raymond G. *The Politics of English Dissent*. New York: New York UP, 1956.

Cowling, Maurice. 'The Use of Political Philosophy in Mill, Green and Bentham,' *Historical Studies*, 5 (1965), pp. 141–52.

Crimmins, J. E., ed. *Religion, Secularization, and Political Thought. Thomas Hobbes to J. S. Mill*. London: Routledge, 1989.

Cross, F. L., ed. *Oxford Dictionary of the Christian Church*, 2nd ed. Oxford: Clarendon, 1974. S.v. 'Atonement,' 'J. Boehme,' 'Christian Socialism,' 'Christology,' 'Evangelicalism,' 'A. C. Fraser,' 'C. Gore,' 'T. H. Green,' 'H. Grotius,' 'H. S. Holland,' 'Incarnation,' 'W. R. Inge,' 'B. Jowett,' 'H. Lotze,' 'Lux Mundi,' 'J. Martineau,' 'F. D. Maurice,' 'Moravian Brethren,' 'F. W. Schelling,' 'F. Schlegel,' 'F. Schleiermacher,' 'N. Zinzendorf'.

Cunningham, Hugh. 'The Language of Patriotism, 1750–1914,' *History Workshop Journal*, 12 (1981), pp. 8–33.

Cunningham, William. *The Common Weal. Six Lectures on Political Philosophy*. CUP, 1917.

David, Deirdre. *Intellectual Women and Victorian Patriarchy. Harriet Martineau, Elizabeth Barrett Browning, George Eliot*. Ithaca, NY: Cornell UP, 1987.

Davidoff, Leonore, and Catherine Hall. *Family Fortunes. Men and Women of the English Middle Class, 1780–1850*. Chicago: UP Chicago, 1987.

Davie, Donald. *A Gathered Church. The Literature of the English Dissenting Interest, 1700–1930*. The Clark Lectures 1976. OUP, 1978.

Davies, Horton. *Worship and Theology in England. Vol. Three: From Watts and Wesley to Maurice, 1690–1850*. Princeton, NJ: Princeton UP, 1961.

—, *Worship and Theology in England. Vol. Four: From Newman to Martineau, 1830–1900*. Princeton UP, 1962.

Davis, David Brion. *The Problem of Slavery in the Age of Revolution, 1770–1823*. Ithaca, NY: Cornell UP, 1975.

Davis, H. W. C. *A History of Balliol College*. Revised R. H. C. Davis and R. Hunt. Oxford: Clarendon, 1963.

Davis, Richard W. *Dissent in Politics, 1780–1830: the Political Life of William Smith, M.P.* London: Epworth, 1971.

Denker, Alfred. 'Kant und Fichte: Kann die Religion vernuenftig sein?,' *Fichte-Studien*, 8 (1995), pp. 1–13.

Dennis, Norman, and A. H. Halsey. *English Ethical Socialism. Thomas More to R. H. Tawney*. Oxford: Clarendon, 1988.

Den Otter, Sandra M. *British Idealism and Social Explanation. A Study in Late Victorian Thought*. Oxford: Clarendon, 1996.

Derry, J. W. *The Radical Tradition. Tom Paine to Lloyd George*. London: Macmillan, 1967.

Dewey, John. *Lectures on Psychology and Political Ethics: 1898*, ed. D. F. Koch. New York: Hafner Press, 1976.

Dickey, Laurence. *Hegel. Religion, Economics, and the Politics of the Spirit, 1770–1807*. CUP, 1987.

—, 'The Pocockian Moment,' *JBS*, 26 (1987), pp. 93–9.

Dickinson, H. T. *Liberty and Property: Political Ideology in Eighteenth–Century Britain*. London: Weidenfeld and Nicolson, 1977.

Dictionary of the History of Ideas, ed. P. Wiener. New York: Scribner's, 1973. S.v. 'Liberalism,' by J. Plamenatz.

Dimova-Cookson, Maria. *T. H. Green's Moral and Political Philosophy: A Phenomenological Approach*. Basingstoke, Hants.: Palgrave, 2001.

Dingle, A. E. *The Campaign for Prohibition in England: the United Kingdom Alliance, 1872–1895*. London: Croom Helm, 1980.

Dinwiddy, J. R. *Radicalism and Reform in Britain, 1780–1850*. London: Hambledon, 1992.

Dockhorn, Klaus. *Die Staatsphilosophie des englischen Idealismus, ihre Lehre und Wirkung.* Koeln: H. Poppinghaus, 1937.

Duncan, Graeme. *Marx and Mill. Two Views of Social Conflict and Social Harmony.* CUP, 1973.

Dunn, John. *The Political Thought of John Locke.* CUP, 1969.

Dutton, D. J. 'The Unionist Party and Social Policy, 1906–1914,' *HJ*, 24 (1981), pp. 871–84.

Dworkin, R. *Taking Rights Seriously.* Cambridge, MA: Harvard UP, 1977.

Eberle, Christopher J. *Religious Conviction in Liberal Politics.* CUP, 2002.

Edwards, D. L. 'Inge, William Ralph' in *Twentieth-Century Culture. A Biographical Companion,* ed. Alan Bullock and R. B. Woodings. New York: Harper and Row, 1983.

Eisen, Sidney. 'Frederic Harrison and Herbert Spencer: Embattled Unbelievers,' *VS*, 12 (1968), pp. 33–56.

Eisenach, Eldon J. *Two Worlds of Liberalism. Religion and Politics in Hobbes, Locke, and Mill.* Chicago: UP Chicago, 1981.

Elliot-Binns, L. E. *English Thought 1860–1900. The Theological Aspect.* London: Longmans, 1956.

Emy, H. V. *Liberals, Radicals and Social Politics 1892–1914.* CUP, 1973.

Engel, A, J. *From Clergyman to Don: The Rise of the Academic Profession in Nineteenth Century Oxford.* OUP, 1983.

Ensor, R. C. K. *England, 1870–1914.* Oxford: Clarendon, 1936.

Epstein, James. *The Lion of Freedom: Feargus O'Connor and the Chartist Movement, 1832–1842.* London: Croom Helm, 1982.

Erb, Peter C., ed. *Pietists. Selected Writings.* New York: Paulist Press, 1983.

Evans, E. J. *The Forging of the Modern State. Early Industrial Britain, 1793–1870.* London: Longman, 1983.

Faber, G. *[Benjamin] Jowett: A Portrait With Background.* Cambridge, MA: Harvard UP, 1958.

Fairfield, Paul. *Moral Selfhood and the Liberal Tradition: the Politics of Individuality.* Toronto: Toronto UP, 2000.

Farnell, Lewis. *An Oxonian Looks Back.* London: Hopkinson, 1934.

Fasnacht, G. E. *Acton's Political Philosophy.* London: Hollis and Carter, 1952.

Feinberg, J. *Rights, Justice, and the Bounds of Liberty.* Princeton, NJ: Princeton UP, 1980.

Ferreira, P. 'Caird on Kant and the Refutation of Skepticism' in *Anglo-American Idealism, 1865–1927,* ed. William J. Mander. Westport, CT: Greenwood, 2000.

Fforde, Matthew. *Conservatism and Collectivism 1886–1914.* Edinburgh: Edinburgh UP, 1990.

Finlayson, G. B. A. M. 'The Politics of Municipal Reform, 1835,' *EHR*, 81 (1966), pp. 673–92.

Finn, Margot C. *After Chartism. Class and Nation in English Radical Politics, 1848–1874.* CUP, 1993.

Fisher, H. A. L. *Life of James Bryce.* 2 vols. New York: Macmillan, 1927.

Fitzgerald, Penelope. *The Blue Flower.* New York: Houghton Mifflin, 1995.

Fitzpatrick, M. 'Heretical Religion and Radical Political Ideas in Late Eighteenth Century England' in *The Transformation of Political Culture. England and Germany in the Late Eighteenth Century,* ed. E. Hellmuth. Studies of the German Historical Institute London. OUP, 1990.

Flick, Carlos. *The Birmingham Political Union and the Movement for Reform in Britain, 1830–1839.* Hamden, CT: Archon, 1978.

Formisano, Ronald. 'The Concept of Political Culture,' *Journal of Interdisciplinary History*, 31 (2001), pp. 393–426.

Forrester, Duncan B. *Christian Justice and Public Policy.* CUP, 1997.

Foster, R. F. *Modern Ireland 1600–1972*. London: Penguin, 1989.

Foucault, Michel. *The Order of Things* [*Les mots et les choses*], trans. A. Sheridan. London: Tavistock, 1970.

Fowler, W. S. 'The Influence of Idealism Upon State Provision of Education,' *VS*, 4 (1961), pp. 337–44.

Fox, Alan. *History and Heritage: The Social Origins of the British Industrial Relations System*. London: Allen and Unwin, 1985.

Francis, Mark. 'Herbert Spencer and the Myth of Laissez-faire,' *Journal of the History of Ideas*, 39 (1978), pp. 317–28.

—, 'The Use and Abuse of Paradigms in the History of Political Thought,' *Politics*, 18 (1983), pp. 93–9.

—, and John Morrow. *A History of English Political Thought in the Nineteenth Century*. New York: St Martin's, 1994.

Freeden, Michael. *Ideologies and Political Theory: A Conceptual Approach*. Oxford: Clarendon, 1996.

—, 'Liberal Community: An Essay in Retrieval' in *The New Liberalism: Reconciling Liberty and Community*, ed. Avital Simhony and D. Weinstein. CUP, 2001.

—, *Liberalism Divided: A Study in British Political Thought, 1914–1939*. Oxford: Clarendon, 1986.

—, *The New Liberalism. An Ideology of Social Reform*. Oxford: Clarendon, 1978.

Freeman, Kenneth D. *The Role of Reason in Religion: A Study of Henry Mansel*. The Hague: M. Nijhoff, 1969.

Gallagher, Catherine. *The Industrial Transformation of English Fiction. Social Discourse and Narrative Form*. Chicago: UP Chicago, 1985.

Gamble, Andrew. 'Wallas, Graham' in *Twentieth-Century Culture. A Biographical Companion*, ed. A. Bullock and R. B. Woodings. New York: Harper and Row, 1983

Garrard, John A. 'The History of Local Political Power: Some Suggestions for Further Analysis,' *Political Studies*, 25 (1977), pp. 252–69.

Gash, Norman. *Politics in the Age of Peel. A Study in the Technique of Parliamentary Representation 1830–1850*. London: Longman, 1953; reprint, New York: Norton, 1971.

Gaus, Gerald F. 'Bosanquet's Communitarian Defense of Economic Individualism' in *The New Liberalism: Reconciling Liberty and Community*, ed. Avital Simhony and D. Weinstein. CUP, 2001.

—, 'Ideological Dominance Through Philosophical Confusion: Liberalism in the Twentieth Century' in *Reassessing Political Ideologies: the Durability of Dissent*, ed. M. Freeden. London: Routledge, 2001.

—, *The Modern Liberal Theory of Man*. London: Croom Helm, 1983.

Gay, Peter. 'The Manliness of Christ' in *Religion and Irreligion in Victorian Society. Essays in Honour of R. K. Webb*, ed. Richard W. Davis and R. J. Helmstadter. London: Routledge, 1992.

Gerrish, B. A. *Tradition and the Modern World. Reformed Theology in the Nineteenth Century*. Chicago: UP Chicago, 1978.

Gibbins, John. 'Liberalism, Nationalism and the English Idealists,' *History of European Ideas*, 15 (1992), pp. 491–7.

Gilbert, Alan. *Religion and Society in Industrial England. Church, Chapel and Social Change, 1740–1914*. London: Longman, 1976.

Gilbert, Bentley B. *David Lloyd George: a Political Life. The Architect of Change, 1863–1912*. London: Batsford, 1987.

—, *The Evolution of National Insurance in Great Britain. The Origins of the Welfare State*. London: M. Joseph, 1966

Gildea, Robert. *Barricades and Borders. Europe 1800–1914*, 2nd ed. OUP, 1996.

Gill, F. C. *The Romantic Movement and Methodism. A Study of English Romanticism and the Evangelical Revival.* London: Epworth, 1954.

Glaser, John F. 'English Nonconformity and the Decline of Liberalism,' *AHR*, 63 (1957), pp. 352–8.

Goldman, Lawrence, ed. *The Blind Victorian. Henry Fawcett and British Liberalism.* CUP, 1989.

—, *Dons and Workers: Oxford and Adult Education since 1850.* Oxford: Clarendon, 1995.

—, 'A Peculiarity of the English? The Social Science Association and the Absence of Sociology in Nineteenth–Century Britain,' *Past and Present*, 114 (1987), pp. 133–71.

Gomez, F. G. 'The Endowed Schools Act, 1869. A Middle Class Conspiracy?,' *Journal of Educational Administration and History*, 6 (1974), pp. 9–18.

Gordon, Peter, and White, J. *Philosophers as Educational Reformers: the Influence of Idealism on British Educational Thought and Practice.* London: Routledge and Kegan Paul, 1979.

Gosse, Edmund. *The Life of Algernon Charles Swinburne.* London: Macmillan, 1917.

Gossman, Norbert J. 'Republicanism in Nineteenth Century England,' *International Review of Social History*, 8 (1962), pp. 47–60.

Graff, Gerald. 'Arnold, Reason, and Common Culture' in *Culture and Anarchy*, ed. S. Lipman with commentaries by M. Cowling, G. Graff and others. New Haven, CT: Yale UP, 1994.

—, *Professing Literature. An Institutional History.* Chicago: UP Chicago, 1987.

Gray, John. 'Spencer on the Ethics of Liberty and the Limits of State Interference,' *HPT*, 3 (1982), pp. 465–81.

Gray, Robert. 'The Deconstructing of the English Working Class' [review article],' *Social History*, 11 (1986), pp. 363–73.

Gray, T. S. 'Herbert Spencer's Theory of Social Justice — Desert or Entitlement?,' *HPT*, 2 (1981), pp. 161–86.

Greaves, Richard L. *The Puritan Revolution and Educational Thought. Background for Reform.* New Brunswick, NJ: Rutgers UP, 1969.

Green, E. H. H. *The Crisis of Conservatism: The Politics, Economics and Ideology of the British Conservative Party, 1880–1914.* London: Routledge, 1995.

—, *Ideologies of Conservatism. Conservative Political Ideas in the Twentieth Century.* OUP, 2002.

Green, Ronald M. *Religion and Moral Reason: A New Method for Comparative Study.* OUP, 1988.

Greengarten, I. M. *Thomas Hill Green and the Development of Liberal–Democratic Thought.* Toronto: Toronto UP, 1981.

Greenleaf, W. H. *The British Political Tradition, Volume II: The Ideological Heritage.* London: Methuen, 1983.

—, 'Laski and British Socialism,' *HPT*, 2 (1981), pp. 573–91.

Grosskurth, Phyllis. *John Addington Symonds. A Life.* London: Longmans, 1964.

—, ed. *The Memoirs of John Addington Symonds.* London: Hutchinson, 1984.

Gulley, Elsie. *Joseph Chamberlain and English Social Politics.* New York: Columbia UP, 1926.

Haakonssen, K., ed. *Enlightenment and Religion: Rational Dissent in Eighteenth–Century Britain.* CUP, 1996.

—, *The Science of a Legislator. The Natural Jurisprudence of David Hume and Adam Smith.* CUP, 1981.

Habermas, Jürgen. *Strukturwandel der Öffentlichkeit*, 2. Ausgabe. Neuwied: Luchterhand, 1965.

Halévy, Elie. *The Birth of Methodism in England*, trans. B. Semmel. Chicago: UP Chicago, 1971.

—, *England in 1815*, 2nd ed., trans. E. I. Watkin and D. A. Barker. London: Ernest Benn, 1949.

—, *The Growth of Philosophic Radicalism*, trans. Mary Morris. London: Benn, 1928; reprint, Boston: Beacon, 1955.

—, *The Rule of Democracy (1905–1914)*, 2nd ed., trans. E. I. Watkin. London: Benn, 1961.

Hamer, D. A. *Liberal Politics in the Age of Gladstone and Rosebery. A Study in Leadership and Policy*. Oxford: Clarendon, 1972.

—, *The Politics of Electoral Pressure. A Study in the Techniques of Victorian Reform Agitations*. Hassocks, Sussex: Harvester, 1977.

Hammond, J. L., and B. Hammond. *Lord Shaftesbury*, 2nd ed. London: Constable, 1923.

Hanham, H. J. *Elections and Party Management. Politics in the Time of Disraeli and Gladstone*, revised ed. Hassocks, Sussex: Harvester, 1978.

Hansen, Philip. 'T. H. Green and the Limits of Liberalism: A Response to Professor Lawless,' *Canadian Journal of Political and Social Theory*, 2 (1978), pp. 156–8.

—, 'T. H. Green and the Moralization of the Market,' *Canadian Journal of Political and Social Theory*, 1 (1977), pp. 91–117.

Hanson, T. B. *The Saffron Wave. Democracy and Hindu Nationalism in Modern India*. Princeton, NJ: Princeton UP, 1999.

Hare, R. M. *The Language of Morals*. OUP, 1952.

Harlan, David. 'Intellectual History and the Return of Literature,' *AHR*, 94 (1989), pp. 581–601.

Harpham, Edward J. 'Liberalism, Civic Humanism, and the Case of Adam Smith,' *American Political Science Review*, 78 (1984), pp. 764–74.

Harris, F. P. *Neo-Idealist Political Theory*. New York: King's Crown, 1944.

Harris, Horton. *David Friedrich Strauss and His Theology*. CUP, 1973.

Harris, José. 'Political Thought and the Welfare State 1870–1940: An Intellectual Framework for British Social Policy,' *Past and Present*, 135 (1992), pp. 116–41.

—, *William Beveridge: A Biography*. Oxford: Clarendon, 1977.

Harris, Paul. 'Moral Progress and Politics: the Theory of T. H. Green,' *Polity*, 21 (1989), pp. 538–627.

Harris, Paul, and J. Morrow. 'Did Nettleship Corrupt Green's Lectures? – A Comment on Smith,' *HPT*, 6 (1985), pp. 643–6.

Harrison, Brian. *Drink and the Victorians. The Temperance Question in England 1815–1872*. Pittsburgh, PA: Pittsburgh UP, 1971.

—, *Separate Spheres: The Opposition to Women's Suffrage in Britain*. New York: Holmes and Meier, 1978.

—, 'Teetotal Chartism,' *History*, 58 (1973), pp. 193–203.

—, '"A World of Which We Had No Conception": Liberalism and the English Temperance Press,' *VS*, 13 (1969), pp. 125–58.

Harrison, Brian, and P. Hollis. 'Chartism, Liberalism and the Life of Robert Lowery,' *EHR*, 82 (1967), pp. 503–35.

Harrison, J. F. C. *Late Victorian Britain 1875–1901*. London: Fontana, 1990.

Hart, H. L. A. 'Are There Any Natural Rights?,' *Philosophical Review*, 64 (1955), pp. 175–91.

—, *Essays on Bentham*. Oxford: Clarendon, 1982.

Harvie, Christopher. 'Gladstonianism, the Provinces, and Popular Culture, 1860–1906' in *Victorian Liberalism. Nineteenth–Century Political Thought and Practice*, ed. R. Bellamy. London: Routledge, 1990.

—, *The Lights of Liberalism: University Liberals and the Challenge of Democracy, 1860–86*. London: Allen Lane, 1976.

Havard, William. *Henry Sidgwick and Later Utilitarian Political Philosophy* Gainesville, FL: Florida UP, 1959.

Havighurst, Alfred F. *Britain in Transition. The Twentieth Century*, 4th ed. Chicago: UP Chicago, 1985.

—, *Radical Journalist. H. W. Massingham (1860–1924)*. CUP, 1974.

Hawkins, Angus. '"Parliamentary Government" and Victorian Political Parties, c. 1830–c.1880,' *EHR*, 104 (1989), pp. 638–69.

Helmstadter, Richard J. 'The Nonconformist Conscience' in *The Conscience of the Victorian State*, ed. P. Marsh. Syracuse, NY: Syracuse UP, 1979.

—, and Bernard Lightman, eds. *Victorian Faith in Crisis. Essays on Continuity and Change in Nineteenth–Century Religious Belief*. Palo Alto, CA: Stanford UP, 1990.

Hempton, David. *Methodism and Politics in British Society 1750–1850*. Palo Alto, CA: Stanford UP, 1984.

—, *Religion and Political Culture in Britain and Ireland. From the Glorious Revolution to the Decline of Empire*. CUP, 1996.

Hennock, E. P. *Fit and Proper Persons. Ideal and Reality in Nineteenth–Century Urban Government*. London: Arnold, 1973.

—, 'Poverty and Social Theory in England: the Experience of the 1880s,' *Social History*, 1 (1976), pp. 67–82.

Hetherington, Henry, and J. H. Muirhead. *Social Purpose: A Contribution to a Philosophy of Civic Society*. London: Allen and Unwin, 1922 [1918].

Heyck, Thomas William. *The Dimensions of British Radicalism. The Case of Ireland 1874–95*. Urbana, IL: UP Illinois, 1974.

—, *The Transformation of Intellectual Life in Victorian England*. London: Croom Helm, 1982.

Hill, Christopher. *Collected Essays*. Vols. 1–2. Amherst, MA: UP Massachusetts, 1985–6.

Hilton, Boyd. *The Age of Atonement: The Influence of Evangelicalism on Social and Economic Thought, 1785–1865*. Oxford: Clarendon, 1995 [1988].

—, 'The Role of Providence in Evangelical Social Thought' in *History, Society and the Churches. Essays in Honour of Owen Chadwick*, ed. Derek Beales and Geoffrey Best. CUP, 1985.

Himmelfarb, Gertrude. *On Liberty and Liberalism. The Case of John Stuart Mill*, revised ed. San Francisco: ICS Press, 1990.

—, *Poverty and Compassion. The Moral Imagination of the Late Victorians*. New York: Vintage–Random, 1992.

Hinchliff, Peter. *Benjamin Jowett and the Christian Religion*. Oxford: Clarendon, 1987.

Hirsch, E. D., Jr. *Wordsworth and Schelling: A Typological Study of Romanticism*. New Haven, CT: Yale UP, 1960.

Hobhouse, Leonard T. *The Metaphysical Theory of the State*. London: Allen and Unwin, 1918.

Hobsbawm, E. J. 'Labour History and Ideology,' *Journal of Social History*, 7 (1974), pp. 372–81.

Hobson, John A. *Confessions of an Economic Heretic*. London: Allen and Unwin, 1938; reprint, ed. with an introduction by Michael Freeden, Hassocks, Sussex: Harvester, 1976.

Holborn, Hajo. *A History of Modern Germany, Volume 2: 1648–1840*. New York: Knopf, 1964; reprint, Princeton, NJ: Princeton UP, 1982.

—, *A History of Modern Germany, Volume 3: 1840–1945*. New York: Knopf, 1964; reprint, Princeton UP, 1982.

Hollinger, David. 'The Return of the Prodigal: The Persistence of Historical Knowing,' *AHR*, 94 (1989), pp. 601–21.

—, 'The "Secularization" Question and the United States in the Twentieth Century,' *Church History*, 70 (2001), pp. 132–43.

Hollis, Patricia. *Ladies Elect. Women in English Local Government, 1865–1914*. Oxford: Clarendon, 1987.

—, ed. *Women in Public, 1850–1900: Documents of the Victorian Women's Movement*. London: Allen and Unwin, 1979.

Holloway, Harry. 'Mill and Green on the Modern Welfare State,' *Western Political Quarterly*, 13 (1960), pp. 389–405.

Holmes, Colin J. 'Laissez–Faire in Theory and Practice, Britain 1800–75,' *Journal of European Economic History*, 5 (1976), pp. 671–88.

Honan, Park. *Matthew Arnold. A Life*. Cambridge, MA: Harvard UP, 1983.

Honderich, T., ed. *Oxford Companion to Philosophy*. Oxford: Blackwell, 1995. S.v. 'T. H. Green,' 'idealism, philosophical,' 'liberalism'.

de S. Honey, J. R. *Tom Brown's Universe: the Development of the Victorian Public School in the Nineteenth Century*. New York: Quadrangle, 1977.

Hont, Istvan, and Michael Ignatieff, eds. *Wealth and Virtue. The Shaping of Political Economy in the Scottish Enlightenment*. CUP, 1983.

Hook, Sidney. *From Hegel to Marx: Studies in the Intellectual Development of Karl Marx*. New York, 1936; reprint, New York: Columbia UP, 1994.

Hooper, A. 'From Liberal Radicalism to Conservative Corporatism: the pursuit of "Radical business" in "Tory" Livery. Joseph Chamberlain, Birmingham, and British Politics, 1870–1930' in *Victorian Liberalism. Nineteenth-Century Political Thought and Practice*, ed. R. Bellamy. London: Routledge, 1990.

Hoover, Kenneth R. 'Liberalism and the Idealist Philosophy of Thomas Hill Green,' *Western Political Quarterly*, 26 (1973), pp. 550–65.

Horton, R. F. *An Autobiography*. London: Allen and Unwin, 1917.

Houghton, Walter E. *The Victorian Frame of Mind 1830–1870*. New Haven, CT: Yale UP, 1957.

—, ed. *The Wellesley Index to Victorian Periodicals 1824–1900*. Toronto: Toronto UP, 1966–88.

Howse, Ernest Marshall. *Saints in Politics: the 'Clapham Sect' and the Growth of Freedom*. Toronto: UP Toronto, 1952; reprint, London: Allen and Unwin, 1971.

Hudelson, Richard. *Modern Political Philosophy*. Armonk, NY: M. E. Sharpe, 1999.

Hughes, H. Stuart. *Consciousness and Society. The Reorientation of European Social Thought*, revised ed. New York: Vintage–Random, 1977.

Hurst, M. C. *Joseph Chamberlain and West Midland Politics, 1886–1895*. Dugdale Society Occasional Papers 15. OUP, 1962.

Hutton, T. W. *King Edward's School Birmingham, 1552–1952*. Oxford: Blackwell, 1952.

Hylton, Peter. *Russell, Idealism, and the Emergence of Analytic Philosophy*. Oxford: Clarendon, 1990.

—, 'The Nature of the Proposition and the Revolt Against Idealism' in *Philosophy in History. Essays in the Historiography of Philosophy*, ed. R. Rorty, J. B. Schneewind, and Q. Skinner. CUP, 1984.

Ingham, S. M. 'The Disestablishment Movement in England, 1868–74,' *Journal of Religious History*, 3 (1964), pp. 38–60.

Inglis, Fred. *Radical Earnestness. English Social Theory 1880–1980*. Oxford: M. Robertson, 1982.

Inglis, K. S. *Churches and the Working Classes in Victorian England*. London: Routledge and Kegan Paul, 1963.

—, 'English Nonconformity and Social Reform, 1880–1900,' *Past and Present*, 13 (1958), pp. 73–88.

International Encyclopedia of the Social Sciences. New York: Macmillan/Free Press, 1969. S.v. 'T. H. Green,' by Anthony Quinton

Irwin, T. 'Morality and Personality: Kant and Green' in *Self and Nature in Kant's Philosophy*, ed. Allen W. Wood. Ithaca, NY: Cornell UP, 1984.

Irvine, William. *Apes, Angels, and Victorians. Darwin, Huxley, and Evolution.* New York: McGraw–Hill, 1955; reprint, Cleveland, OH: Meridian–World, 1959.

Isaac, Jeffrey C. 'Republicanism Versus Liberalism? A Reconsideration,' *HPT*, 9 (1988), pp. 349–77.

Izenberg, G. N. *Impossible Individuality. Romanticism, Revolution, and the Origins of Modern Selfhood, 1787–1802.* Princeton, NJ: Princeton UP, 1992.

James, D. G. *Henry Sidgwick: Science and Faith in Victorian England.* OUP, 1970.

Jenkins, Roy. *Asquith. Portrait of a Man and an Era.* New York: Chilmark Press, 1964.

Jenkins, T. A. *Gladstone, Whiggery and the Liberal Party, 1874–1886.* Oxford: Clarendon, 1988.

Jenks, Craig. 'T. H. Green, the Oxford Philosophy of Duty and the English Middle Class,' *British Journal of Sociology*, 28 (1977), pp. 481–97.

Johnson, Mark D. *The Dissolution of Dissent, 1850–1918.* New York: Garland, 1987.

Jones, Gareth Stedman. 'The Determinist Fix: Some Obstacles to the Further Development of the Linguistic Approaches to History in the 1990s,' *History Workshop Journal*, 42 (1996), pp. 19–35.

—, *Languages of Class: Studies in English Working–Class History 1832–1982.* CUP, 1983.

—, *Outcast London: A Study in the Relationship Between Classes in Victorian Society.* London: Clarendon, 1971.

Jones, Henry, and J. H. Muirhead. *The Life and Philosophy of Edward Caird.* Glasgow: Privately printed, 1921.

Jones, Howard Mumford. *Revolution and Romanticism.* Cambridge, MA: Harvard UP, 1974.

Jones, John. *Balliol College. A History: 1263–1939.* OUP, 1988.

Jones, Peter d'A. *The Christian Socialist Revival, 1877–1914.* Princeton, NJ: Princeton UP, 1968.

Joyce, Patrick. *Democratic Subjects. The Self and the Social in Nineteenth–Century England.* CUP, 1994.

—, *Visions of the People: Industrial England and the Question of Class, 1848–1914.* CUP, 1991.

—, *Work, Society and Politics: the Culture of the Factory in Late Victorian England.* New Brunswick, NJ: Rutgers UP, 1980.

Judson, Margaret A. *From Tradition to Political Reality. A Study of Ideas Set Forth in Support of the Commonwealth Government in England, 1649–1653.* Hamden, CT: Archon, 1980.

Kadish, Alon. *Apostle Arnold. The Life and Death of Arnold Toynbee.* Durham, NC: Duke UP, 1986.

Kahan, Alan S. *Aristocratic Liberalism. The Social and Political Thought of Jacob Burckhardt, John Stuart Mill, and Alexis de Tocqueville.* OUP, 1992.

Kateb, Georg. *The Inner Ocean: Individualism and Democratic Thought.* Ithaca, NY: Cornell UP, 1992.

Kaufman, G. D. *Systematic Theology: A Historicist Perspective.* New York: Scribner's, 1968.

Kautz, S. *Liberalism and Community.* Ithaca, NY: Cornell UP, 1995.

Kaye, Elaine. *Mansfield College, Oxford. Its Origin, History, and Significance.* OUP, 1996.

Kelley, Robert. *The Transatlantic Persuasion: The Liberal–Democratic Mind in the Age of Gladstone.* New York: Knopf, 1969.

Kelly, G. A. *Idealism, Politics and History. Sources of Hegelian Thought.* CUP, 1969.

Kenny, A. J. P., ed. *Rationalism, Empiricism, and Idealism.* OUP, 1986.

Kent, Christopher. *Brains and Numbers: Elitism, Comtism and Democracy in Mid–Victorian England.* Toronto: Toronto UP, 1978.

—, 'Higher Journalism and the Mid–Victorian Clerisy,' *VS*, 13 (1969), pp. 181–98.

Kent, J. *William Temple: Church, State and Society in Britain, 1880–1950.* CUP, 1992.

Kenyon, J. 'R.W. Dale and Christian Worldliness' in *The View From the Pulpit. Victorian Ministers and Society*, ed. Paul T. Phillips. Toronto: Macmillan Canada, 1978.

Kenyon, J. P. *The Stuart Constitution 1603–1688. Documents and Commentary.* CUP, 1969.

Kiernan, Victor. 'Evangelicalism and the French Revolution,' *Past and Present*, 1 (1952), pp. 44–56.

King, W. M. 'Hugh Price Hughes and the British "Social Gospel",' *Journal of Religious History*, 13 (1984), pp. 66–82.

Kinzer, Bruce, ed. *The Gladstonian Turn of Mind.* Toronto: Toronto UP, 1985.

Kirk, Neville. *The Growth of Working Class Reformism in Mid–Victorian England.* Urbana, IL: Illinois UP, 1985.

Kitson Clark, George. *Churchmen and the Condition of England, 1832–1885. A Study in the Development of Social Ideas and Practice from the Old Regime to the Modern State.* London: Methuen, 1973.

Kleingeld, Pauline. 'Kant, History, and the Idea of Moral Development,' *History of Philosophy Quarterly*, 16 (1999), pp. 59–80.

Kloppenberg, James. Review of *The Political Philosophy of the British Idealists*, by P. Nicholson, *Albion*, 24 (1992), pp. 150–2.

—, *Uncertain Victory. Social Democracy and Progressivism in European and American Thought, 1870–1920.* OUP, 1986.

Knapp, V. J. 'T. H. Green and the Exorability of Property,' *Agora*, 1 (1969), pp. 57–65.

Knickerbocker, F. W. *Free Minds: John Morley and His Friends.* Cambridge, MA: Harvard UP, 1943.

Knights, Ben. *The Idea of the Clerisy in the Nineteenth Century.* CUP, 1978.

Knoepflmacher, U. C. *Religious Humanism and the Victorian Novel.* Princeton, NJ: Princeton UP, 1965.

Knox, R. A. *Enthusiasm. A Chapter in the History of Religion.* Oxford: OUP, 1950; reprint, New York: Galaxy, 1961.

Koepf, Ulrich, ed. *Historisch-kritische Geschichtsbetrachtung: Ferdinand Christian Baur und seine Schueler: 8. Blaubeurer Symposion.* Sigmaringen: J. Thorbecke, 1994.

Koss, Stephen. *Nonconformity in Modern British Politics.* Hamden, CT: Archon, 1975.

Kramnick, Isaac. *Republicanism and Bourgeois Radicalism: Political Ideology in Late Eighteenth–Century England and America.* Ithaca, NY: Cornell UP, 1990.

Kuklick, Bruce. *Churchmen and Philosophers: From Jonathan Edwards to John Dewey.* New Haven, CT: Yale UP, 1985.

Kymlicka, Will. *Liberalism, Community and Culture.* Oxford: Clarendon, 1989.

LaCapra, Dominick. *Rethinking Intellectual History: Texts, Contexts, Language.* Ithaca, NY: Cornell UP, 1983.

Lamont, William. *Puritanism and Historical Controversy.* Montreal: McGill–Queen's UP, 1996.

—, *Richard Baxter and the Millennium.* London: Croom Helm, 1979.

Lancaster, Bill. *Radicalism, Cooperation and Socialism: Leicester Working–Class Politics 1860–1906.* Leicester: Leicester UP, 1987.

Lang, Timothy. *The Victorians and the Stuart Heritage. Interpretations of a Discordant Past.* CUP, 1995.

Langford, Paul. *A Polite and Commercial People. England 1727–1783.* OUP, 1989; reprint, OUP, 1992.

Larsen, T. *Friends of Religious Equality. Nonconformist Politics in Mid–Victorian England.* Woodbridge, Suffolk: Boydell, 1999.

LaSelva, Samuel V. '"A Single Truth": Mill on Harm, Paternalism and Good Samaritanism,' *Political Studies*, 36 (1988), pp. 486–96.

Laslett, Peter, ed. *Philosophy, Politics and Society.* Oxford: Blackwell, 1956.

Lawless, Andrew. 'T. H. Green and the British Liberal Tradition,' *Canadian Journal of Political and Social Theory*, 2 (1978), pp. 142–55.

Lawrence, Jon. 'Popular Radicalism and the Socialist Revival in Britain,' *JBS*, 31 (1992), pp. 163–86.

—, *Speaking for the People. Party, Language and Popular Politics in Britain, 1867–1914.* CUP, 1998.

Lehmann, Hartmut. '"Community" and "Work" As Concepts of Religious Thought in Eighteenth-Century Württhemberg Pietism' in *Protestant Evangelicalism: Britain, Ireland, Germany and America, c.1750–c.1950. Essays in Honour of W. R. Ward*, ed. Keith Robbins. Studies in Church History 7. Oxford: Blackwell, 1990.

—, 'Pietistic Millenarianism in Late Eighteenth-Century Germany' in *The Transformation of Political Culture. England and Germany in the Late Eighteenth Century*, ed. E. Hellmuth. Studies of the German Historical Institute London. OUP, 1990.

Leighton, D. P. 'Municipal Progress, Democracy and Radical Identity in Birmingham, 1838–1886,' *Midland History*, 25 (2000), pp. 115–42.

Leventhal, F. M. *The Last Dissenter: H. N. Brailsford and His World*. Oxford: Clarendon, 1985.

—, *Respectable Radical. George Howell and Victorian Working Class Politics*. Cambridge, MA: Harvard UP, 1971.

Lewis, H. D. 'Individualism and Collectivism: A Study of T. H. Green,' *Ethics*, 63 (1952), pp. 44–63.

—, *Morals and Revelation*. London: Allen and Unwin, 1951.

—, '"Self-Satisfaction" and the "True Good" in Green's Moral Theory,' *Proceedings of the Aristotelian Society*, n.s. 42 (1941–2), pp. 151–82.

—, 'Was Green a Hedonist?,' *Mind*, n.s. 45 (1936), pp. 193–8.

Liedtke, R., and S. Wendehorst, eds. *The Emancipation of Catholics, Jews and Protestants: Minorities and the Nation State in Nineteenth-Century Europe*. Manchester: Manchester UP, 1999.

Lincoln, Anthony. *Some Political and Social Ideas of English Dissent, 1763–1800*. CUP, 1938.

Lindsay, A. D. 'Introduction,' *[T. H. Green] Lectures on the Principles of Political Obligation*. London: Longmans, Green and Co., 1955.

—, *The Modern Democratic State*. OUP, 1943.

Loewith, Karl. *From Hegel to Nietzsche: the Revolution in Nineteenth Century Thought*, translated by D. E. Green. New York, 1946; reprint, New York: Columbia UP, 1991.

Lopatin, Nancy D. *Political Unions, Popular Politics and the Great Reform Act*. New York: Macmillan–St. Martin's, 1999.

Lovejoy, A. O. *Essays in the History of Ideas*. Baltimore: Johns Hopkins UP, 1948.

Lubenow, William C. *The Politics of Government Growth: Early Victorian Attitudes Toward State Intervention, 1833–1848*. Newton Abbot: David and Charles, 1971.

Lynd, Helen Merrell. *England in the Eighteen Eighties: Toward a Social Basis for Freedom*. OUP, 1945; reprint, London: Frank Cass, 1968.

McBriar, A. M. *An Edwardian Mixed Doubles: The Bosanquets versus the Webbs; A Study in British Social Policy*. Oxford: Clarendon, 1987.

McCann, W. P. 'Trade Unionists, Artisans and the 1870 Education Act,' *British Journal of Educational Studies*, 18 (1970), pp. 134–50.

McCardle, A. W. *Friedrich Schiller and Swabian Pietism*. New York: Peter Lang, 1986.

McClelland, J. S. *A History of Western Political Thought*. London: Routledge, 1996.

Maccoby, Simon. *English Radicalism [1832–86]*. Vols. 3–4. London: Allen and Unwin, 1935–8.

MacDonagh, Oliver. *Early Victorian Government, 1830–1870*. London: Weidenfeld and Nicolson, 1977.

Machin, G. I. T. *The Catholic Question in English Politics, 1820–1830*. Oxford: Clarendon, 1964.

—, 'Disestablishment and Democracy, c. 1840–1930' in *Citizenship and Community. Liberals, Radicals and Collective Identities in the British Isles, 1865–1931*, ed. Eugenio F. Biagini. CUP, 1996.

—, 'Gladstone and Nonconformity in the 1860s: the Formation of an Alliance,' *HJ*, 17 (1974), pp. 347–64.

MacIntyre, Alasdair. *After Virtue. A Study in Moral Theory*, 2nd ed. Notre Dame, IN: Notre Dame UP, 1984.

—, *Secularisation and Moral Change*. London: OUP, 1967.

—, *Three Rival Versions of Moral Enquiry*. Gifford Lectures 1988. Notre Dame, IN: Notre Dame UP, 1990.

Mack, E. C. *Public Schools and British Opinion Since 1860*. New York: Columbia UP, 1941.

McKendrick, Neil. 'The Consumer Revolution of Eighteenth Century England' in *The Birth of Consumer Society. The Commercialization of Eighteenth–Century England*, ed. McKendrick, John Brewer, and J. H. Plumb. London: Hutchinson, 1983.

MacKillop, I. D. *The British Ethical Societies*. CUP, 1986.

Mackinnon, D. M. *A Study in Ethical Theory*. London: Adam and Charles Black, 1957.

Mackintosh, Hugh Ross. *Types of Modern Theology: Schleiermacher to Barth*. London: Nisbet and Co., 1937.

McLeod, Hugh. *Class and Religion in the Late Victorian City*. Hamden, CT: Archon, 1974.

—, 'Religion in Nineteenth–Century Britain [review essay],' *JBS*, 38 (1999), pp. 385–91.

McMenamin, Iain. '"Self–Choosing" and "Right–Acting" in the Nationalism of Giuseppe Mazzini,' *History of European Ideas*, 23 (1997), pp. 221–34.

Macpherson, C. B. *Democratic Theory. Essays in Retrieval*. Oxford: Clarendon Press, 1973.

—, *The Political Theory of Possessive Individualism. Hobbes to Locke*. Oxford: Clarendon, 1962; reprint, OUP, 1988.

McWilliam, R. 'Radicalism and Popular Culture: the Tichbourne Case and the Politics of "Fair Play", 1867–1886' in *Currents of Radicalism. Popular Radicalism, Organized Labour, and Party Politics in Britain, 1850–1914*, ed. Eugenio F. Biagini and A. J. Reid. CUP, 1991.

Magnus, Philip. *Gladstone. A Biography*. London: J. Murray, 1954.

Mandelbaum, Maurice. *History, Man, and Reason. A Study of Nineteenth Century Thought*. Baltimore: Johns Hopkins UP, 1971.

Mander, William J., ed. *Anglo-American Idealism, 1865–1927*. Westport, CT: Greenwood, 2000.

—, 'Caird's Developmental Idealism' in *Anglo-American Idealism, 1865–1927*, ed. Mander. Westport, CT: Greenwood, 2000.

de Marchi, N. B. 'The Success of Mill's *Principles*,' *History of Political Economy*, 6 (1974), pp. 119–57.

Marcuse, Herbert. *Reason and Revolution. Hegel and the Rise of Social Theory*. OUP, 1941.

Marler, J. *History of the Oxford Boys' High School*. N.d. Typescript in Oxford Central Library.

Marsh, Peter. 'Backward versus Radical Conservatives [review essay],' *JBS*, 38 (1999), pp. 261–6.

—, *Joseph Chamberlain. Entrepreneur in Politics*. New Haven, CT: Yale UP, 1994.

Marshall, Alfred. *Principles of Economics*, 8th ed. London: Macmillan, 1927.

Martin, Rex. 'Green on Natural Rights in Hobbes, Spinoza and Locke' in *The Philosophy of T. H. Green*, ed. Andrew Vincent. Aldershot, England: Gower, 1986.

Mason, John W. 'Political Economy and the Response to Socialism in Britain, 1870–1914,' *HJ*, 23 (1980), pp. 565–87.

Matsumura, Takao. *The Labour Aristocracy Revisited. The Victorian Flint Glass Makers 1850–80*. Manchester: Manchester UP, 1983.

Matthew, H. C. G. *Gladstone. 1809–1874*. Oxford: Clarendon, 1986.

—, ed. *The Gladstone Diaries*. 14 vols. Oxford: Clarendon, 1968–94.

Mayfield, David, and Susan Thorne. 'Social History and its Discontents: Gareth Stedman Jones and the Politics of Language,' *Social History*, 17 (1992), pp. 165–88.

Mazower, Mark. *The Balkans. A Short History*. New York: Modern Library, 2000.

Meacham, Standish. *Toynbee Hall and Social Reform, 1880–1914: the Search for Community*. New Haven, CT: Yale UP, 1987.

Meadowcroft, James. *Conceptualizing the State. Innovation and Dispute in British Political Thought 1880–1914*. Oxford: Clarendon, 1995.

Meerbote, R. 'Commentary [on Irwin]' in *Self and Nature in Kant's Philosophy*, ed. Allen W. Wood. Ithaca, NY: Cornell UP, 1984.

Mehta, U. S. *Liberalism and Empire: A Study in Nineteenth Century British Liberal Thought*. Chicago: Chicago UP, 1999.

Mehta, V. R. 'The Origins of English Idealism in Relation to Oxford,' *Journal of the History of Philosophy*, 13 (1975), pp. 177–87.

—, 'T. H. Green and the Problem of Political Obligation,' *Indian Political Science Review*, 7 (1973), pp. 115–24.

Meisel, Joseph S. *Public Speech and the Culture of Public Life in the Age of Gladstone*. New York: Columbia UP, 2001.

Miller, D., ed. *Liberty*. OUP, 1991.

Milne, A. J. M. *Ethical Frontiers of the State: an Essay in Political Philosophy*. New York: Macmillan/St. Martins, 1998.

—, 'The Idealist Critique of Utilitarian Social Philosophy,' *Archives Europèennes de sociologie*, 8 (1967), pp. 318–31.

—, *The Social Philosophy of English Idealism*. London: Allen and Unwin, 1962.

Mink, Louis O. *Mind, History and Dialectic. The Philosophy of R. G. Collingwood*. Bloomington, IN: Indiana UP, 1969.

Minor, Robert N. *Radhakrishnan: a Religious Biography*. Albany: SUNY Press, 1986.

Monsman, Gerald C. 'Old Mortality at Oxford,' *Studies in Philology*, 67 (1970), pp. 359–89.

Montagné, Paul. *Un Radical Religieux en Angleterre au XIXe Siècle ou la Philosophie de Thomas Hill Green*. Toulouse: Ouvrière, 1927.

Moore, G. E. *Philosophical Studies*. London: Routledge and Kegan Paul, 1948 [1922].

Morefield, Jeannie. 'Hegelian Organicism, British New Liberalism and the Return of the Family State,' *HPT*, 23 (2002), pp. 141–70.

Morgan, Kenneth O. *Keir Hardie. Radical and Socialist*. London: Weidenfeld and Nicolson, 1975.

—, *The People's Peace. British History 1945–1989*. OUP, 1990.

Morley, John. *Nineteenth Century Essays*. Ed. and with intro. by Peter Stansky. Chicago: UP Chicago, 1970.

Morrell, J., and A. Thackray. *Gentlemen of Science: Early Years of the B.A.A.S.*. Oxford: Clarendon, 1981.

Morrow, John. 'Ancestors, Legacies and Traditions: British Idealism in the History of Political Thought,' *HPT*, 6 (1985), pp. 491–515.

—, *Coleridge's Political Thought: Property, Morality and the Limits of Traditional Discourse*. New York: St. Martin's, 1990.

—, *A History of Political Thought. A Thematic Introduction*. New York: New York UP, 1998.

—, 'Introduction', *History of the Commonwealth of England: William Godwin*. Bristol: Thoemmes, 2003, pp. v–xxxiv.

—, 'Liberalism and British Idealist Political Philosophy: A Reassessment,' *HPT*, 5 (1984), pp. 91–108.

—, 'Private Property, Liberal Subjects, and the State' in *The New Liberalism: Reconciling Liberty and Community*, ed. Avital Simhony and D. Weinstein. CUP, 2001.

—, 'Property and Personal Development: an Interpretation of T. H. Green's Political Philosophy,' *Politics*, 18 (1983), pp. 84–92.

Muirhead, John Henry, ed. *Bernard Bosanquet and His Friends – Letters*. London: George Allen and Unwin, 1935.

Mukhopadhyay, Amal Kumar. *The Ethics of Obedience: A Study of the Philosophy of T. H. Green*. Calcutta: World Press, 1967.

Mure, G. R. G. *Idealist Epilogue*. Oxford: Clarendon, 1978.

—, Review of *La nature et l'esprit dans la philosophie de T. H. Green*, by J. Pucelle, *Philosophy*, 37 (1962), pp. 279–80.

Murphey, Howard R. 'The Ethical Revolt Against Orthodox Christianity in Early Victorian England,' *AHR*, 60 (1955), pp. 800–17.

Murray, Robert H. *Studies in the English Social and Political Thinkers of the Nineteenth Century*. 2 vols. Cambridge: W. Heffer and Sons, 1929.

Musson, A. E., ed. *Science, Technology, and Economic Growth in the Eighteenth Century*. London: Methuen, 1972.

Nandy, Ashis. 'Telling the Story of Communal Conflicts in South Asia,' *Ethnic and Racial Studies*, 25 (2002), pp. 1–19.

Neal, Patrick. 'In the Shadow of the General Will: Rawls, Kant and Rousseau on the Problems of Political Right,' *Review of Politics*, 49 (1987), pp. 389–409.

Nesbitt, Darin R. 'Recognizing Rights: Social Recognition in T. H. Green's System of Rights,' *Polity*, 33 (2001), pp. 423–37.

Nettleship, L. E. 'William Freemantle, Samuel Barnett and the Broad Church Origins of Toynbee Hall,' *Journal of Ecclesiastical History*, 33 (1982), pp. 564–79.

Newbould, Ian. *Whiggery and Reform, 1830–1841: the Politics of Government*. Palo Alto, CA: Stanford UP, 1990.

Newsome, David. *Godliness and Good Learning: Four Studies on a Victorian Ideal*. London: Cassell, 1961.

Nicholls, David. *Deity and Domination: Images of God and the State in the Nineteenth and Twentieth Centuries*. London: Routledge, 1994 [1989].

—, 'The English Middle Class and the Ideological Significance of Radicalism', *JBS*, 24 (1985), pp. 415–33.

—, 'Positive Liberty, 1880–1914,' *American Political Science Review*, 65 (1962), pp. 114–28.

Nicholson, Peter. 'Kant, Revolutions and History' in *Essays on Kant's Political Philosophy*, ed. H. L. Williams. Chicago: Chicago UP, 1992.

—, 'A Moral View of Politics: T. H. Green and the British Idealists,' *Political Studies*, 35 (1987), pp. 116–22.

—, *The Political Philosophy of the British Idealists*. CUP, 1990.

—, 'T. H. Green and State Action: Liquor Legislation,' *HPT*, 6 (1985), pp. 517–50. Reprinted in *The Philosophy of T. H. Green*, ed. Andrew Vincent. Aldershot, England: Gower, 1986.

—, 'Thomas Hill Green: *Lectures on the Principles of Political Obligation*' in *The Political Classics: Green to Dworkin*, ed. M. Forsyth and M. Keens-Soper. OUP, 1996.

Nord, Deborah Epstein. *The Apprenticeship of Beatrice Webb*. Ithaca, NY: Cornell UP, 1985.

Norman, E. R. *The Victorian Christian Socialists*. CUP, 1987.

Nozick, R. *Anarchy, State, and Utopia*. New York: Basic Books, 1974.

Oakeshott, Michael. *'On History' and Other Essays*. Totowa, NJ: Barnes and Noble, 1983.

Offer, Avner. *Property and Politics, 1870-1914: Landownership, Law, Ideology and Urban Development in England*. CUP, 1981.

Okin, Susan Moeller. *Women in Western Political Thought*. Princeton, NJ: Princeton UP, 1979.

O'Leary, C. *The Elimination of Corrupt Practices in British Elections, 1868-1911*. OUP, 1962.

Oman, Charles. *Memories of Victorian Oxford*. London: Methuen, 1941.

O'Sullivan, Noel Kerry. *Conservatism*. New York: St Martin's, 1976.

—, *The Problem of Political Obligation in the Writings of T. H. Green, Bernard Bosanquet and Michael Oakeshott*. New York: Garland, 1987.

Oxford Universal Dictionary, 3rd revised ed. Oxford: Clarendon, 1944 [official abridgement of the *Oxford English Dictionary*].

Pagden, Anthony, ed. *The Languages of Political Theory in Early Modern Europe*. CUP, 1987.

Paget, Steven, ed. *Henry Scott Holland. Memoir and Letters*. London: J. Murray, 1921.

Panagakou, Stamatoula. 'Religious Consciousness and the Realisation of the True Self: Bernard Bosanquet's Views on Religion in "What Religion Is",' *Bradley Studies*, 5, no. 2 (1999), pp. 139-61.

Pant, Nalini. 'Political Authority and Individual Liberty in Rousseau and Green: An Autopsy,' *Journal of Political Studies*, 7 (1974), pp. 70-7.

Parry, J. P. *Democracy and Religion: Gladstone and the Liberal Party,1867-1875*. CUP, 1986.

—, 'Religion and the Collapse of Gladstone's First Government, 1870-74,' *HJ*, 25 (1982), pp. 71-101.

—, *The Rise and Fall of Liberal Government in Victorian Britain*. New Haven, CT: Yale UP, 1993.

—, 'The State of Victorian Political History [review article],' *HJ*, 26 (1983), pp. 469-84.

Parsons, G., ed. *Religion in Victorian Britain. Volume 2: Controversies*. Manchester: Manchester UP, 1988.

Payne, P. L. *British Entrepreneurship in the Nineteenth Century*. London: Macmillan, 1974.

—, 'The Emergence of the Large-Scale Company in Great Britain, 1870-1914,' *Economic History Review*, 2nd ser., 20 (1967), pp. 519-42.

Pedersen, Susan. 'Eleanor Rathbone (1872-1946): the Victorian Family Under the Daughter's Eye' in *After the Victorians. Private Conscience and Public Duty in Modern Britain. Essays in Memory of John Clive*, ed.Pedersen and Peter Mandler. London/New York: Routledge, 1994.

Peel, J. D. Y. *Herbert Spencer: the Evolution of a Sociologist*. New York: Basic Books, 1971.

Pelling, Henry. *The Origins of the Labour Party, 1880-1900*, 2nd ed. Oxford: Clarendon, 1965.

Pennar Davies, W. T. *Mansfield College: Its History, Aims and Achievements*. Oxford: Privately printed, 1947.

Peperzak, A. T. *Reason in Faith: On the Relevance of Christian Spirituality for Philosophy*. Mahway, NJ: Paulist Press, 1999.

Perkin, Harold. *The Rise of Professional Society. England Since 1880*. London: Routledge, 1989.

—, *The Structured Crowd. Essays in English Social History*. Brighton: Harvester, 1981.

Perry, Marvin. *An Intellectual History of Modern Europe*. Boston: Houghton Mifflin, 1993.

Peterson, William S. 'Gladstone's Review of *Robert Elsmere*: Some Unpublished Correspondence,' *Review of English Studies*, 21 (1970), pp. 442-61.

Petrella, Frank. 'Individual, Group, or Government? Smith, Mill, and Sidgwick,' *History of Political Economy*, 2 (1970), pp. 152–76.

Pettit, Philip. *Republicanism: A Theory of Freedom and Government*. Oxford: Clarendon, 1997.

Phillips, Paul T. *The Sectarian Spirit: Sectarianism, Society, and Politics in Victorian Cotton Towns*. Toronto: Toronto UP, 1982.

Pierson, Stanley. *Marxism and the Origins of British Socialism*. Ithaca: Cornell UP, 1973.

Plamenatz, J. P. *Consent, Freedom and Political Obligation*. OUP, 1938.

—, *Mill's 'Utilitarianism' Reprinted with a Study of the English Utilitarians*. Oxford: Blackwell, 1949.

Plant, Raymond. *Politics, Theology and History*. CUP, 2001.

Plowright, John. 'Political Economy and Christian Polity: the Influence of Henry George in England Reassessed,' *VS*, 30 (1987), pp. 235–52.

Pocock, J. G. A. *The Machiavellian Moment: Florentine Political Thought and the Atlantic Republican Tradition*. Princeton, NJ: Princeton UP, 1975.

—, *Politics, Language, and Time: Essays on Political Thought and History*. Chicago: Chicago UP, 1971; reprint, 1989.

—, *Virtue, Commerce, and History: essays on political thought and history, chiefly in the eighteenth century*. CUP, 1985.

Pollock, Frederick. 'Sir Courtenay Peregrine Ilbert, G.C.B.,' *Proceedings of the British Academy*, 11 (1924–5), pp. 441–5.

Pombeni, Paolo. 'Starting in Reason, Ending in Passion. Bryce, Lowell, Ostrogorski and the Problem of Democracy,' *HJ*, 37 (1994), pp. 319–41.

Porter, Roy. *English Society in the Eighteenth Century*. London: Penguin, 1982.

Powell, David. 'The Liberal Ministries and Labour, 1893–1895,' *History*, 68 (1983): pp. 408–26.

Prest, J. M. 'The Death and Funeral of T. H. Green,' *Balliol College Annual Record 1998*, pp. 23–6.

—, ed. *Jowett's Correspondence with Earl Russell in 1867*. Oxford: Oxonian Press, 1965.

—, *Liberty and Locality. Parliament, Permissive Legislation, and Ratepayers' Democracies in the Nineteenth Century*. Oxford: Clarendon, 1990.

Price, Richard. 'Historiography, Narrative, and the Nineteenth Century', *JBS*, 35 (1996), pp. 220–56.

Prichard, H. A. *Moral Obligation. Essays and Lectures*. Oxford: Clarendon, 1949.

Prickett, Steven. *Romanticism and Religion: the Tradition of Coleridge and Wordsworth in the Victorian Church*. CUP, 1976.

Pucelle, Jean. *La nature et l'esprit dans la philosophie de T. H. Green*. 2 vols. Louvain: Nauwelaerts, 1961–5.

Pugh, M. 'The Limits of Liberalism: Liberals and Women's Suffrage, 1867–1914' in *Citizenship and Community. Liberals, Radicals and Collective Identities in the British Isles, 1865–1931*, ed. Eugenio F. Biagini. CUP, 1996.

Punter, D. *Blake, Hegel and Dialectic*. Amsterdam: Rodopi B. V., 1982.

Quinn, E. V. and John Prest, eds. *Dear Miss Nightingale. A Selection of Benjamin Jowett's Letters to Florence Nightingale, 1860–1893*. Oxford: Clarendon, 1987.

Quinton, Anthony. 'Absolute Idealism,' *Proceedings of the British Academy*, 57 (1971), pp. 303–29.

—, 'Collingwood, Robin George' in *Twentieth-Century Culture. A Biographical Companion*, ed. Alan Bullock and R. B. Woodings. New York: Harper and Row, 1983.

Rait, R. S. 'Dicey, Albert Venn' in *Dictionary of National Biography: 1922–1930, fourth supplement*.

—, ed. *Memorials of A. V. Dicey. Being Chiefly Letters and Diaries*. London: Macmillan, 1925.

Randall, J. H., Jr. *Philosophy After Darwin [Collected Essays]*, ed. B. J. Singer. New York: Columbia UP, 1977.

Rawls, John. *A Theory of Justice*. Cambridge, MA: Harvard UP, 1971.

Razavi, Mehdi Amin, and David Ambuel, eds. *Philosophy, Religion and the Question of Intolerance*. Albany, NY: SUNY Press, 1997.

Reader, W. J. *Professional Men. The Rise of the Professional Classes in Nineteenth–Century England*. London: Weidenfeld and Nicolson, 1966.

Reardon, B. M. G. *From Coleridge to Gore. A Century of Religious Thought in Britain*. London: Longman, 1971.

—, *Religion in the Age of Romanticism. Studies in Early Nineteenth Century Thought*. CUP, 1985.

—, 'T. H. Green as a Theologian' in *The Philosophy of T. H. Green*, ed. Andrew Vincent. Aldershot, England: Gower, 1986.

Reid, F. 'Keir Hardie's Conversion to Socialism' in *Essays in Labour History 1886–1923*, ed. Asa Briggs and John Saville. Hamden, CT: Archon, 1971.

Reiss, H. S., ed. *The Political Thought of the German Romantics 1793–1815*. New York: Macmillan, 1955.

Reventlow, Henning Graf, and W. Farmer, eds. *Biblical Studies and the Shifting of Paradigms, 1850–1914*. Sheffield: Sheffield Academic Press, 1995.

Rich, Paul. 'T. H. Green, Lord Scarman and the Issue of Ethnic Minority Rights in English Liberal Thought,' *Ethnic and Racial Studies*, 10 (1987), pp. 149–68.

Richards, N. J. 'British Nonconformity and the Liberal Party 1868–1906,' *Journal of Religious History*, 9 (1977), pp. 387–401.

—, 'Religious Controversy and the School Boards, 1870–1902,' *British Journal of Educational Studies*, 18 (1970), pp. 180–96.

Richter, Melvin. *The History of Political and Social Concepts: A Critical Introduction*. OUP, 1995.

—, 'Intellectual and Class Alienation: Oxford Idealist Diagnoses and Prescriptions,' *European Journal of Sociology*, 7 (1966), pp. 1–26.

—, *The Politics of Conscience: T. H. Green and His Age*. London: Weidenfeld and Nicolson, 1964.

—, 'Reconstructing the History of Political Languages,' *History and Theory*, 29 (1990), pp. 38–70.

—, 'T. H. Green and His Audience: Liberalism as a Surrogate Faith,' *Review of Politics*, 18 (1956), pp. 444–72.

Riedel, Manfred. *Zwischen Tradition und Revolution: Studien zu Hegels Rechtsphilosophie*. Stuttgart: Klett–Cotta, 1982.

Ringer, Fritz. *The Decline of the German Mandarins. The German Academic Community, 1890–1933*. Cambridge, MA: MIT UP, 1969.

—, *Max Weber's Methodology: the Unification of the Cultural and Social Sciences*. Cambridge, MA: Harvard UP, 1997.

Ritter, Joachim. *Hegel und die französische Revolution*. Frankfurt: Suhrkamp, 1965.

Roach, John. 'Liberalism and the Victorian Intelligentsia,' *Cambridge Historical Review*, 13 (1957), pp. 58–81.

Robbins, Keith. *John Bright*. London: Routledge Kegan Paul, 1979.

—, *Nineteenth–Century Britain. England, Scotland and Wales: the Making of a Nation*. OUP, 1988.

Robbins, Peter. *The British Hegelians, 1875–1925*. New York: Garland, 1982.

Roberts, David. *The Early Victorian Origins of the British Welfare State*. New Haven, CT: Yale UP, 1960.

—, *Paternalism in Early Victorian England*. New Brunswick, NJ: Rutgers UP, 1979.

Robertson, J. M. *The Meaning of Liberalism*. London, 1925; reprint, Port Washington, NY: Kennikat, 1971.

Robson, R., ed. *Ideas and Institutions of Victorian Britain. Essays in Honour of George Kitson Clark.* London: G. Bell and Sons, 1967.

Rodman, John. 'What Is Living and What Is Dead in the Philosophy of T. H. Green,' *Western Political Quarterly,* 26 (1973), pp. 566–86.

Rogers, Arthur Kenyon. *English and American Philosophy Since 1800. A Critical Survey.* New York: Macmillan, 1922.

Rorty, Richard. *Philosophical Papers. Volume Two* (CUP, 1991).

—, *Philosophy and the Mirror of Nature.* Princeton, NJ: Princeton UP, 1979.

Rosenblum, Nancy. *Another Liberalism.* Cambridge, MA: Harvard UP, 1987.

—, *Bentham's Theory of the Modern State.* Cambridge, MA: Harvard UP, 1978.

—, ed. *Liberalism and the Moral Life.* Cambridge, MA: Harvard UP, 1989.

Rostow, W. W. *British Economy of the Nineteenth Century.* Oxford: Clarendon, 1948.

Rothblatt, Sheldon. *Revolution of the Dons: Cambridge and Society in Victorian England.* New York: Basic, 1968.

Routh, D. A. 'The Philosophy of International Relations: T. H. Green versus Hegel,' *Politica,* 3 (1938), pp. 223–35.

Rowbotham, Sheila. 'The Call to University Extension Teaching 1873–1900,' *University of Birmingham Historical Journal,* 12 (1969), pp. 57–71.

Rowland, W. J. 'Some Free Church Pioneers of Social Reform,' *Congregational Quarterly,* 35 (1957), pp. 134–45.

Royle, Edward. *Radicals, Secularists and Republicans. Popular Freethought in Britain, 1866–1915.* Manchester: Manchester UP, 1980.

Rubinstein, William D. *Men of Property: the Very Wealthy in Britain Since the Industrial Revolution.* London: Croom Helm, 1987.

de Ruggerio, Guido. *The History of European Liberalism,* trans. R. G. Collingwood. OUP, 1927.

Rupp, E. G. *Religion in England, 1688–1791.* OUP, 1986.

Russell, A. K. *Liberal Landslide. The General Election of 1906.* Newton Abbot, Devon: David and Charles, 1973.

Ryan, Alan, ed. *John Stuart Mill and Jeremy Bentham. 'Utilitarianism' and Other Essays.* London: Penguin, 1987.

—, *The Philosophy of John Stuart Mill,* 2nd ed. London: Macmillan, 1987.

Sabine, George H. *A History of Political Theory.* London: Harrap, 1937.

Salter, F. R. *Dissenters and Public Affairs in Mid–Victorian England.* London: Dr. Williams's Trust, 1967.

—, 'Political Nonconformity in the Eighteen–Thirties,' *Transactions of the Royal Historical Society,* 5th ser. 3 (1953), pp. 125–43.

Sampson, R. V. 'The Limits of Religious Thought: the Theological Controversy' in *1859: Entering an Age of Crisis,* ed. P. Appleman, W. A. Madden and M. Wolff. Bloomington, IN: Indiana UP, 1959.

de Sanctis, Alberto. *La democrazia 'Puritana' di Thomas Hill Green.* Florence: Centro Editoriale Toscana, 2002.

Sandel, Michael. *Liberalism and the Limits of Justice.* CUP, 1982.

Sansom, T. R. 'From God to Man? F. D. Maurice and Changing Ideas of God and Man' in *Religion, Secularization, and Political Thought. Thomas Hobbes to J. S. Mill,* ed. J. E. Crimmins. London: Routledge, 1989.

Sawer, Marian. 'The Ethical State: Social Liberalism and the Critique of Contract,' *Australian Historical Studies,* 114 (2000), pp. 67–90.

—, 'Reclaiming the State: Feminism, Liberalism and Social Liberalism,' *Australian Journal of Politics and History,* 40 [special issue] (1994), pp. 159–72.

Scally, R. J. *The Origins of the Lloyd George Coalition. The Politics of Social Imperialism, 1900–1918.* Princeton, NJ: Princeton UP, 1975.

Schneewind, J. B. 'Moral Problems and Moral Philosophy in the Victorian Period,' *VS*, 9 [supplement] (1965), pp. 29–46.

—, *Sidgwick's Ethics and Victorian Moral Philosophy*. Oxford: Clarendon, 1977.

Schreuder, D. M. 'Gladstone and the Conscience of the State' in *The Conscience of the Victorian State*, ed. Peter Marsh. Syracuse, NY: Syracuse UP, 1979.

—, 'Gladstone and Italian Unification: The Making of a Liberal?,' *EHR*, 85 (1970), pp. 475–501.

Schueller, H. M., and R. L. Peters, eds. *Letters of John Addington Symonds*. 3 vols. Detroit: Wayne State UP, 1967–9.

Schuffenhauer, Werner. *Feuerbach und der junge Marx. Zur Entstehungsgeschichte der marxistischen Weltanschauung*. Berlin: Deutscher Verlag der Wissenschaften, 1965.

Schwaiger, Georg, ed. *Historische Kritik in der Theologie: Beitraege zu ihre Geschichte*. Goettingen: Vandenhoeck & Ruprecht, 1980.

Scotland, N. 'The National Agricultural Labourers' Union and the demand for a stake in the soil, 1872–1896' in *Citizenship and Community. Liberals, Radicals and Collective Identities in the British Isles, 1865–1931*, ed. Eugenio F. Biagini. CUP, 1996.

Scott, W. R. 'Alfred Marshall,' *Proceedings of the British Academy*, vol. 11 (1924–25), pp. 446–57.

Searle, G. E. *The Quest for National Efficiency: A Study in British Politics and Political Thought, 1899–1914*. Los Angeles and Berkeley: California UP, 1971.

Seccombe, Wally. 'Patriarchy Stabilized: the Construction of the Male Breadwinner Wage Norm in Nineteenth–Century Britain,' *Social History*, 11 (1986): pp. 53–76.

Seed, John. 'Theologies of Power: Unitarianism and the Social Relations of Religious Discourse, 1800–50' in *Class, Power and Social Structure in British Nineteenth–Century Towns*, ed. R. J. Morris. Leicester: Leicester UP, 1986.

—, 'Unitarianism, Political Economy and the Antinomies of Liberal Culture in Manchester, 1830–50,' *Social History*, 7 (1982), pp. 1–25.

Selbie, W. B. 'Fifty Years at Oxford,' *Congregational Quarterly*, 14 (1936), pp. 282–90.

Sell. A. P. F. *Philosophical Idealism and Christian Belief*. New York: St. Martin's, 1995.

—, *The Philosophy of Religion, 1875–1980*. London: Croom Helm, 1988.

Semmel, Bernard. *The Governor Eyre Controversy*. London: MacGibbon and Kee, 1962.

—, *John Stuart Mill and the Pursuit of Virtue*. New Haven, CT: Yale UP, 1984.

—, *The Methodist Revolution*. New York: Basic, 1973.

Sen, Amartya. *Inequality Reexamined*. Delhi: OUP, 1992.

Shanley, Mary Lyndon. *Feminism, Marriage, and the Law in Victorian England, 1850–1895*. London: I. B. Tauris, 1989.

Shannon, Richard. *The Age of Salisbury, 1881–1902: Unionism and Empire*. London and New York: Longman, 1996.

—, *The Crisis of Imperialism 1865–1915*. London: Hart–Davis, MacGibbon, 1974; reprint, London: Palladin–Granada, 1976.

—, *Gladstone. Volume One: 1809–1865*. London: Hamilton, 1982.

—, *Gladstone and the Bulgarian Agitation 1876*. London: Thomas Nelson, 1963.

Shaw, Christopher. 'Eliminating the Yahoo: Eugenics, Social Darwinism and Five Fabians,' *HPT*, 8 (1987), pp. 521–44.

Sheehan, James J. *German Liberalism in the Nineteenth Century*. Chicago: UP Chicago, 1978.

Shiman, L. L. *The Crusade Against Drink in Victorian England*. New York: St Martin's, 1988.

Simhony, Avital. 'Beyond Negative and Positive Freedom: T. H. Green's View of Freedom,' *Political Theory*, 21 (1993), pp. 28–54.

—, 'Idealist Organicism: Beyond Holism and Individualism,' *HPT*, 12 (1991), pp. 515–35.

—, and D. Weinstein, eds. *The New Liberalism: Reconciling Liberty and Community*. CUP, 2001.

—, 'T. H. Green: The Common Good Society,' *HPT*, 14 (1993), pp. 225–47.

—, 'T. H. Green's Complex Good' in *The New Liberalism: Reconciling Liberty and Community*, eds. Simhony and D. Weinstein. CUP, 2001.

—, 'T. H. Green's Theory of the Morally Justified Society,' *HPT*, 10 (1989), pp. 405–20.

Skinner, Quentin. *Foundations of Modern Political Thought. Volume I: the Renaissance*. CUP, 1978.

—, *Liberty Before Liberalism*. CUP, 1998.

—, 'Meaning and Understanding in the History of Ideas,' *History and Theory*, 8 (1969), pp. 3–53.

Skorupski, John. 'Desire and Will in Sidgwick and Green,' *Utilitas*, 12 (2000), pp. 307–28.

Smiechen, James A. *Sweated Industries and Sweated Labor: The London Clothing Trades, 1860–1914*. Urbana, IL: Illinois UP, 1984.

Smith, Bruce James. *Politics and Remembrance: Republican Themes in Machiavelli, Burke, and Tocqueville*. Princeton, NJ: Princeton UP, 1985.

Smith, Craig A. 'The Individual and Society in T. H. Green's Theory of Virtue,' *HPT*, 2 (1981), pp. 187–201.

—, 'T. H. Green's Philosophical Manuscripts: An Annotated Catalogue,' *Idealistic Studies*, 9 (1979), pp. 178–84.

Smith, Dennis. *Conflict and Compromise. Class Formation in English Society 1830–1914. A Comparative Study of Birmingham and Sheffield*. London: Routledge Kegan Paul, 1982.

Smith, G. W. Review of *The Political Philosophy of the British Idealists*, by P. Nicholson, *Political Theory*, 19 (1991), pp. 306–9.

Smith, Paul. *Disraelian Conservatism and Social Reform*. London: Macmillan, 1967.

Smith, Quentin. *Ethical and Religious Thought in Analytic Philosophy of Language*. New Haven, CT: Yale UP, 1998.

Soffer, Reba N. *Discipline and Power. The University, History, and the Making of an English Elite, 1870–1930*. Palo Alto, CA: Stanford UP, 1994.

—, 'The Revolution in English Social Thought 1880–1914,' *AHR*, 75 (1970), pp. 1938–64.

Somervell, D. C. *English Thought in the Nineteenth Century*, 6th ed. London: Methuen, 1950.

Southgate, Donald. *The Passing of the Whigs, 1832–86*. London: Macmillan, 1962.

Sparrow, John H. *Mark Pattison and the Idea of a University*. CUP, 1967.

Stack, D. A. 'The First Darwinian Left: Radical and Socialist Responses to Darwin, 1859–1914,' *HPT*, 21 (2000), pp. 682–710.

Stapleton, Julia. 'Dicey and His Legacy,' *HPT*, 16 (1995), pp. 234–55.

—, ed. *Liberalism, Democracy, and the State in Britain: Five Essays, 1862–1891*. Bristol: Thoemmes, 1997.

—, *Political Intellectuals and Public Identities in Britain Since 1850*. Manchester: Manchester UP, 2001.

—, 'Political Thought, Elites, and the State in Modern Britain [review essay],' *HJ*, 42 (1999), pp. 251–68.

Stern, Fritz. *The Politics of Cultural Despair: a Study in the Rise of the Germanic Ideology*. Berkeley, CA: California UP, 1961.

Stoeffler, F. E. 'Pietism' in *Encyclopedia of Religion*, ed. M. Eliade. New York: Macmillan, 1987.

Stokes, Eric. *The English Utilitarians and India*. Oxford: Clarendon, 1959.

Storey, John. 'Matthew Arnold: The Politics of An Organic Intellectual,' *Literature and History*, 11 (1985), pp. 217–28.

Strachey, John St Loe. *The Adventure of Living: A Subjective Autobiography (1860–1922)*. London: Hodder and Stoughton, 1922.

Stuurman, Siep. 'The Canon of the History of Political Thought: Its Critique and a Proposed Alternative,' *History and Theory*, 39 (2000), pp. 147–66.

Sutherland, Gillian. 'The Movement for the Higher Education of Women: its Social and Intellectual Context in England, ca 1840–80' in *Politics and Social Change in Modern Britain. Essays Presented to A. F. Thompson*, ed. P. J. Waller. Hassocks, Sussex: Harvester, 1987.

—, *Policy-Making in Elementary Education, 1870–1895*. OUP, 1973.

Sutherland, John. *Mrs. Humphry Ward. Eminent Victorian, Pre-Eminent Edwardian*. OUP, 1991.

Sweet, William. *Idealism and Rights. The Social Ontology of Human Rights in the Political Thought of Bernard Bosanquet*. Lanham, MD: UP America, 1997.

Symonds, R. *Oxford and Empire: the Last Lost Cause?* London: Macmillan, 1986; reprint, Oxford: Clarendon, 1991.

Tawney, R. H. *Religion and the Rise of Capitalism. A Historical Study*. New York: Harcourt, Brace and World, 1926; reprint, Gloucester, MA: P. Smith, 1962.

Taylor, A. E. 'Francis Herbert Bradley,' *Proceedings of the British Academy*, 11 (1924–25), pp. 458–68.

Taylor, Barbara. 'Religion, Radicalism, and Fantasy,' *History Workshop Journal*, (1995), pp. 102–11.

Taylor, Charles. *Hegel and Modern Society*. CUP, 1979.

Taylor, Michael, ed. *Herbert Spencer and the Limits of the State. The Late Nineteenth-Century Debate Between Liberalism and Collectivism*. Bristol: Thoemmes Press, 1996.

—, *Men Versus the State. Herbert Spencer and Late Victorian Individualism*. Oxford: Clarendon, 1992.

Taylor, Miles. 'The Beginnings of Modern British Social History?,' *History Workshop Journal*, 43 (1997), pp. 155–76.

—, *The Decline of British Radicalism, 1847–1860*. Oxford: Clarendon, 1995.

Temmel, M. R. 'Liberal Versus Liberal, 1874: W. E. Forster, Bradford and Education,' *HJ*, 18 (1975), pp. 611–22.

Terrill, Ross. *R. H. Tawney and His Times. Socialism as Fellowship*. Cambridge, MA: Harvard UP, 1973.

Tholfsen, Trygve. *Working-Class Radicalism in Mid Victorian Britain*. London: Croom Helm, 1976.

Thomas, Donald. *Swinburne. The Poet in his World*. OUP, 1979.

Thomas, Geoffrey. *The Moral Philosophy of T. H. Green*. Oxford: Clarendon, 1987.

Thomas, William. *The Philosophic Radicals*. Oxford: Clarendon, 1979.

Thompson, Dennis F. *John Stuart Mill and Representative Government*. Princeton, NJ: Princeton UP, 1976.

Thompson, D. M. 'The Liberation Society 1844–1868' in *Pressure from Without in Early Victorian England*, ed. Patricia Hollis. New York: St Martin's, 1974.

Thompson, E. P. *The Making of the English Working Class*. London, 1963; reprint, New York: Vintage-Random, 1966.

Thompson, F. M. L. *The Rise of Respectable Society: A Social History of Victorian Britain, 1830–1900*. London: Fontana, 1988.

Thompson, Paul. *Socialists, Liberals and Labour: the Struggle for London, 1885–1914*. London: Routledge and Kegan Paul, 1967.

Tillyard, F. 'The Oxford Nonconformists' Union, 1883–1886,' *Congregational Quarterly*, 25 (1947), pp. 133–7.

Toews, John E. *Hegelianism: the Path Toward Dialectical Humanism, 1805–1841*. CUP, 1980.

Tuck, Richard. *Natural Rights Theories. Their Origin and Development*. CUP, 1979.

Turner, Frank M. *Between Science and Religion: The Reaction to Scientific Naturalism in Late Victorian England.* New Haven, CT: Yale UP, 1974.

—, *The Greek Heritage in Victorian Britain.* New Haven, CT: Yale UP, 1981.

Tyler, Colin. *Thomas Hill Green and the Philosophical Foundations of Politics: An Internal Critique.* Lewiston, NY: Edwin Mellen Pess, 1997.

Tyrrell, Alex. *Joseph Sturge and the Moral Radical Party in Early Victorian Britain.* London: Croom Helm, 1987.

Ulam, Adam B. *Philosophical Foundations of English Socialism.* Cambridge, MA: Harvard UP, 1951.

Vernon, James. *Politics and the People. A Study in English Political Culture, c.1815–1867.* CUP, 1993.

—, ed. *Re-Reading the Constitution. New Narratives in the Political History of England's Long Nineteenth Century.* CUP, 1996.

Vernon, R. 'J. S. Mill and the Religion of Humanity' in *Religion, Secularization, and Political Thought. Thomas Hobbes to J. S. Mill*, ed. J. E. Crimmins. London: Routledge, 1989.

Vincent, Andrew. 'Classical Liberalism and its Crisis of Identity,' *HPT*, 11 (1990), pp. 143–61.

—, 'The New Liberalism in Britain, 1880–1914,' *Australian Journal of Politics and History*, 36 (1990), pp. 388–405.

—, ed. *The Philosophy of T.H. Green.* Aldershot, England: Gower, 1986.

—, 'The Poor Law Reports of 1909 and the Social Theory of the Charity Organisation Society,' *VS*, 27 (1984), pp. 43–63.

—, 'The State and Social Purpose in Idealist Political Philosophy,' *History of European Ideas*, 8 (1987), pp. 333–47.

Vincent, Andrew, and Raymond Plant. *Philosophy, Politics and Citizenship: The Life and Thought of the British Idealists.* Oxford: Blackwell, 1984.

Vincent, David. *Literacy and Popular Culture. England 1750–1914.* CUP, 1989.

Vincent, John. *The Formation of the British Liberal Party, 1857–68*, 2nd. ed. Hassocks, Sussex: Harvester, 1976.

Vogel, Ursula. 'Liberty is Beautiful: Von Humboldt's Gift to Liberalism,' *HPT*, 3 (1982), pp. 77–101.

Von Arx, J. P. *Progress and Pessimism: Religion, Politics and History in Late Nineteenth–Century Britain.* Cambridge, MA: Harvard UP, 1985.

Wahrman, Dror. *Imagining the Middle Class. The Political Representation of Class in Britain, c.1780–1840.* CUP, 1995.

Walcott, Fred G. *The Origins of 'Culture and Anarchy'. Matthew Arnold and Popular Education in England.* Toronto: Toronto UP, 1970.

Waldron, Jeremy. 'Theoretical Foundations of Liberalism,' *Philosophical Quarterly*, 37 (1987), pp. 127–50.

Walkowitz, Judith R. *City of Dreadful Delight. Narratives of Sexual Danger in Late–Victorian London.* Chicago: UP Chicago, 1992.

—, *Prostitution and Victorian Society: Women, Class, and the State.* CUP, 1980.

Wallace, Elizabeth. *Goldwin Smith, Victorian Liberal.* Toronto: Toronto UP, 1957.

Walsh, W. H. 'Green's Criticism of Hume' in *The Philosophy of T. H. Green*, ed. Andrew Vincent. Aldershot, England: Gower, 1986.

—, 'Green, Thomas Hill' in *Encyclopedia of Philosophy*, ed. P. Edwards. New York: Macmillan, 1967.

—, *Kant's Criticism of Metaphysics.* Chicago: UP Chicago, 1975.

Walzer, Michael. *The Revolution of the Saints: A Study in the Origins of Radical Politics.* Cambridge, MA: Harvard UP, 1965.

Ward, Humphry, Mrs. [Mary Augusta Arnold Ward]. *A Writer's Recollections.* London: W. Collins, 1918.

Ward, W. R. *The Protestant Evangelical Awakening*. CUP, 1992.

—, *Victorian Oxford*. London: Frank Cass and Co., 1965.

—, 'The Way of the World: the Rise and Decline of Protestant Social Christianity in Britain,' *Kirchliche Zeitgeschichte*, 1 (1988), pp. 293–305.

—, 'Zinzendorf and Money,' *Studies in Church History*, 24 (1987), pp. 283–305.

Warnock, Geoffrey. *English Philosophy Since 1900*. OUP, 1958.

—, Review of G. Thomas, *The Moral Philosophy of T. H. Green*, *Times Literary Supplement*, 3 June1988, p. 606.

Waszek, Norbert. *The Scottish Enlightenment and Hegel's Account of 'Civil Society'*. The Hague: M. Nijhoff, 1988.

Waterhouse, Rachel. *The Birmingham and Midland Institute 1854–1954*. Birmingham: Birmingham Mail Ltd., 1954.

Waterman, A. M. C. *Revolution, Economics and Religion: Christian Political Economy, 1798–1833*. CUP, 1991.

Watson, David. 'Social Theory and National Culture: The Case of British and American Absolute Idealism, 1860–1900,' *Social Science History*, 5 (1981), pp. 251–74.

Watts, Michael. *The Dissenters: Reformation to French Revolution*. Oxford: Clarendon, 1978.

Wearmouth, R. F. *Methodism and the Struggle of the Working Classes, 1850–1900*. Leicester: Leicester UP, 1954.

Webb, R. K. 'The Limits of Religious Liberty: Theology and Criticism in Nineteenth Century England' in *Freedom and Religion in the Nineteenth Century*, ed. Richard J. Helmstadter. Palo Alto, CA: Stanford UP, 1997.

—, *Modern England. From the Eighteenth Century to the Present*, 2nd ed. New York: Harper and Row, 1980.

Weiler, Peter. *The New Liberalism: Liberal Social Theory in Great Britain*. New York: Garland, 1982.

Weinstein, David. 'Between Kantianism and Consequentialism in T. H. Green's Moral Philosophy,' *Political Studies*, 41 (1993), pp. 618–35.

—, 'The New Liberalism and the Rejection of Utilitarianism' in *The New Liberalism: Reconciling Liberty and Community*, ed. A. Simhony and Weinstein. CUP, 2001.

—, 'The New Liberalism of L. T. Hobhouse and the Reenvisioning of Nineteenth-Century Utilitarianism,' *Journal of the History of Ideas*, 57 (1996), pp. 487–507.

Weinstein, W. L. 'The Concept of Liberty in Nineteenth Century English Political Thought,' *Political Studies*, 13 (1965), pp. 145–62.

Weischedel, W. *Der Gott der Philosophen*. Darmstadt: Wissenschaftliche Buchgesellschaft, 1983.

Weithman, Paul J., ed. *Religion and Contemporary Liberalism*. Notre Dame, IN: Notre Dame UP, 1997.

Weldon, T. D. *The Vocabulary of Politics*. London: Penguin, 1957.

Wempe, Ben. *Beyond Equality: A Study of T. H. Green's Theory of Positive Freedom*. Delft, Netherlands: Eburon, 1986.

Wendehorst, S., 'Emancipation as Path to National Integration', in *The Emancipation of Catholics, Jews and Protestants: Minorities and the Nation-State in Nineteenth-Century Europe*, ed. R. Liedtke and S. Wendehorst. Manchester: Manchester UP, 1999.

Wiener, Martin. *Between Two Worlds. The Political Thought of Graham Wallas*. Oxford: Clarendon, 1971.

—, *English Culture and the Decline of the Industrial Spirit*. CUP, 1981.

Wilkinson, William J. *Tory Democracy*. New York: Columbia UP, 1925; reprint, New York: Farrar, Straus and Giroux, 1980.

Willey, Basil. *Nineteenth Century Studies. Coleridge to Matthew Arnold*. New York: Columbia UP, 1949.

—, *The Seventeenth Century Background*. London: Chatto and Windus, 1934.

Williams, H. G. 'Arthur Acland, Tom Ellis and Welsh Education: A Study in the Politics of Idealism,' *Welsh History Review*, 17 (1995), pp. 387–410.

Williams, Raymond. *Culture and Society: 1780–1950*, new ed. New York: Columbia UP, 1983.

Willis, Kirk. 'The Introduction and Critical Reception of Hegelian Thought in Britain, 1830–1900,' *VS*, 32 (1988), pp. 85–111.

Wilson, A. N. *God's Funeral*. New York: W. W. Norton, 1999.

Wolfe, Willard. *From Radicalism to Socialism*. New Haven: Yale UP, 1975.

Wollheim, Richard. *F. H. Bradley*. London: Penguin, 1959.

Woloch, Isser. *Eighteenth-Century Europe. Tradition and Progress, 1715–1789*. New York: Norton, 1982.

Wolpert, Stanley. *A New History of India*, 2nd ed. OUP, 1982.

Wood, Allen W., ed., *Self and Nature in Kant's Philosophy*. Ithaca, NY: Cornell UP, 1984.

—, 'Unsocial Sociability: the Anthropological Basis of Kantian Ethics,' *Philosophical Topics*, 19 (1991), pp. 325–51.

Wright, T. R. *The Religion of Humanity: the Impact of Comtean Positivism on Victorian Britain*. CUP, 1986.

Yeo, R. 'Science and Intellectual Authority in Mid Nineteenth-Century Britain: Robert Chambers and *Vestiges of the Natural History of Creation*' in *Energy and Entropy. Science and Culture in Victorian Britain*, ed. Patrick Brantlinger. Bloomington, IN: Indiana UP, 1989.

Zeldin, Theodore, ed. *Conflicts in French Society. Anticlericalism, Education and Morals in the Nineteenth Century*. London: Allen and Unwin, 1970.

VI
THESES AND DISSERTATIONS

Copeland, John Wilson. 'Green, Bradley, and Sidgwick on the Ultimate Good.' Ph.D. diss., Cornell University, 1953.

Hebrank, H. G. 'Manchester and the Struggle for Nondenominational Education, 1847–1870.' Ph.D. diss., University of Minnesota, 1976.

Lawless, Mervyn Andrew. 'Liberty and Class Conflict in the Nineteenth-Century British Liberal State: T. H. Green's concept of freedom in relationship to the development of the liberal tradition in Britain.' Ph.D. diss., University of London, 1976.

Lynn, Paul. 'Thomas Hill Green (1836–82) and His Involvement in Victorian Education.' B.Ed. thesis, University of Manchester, 1976.

Matross, G. N. 'T. H. Green and the Concept of Rights.' Ph.D. diss., University of Kansas, 1972.

Mehta, V. R. 'T. H. Green's Ideas in Relation to his Time, with Special Reference to his Social and Political Thought.' D.Phil. thesis, Cambridge University, 1971.

Orr, Robert R. 'The Neo-Idealist Origins of British Social Democracy.' Ph.D. diss., University of Maine, 1979.

Simchoni [Simhony], Avital. 'The Political and Social Thought of the British Idealists.' D.Phil. thesis, Oxford University, 1980.

Smith, C. A. 'A Critical Study of T. H. Green's Theory of Political Obligation.' Ph.D. diss., London School of Economics, 1977.

Townsend, H. G. 'The Principle of Individuality in the Philosophy of Thomas Hill Green.' Ph.D. diss., Cornell University, 1914.

Vogeler, A. R. 'Disestablishmentarianism: The Liberationist Crusade Against the Church of England.' Ph.D. diss., Columbia University, 1973.

Watson, David John. 'Idealism and Social Theory: A Comparative Study of British and American Adaptations of Hegel, 1860–1914.' Ph.D. diss., University of Pennsylvania, 1975.

VII
UNPUBLISHED CONFERENCE PAPERS

Armour, Leslie. 'Green's Idealism and the Metaphysic of Ethics.' Paper presented to the conference 'T. H. Green and Contemporary Philosophy,' Harris Manchester College, Oxford, 2–4 September 2002.

Leighton, Denys. 'T. H. Green and the Social Aspects of Evangelicalism,' Middle Common Room Occasional Paper, Mansfield College, Oxford, 30 May 1991.

de Sanctis, Alberto. 'T. H. Green and the "Force of Circumstances": Can Uncommon Individuality Be Consistent with Democracy?' Paper presented to the Political Studies Association (UK), London, 50th Annual Conference, 10–13 April 2000.

Index

Vaughan, David James ('Uncle David'), 45, 144, 146-9, 171, 307n
Vaughan, Robert, 177 and n, 199
Venn, John, 145
Vernon, James, 237
Vico, Giambatista, 63n
Victoria, Queen, 220n
Vincent, Andrew, 37-8, 130, 132, 282, 320
Vincent, Henry, 192
Vincent, John, 9, 194 and n, 293, 322
virtu and virtue, 79, 95n, 101, 106, 108,123-6, 138n, 156n, 222, 260, 283, 290, 292-3, 322
Voltaire, 138n, 145n, 158, 198, 319
Volunteer Movement, 12-13, 103n

W

Wadsworth, S., 225
Wahrman, Dror, 237
Wales, 196, 203n, 226, 242n, 255, 263n, 296, 306
Walkowitz, Judith, 23n, 244, 245n, 256
Wallace, William, 62n, 68n, 86n, 281
Wallas, Graham, 57, 74, 275
Walsh, W. H., 104n
Ward, Mrs. (Thomas) Humphry, 10, 41n, 82, 231n, 250-1, 277 and n, 286- 7, 302, 307-9; _Robert Elsmere_, 10, 82, 251 and n, 274n
Ward, Thomas Humphry, 82, 287n
Ward, W. G., 41n
Watts, Isaac, 195
Webb, Beatrice, 227, 230, 250, 251n, 277, 295-6, 307n
Webb, Robert K., 147
Webb, Sidney, 230, 233, 238, 247, 264, 277, 283, 293, 295-6, 298n, 299
Weber, Max, ix, 25, 69, 156n, 200n, 317-18
Wempe, Ben, 11, 37, 42n, 51n, 52
Wesley, Charles, 140, 157-8
Wesley, John, 140, 154, 157-9, 172, 185, 196, 271
Westcott, F. B., 147, 260, 261n
Whewell, William, 96
Whig idea of history and Whiggism, 4, 173, 174 and n, 188, 198, 235n, 238- 40
Whigs, 8, 12, 23, 134n, 146, 196, 198-9, 240, 263
Whitechapel, 148, 229
Whitefield, George, 140

Whyte's Professorship of Moral Philosophy (_see also_ University of Oxford), 79, 57, 61
Wicksteed, Philip Henry, 75, 275 and n
Wiener, Martin, 227n
Wilberforce, Samuel, 42-3, 167
Wilberforce, William, 145 and n, 269
Wilde, Oscar, 125n
Wilkinson, Ellen, 216n
Williams, Raymond, 184n
Wilson, A. N., 6 and n, 71n, 132
Wilson, John, 91 and n
Winch, Donald, 26
Windelband, Wilhelm, 69
Winstanley, Gerrard, 161 and n
Wittgenstein, Ludwig, 33
Wolff, Christian, 156
Wolff, F. A., 240n
Wollstonecraft, Mary, 303n
women, in ancient Greece, 15, 108-9; and charity work, 74, 231n, 250, 277, 280, 302-3; education of, 61 and n, 214 and n, 287, 304, 307-9; and labour, 191, 231, 245 and n; legal and political rights of, 126, 263, 282, 291, 302-6; and morality, 108-9, 245-6, 256 and n; and property, 119n, 304-6
Woolf, Virginia, 83
Wordsworth, William, 63-4, 150, 159, 323
Workers' Educational Association, 275, 280, 297
World Council of Churches, 280, 313
Wyggeston Girls' School, 307n

Z

Zeller, Edouard, 69 and n, 70
Zinzendorf, Nikolaus Ludwig von, Count, 156-7
Zunz, Leopold, 68n